Lecture Notes in Computer Science   13999

Founding Editors

Gerhard Goos
Juris Hartmanis

Editorial Board Members

The series Lecture Notes in Computer Science (LNCS), including its subseries Lecture Notes in Artificial Intelligence (LNAI) and Lecture Notes in Bioinformatics (LNBI), has established itself as a medium for the publication of new developments in computer science and information technology research, teaching, and education.

LNCS enjoys close cooperation with the computer science R & D community, the series counts many renowned academics among its volume editors and paper authors, and collaborates with prestigious societies. Its mission is to serve this international community by providing an invaluable service, mainly focused on the publication of conference and workshop proceedings and postproceedings. LNCS commenced publication in 1973.

Amanda Bienz · Michèle Weiland ·
Marc Baboulin · Carola Kruse
Editors

High Performance Computing

ISC High Performance 2023 International Workshops
Hamburg, Germany, May 21–25, 2023
Revised Selected Papers

 Springer

Editors
Amanda Bienz
University of New Mexico
Albuquerque, NM, USA

Michèle Weiland 🆔
University of Edinburgh
Edinburgh, UK

Marc Baboulin 🆔
Université Paris-Saclay
Gif sur Yvette, France

Carola Kruse 🆔
CERFACS
Toulouse, France

ISSN 0302-9743 ISSN 1611-3349 (electronic)
Lecture Notes in Computer Science
ISBN 978-3-031-40842-7 ISBN 978-3-031-40843-4 (eBook)
https://doi.org/10.1007/978-3-031-40843-4

This Springer imprint is published by the registered company Springer Nature Switzerland AG
The registered company address is: Gewerbestrasse 11, 6330 Cham, Switzerland

Preface

The 38th edition of the ISC High Performance conference (ISC-HPC 2023) was held in Hamburg, Germany. This edition was held in-person during the period from May 21 to May 25, 2023. As with the previous editions, the HPC community responded enthusiastically, as manifested by over 3,000 attendees from over 50 countries.

As in past years, ISC 2023 was accompanied by the ISC High Performance workshop series. In total, 10 workshops chose the option to contribute to this edition of proceedings: 2nd International Workshop on Malleability Techniques Applications in High-Performance Computing, 4th ISC HPC International Workshop on "Monitoring & Operational Data Analytics", 7th Workshop on In Situ Visualization, 18th Workshop on Virtualization in High-Performance Cloud Computing, First International workshop on RISC-V for HPC, HPC I/O in the Data Center, HPC on Heterogeneous Hardware (H3), Second Combined Workshop on Interactive and Urgent Supercomputing, Second workshop on Communication, I/O, and Storage at Scale on Next-Generation Platforms - Scalable Infrastructures, and WOCC'23-International Workshop on Converged Computing of Cloud, HPC and Edge. Also, 10 other workshops opted for a presentation-only format (workshops without proceedings).

Each of the 70 submitted papers received on average 3 reviews, either single- or double-blind. In total, 52 high-quality papers were accepted, among which 49 were submitted for publication. They all underwent thorough review by their respective workshops' Program Committees. Each chapter of this proceedings book contains the accepted and revised papers for a single workshop. For some workshops, an additional preface describes the review process and provides a summary of the outcomes.

We will gather next year in Hamburg, Germany, for another successful ISC High Performance workshops series. Until then, we want to thank our workshop committee members, workshop organizers, and all contributors and attendees of the ISC 2023 workshops, and we are proud to present the latest findings on the topics related to the research, development, and applications of large-scale, high-performance systems.

September 2023

Amanda Bienz
Michèle Weiland
Marc Baboulin
Carola Kruse

Organization

Workshop Committee

Amanda Bienz (Chair)	University of New Mexico, USA
Michèle Weiland (Deputy Chair)	University of Edinburgh, UK
Marc Baboulin	Université Paris-Saclay, France
Carola Kruse	CERFACS, France
Cody Balos	Lawrence Livermore National Laboratory, USA
Harun Bayraktar	NVIDIA, USA
Natalie Beams	University of Tennessee, USA
George Bosilca	University of Tennessee, USA
Jon Calhoun	Clemson University, USA
Lisa Claus	Lawrence Berkeley National Laboratory, USA
Terry Cojean	Karlsruhe Institute of Technology, Germany
Edoardo Di Napoli	Jülich Supercomputing Centre, Germany
Markus Götz	Karlsruhe Institute of Technology, Germany
Sidharth Kumar	University of Alabama, USA
Carl Pearson	Sandia National Labs, USA

Proceedings Chairs

Marc Baboulin (Chair)	Université Paris-Saclay, France
Carola Kruse (Deputy Chair)	CERFACS, France

Contents

HPC I/O in the Data Center (HPC IODC)

**Workshop on Converged Computing of Cloud, HPC, and Edge
(WOCC'23)**

HPC on Heterogeneous Hardware (H3)

2nd International Workshop on Malleability Techniques Applications in High-Performance Computing (HPCMALL)

From Static to Malleable: Improving Flexibility and Compatibility in Burst Buffer File Systems

Marc-André Vef[1]([✉])([iD]), Alberto Miranda[2]([iD]), Ramon Nou[2]([iD]),
and André Brinkmann[1]([iD])

[1] Johannes Gutenberg University Mainz, Mainz, Germany
{vef,brinkman}@uni-mainz.de
[2] Barcelona Supercomputing Center, Barcelona, Spain
{alberto.miranda,ramon.nou}@bsc.es

Abstract. Numerous burst buffer file systems have been developed in recent years in the context of high-performance computing (HPC). These file systems aim to combat I/O bottlenecks and cross-application interference that arise in parallel file systems due to competing and uncoordinated I/O patterns. While burst buffer file systems have demonstrated linear scaling for metadata and data workloads, their configurations are currently static and cannot adapt to changing requirements from applications or the HPC system. User space file system implementations have emerged as a promising solution since they can be customized to meet specific application I/O requirements. However, developing file systems in user space comes with significant challenges, such as the lack of mature I/O interfaces that can hurt application compatibility.

This paper explores the challenges that have shaped the design of GekkoFS, an exemplary user space burst buffer file system, and presents an overhauled file system architecture to improve application compatibility and provide a foundation for additional malleability techniques, molding the file system to the application's requirements. We also evaluate this new architecture and show its performance overhead that remains well above the storage capability of commonly used node-local storage devices. Overall, the paper demonstrates the potential benefits of this architecture for user space file system implementations and presents a path forward for their continued development.

Keywords: Burst buffer file systems · distributed file systems · I/O malleability · user space file systems

1 Introduction

High-performance computing (HPC) is increasingly being utilized by data-driven applications that process massive amounts of data [24]. These new I/O access patterns and the resulting higher I/O pressure on the HPC system's backend

© The Author(s), under exclusive license to Springer Nature Switzerland AG 2023
A. Bienz et al. (Eds.): ISC High Performance 2023 Workshops, LNCS 13999, pp. 3–15, 2023.
https://doi.org/10.1007/978-3-031-40843-4_1

parallel file systems (PFSs) have led to the design of *burst buffer file systems* [5]. These file systems can be created *ad-hoc* within the scope of an HPC compute job. The goals of such file systems are manifold: applications can use their own dedicated file system, making them less vulnerable to changes in PFS I/O performance. Additionally, depending on how many nodes are used by the burst buffer file system and which storage devices are available, applications can experience significantly higher I/O throughput compared to what the PFS can offer [23,28]. Examples of such file systems include GekkoFS [24], BurstFS [28], UnifyFS [15], BeeGFS BeeOND [4], and others [8,11,14,21]. Each file system targets slightly different use cases, with some running entirely in user space, e.g., GekkoFS or Hercules IMSS [11], and others requiring a kernel component, e.g., BeeGFS.

User space implementations have the benefit of not being held back by the data structures required by the kernel's *virtual file system* (VFS). They can modify or extend the POSIX API with additional I/O calls, e.g., similar to object storage interfaces, or provide various hints to the file system. However, although these extended APIs can be useful for newly developed applications, they are challenging to use in existing applications due to their complex code base, which may have been developed over decades [9]. In such cases, modifying the I/O layer can be a daunting and time-consuming task that may not always be possible. Therefore, user space file systems should still strive to offer a compatible POSIX API. Unfortunately, there are only a limited set of techniques available for user space file systems, each with its own unique challenges and drawbacks.

On the other hand, burst buffer file systems can be optimized to meet the requirements of a single application since they are often accessed by one application. These optimizations can include data distribution patterns that align with the application's data access patterns, changes to cache consistency guarantees, or complete modifications to I/O protocols that relax POSIX expectations. Recent studies suggest that not all I/O functions or strong consistency file system semantics are required by applications [16,26,27], making such mechanisms helpful for boosting performance. User space implementations are particularly effective for these use cases since they can incorporate these optimizations into the file system without kernel restrictions.

Nevertheless, these file systems and their configurations are still *static* and must be determined when the file system is launched. With more intelligent HPC systems that can react to available resources, as proposed by the ADMIRE EURO-HPC project[1], file systems should become *malleable*. This means they could dynamically change their configurations and algorithms, such as adjusting consistency guarantees or the number of used I/O servers. However, transitioning from a static to a malleable file system has its challenges and may require significant architectural design changes.

In this paper, we examine the major challenges in designing a distributed file system in user space supporting both the standard POSIX I/O interfaces and future malleability techniques in Sect. 2. To demonstrate how to address some of these challenges, we modify the user space GekkoFS burst buffer file system to fit

---

[1] https://www.admire-eurohpc.eu/.

our requirements by introducing a new component into its design – *the GekkoFS proxy* – with the goal of improving both application compatibility and providing a platform for malleability in Sect. 3. We evaluate this new architecture and compare it to the original GekkoFS design in Sect. 4. Section 5 concludes this paper.

2   Challenges in User Space File System Design

Developing file systems in user space is challenging due to the lack of proper mechanisms in the Linux kernel to integrate those file systems into the existing VFS namespace and overall kernel facilities. Note, however, that the potential performance benefits of not crossing the kernel barrier have pushed many developers of HPC file systems and I/O libraries towards this approach, despite its many drawbacks. When compared to kernel file systems, which are known for longer and more complex development cycles [7], user space file systems benefit from simpler and shorter development cycles, as well as from the many tools available to develop and debug user space programs. User space file systems have also been shown to add lower performance overhead per I/O call [6,18], especially for modern *non-volatile main memory* (NVMM) devices [18], and can be designed beyond the constraints of VFS interfaces and data structures. In this section, we discuss the major challenges we found when implementing such file systems.

I/O Interface. The first decision to be made when designing a user space file system, is which I/O interface will be offered to its client applications. If the file system designers wish to offer a POSIX-compliant I/O interface (e.g., one based on `open()`, `read()`, `lseek()`, etc.), they generally have three options available:

1. Using FUSE (*Filesystem in Userspace*) [1] to implement the file system.
2. Statically linking the application to the file system as an I/O library (which may include a custom I/O interface).
3. Intercepting I/O requests before they reach the kernel.

Brinkmann et al. [5] discussed these options in detail and found that while FUSE has seen many improvements and extensions in recent years [13,29], its performance overhead is still considered too high, especially for latency-sensitive requests like metadata operations [22]. Additionally, while FUSE allows for user space file system implementations, they are still connected to the VFS, which means that the same restrictions as kernel space file systems apply to them. Therefore, most user space file system implementations use options 2 and 3. However, each option has its own limitations.

Static linking has the advantage that the provided I/O library can offer custom non-POSIX I/O interfaces that may benefit certain applications [10]. Nevertheless, it has the obvious drawback that it forces legacy applications to be recompiled or even rewritten to some extent in order to use these interfaces.

Intercepting I/O requests is typically done by using the `LD_PRELOAD` environment variable, which instructs the dynamic loader `ld.so` to prioritize the provided library during symbol resolution. This allows placing an interposition library between the application and the *libc* standard library, which can be used to serve I/O operations as required. Libraries based on GOTCHA [19] are similar to interposition libraries, as they can be used via LD_PRELOAD but can also be directly linked to the application as an I/O library. Linking I/O libraries directly is generally easier for application compatibility but requires some additional actions by the application user when compiling it.

A different option is to interpose I/O system calls directly by using the *syscall_intercept* API from Intel®'s *persistent memory developer kit* (PMDK) [2]. While *syscall_intercept*-based libraries are still used with LD_PRELOAD, the interception mechanism is not positioned between the application and libc, but in the last step before the kernel's system call layer is called. This is done by hot-patching the machine code in the process memory during runtime and inserting a trampoline jmp instruction to the corresponding library function. Libraries based on *syscall_intercept* can improve application compatibility and reduce development because only system calls need to be handled instead of all libc I/O functions in their various versions. Other benefits of using *syscall_intercept* are that other I/O libraries (and their corresponding functions) which would need to be intercepted otherwise, work out of the box, e.g., the MPI I/O API. Nonetheless, note that any method based on LD_PRELOAD means that the file system client code will live embedded within the context of each application process and will also destroyed when a process is terminated. This leads to several challenges from a design perspective and also restricts the applicability of any malleable techniques to a single process only.

Threads and fork() Do Not Mix. As mentioned, LD_PRELOAD-based techniques directly inject code from the user space file system interface into the application's client code. This can have unexpected consequences if the file system code is multithreaded and the application code needs to create new processes using the fork() family of system calls (namely fork(), vfork(), and clone()).

Whenever a thread is created using pthread_create(), a new kernel task is created within the context of the calling process that shares the process space: memory, file descriptors, ownership, etc. When a process executes a fork() system call, however, a separate copy of the *currently running* kernel task is created. This means that any additional threads besides the one currently executing the fork() are lost and, hence, any locks held by them will be permanently left in a locked state, probably leading to an application-level deadlock. While locks may be the more evident problem, any shared resources such as sockets or memory allocations will also disappear, leading to often obscure and unpredictable errors. While there are some provisions to mitigate this situation, such as using pthread_atfork() to register pre- and post- fork() handlers, it is not always possible to ensure that all affected resources are in a sensible state (consider for instance any connected sockets created by 3rd party communication libraries) and, even when it is, ensuring so may incur a performance penalty too large for the goals of the user space file system.

These problems are not specific to user space file systems and may occur in normal application code as well if the shared state between threads is not managed before a `fork()`. Even so, this problem is specially important for LD_PRELOAD-based file systems, since they can unwittingly introduce errors in applications due to the injection of the file system client libraries themselves.

File Descriptor Management. Any user space file system client injected directly into application code with LD_PRELOAD will share the resources assigned to the process upon which it was injected, which includes the process' file descriptors (`fds`). This has an immediately intrusive effect in the client process: If the file system client keeps many open `fds` (e.g., to maintain live sockets to the file system's I/O servers) the number of open files and/or connections that the application will be able to use will be drastically reduced.

Other issues can be more subtle: a specific application code may depend on a certain (hardcoded) numeric range of `fds` to be available. Since `fds` are assigned in a monotonically increasing manner by the kernel as long as they are not closed, the injected file system code might have unwittingly occupied that specific range. This can lead to unpredictable errors and data corruption due to the application reading and writing data from `fds` that should be meant for internal file system use. Since the Linux kernel does not offer specific user space APIs that allow a process to manipulate its table of open files (outside the POSIX I/O API itself), user space file system clients must implement a `fd` management strategy to prevent these issues. This is further complicated by the fact that some kernel modules (such as `ib_uverbs`) may create `fds` in kernel space and return them to user space via `fnctl()` or `ioctl()`. Since these interfaces are by design device-dependent, there is no generic way for the injected file system code to handle this, and the code will need to be patched in a case-by-case basis.

File System Malleability. Since user space file systems are not restricted by the kernel, they can offer configuration options to modify their behavior. For instance, GekkoFS offers options such as selecting a specific metadata backend, choosing the data distribution algorithm, enabling symlink support, and altering file system protocols among others. Nonetheless, such configurations must be set before the file system is launched and cannot be changed afterwards, remaining static for the application's lifetime. In the next section, we propose an architecture that takes this limitation into account, and attempts to offer a malleable platform for user space file systems based on I/O interception mechanisms.

3   Revising GekkoFS's Architecture

This section proposes a revised client architecture for user space file systems that addresses the limitations described above. We start by examining the architecture of a real burst buffer file system (GekkoFS), and extend it to support malleability reconfigurations, discussing the final architecture's advantages and limitations. The primary goal of this redesign is to improve the compatibility of user space file systems while establishing a framework that can support various malleability techniques. While the proposed architecture is GekkoFS-specific, the design is generic enough that it can be adopted by other user space file systems.

While examining GekkoFS's current design, we discovered that GekkoFS I/O servers are already equipped for supporting malleable mechanisms to a certain extent. Due to GekkoFS's decoupled architecture, adding mechanisms such as increasing or removing server nodes during runtime is relatively straight-forward. GekkoFS's original design already supports this use case without any issues, as long as the file system is empty. Changing the number of server nodes, however, would work but in an inefficient manner: Since a file's data and metadata server node are computed by generating hash keys, these keys would change, and most of the data in the file system would need to be redistributed. While there are techniques to address this [17], applying them is out of the scope of this paper.

On the other hand, the GekkoFS client design is currently not suitable for supporting a broad set of malleability techniques. Since GekkoFS clients are restricted to an application process's lifespan, it is not possible to implement relaxed cache consistency protocols and align them more closely with NFSv4 semantics [12] on a node-level, for example. Temporarily relaxing cache consistency guarantees, such as during the write burst of bulk-synchronous applications [5], could considerably improve performance, particularly for small I/O requests that are latency-sensitive. Overall, a GekkoFS client design that supports these use cases would complement a minimal *syscall_intercept* or `libc` interposition library, by outsourcing more complex client code to another client process that operates on node-granularity. Therefore, as a part of this overhaul, a new file system component is added – the *GekkoFS proxy*.

Goals. We define the following goals for GekkoFS's revised design: 1. minimize the complexity of the *syscall_intercept* library to mitigate aforementioned challenges; 2. design a new component that consolidates the communication of all GekkoFS clients and serves as a gateway to remote nodes, while also allowing for future malleable mechanisms; and 3. maintain the overall file system performance, minimizing extra overheads when compared to GekkoFS's original design.

Design. Figure 1 illustrates the GekkoFS architecture with the newly introduced GekkoFS proxy. The proxy acts as a gateway between the client and daemons, forwarding all communication between the two components. The client communicates with the proxy via cross-memory attach (CMA) [25], which is supported by GekkoFS's current *remote-procedure call* (RPC) framework *Mercury* [20]. Mercury's communication mode via shared memory uses single-copy transfers between two processes without the need to pass through the kernel space. The proxy communicates with the GekkoFS daemons via the respective native network protocol, e.g., Omni-Path or Infiniband, using *remote direct memory access* (RDMA) for bulk transfers, i.e., read and write operations.

As a result, the GekkoFS client complexity is considerably reduced, removing GekkoFS's dependency on low-level network libraries such as `libfabric` for

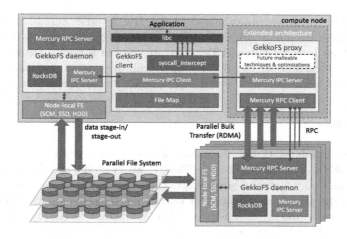

Fig. 1. GekkoFS architecture and its components with GekkoFS the proxy.

remote communication. Since these libraries are typically multithreaded, this also takes care of any issues with fork() system calls. This also reduces the number of opened fds by the low-level network libraries, which, coupled with forcibly allocating internal file system fds to a separate numeric range inaccessible by the application, successfully mitigates most fd challenges. A full solution, e.g. offering kernel extensions for correct fd management, is left for future work.

Since all file system communication now passes through the proxy, other advanced file system features can be implemented. For instance, with caching on the proxy, relaxed consistency models can be implemented that define how long data remains at the proxy before being distributed to the daemons. One of the supported cache consistencies could be similar to NFSv4 [12], providing *close-to-open* semantics where data is distributed once a file is closed. Therefore, multiple client processes on the same node can operate on a distributed file at local speeds. Other use cases could involve batching, which bundles many small I/O requests at the proxy before sending a corresponding remote request instead of serving each I/O request individually, or encryption. The applied strictness of these features could be steered through an API accepting external malleable requests. We plan to investigate the performance implications in future work.

Nevertheless, using the GekkoFS proxy adds one additional communication step in the form of *inter-process communication* (IPC) for each file system operation sent to the daemon. This increases the latency for each operation, which may affect both data and metadata throughput. For metadata operations, e.g., file creation, the corresponding request is served by sending a single RPC to the proxy, which is then directly forwarded to the responsible daemon determined by hashing the file's path [24]. For data operations, such as a write operation, the entire client's buffer is first transferred to the GekkoFS proxy using CMA and then distributed to the processing daemons. On the proxy, the Margo-driven RPC operations, which send RPCs to remote GekkoFS daemons, run within the context of the Argobots-provided Margo IPC handler threads that process incoming GekkoFS client IPCs. This avoids copying bulk buffers between two Argobots *User-level threads* (ULTs) that are part of separate thread pools. In short, the GekkoFS proxy can reduce the overall file system performance due to the additional communication steps. We evaluate the potential overheads next.

4   Evaluation

This section evaluates the performance of our new architecture and compares it to GekkoFS's original design. Specifically, we evaluate workloads, small I/O operations on many files, and general I/O throughput. We chose these workloads to measure the potential overhead of both latency-sensitive (RPC) operations (metadata) and throughput-sensitive (RDMA) operations (data). The expectation is that GekkoFS's performance with the proxy does not exceed its original design when the native Omni-Path protocol is used but remains close to it.

Experimental Setup. We ran the experiments on the MOGON II supercomputer at the Johannes Gutenberg University in Mainz, Germany. It consists of 1,876 nodes in total, with 822 nodes using Intel 2630v4 Intel Broadwell processors (two sockets each) and 1046 nodes using Xeon Gold 6130 Intel Skylake processors (four sockets each) which were used in all experiments. MOGON II uses a 100 Gbit/s Intel Omni-Path interconnect to establish a fat tree between all compute nodes with each node using a Intel SATA SSD DC S3700 Series as a scratch environment (*XFS* formatted).

Each data point in this section's evaluation figures represent the average of ten iterations unless otherwise specified. Further, unless otherwise specified, the GekkoFS daemons are using shared memory as their data backend. The used abbreviations of the compared network configurations are defined as follows:

1. GekkoFS without proxy using the native Omni-Path protocol (psm2) presenting GekkoFS's maximum performance (GKFS_MAX).
2. GekkoFS without the proxy using the TCP/IP protocol over Omni-Path (GKFS_TCP) providing a fallback in cases psm2 cannot be used.
3. GekkoFS with the proxy using the native Omni-Path protocol (psm2) for communication between the proxy and the daemons (GKFS_PROXY).
4. GekkoFS using the node-local SATA SSDs (GKFS_SSD) which is the most common GekkoFS operating mode.

Metadata Performance. Several microbenchmarks were run with mdtest [3] to evaluate the metadata performance. We used 16 processes per node with each process creating, stating, and removing 100,000 zero-byte files in a single directory. Figure 2 presents the average metadata performance difference for all three configurations for up to 64 nodes. Overall, GKFS_PROXY achieved between ~86% and ~95% of GKFS_MAX's throughput for the file create case. GKFS_TCP, on the other hand, only reached between ~16% and ~30% of GKFS_MAX's throughput.

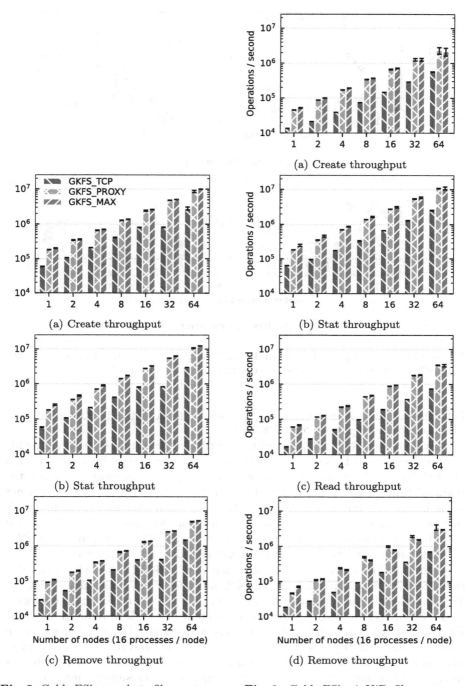

(a) Create throughput

(a) Create throughput

(b) Stat throughput

(b) Stat throughput

(c) Read throughput

(c) Remove throughput

(d) Remove throughput

Fig. 2. GekkoFS's zero-byte file create, stat, and remove throughput using the GekkoFS proxy.

Fig. 3. GekkoFS's 4 KiB file create, stat, read, and remove throughput using the GekkoFS proxy.

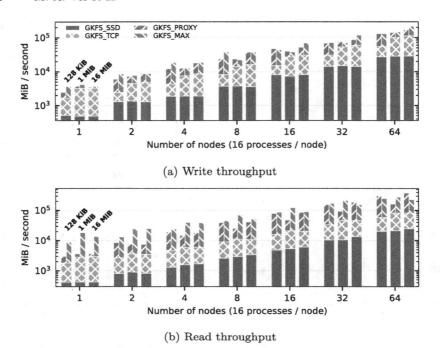

(a) Write throughput

(b) Read throughput

Fig. 4. GekkoFS's sequential write and read throughput for up to 64 nodes using the GekkoFS proxy compared to other network protocols for various I/O sizes.

For the stat and remove cases, the behavior was similar, showing significant performance discrepancies for GKFS_TCP.

Another set of mdtest experiments investigated the throughput when the file size was set to 4 KiB. This represents an extreme scenario where each process created 100,000 small files in a single directory. Therefore, mdtest includes the required time of the 4 KiB write operation for each file in the file creates per second. The benchmark also reads all files, reporting the amount of file reads per second. Similar to the zero-byte file benchmarks above, GKFS_TCP showed considerable performance differences compared with GKFS_PROXY and GKFS_MAX, reaching only ~20% to ~25% of GKFS_MAX's throughput in the write and read file operations per second. For the same cases, GKFS_PROXY achieved at least 85% of GKFS_MAX's throughput. Figure 3 depicts all experiments in detail and includes the file creates/writes, stats, reads, and removals per second for up to 64 nodes.

In summary, although metadata performance is slightly reduced with the GekkoFS proxy, it remains close to the original design, e.g., achieving close to 9 million file creates per second for 64 nodes. Note however that future (now possible) features, such as batching of small requests, could lead to a higher metadata throughput without noticeably impacting consistency guarantees.

Data Performance. Several experiments investigated the GekkoFS proxy's data performance via the IOR [3] microbenchmark. In each experiment, 16 processes were run per node, with each process sequentially writing and reading a 1 GiB file to and from memory. To investigate the throughput for different I/O sizes, IOR was run with three separate I/O sizes: 128 KiB, 1 MiB, and 16 MiB (Fig. 4).

Notice that each data point depicts the maximum achieved bandwidth over ten iterations instead of the average. This is because the experiments showed that bulk transfers via RDMA could vary significantly depending on the overall cluster state and the network usage of other applications. Generally, this effect was more pronounced with more nodes with a relative standard deviation of up to 30% for some 64 node experiments in which the native network protocols were used. When the same experiments were run using the node-local SSDs for the daemon's data backend, the relative standard deviation remained below 5% in all three GekkoFS configurations. This indicates disruptions on the network that are otherwise hidden when using a much slower data backend.

Further, compared to the earlier figures, the GKFS_SSD case is included. GKFS_SSD presents the case where each process writes and reads 4 GiB to the node-local SSD while over 90% of the memory available memory was in use by another process to prevent buffer caching of the node-local file system. Nevertheless, the experiments showed that the maximum I/O throughput for GKFS_TCP, GKFS_PROXY, and GKFS_MAX were, in fact, similar when an SSD was used as the data backend. This demonstrates that in this setup, using the proxy has no impact on I/O performance. Figure 4 shows GKFS_TCP's high throughput discrepancies compared with GKFS_MAX and GKFS_PROXY, depending on the number of nodes and I/O sizes. In contrast to the metadata experiments, however, GKFS_MAX and GKFS_PROXY performed similarly.

5 Conclusion

In this paper, we have introduced the challenges of developing and designing user space burst buffer file systems. Using GekkoFS as an example, we have discussed the critical issues of LD_PRELOAD as an interception mechanism. We have proposed a new architecture for GekkoFS that overcomes these challenges and provides a platform for possible future malleability techniques, such as node-granular caching. Finally, we have evaluated the new architecture for latency- and throughput-sensitive operations and have concluded that the proxy only induces minor overheads, maintaining most of the file system's performance.

Acknowledgements. This research was conducted using the supercomputer Mogon II and services offered by Johannes Gutenberg University Mainz. The authors gratefully acknowledge the computing time granted on Mogon II.

This work was partially funded by the European Union's Horizon 2020 and the German Ministry of Education and Research (BMBF) under the "Adaptive multi-tier intelligent data manager for Exascale (ADMIRE)" project; Grant Agreement number: 956748-ADMIRE-H2020-JTI-EuroHPC-2019-1. Further, this work was partially supported by the Spanish Ministry of Economy and Competitiveness (MINECO) under grants PID2019-107255GB, and the Generalitat de Catalunya under contract 2021-SGR-00412. This publication is part of the project ADMIRE PCI2021-121952, funded by MCIN/AEI/10.13039/501100011033.

References

1. Fuse (filesystem in userspace) (2002). https://github.com/libfuse/libfuse
2. Persistent memory development kit (2014). https://pmem.io/pmdk/
3. Ior and mdtest (2020). https://github.com/hpc/ior
4. BeeGFS: Beeond: Beegfs on demand (2018). https://www.beegfs.io/wiki/BeeOND
5. Brinkmann, A., et al.: Ad hoc file systems for high-performance computing. J. Comput. Sci. Technol. **35**(1), 4–26 (2020). https://doi.org/10.1007/s11390-020-9801-1
6. Didona, D., Pfefferle, J., Ioannou, N., Metzler, B., Trivedi, A.: Understanding modern storage APIs: a systematic study of libaio, SPDK, and io_uring. In: SYSTOR 2022: The 15th ACM International Systems and Storage Conference. ACM (2022)
7. Dilger, A.: Lustre metadata scaling (2012)
8. Dun, N., Taura, K., Yonezawa, A.: GMount: an ad hoc and locality-aware distributed file system by using SSH and FUSE. In: 9th IEEE/ACM International Symposium on Cluster Computing and the Grid (CCGrid) (2009)
9. Fischer, P., Lottes, J., Tufo, H.: Nek5000. Technical report, Argonne National Lab. (ANL), Argonne, IL, United States (2007)
10. Folk, M., Heber, G., Koziol, Q., Pourmal, E., Robinson, D.: An overview of the HDF5 technology suite and its applications. In: Proceedings of the 2011 EDBT/ICDT Workshop on Array Databases. ACM (2011)
11. Garcia-Blas, J., Singh, D.E., Carretero, J.: IMSS: in-memory storage system for data intensive applications. In: Anzt, H., Bienz, A., Luszczek, P., Baboulin, M. (eds.) ISC High Performance 2022. LNCS, vol. 13387, pp. 190–205. Springer, Cham (2022). https://doi.org/10.1007/978-3-031-23220-6_13
12. Haynes, T.: Network file system (NFS) version 4 minor version 2 protocol. RFC 7862 (2016)
13. Huai, Q., Hsu, W., Lu, J., Liang, H., Xu, H., Chen, W.: XFUSE: an infrastructure for running filesystem services in user space. In: 2021 USENIX Annual Technical Conference, USENIX ATC 2021. USENIX Association (2021)
14. Isaila, F., Blas, J.G., Carretero, J., Liao, W., Choudhary, A.N.: AHPIOS: an MPI-based ad hoc parallel I/O system. In: 14th International Conference on Parallel and Distributed Systems (ICPADS) (2008)
15. L.L.N. Laboratory: Unifyfs (2019). https://github.com/LLNL/UnifyFS
16. Lensing, P.H., Cortes, T., Brinkmann, A.: Direct lookup and hash-based metadata placement for local file systems. In: 6th Annual International Systems and Storage Conference, SYSTOR 2013. ACM (2013)
17. Miranda, A., Effert, S., Kang, Y., Miller, E.L., Brinkmann, A., Cortes, T.: Reliable and randomized data distribution strategies for large scale storage systems. In: 18th International Conference on High Performance Computing. IEEE (2011)
18. Moti, N., et al.: Simurgh: a fully decentralized and secure NVMM user space file system. In: SC 2021: The International Conference for High Performance Computing, Networking, Storage and Analysis. ACM (2021)

19. Poliakoff, D., LeGendre, M.: Gotcha: an function-wrapping interface for HPC tools. In: Bhatele, A., Boehme, D., Levine, J.A., Malony, A.D., Schulz, M. (eds.) ESPT/VPA 2017-2018. LNCS, vol. 11027, pp. 185–197. Springer, Cham (2019). https://doi.org/10.1007/978-3-030-17872-7_11
20. Soumagne, J., et al.: Mercury: enabling remote procedure call for high-performance computing. In: IEEE International Conference on Cluster Computing, CLUSTER (2013)
21. Tatebe, O., Obata, K., Hiraga, K., Ohtsuji, H.: CHFS: parallel consistent hashing file system for node-local persistent memory. In: HPC Asia 2022: International Conference on High Performance Computing in Asia-Pacific Region (2022)
22. Vangoor, B.K.R., Tarasov, V., Zadok, E.: To FUSE or not to FUSE: performance of user-space file systems. In: 15th USENIX Conference on File and Storage Technologies (FAST) (2017)
23. Vef, M., et al.: GekkoFS - a temporary burst buffer file system for HPC applications. J. Comput. Sci. Technol. **35**(1), 72–91 (2020). https://doi.org/10.1007/s11390-020-9797-6
24. Vef, M., et al.: GekkoFS - a temporary distributed file system for HPC applications. In: IEEE International Conference on Cluster Computing, CLUSTER 2018, Belfast, UK, 10–13 September 2018. IEEE Computer Society (2018)
25. Vienne, J.: Benefits of cross memory attach for MPI libraries on HPC clusters. In: Annual Conference of the Extreme Science and Engineering Discovery Environment, XSEDE 2014, Atlanta, GA, USA, 13–18 July 2014, pp. 33:1–33:6 (2014)
26. Wang, C.: Detecting data races on relaxed systems using recorder (2022)
27. Wang, C., Mohror, K., Snir, M.: File system semantics requirements of HPC applications. In: HPDC 2021: The 30th International Symposium on High-Performance Parallel and Distributed Computing, Virtual Event. ACM (2021)
28. Wang, T., Mohror, K., Moody, A., Sato, K., Yu, W.: An ephemeral burst-buffer file system for scientific applications. In: Proceedings of the International Conference for High Performance Computing, Networking, Storage and Analysis, SC 2016 (2016)
29. Zhu, Y., et al.: Direct-FUSE: removing the middleman for high-performance FUSE file system support. In: Proceedings of the 8th International Workshop on Runtime and Operating Systems for Supercomputers, ROSS@HPDC 2018. ACM (2018)

Malleable Techniques and Resource Scheduling to Improve Energy Efficiency in Parallel Applications

Alberto Cascajo$^{(\boxtimes)}$ 🆔, Alvaro Arbe, Javier Garcia-Blas🆔, Jesus Carretero🆔, and David E. Singh🆔

University Carlos III of Madrid. Computer Science and Engineering Department, Madrid, Spain
{acascajo,fjblas,jcarrete,dexposit}@inf.uc3m.es

Abstract. The high energy consumption of computing platforms has become one of the major problems in high-performance computing (HPC). Computer energy consumption represents a significant percentage of the CO_2 emissions that occur each year in the world, therefore, it is crucial to develop energy efficiency techniques in order to reduce the energy consumption in HPC systems. In this work, we present a resource scheduler capable of choosing, using real-time data, the optimal number of processes of running applications. The solution takes advantage of the use the FlexMPI runtime to dynamically reconfigure the application number of processes and DVFS to modify the frequency of cores of the platform. The scheduling algorithms presented in this work include one that minimizes the application energy and another more holistic one that allows the user to balance between energy and execution time minimization. This work presents a description of the methodologies and a experimental evaluation on a real platform.

Keywords: Energy efficiency · Scheduling · High-Performance Computing · DVFS

1 Introduction

For many years, energy consumption in HPC systems has been a challenging topic. Data centers account for around 4% of global electricity consumption and between 73 and 140 million MWh per year [8]. It is estimated that from 2010 to 2018, the demand for work in data centers has increased by 550% while consumption has only increased by 6% because of the advances in energy efficiency that has been carried out [1]. Current supercomputers such as Frontier [9] and

This work was partially supported by the EuroHPC project "Adaptive multi-tier intelligent data manager for Exascale" under grant 956748 - ADMIRE - H2020-JTI-EuroHPC-2019-1 and by the Agencia Española de Investigación under Grant PCI2021-121966.

A. Bienz et al. (Eds.): ISC High Performance 2023 Workshops, LNCS 13999, pp. 16–27, 2023.
https://doi.org/10.1007/978-3-031-40843-4_2

Fugaku, even being much more efficient than the previous ones, require more than 20 MWh during peak loads. Therefore, Green Computing has become a recent trend in computer science, which aims to reduce the energy consumption and carbon footprint produced by computers on distributed platforms such as clusters, grids, and clouds [6].

From the environmental and economic point of view, it can be seen that multiple works address the development of energy efficient HPC systems since they make it possible to reduce high consumption (e.g. Frontier, the most efficient supercomputer in the world and was placed at the top of the GREEN500). The advances that have been made in this area are highly relevant since they enable the reduction of CO2 emissions from computing [10].

While traditional scheduling solutions attempt to minimize processing time without taking into account the energetic, energy-aware scheduling of jobs has become a trend in computing facilities. Most of those solutions are based on job grouping and migration, considering that the number of resources needed for a workload can be minimized [2]. Other solutions propose real-time dynamic scheduling systems to execute applications efficiently optimizing energy consumption [5]. Those solutions are not usually addressed on supercomputers, where jobs are statically allocated and elasticity or migrations mechanisms are not available. In supercomputers, techniques like varying CPU frequencies [3] or allocating jobs to CPU or heterogeneous devices [4] are more popular to increase the energy efficiency of the system without compromising the application makespan.

The main goal of this work is to increase energy efficiency in HPC platforms by means of malleability and dynamic energy-aware application scheduling. Malleability is a promising technique to reduce the energy consumption of parallel applications by adjusting dynamically the resources to the computation requirements of each application. In this work, we present a resource scheduler capable of choosing, using real-time data, the application processes that reduce energy consumption under different constraints. We use the FlexMPI [7] runtime to dynamically adapt and reconfigure the applications while it is able to adapt the frequency of the CPUs in the platform. Scheduling algorithms range from the simplest one that minimizes the energy consumption over all possible configurations, to the most sophisticated one, which uses a cost function that allows the user to prioritize the minimization of execution time or energy consumption. We use mathematical methods to predict the application workload and execution phases, which enable the resource scheduler to refine its decisions. We also provide a set of use cases integrated with the FlexMPI runtime that can be used as benchmarks. Additionally, Using these use cases, we support an energy profile modeler that estimates the application energy consumption, an energy-aware malleable scheduler that is able to run the use cases in an efficient way, and a practical evaluation on a real platform.

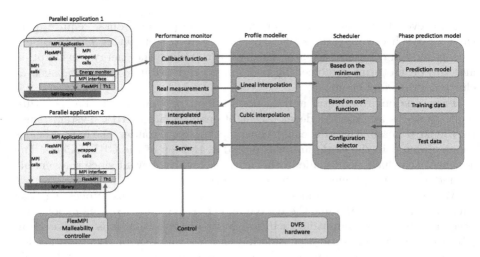

Fig. 1. Overview of the system architecture.

2   Energy-Aware FlexMPI System Architecture

Figure 1 depicts the proposed energy-aware system architecture based on the FlexMPI framework. The first component includes the *Parallel applications*. Applications also respond to FlexMPI commands. These calls are sent by the root process after they have been received from the controller. Energy is measured by the root process and sent to the controller, which forwards it to the scheduler. The root application is made up of a single thread and it is in charge of executing and controlling FlexMPI. The *performance monitor* is the component that collects the energy metrics and forwards them to the scheduler. It is also the part that is in charge of receiving the new configurations from the scheduler and forwarding them to the controller. It is the intermediate piece between FlexMPI and another component developed in MATLAB that runs on a different compute node. The *Malleability scheduler* is the element that is in charge of analyzing the available information (energy, minimum points, workload predictions, and phases) continuously and determining what is the ideal configuration to apply in every reconfiguration point. This information is received from the monitor (integrated with FlexMPI), the profiler, and the prediction model. The *Profile modeler* collects energy time series and uses them to model the energy that the applications consume under different configurations (number of processes). The reconstruction is done using mathematical methods (i.e., interpolation) and the results are sent to the scheduler.

The FlexMPI controller is in charge of receiving the desired malleability configurations, sending the malleability commands to the processes (expanding or shrinking them) and updating the frequency and voltage of the processors. This component interacts with two elements: the FlexMPI malleability driver [7] and the Dynamic voltage and frequency scaling (DVFS). DVFS is a technique used to reduce energy in digital systems by reducing the voltage of the nodes.

3   Malleable Resource Scheduling for Energy Saving

There are two principal components in the proposed architecture: an energy-aware scheduler that determines the application configuration and DVFS value in run-time and an energy profile modeler that supports the scheduler support-making process. This section describes both of them.

3.1   Malleability Scheduler

The malleability scheduler is in charge of analyzing all the available information in real-time (energy, execution times, application phases, etc.). The scheduler calculates which is the best configuration (frequency and the number of processes) to apply in order to reduce energy or execution time.

From the scheduler's point of view, in order to make the best decision, it is necessary to collect both the system and application performance from historical records, data from the current execution, and predictions of future performance based on models. Note that in the proposed framework runtime energy and performance metrics are collected by FlexMPI because it integrates a performance and energy monitor, and these measurements are sent to the scheduler for decision-making.

In the cost function depicted in Eq. 3.1, $E(NP, freq)$ and $T(NP, freq)$ are the energy and execution time of a specific configuration of the number of processes and frequency (NP and $freq$, respectively) and E_{max} and T_{max} are the maximum existing values of both parameters. W_1 and W_2 are normalized weights, with $W_1 + W_2 = 1$. The scheduling algorithm can find multiple solutions (by minimizing the cost function) according to the weight parameters. For instance, when the user desires to balance the energy and execution time values, then both weights should be similar. If it is necessary to minimize the energy, then W_1 should be higher (and *vice-versa* if the goal is to only minimize the execution time).

$$C(NP, freq) = W_1 \frac{E(NP, freq)}{E_{max}} + W_2 \frac{T(NP, freq)}{T_{max}} \qquad (3.1)$$

The scheduling algorithm consists of finding the minimum value of the cost function across all the existing combinations of the number of processes and DVFS values. Given that not all energy data is available, we propose an energy profile modeler that reduces the complexity and the amount of monitoring information needed by the scheduler.

3.2   Energy Profile Modeller

This section introduces the mathematical method employed to implement the energy modeler. This method approximates the information related to the energy consumption of the application, allowing the system to configure the most appropriate setup, based on the number of processes and DVFS values (NP and *freq*).

Existing combinations can be seen as two surfaces, with the x and y axis ranging the possible NP and $freq$ values, and the z-axis with the corresponding application energy or execution time.

The main idea behind this proposal is to monitor the application performance by using a limiting number of configurations under certain NP and $freq$ values. We denote each measurement as a sample. For each sample, the application's energy consumption and execution time are collected. The mathematical interpolation method reconstructs the energy and execution time surfaces by means of linear interpolation techniques. Algorithm 1 describes the interpolation process. Initially, we collect samples using the maximum and minimum number of processes while considering multiple ranges of $freq$ values. We have observed that the overhead of updating the DVFS values is negligible. In contrast, adapting the number of processes has a more relevant impact, not only related to the process creation or destruction but also to data redistribution. In the following iterations, new samples are collected based on the maximum difference between the application sample and the model. This process enables the refinement of the interpolation process. Algorithm 2 depicts the interpolation algorithm that reconstructs the curve surfaces based on the existing samples.

3.3 FlexMPI Support

In this work, we leverage malleable support provided by FlexMPI to collect multiple sample points (number of processes and DVFS values) during the application execution. The system performs two operations. First, the system collects the performance metrics of the current configuration of the execution. Second, once it has enough information for that configuration, by using malleability, it reconfigures the application to analyse another sample (expanding or shrinking the number of processes and changing the DVFS value). Following this approach, the system is able to execute multiple analyses during one execution of the real use case. By means of leveraging malleability, our proposal is able to build the models in the early execution stages, reducing data collection time and making the models available during the first application execution. Note that this approach is also beneficial due to a lower energy consumption compared with running independent use cases varying both the processes number and DVFS value. We assume that the performance behaviour at the beginning of the application represents the situation in the whole execution.

4 Evaluation

The evaluation has been carried out in a baremetal cluster consisting of compute nodes with Intel(R) Xeon(R) Gold 6212U with 24 cores and 330 GB of RAM. The connection between nodes is by 10 Gbps Ethernet. A FlexMPI-based implementation of the Jacobi algorithm method is used. Our implementation includes a set of tunable parameters that modify the behavior of the code, generating different performance profiles of CPU, I/O, and network usage. Due to this, we

Algorithm 1. First iteration - Curve interpolation algorithm.

1: $num\_used \leftarrow 2$
2: $flag\_used \leftarrow array_24(0)$
3: $extreme \leftarrow 1$
4: $extreme \leftarrow 24$
5: $flag\_used(extreme1) \leftarrow 1$
6: $flag\_used(extreme2) \leftarrow 24$
7: $write(server, extreme1)$
8: $energy\_matrix(extreme1) \leftarrow read(server)$
9: $write(server, extreme2)$
10: $energy\_matrix(extreme2) \leftarrow read(server)$
11: $energy\_interpol \leftarrow interp2(energy\_matrix(extreme1), energy\_matrix(extreme2))$
12: $figure(energy\_interpol)$
13: $writeInFile(energy\_interpol)$
14: $s \leftarrow 0$
15: $ind \leftarrow 1$
16: $max \leftarrow 0$
17: **for** $s > extreme1$ **and** $s < extreme2$ **do**
18:    **if** $s\ not\ in\ flag\_used$ **then**
19:       $dif1 \leftarrow abs\_val(energy\_interpol(s) - energy\_matrix(extreme1))$
20:       $dif2 \leftarrow abs\_val(energy\_interpol(s) - energy\_matrix(extreme2))$
21:       $dif \leftarrow min(dif1, dif2)$
22:       **if** $max < dif$ **then**
23:          $max \leftarrow dif$
24:          $ind \leftarrow s$
25:       **end if**
26:    **end if**
27: **end for**
28: $flag\_used(ind) \leftarrow 1$
29: $num\_used \leftarrow num\_used + 1$

have designed a set of configurations that cover a wide range of performance patterns. Following we describe the main use cases:

- Use case 1 (UC1): CPU-intensive application with high data locality.
- Use case 2 (UC2): CPU-intensive application with low data locality.
- Use case 3 (UC3): Combination of CPU and communication intensive phases.
- Use case 4 (UC4): Combination of CPU and I/O intensive phases.
- Use case 5 (UC5): Combination of CPU, I/O, and communication intensive phases.

To obtain execution profiles, the application has been run in multiple iterations. Each iteration includes all the executions combining the entire frequency range (from 1.2 GHz to 2.4 GHz) and all the available cores (from 1 to 24). The energy metric represents the average energy of the existing samples.

In Fig. 2, we can observe that the energy profile for UC1, which is very similar to the energy profile from UC2 and UC4 (note that we do not include all the figures due to the available space). We can state that increasing the number of processes reduces the overall consumed energy. However, there is a point where the reduction is very small and the profile looks like a flat surface. Figure 3 plots

Algorithm 2. Second iteration - Curve refinement algorithm.

```
1: while num_used < 4 do
2:     extreme1 ← 1
3:     extreme2 ← 1
4:     max ← 0
5:     ind ← 1
6:     while extreme2 < 24 do
7:         extreme2 ← extreme2 + 1
8:         if flag_used(ind)! = 1 then
9:             if extreme1 + 1 == extreme then
10:                extreme1 ← extreme2
11:            else
12:                write(server, extreme1)
13:                energy_matrix(extreme1) ← read(server)
14:                write(server, extreme2)
15:                energy_matrix(extreme2) ← read(server)
16:                energy_interpol_m ← interp2(energy_matrix(extreme1), energy_matrix(extreme2))
17:                ind ← find_max_diff(energy_matrix, energy_interpol_m, extreme1, extreme2)
18:                energy_interpol(extreme1 : extreme2) ← energy_interpol_m
19:                extreme1 ← extreme2
20:                flag_used(ind) ← 1
21:                max ← 0
22:            end if
23:        end if
24:    end while
25:    figure(energy_interpol)
26:    writeInFile(energy_interpol)
27:    num_used ← num_used + 1
28: end while
```

the energy profile for the fifth use case UC5, which is a combination of UC3 and UC4, and that is the reason why it is also very similar to UC3. This profile includes features of UC4 by the end of the figure because the I/O intensity is dominant. As the frequency increases, the energy consumption increases as well, and the minimum energy point is with a frequency of 1.4 GHz. When we consider the number of processes, we can see that the more processes are included, the higher the energy consumption. The minimum frequency point is 1.4 GHz.

4.1 Energy Modeller Accuracy

In this section, we analyze the experimental results of the energy profile modeler. The comparison between the real and the interpolated models takes into account: (1) how the surface is refined during the modeler iterative process, and (2) the differences between the real and the model surfaces. In these examples, the interpolation is only done in four iterations because the results after the fourth iteration were very similar to the original one.

Figures 4 and 5 plot the interpolated energy profile model for UC1. It is important to highlight that in the first iteration, the profile is a plane using only two points. Then it is divided into two for the second iteration by taking a midpoint, and, including more data from new iterations, it becomes more like the actual CPU profiles. If we consider differences with the real profile, we can see that in the first iteration, there are differences between 100 J and 400 J. For four iterations, the maximum difference is 180 J between process numbers 2 and 4 and decreases to 0.03 J between 4 and 20 processes.

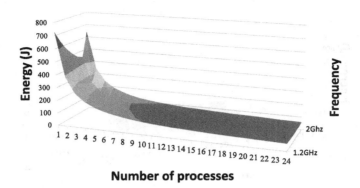

Fig. 2. Generalized energy profile to represent the use cases UC1, UC2 and UC4. Note that the colors on the graphs identify the energy range to which the points belong.

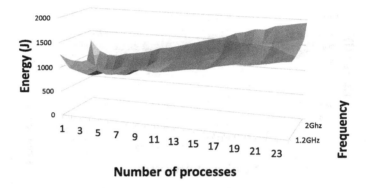

Fig. 3. Generalized energy profile that represents the use cases UC3 and UC5. Note that the colors on the graphs identify the energy range to which the points belong.

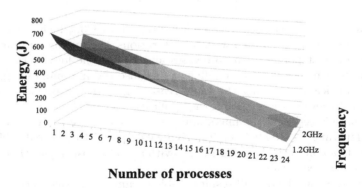

Fig. 4. Interpolated energy profile with 1 iteration refinement for use cases UC1, UC2 and UC4. Quantitative results are included in Tables 1 to 4.

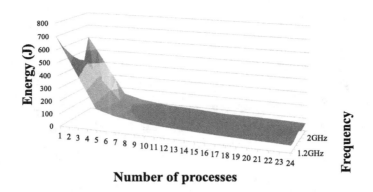

Fig. 5. Interpolated energy profile with 4 iteration refinement for use cases UC1, UC2 and UC4. Quantitative results are included in Tables 1 to 4.

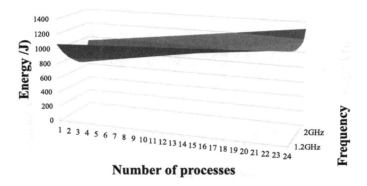

Fig. 6. Interpolated energy profile with 1 iteration refinement for use cases UC3 and UC5. Quantitative results are included in Tables 1 to 4.

In Figs. 6 and 7, we can see the modeler surface for UC3, which is very similar to UC5. Considering the profile with four iterations, the maximum difference is 190 J at the lowest points of the processes and 13 J at the lowest. In this case, the difference can have a greater influence because the minimum energy point location is unclean. Following the same reasoning as in the previous analysis, considering the lowest energy point, the application spends an energy of 531.51 J per iteration. Considering the maximum saving, we observe a saving of 59.50% per iteration (max. 1310.59 J per iteration). Compared to the real surface the model selects a non-optimal configuration with a 9.50% cost higher than the one obtained by the real surface.

In order to show the overall results, Table 1 summarizes the scheduling metrics based on minimizing only energy consumption. Table 2 depicts the scheduling results based on the cost function that provides the same weight to both energy and execution time. Next, Table 3 shows the scheduling results based on

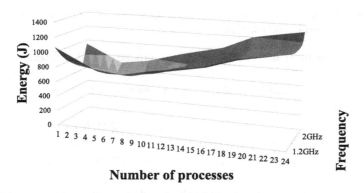

Number of processes

Fig. 7. Interpolated energy profile with 4 iteration refinement for use cases UC3 and UC5. Quantitative results are included in Tables 1 to 4.

Table 1. Summary table of scheduling results based on minimizing energy.

Profile	Configuration	Saving (%)	Interpolated conf.	Interpolated saving (%)
UC1	$24procs + 2.2\,GHz$	93.0	$24procs + 2\,GHz$	92.6
UC2	$24procs + 2.2\,GHz$	92.7	$10procs + 2.4\,GHz$	85.0
UC3	$3procs + 2.2\,GHz$	59.5	$5procs + 2.2\,GHz$	54.3
UC4	$8procs + 2\,GHz$	81.0	$7procs + 2.2\,GHz$	80.8
UC5	$3procs + 2\,GHz$	77.1	$1procs + 2.2\,GHz$	74.6

Table 2. Summary table of scheduling results based on cost function with more weight in energy.

Profile	Configuration	Saving (%)	Interpolated conf.	Interpolated saving (%)
UC1	$24procs + 2.2\,GHz$	93.0	$24procs + 2.2\,GHz$	93.0
UC2	$24procs + 2.2\,GHz$	92.7	$24procs + 1.6\,GHz$	92.4
UC3	$4procs + 2.2\,GHz$	59.0	$5procs + 2.2\,GHz$	54.4
UC4	$8procs + 2\,GHz$	81.0	$7procs + 2.2\,GHz$	80.8
UC5	$3procs + 2\,GHz$	77.1	$7procs + 2.2\,GHz$	73.2

the cost function, considering more importance to energy. Finally, Table 4 shows the scheduling results based on the cost function prioritizing execution time.

Regarding the interpolation, for some profiles, the energy saving is the same, and for others is a bit lower than the real one. However, we can compensate for the difference because the interpolation applies early to the best configuration. On the other hand, the scheduling results obtained using the cost function show similar savings to the energy minimization. However, taking into account that

Table 3. Summary table of scheduling results based on cost function with the same weight in energy and execution time.

Profile	Configuration	Saving (%)	Interpolated conf.	Interpolated saving (%)
UC1	$24procs + 2.2\,GHz$	93.0	$24procs + 2.2\,GHz$	93.0
UC2	$24procs + 2.2\,GHz$	92.7	$12procs + 2.4\,GHz$	87.7
UC3	$4procs + 2.2\,GHz$	59.0	$5procs + 2.2\,GHz$	54.3
UC4	$8procs + 2\,GHz$	81.0	$7procs + 2.2\,GHz$	80.8
UC5	$3procs + 2\,GHz$	77.1	$7procs + 2\,GHz$	73.2

Table 4. Summary table of scheduling results based on cost function with more weight in execution time.

Profile	Configuration	Saving (%)	Interpolated conf.	Interpolated saving (%)
UC1	$24procs + 2.2\,GHz$	93.0	$24procs + 2.2\,GHz$	93.0
UC2	$24procs + 2.2\,GHz$	92.7	$24procs + 2.2\,GHz$	92.7
UC3	$4procs + 2.2\,GHz$	59.0	$5procs + 2.2\,GHz$	54.4
UC4	$8procs + 2\,GHz$	81.0	$7procs + 2.2\,GHz$	80.8
UC5	$3procs + 2.2\,GHz$	76.5	$7procs + 2\,GHz$	73.2

some results are equal, even a bit lower, we consider it better to use this method because it allows the user to adjust the target of the cost function: saving energy or execution time.

5   Conclusion

In this work, we have introduced a dynamic energy-profile scheduler for MPI-based applications that integrates FlexMPI runtime and application modeling at run-time. The scheduler exploits the previous models to determine the best configuration (DVFS value and number of processes) for each application to reduce energy consumption. Finally, we have completed an evaluation on a real platform, which demonstrates that our proposal can minimize either the energy consumption and the execution time of the scheduled application. Finally, we are working on a machine learning model capable of predicting at near/real-time given the execution information (wall-clock time, energy, data used) that phase of the application execution is the next. With this information, we will be able to enrich the scheduler with global vision of which phase is going to be executed in the future improving the scheduling decisions.

References

1. A carbon crisis looms over supercomputing. how do we stop it?. https://www. hpcwire.com/2021/06/11/a-carbon-crisis-looms-over-supercomputing-how-do-we-stop-it/
2. Agrawal, P., Rao, S.: Energy-aware scheduling of distributed systems. IEEE Trans. Autom. Sci. Eng. **11**(4), 1163–1175 (2014)
3. Auweter, A., et al.: A case study of energy aware scheduling on SuperMUC. In: Kunkel, J.M., Ludwig, T., Meuer, H.W. (eds.) ISC 2014. LNCS, vol. 8488, pp. 394–409. Springer, Cham (2014). https://doi.org/10.1007/978-3-319-07518-1_25
4. Chen, J., He, Y., Zhang, Y., Han, P., Du, C.: Energy-aware scheduling for dependent tasks in heterogeneous multiprocessor systems. J. Syst. Architect. **129**, 102598 (2022)
5. Juarez, F., Ejarque, J., Badia, R.M.: Dynamic energy-aware scheduling for parallel task-based application in cloud computing. Futur. Gener. Comput. Syst. **78**, 257–271 (2018)
6. Lin, W., Shi, F., Wu, W., Li, K., Wu, G., Mohammed, A.A.: A taxonomy and survey of power models and power modeling for cloud servers. ACM Comput. Surv. (CSUR) 53, 1–41 (2020). https://doi.org/10.1145/3406208,https://dl.acm.org/doi/doi:10.1145/3406208
7. Martín, G., Marinescu, M.-C., Singh, D.E., Carretero, J.: FLEX-MPI: an MPI extension for supporting dynamic load balancing on heterogeneous non-dedicated systems. In: Wolf, F., Mohr, B., an Mey, D. (eds.) Euro-Par 2013. LNCS, vol. 8097, pp. 138–149. Springer, Heidelberg (2013). https://doi.org/10.1007/978-3-642-40047-6_16
8. PROJECT, T.S.: Impact environnemental du numÉrique : Tendances À 5 ans et gouvernance de la 5G (2021). https://theshiftproject.org/wp-content/uploads/2021/03/Note-danalyse-Numerique-et-5G-30-mars-2021.pdf
9. Schneider, D.: The Exascale era is upon us: the frontier supercomputer may be the first to reach 1,000,000,000,000,000,000 operations per second. IEEE Spectr. **59**, 34–35 (2022). https://doi.org/10.1109/MSPEC.2022.9676353
10. Ábrahám, E., et al.: Preparing HPC applications for Exascale: challenges and recommendations. In: Proceedings - 2015 18th International Conference on Network-Based Information Systems, NBiS 2015, pp. 401–406 (2015). https://doi.org/10.1109/NBIS.2015.61

Towards Achieving Transparent Malleability Thanks to MPI Process Virtualization

Hugo Taboada[1,2]([✉]), Romain Pereira[1,3], Julien Jaeger[1,2],
and Jean-Baptiste Besnard[4]

[1] CEA, DAM, DIF, 91297 Arpajon, France
hugo.taboada@cea.fr
[2] Université Paris-Saclay, CEA, Laboratoire en Informatique Haute Performance
pour le Calcul et la simulation, 91680 Bruyères-le-Châtel, France
[3] INRIA, EPI AVALON, ENS Lyon, LIP, Lyon, France
[4] ParaTools SAS, Bruyères-le-Châtel, France

Abstract. The field of High-Performance Computing is rapidly evolving, driven by the race for computing power and the emergence of new architectures. Despite these changes, the process of launching programs has remained largely unchanged, even with the rise of hybridization and accelerators. However, there is a need to express more complex deployments for parallel applications to enable more efficient use of these machines. In this paper, we propose a transparent way to express malleability within MPI applications. This process relies on MPI process virtualization, facilitated by a dedicated privatizing compiler and a user-level scheduler. With this framework, using the MPC thread-based MPI context, we demonstrate how code can mold its resources without any software changes, opening the door to transparent MPI malleability. After detailing the implementation and associated interface, we present performance results on representative applications.

Keywords: MPI · Malleability · Compiler

1 Introduction

The field of High-Performance Computing (HPC) is witnessing an increasing complexity in hardware, with hybridized architectures combining distributed and shared-memory parallelism along with accelerators. This requires programs to incorporate multiple programming models, potentially with diverse computing abstractions, to fully utilize the capabilities of the underlying computing substrate. This complexity has consequences both on the programs themselves and on their efficient utilization of the hardware. Programs in HPC are typically large simulation codes, often consisting of millions of lines of code. Therefore, adapting to new architectures is a planned and complex process. The chosen technology should be able to remain relevant for a sufficient duration to avoid

© The Author(s), under exclusive license to Springer Nature Switzerland AG 2023
A. Bienz et al. (Eds.): ISC High Performance 2023 Workshops, LNCS 13999, pp. 28–41, 2023.
https://doi.org/10.1007/978-3-031-40843-4_3

tying the codebase to a particular technology or vendor, necessitating parallelism abstractions [4]. The process is often piece-wise, leading to incomplete parallelism and parallel limitations due to fork-join patterns. Parallel runtimes play a crucial role in abstracting hardware changes. However, due to increasing hardware constraints, low-level behaviours start to impact applications. OpenMP is successful in porting *existing* code to new architectures in a piece-wise manner by adding `#pragma parallel for`. However, the slower adoption of recent OpenMP advances suggests that this is less effective for tasks and OpenMP targets, despite the preservation of optional pragmas. On the MPI side, the programming model is deeply embedded in most of the HPC payloads due to its robustness and ability to constantly evolve to handle new hardware while providing bare-metal performance. However, this strength is also a weakness as it encloses parallelism expression in a relatively low-level and fine-grained form. The end-users are directly using what could have become the "assembly" of a higher-level abstraction.

Our paper highlights the imminent complexity barrier that HPC is facing due to architectural evolutions and technical debt accumulated by HPC applications. Although runtimes have evolved and new abstractions have been provided, they often do not translate to applications [5, 19]. The empirical nature of the usage of supercomputers, driven by domain-specific scientists who are mainly interested in their results and given virtually unlimited computing power with little or no quota, has resulted in heuristics of doing good science that prioritize final results over efficient use of parallel machines. However, with the rise of GPUs and multi-level parallelism, the need for efficient use of parallel machines is more pressing than ever. Ideally, the solution would be to rewrite applications using new abstractions to address new hardware. However, this requires teaching domain-specific scientists how to code in parallel abstractions or providing them with tools that hide the complexity of parallelism. Several languages, including domain-specific ones, have tried to define more expressive ways of parallelizing programs [4, 17, 29]. Acknowledging the existence of inefficient (by design) and potentially transitively inefficient parts of parallel programs, the question of malleability then becomes preponderant.

2 Fast is Not Efficient

Time to result is not a correct heuristic to define how efficient a computation is. Indeed, from the well-known parallel efficiency formula, one may add computing resources to a computation while contributing only at the margin to the final result. As a consequence, sometimes a slower run is making much better use of the underlying hardware while leaving space for other runs on the freed resources [3, 10]. Malleability is the systematic and automated application of such reasoned running configuration for a given heuristic. And for more optimized applications, co-scheduling also provides opportunities for resource sharing for example during alternating phases of computing or to cope with load imbalance. In this work, we propose to implement transparent application co-location using the MPC thread-based MPI and a specialized compiler enabling the conversion of MPI+OpenMP applications to threads.

3   The Multi-processor Computing Runtime

MPC is a thread-based implementation of MPI, where MPI processes run in threads instead of traditional UNIX processes. This approach has various benefits, including reduced memory usage, faster launch times, and improved intranode messaging (see Sect. 6). Moreover, MPC has its own implementation of OpenMP and a user-level scheduler that is necessary for transparently running programs in co-routines, as discussed in Sect. 3.2. Additionally, MPC provides a specialized compiler that facilitates the porting of regular MPI+OpenMP codes to a thread-based context.

3.1   MPC Compiler Additions: Privatization

The process of converting global variables to Thread-Local Storage (TLS) variables using MPC's privatizing compiler [6] is crucial to enable the thread-based execution of regular MPI programs inside threads. This is necessary because global variables can cause conflicts when loaded in the same address space. The MPC privatizing compiler converts these global variables to MPC's TLS variables, which enables loading the same program multiple times in a single address space without any conflicts. The privatizing compiler is based on a modified version of GCC and includes a pass that converts global variables and other TLS levels (such as OpenMP thread-locals) to MPC's TLS. This pass has been implemented in a component called libextls (extended TLS) [6].

After a program has been privatized, it can be executed in the context of a thread, initially to meet the needs of a thread-based MPI. However, as we will discuss later in this paper, we aim to expand this concept to hybrid computing, where various executables are loaded in the same address space. In such a setup, the MPC runtime (MPI and OpenMP) can better address performance differences between the different applications.

3.2   User-Level Threads

Once MPI processes are threads, it becomes interesting to consider their execution inside user-level threads. This is a convenient way to hide waiting time, replacing it with context switches [31]. When a *task* is delayed, the resources can be used productively by moving to another task, instead of remaining in a busy loop. MPC is built around the concept of co-routines, and to make this approach viable, it is crucial to not only privatize threads but also to wrap the complete Pthread interface to capture potentially blocking calls, redirecting them to the scheduling loop inside MPC. Otherwise, a lock could be held by a pending task. Using MPC's $m{:}n$ scheduler, it is already possible to run two programs on the same resources in an oversubscribed fashion, meaning that the two programs will alternate on the underlying Pthread (co-routines).

By extending this idea to malleable programs, two programs can run on the same resources [25]. In addition, since MPI programs are now running inside threads, it is possible to move them on the node, changing their affinities. This is analogous to changing the target pending list in the scheduler without having to handle data dependencies, which can be complex in the case of regular MPI processes, but trivial in shared-memory. This extended support for threads and the user-level scheduler provides opportunities for fine-grained control over cross-scheduling of runtimes [13,18,32].

3.3 OpenMP Runtime

The MPC framework includes an OpenMP runtime that utilizes the same user-level thread and privatization infrastructures as the MPI runtime. This runtime is designed to be compatible with both GOMP and Intel/LLVM ABIs, enabling it to run OpenMP programs generated by different compilers. One significant advantage of co-locating both OpenMP and MPI threads in the same scheduler is the potential for runtime-stacking [11,28]. This refers to the idea of combining multiple runtimes for improved scheduling. Recent research has shown that it is possible to convert MPI waiting time into OpenMP task progress [32]. We aim to utilize this feature, in conjunction with privatization, in our co-scheduling approach, which relies on MPI process virtualization.

4 MPI Process Virtualization

MPI process virtualization is the process of converting MPI processes into threads within compute nodes [6,31]. This approach allows for new scheduling opportunities for parallel applications by implementing cross-job malleability at the node level, instead of relying on a single scheduler. In this section, we will provide an overview of this concept. We will discuss how it involves using a node-level scheduler, specifically MPC, to enable job malleability, resource sharing, and mitigation. Additionally, we will explore the compilation aspect of gathering multiple programs in the same binary and the executive part of leveraging OpenMP tasking, building on previous work [32], to optimize performance.

4.1 The Need for Node-Level Schedulers

As shown in Fig. 1a, a traditional HPC scheduler allocates resources based on UNIX processes. Typically, there is a one-to-one correspondence between UNIX processes and MPI processes. In contrast, our approach using MPC involves colocating and co-scheduling multiple programs within a single address space on each node, as illustrated in Fig. 1b. One advantage of this approach is that it requires fewer processes to run a given program. This is because there is no longer a direct mapping between UNIX and MPI processes; MPI processes

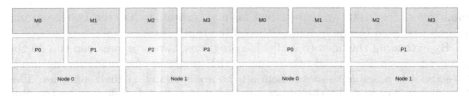

(a) Process-based MPI.   (b) Virtualized MPI processes.

Fig. 1. Comparison between regular scheduling approach and virtualized MPI processes.

are now threads. Furthermore, the work we present in this paper has indirect implications for malleability pivoting with a centralized scheduler (e.g., using the Process Management Interface or PMIx), as it can now be partially a local scheduling decision that is fully dynamic and arbitrary. Our two-level scheduling approach can leand to multiple profitable scenarios that have been explored in the literature:

- **Resource sharing** [1,12,16,22,24,30]: two applications residing in the same address space can dynamically exchange their resources without the need for copying or remapping of data. This allows the underlying scheduler to balance the compute resources from all collocated applications without complex code adaptation. For instance, two applications that require linear algebra computations on the node could have their respective tasks scheduled on the GPUs with a global view of the system, potentially achieving higher utilization than when allocating GPUs to each program separately.
- **Overprovisioning** [8,21,25,36]: in this configuration we run multiple applications per core, forcing them to alternate on the resources. In this case, the waiting time is directly recovered by the yield mechanism of the user-level scheduler, hiding latency. This case is of course bound to the availability of enough memory on the node.
- **Specialization** [14,15,35]: this opens the way to define in-process services providing facilities such as I/O to all programs running on the node in a very efficient manner (true zero-copy). Doing so may open the way to machines with smaller service islands, I/O being part of the job themselves with dedicated resources. This provides strong advantages to in-situ scenarios.

Overall, the main advantage of this two-level scheduler model is that scheduling decisions at the node level is now local, and there is no need to rely on an external component, except when more resources are needed. In the context of this work, we consider that we have colocated multiple applications in the same address space, and they now share their CPUs. Moving an application is now equivalent to moving a simple thread.

Therefore, as shown in Fig. 2, malleability inside the node becomes practical for any MPI+OpenMP application without requiring specific porting or modification. This is due to MPC's privatizing compiler that ensures applications

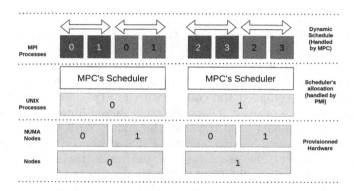

Fig. 2. Illustation of node-level malleability in the context of virtualized MPI processes.

can run inside threads, and we can simply adjust the resources allocated to each of these applications while sharing all the runtime components between the two programs. In the next section, we will describe how an application can be converted to a virtualized program inside MPC.

4.2   Virtualizing Programs

The process of virtualizing an existing program is very similar to the one done inside MPC for privatization purposes, which involves running the same program image multiple times in a single process [6]. It consists of compiling the program with a modified compiler that converts global variables and thread-local variables to the extended TLS hierarchy of MPC, which features an additional "process" level that matches each MPI process in the final runtime memory image. This process preserves TLS optimizations [6]. As shown in Fig. 1b, once this is done, and because the **main** function of the application has been renamed using a preprocessor directive, MPC simply launches N threads with their respective pinning, TLS context, and ranks to mimic the execution of the process in MPI, except that it is now in threads. This process has been reliably used by MPC to run C, Fortran, and C++ applications, with C++ being the most complex due to potential dynamic initializers, global objects, and templates. The idea of virtualizing MPI processes is not new and has a long research history [20,25,31]. AMPI [31], FG-MPI [26] and the Charm++ [24] runtimes have demonstrated many benefits of virtualized MPI processes, such as load-balancing [31] and dynamicity [23]. The closest related work to the idea we present in this paper is Adaptive Jobs [23]. This work moves the scheduler inside virtualized MPI processes and proposes to allocate programs in these address spaces. Conversely, in our approach, we stay much closer to the existing parallelism interfaces and runtimes, with the goal of transparently running *existing* programs in a virtualized configuration. This is only possible because MPC features its own OpenMP implementation and a Pthread interface to redirect locking calls to the user-level scheduler. When multiple programs are living in the same address space, there are opportunities for *runtime stacking*, and it is this aspect that we aim to highlight in this paper.

Returning to our initial goal of generalizing the approach to multiple programs, we needed to load multiple privatized programs in the same address space. To achieve this, we compiled the codes with the `-fpic -rdynamic -shared` flags, making the code position independent (as shared libraries) and exposing symbols in the final binary (and therefore the main). With this done, we were able to dynamically open binaries and their shared library dependencies with the help of the loader. The programs now run inside the same process, and we eventually replace their `MPI_COMM_WORLD` with a subset of the actual world, matching the actual program splitting. As MPC is also an MPI runtime, doing so is straightforward, as it simply involves replacing the communicator in the MPI process context. Note that this last step can become even more transparent using the session model, in which the application builds its `COMM_WORLD`, enabling explicit redirection. There are of course security issues when colocating programs in a single address space, and therefore such a scenario can only be envisioned for binaries belonging to the same user, and not as a way to run general programs in such a configuration. Memory segmentation from the Operating System and the zero-page mechanism are essential security measures to ensure perfect impermeability in between address spaces. Besides, signals are also handled by the controlling process and therefore, events such as `SIGINT` cannot be handled individually in such a configuration.

4.3   Co-scheduling Multiple Programs in a Single Process

Thanks to the nature of the MPC thread-based MPI+OpenMP runtime, multiple programs can run within a single UNIX process. Now comes the question of *co-scheduling* [2] each program to guarantee efficient progression of each application. The first possibility is through cores oversubscription with kernel threads (e.g., *pthreads*), letting the operating system preemptively schedule threads of each program. With n cores and $m > n$ threads, this is the $m{:}n$ co-scheduling approach. Oversubscription has been widely adopted in runtimes for overlapping synchronization idleness on cores, on AMPI [31] or LLVM OpenMP [34] for instance. Yet, it can degrade performances when a high number of asynchronous operations concurrently progresses [21,36], one source of overheads being the operating system [7,33]. The second possibility is an $n{:}n$ approach: each core is assigned a single kernel thread, and the scheduling decision is taken by the MPC user space scheduler. In particular, recent work on the MPC OpenMP *task* scheduler has shown improvement over the LLVM $m{:}n$ approach for target tasks offloading [18].

The final goal of our work, which we are yet to reach, is to deploy a co-scheduling approach as depicted on Listing 1.1. Line 1 to 6 corresponds to program dynamic loading, line 10 the $n{:}n$ threads binding is created. From lines 11 to 19, each program starts execution within an OpenMP task with its own *fiber*, which is an MPC extension hinting at the OpenMP runtime to execute tasks on their stack, enabling more scheduling flexibility. Descendant MPI processes, OpenMP parallel regions, and tasks created by each program will then run as part of a single MPC OpenMP task scheduler responsible for co-scheduling. Note that our execution model assumes tasks can migrate between *teams* which is not compliant with current OpenMP specifications and therefore still requires dedicated work. Recent work on Free Agent Threads [27] provided a solution to this limitation, improving the malleability of OpenMP tasking. Our execution model also relies on runtimes interoperability [32] so that a task blocking within an MPI call is automatically preempted instead of retaining its core.

Listing 1.1. Pseudo-code of the launcher wrapper

```
1   extern struct program_t {
2       int argc;
3       char ** argv;
4       int (*main)(int, char **);
5   } * programs;
6   extern int n_programs;
7
8   int main(void)
9   {
10      # pragma omp parallel
11      # pragma omp single
12      {
13          for (int i = 0 ; i < n_programs ; ++i)
14          {
15              program_t * p = programs + i;
16              #pragma omp task fiber
17                  p->main(p->argc, p->argv);
18          }
19      }
20      return 0;
21  }
```

5   Co-scheduling Experiment

In this section, we present the results of our initial experiments, which involved running applications on the same node in order to identify optimal execution times. The purpose of this setup was to identify potential "sweet spots" for execution time, which could eventually become more dynamic as shared-memory models used within applications become more flexible, particularly in terms of their ability to be invasive. However, it is important to note that the results presented here are limited by the static nature of the allocation used in our experiments.

In Fig. 3a, we show the scalability of the various kernels, which have different problem sizes and exhibit different strong scaling behavior. The smaller kernels exhaust their parallelism more quickly than the larger ones. This behavior is

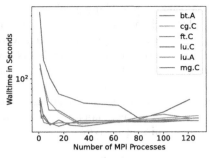
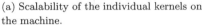
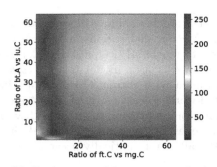

(a) Scalability of the individual kernels on the machine.

(b) Combination of four programs bt.A, lu.C, ft.C and mg.C over the machine (walltimes)

Fig. 3. Walltime for various resource breakdowns for co-located NAS MPI benchmarks.

also present in the individual nodes of larger simulations, particularly when considering dynamic behavior over time.

To further investigate co-location, we selected four of these benchmarks (bt.A, lu.C, ft.C, and mg.C) and ran them on a single node. As expected from the scaling behavior, there are sweet spots of scheduling for these four programs, which are indicated by the lower values in Fig. 3b. This suggests that dynamically reshaping jobs over time to follow these sweet spots could lead to improved performance. However, this can be difficult to accomplish through models alone, which is why our future work will focus on developing a node-level shared runtime to support malleability.

Co-locating programs is not a new idea, and several MPI runtimes and experiments dedicated to malleability have demonstrated similar gains to the ones we present here [2,9,24,30]. However, one of the main motivations for our work is that MPC can convert existing programs to shared-address space transparently, while still supporting regular MPI and OpenMP. This simplifies the process of making programs malleable and expands the range of applications that can benefit from this approach.

6   Networking Performance

As a thread-based MPI, MPC is capable of exchanging MPI messages between MPI Processes (now threads) running in the same process. In addition, it also supports all intermediate configurations, including a regular process-based execution. Besides, MPC has support for standard HPC networks, including SHM, Infiniband, Portals 4 BXI [?] interconnect and libFabric. It means co-scheduled programs can run distributed as regular MPI applications, malleability would only occur at the level of nodes, in between colocated programs thanks to the shared runtimes (mostly OpenMP for compute).

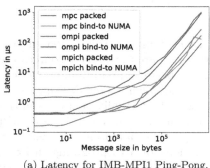
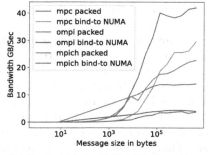

(a) Latency for IMB-MPI1 Ping-Pong.   (b) Bandwidth for IMB-MPI1 Ping-Pong.

Fig. 4. Comparison of MPC, OpenMPI and MPICH over various biding configuration using the IMB-MPI1 Ping-Pong benchmark.

Figure 4 presents the performance results of running the Intel IMB-MPI1 Ping-Pong benchmark between two processes co-located on the same node. This simple benchmark allows us to assess the relative bandwidth and latency performance between co-located programs. The tests were conducted on a bi-socket AMD EPYC 7413 machine with a total of 48 cores. The "packed" configuration means processes are running on nearby cores, while the "scattered" configuration means processes are spread across the two NUMA nodes. We measured the performance using MPC 4.1.0, OpenMPI 4.1.5, and MPICH 4.1, all of which were installed through spack using the default configuration flags.

In Fig. 4a, we observe that MPC has lower latencies for larger messages. However, for smaller messages, other runtimes, particularly OpenMPI, can perform better. The main reason for this is that in MPC, the THREAD_MULTIPLE support is always on, due to its thread-based nature, which leads to locking requirements and impacts the micro-optimizations needed to reach performance levels comparable to OpenMPI. However, thanks mostly to the improved bandwidth as messages are moved through direct memcpy (as shown in Fig. 4b), MPC yields lower latencies for larger messages. Other runtimes may use SHM fragments or more optimal Cross-Memory Attach (CMA) to transfer such large buffers, which are less direct than a regular *memcpy*.

Overall, we have demonstrated that running programs in shared memory with MPC can result in improved messaging bandwidth in some cases. This improvement is more pronounced for larger messages, but smaller messages still suffer from locking overhead. To address this limitation, we are currently in the process of fully rewriting the networking stack in the MPC runtime. Our goal is to improve performance and reduce overhead for all message sizes, further enhancing the benefits of running programs in shared memory with MPC.

7 Conclusion

High-performance computing architectures are evolving towards increased flexibility in utilizing node-level resources. However, shared-memory resources are often underutilized due to a lack of collaboration between programming models. For instance, MPI may get stuck in a busy-wait loop while OpenMP may have pending tasks. To address this issue, we utilized the virtualization capabilities of the MPC thread-based MPI + OpenMP runtime to transparently port MPI applications to a space where they can be adapted to shared memory with less effort. This process is analogous to what MPC does for MPI programs, utilizing its Extended TLS model. In this work, we presented two types of co-scheduling: oversubscription to eliminate busy waiting by using context yields and a unified scheduler that balances computing on a whole node, including between different virtualized programs. We also showcased the OpenMP code that we plan to use to achieve this.

We then conducted co-scheduling experiments that showed the potential for dynamic scheduling at the node level to compensate for imbalance and inefficiencies by opening a common task-oriented scheduler to all runtimes. Eventually, we have shown that by running in shared memory there were opportunities to improve MPI messaging performance. Going forward, we plan to further develop this work on the OpenMP side, seeking a practical way to define node-wide task stealing, which is currently not feasible between different parallel regions. This would enable OpenMP programs co-located in the same node (and virtualized in the same process) to dynamically balance their computations.

References

1. Acun, B., et al.: Parallel programming with migratable objects: Charm++ in practice. In: SC 2014: Proceedings of the International Conference for High Performance Computing, Networking, Storage and Analysis, pp. 647–658. IEEE (2014)
2. Aguilar Mena, J., Shaaban, O., Beltran, V., Carpenter, P., Ayguade, E., Labarta Mancho, J.: OmpSs-2@Cluster: distributed memory execution of nested OpenMP-style tasks. In: Cano, J., Trinder, P. (eds.) Euro-Par 2022. LNCS, vol. 13440, pp. 319–334. Springer, Cham (2022). https://doi.org/10.1007/978-3-031-12597-3_20
3. Arima, E., Comprés, A.I., Schulz, M.: On the convergence of malleability and the HPC PowerStack: exploiting dynamism in over-provisioned and power-constrained HPC systems. In: Anzt, H., Bienz, A., Luszczek, P., Baboulin, M. (eds.) ISC High Performance 2022. LNCS, vol. 13387, pp. 206–217. Springer, Cham (2023). https://doi.org/10.1007/978-3-031-23220-6_14
4. Beckingsale, D.A., et al.: RAJA: portable performance for large-scale scientific applications. In: 2019 IEEE/ACM International Workshop on Performance, Portability and Productivity in HPC (P3HPC), pp. 71–81. IEEE (2019)
5. Bernholdt, D.E., et al.: A survey of MPI usage in the us exascale computing project. Concurr. Comput. Pract. Exp. **32**(3), e4851 (2020)
6. Besnard, J.B., et al.: Introducing task-containers as an alternative to runtime-stacking. In: Proceedings of the 23rd European MPI Users' Group Meeting, pp. 51–63 (2016)

7. Bierbaum, J., Planeta, M., Hartig, H.: Towards efficient oversubscription: on the cost and benefit of event-based communication in MPI. In: 2022 IEEE/ACM International Workshop on Runtime and Operating Systems for Supercomputers (ROSS), Los Alamitos, CA, USA, pp. 1–10. IEEE Computer Society (2022). https://doi.org/10.1109/ROSS56639.2022.00007. https://doi.ieeecomputersociety.org/10.1109/ROSS56639.2022.00007

8. Bierbaum, J., Planeta, M., Härtig, H.: Towards efficient oversubscription: on the cost and benefit of event-based communication in MPI. In: 2022 IEEE/ACM International Workshop on Runtime and Operating Systems for Supercomputers (ROSS), pp. 1–10. IEEE (2022)

9. Bungartz, H.J., Riesinger, C., Schreiber, M., Snelting, G., Zwinkau, A.: Invasive computing in HPC with X10. In: Proceedings of the Third ACM SIGPLAN X10 Workshop, pp. 12–19 (2013)

10. Cantalupo, C., et al.: A strawman for an HPC PowerStack. Technical report, Intel Corporation, United States; Lawrence Livermore National Lab. (LLNL) (2018)

11. Carribault, P., Pérache, M., Jourdren, H.: Enabling low-overhead hybrid MPI/OpenMP parallelism with MPC. In: Sato, M., Hanawa, T., Müller, M.S., Chapman, B.M., de Supinski, B.R. (eds.) IWOMP 2010. LNCS, vol. 6132, pp. 1–14. Springer, Heidelberg (2010). https://doi.org/10.1007/978-3-642-13217-9_1

12. Cores, I., González, P., Jeannot, E., Martín, M.J., Rodríguez, G.: An application-level solution for the dynamic reconfiguration of MPI applications. In: Dutra, I., Camacho, R., Barbosa, J., Marques, O. (eds.) VECPAR 2016. LNCS, vol. 10150, pp. 191–205. Springer, Cham (2017). https://doi.org/10.1007/978-3-319-61982-8_18

13. Dionisi, T., Bouhrour, S., Jaeger, J., Carribault, P., Pérache, M.: Enhancing load-balancing of MPI applications with workshare. In: Sousa, L., Roma, N., Tomás, P. (eds.) Euro-Par 2021. LNCS, vol. 12820, pp. 466–481. Springer, Cham (2021). https://doi.org/10.1007/978-3-030-85665-6_29

14. Dorier, M., Dreher, M., Peterka, T., Wozniak, J.M., Antoniu, G., Raffin, B.: Lessons learned from building in situ coupling frameworks. In: Proceedings of the First Workshop on In Situ Infrastructures for Enabling Extreme-Scale Analysis and Visualization, pp. 19–24 (2015)

15. Duro, F.R., Blas, J.G., Isaila, F., Carretero, J., Wozniak, J., Ross, R.: Exploiting data locality in Swift/T workflows using Hercules. In: Proceedings of NESUS Workshop (2014)

16. El Maghraoui, K., Desell, T.J., Szymanski, B.K., Varela, C.A.: Dynamic malleability in iterative MPI applications. In: Seventh IEEE International Symposium on Cluster Computing and the Grid (CCGrid 2007), pp. 591–598. IEEE (2007)

17. Fanfarillo, A., Burnus, T., Cardellini, V., Filippone, S., Nagle, D., Rouson, D.: OpenCoarrays: open-source transport layers supporting coarray Fortran compilers. In: Proceedings of the 8th International Conference on Partitioned Global Address Space Programming Models, pp. 1–11 (2014)

18. Ferat, M., Pereira, R., Roussel, A., Carribault, P., Steffenel, L.A., Gautier, T.: Enhancing MPI+OpenMP task based applications for heterogeneous architectures with GPU support. In: Klemm, M., de Supinski, B.R., Klinkenberg, J., Neth, B. (eds.) IWOMP 2022. LNCS, vol. 13527, pp. 3–16. Springer, Cham (2022). https://doi.org/10.1007/978-3-031-15922-0_1

19. Hori, A., et al.: An international survey on MPI users. Parallel Comput. **108**, 102853 (2021)

20. Hori, A., et al.: Process-in-process: techniques for practical address-space sharing. In: Proceedings of the 27th International Symposium on High-Performance Parallel and Distributed Computing, pp. 131–143 (2018)
21. Iancu, C., Hofmeyr, S., Blagojević, F., Zheng, Y.: Oversubscription on multicore processors. In: 2010 IEEE International Symposium on Parallel & Distributed Processing (IPDPS), pp. 1–11. IEEE (2010)
22. Iserte, S., Mayo, R., Quintana-Orti, E.S., Pena, A.J.: DMRlib: easy-coding and efficient resource management for job malleability. IEEE Trans. Comput. **70**(9), 1443–1457 (2020)
23. Kalé, L.V., Kumar, S., DeSouza, J.: A malleable-job system for timeshared parallel machines. In: 2nd IEEE/ACM International Symposium on Cluster Computing and the Grid (CCGRID 2002), pp. 230–230. IEEE (2002)
24. Kale, L.V., Zheng, G.: Charm++ and AMPI: adaptive runtime strategies via migratable objects. In: Advanced Computational Infrastructures for Parallel and Distributed Applications, pp. 265–282 (2009)
25. Kamal, H., Wagner, A.: Added concurrency to improve MPI performance on multicore. In: 2012 41st International Conference on Parallel Processing, pp. 229–238. IEEE (2012)
26. Kamal, H., Wagner, A.: FG-MPI: Fine-grain MPI for multicore and clusters. In: 2010 IEEE International Symposium on Parallel & Distributed Processing Workshops and Phd Forum (IPDPSW), pp. 1–8 (2010). https://doi.org/10.1109/IPDPSW.2010.5470773
27. Lopez, V., Criado, J., Peñacoba, R., Ferrer, R., Teruel, X., Garcia-Gasulla, M.: An OpenMP free agent threads implementation. In: McIntosh-Smith, S., de Supinski, B.R., Klinkenberg, J. (eds.) IWOMP 2021. LNCS, vol. 12870, pp. 211–225. Springer, Cham (2021). https://doi.org/10.1007/978-3-030-85262-7_15
28. Loussert, A., Welterlen, B., Carribault, P., Jaeger, J., Pérache, M., Namyst, R.: Resource-management study in HPC runtime-stacking context. In: 2017 29th International Symposium on Computer Architecture and High Performance Computing (SBAC-PAD), pp. 177–184. IEEE (2017)
29. Marowka, A.: On the performance portability of OpenACC, OpenMP, Kokkos and RAJA. In: International Conference on High Performance Computing in Asia-Pacific Region, pp. 103–114 (2022)
30. Martín, G., Marinescu, M.-C., Singh, D.E., Carretero, J.: FLEX-MPI: an MPI extension for supporting dynamic load balancing on heterogeneous non-dedicated systems. In: Wolf, F., Mohr, B., an Mey, D. (eds.) Euro-Par 2013. LNCS, vol. 8097, pp. 138–149. Springer, Heidelberg (2013). https://doi.org/10.1007/978-3-642-40047-6_16
31. Pei, Y., Bosilca, G., Yamazaki, I., Ida, A., Dongarra, J.: Evaluation of programming models to address load imbalance on distributed multi-core CPUs: a case study with block low-rank factorization. In: 2019 IEEE/ACM Parallel Applications Workshop, Alternatives To MPI (PAW-ATM), pp. 25–36 (2019). https://doi.org/10.1109/PAW-ATM49560.2019.00008
32. Pereira, R., Roussel, A., Carribault, P., Gautier, T.: Communication-aware task scheduling strategy in hybrid MPI+OpenMP applications. In: McIntosh-Smith, S., de Supinski, B.R., Klinkenberg, J. (eds.) IWOMP 2021. LNCS, vol. 12870, pp. 197–210. Springer, Cham (2021). https://doi.org/10.1007/978-3-030-85262-7_14
33. Radojkovic, P., et al.: Measuring operating system overhead on CMT processors. In: 2008 20th International Symposium on Computer Architecture and High Performance Computing, pp. 133–140 (2008). https://doi.org/10.1109/SBAC-PAD.2008.19

34. Tian, S., Doerfert, J., Chapman, B.: Concurrent execution of deferred OpenMP target tasks with hidden helper threads. In: Chapman, B., Moreira, J. (eds.) LCPC 2020. LNCS, vol. 13149, pp. 41–56. Springer International Publishing, Cham (2022). https://doi.org/10.1007/978-3-030-95953-1_4
35. Vef, M.A., et al.: GekkoFS-a temporary distributed file system for HPC applications. In: 2018 IEEE International Conference on Cluster Computing (CLUSTER), pp. 319–324. IEEE (2018)
36. Wende, F., Steinke, T., Reinefeld, A.: The impact of process placement and oversubscription on application performance: a case study for exascale computing (2015)

A Case Study on PMIx-Usage
for Dynamic Resource Management

Dominik Huber[1]([⊠])[iD], Martin Schreiber[1,2][iD], and Martin Schulz[1][iD]

[1] Technical University Munich, Boltzmannstraße 3, 85748 Garching, Germany
{domi.huber,martin.schreiber,schulzm}@tum.de
[2] Université Grenoble Alpes, 621 Av. Centrale, 38400 Saint-Martin-d'Hères, France
martin.schreiber@univ-grenoble-alpes.fr

Abstract. With the increasing scale of HPC supercomputers efficient resource utilization on such systems becomes even more important. In this context, dynamic resource management is a very active research field, as it is expected to improve several metrics of resource utilization on HPC systems, such as job throughput and energy efficiency.

However, dynamic resource management is complex and requires significant changes to various layers of the software stack including resource- and process management, programming models and applications. So far, approaches for resource management are often specific to a particular implementation of the resource management and process management software, thus hindering interoperability, composability and comparability of such approaches.

In this paper, we discuss the usage of the Process Management Interface - Exascale (PMIx) Standard for interactions between the process manager and the resource manager. We describe an architecture that allows the resource manager to connect to the process manager as PMIx Tool to have access to a set of PMIx services useful for resource management.

In a concrete case-study we connect a python- and PMIx-based resource manager to PRRTE and assess the applicability of this architecture for debugging and exploration of dynamic resource management techniques. We conclude that a PMIx-based architecture can simplify the process of exploring new dynamic and disruptive resource management mechanisms while improving composability.

Keywords: Dynamic Resource Management · Process Management · PMIx

1 Introduction

HPC supercomputers are just entering the exascale era, which comes with a myriad of challenges such as energy efficiency, scalability of system software and resiliency [17]. To tackle these challenges, hardware technology, as well as system software and HPC applications need to be rethought under these new

A. Bienz et al. (Eds.): ISC High Performance 2023 Workshops, LNCS 13999, pp. 42–55, 2023.
https://doi.org/10.1007/978-3-031-40843-4_4

circumstances. In the area of system software, new ways have to be explored to make this software scalable and to improve the overall efficiency of resource utilization on the system.

In this context, hierarchical resource management software and dynamic resource management (where we consider malleability to be a subset of this) are very active research areas. In the last years, a large amount of research has been done ranging from theoretical work on dynamic resource scheduling [5,18,19] and simulations of dynamic scheduling strategies [8,9,20], to concrete implementations of mechanisms for dynamic resource management software [3,7,16,22,23] as well as runtime systems, programming models and applications (see, e.g., [4] for an overview of work). In these works, various benefits of dynamic resource management have been demonstrated. However, despite this large amount of research in this area, different dynamic resource management approaches often remain isolated from each other due to a lack of interoperability between the different solutions for the components in the system software stack as well as a high specialization on just one or a few applications.

To this end, we study the usage of PMIx [2] to increase the interoperability in the system software stack. PMIx is a programming interface standard providing an abstract interface for various services required on parallel and distributed systems, such as a distributed key-value store or an event notification system. Thus, PMIx can enable implementation-independent interactions between different system components. Despite providing an extensive API for the interaction between various components in the system software stack, so far PMIx has not been widely adopted. In most resource managers/process managers its usage is restricted to the small subset of its API required for bootstrapping parallel applications. One exceptions is the PMIx Reference Runtime Environment (PRRTE) [6], which provides a fully PMIx-enabled runtime environment. In the context of containerization techniques PMIx has also been used for the separation of application and runtime containers for running unprivileged HPC applications [15] and for enabling on-node resource management for containerized HPC workloads integrated into a hierarchical setup [24].

This work illustrates how PMIx could be used for portable interactions between the *Resource Manager (RM)* and the *Process Manager (PM)*. Here, we refer to the RM as the global system software responsible for managing and scheduling resources of the system. In contrast, we refer to the PM as the software managing the lifecycle of jobs and processes on the resources assigned by the resource manager.

We start by giving an overview of an architecture that allows PMIx-based interaction between the RM and the PM in Sect. 2. Then, in Sect. 3, we describe various possible PMIx-based interactions this architecture could provide for resource management, based on the specifications in the PMIx Standard 4.1 [21]. Subsequently, Sect. 4 presents a concrete case study of such a architecture, where we connect a Python- and PMIx-based dynamic RM to a modified version of the PMIx Reference Runtime Environment (PRRTE) to provide a testbed for dynamic resource management research. We conclude the paper by discussing and summarizing the key insights we gained from our case study in Sect. 5 and Sect. 6.

2   Overview of a PMIx-Based Architecture

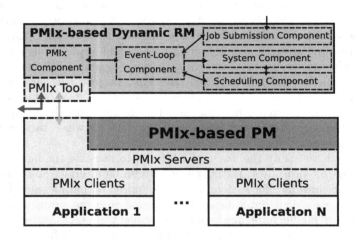

Fig. 1. Overview of an architecture for PMIx-based interactions between the Resource Manager (RM) and the Process Manager (PM). The bottom part represents the PM, which manages the execution of one or more applications. It operates PMIx servers to expose certain services to the application processes or other software components via the PMIx Client and PMIx Tool interface. The top part represents a RM manager consisting of various components. The PMIx component is responsible for managing the PMIx-based connection and interaction with the PM (yellow arrow) and possibly other system components (blue arrow) using the PMIx Tool interface. Note, that although the PM could potentially manage multiple applications across multiple nodes, the RM only needs to connect to one of the PM's PMIx servers, which facilitates the scalability of the approach. (Color figure online)

In this section we introduce a possible, basic architecture that enables PMIx-based interaction between the RM and the PM. An overview of this architecture is given in Fig. 1. The following subsections describe the three basic components in our architecture: PMIx, the PMIx-based PM and the PMIx-based RM.

2.1   PMIx

The central component in our architecture is PMIx. The PMIx standard defines PMIx as an "*application programming interface standard that provides libraries and programming models with portable and well-defined access to commonly needed services in distributed and parallel computing systems*" [21, p. 1]. This is achieved by providing an abstraction from the concrete system component using three generic roles: PMIx Server, PMIx Client and PMIx Tool. In the following we briefly introduce these PMIx roles.

PMIx Server: A process can initialize PMIx as PMIx Server using the `PMIx_server_init` function. Subsequently, PMIx Clients and PMIx Tools can connect to this PMIx Server, which gives them access to the PMIx services defined by the PMIx Standard. While some PMIx services can be serviced solely by the PMIx Server library implementation, usually interaction with the process that initialized the PMIx server library is required. To this end, during the initialization call, the process passes callback functions which enables the PMIx server library to pass on requests to be serviced by this process. The behavior of these callback functions is defined by the PMIx Standard, however, the concrete implementation needs to be provided by the hosting process. Thus, the PMIx server role provides an abstraction that can be used by system software components such as the PM to expose certain services.

PMIx Client: A process can initialize PMIx as PMIx Client using the `PMIx_Client_init` function, which establishes a connection with a local PMIx server. PMIx Clients are usually application processes launched by the process that hosts the PMIx server. Through the PMIx Client interface the launched processes have access to various PMIx services such as process synchronization and a distributed key-value store. In many MPI implementations MPI Processes use the PMIx Client role to interact with the MPI runtime environment, e.g., to exchange process wire-up information during MPI initialization.

PMIx Tool: A process can initialize PMIx as a PMIx Tool using the `PMIx_Tool_init` function. The PMIx Tools Interface is a superset of the PMIx Client Interface, providing additional functionality for establishing connections to PMIx servers and for I/O forwarding. PMIx Tools are able to connect to PMIx Servers on local as well as on remote hosts and are usually used for HPC tools, such as debuggers and launchers. We will use this interface for the connection between the RM and PM.

2.2   PMIx-Based Process Manager

PMs for distributed applications mange the lifecycle of applications and their processes. This involves launching and monitoring of application processes as well as process termination and cleanup. For this, PMs usually create an overlay-network of daemons on the compute nodes where the applications are running on. Beyond these basic functionalities, PMs often provide a varying degree of runtime services for applications.

Figure 1 (bottom) illustrates the concept of a PMIx-based PM. A PMIx-based PM is a PM that follows the PMIx Standard to provide its process management functionalities. For this, daemon processes usually initialize PMIx as a PMIx Server, i.e., the PM runs one PMIx Server per compute node. When launching applications, the application processes connect to the PMIx Server on their local node as PMIx Clients, giving them access to services of the PM exposed via PMIx.

2.3 PMIx-Based Resource Manager

The RM is responsible for the efficient execution of jobs on the system's resources. Figure 1 (top) illustrates the concept of a PMIx-based RM. A simple, PMIx-based RM could consist of the following components:

Event Loop Component: The event loop is the central component of the RM. It allows for thread-safe, serialized processing of events from different event sources. Events can be periodic, such as periodic invocations of the scheduling component, as well as non-periodic invocations, such as events triggered by notifications from the PM, e.g., to update the system state in the system component.

Job Submission Component: This component allows the submission of jobs to be executed on the system. While on production systems jobs usually are submitted *interactively* by users, for investigating novel resource management strategies it is preferable to *simulate* job submissions, e.g., by providing a job mix file with jobs and job arrival times. Submitted jobs are included in the job queue of the system component and are considered by the scheduling component.

PMIx Component: The PMIx component manages the connections and interactions with PMIx-enabled system software components. To this end, the PMIx Tools interface is used to connect, e.g., to the PMIx-based PM (dark yellow arrow in Fig. 1). This allows for various interactions, which are described in the next section. The PMIx Standard also allows tools to be connected to multiple PMIx servers. Thus, the PMIx component could possibly manage multiple connections (indicated by the blue arrow in Fig. 1), e.g., to multiple PMIx-enabled PMs or to a parent RM instance in a hierarchical resource management setup.

System State Component: The system state component provides a *representation of the current state of the system under management.* This includes for instance information about the usage of system resources such as compute nodes as well as information about currently running jobs and jobs in the job queue. Here, the PMIx component allows for tight interaction with other system software components to collect information about the current system state.

Resource Management Component: The resource management component is responsible for scheduling job execution and dynamic resource management during a job's lifetime based on the information of the system component.

To this end, an *instance of a resource management component* can be assigned to an *instance of the system state component.* This design allows to (dynamically) change the resource management strategy of the system and to facilitate the exploration of such strategies within a Python environment.

3   PMIx-Based Interactions for Resource Management

The architecture described in the last section provides the PMIx-based RM access to various PMIx functionalities of the PMIx Tool Interface. This section summaries some of these PMIx services and describes how they can be used by such an RM to interact with the PM. However, it is important to note that a PMIx-based PM might not provide support for all of these PMIx services listed below, or it might not support all of the attributes the PMIx standard defines for these services. For our case study in Sect. 4 we used a subset of these services.

3.1   Controlling Job Execution

An important area of interaction between the RM and PM are functionalities for controlling job executions. PMIx provides several functions related to job execution.

- `PMIx_Spawn`: Launches the specified number of instances of the given executable(s) on the specified resources. PMIx specifies various attributes that can be passed to further control properties of the job, such as I/O forwarding, event generation and logging. The RM can make use of this function to start jobs based on the scheduling decisions.
- `PMIx_Abort`: Aborts the specified processes. The RM could for instance use this function to abort jobs exceeding their time limit.
- `PMIx_Job_control`: Requests job control actions. Control actions include for instance, pausing, restarting or terminating processes, checkpointing and directory cleanup. The RM could use such control actions to enforce, e.g., fault tolerance or dynamic job co-scheduling strategies.

3.2   Retrieving System, Job and Process Information

Another requirement for the RM is to have access to system and application information relevant for the efficient management of the system resources. PMIx provides various functionalities to retrieve information about supported operations, system soft- and hardware as well as jobs, applications and processes. The RM can make use of these functions to retrieve information for its system state component, which can then be considered by its resource management component.

- `PMIx_Query_info`: Queries general information about the system. The PMIx Standard defines a rich set of query keys to be used to query system information. This includes queries for function and attribute supported by the PMIx implementation and host environment, names of running jobs, memory usage of daemons and application processes and statuses of jobs and application processes. The RM can make use of the query functionality to adjust its execution to the support level of the PM and to retrieve information for its system component.

- PMIx_Get: Retrieves key-value pairs associated with the specified process. This can be information about the process itself, as well as the session, job, application or node the process is associated with. The RM can use this functionality to retrieve information to be included in its system component, such as the mapping of a job's processes, or the memory size and CPU set of compute nodes.
- PMIx_Compute_distances: Computes relative distances from the specified process location to local devices such as GPUs, or network devices. This information could be included in the RM's system component to provide additional input to the resource management component, e.g., when dynamically assigning accelerators to jobs.
- PMIx_Fabric_(de)register: Registers access to fabric related information such as a cost matrix. The RM could include this information in its system component and use it in its scheduling decisions, e.g., to improve locality of communication.

3.3 Event Notification System and Logging

Finally, the last feature which is missing for the interaction between the RM and PM is the exchange of events. PMIx provides functionalities for event notification and logging. This allows the RM to record and react to changes of the system state and to inform the PM about reconfiguration decisions.

- PMIx_register_event/PMIx_Notify_event: Event Notifications are an important building block for the interaction between the RM and PM. Processes can use the PMIx_register_event function to register callbacks for particular event codes. The PMIx_Notify_event function can be used to send notifications of an event, thus triggering registered callbacks. The RM could for instance register callbacks for events triggered by the PM, such as job completion, node failures or reconfiguration requests. The PM could register callback for events triggered by the RM, such as job reconfiguration decisions.
- PMIx_Log: This function can be used to log data, such as events, to a data service. This can be useful to record and analyze the interactions between the RM and PM.

4   Case Study

In this section we present a case study of connecting a Python- and PMIx-based RM to a PMIx-based PM for debugging and exploration of dynamic resource management techniques. The code we develop and use in our work is included in a public repository [12]. The main objectives of this case study are a) to provide a proof-of-concept of a setup with a PMIx-based interaction between the RM and PM and b) reporting our experiences of using this setup to explore dynamic resource management techniques. We first describe our concrete setup and implementation in Sect. 4.1 followed by an evaluation based on a simple test case for dynamic resource management in Sect. 4.2.

4.1   Setup

In our setup, we closely follow the design described in Sect. 2 and we use a small subset of the possible interactions outlined in Sect. 3.

PMIx-Based Process Manager. For the PMIx-based PM we use a modified implementation of the PMIx Reference Runtime Environment (PRRTE). PRRTE is a fully PMIX-enabled PM for parallel and distributed applications and it is the native runtime environment of the Open MPI [11] implementation. It is capable of running and managing multiple jobs simultaneously, where each job can consist of multiple executables.

The PRRTE implementation we use in our setup is based on an implementation from prior work [10,13], which introduced dynamic MPI features to Open MPI, OpenPMIx and PRRTE. We extended the implementation from the prior version in two ways. First, we improve the flexibility of the dynamic MPI interface which will be described in a forthcoming publication. Second, we add support for connections with a PMIx-based RM. For this, we extend PRRTE's Resource Allocation Subsystem (RAS) framework and implement a RAS module for the interactions with our PMIx-based RM. This setup allows for single-application jobs to be reconfigured with node granularity based on the RM's resource management decisions, i.e., only full nodes can be added to or removed from applications.

Dynamic Resource Manager. We develop the (dynamic) RM entirely in Python to lay the fundament for future work on the fast prototyping of dynamic resource managers. So far we only investigate the basics of it. The user can specify the hostnames to be included in the managed system, the interval of the resource management loop and the file containing the job mix to be executed. At startup, it starts PRRTE using the

```
prterun --host hostnames --daemonize --mca ras timex --report-pid filename
```
command, which starts PRRTE on the specified hosts, daemonizes the DVM daemons into the background, selects our new RAS module and writes the PID of the PRRTE master process into the specified file. The design of the resource manager follows the component design from Sect. 2.3:

- **Job Submission Component:** The job submission component parses an input file containing a job mix. Each line is a job description in json format, containing the name of the job, the mpirun command to be executed and the arrival time.
- **PMIx Component:** The PMIx component makes use of the PMIx Python package that provides Python bindings for the PMIx Interface. PMIx is initialized as PMIx Tool and the connection to PRRTE is established using the PID reported by the prterun command. The interaction with PRRTE is based on only a small subset of the functionalities outlined in Sect. 3:
  - PMIx_Spawn is used to launch new jobs from the job queue.

- PMIx_Query is used to query the names of compute nodes, running jobs and process sets.
- PMIx_Get is used to query the mapping of processes on nodes.
- PMIx_register_event is used to register callbacks for events such as job termination, process set definition, job reconfiguration requests and finalization of job reconfigurations.
- PMIx_Notify_event is used to notify PRRTE about job reconfiguration decisions of the scheduler.

- **Event Loop Component:** For the event loop component the *asyncio* Python package [1] is used. We use a periodic event that checks for new submissions based on the information from the job submission component and executes the resource management policy. Based on the results of the resource management decision, it makes use of the PMIx component to launch new jobs or to communicate job reconfiguration decisions to the PM. Here, we like to briefly mention that the periodic event could lead to delayed resource management decisions, but could be replaced with events related to updates to the system-state components. However, this is not required in the present work.

- **System State Component:** The system state component stores a small set of information about the current system state. In our setup, the system state is characterized by the nodes available in the system, the jobs executing on these nodes, the processes included in each job and the current job reconfiguration requests. Moreover, the system state component provides a resource management function, which produces resource management decisions based on the currently assigned policy instance.

- **Resource Management Component:** The resource management component provides the resource management policy class with an abstract resource management function definition, allowing for different instances of such policies. A resource management policy instance can be assigned to the system state component dynamically.

4.2   Evaluation

We evaluate the applicability of our setup based on a concrete example. This example show-cases the usage of our setup in the context of debugging and exploring dynamic job reconfiguration and in particular resource management strategies.

Test System. As a test system we use a Docker-swarm based environment [14] to simulate the nodes of a compute cluster. For our tests we simulate a 4-node system, where each node has 8 cores and runs a CentOS based docker image. Such a docker based setup is optimal for fast debugging and exploration as it allows to simulate a multi-host environment on a local machine. Thus it is a convenient and efficient environment for the functionality experiments, which are the main goal of the present work. However, this setup is obviously not suited for any kind of realistic performance measurements, as it usually leads to oversubscription to simulate multiple nodes on a single machine.

Test Case. In our test case we compare the resource management of jobs exhibiting dynamically varying resource requirements with and without dynamic reconfiguration. We use a simple loop-based test application, which executes a 50 ms sleep command followed by an MPI Barrier in every iteration. In the static case (without reconfiguration) the number of processes remains the same for each iteration. In the dynamic case (with reconfiguration), the application can request a reconfiguration to add or remove processes before entering the next loop iteration. Here, we use a blocking approach, i.e., dynamic applications block until their reconfiguration request can be fulfilled. While such a blocking approach can obviously lead to deadlocks, it is sufficient for the functionality tests of the interactions between RM and PM, which are the main objective of this test case.

We execute test runs for two different job mix files containing two dynamic and two static jobs respectively. Table 1 lists the number of processes in each iteration for the dynamic and static jobs. In both cases, the arrival time for *job1* and *job2* is after 3.6 and 5.7 s, respectively. For the resource management we use a simple approach, which first attempts to start jobs from the job queue whenever there are enough system resources available. If no jobs can be launched, it checks if any job reconfiguration request can be fulfilled. The duration of the resource management loop is 0.3 s. We plan to replace this by events triggered by changes of the system state.

Table 1. Number of processes in each iteration.

Iteration	0–10	11–20	21–30	31–40	41–50	51–60	61–70
Job1 (dynamic)	8	16	8	24	8	32	8
Job2 (dynamic)	8	16	8	24	8	–	–
Job1 (static)	32	32	32	32	32	32	32
Job2 (static)	24	24	24	24	24	–	–

Results. Figure 2 shows a side-by-side comparison of the node occupation in the system at the beginning of each iteration of the resource management loop for the dynamic and static test run. In the static case *job1* occupies all nodes of the system during its entire runtime, thus preventing any other jobs to be started. In the dynamic case, *job1* grows step wise, which allows *job2* to be launched in iteration 19 and to be executed simultaneously. This allows for a higher job throughput in the dynamic case (37 resource management iterations vs. 46 resource management iterations). However, the individual time-to-completion of the jobs is higher in the dynamic case with 37 vs. 27 and 21 vs. 18 for *job1* and *job2* respectively. This is mainly due to the dynamic jobs blocking until resources are available for the requested reconfiguration. When comparing the node-hours (in terms of resource management iterations), the dynamic setup still provides benefits from the application perspective, with 69 vs. 108 and 35 vs. 72 iterations for *job1* and *job2*, respectively.

5   Discussion

Our case study demonstrated the applicability of the architecture described in Sect. 2 to enable PMIx-based interaction between the RM and PM and provides examples of concrete interactions for dynamic resource management using a subset of the functionalities described in Sect. 3. Based on the specifications in the PMIx standard, this architecture, in future work, can be integrated into a hierarchical resource management strategy, as described in Sect. 2.3.

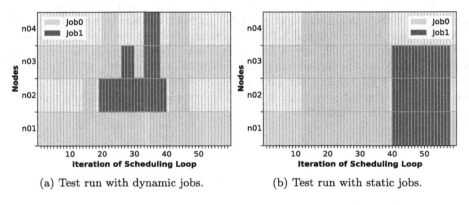

(a) Test run with dynamic jobs.   (b) Test run with static jobs.

Fig. 2. Node occupation during each iteration of the resource management loop using dynamic jobs (left) and static jobs (right).

We have shown how connecting a Python- and PMIx-based RM to a PMIx-based PM facilitates fast prototyping, debugging and exploration of dynamic resource management strategies. To this end, PMIx provides various benefits: First, it already provides a rich interface for managing and controlling resources and job executions, where we assessed its usability for at-least a basic PMIx-based setup for resource management. It maintains a separation-of-concerns between resource management and process management by acting as a messenger between these components. Thus, it reduces the time spent for implementing the communication protocol and allows to focus on exploring novel dynamic resource management strategies where we are convinced that these novel methods are required for convincing cases to make dynamic resource utilization a success. Second, it defines python bindings which allows for fast development and for the direct integration of python package for visualization, data analysis and mathematical models. This facilitates the debugging and comparison when exploring new techniques for dynamic resource management. Third, the usage of PMIx potentially allows for interchangeability of different RMs and PM that support PMIx, which could simplify the transfer from exploratory setups to production environments.

Our case study provided some valuable insight into various aspects of the usage of PMIx for resource management, however, it is also limited in some aspects:

Our tests were run inside of a docker environment and based on small-scale examples. While this is a convenient setup for development, debugging and prototyping, it can only provide limited insight into performance behavior and hardware related aspects. Thus, not all results from this setup are fully transferable to real HPC systems and large-scale experiments.

Moreover, while the specifications in the PMIx standard indicate that this architecture could be easily integrated into hierarchical resource management, in our case study we so far only provided a proof-of-concept for the case where the RM manages the resources assigned to the connected PM. A setup with deeper hierarchies remains to be demonstrated in future work.

6   Summary

The increase of the scale of HPC supercomputers introduces new challenges for system hardware and software. One of these challenges is to ensure efficient usage of the system's resources. To this end, scalable, dynamic resource management has gained significant interest over the last years. While there has been a large amount of work towards enabling dynamic resource management in different components of the system software stack, these attempts are often tailored towards particular implementations of these components and are often isolated from each other.

In this paper we investigated the usage of PMIx to facilitate portable interaction between the Resource Manager and Process Manager and to simplify the exploration of new resource management techniques. We first described a generic setup to enable a PMIx-based connection between the resource and process manager and describe possible interactions for resource management based on the PMIx Standard. We then described a case study based on a concrete implementation of the described setup and demonstrated its applicability to debug and explore dynamic resource management mechanisms and strategies. We see this as a proof of concept of a PMIx-based interaction between the resource manager and process manager which we expect to be an important building block for research on dynamic resource management.

In future work we will work on extending our implementation to support a hierarchical setup and use it to explore more sophisticated interactions and resource management strategies on real HPC systems.

Acknowledgements. We like to gratefully acknowledge Ralph Castain and Isaías Comprés for the discussions as part of the meetings of the PMIx Tools working group.

This project has received funding from the Federal Ministry of Education and Research and the European HPC Joint Undertaking (JU) under grant agreement No. 955701, Time-X and No. 955606, DEEP-SEA. The JU receives support from the European Union's Horizon 2020 research and innovation program and Belgium, France, Germany, Switzerland.

References

1. asyncio - asynchronous i/o. https://docs.python.org/3/library/asyncio.html
2. Castain, R.H., Solt, D., Hursey, J., Bouteiller, A.: PMIx: process management for exascale environments. Parallel Comput. **79**, 9–29 (2018). https://doi.org/10.1016/j.parco.2018.08.002
3. Ahn, D.H., Garlick, J., Grondona, M., Lipari, D., Springmeyer, B., Schulz, M.: Flux: a next-generation resource management framework for large HPC centers. In: 2014 43rd International Conference on Parallel Processing Workshops, pp. 9–17 (2014). https://doi.org/10.1109/ICPPW.2014.15
4. Aliaga, J., Castillo, M., Iserte, S., Martin-Alvarez, I., Mayo, R.: A survey on malleability solutions for high-performance distributed computing. Appl. Sci. **12**, 5231 (2022). https://doi.org/10.3390/app12105231
5. Bampis, E., Dogeas, K., Kononov, A., Lucarelli, G., Pascual, F.: Scheduling malleable jobs under topological constraints. In: 2020 IEEE International Parallel and Distributed Processing Symposium (IPDPS), Los Alamitos, CA, USA, pp. 316–325. IEEE Computer Society (2020). https://doi.org/10.1109/IPDPS47924.2020.00041
6. PMIx Administrative Steering Committee: PMIx-based reference runtime environment (PRRTE) (2023). https://github.com/pmix/prrte. Accessed 21 Apr 2023
7. Dai, Y., et al.: Towards scalable resource management for supercomputers. In: SC22: International Conference for High Performance Computing, Networking, Storage and Analysis, Los Alamitos, CA, USA, pp. 324–338. IEEE Computer Society (2022). https://www.google.com/url?sa=t&source=web&rct=j&opi=89978449&url=https://ieeexplore.ieee.org/document/10046103/&ved=2ahUKEwjb7PnelsGAAxXEOewKHfDhBpkQFnoECA4QAQ&usg=AOvVaw2gVV4Lq8_DZ9_6NCvwbPNC
8. Dupont, B., Mejri, N., Da Costa, G.: Energy-aware scheduling of malleable HPC applications using a Particle Swarm optimised greedy algorithm. Sustain. Comput. Inform. Syst. **28**, 100447 (2020). https://doi.org/10.1016/j.suscom.2020.100447
9. Fan, Y., Rich, P., Allcock, W.E., Papka, M.E., Lan, Z.: Hybrid workload scheduling on HPC systems. CoRR abs/2109.05412 (2021)
10. Fecht, J., Schreiber, M., Schulz, M., Pritchard, H., Holmes, D.J.: An emulation layer for dynamic resources with MPI sessions. In: HPCMALL 2022 - Malleability Techniques Applications in High-Performance Computing, Hambourg, Germany (2022). https://hal.science/hal-03856702
11. Graham, R.L., Woodall, T.S., Squyres, J.M.: Open MPI: a flexible high performance MPI. In: Wyrzykowski, R., Dongarra, J., Meyer, N., Waśniewski, J. (eds.) PPAM 2005. LNCS, vol. 3911, pp. 228–239. Springer, Heidelberg (2006). https://doi.org/10.1007/11752578_29

12. Huber, D.: Dynamic processes development repository. https://gitlab.inria.fr/dynres/dyn-procs
13. Huber, D., Streubel, M., Comprés, I., Schulz, M., Schreiber, M., Pritchard, H.: Towards dynamic resource management with MPI sessions and PMIx. In: Proceedings of the 29th European MPI Users' Group Meeting, EuroMPI/USA 2022, pp. 57–67. Association for Computing Machinery, New York (2022). https://doi.org/10.1145/3555819.3555856
14. Hursey, J.: PMIx docker swarm toy box (2021). https://github.com/jjhursey/pmix-swarm-toy-box
15. Hursey, J.: A separated model for running rootless, unprivileged PMIx-enabled HPC applications in Kubernetes. In: 2022 IEEE/ACM 4th International Workshop on Containers and New Orchestration Paradigms for Isolated Environments in HPC (CANOPIE-HPC), pp. 36–44 (2022). https://doi.org/10.1109/CANOPIE-HPC56864.2022.00009
16. Iserte, S., Mayo, R., Quintana-Ortí, E.S., Beltran, V., Peña, A.J.: DMR API: improving cluster productivity by turning applications into malleable. Parallel Comput. **78**, 54–66 (2018). https://doi.org/10.1016/j.parco.2018.07.006
17. Lucas, R., et al.: DOE advanced scientific computing advisory subcommittee (ASCAC) report: top ten exascale research challenges (2014). https://doi.org/10.2172/1222713
18. Marchal, L., Simon, B., Sinnen, O., Vivien, F.: Malleable task-graph scheduling with a practical speed-up model. IEEE Trans. Parallel Distrib. Syst. **29**(6), 1357–1370 (2018). https://doi.org/10.1109/TPDS.2018.2793886
19. Nagarajan, V., Wolf, J., Balmin, A., Hildrum, K.: Malleable scheduling for flows of jobs and applications to MapReduce. J. Sched. **22**(4), 393–411 (2018). https://doi.org/10.1007/s10951-018-0576-y
20. Özden, T., Beringer, T., Mazaheri, A., Fard, H.M., Wolf, F.: ElastiSim: a batch-system simulator for malleable workloads. In: Proceedings of the 51st International Conference on Parallel Processing, ICPP 2022. Association for Computing Machinery, New York (2023). https://doi.org/10.1145/3545008.3545046
21. PMIx Administrative Steering Committee (ASC): Process management interface for exascale (PMIx) standard version 4.1 (2021). https://pmix.github.io/uploads/2021/10/pmix-standard-v4.1.pdf
22. Prabhakaran, S.: Dynamic resource management and job scheduling for high performance computing. Ph.D. thesis, Technische Universität Darmstadt, Darmstadt (2016). http://tuprints.ulb.tu-darmstadt.de/5720/
23. Schreiber, M., Riesinger, C., Neckel, T., Bungartz, H.-J., Breuer, A.: Invasive compute balancing for applications with shared and hybrid parallelization. Int. J. Parallel Prog. **43**(6), 1004–1027 (2014). https://doi.org/10.1007/s10766-014-0336-3
24. Vallee, G., Gutierrez, C.E.A., Clerget, C.: On-node resource manager for containerized HPC workloads. In: 2019 IEEE/ACM International Workshop on Containers and New Orchestration Paradigms for Isolated Environments in HPC (CANOPIE-HPC), pp. 43–48 (2019). https://doi.org/10.1109/CANOPIE-HPC49598.2019.00011

Malleable and Adaptive Ad-Hoc File System for Data Intensive Workloads in HPC Applications

Genaro Sanchez-Gallegos[ID], Javier Garcia-Blas[(✉)][ID], Cosmin Petre[ID], and Jesus Carretero[ID]

University Carlos III of Madrid, Leganes, Spain
{gesanche,cpetre}@pa.uc3m.es, {fjblas,jcarrete}@inf.uc3m.es

Abstract. Advancement in storage technologies, such as NVMe and persistent memory, enables the acceleration of I/O operations in HPC systems. However, relying solely on ultra-fast storage devices is not cost-effective, leading to the need for multi-tier storage hierarchies to move data based on its usage. Ad-hoc file systems have been proposed as a solution, as they can exploit local storage resources and adapt the storage level to the needs of any particular applications. They allow to create a temporary file system that adapts to the application deployment in the HPC environment based on profiling of the application or hints from the users. Even assuming that the initial deployment fits well to the application, the I/O behaviour of an HPC application might change along the different execution phases of each application, thus changing I/O requirements. Ad-hoc file systems may supply those needs of the different phases by applying malleability techniques to extend or shrink the ad-hoc files system deployment on runtime following application I/O demands. This work presents the design, implementation, and evaluation of malleability techniques into the Hercules distributed ad-hoc in-memory file system. Those techniques allow to adapt (expand or shrink) the number of data nodes following a desired QoS metric. Our approach eliminates the necessity of migrating large amounts of data between data nodes. We are based on ruled-based distribution policies, which modify the placement mechanism with a low impact. Rules are orchestrated in terms of predefined thresholds. In the developed prototype, malleability techniques are applied to each deployment of the Hercules systems. Preliminary evaluation results show the feasibility of our solution.

Keywords: HPC I/O · Data intensive · Malleability · In-memory storage

This work was partially supported by the EuroHPC project "Adaptive multi-tier intelligent data manager for Exascale" under grant 956748 - ADMIRE - H2020-JTI-EuroHPC-2019-1 and by the Agencia Española de Investigación under Grant PCI2021-121966. This work was also partially supported by the Spanish Ministry of Science and Innovation Project "New Data Intensive Computing Methods for High-End and Edge Computing Platforms (DECIDE)" Ref. PID2019-107858GB-I00. Finally, we would like to thanks Marco Aldinuchi for providing the computing system.

A. Bienz et al. (Eds.): ISC High Performance 2023 Workshops, LNCS 13999, pp. 56–67, 2023.
https://doi.org/10.1007/978-3-031-40843-4_5

1 Introduction

Current scientific and engineering applications running on today's large-scale supercomputers are usually characterised by a data-intensive nature. A single application's workflow easily generates tens of terabytes of data, mostly produced by online operations [2]. Advancement in storage technologies, such as NVMe and persistent memory, enables the acceleration of I/O operations in HPC systems. However, relying solely on ultra-fast storage devices is not cost-effective, leading to the need for multi-tier storage hierarchies to move data based on its usage. Another weakness of existing HPC I/O systems is the semantic gap between the application requests and the way they are managed by the storage backend, as HPC I/O backend systems are installed to cope with all kind of applications that may be executed in a supercomputer and are not flexible enough to adapt to the applications' behaviour, specially for emerging data workloads, such as AI applications, data-intensive workflows, and domain-specific libraries. I/O patterns mainly dominated by reading files, using a large number of small files, or random access into files do not perform well in current HPC I/O systems, that have been designed for applications accessing a few very large files mostly sequentially [4].

Due to the appearance of these data-demanding high-performance applications, multiple software solutions have been introduced in an attempt to cope with challenges along the entire I/O software stack [6], such as high-level I/O libraries, parallel file systems, and I/O middleware, with a final objective consisting on reducing the amount of file system calls and offloading I/O functionalities from compute nodes, respectively. Those optimisations are even more important for data-intensive workflows, consisting of interdependent data processing tasks often connected in a DAG-style sequence, which communicate through intermediate storage abstractions, typically files. Therefore, developing methods that can manage the network and storage resources accordingly is a must [8].

Ad-hoc file systems have been proposed as a feasible solution, as they can exploit local storage resources and adapt the storage level to the needs of any particular applications [9,13]. They enable the creation of a temporary file system that adapts to the application deployment in the HPC environment based on profiling of the application or hints from the users. However, even assuming that the deployment of the ad-hoc file system fits well the initial application's I/O needs, the I/O behaviour of an HPC application might change along the different execution phases, thus changing I/O requirements, *e.g.*, workflows, machine learning applications, or large-scale simulations where the output of data depends on the simulation steps [11].

Applying malleability techniques, Ad-hoc file systems would be a possible solution to adapt the storage system to the I/O needs of the different phases of an application. Malleability would allow to extend or shrink the ad-hoc files system deployment on runtime following application I/O demands [3,12]. This work presents the design, implementation, and evaluation of malleability techniques into the Hercules distributed ad-hoc in-memory file system. Those techniques allow to adapt (expand or shrink) the number of data nodes following a desired QoS metric. Our approach eliminates the necessity of migrating large amounts of data between data nodes. We are based on ruled-based distribution policies, which modify the placement mechanism with a low impact and are orchestrated in terms of predefined thresholds. In the developed prototype, malleability techniques are applied to each deployment of the Hercules systems; preliminary evaluation results show the feasibility of our solution.

The outline of the paper is as follows. Section 2 present some background for ad-hoc file systems and malleability techniques. Section 3 shows the main features and design ideas of Hercules ad-hoc file system. Section 4 introduces the malleability techniques proposed in this paper. Section 5 presents the experiments made, and their results. Finally, Sect. 6 shows the main conclusions of the work.

2 Related Work

FlexMPI [12] is a runtime that provides dynamic load balancing and malleability capabilities for MPI applications. FlexMPI provides a coordinated way of using CLARISSE [5] and FlexMPI control mechanisms based on two different optimization strategies, with the aim of improving both the application I/O and overall system performance. The applications are analyzed using the monitoring components of CLARISSE and FlexMPI. These modules send the data to an external framework that gathers the information from all applications executed in the system, considering the CPU, communication, and I/O performances.

Ceph [1] presents BlueStore, a distributed file system implementing a storage backend deployed directly on raw storage devices. BlueStore works with an ordered key-value technique, with transactions as a write-ahead log. To face slow metadata operations (*e.g.*, directory enumeration (*readdir*) on large directories), they distribute objects among directories, sort some selected directories' contents, and kept directories with a small size by splitting them when the number of entries grows. BlueStore implements its own interface's specification with basic system calls (*open, mkdir, and pwrite*). Data is found using a space allocator that connects with a metadata service to determine available space.

Another interesting approach is Pufferscale [3], which studies the factors that affect rescaling operations and implements a rescaling manager for microservice-based distributed storage system. HEPnOS [10] is the High-Energy Physics's new Object Store, a distributed storage system specially designed for HEP experiments and workflows for the FermiLab. HEPnOS optimizes data accesses by storing small objects within their metadata, in a way similar to file systems storing data in their nodes when the data are small enough. Benchmarks should be executed on a given platform to establish the threshold below which embedding data inside metadata is advantageous. HEPnOS bypasses Mercury's serialization mechanism and relies on Boost. Serialization instead, in order to enable serializing C++ objects with minimal changes to the user code.

Finally, a similar approach that takes advantage of in-memory burst buffer is UnifyFS [7]. This file system accelerates scientific I/O based on scalable metadata indexing, co-located I/O delegation, and server-side read clustering and pipelining. However, the current version lacks of directory-based operations and data consistency. Note that Hercules delegates the data replication to each distribution policy.

3   Hercules Ad-Hoc File System

As shown in Fig. 1, the architectural design of Hercules follows a client-server design model. Hercules is an ad-hoc file system that can be deployed by each application, which is responsible for the metadata and data server entities deployment. Each application process will be connected to Hercules through a frontend layer. This way, each application can adjust the dimensions of each Hercules deployment to fit its I/O needs. That means that there could be many deployments of Hercules in the same computer system, as we are going to show, but they will be independent to protect data isolation.

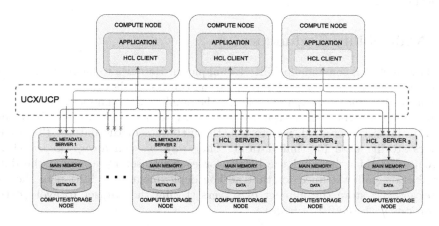

Fig. 1. Architecture of an Hercules deployment following a client-server design model, where the clients (applications) communicates to the metadata and data servers through UCX/UCP framework.

The development of the present work was strictly conditioned by a set of well-defined objectives. Firstly, Hercules provides flexibility in terms of deployment. To achieve this, multiple location server conforming an instance counts with a dispatcher thread and a pool of worker threads. The dispatcher thread distributes the incoming workload between the worker threads with the aim of balancing the workload in a multi-threaded scenario. Main entities conforming the architectural design are Hercules clients (frontend), Hercules data (1 to M) and metadata (1 to N) nodes (backend). Addressing the interaction between these components, the Hercules frontend exclusively communicates with the Hercules metadata servers whenever a metadata-related operation is performed, such as *create* and *open*. Data-related operations will be handled directly by the corresponding storage server calculated in the frontend side. Thus, global data mapping is not needed at all levels. Finally, Hercules offers to the application a set of data distribution policies at dataset level, increasing the application's awareness about the data location A dataset is a collection of data elements with a fixed size that are distributed among the storage servers of a single Hercules instance, according to a specific data distribution policy. As a result, the storage system will increase awareness in terms of data distribution at the client side, providing benefits such as data locality exploitation and load balancing.

In Hercules, applications are able to determine critical parameters like the data distribution policy, which is settled at dataset level and establish how data blocks are distributed among Hercules data nodes. Currently, Hercules counts with the following policies: ROUND ROBIN, BUCKETS, HASHED, CRC16bits, CRC64bits, and LOCAL. Data distribution policy can be setup specifically for each ad-hoc deployment of Hercules. This policy is established for all datasets of that ad-hoc deployment. In this work, we use the ROUND ROBIN data distribution policy as default.

4   Malleability Techniques

We have included some malleability techniques in Hercules to facilitate dynamic modifications of the number of data nodes on runtime. Following the application I/O needs, Hercules can expand or shrink the number of data nodes to increase or reduce I/O throughput of the application. In any ad-hoc deployment of Hercules, when a dataset is created, we store in the metadata of the dataset the list of servers storing data for that dataset. That way, we can always know where Hercules should write/read the blocks for each dataset by applying the data distribution policy defined for that ad-hoc deployment. In addition to the list of servers, we store the number of servers storing the dataset to avoid extra operations with the list of nodes.

4.1   Firing Malleability Operations

In Hercules, malleability operations can be started by two alternatives sources: external controller or internal heuristic. We provide an API to enable an *external controller* to pass as argument the new number of servers and the list of new data nodes to be added/removed from an Hercules ad-hoc deployment. In this case, Hercules will expand/shrink that deployment following the controller commands. Additionally, Hercules provides an *internal heuristic* to determine whether a malleability operation should be carried out. In our system, an application can define a recommended I/O throughput (RIO) for the I/O system. As an application executes, Hercules is tracking the actual throughput provided by the I/O system to the application (AIO), with three possible results: near the RIO (N_{io}), below the RIO (B_{io}), and above the RIO (A_{io}). The distance to the throughput is currently computed using a time series of the throughput obtained by the write/read throughput of the consecutive operations of the application on the different datasets. The distance for an I/O operation is computed as the difference between the RIO and the AIO:

$$d_i = AIO_i - RIO_i, \forall\ i\ 1..n \tag{1}$$

We use a sliding window with a size k to decide which is the behaviour of the system based on the average distance for the sliding window values:

$$avg_d = \text{average}(d_j, d_{j+1}, \ldots, d_{j+k}) \tag{2}$$

We also used a predefined throughput tolerance threshold (T_{io}) to determine the near, below or above situation of the I/O throughput, as shown below:

$$state = \begin{cases} -1, & \text{if } avg_d > (RIO + T_{io}) \\ 0, & \text{if } avg_d \in [RIO - T_{io}, RIO + T_{io}] \\ 1, & \text{if } avg_d < (RIO - T_{io}) \end{cases}$$

where a *state* equals to -1 means B_{io}, 0 is N_{io} and 1 is A_{io}.

The sliding window size can be adjusted to fit the behaviour of applications with changing I/O demands. So, Hercules will take three possible decisions:

- Keeping the same number of servers (N_{io}),
- On-line *commissioning* for expanding the file system servers (B_{io}), or
- Off-line decommissioning for shrinking the file system servers (A_{io}).

Following the former definitions, an Hercules dataset can be in three stages: *commissioning, decommissioning, or ready* (initial status), which is also reflected in the metadata entry.

4.2   Expanding the Hercules File System

To expand a deployment of Hercules, we have designed an on-line *commissioning* mechanism for increasing the file system servers that avoids blocking I/O operations while resources are got. When B_{io} is activated, Hercules asks for new server nodes to the resource manager of the system (RMS) and keep on working until the resources are available; the deployment status is set as *commissioning*.

When the resources are obtained, new servers are connected to the ad-hoc deployment, and they will be used for new datasets, that will include in the metadata the new number of servers and the increased list of servers; the deployment status is set as *ready* and new datasets will start using the extended deployment. Already existing datasets keep on using the servers previously allocated for the existing blocks, and will start using the extended deployment for new blocks. A dataset of an extended deployment will be then defined as a list of block intervals, when the number of intervals depends on the number of malleability operations made. It will usually be small, as we do not foresee to have many malleability operations on an ad-hoc deployment.

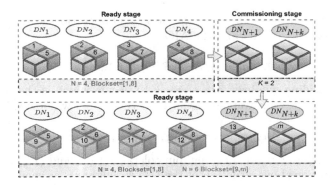

Fig. 2. Extending an Hercules deployment. Applied a ROUND ROBIN policy for block-set distribution.

One important question is to calculate the number of servers to be added to the current deployment. Again, if an external controller indicates the number and the list, Hercules will just add those processes to the current deployment. If our internal heuristic is used, the distance metric is applied to calculate the number of new servers to be requested to the RMS. More specifically, we use the average distance to compute an estimation of the throughput to increase the number of servers.

Figure 2 shows the *ready* and *commissioning* stages of the malleability process. As you can see, on the *ready* stage Hercules works with four file system servers (see $DN_{1...4}$, where DN is a Data Node where a file system server is running), and by using the ROUND ROBIN data distribution policy, the datasets 1 to 8 are distributed along them. Then, after the *commissioning* stage, two extra file system servers are added (see $DN_{N+1...N+k}$), which are used by Hercules following the same policy. Thus mechanism allows to use the new servers without overhead to migrate data if not needed. The only thing to do is to discriminate block location considering the interval associated to the servers commissioned when the block was created.

We are already working to provide an offline migration mechanism to consolidate formerly existing datasets to use all nodes of an extended deployment. This mechanism will be executed if the application makespan is long enough to compensate the overhead of the migration. The basic idea consists of expanding the interval allocated to reduced server sets to the extended one, avoiding locking the blocks, except in the very moment of copying each block individually.

4.3   Shrinking the Hercules File System

Figure 3 depicts the execution workflow in case of an off-line decommission. Once the target data node is select (red box in the figure), datasets using this data node

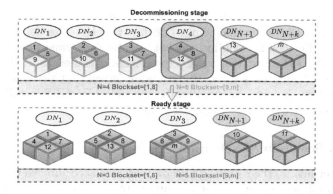

Fig. 3. Shrinking in Hercules. Blue and green blocks represent the previously extended dataset, and purple blocks correspond with a different dataset. (Color figure online)

are marked as decommissioning state, so updates are blocked up to decommission/data balancing is completed. Data balancing is needed to speed up decommission operations and to stabilise the duration and performance of all re-scaling operations.

Malleability follows a bottom-up approach. Once decommissioning is started, metadata nodes notify to clients that both the number and layout of data nodes have changed. Then, clients wait up to receive a final message informing that decommission/data balancing is completed. During this procedure, data nodes migrate data blocks to the new corresponding data node. This data redistribution aims to reduce the data staging costs and also to maintain the data distribution policy. Hercules provides two alternatives for performing data balancing: 1) a total redistribution of data blocks that requires a costly data movement between all data nodes; 2) partial redistribution, which aims to minimise data movement in case of dealing with small files (as shown in Fig. 3).

5   Experimental Evaluation

In this section we describe the experiments conducted to evaluate Hercules performance, the evaluation environment setup, and the results obtained from the tests made. The hardware used to carry out the experiments consists of a 64-nodes cluster running Ubuntu 20.04.5 LTS. Each node is equipped with two Intel Xeon CPU E5-2697 v4 16-Core processors with a total of 32 physical cores and a clock speed per core of 2.6 GHz. Network topology is created with three switches conforming a fat-tree network of two levels. All the compute nodes are connected through Intel Omni-path network reaching a peak performance of 100 Gbps. The software employed is UCX 1.15, OpenMPI 4.1 and *glib*. UCX exposed OPA network using *ibverbs* library, reaching a similar bandwidth comparing with the native OpenMPI installation.

Experimental results were obtained using the IOR benchmark, a widely-used solution for measuring I/O performance at scale. The evaluation metrics shown in this paper correspond with the average value of 10 consecutive executions. This subsection shows the evaluation results of comparing Hercules doing malleability operations (on-line commissioning) against a static deployment by using 2 to 16 data nodes. We performed two set of experiments classified as weak and strong scalability. We show results up to 16 data nodes given that this number reaches the bandwidth peak performance. Finally, the global BeeGFS installation offers a maximum of 7.5 GB/s (one single data node).

5.1 Weak Scalability Evaluation

In those experiments, the resulting file size increases according to the number of clients deployed, since every client is writing 100 MB to a shared file. We have evaluated on-line commissioning (see Sect. 4.2) and the malleability has been configured to use up to 16 data nodes. For example, in a configuration of 4 data nodes, a static configuration will perform all the operations with this value, but with the malleability configuration this value is taken as a lower bound (the initial data nodes) and then, during execution time, the system will allocate more nodes (with a maximum of 16) depending on I/O needs.

Figures 4a and 4b plot the throughput for both write and read operations using a block size of 256 KB. In general, for write operations, Hercules gets a better performance by using *malleability* compared with their corresponding *static* configuration. When we set the lower bound to 2 data nodes, malleability configuration has a performance gain of 57.54% in the best case and 1.10% in the most limiting case (16 clients/16 servers). We can observe that when the number of data nodes increase, the difference between the malleability's throughput and static's throughput decrease, as we are closer to the number of available data nodes. When we reach the maximum number of nodes, the system lacks of resources to be expanded, thus malleability generates a small overhead. We have forced this situation when comparing a 16/16 deployment, appreciating an overhead of 1.10% due to malleability operations. For read operations, we can observe a different behaviour; the performance gain is 24.48% and 4.99% for 2 and 4 data nodes respectively, for 8 data nodes there is no difference (less than 0.0003%) and in the last one malleability has a gain of 1.12% for a 16/16 deployment. This is due to the data locality in the experiments and cannot be associated to malleability effects. In the case of read operations, we saturate the network with a small number of data nodes.

Figures 4c and 4d show the throughput for write and read operations using a block size of 1 MB. We can observe in both situations (malleability and static) an increment in the general throughput compared with a 256 KB block size. For write operations, Hercules has a performance gain from 54.72% to 22.96% with 2 to 8 data nodes and a loss of 3.87% with 16 data nodes, again caused by the overhead of implementing malleability operations. In case of read operations with 2 data nodes, Hercules obtains a performance gain of 23.53%, getting the best performance with 8 data nodes with a performance gain of 1.26%.

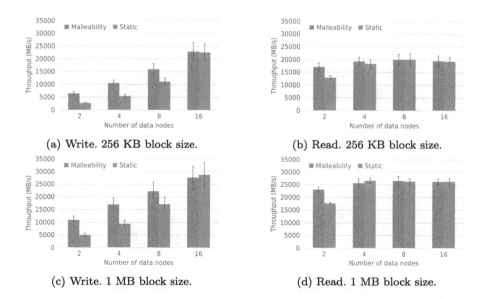

(a) Write. 256 KB block size.   (b) Read. 256 KB block size.

(c) Write. 1 MB block size.   (d) Read. 1 MB block size.

Fig. 4. Weak scalability evaluation when fixing 16 compute nodes and 1 process per compute node.

5.2 Strong Scalability Evaluation

For strong scalability tests, we set the size in 1 GB, then we divide it between the number of clients to get how many MB should be writing per client. Figures 5a and 5b show the throughput for write and read operations using a block size of 256 KB. For write operations, we can observe a performance gain from 57.83% to 30.12% with 2 to 8 data nodes by using malleability. Additionally, we get an overhead of 3.02% when there are 16 data nodes compared with the static situation. Whereas, for read operations we can see that only with 2 data nodes, Hercules implementing malleability get a notable performance gain of 18.64%, while for 4 and 16 data nodes the performance gain is 1.10% and 0.85% respectively, and for 8 data nodes there is a loss of 0.38%. Figures 5c and 5d show the throughput for write and read operations using a block size of 1 MB. For write operations, we can depict the same behaviour compared with the 256 KB block size configuration, with the difference that using a bigger block (1 MB) the overall throughput increase with an average speedup of 1.47x. In this experiment, malleability has a performance gain from 51.98% to 4.42% for 2 to 16 correspondingly. For read operations, we get an average speedup of 1.10x comparing with the 256 KB block size's configuration, obtaining a performance gain of 13.27% and 9.07% with 2 and 16 data nodes.

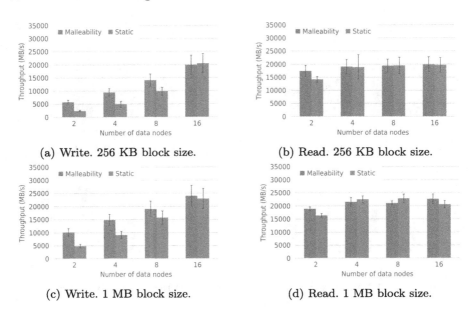

(a) Write. 256 KB block size.

(b) Read. 256 KB block size.

(c) Write. 1 MB block size.

(d) Read. 1 MB block size.

Fig. 5. Strong scalability evaluation when fixing 16 compute nodes and 1 process per compute node. Shared file of 1 Gbyte.

6 Conclusions

This work presented the design, implementation, and evaluation of malleability techniques into the Hercules distributed ad-hoc in-memory file system. Malleability techniques allow to adapt (expand or shrink) the number of data nodes following a desired QoS metric. Our approach eliminates the necessity of migrating large amounts of data between data nodes. We are based on ruled-based distribution policies, which modify the placement mechanism with a low impact. Rules are orchestrated in terms of predefined thresholds. In the developed prototype, malleability techniques are applied to each deployment of the Hercules systems. Preliminary evaluation results show the feasibility of our solution and the increase of performance obtained when there are resources available to expand the system. Future work is going on to compute distance metrics with a larger number of experiments to elaborate heuristics to take better decisions and to predict the need of commissioning and decommissioning data server nodes. Additionally, we plan to measure the impact of I/O malleability on metadata nodes. Storage on metadata nodes follows a similar design of data nodes, so its implementation is straightforward.

References

1. Aghayev, A., Weil, S., Kuchnik, M., Nelson, M., Ganger, G.R., Amvrosiadis, G.: File systems unfit as distributed storage backends: lessons from 10 years of Ceph evolution. In: Proceedings of the 27th ACM Symposium on Operating Systems Principles, pp. 353–369 (2019)
2. Ahn, D.H., et al.: Flux: overcoming scheduling challenges for exascale workflows. Futur. Gener. Comput. Syst. **110**, 202–213 (2020)
3. Cheriere, N., Dorier, M., Antoniu, G., Wild, S.M., Leyffer, S., Ross, R.: PufferScale: rescaling HPC data services for high energy physics applications. In: 2020 20th IEEE/ACM International Symposium on Cluster, Cloud and Internet Computing (CCGRID), pp. 182–191. IEEE Computer Society, Los Alamitos (2020)
4. Chowdhury, F., et al.: I/O characterization and performance evaluation of BeeGFS for deep learning. In: Proceedings of the 48th International Conference on Parallel Processing, ICPP 2019. Association for Computing Machinery (2019)
5. Isaila, F., Carretero, J., Ross, R.: CLARISSE: a middleware for data-staging coordination and control on large-scale HPC platforms. In: 2016 16th IEEE/ACM International Symposium on Cluster, Cloud and Grid Computing (CCGrid), pp. 346–355 (2016)
6. Isaila, F., Garcia-Blas, J., Carretero, J., Ross, R., Kimpe, D.: Making the case for reforming the I/O software stack of extreme-scale systems. Adv. Eng. Softw. **111**, 26–31 (2017). Advances in High Performance Computing: on the path to Exascale software
7. Moody, A., et al.: UnifyFS: a distributed burst buffer file system - 0.1.0 (2017). https://www.osti.gov/biblio/1408515
8. Narasimhamurthy, S., et al.: SAGE: percipient storage for exascale data centric computing. Parallel Comput. **83**, 22–33 (2019)
9. Rodrigo Duro, F.J., Marozzo, F., García Blas, J., Carretero Pérez, J., Talia, D., Trunfio, P.: Evaluating data caching techniques in DMCF workflows using Hercules (2015)
10. Ross, R.B., et al.: Mochi: composing data services for high-performance computing environments. J. Comput. Sci. Technol. **35**, 121–144 (2020)
11. Rosti, E., Serazzi, G., Smirni, E., Squillante, M.S.: Models of parallel applications with large computation and I/O requirements. IEEE Trans. Softw. Eng. **28**(3), 286–307 (2002)
12. Singh, D.E., Carretero, J.: Combining malleability and I/O control mechanisms to enhance the execution of multiple applications. J. Syst. Softw. **148**, 21–36 (2019)
13. Vef, M., et al.: GekkoFS - a temporary distributed file system for HPC applications. In: 2018 IEEE International Conference on Cluster Computing, pp. 319–324 (2018)

Towards Smarter Schedulers: Molding Jobs into the Right Shape via Monitoring and Modeling

Jean-Baptiste Besnard[1]([✉]), Ahmad Tarraf[2], Clément Barthélemy[3], Alberto Cascajo[4], Emmanuel Jeannot[3], Sameer Shende[1], and Felix Wolf[2]

[1] ParaTools SAS, Bruyères-le-Châtel, France
`jbbesnard@paratools.fr`
[2] Department of Computer Science, Technical University of Darmstadt, Darmstadt, Germany
[3] INRIA Bordeaux, Bordeaux, France
[4] Computer Science Department, University Carlos III of Madrid, Madrid, Spain

Abstract. High-performance computing is not only a race towards the fastest supercomputers but also the science of using such massive machines productively to acquire valuable results – outlining the importance of performance modelling and optimization. However, it appears that more than punctual optimization is required for current architectures, with users having to choose between multiple intertwined parallelism possibilities, dedicated accelerators, and I/O solutions. Witnessing this challenging context, our paper establishes an automatic feedback loop between how applications run and how they are launched, with a specific focus on I/O. One goal is to optimize how applications are launched through moldability (launch-time malleability). As a first step in this direction, we propose a new, always-on measurement infrastructure based on state-of-the-art cloud technologies adapted for HPC. In this paper, we present the measurement infrastructure and associated design choices. Moreover, we leverage an existing performance modelling tool to generate I/O performance models. We outline sample modelling capabilities, as derived from our measurement chain showing the critical importance of the measurement in future HPC systems, especially concerning resource configurations. Thanks to this precise performance model infrastructure, we can improve moldability and malleability on HPC systems.

Keywords: Monitoring · Performance Modeling · MPI · IO · Malleability

1 Introduction

A few decades ago, programmers did not have to change their code to gain efficiency, as the benefits of the sequential Moore's law were not depleted, and it was possible to run the same code faster without any effort. However, as outlined

A. Bienz et al. (Eds.): ISC High Performance 2023 Workshops, LNCS 13999, pp. 68–81, 2023.
https://doi.org/10.1007/978-3-031-40843-4_6

in the well-known quotation "free lunch is over", power dissipation constraints have forced us to rely on multiple cores per socket and thus transitively led to compulsory shared-memory parallelism. With applications running in MPI+X (with X typically being OpenMP) to address inter- and intra-node parallelism, the execution space already grew substantially. Indeed, if MPI is suitable for memory locality as it works in distributed address space by nature, it is not the case for OpenMP which then required careful handling at a time OpenMP places were not devised. As a consequence, one of the practical ways was to run one MPI process per NUMA node and then rely on shared-memory parallelism inside each memory region. If we now continue our journey towards current hardware, the pressure on energy consumption has advocated for simpler (or specialized) cores, leading to the democratization of GPUs or, more commonly, accelerators. It means that from now on, a non-negligible part of the computation has to run on specialized hardware, which leads to data movements inside the node, from and to the accelerator. And again, these data movements are typically associated with at least affinity preferences (NUIOA) [15] or capacity constraints (stacked HBM, memory-mapped GPU memory, split address space, etc.). We are now at a point where the layering of runtime configurations and constraints are difficult to untangle – generally leading to inefficient use of parallel systems simply because of the difficulty of exploring the execution space.

Starting from this convoluted scenario, we can add a layer of complexity now unfolding in the HPC field: the horizontalization of computing [13, 32]. Indeed, HPC software tends to be relatively monolithic, often due to the bulk-synchronous bias of MPI. It means features end up stacked in the same binary as shared libraries and the program alternates between the various functions over time. However, due to complexity constraints, this is probably about to evolve towards a specialization of the software components [35], if not simply as a mirror of the underlying hardware specialization. As a result, the program is likely to become more composite, creating several pieces communicating in workflows [1] or collocated in situ during the run. Similarly to what has been advocated around power constraints in PowerStack [2, 6, 32], we consider this process cannot be manual and should be generalized. The programmer should define the workflow (i.e., dependencies), and computational needs (memory, device) but addressing how to run shall be automated.

2 From Ad-Hoc to Always-On Monitoring

Understanding and examining an application's performance is crucial not only for efficient system utilization but also for identifying performance bottlenecks at an early stage, including during the execution. Given the complexity of these systems, performance limitations at any level can significantly impact the application's performance. E.g., Parallel file systems (PFSs) like Lustre and GPFS, form the storage backbone of HPC clusters and have been developed for over two decades. As they have been extensively optimized to support traditional compute-bound HPC applications, which sequentially read and write large data files [7], PFS cannot handle all types of workloads effectively (e.g., Deep learning workloads). This aspect can have such an impact that the I/O performance for identical workloads can differ by more than 200 times depending on the time when the workloads are executed [23]. In general, performance variability, which is the difference between execution times across repeated runs in the same execution environment, is far from being eliminated and will remain an active research area as several studies have suggested [26,27].

Still, monitoring and modeling the performance of an application is an aspect that future systems require for optimal throughput. In light of heterogeneous computing and the current trends toward using programming models focusing on job malleability, characterizing an application's performance is crucial for application developers, as well as for system optimization. Considering malleability, e.g., a balance between the compute and I/O resources is required to utilize the different underlying components of a system effectively. Without detailed knowledge in both aspects, resource management of malleable jobs would be closer to random guessing. Once the monitoring data is available, performance models can be systematically generated to drive scheduling.

In this context, we present a monitoring infrastructure developed in the ADMIRE project, with a particular focus on the trade-offs the infrastructure relies on to provide always-on low overhead measurement capabilities. In the second part, we generate performance models with *Extra-P* [5], which exceed the computational aspect and consider also I/O. Then, we apply these monitoring and modeling capabilities to actual applications with the goal of defining dynamically what is the best configuration to launch them, either for efficiency or finding the best I/O configuration. Finally, we discuss how this work sets the basis for systems only featuring self-configured jobs and approaches like malleability.

3   On Performance and Execution Spaces

The execution space for applications can be complex due to current hardware. Indeed, what used to be mono-variadic (i.e., only the number of MPI processes) is now becoming a much more intricate space [3]. With compulsory shared-memory parallelism and accelerators, programs have to obey several constraints to run in their optimal configuration. From the user perspective, supercomputers are means for producing results, and therefore, end-users often optimize for *time-to-result*. This leads to running at the largest scale possible to minimize this *time-to-result*. However, looking closely at existing parallel execution descriptors, such a heuristic doesn't necessarily lead to efficient execution.

Overall, there are two main ways of running a parallel program on an HPC system. On one hand, one wants to accelerate computing, leading to **strong scaling** "If I double the dedicated resources I want my execution time to be divided by two". Strong scaling is limited by the sequential part of the program and facilitated by larger problem sizes. On the other hand, **weak scaling** "If I double both the problem size and resources, I want to run for the same time";

leads to payloads where the problem size increases with the number of cores [4]. Understanding how a program behaves is thus correlated with the ability to track down multiple executions of the same program, and more precisely the same test case in several configurations. Indeed, in current HPC machines, a program is bound to run in a non-linear space; The same problem can be solved on MPI, MPI+OpenMP, and even with accelerators such as GPUs. This leads to a combinatorial space where previously mentioned scalability rules are still valid. Exploring this space empirically is now impractical and therefore auto-mated measurement and modeling capabilities are needed to obtain the correct configuration for its target problem – we foresee the process in the context of *smart schedulers*.

4   The Need for Smarter Schedulers

As mentioned, the job execution space is getting increasingly larger [3]. In addi-tion, programs are getting more horizontal, running either as workflows or cou-pled computation (in-situ [13] or services oriented [35]), which increases further the combinatorial aspect. Consequently, we are convinced that manually launch-ing programs is not realistic anymore as the target space is too large to be empir-ically explored. As programming models are facing difficulties hiding hardware complexity, requiring changes in programs (i.e. hybridization), the same is true for launch configurations which now suffer from this lack of abstraction.

As outlined in the second part of the paper, thanks to a monitoring infras-tructure, it should be possible to build models of running applications to drive launch configurations over time. This major shift in how programs are launched naturally requires a change in habits – efficient resource usage not being an option anymore. It is important to note that our approach is not exclusive to our particular implementation and that by design it has to fit in a larger shared effort between standards and runtimes [19].

So, taking all of this into account, a smarter scheduler would enable a large set of optimizations [29] over several system components, including:

- **improved backfilling:** by leveraging model projection, jobs can be molded to improve their chance of being backfilled, improving platform utilization.
- **automated job configuration:** choose the configuration for jobs too max-imize efficiency. This is elaborated in Sect. 7.1.
- **reconfiguration:** if a job can run on both CPU and GPU, the scheduler may choose depending on availability while being aware of the efficiency difference.
- **job horizontalization:** as the service island in machines probably get smaller, the scheduler could be the pivot to *service* side components such as I/O back-end [8] on demand. This is a core aspect in the ADMIRE project, which features ad-hoc filesystems [35].

After, contextualizing our approach with related work, the following sections illustrate a possible implementation of such a smarter scheduler. After introduc-ing the monitoring and modeling architecture (Sect. 6), we show how it can be applied to two use cases (Sect. 7).

5 Related Work

The concept of running parallel programs in the right configuration is not new, and several attempts have been made to provide such a feature, commonly known as *auto-tuning* [3,16,17,37], which involves exploring the execution space of a program to find optimal configurations. Our contribution follows the same approach but with a unique focus on systematizing it at the scheduler level. This systematization introduces specific monitoring requirements, such as always-on monitoring and data management challenges. A similar effort to our ADMIRE project is PowerStack [38], which focuses on power optimization rather than I/O. In the PowerStack framework, similar needs for measurement and performance models are identified, with the ultimate goal of optimizing overall resource usage. However, our approach differs in its generalization to all launch parameters including I/O backend, combining moldability and at-term malleability to leverage performance models. We believe that moldability gains have not been depleted yet by current approaches, despite being simpler to implement compared to malleability. In terms of the monitoring approach, a closely related contribution is the Data-Center Data-Base (DCDB) [25], which shares many aspects with our model. In our approach, as we will further outline, Prometheus manages this role and aggregation is done directly on the node, including from the target application, Overall, our methodology is similar in that it systematically manages application metrics by design.

In HPC systems, the resources are managed by the Resource Management System (RMS), which is responsible for multiplexing resources between multiple users and jobs. This component becomes more crucial in dynamic environments running moldable and malleable applications. Typical RMSs can configure the resources for a job before the execution, whereas dynamic applications require an RMS capable of reshaping the resource allocations at runtime [10,34]. Several efforts are looking into this, including the PMIX standard [19] but such support for malleability is not mainstream. Authors in [20] proposed CooRMv2, an RMS that is able to give more/fewer resources to the executing jobs based on their requests. This approach relies on pre-allocated resources estimated from peak usage, which can result from underutilization. D'Amico et Al. [11] proposed a new job scheduling policy for malleable applications to increase the response of the jobs. This approach differs by using shared computing nodes for all possible jobs, instead of exclusive node allocations. While this reduces job response time, interference between jobs in the same node could affect the results (CPU, memory, I/O, etc.). Developing smart schedulers for dynamic environments in HPC can yield many benefits for all (researchers and developers). The executions could be more efficient, reduce job completion times, and improve the global system performance.

6 ADMIRE Monitoring Infrastructure

Our proposal aims to measure how applications run to fine-tune them before or during their execution. With a particular focus on I/O, the project features several ad-hoc file systems [14,22,35], each with its specificities. By building this feedback loop between the expression of a job and its parameters, the project aims at defining a new way of using parallel machines due to a generalized auto-tuning approach crossing all layers of the parallel machine. These measurements can then be leveraged to reconfigure the run when it starts (i.e. moldability), either choosing the right scale to run or the right ad-hoc file system. This can also be done at runtime (i.e. malleability). However, we focus on moldability in this paper since it is already benefiting from this infrastructure, which fulfils the malleability constraints. Among these constraints, we have first the ability to model all runs, enforcing *always-on* measurements. Transitively, the measure has to be *low-overhead* not to impact performance. A second aspect related to programmability is that it should be non-intrusive by default as malleability supposes a holistic view of the system. Consequently, the ADMIRE monitoring infrastructure focused on the interception of the parallel programming interfaces, voluntarily leaving the applicative side apart. We developed instrumentation layers for MPI, and for the ad-hoc file systems part of the project. Similarly, to capture the I/O syscalls, we have modified *strace* to attach and detach from running programs to provide on-demand data. The goal in maintaining this data variety in the system is to provide a large set of information to feed potential models guiding the dynamicity decisions. To do so, the time series for each node and profiles per job are generated by a dedicated component relying on the *TAU metric proxy*.

6.1   TAU Metric Proxy

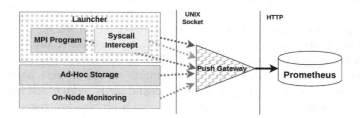

Fig. 1. Interconnection with the aggregating push gateway to implement on-node always on counter tracking.

As time-based metrics are critical when making dynamic decisions (i.e., as such decisions have to be done over time), we decided early in the project to store them in a dedicated Time-Series Database (TSDB). One of the most prominent ones is Prometheus, which has a significant record of usage in production while remaining simple and heavily interfaceable thanks to its HTTP-based interface. Prometheus *pulls* data from a variety of *exporters*, which are practically HTTP servers embedded in the various components of interest. The database then regularly accumulates values over time to store as time series. While this scheme is excellent for composability, it faces challenges in the HPC context as it is not affordable to open an HTTP listening socket in each MPI process and to dynamically track all running processes. To solve this problem, we had to design a *push gateway* which allows components to push data inside Prometheus. Note that there were existing push gateways but none of them was designed for HPC as they rely on HTTP. As shown in Fig. 1, the *TAU metric proxy* is an aggregating push gateway based on UNIX sockets, capable of handling hundreds of local clients. The client-side library is a single C file that allows forwarding the counters in an opt-in manner. The performance counters are stored in memory at the client level, and polling threads send them periodically over the UNIX socket to the push gateway for decoupling. When reaching the server, two arrays accumulate the values, one for the given job and another for the whole node. In addition, a global summative system view at high frequency is provided by a Tree-Based overlay Network (TBON) thanks to the LIMITLESS [9] monitoring infrastructure, which is coupled to the proxy. This architecture allows several distinct components to contribute to node-level counters in a scalable manner, in Fig. 1, we have the application, its launcher, the strace wrapper, the ad-hoc file system and node-level monitoring pushing data concurrently. Conjointly, the Prometheus time-series database polls the metric-proxy HTTP server which holds the aggregated state for the node, inserting new points and time series inside the database for data persistence. At a given moment, the metric proxy only holds a single value for all the counters and exposes them dynamically when receiving an HTTP request using the OpenMetric Format. In addition, the measurement chain can only handle counters due to the summative nature of the measurements, a common design approach when creating Prometheus collectors as storage relies on delta encoding. In addition, PromQL, the language allowing arbitrarily complex queries to the performance database includes means of computing derivative (`rate` function) to infer dynamic behaviours over time.

To complement this node-level view with a per-job one, when all participants of a given job have disconnected, the per-job array is released and stored in the file system according to the *Slurm* job-id. We run a metric proxy on each node, meaning that we maintain performance counters on a per-node basis. Per-job profiles are also generated on a per-node basis and lazily aggregated from the file system to create a single summed-up profile. Such profiles are generated for all jobs and stored in a dedicated *profile storage directory*. Conjointly, we designed a Python library to read and compare values from these profiles. Besides, each profile contains meta-data describing the associated job, including time span, allocation parameters, and spanning nodes.

6.2 Performance Modeling

Performance modeling has a long research history [5,17,28,31,36]. These models were usually used to generate scalability models that show how the runtime scales in accordance with one or more execution parameters, one of them often being the number of processors. Extra-P, for example, is an automatic performance-modeling tool that generates empirical performance models. A performance model is a mathematical formula that expresses a performance metric of interest (e.g., execution time or energy consumption) as a function of one or more execution parameters (e.g., size of the input problem or the number of processors). The tool has a long research history, with recent updates adding noise-resilient empirical performance modeling capabilities to use cases such as Deep Neural Networks [31] or statistical meaningfulness [30].

To generate performance models, Extra-P requires repeated performance measurements. It is suggested that at least five measuring points per parameter should be performed. By profiling an application, the required data for model generation can be collected. Moreover, by continuously passing data from the Prometheus database, it is possible to continuously improve the models. So far, Extra-P has been used to model the call path of the application, focusing on computational and communication aspects but excluding I/O. Though recent terms, such as the storage wall [18], try to quantify the I/O performance bottleneck from the application scalability perspective. Indeed, due to the fact that I/O subsystems have not kept up with the rapid enhancement of the remaining resource on an HPC Cluster, I/O bottlenecks are often encountered due to various aspects (I/O contention, hardware restrictions, etc.). Thus, there is a need to analyze the scalability behaviour in regard to I/O as well. Thus, instead of developing a new tool, we used Extra-P to generate performance models for various I/O metrics. This is done by providing the I/O data in an Extra-P compatible format. Moreover, when using the JSON Lines format, the continuously collected I/O monitoring data can be appended to such a file, allowing us to refine the performance models whenever more data is available. This becomes especially interesting if several I/O metrics are captured alongside significant computational metrics. By generating several performance models, we can judge the computational I/O intensity of an application regarding the number of processors. Moreover, if we model, e.g. the write bandwidth over the number of nodes or MPI ranks, we can depict which roofline in Fig. 2a is encountered and can hence decide on using burst buffers to counter such a scenario.

In the context of a *smart scheduler*, Extra-P is used to generate either offline or online models corresponding to all executions on a system. These models are then leveraged to guide decisions with respect to optimization criteria as mentioned in Sect. 4.

7   Use-Cases

This section shows two examples of heuristics driving job configuration. We start with an auto-tuning job configuration to maintain running jobs within a given time frame. As a second example, we show how job requirements in terms of I/O can be extracted from relatively compact metrics linked to bandwidth and I/O operations per second (IOPS).

7.1   Deadline Scheduling of Moldable Jobs

In this section we focus on moldability. However, this approach can be extended for malleability, i.e. changing configuration at runtime. The reason we consider this use case as relevant is that we are convinced that the moldability gains have

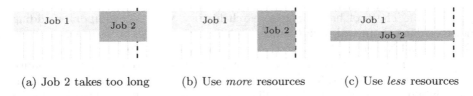

(a) Job 2 takes too long   (b) Use *more* resources   (c) Use *less* resources

Fig. 2. Molding job 2 to fit a deadline. Job 1 is fixed. There are two possibilities: either use more resources to accelerate job 2, i.e. scale up; or use fewer resources to take advantage of the scheduler backfilling policy. Solution (c) is better because it reaches the deadline using less resources, which is more efficient.

not been depleted. To validate and implement our moldability goals, we base our first implementation of a *smart scheduler* on a simple shell script wrapping the Slurm command line. More precisely, let us assume that the user wants to run a job with a given *deadline* (e.g. the job needs to be done by Monday morning or the end of the night). The tool will (1) extract this deadline parameter, (2) compute the number of cores required to reach the deadline given the Extra-P scaling model and (3) launch the job with this configuration. The monitoring infrastructure will then generate a profile of this run that will, in turn, be used to refine the scaling model and improve prediction for subsequent runs. As of now, this solution is incomplete because it does not take into account the time spent in the Slurm scheduler queue. Ideally, the tool would balance the expected performance of the application with the wait time incurred when asking for a larger set of resources, allowing it to finish on time, but not earlier, improving the job efficiency as described in Fig. 2. Some schedulers such as Slurm and OAR provide interfaces to query the expected wait time of an application in the queue, but can only rely on estimates provided by application users, which are usually inaccurate [24]. Several approaches have been proposed to obtain better estimates of the queuing time, using e.g. statistical analysis [21] or based on simulating the scheduler behavior [33]. Finally, note that this approach is not restricted to deadline scheduling, any launch parameter could be extracted and redefined before the run.

7.2   Characterising I/O Applicative Requirements

Typically, the file system (FS) is a shared resource in HPC, which makes it subject to contention. To outline the potential performance effect of I/O, we have implemented a dedicated I/O benchmark to measure peak performance in terms of bandwidth and I/O operations per second (IOPS). As shown in Fig. 3, FSs can have very different responses in the function of both their nature and of the contention level. Measurements were run on the same two bi-socket nodes connected in Infiniband (100 Gb/s ConnectX-4) for the three FSs. As mentioned in Sect. 6.2, characterizing the scalability behavior of an application in terms of I/O can bring various advantages, especially for choosing the appropriate configuration that uses the different resources on an HPC cluster.

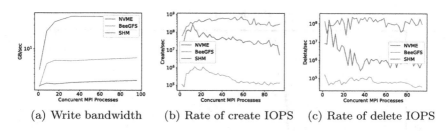

(a) Write bandwidth   (b) Rate of create IOPS   (c) Rate of delete IOPS

Fig. 3. Experimental FS peak performance in function of MPI processes.

Generally speaking, I/O subsystems present a similar performance behaviour driven by two main parameters, bandwidth, and IOPS. The Bandwidth increases with the number of nodes, as does the bisection bandwidth between compute and storage (more network links), up to a point where the back-end storage capabilities are saturated, leading to peak bandwidth. As far as IOPS are concerned, we observe such an increase, a plateau, and often contention, as the POSIX coherency requirements do imply a form of locking on meta-data operations. As we further develop, we rely on a derivation of these two rooflines [12,36] to implement a multi-variadic saturation diagram, guiding our FS choices.

In Fig. 3, the peak performance measurements on a dual socket 64-core AMD Milan featuring multiple FSs (SHM, BeeGFs, local NVME) are shown. We can observe behaviours matching the roofline models. In particular, each file system parametrizes a given roofline, and thus, such compact representation can be leveraged to characterize I/O trade-offs between FS.

We summarize our I/O parametrization implementation in Fig. 4, based on the peak values shown in Fig. 3. Metadata operations in BeeGFS, like in most HPC-oriented file systems, have lower efficiency compared to bandwidth. On the other hand, the single local NVME has better metadata performance but cannot match the performance of a whole storage array. In comparison, SHM is significantly faster. This diagram provides a practical way to quantify the performance differences between file systems and see what limits the I/O performance for a given program, whether it is IOPS or bandwidth. We also overlaid the execution coordinates of multiple applications using average bandwidth and average IOPS, creating a combined resource saturation diagram that can be used to measure the sensitivity of a program to I/O. The I/O benchmarks showed variable performance, whereas LULESH (with visualization activated) and BT-IO (class C) mainly remained fixed in this diagram. We are currently using models backed up by Extra-P to project the total dataset size and execution times to compute this mapping and anticipate saturation for a given file system, which can guide moldability. In particular, we anticipate that machine learning payloads may lead to higher IOPS, leading to patterns diverging from HPC applications.

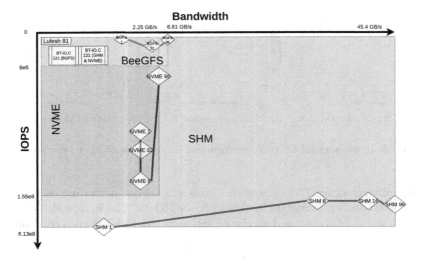

Fig. 4. Resource saturation diagram over bandwidth and IOPS. All scales are logarithmic. Applications are mapped as per average bandwidth and IOPS.

8   Conclusion and Future Work

To enable productivity and ease of use of HPC platforms, and in light of the increasingly complex launch configuration space of applications, there is a need for potential abstractions and automation. The concept of the *smart scheduler* has been discussed in this paper as a means of abstracting the use of HPC systems through monitoring and dynamic job configuration (moldability and malleability), it fits in a larger effort transversal to the whole execution chain. We briefly described the ADMIRE monitoring infrastructure and highlighted its capabilities for always-on monitoring, real-time performance tracking, and job profile generation. Additionally, we presented two use cases demonstrating dynamic job configuration and I/O tuning at launch time. Currently, we are integrating the ADMIRE infrastructure to leverage the concept of *smart scheduler*. This integration is expected to provide practical results shortly. Overall, the main contribution of the paper is offering a new approach to managing the complexity of HPC systems to enable their efficient use.

While we focused on moldability in this paper, the monitoring approach is also especially suited for malleability, as it provides key information (e.g., compute and I/O loads) that can be utilized. Hence, our future work focuses on using the described approach scheduling algorithms that consider malleable jobs, to effectively utilizes the different components of the HPC cluster and enhance the system throughput. Moreover, since in such a context, it can be valuable to know some key aspects like the periodicity of I/O phases (in case they are periodic), future work also centers on adding predictive capabilities to this infrastructure to boost the malleable decisions.

Acknowledgment. This work has been partially funded by the European Union's Horizon 2020 under the ADMIRE project, grant Agreement number: 956748-ADMIRE-H2020-JTI-EuroHPC-2019-1.

References

1. Ahn, D.H., Garlick, J., Grondona, M., Lipari, D., Springmeyer, B., Schulz, M.: Flux: a next-generation resource management framework for large HPC centers. In: 2014 43rd International Conference on Parallel Processing Workshops, pp. 9–17. IEEE (2014)
2. Arima, E., Comprés, A.I., Schulz, M.: On the convergence of malleability and the HPC PowerStack: exploiting dynamism in over-provisioned and power-constrained HPC systems. In: Anzt, H., Bienz, A., Luszczek, P., Baboulin, M. (eds.) ISC High Performance 2022. LNCS, vol. 13387, pp. 206–217. Springer, Cham (2023). https://doi.org/10.1007/978-3-031-23220-6_14
3. Balaprakash, P., et al.: Autotuning in high-performance computing applications. Proc. IEEE **106**(11), 2068–2083 (2018)
4. Besnard, J.B., Malony, A.D., Shende, S., Pérache, M., Carribault, P., Jaeger, J.: Towards a better expressiveness of the speedup metric in MPI context. In: 2017 46th International Conference on Parallel Processing Workshops (ICPPW), pp. 251–260. IEEE (2017)
5. Calotoiu, A., Hoefler, T., Poke, M., Wolf, F.: Using automated performance modeling to find scalability bugs in complex codes. In: Proceedings of the International Conference on High Performance Computing, Networking, Storage and Analysis, p. 45 (2013). tex.organization: ACM Citation Key: CA13
6. Cantalupo, C., et al.: A strawman for an HPC PowerStack. Technical report, Intel Corporation, United States; Lawrence Livermore National Lab. (LLNL) (2018)
7. Carns, P.H., et al.: Understanding and improving computational science storage access through continuous characterization. ACM Trans. Storage **7**(3), 8:1–8:26 (2011). https://doi.org/10.1145/2027066.2027068
8. Carretero, J., Jeannot, E., Pallez, G., Singh, D.E., Vidal, N.: Mapping and scheduling HPC applications for optimizing I/O. In: Proceedings of the 34th ACM International Conference on Supercomputing, pp. 1–12 (2020)
9. Cascajo, A., Singh, D.E., Carretero, J.: LIMITLESS-light-weight monitoring tool for large scale systems. Microprocess. Microsyst. **93**, 104586 (2022)
10. Cera, M.C., Georgiou, Y., Richard, O., Maillard, N., Navaux, P.O.A.: Supporting malleability in parallel architectures with dynamic CPUSETs mapping and dynamic MPI. In: Kant, K., Pemmaraju, S.V., Sivalingam, K.M., Wu, J. (eds.) ICDCN 2010. LNCS, vol. 5935, pp. 242–257. Springer, Heidelberg (2010). https://doi.org/10.1007/978-3-642-11322-2_26
11. D'Amico, M., Jokanovic, A., Corbalan, J.: Holistic slowdown driven scheduling and resource management for malleable jobs. In: ACM International Conference Proceeding Series (2019). https://doi.org/10.1145/3337821.3337909
12. Denoyelle, N., Goglin, B., Ilic, A., Jeannot, E., Sousa, L.: Modeling large compute nodes with heterogeneous memories with cache-aware roofline model. In: Jarvis, S., Wright, S., Hammond, S. (eds.) PMBS 2017. LNCS, vol. 10724, pp. 91–113. Springer, Cham (2018). https://doi.org/10.1007/978-3-319-72971-8_5

13. Dorier, M., Dreher, M., Peterka, T., Wozniak, J.M., Antoniu, G., Raffin, B.: Lessons learned from building in situ coupling frameworks. In: Proceedings of the First Workshop on In Situ Infrastructures for Enabling Extreme-Scale Analysis and Visualization, pp. 19–24 (2015)
14. Duro, F.R., Blas, J.G., Isaila, F., Carretero, J., Wozniak, J., Ross, R.: Exploiting data locality in Swift/T workflows using Hercules. In: Proceedings of NESUS Workshop (2014)
15. Goglin, B., Moreaud, S.: Dodging non-uniform I/O access in hierarchical collective operations for multicore clusters. In: 2011 IEEE International Symposium on Parallel and Distributed Processing Workshops and Phd Forum, pp. 788–794. IEEE (2011)
16. Gupta, R., Laguna, I., Ahn, D., Gamblin, T., Bagchi, S., Lin, F.: STATuner: efficient tuning of CUDA kernels parameters. In: Supercomputing Conference (SC 2015), Poster (2015)
17. Hoefler, T., Gropp, W., Kramer, W., Snir, M.: Performance modeling for systematic performance tuning. In: State of the Practice Reports, SC 2011, pp. 1–12. Association for Computing Machinery, New York (2011). https://doi.org/10.1145/2063348.2063356
18. Hu, W., Liu, G., Li, Q., Jiang, Y., Cai, G.: Storage wall for exascale supercomputing. Front. Inf. Technol. Electron. Eng. **17**(11), 1154–1175 (2016). https://doi.org/10.1631/FITEE.1601336
19. Huber, D., Streubel, M., Comprés, I., Schulz, M., Schreiber, M., Pritchard, H.: Towards dynamic resource management with MPI sessions and PMIx. In: Proceedings of the 29th European MPI Users' Group Meeting, pp. 57–67 (2022)
20. Klein, C., Pérez, C.: An RMS for non-predictably evolving applications. In: Proceedings - IEEE International Conference on Cluster Computing, ICCC, pp. 326–334 (2011). https://doi.org/10.1109/CLUSTER.2011.56
21. Kumar, R., Vadhiyar, S.: Identifying quick starters: towards an integrated framework for efficient predictions of queue waiting times of batch parallel jobs. In: Cirne, W., Desai, N., Frachtenberg, E., Schwiegelshohn, U. (eds.) JSSPP 2012. LNCS, vol. 7698, pp. 196–215. Springer, Heidelberg (2013). https://doi.org/10.1007/978-3-642-35867-8_11
22. Martí Fraiz, J.: dataClay: next generation object storage (2017)
23. Miranda, A., Jackson, A., Tocci, T., Panourgias, I., Nou, R.: NORNS: extending Slurm to support data-driven workflows through asynchronous data staging. In: 2019 IEEE International Conference on Cluster Computing (CLUSTER), USA, pp. 1–12. IEEE (2019). https://doi.org/10.1109/CLUSTER.2019.8891014
24. Mu'alem, A.W., Feitelson, D.G.: Utilization, predictability, workloads, and user runtime estimates in scheduling the IBM SP2 with backfilling. IEEE Trans. Parallel Distrib. Syst. **12**(6), 529–543 (2001). https://doi.org/10.1109/71.932708
25. Netti, A., et al.: DCDB wintermute: enabling online and holistic operational data analytics on HPC systems. In: Proceedings of the 29th International Symposium on High-Performance Parallel and Distributed Computing, pp. 101–112 (2020)
26. Nikitenko, D.A., et al.: Influence of noisy environments on behavior of HPC applications. Lobachevskii J. Math. **42**(7), 1560–1570 (2021). https://doi.org/10.1134/S1995080221070192
27. Patki, T., Thiagarajan, J.J., Ayala, A., Islam, T.Z.: Performance optimality or reproducibility: that is the question. In: Proceedings of the International Conference for High Performance Computing, Networking, Storage and Analysis, Denver Colorado, pp. 1–30. ACM (2019). https://doi.org/10.1145/3295500.3356217

28. Petrini, F., Kerbyson, D., Pakin, S.: The case of the missing supercomputer performance: achieving optimal performance on the 8,192 processors of ASCI Q. In: SC 2003: Proceedings of the 2003 ACM/IEEE Conference on Supercomputing, p. 55 (2003). https://doi.org/10.1145/1048935.1050204
29. Prabhakaran, S., Neumann, M., Rinke, S., Wolf, F., Gupta, A., Kale, L.V.: A batch system with efficient adaptive scheduling for malleable and evolving applications. In: 2015 IEEE International Parallel and Distributed Processing Symposium, pp. 429–438. IEEE (2015)
30. Ritter, M., Calotoiu, A., Rinke, S., Reimann, T., Hoefler, T., Wolf, F.: Learning cost-effective sampling strategies for empirical performance modeling. In: 2020 IEEE International Parallel and Distributed Processing Symposium (IPDPS), pp. 884–895 (2020). https://doi.org/10.1109/IPDPS47924.2020.00095
31. Ritter, M., et al.: Noise-resilient empirical performance modeling with deep neural networks. In: 2021 IEEE International Parallel and Distributed Processing Symposium (IPDPS), pp. 23–34 (2021). https://doi.org/10.1109/IPDPS49936.2021.00012
32. Schulz, M., Kranzlmüller, D., Schulz, L.B., Trinitis, C., Weidendorfer, J.: On the inevitability of integrated HPC systems and how they will change HPC system operations. In: Proceedings of the 11th International Symposium on Highly Efficient Accelerators and Reconfigurable Technologies, pp. 1–6 (2021)
33. Smith, W., Taylor, V., Foster, I.: Using run-time predictions to estimate queue wait times and improve scheduler performance. In: Feitelson, D.G., Rudolph, L. (eds.) JSSPP 1999. LNCS, vol. 1659, pp. 202–219. Springer, Heidelberg (1999). https://doi.org/10.1007/3-540-47954-6_11
34. Sudarsan, R., Ribbens, C.J.: ReSHAPE: a framework for dynamic resizing and scheduling of homogeneous applications in a parallel environment. In: Proceedings of the International Conference on Parallel Processing (2007). https://doi.org/10.1109/ICPP.2007.73
35. Vef, M.A., et al.: GekkoFS-a temporary distributed file system for HPC applications. In: 2018 IEEE International Conference on Cluster Computing (CLUSTER), pp. 319–324. IEEE (2018)
36. Williams, S., Waterman, A., Patterson, D.: Roofline: an insightful visual performance model for multicore architectures. Commun. ACM 52(4), 65–76 (2009). https://doi.org/10.1145/1498765.1498785
37. Wood, C., et al.: Artemis: automatic runtime tuning of parallel execution parameters using machine learning. In: Chamberlain, B.L., Varbanescu, A.-L., Ltaief, H., Luszczek, P. (eds.) ISC High Performance 2021. LNCS, vol. 12728, pp. 453–472. Springer, Cham (2021). https://doi.org/10.1007/978-3-030-78713-4_24
38. Wu, X., et al.: Toward an end-to-end auto-tuning framework in HPC PowerStack. In: 2020 IEEE International Conference on Cluster Computing (CLUSTER), pp. 473–483. IEEE (2020)

Probabilistic Job History Conversion and Performance Model Generation for Malleable Scheduling Simulations

Isaías Comprés[1]([✉]), Eishi Arima[1], Martin Schulz[1], Tiberiu Rotaru[2], and Rui Machado[2]

[1] Technical University of Munich, Garching, Germany
{isaias.compres,eishi.arima,martin.w.j.schulz}@tum.de
[2] Fraunhofer ITWM, Kaiserslautern, Germany
{rotaru,rui.machado}@itwm.fraunhofer.de

Abstract. Malleability support in supercomputing requires several updates to system software stacks. In addition to this, updates to applications, libraries and the runtime systems of distributed memory programming models are also necessary. Because of this, there are relatively few applications that have been extended or developed with malleability support. As a consequence, there are no job histories from production systems that include sufficient malleable job submissions for scheduling research. In this paper, we propose a solution: a probabilistic job history conversion. This conversion allows us to evaluate malleable scheduling heuristics via simulations based on existing job histories. Based on a configurable probability, job arrivals are converted into malleable versions, and assigned a malleable performance model. This model is used by the simulator to evaluate its changes at runtime, as an effect of malleable operations being applied to it.

Keywords: Malleability · Supercomputing · Scheduling · Job History

1 Introduction

Adding malleability support requires extensive changes to supercomputing software stacks. Programming models, runtime systems, process managers, tools, monitoring systems, and others, have been designed for rigid node allocations and require non-trivial updates to their implementations. New scheduling research efforts are necessary, given the additional flexibility of updating job node counts at runtime. Furthermore, other types of resources that have been managed statically, can be managed dynamically, for example, energy budgets.

Adding scheduling support for new system features, such as malleability and dynamic power management, introduce additional challenges. For example, the

This work has received funding under the European Commission's EuroHPC and Horizon 2020 programmes under grant agreements no. 955606 (DEEP-SEA) and 956560 (REGALE).

scheduling heuristic needs to be developed concurrently with system software, and there is no real job history data available from production systems.

We propose a solution to overcome the lack of real job history data: a probabilistic conversion of existing job histories and performance model generation. We support parameter sweeps to enable making conclusions based on varying scenarios. For example, the arrival rate of malleable jobs can be adjusted and its effect on the makespan or node utilization can be evaluated. These are our presented contributions:

1. The probabilistic job history conversion and performance modeling.
2. An extension to the First-Come First-Serve (FCFS) with backfilling heuristic that adds malleability support.
3. A Slurm-based framework for malleable scheduling research.

We introduce these contributions in detail, together with some background information about the general scheduling problem as it applies to supercomputing. Afterwards, we present simulation results based on the conversion of a Standard Workload Format (SWF) job history that is publicly available. Finally, we state our conclusion and share our future work plans.

2   Related Work and Concepts

Malleability in scheduling has been an active area of research for years, and has been well documented in survey works [5]. These works [14,18] have identified and described the challenges, but also the potential benefits that malleable allocations can provide for both applications and systems. In this work, we focus on presenting a research technique that can be used during scheduling research, instead of focusing on a specific technique or heuristic. We implement an extension to the First-Come First-Serve (FCFS) with backfilling heuristic, that can be used as a baseline to compare with future more elaborate scheduling solutions.

There are also several works that focus on the development of runtime systems for new programming models, or extensions to existing ones. Their process scheduling approaches are also important, and may perform scheduling decisions at the job allocation or node level [12,17,28]. The topic of other malleable resources, such as I/O, has also been investigated [9] and its importance demonstrated. Some other works have also explored the integration of supercomputing and schedulers of other fields [4,10], such as machine learning or cloud computing, via malleability support. In this work, we do not offer a solution to the malleable programming problem. Instead, we provide a mechanism to perform parameter sweeps on performance models that represent malleable jobs.

The Standard Workload Format (SWF) [15] has been used extensively for research on batch scheduling. This format has been stable, with only a few suggestions for extensions in recent years [13]. In this work, we do not extend the format itself, but provide a probabilistic conversion of job arrivals.

For our evaluation, we develop a simulator directly in top of Slurm [16] and that is directly based on its existing heuristics. There are also malleable scheduler simulators that are not based on Slurm [20,21,24,25]. While there have been similar Slurm-based simulators in the past [11,19], we decided to develop our own, as the approach is different: for one, our simulator directly works on Slurm's 's code base and its native algorithms, enabling simulations that represent its behaviour when deployed. Furthermore, it does not emulate the event handling that occurs between the Slurm controller and its node daemons, offering higher simulation performance. The job conversion and modeling techniques presented in this work can also be applied to other simulators.

Since power limits have become important design constraints when building supercomputers, research around power-aware supercomputing has been very active in recent years. The Energy Efficient HPC (EEHPC) Working Group (WG) established a comparative power measurement methodology which is used for the Green500 ranking today [29]. The feasibility of power management in over-provisioned supercomputing systems have been explored [22], and various power management techniques have been proposed and implemented [23,26,27]. The PowerStack initiative community [2] was launched based on these studies. In this work, we propose performance modeling that covers the interaction of malleability and power management for simulation purposes.

3   Supercomputing Job Scheduling Problem and Malleability

The general problem of scheduling in HPC is a particular case of the multiprocessor scheduling problem. It is an optimization problem that has been widely analyzed. Equation 1 is a simplified representation of it.

Let J be a set of jobs j_i where the subscript $i \in \mathbb{N}$ identifies each job uniquely. Similarly, let N be a set of m nodes n_k where the subscript $\{k \mid k \in \mathbb{N} \wedge k < m\}$ identifies each node uniquely. One or more nodes in N can perform the tasks in J in some manner. If $\tau(j_i)$ is the maximum execution time and $\rho(j_i)$ the number of nodes required to perform a job j_i, then we can define the following optimization problem:

$$\begin{aligned} \text{given inputs} \quad & J = \{j_i \mid \tau(j_i) < \infty \wedge \rho(j_i) \leq m\}, \\ & N = \{n_k \mid k < m\} \\ \text{compute a} \quad & S = \{j_i \mapsto \varrho_i\} \\ \text{that optimizes } & objective(M) \end{aligned} \tag{1}$$

The output is a schedule S, which is a set of mappings from each individual job j_i into an allocation ϱ_i of size $\rho(j_i)$, where $\varrho_i \subset N$, has a starting time, and duration $\tau(j_i)$. Jobs where $\rho(j_i) > m$ are impossible to schedule and therefore not considered, while $\tau(j_i)$ may have a maximum value based on system policy.

Changes to the schedule S result in changes to the metrics in the set M. The $objective()$ function takes the set of metrics M as input, and produces an evaluation of the quality of the schedule that is usually represented as a single real number.

When malleability is supported by the system, there are some changes to the general problem:

- Each running malleable job can have its mapping $j_i \mapsto \varrho_i$ updated before completion, essentially becoming time dependent.
- The optimization process includes evaluations of $objective(M)$ on each update to malleable job mappings.

In general, the ability to update resource mappings give schedulers additional opportunities to improve system metrics. These additional opportunities will depend on the mix of rigid and malleable job arrivals.

3.1   Scheduler Implementation in Slurm

Like most schedulers for supercomputing today, Slurm implements a form of priority-based First-Come First-Served (FCFS) scheduling with backfilling. Specifically, Slurm implements the EASY backfilling algorithm, where only the highest priority job has a guaranteed start time. Each of these have a dedicated thread with a configurable period of execution.

3.2   Malleable Scheduler Extension

The priority-based FCFS batch scheduling with backfilling heuristic has been very effective at keeping the node utilization metric of HPC systems within expectations. Because this heuristic has been so effective, we have preserved its core design completely unmodified. In addition to this, we do not interfere at all with the two passes of Slurm's scheduler: the FCFS pass and the backfilling pass. Because of this, all policies will be applied correctly and the execution of traditional rigid jobs will remain identical. Any Slurm deployment that has been well tested, validated, and may be under a support contract will operate exactly the same as before. This is the general engineering goal of our malleability prototype.

We introduce an additional thread, with its own configurable period, as our malleability extension. This follows the existing design of periodic and asynchronous operations on the scheduling data structures.

To explain how the malleable extension works, an example scenario where a queue has been populated with seven jobs is provided in Fig. 1. Assuming the algorithm is starting with an empty machine, the first decision is to start Job 0 at T0. Next, since there are not enough resources for Job 1 and it is the highest priority job at the moment, a reservation is created at time T1. The creation of job 1's reservation introduces a large gap of idle nodes between T0 and T1. Job 2 fits within the gap, and is therefore started at T0; however, Job 3 does not fit in the remaining space, and therefore a reservation is created for it at T2. Job 4 fits in the T0-T1 gap, and is therefore started. Job 5 and 6 do not fit in the remaining gap, therefore reservations are created for them at T2. This schedule is the output of both the FCFS pass and the backfill pass, but for simplicity we have presented them together. The start of Jobs 2 and 4 were backfill operations.

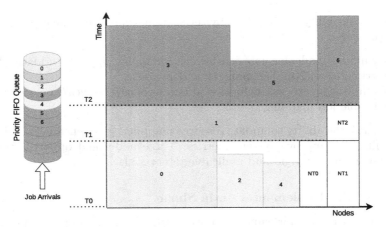

Fig. 1. Queue, reservations and node-time data structures.

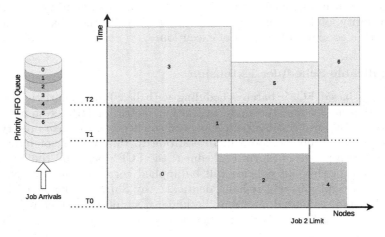

Fig. 2. Updated job allocations after Job 2 doubles its allocation size.

At this point, the existing scheduler has exhausted all opportunities available, taking into consideration priorities and other policies that are reflected in the queue order and the availability of the compute nodes. The malleability extension can detect additional opportunities for the scheduler. It identifies node availability in the node-time blocks. In Fig. 1, there are three node-time blocks based on the discussed scenario.

If resources are acquired, some or all of the available nodes in the node-time gaps can be occupied by running malleable jobs. This is illustrated in Fig. 2. In this scenario, Job 2 acquires extra nodes until its upper limit of scalability.

We have implemented a simulator within the malleable scheduler implementation. This has the advantage of evaluating the actual Slurm implementation and our own deployable extension. As usual in simulations, there is a main time loop. The simulator has a resolution of one second. The following operations are simulated, if necessary, on each step: job completions, job arrivals, FIFO pass, backfilling pass, and malleable pass. On each step, system metrics and outputs are generated when necessary.

4 Probabilistic Job History Conversion and Performance Model Generation

Job arrivals are determined by the SWF input. The SWF input specifies the arrival time, in seconds (offset from zero), as recorded. The input also includes the number of resources requested, the wall clock time (guessed completion time) provided by the user, and the actual run time recorded.

4.1 Scalability Modeling for Allocation Size Updates

To determine the resource allocation size, we use the well-known Amdahl's law [6] that governs the strong-scaling behavior of parallel applications. Let the serial portion of an application be α $(0 < \alpha \leq 1)$, and let the number of nodes be n, then the parallel speed-up from the serial execution $S(n)$ and the parallel efficiency $PE(n)$ are denoted as follows:

$$S(n) = n/((n-1)\alpha + 1) \tag{2}$$
$$PE(n) = S(n)/n = 1/((n-1)\alpha + 1) \tag{3}$$

We estimate the scalability of each job by using the model and the number of nodes stated in the SWF file N. Suppose the job runs with N nodes and the parallel efficiency equals to β $(0 < \beta < 1)$, then the following equation stands:

$$PE(N) = 1/((N-1)\alpha + 1) = \beta \tag{4}$$

We can identify the parameter α, and the speed-up can be described without α:

$$S(n) = \begin{cases} n\beta(N-1)/(n(1-\beta) + \beta N - 1) & (N \neq 1) \\ 1 & (N = 1) \end{cases} \tag{5}$$

Note that we consider the job was completely serial $(\alpha = 1)$ when it was executed with a single node $(N = 1)$ in the SWF file. In our simulations, we randomly pick up the parameter β from a given range $[0.5 - \Delta\beta/2, 0.5 + \Delta\beta/2]$ $(0 < \Delta\beta < 1)$. The parameter β depends on the job and represents its parallel efficiency. We handle the variation probabilistically and can control the range with the parameter $\Delta\beta$.

Figure 3 shows the shape of the parallel speed-up curve depending on the two parameters (β, N). The horizontal axis indicates the number of nodes n, while the vertical axis represents the speed-up $S(n)$. The curve is set when the job is converted into malleable, via the provided N from the SWF input, and the generated β, while n can be adjusted by the scheduler during its runtime. In essence, the original node requirement N of the job determines its scalability potential, with some variability introduced by the generated β.

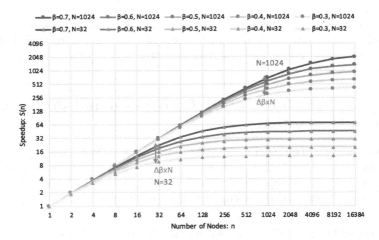

Fig. 3. Speed-up $S(n)$ as a function of node allocation n for different parameter setups (β, N)

4.2   Power-Performance Modeling for Power Cap Updates

For power-performance modeling, we utilize the well-known roofline model [33]. The shape of the roofline is adjusted based on the power cap. Let B be the node memory bandwidth, F the maximum node FLOPS at the maximum clock frequency, γ the job arithmetic intensity, f the current clock frequency, and f_{max} the maximum clock frequency. Then, the node performance of the job $Perf(f)$ as well as the relative node performance $NP(f)$ normalized to that of $f = f_{max}$ are described as follows:

$$Perf(f) = \min(B\gamma, Ff/f_{max}) \tag{6}$$

$$NP(f) = Perf(f)/Perf(f_{max})$$
$$= \min(B\gamma, Ff/f_{max})/\min(B\gamma, F) \tag{7}$$

The clock frequency f is set depending on the power cap. To this end, we utilize the well-known power model used for semiconductor chips: power is proportional to the clock frequency, and the square of the supply voltage [31]. The supply voltage is proportional to the clock frequency, given by the Shmoo plot [30]. We model power $Pow(f)$ as follows:

$$Pow(f) = C_3 f^3 + C_1 f + C_0 \tag{8}$$

Given the power cap P_{cap}, the clock frequency is set f while meeting $Pow(f) \leq P_{cap}$. Given the clock frequency, we set the performance at the power cap with Eq. 6 and 7.

We setup a test scenario with the hardware parameters based on the AMD Ryzen Threadripper 5975WX by using publicly available known data [1,8,32]. The setups are listed in Table 1. Note the coefficients C in Eq. 8 are identified

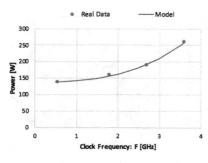

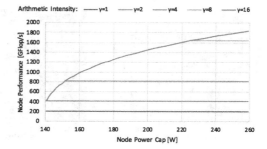

Fig. 4. Power as a function of clock frequency.

Fig. 5. Performance as a function of node power cap.

by applying the least square method to the catalog sheet data [1, 32]. Figure 4 illustrates the result—the model fits very well to the real data of power and clock frequency combinations. We show the performance as a function of node power caps in Fig. 5, which is obtained by combining Eq. (6) and Eq. (8). The impact of power capping on performance depends on the arithmetic intensity (γ) of the workload. For memory intensive jobs (e.g., $\gamma = 1$), the performance impact of power capping is low, while for compute intensive ones (e.g., $\gamma = 16$), the impact is considerable. Note that $\gamma = 0.25$ stands for SpMV (memory intensive), and $\gamma = 32$ stands for DGEMM (compute intensive) [7].

4.3 Model-Based Job Characterization

We then classify jobs with respect to the scalability α (fixed when β and N are determined) as well as the arithmetic intensity γ and check the performance impact of resource/power allocations for the different classes, in order to gain insights for the resource/power allocations to malleable jobs. Here, we consider the speed-up or relative performance that is normalized to the single-node performance without the node power cap. This is a function of the number of nodes n as well as the node power cap setup P_{cap}. Let the function be $S'(n, P_{cap})$, then the following equation stands:

$$S'(n, P_{cap}) = S(n) \times NP(Pow^{-1}(P_{cap})) \qquad (9)$$

Figure 6, 7, 8 and 9 show the speed-up or relative performance $S'(n, P_{cap})$ as a function of the resource/power allocations, i.e., the number of nodes n and the node power cap P_{cap}, for 4 different job parameter setups, i.e., $(\alpha, \gamma) = (0.1, 1)$, $(0.1, 16)$, $(0.01, 1)$, $(0.01, 16)$. The horizontal axis indicates the node power cap P_{cap}, while the vertical axis represents the number of nodes assigned to the job n. The green-colored curve in each figure is the 8 KW job power budget boundary, i.e., $n \times P_{cap} = 8$ KW. Here, we assume the job power budget is evenly distributed to n nodes so that the node performance becomes uniform among the assigned nodes[1]. Figure 6 shows a *non-scalable* and *memory intensive* job,

---

[1] We do not take the impact of manufacturing process variations into account here.

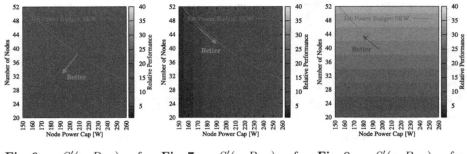

Fig. 6. $S'(n, P_{cap})$ for **Fig. 7.** $S'(n, P_{cap})$ for **Fig. 8.** $S'(n, P_{cap})$ for
$(\alpha, \gamma) = (0.1, 1)$ $(\alpha, \gamma) = (0.1, 16)$ $(\alpha, \gamma) = (0.01, 1)$

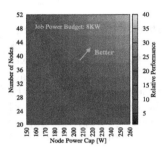

Fig. 9. $S'(n, P_{cap})$ for (α, γ)
$= (0.01, 16)$

Table 1. Parameter/Coefficients Setups Based on AMD Ryzen Threadripper 5975W [1,8,32]

Param	Number
F	32Cores x3.6 GHz x16flop/core/cycle = 1843.2 GFlop/s
B	DDR4-3200 x8ch = 204.8 GB/s
f_{max}	3.6 GHz (260 W@3.6 GHz)
C_*	$C_3 = 2.36\,[\mathrm{W/GHz^3}]$, $C_1 = 3.61\,[\mathrm{W/GHz}]$, $C_0 = 136\,[\mathrm{W}]$

and shifting the job power budget boundary toward the down-left area does not cause any noticeable performance impact. Figure 7 depicts a *non-scalable* but *compute intensive* job, and we should reduce the number of nodes but increase the node power cap under the given 8 KW job power budget. Figure 8 illustrates a *scalable* but *memory intensive* job, and we should allocate more nodes but decrease the node power cap while keeping the given 8 KW job power budget. Figure 9 represents a *scalable* and *compute intensive* job, and it is better to move the power budget boundary toward the upper-right area as it can gain speed-up efficiently. The resource and power allocation policy for malleable jobs should follow the above principles while taking the available nodes/power into account.

5   Power Capping with Malleability Simulation Case Study

In Fig. 10, we present the instantaneous node utilization baseline and its improvement when malleability is enabled. This is one of the many parameter sweeps withing node scaling and power capping dimensions. This particular scenario is based on the *KIT-FH2* SWF log from the Parallel Workloads Archive website [3]. Since we have SWF input support, simulations can be made with any of

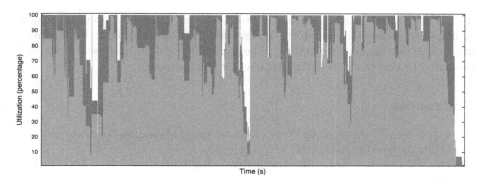

Fig. 10. Instantaneous node utilization baseline (green) and with malleability (gray) enabled. (Color figure online)

these logs, with minor modifications to the header. This system was configured with 1152 nodes, with 20 cores each, and we have configured the simulator to mach the node count and cores per node settings. For this run we have set a node power cap of 200 W, and the probability of malleable job arrivals was set to 20%.

In order to include observable detail in the plot, we have limited the view to the final week of simulated time (this makes the increase in the makespan seem larger). As can be observed, the node utilization metric has improved versus the baseline, but the makespan has increased slightly. The increase in the makespan is negligible, while node utilization was improved from approximately 87% to slightly greater than 93%. Node utilization varies based on the configured probabilities and distributions in the parameter sweep setup. In this particular simulation run, certain node utilization minimums were not improved significantly, due to lower job submissions recorded in the log.

The combination of compute node malleability, with dynamic power management, create these additional opportunities for schedulers to take advance of. Although we apply a power model to converted malleable jobs, our current scheduler is not power aware; therefore, the simulation is performed with the same node power cap across all jobs. These benefits will depend largely on the hardware platform, node configuration, network performance, and the types of workloads and submission patterns generated by the users of the target system.

6   Conclusion and Future Work

A probabilistic malleable conversion of job histories, together with performance model generation, was presented. With this approach, we overcome the lack of real malleable job histories, that would otherwise hinder the development of schedulers with malleability support. We plan to further develop the scheduler with better malleability strategies, and add power and energy awareness to it. Future over provisioned and power constrained supercomputing deployments, with malleability support, are foreseen, and therefore further scheduling research in this field is well justified. The techniques and Slurm-based framework presented in this work are valuable tools for this purpose.

References

1. AMD ryzen™ threadripper™ pro 5975wx. https://www.amd.com/en/product/11791. Accessed 13 Mar 2023
2. The HPC powerstack. https://hpcpowerstack.github.io/index.html. Accessed 16 Mar 2023
3. Logs of real parallel workloads from production systems. https://www.cs.huji.ac.il/labs/parallel/workload/logs.html. Accessed 18 Mar 2023
4. Ahn, D.H., et al.: Flux: overcoming scheduling challenges for exascale workflows. In: 2018 IEEE/ACM Workflows in Support of Large-Scale Science (WORKS), pp. 10–19 (2018)
5. Aliaga, J.I., Castillo, M., Iserte, S., Martín-Álvarez, I., Mayo, R.: A survey on malleability solutions for high-performance distributed computing. Appl. Sci. **12**(10), 5231 (2022)
6. Amdahl, G.M.: Computer architecture and Amdahl's law. Computer **46**(12), 38–46 (2013)
7. Barba, L.A., Yokota, R.: How will the fast multipole method fare in the exascale era. SIAM News **46**(6), 1–3 (2013)
8. Burd, T., et al.: Zen3: the AMD 2 nd-generation 7nm x86-64 microprocessor core. In: 2022 IEEE International Solid-State Circuits Conference (ISSCC), vol. 65, pp. 1–3. IEEE (2022)
9. Cascajo, A., Singh, D.E., Carretero, J.: Detecting interference between applications and improving the scheduling using malleable application proxies. In: Anzt, H., Bienz, A., Luszczek, P., Baboulin, M. (eds.) ISC High Performance 2022. LNCS, vol. 13387, pp. 129–146. Springer, Cham (2022). https://doi.org/10.1007/978-3-031-23220-6_9
10. Chacko, J.A., Ureña, I.A.C., Gerndt, M.: Integration of apache spark with invasive resource manager. pp. 1553–1560 (2019)
11. Chadha, M., John, J., Gerndt, M.: Extending slurm for dynamic resource-aware adaptive batch scheduling (2020)
12. Comprés, I., Mo-Hellenbrand, A., Gerndt, M., Bungartz, H.J.: Infrastructure and API extensions for elastic execution of MPI applications. In: Proceedings of the 23rd European MPI Users' Group Meeting, EuroMPI 2016, pp. 82–97. Association for Computing Machinery, New York (2016)
13. Corbalan, J., D'Amico, M.: Modular workload format: extending SWF for modular systems. In: Klusáček, D., Cirne, W., Rodrigo, G.P. (eds.) JSSPP 2021. LNCS, vol. 12985, pp. 43–55. Springer, Cham (2021). https://doi.org/10.1007/978-3-030-88224-2_3
14. Fan, Y., Lan, Z., Rich, P., Allcock, W., Papka, M.E.: Hybrid workload scheduling on HPC systems. In: 2022 IEEE International Parallel and Distributed Processing Symposium (IPDPS), pp. 470–480 (2022). https://doi.org/10.1109/IPDPS53621.2022.00052
15. Feitelson, D.G., Tsafrir, D., Krakov, D.: Experience with using the parallel workloads archive. J. Parallel Distrib. Comput. **74**(10), 2967–2982 (2014)

16. Georgiou, Y., Hautreux, M.: Evaluating scalability and efficiency of the resource and job management system on large HPC clusters. In: Cirne, W., Desai, N., Frachtenberg, E., Schwiegelshohn, U. (eds.) JSSPP 2012. LNCS, vol. 7698, pp. 134–156. Springer, Heidelberg (2013). https://doi.org/10.1007/978-3-642-35867-8_8

17. Huber, D., Streubel, M., Comprés, I., Schulz, M., Schreiber, M., Pritchard, H.: Towards dynamic resource management with MPI sessions and PMIX. In: Proceedings of the 29th European MPI Users' Group Meeting, EuroMPI/USA 2022, pp. 57–67. Association for Computing Machinery, New York (2022)

18. Iserte, S., Mayo, R., Quintana-Ortí, E.S., Peña, A.J.: DMRlib: easy-coding and efficient resource management for job malleability. IEEE Trans. Comput. **70**(9), 1443–1457 (2021). https://doi.org/10.1109/TC.2020.3022933

19. Jokanovic, A., D'Amico, M., Corbalan, J.: Evaluating SLURM simulator with real-machine SLURM and vice versa. In: 2018 IEEE/ACM Performance Modeling, Benchmarking and Simulation of High Performance Computer Systems (PMBS), pp. 72–82 (2018)

20. Legrand, A., Marchal, L., Casanova, H.: Scheduling distributed applications: the SimGrid simulation framework, pp. 138–145 (2003)

21. Özden, T., Beringer, T., Mazaheri, A., Fard, H.M., Wolf, F.: ElastiSim: a batch-system simulator for malleable workloads. In: Proceedings of the 51st International Conference on Parallel Processing (ICPP), Bordeaux, France. ACM (2022)

22. Patki, T., et al.: Exploring hardware overprovisioning in power-constrained, high performance computing. In: ICS, pp. 173–182 (2013)

23. Patki, T., et al.: Practical resource management in power-constrained, high performance computing. In: HPDC, pp. 121–132 (2015)

24. Prabhakaran, S., Iqbal, M., Rinke, S., Windisch, C., Wolf, F.: A batch system with fair scheduling for evolving applications. In: 2014 43rd International Conference on Parallel Processing, pp. 351–360 (2014)

25. Prabhakaran, S., Neumann, M., Rinke, S., Wolf, F., Gupta, A., Kale, L.V.: A batch system with efficient adaptive scheduling for malleable and evolving applications. In: 2015 IEEE International Parallel and Distributed Processing Symposium, pp. 429–438 (2015)

26. Sakamoto, R., et al.: Analyzing resource trade-offs in hardware overprovisioned supercomputers. In: IPDPS, pp. 526–535 (2018)

27. Sarood, O., et al.: Maximizing throughput of overprovisioned HPC data centers under a strict power budget. In: SC, pp. 807–818 (2014)

28. Schreiber, M., Riesinger, C., Neckel, T., Bungartz, H.J.: Invasive compute balancing for applications with hybrid parallelization. In: 2013 25th International Symposium on Computer Architecture and High Performance Computing, pp. 136–143 (2013)

29. Scogland, T.R., et al.: A power-measurement methodology for large-scale, high-performance computing. In: ICPE, pp. 149–159 (2014)

30. Singh, T., et al.: Zen: an energy-efficient high-performance ×86 core. IEEE J. Solid-State Circ. **53**(1), 102–114 (2017)

31. Suleiman, D., Ibrahim, M., Hamarash, I.: Dynamic voltage frequency scaling (DVFS) for microprocessors power and energy reduction. In: 4th International Conference on Electrical and Electronics Engineering, vol. 12 (2005)

32. Wallossek, I.: Chagall lives! AMD Ryzen threadripper PRO 5995WX and its 4 brothers 5975WX, 5965WX, 5955WX and 5945WX with technical data (2021). https://www.igorslab.de/en/chagall-lives-at-ryzen-threadripper-pro-5995wx-and-his-4-brothers-with-interesting-technical-data/. Accessed 13 Mar 2023
33. Williams, S., Waterman, A., Patterson, D.: Roofline: an insightful visual performance model for multicore architectures. Commun. ACM **52**(4), 65–76 (2009)

18th Workshop on Virtualization in High-Performance Cloud Computing (VHPC 23)

Improving Live Migration Efficiency in QEMU: A Paravirtualized Approach

Filippo Storniolo⬤, Luigi Leonardi(✉)⬤, and Giuseppe Lettieri⬤

University of Pisa, Pisa, Italy
f.storniolo@studenti.unipi.it, luigi.leonardi@phd.unipi.it,
giuseppe.lettieri@unipi.it

Abstract. Virtual Machines are the key technology in cloud computing. In order to upgrade, repair or service the physical machine where a Virtual Machine is hosted, a common practice is to live-migrate the Virtual Machine to a different server. This involves copying all the guest memory over the network, which may take a non-negligible amount of time. In this work, we propose a technique to speed up the migration time by reducing the amount of guest memory to be transferred with the help of the guest OS. In particular, during live-migration, a paravirtualized driver running in the guest kernel obtains, and sends to the Virtual Machine Monitor, the list of guest page frames that are currently unused. The VMM can then safely skip these pages during the copy. We have integrated this technique in the live-migration implementation of QEMU [3], and we show the effects of our work in some experiments comparing the results against QEMU default implementation and VirtIO-Balloon.

Keywords: Paravirtualization · Virtualization · Live Migration · QEMU

1 Introduction

Most of the cloud computing infrastructure relies on Virtual Machines (VMs) and usually has strong requirements on downtime periods to be as low as possible. This is not an easy task to achieve because Physical Machines (PMs) or Host Machines, i.e. where the VMs are hosted, may require maintenance for several reasons: hardware failures, periodic checks or upgrades. If one of such machines is turned off without any precaution, all the VMs, and the services running on them, become suddenly unavailable. One possible solution is to move all the hosted VM(s) to another computer before shutting down the PM. This should be completed as fast as possible to reduce downtime for the users. Migrating VMs be also be useful for load balancing [1,16]: a VM that is running on an overloaded server and experiencing degraded performance, can be moved to a lightly loaded server. Finally, a server experiencing a low load can be turned off, after copying its VMs to another machine, thus saving power. Overall, migration can be used for optimizing the usage of all available PMs.

A. Bienz et al. (Eds.): ISC High Performance 2023 Workshops, LNCS 13999, pp. 97–106, 2023.
https://doi.org/10.1007/978-3-031-40843-4_8

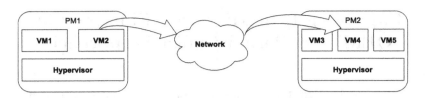

Fig. 1. Example of Live Migration of VM2 from PM1 to VM4 in PM2

Live Migration [4] is a technique that is available in most of the hypervisor like Xen [2] or KVM [9] and for containers like Linux Containers LXC [5,13] or Docker [17]. Because most of the migration time is spent for the data copy of the *guest* context to the *target* VM, the idea is to perform it while keeping the *source* machine running. It is not possible to copy the entire state because the running machine constantly modifies (a part of) its memory known as its *working set*, so the VM needs to be shut down at some point to copy this set (stop and copy). However, since the size of the *working set* is smaller than the entire *guest* state, the downtime is greatly reduced. Optimizing the downtime or the migration time is not an easy task and there are several routes that have been explored: in [8] the authors introduced a novel stopping condition based on the rate of page transmission during migration, Svärd et al. in [14] explained how delta compression techniques can reduce the amount of data to be sent (Fig. 1).

The migration process can be further optimized by skipping all the guest pages that are marked as free, but because of the *semantic gap* that exists between the *host* and the *guest* system, the VMM is unaware of the status of each memory frame inside the VM. This gap can be overcome using VM Introspection [6] (VMI) that consists in analyzing the guest memory content from the hypervisor. Using the latter tecnique Wang et al. [15] implemented this optimization by ignoring caches and free pages, drastically reducing the data transferred by $\approx 70\%$. However, this promising method has some limitations: in the case of a VM with an encrypted RAM, as found in modern confidential computing environment, the method cannot be used, since the hypervisor cannot decrypt the guest memory. This limitation can be address by paravirtualization: the virtualized system, or at least some part of it, is aware that is running inside a VM and is willing to exchange information with the Hypervisor(HV). One example is Ballooning [7]: with the latter technology the HV can reclaim part of the guest's memory by "inflating" the balloon before starting the migration: this limits the amount of RAM available for the guest, and therefore also the amount of data to be transferred. However, this does not come for free: reducing the guest's memory to give it back to the hypervisor, implies that the guest cannot use that memory until it is released by the host. In fact, the hypervisor may use the regained memory to run a new VM, for example, and if the guest could use that portion of memory, it could read/write the memory of another VM. In this work we propose a paravirtualized driver that sends to the HV the list of page frames that are free when the migration starts. In our solution, the guest still owns the memory for the duration of the migration and can use it as needed. A similar solution has been proposed for the Xen hypervisor [12]. We provide and evaluate a complete implementation for the QEMU hypervisor [3] by reusing a generic paravirtualization device [10].

The rest of the paper is organized as follows: Sect. 2 provides the necessary background on the existing technologies (Linux memory management, live migration and Ballooning in QEMU); Sect. 3 describes our proposed paravirtualized migration; Sect. 4 shows the results of some experiments and Sect. 5 concludes.

2 Background

2.1 Linux Physical Memory

Linux physical memory is organized in blocks of physical pages with different sizes. Each block is built from a set of consecutive physical pages, the number of which is always a power of 2. The power exponent is usually called *order* and it can vary from 0 to 10. This means that the size of the smallest and the biggest block of physical pages is respectively 4 KiB (that is the size of a single physical page) and 4 MiB (that is the size of 2^{10} consecutive physical pages) (Fig. 2).

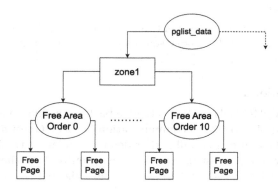

Fig. 2. Linux Physical Memory Structure

Whenever the Kernel needs to allocate memory for some processes, it needs to find a list of free blocks of physical pages. This information can be searched through a hierarchy of data structures. From top to bottom, the first layer is represented by the *node* data structure. There are as many nodes as the number of NUMA nodes, so in UMA machines just one node is present. Each node is responsible for a certain number of *zones*, which in turn handle an array of *free area* data structures: each of these contains a pointer to a list of free blocks of pages with the same order. Since memory allocation can occur concurrently, a synchronization mechanism to protect the critical section is required. For this reason, each *zone* contains a spin-lock.

2.2   QEMU Live-Migration

QEMU [3] is a widely used hypervisor originally based on binary-translation and later extended to hardware-assisted virtualization [9]. QEMU implements the so called *Pre-Copy live-migration*, since the memory is transferred before the *Guest* runs in the new environment. In fact—when the migration task is terminated—the Guest is ready to run as if nothing had ever happened.

QEMU implements this technique using three stages.

– In the first stage all the Guest RAM is marked as dirty.

– The second stage is an iterative one: when the latter starts, the Hypervisor keeps sending to the new Virtual Machine on the destination Host all the dirty memory. However, the Hypervisor may send the same portion of memory more than once, since the Guest kernel and the Guest processes may still perform write operations on memory, making it dirty again. In order to end the second stage, watermarks or specific ending conditions must be chosen and reached (such as watermarks on the minimum amount of memory left to be transferred or a maximum number of iterations).

– During the third and final stage, the Hypervisor momentarily stops the Guest in order to transfer the last portion of dirty memory, the CPU and the other peripherals state.

Metrics such as setup time (time spent in the first stage), downtime (time spent in the third stage) and total memory sent can be read by checking the migration state on the QEMU Monitor.

2.3   VirtIO Balloon

The idea behind VirtIO Balloon [11] is to give back to the hypervisor the unused memory of a Guest. To do that, a communication between Guest and Hypervisor is required. The balloon can be inflated or deflated. Inflating the balloon means increasing the portion of guest memory that is given back to the Host and can no longer be used by the guest kernel. Deflating the balloon is the opposite operation. The bigger the balloon, the lower is the amount of memory that the Guest can use, but this means that the Host has regained more memory.

VirtIO Balloon can inflate/deflate the balloon in two different ways:

– *static:* the administrator manually resizes (by inflating or deflating the balloon) the guest memory through the QEMU Monitor.
– *automatic:* the HV and the guest kernel communicate to dynamically resize the guest memory depending on the guest and host needs.

VirtIO Balloon can be used to speed up live-migration. To do so in QEMU, the balloon can be inflated from the QEMU Monitor so that the memory that the guest kernel can use is smaller. Now the hypervisor can copy just the memory that the guest can actually use. The balloon can then be deflated once the migration is complete. Note that, for the entire duration of the migration process, the guest kernel cannot use the memory contained in the balloon.

3 Paravirtualized Migration

In Linux all the memory is divided in pages. These pages can be either allocated for different purposes, or can be marked as free. The HV, because of the semantic gap, is unaware of the status of each page and, while performing a migration, must copy all of them. Our idea to reduce the amount of data transferred is to communicate to the HV the list of free pages, along with their physical addresses, during the first state of the migration, so that the HV can skip them during the first iteration of the second stage.

To provide communication between the Guest OS, the Hypervisor and the Host OS the mechanism described in [10] has been exploited. It involves the use of a virtual device, attached to QEMU, that provides a TCP socket for the host system, and a readable buffer for the device-driver. In this way, the host system, using the socket, is able to send a message to the device, while the HV and the guest OS can communicate using the device buffer.

On the other hand, to send back information from the guest to the host, the guest OS can write—with the help of the device driver—inside a buffer available in the device. Since the device is virtual all the information written can be then sent to the host via the socket.

One example of communication is when the *host* system wants to enable or disable the new migration mechanism. In this case, it just needs to send a message to the device so that it will store this information until the migration procedure starts.

If migration optimization is enabled, the following steps show the entire process of our mechanism:

1. The migration thread raises a specific IRQ on the virtual device in order to communicate to the device driver that a migration is occurring. It then waits until the device driver terminates its task.
2. The device driver handles the IRQ. It acquires each zone spinlock and communicates to the HV the physical addresses of the Free Blocks of Physical Pages (FBPP from now on) with their relative sizes, causing a VM Exit.
3. The virtual device can now wake up the migration thread and it waits until the migration's first stage is terminated.
4. The migration thread can now read the guest physical addresses of FBPP from the device buffer. Since the HV is a Host's process, it needs to translate the Guest Physical Addresses to Host Physical Addresses. Once the translation is performed, it can remove every FBPP from the list of dirty pages. Then it will wake up the thread in charge of the device's emulation, and it will start the migration's second stage.
5. The VM Exit is concluded, so the device driver can now release the spinlocks.

The Guest cannot allocate, nor deallocate memory during this stage, but it can do it freely during the other stages, and in particular while memory is being transferred, since any modifications to the Guest kernel's memory-allocation data structures will be caught by the normal dirty-pages tracking mechanism.

4   Experimental Results

All the experiments where run on an Intel i7 8700K with 16 GiB DDR4 RAM. The Guest VM was assigned 4 virtual CPUs and 8 GiB of memory. Both the host and the guest were running v5.11.22 of the Linux kernel. To evaluate performance, we tested different scenarios varying the amount of free memory and the live-migration methodology: The improved live-migration mechanism has been compared against the current QEMU migration implementation with and without the use of VirtIO Balloon.

Our expectation in terms of performance was a decrease in the amount of transferred memory at the cost of a slight increase in setup time. The reduction in terms of transferred memory comes from the avoidance of sending the free memory pages from the VM in the source PM to the VM in the destination PM. On the other hand, this improvement does not come for free, since the list of the FBPP must be evaluated during the first live-migration stage, increasing the setup time. However, we expect that this is largely offset by the time saved from not sending a large portion of memory.

In the first testing session, we compared our optimized live-migration implementation with the QEMU native one.

Three scenarios with different memory loads have been tested. In order to simulate these scenarios, we used a program that used a fixed amount of memory and kept it allocated for the whole migration process.

- *No Load:* No memory from the program was allocated during the migration process.
- *Mid Load:* 4 GiB of memory from the program were allocated during the migration process.
- *High Load:* 6 GiB of memory from the program were allocated during the migration process.

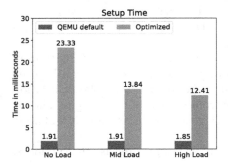

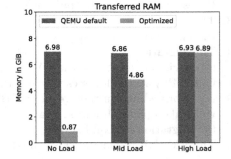

Fig. 3. Setup time with and without the optimization in low mid and high load.

Fig. 4. Transferred RAM with and without the optimization in low mid and high load.

Figure 3 show that, in each scenario, we experienced a higher setup time compared to the standard QEMU migration, as expected. The setup time is about 25 milliseconds and tends to decrease when the load on memory increases. In fact, when a big amount of memory has already been allocated by the kernel, the number of FBPP is lower, so the driver of the emulated guest device that is running into the guest kernel finishes its job faster. Experiments also show that in the high load scenario, setup time is still not comparable to the one obtained by the QEMU default migration, since in this case there is still the overhead caused by synchronization between the migration thread and the guest device driver.

As for the amount of transferred memory, experiments in Fig. 4 show an improvement in the no load and mid load scenario, while there is no difference in the high load one. In fact, in this last case, the amount of free memory is so low that there is no improvement at all since the hypervisor needs to copy the whole memory anyway. On the other hand, when there is a really high portion of free memory, as in no load scenario, the transferred memory reduction is quite significant.

Now let's compute the amount of time spared performing the live migration considering a 1 Gib/s transmission bitrate:

- *no load:* with the standard QEMU migration the hypervisor needs to transfer 6.98 GiB of memory, taking around 55,84 s. The optimized mechanism allows the hypervisor to just send 870.32 MiB of memory, taking just 6.96 s. The added setup time is so small compared to these numbers that it is negligible.
- *mid load:* with the standard QEMU migration the hypervisor needs to transfer 6.86 GiB of memory against the 4.86 GiB with the optimized mechanism. This leads to a spare of 16 s in terms of total migration time. Even in this case, the added setup time is so small that is still negligible.
- *full load:* this is the worst scenario, in fact the amount of transferred RAM is basically equal between the two migration mechanism, implying no improvement in terms of time saved.

Of course having an higher bitrate implies a less evident advantage in terms of time saved. In fact, while an higher bitrate allows the HV to copy the same amount of data in a shorter time, on the other hand it offers no setup time reduction. However, the transferred memory reduction given by this optimization for the no load and mid load scenario is still big enough to be advantageous even with a bitrate of 10 Gib/s.

The following results come from two simulations with different balloon sizes, statically set. In both cases, the guest had no load on memory, in order to maximize the transferred RAM reduction for both migration implementations.

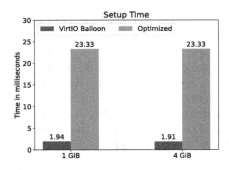
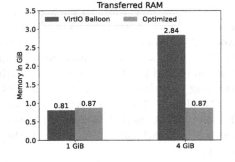

Fig. 5. Setup time using the optimization and VirtIO Balloon in two VM setups (1 GiB and 4 GiB of RAM).

Fig. 6. Transferred RAM using the optimization and VirtIO Balloon in two VM setups (1 GiB and 4 GiB of RAM).

In these two simulations the Guest VM had 1 GiB and 4 GiB of memory respectively. The RAM was reduced by inflating the (VirtIO) balloon and thus given back to the HV.

Figure 5 shows that in each scenario we experienced a higher setup time compared to the standard QEMU migration with the use of VirtIO Balloon. This is expected and the motivation is the same as in the previous scenario.

As for the amount of transferred memory, Fig. 6 shows that there is no significant improvement against the standard QEMU migration using VirtIO Balloon when the guest's memory is shrunk to 1 GiB. In this scenario, the amount of memory left to the guest is basically comparable to the memory without the free pages. In other words the balloon reduced the amount of free pages, making our optimization less effective. However, when the balloon size is not as big as the free memory, like in the second scenario, our implementation performs better, allowing us to save around 15.76 s considering a bitrate of 1 Gib/s. Even in this case, the added setup time is so small that is still negligible.

5   Conclusions and Future Work

In conclusion, in this work we improved the QEMU live migration by not sending the guest's free memory. This showed substantial performance gains against the standard migration, especially when the guest is not handling a high memory load. Future work should consider the use of eBPF to monitor, using probes, guest's memory allocation. Doing this, we can reduce the setup time since we would not need to synchronize the guest's device driver and the migration thread for the entire first migration stage. On the other hand, the guest kernel would be able to allocate memory even during the setup time, since the driver would not need to hold the *free_areas* spin-locks for a long time.

Acknowledgments. Work partially supported by the Italian Ministry of Education and Research (MUR) in the framework of the FoReLab project (Departments of Excellence).

References

1. Anjum, A., Parveen, A.: A dynamic approach for live virtual machine migration using OU detection algorithm. In: 2022 6th International Conference on Computing Methodologies and Communication (ICCMC), pp. 1092–1097 (2022). https://doi.org/10.1109/ICCMC53470.2022.9753974

2. Barham, P., et al.: Xen and the art of virtualization. SIGOPS Oper. Syst. Rev., **37**(5), 164–177 (2003). ISSN 0163–5980, https://doi.org/10.1145/1165389.945462

3. Bellard, F.: Qemu, a fast and portable dynamic translator. In: USENIX Annual Technical Conference, FREENIX Track, vol. 41, p. 46. California, USA (2005)

4. Clark, C., et al. Live migration of virtual machines. In: Proceedings of the 2nd Conference on Symposium on Networked Systems Design & Implementation-Volume 2, pp. 273–286 (2005)

5. Das, R., Sidhanta, S.: LIMOCE: live migration of containers in the edge. In: 2021 IEEE/ACM 21st International Symposium on Cluster, Cloud and Internet Computing (CCGrid), pp. 606–609 (2021). https://doi.org/10.1109/CCGrid51090.2021.00070

6. Garfinkel, T., et al.: A virtual machine introspection based architecture for intrusion detection. In: Ndss, vol. 3, pp. 191–206. San Diega, CA (2003)

7. Hines, M.R., Gopalan, K.: Post-copy based live virtual machine migration using adaptive pre-paging and dynamic self-ballooning. In: Proceedings of the 2009 ACM SIGPLAN/SIGOPS International Conference on Virtual Execution Environments, pp. 51–60 (2009)

8. Ibrahim, K.Z., Hofmeyr, S., Iancu, C., Roman, E.: Optimized pre-copy live migration for memory intensive applications. In: Proceedings of 2011 International Conference for High Performance Computing, Networking, Storage and Analysis, SC 2011, New York, NY, USA (2011). Association for Computing Machinery. ISBN 9781450307710, https://doi.org/10.1145/2063384.2063437

9. Kivity, A., Kamay, Y., Laor, D., Lublin, U., Liguori, A.: KVM: the Linux virtual machine monitor. In: Proceedings of the Linux symposium, vol. 1, pp. 225–230. Dttawa, Dntorio, Canada (2007)

10. Leonardi, L., Lettieri, G., Pellicci, G.: eBPF-based extensible paravirtualization. In: Anzt, H., Bienz, A., Luszczek, P., Baboulin, M. (eds.) High Performance Computing. ISC High Performance 2022 International Workshops. ISC High Performance 2022. Lecture Notes in Computer Science, vol. 13387, pp. 383–393. Springer, Cham (2022). https://doi.org/10.1007/978-3-031-23220-6_27

11. Liu, H., Jin, H., Liao, X., Deng, W., He, B., Cheng-zhong, X.: Hotplug or ballooning: a comparative study on dynamic memory management techniques for virtual machines. IEEE Trans. Parallel Distrib. Syst. **26**(5), 1350–1363 (2015). https://doi.org/10.1109/TPDS.2014.2320915

12. Ma, Y., Wang, H., Dong, J., Li, Y., Cheng, S.: ME2: efficient live migration of virtual machine with memory exploration and encoding. In: 2012 IEEE International Conference on Cluster Computing, pp. 610–613. IEEE (2012)

13. Stoyanov, R., Kollingbaum, M.J.: Efficient live migration of Linux containers. In: Yokota, R., Weiland, M., Shalf, J., Alam, S. (eds.) ISC High Performance 2018. LNCS, vol. 11203, pp. 184–193. Springer, Cham (2018). https://doi.org/10.1007/978-3-030-02465-9_13

14. Svärd, P., Hudzia, B., Tordsson, J., Elmroth, E.: Evaluation of delta compression techniques for efficient live migration of large virtual machines. In: Proceedings of the 7th ACM SIGPLAN/SIGOPS International Conference on Virtual Execution Environments, VEE 2011, pp. 111–120, New York, NY, USA (2011). Association for Computing Machinery. ISBN 9781450306874, https://doi.org/10.1145/1952682.1952698

15. Wang, C., Hao, Z., Cui, L., Zhang, X., Yun, X.: Introspection-based memory pruning for live VM migration. Int. J. Parallel Prog. **45**, 1298–1309 (2017)

16. Wood, T., Shenoy, P.J., Venkataramani, A., Yousif, M.S.: Black-box and gray-box strategies for virtual machine migration. In: Proceedings of the 4th USENIX Conference on Networked Systems Design & Implementation, NSDI 2007, pp. 17, USA (2007). USENIX Association

17. Xu, B., et al.: Sledge: towards efficient live migration of docker containers. In: 2020 IEEE 13th International Conference on Cloud Computing (CLOUD), pp. 321–328 (2020). https://doi.org/10.1109/CLOUD49709.2020.00052

Performance Losses with Virtualization: Comparing Bare Metal to VMs and Containers

Jonatan Baumgartner[1] (iD), Christophe Lillo[2], and Sébastien Rumley[1](✉) (iD)

[1] School of Engineering and Architecture of Fribourg, HES-SO - University of Applied
Sciences and Arts Western Switzerland, Delémont, Switzerland
sebastien.rumley@hefr.ch
[2] DeepSquare, Gotthardstrasse 26, 6300 Zug, Switzerland
lillo@deepsquare.io

Abstract. The use of virtualization technologies has become widespread with the advent of cloud computing. The purpose of this study is to quantify the performance losses caused by all kind of virtualization/containerization configurations.

A benchmark suite consisting of tools that stress specific components and then four real applications commonly used in computing centers has been designed. A system to schedule the execution of these benchmarks and to collect the results has been developed. Finally, a procedure calling all the benchmark in a consistent and reproducible way either within a container or in a (virtual or not machine) has been implemented. These developments permitted then to compare bare metal with four hypervisors and two container runtimes as well as the mix of containers in the virtual machines.

The results show that the performance differences vary greatly depending on the workload and the virtualization software used. When using the right virtualization software, the estimated the performance losses are around 5% for a container and 10% for a virtual machine. The combination of the two entails the addition of these losses to 15%. In the case of non-optimized software, a performance loss of up to 72% can be observed. We also observed that containers and virtual machines can over-perform bare-metal when it comes to file access.

Overall we conclude that virtualization has become very mature and performance losses seems not to be a concern anymore.

Keywords: virtualization · benchmarking · overhead · measures · automation

1 Introduction

During the last decade, containerized or virtualized applications have gradually replaced bare metal computers. These techniques have been popularized by the groundbreaking arrival of cloud computing in companies and public institutions. Hence it is now common for a company to rely exclusively on virtual machines (in addition to personal computers), hosted in a private cloud, or rented to a cloud company. Companies and institutions also increasingly resort to higher-level virtualization solutions, be it thru Containers as a Service (Caas) or Functions as a Service (FaaS). They can even turn to Kubernetes as a Service (KaaS) solutions to manage container deployment themselves, but without having to manage any of the inferior levels (hardware, OS).

A. Bienz et al. (Eds.): ISC High Performance 2023 Workshops, LNCS 13999, pp. 107–120, 2023.
https://doi.org/10.1007/978-3-031-40843-4_9

Stacking services has become so easy that it is common to find multiple layers of virtualization coexisting. For instance, Switch, a swiss academic IT provider, offers a KaaS solution that itself rely on virtual machines (Switch Engine) [16]. It has also become a frequent practice to perform docker-in-docker operations or install docker inside virtual machines for convenience. Furthermore, there is a growing need for nested virtualization [17], which involves running virtual machines inside another.

Virtualization - of the hardware machine (VM hereafter) or of the OS (container hereafter) - makes a lot of sense when it comes to increasing utilization, guaranteeing reproducibility, or easing the deployment. However, there is no free lunch and these benefits come at a cost, namely in terms of performance overhead. We therefore posit that it is legitimate to ask how important this overhead is.

Moreover, in light of the recent energy crisis and the broader objective of transitioning to carbon-neutral societies, the aspect of electrical consumption of IT is gaining importance. Consequently, we inquire: in an energy sobriety context, can a debauchery of virtualization significantly affect the energy consumption of our computing resources? Stated in another way: how much longer will my virtualized application keep my CPU busy? And in yet other terms: what is the performance overhead introduced by virtualization, compared to running the same application directly on the hardware? Addressing the latter question forms the focus of our research, which we explore and discuss in this paper.

Much research in the past tried to answer this question. One of the main challenges for virtualization is the storage input and output rate [1] but other comparisons can be made between bare-metal and high- or low-level virtualization [2]. Some papers [3–5] are quite old and use obsolete technologies like OpenVZ, LXC or Linux-Vserver. Other studies [6, 7] only concentrate on VMs or containers.

The applications used to benchmark the performances differ. While HPL, STREAM and iPerf are almost always used to test the CPU [1, 6, 9], the memory and the network, there is not one default choice when it comes to measuring storage performances. Several articles focus on a specific real-world application: compiling a Linux kernel, testing the capabilities of a web server with RUBiS [3], or accesssing Cassandra database [10]. Shirinbab et al. [11] found that when comparing VMware to XenServer and KVM, no hypervisor has the best performance for all aspects.

Table 1 compiles the results found in literature [2–4, 9]. We see that if there is a consensus on performance degradation for CPU demanding application, there is much more debate about memory or disk intensive workloads. Some papers report discouraging performances in the range of 50% (meaning virtualization introduces a 50% overhead), while others conclude that it is not so bad (at least 90% of the performance).

Interestingly, we note that if there has been a volley of papers published on virtualization benchmarking in the years 2007–2015, the subject has somehow lost traction in the recent years. In our opinion, this is unfortunate since the virtualization technologies did evolve in the last years, notably on the storage performance side, for example with the apparition of ZFS and its aggressive caching methods in Proxmox [12] or with the implementation of virtiofs in Docker [13]. Another type of improvements is the apparition of lighter Kubernetes distributions like k0s which leave more resources available for the containerized workloads themselves. It is also interesting to check if the most

Table 1. Summarized performances loss found by previous studies.

	BARE METAL	CONTAINER	VM
CPU	100%	90–100%	90–100%
MEMORY	100%	95–100%	69–100%
DISK IO	100%	50–90%	45–100%
NETOWRK	100%	64–100%	47–100%

recent platforms still hardly affect performances in peculiar cases, as the one reported by Morabito et al. [9] (UDP traffic).

In summary, we made the decision to carry out a new campaign of benchmarks, with the goal of reconciling the diverse range of results found in the literature and definitively addressing our research question. Our campaign consisted of comparing various virtualization platforms and combination thereof on three different hardware, running a suite of benchmarks. Altogether we totalized more than 1'000 h of benchmarking, yielding in more than 15'000 measurements. To automate the conduction of the experiment, we have implemented a comprehensive test orchestration framework called LSBS, which we made open source available.

Our benchmarking methodology and test orchestration framework LSBS that implements it is presented in Sect. 2. Section 3 presents the results obtained when conducting the tests on the three different hardware targets. We discuss the collected results in Sect. 4. Section 5 concludes.

2 Methodology

We divided our methodology in three components: the *benchmark suite* itself, consisting of different workloads whose performance are measured; the *benchmark procedure*, responsible for (repetitively) calling the *suite* on every *target* available in every desired virtualization configuration, and finally, a data collection system in which all measurements are centralized.

2.1 Benchmark Suite

We strived to assemble a comprehensive and representative collection of benchmarks. The components of this suite are outlined in Table 2. The suite begins with benchmarks that assess individual "hardware" components (IDs 1–16). The HPCC benchmark suite (IDs 1–4) evaluates the CPU and RAM through the utilization of HPL, DGEMM, RandomAccess, and Stream tests. FIO (IDs 5–12) has been chosen for storage testing, encompassing eight measurements that include random or sequential operations, reads or writes, and recording either the operations per second or the speed. Lastly, for network (IDs 13–16), ping is used to measure latency, and IPerf is employed for network assessment, initially in normal mode, followed by reverse mode, and ultimately in UDP mode.

Table 2. The 20 components of the developed benchmark suite

ID	COMPONENT	BENCHMARK	MEASUREMENT	UNIT
1	CPU	HPL	Rate of operations performed by the CPU while resolving a large double precision linear equation system	FLOPS
2		DGEMM	Rate of floating-point operations performed by the CPU multiplicating large matrixes	FLOPS
3	Memory	RandomAccess	Rate of random integer update in the memory	Up/s
4		Stream	Sustainable memory bandwith	GB/s
5	Storage	FIO	Sequential write iops	Io/s
6			Random write iops	
7			Sequential read iops	
8			Random reand iops	
9			Sequential write speed	Kb/s
10			Random write speed	
11			Sequential read speed	
12			Random reand speed	
13	Network	Ping	time between tested and control system	ms
14		Iperf	Network TCP speed from target to control system	Gb/s
15			Network TCP speed from control to target system	
16			Network UDP speed from target to control system	
17	Compound	Blender	Time used to perform the task	seconds
18		Database		
19		Deep Learning		
20		REST server		

In the second part of the suite (IDs 17–20), 4 real applications are used: the rendering of a Blender scene with Blender 3.3.0 and the Classroom scene; operations on a 48MB SQLite database containing phone calls with their source, destination, and cost; the training of a generative adversarial neural network with 322 images; a REST server which, upon requests, creates a 70 MB random file and then asks the client to download it. We measure the execution times of these test applications.

Running the full suite requires multiple launch commands. Installing the suite also requires multiple operations. To both simplify, expedite and, very importantly, standardize both the installation and conduction processes, we described them as Ansible playbooks. Ansible [14] is a command-line software purposed for software installation automation. These playbooks (install and run) can then be "played" over a freshly installed Ubuntu OS. This methodology applies for bare-metal and VM benchmarking.

For containers benchmarking, we wrote Dockerfiles and built images for each benchmark, as well as Ansible playbooks that installs the container runtime and runs the benchmark suite.

2.2 Benchmarking Procedure

In order to run the benchmark suite not only on multiple hardware target, but also in many different (virtualized or not) configurations, and this in an automated way, we implemented *Linux Servers Benchmarking System* (LSBS). LSBS is an open-source tool [18] specifically designed for orchestrating the benchmarking process. LSBS oversees the installation and execution of benchmarks on one or multiple target *platforms* using the aforementioned Ansible playbooks. Once a benchmark has finished, the results are sent back to LSBS which collects them. LSBS takes one or more machines, virtual or not, as targets, with a fresh OS installed on them. Installations and executions of one or more benchmark batches on one or more targets can then be scheduled.

As we must ensure that the software environment is exactly the same each time and can be reproduced, the installation procedure must be extremely precisely defined. The installation of the container runtimes (Docker, k0s) is fully automated and handled by LSBS thru the aforementioned Ansible playbooks. But for installing the base OS (for bare-metal benchmarking), the type 1 hypervisors (hence hypervisors running directly over the metal), and the Ubuntu 22.04 host OS (for VMs), we defined a detailed manual installation procedure, also available in the LSBS repository. In the future, we plan to automate this part as well, using Metal-as-a-Service approaches [15].

2.3 Results Collection and Visualization System

LSBS provides a webapp front-end, thru which 1) benchmarks runs can be scheduled and monitored (Fig. 1a), 2) raw measurements can be verified (Fig. 2) and 3) comparisons between *platforms* for each hardware and benchmark can be displayed in the form of graphs with built-in statistical tools (Fig. 1b). These tools facilitate benchmarking campaigns, for first order result validation notably.

3   Results

With our benchmark suite and benchmarking tool LSBS at hand, we conducted performances comparisons on three different hardware systems, which are listed in Table 3. These three systems show some diversity in the hardware (CPU, manufacturer) and belong to different generations.

As for virtualization, to thoroughly compare bare metal with VMs and containers, we thrived to use the most popular hypervisors and container runtimes. For hypervisors, we selected: VMware vSphere Hypervisor 7.0 (ESXi), Microsoft Hyper-V server 2019, Proxmox Virtual Environment 7.3 and XCP-ng 8.2. For containers, Docker 20.10

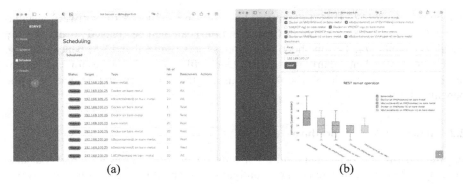

| (a) | (b) |

Fig. 1. LSBS front-end webapp screenshots a) benchmarks scheduling interface. b) results comparison interface, displaying an example result comparing the REST server performance across several *platforms* on the AMD based system (details will be presented below).

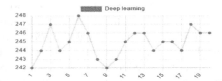

Fig. 2. Example of result checking graph for the bare metal deep learning benchmark on the Intel Core i7-4790k hardware, using LSBS visualization features.

which uses the runC runtime and k0s, a Kubernetes orchestrator that uses the containerd runtime, in version 1.22.

Table 4 lists the 15 combinations that have been tested on each hardware. Essentially, we test 3 container environments (Docker, k0s, *NONE*) across 5 machines (*bare-metal machine*, Proxmox VM, VMWare VM, XCP-ng VM, Hyper-v VM). Grey lines in Table 4 denote combinations that couldn't be tested on the AMD-B550 based system, due to hardware drivers compatibility issues. For this hardware, we thus have only 9 *platforms* to test. Altogether, we ended up with $15 + 15 + 9 = 39$ hardware/virtualization/container combinations - that we call "*platforms*" throughout this document.

Table 3. Systems used for the benchmarks.

CPU	MEMORY	STORAGE	NETWORK
Intel Core i7-4790k 4 cores	24 GB DDR3 1333 MHz	1TB SanDisk SSD Plus	HP NC523SFP 10 Gb/s
2*Intel Xeon E5-2630 v3 $8 + 8 = 16$ cores	128 GB DDR4 1866 MHz	120 GB Intel SSD DC S3500	Intel X540-AT2 10 Gb/s
AMD Ryzen 7 3700X 8 cores	16GB DDR4 3000 MHz	1TB SanDisk SSD Plus	HP NC523SFP 10 Gb/s

Table 4. Tested container/virtualization combinations. Grey lines have not been tested on the AMD based system

		Bare metal
	Docker over	Bare metal
	K0s over	Bare metal
	Ubuntu Proxmox VM over	Bare metal
Docker over	Ubuntu Proxmox VM over	Bare metal
K0s over	Ubuntu Proxmox VM over	Bare metal
	Ubuntu Hyper-v VM over	Bare metal
Docker over	Ubuntu Hyper-v VM over	Bare metal
K0s over	Ubuntu Hyper-v VM over	Bare metal
	Ubuntu XCP-ng VM over	Bare metal
Docker over	Ubuntu XCP-ng VM over	Bare metal
K0s over	Ubuntu XCP-ng VM over	Bare metal
	Ubuntu VMWare VM over	Bare metal
Docker over	Ubuntu VMWare VM over	Bare metal
K0s over	Ubuntu VMWare VM over	Bare metal

As we have 39 *platforms* across the three hardware and given that the benchmarking suite contains 20 benchmarks, we have scheduled 780 batches. Knowing that we asked LSBS to repeat each execution 20 times within a batch, we thus should have collected 39 × 20 benchmarks × 20 repetitions = 15'600 measurements. In practice, a few batches have failed, resulting in a slightly lower number of measurements.

The first phase of result analysis consisted of verifying the consistency of the outcomes across the 20 tests that comprise a single run. This has been done by manually inspecting each of the 39 × 20 = 780 runs on a graph provided by the webapp, as the one visible in Fig. 2. We checked for anomalies, for example an overheating of the CPU with scores that decrease after a while or worse scores at the beginning of the run because other operations could still be running in the background. Upon thorough examination, no evident aberrations have been detected in the gathered data (to the exception of the few missing batches).

Next, we computed, for each benchmark, a reference mark by calculating the mean performance of the workload on the "bare-metal" *platform*, using no virtualization nor containers. Then we normalized our results by this mark. Figure 3 show the result for 3 benchmarks: HPL, database experiment and deep-learning experiment. For HPL (Fig. 3a – higher is better), on the Intel Core i7 computer, performance is rather homogenous, but we see hypervisors outperforming bare-metal (best: XCP-ng with 113% performance of bare-metal), to the exception of Hyper-V. Introducing OS virtualization induces a 10–20% overhead, except on Hyper-V. On the dual Xeon hardware, virtualization induces a massive performance drop. Further investigation of these results are required, but this could be due to the fact that Hypervisors are agnostic to NUMA effects of multi-socket systems.

For database results (Fig. 3b – lower is better), we note that the results are even more homogeneous, except some outlier *platforms* using Docker. On the AMD system, containerized workloads systematically outperform the bare-metal case.

For deep-learning results (Fig. 3c – lower is better), we note again better performances for containerized workloads. We also note a severe performance drop when using Hyper-V on the Intel Core i7 hardware.

In general, we observe that the performance of hypervisor or container runtimes can significantly vary depending on the hardware.

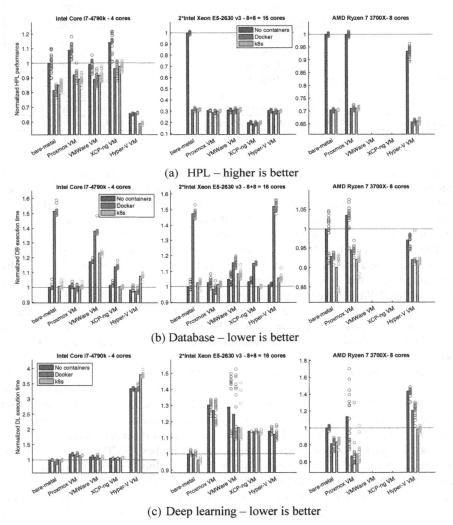

(a) HPL – higher is better

(b) Database – lower is better

(c) Deep learning – lower is better

Fig. 3. Normalized performance measurement for three benchmarks (a,b,c) across the three hardwares (columns). For HPL (a), higher performance is better, while for database (b) and deep-learning (c), lower execution time is better. Circles denote individual measurements.

Table 5. Hypervisor comparison.

Benchmark	Proxmox	VMWare*	Hyper-V	XCP-ng*	Best
CPU	**0.0119**	0.0112	0.0107	*0.0063*	Proxmox
Memory	9.62	9.87	**10.82**	*6.71*	Hyper-V
Storage	35332	*26894*	29827	**36454**	XCP-ng
Network	**167.43**	*150.31*	159.83	163.42	Proxmox
Blender	**36.33**	42.25	*44.33*	41.50	Proxmox
Deep learning	203.19	200.75	*394.69*	**189.00**	XCP-ng
Database	609	*645*	**587**	605	Hyper-V
REST server	*16.5*	15.5	13.5	**13.0**	XCP-ng

Table 6. Container runtimes comparison.

Benchmark	Docker	Containerd	Best
CPU	0.0097	**0.0098**	Containerd
Memory	**7.67**	7.66	Docker
Storage	**38096**	34592	Docker
Network	149.11	**152.84**	Containerd
Blender	39.33	**39.00**	Containerd
Deep learning	**158.83**	162.00	Docker
Database	773.33	**584.33**	Containerd
REST server	11.33	11.33	--

Next, we looked if an hypervisor clearly dominates the others. For that, we aggregated the performance along each benchmark category (except for applications, which we kept individually) and across the different hardwares, without the use of containers. Results are presented in Table 5. We note that no hypervisor seems to clearly emerge once results are averaged over the different hardwares. Each hypervisor is trailing in at least one category (*italic* figures) and only VMWare never achieve a best score (**bold** figures). We performed the same analysis for container runtimes, whose results are visible in Table 6. Here as well, there is no clear winner.

We further aggregated our results to allow a comparison with our initial data extracted from literature (Table 1). Since we concluded that there is no obvious choice in terms of hypervisor or container runtime for comparing performance with bare-metal, we cherry-picked the best hypervisor and the best container runtime of each category according to Tables 5 and 6, and finally we extracted the performances using the worst and best hardware. Results are visible on Table 7.

As we noted before, pure CPU performances seems to suffer a lot from NUMA effects, potentially explaining the poor worst performances. We note, however, that as

Table 7. Performance availability with and without virtualization

Benchmark	Bare metal	Container	Vm
CPU	100%	28–86%	28–108%
Memory	100%	61–91%	51–139%
Storage	100%	64–118%	93–197%
Network	100%	95–112%	90–103%
Blender	100%	96–105%	105–112%
Deep learning	100%	96–110%	93–100%
Database	100%	101–117%	69–96%
Rest server	100%	107–130%	90–93%

we move toward higher level workloads, these penalties tend to disappear. The storage heavily depends on the hypervisor caching methods. For example, Hyper-V offers impressive random performances but has a massive loss on sequential accesses. Proxmox, with the default caching, offers a less impressive random performance boost but has only a maximum 7% loss on sequential operations. On the network side, while containers and VMs both suffer a 0.1ms ping time increase, the speeds heavily depend on the network card drivers. On intel hardwares, the Hyper-V driver has a big performance loss. The strange UDP behavior observed in [9] was not present in our results. Finally, when running "typical" applications, there is not much difference between bare metal, containers, and virtual machines.

Our final analysis consisted of checking whether virtualization overheads are cumulative: if running a workload in a VM reveals a normalized performance of, say, 90%, and running the same workload in a container returns a normalized performance of 85%, can we expect the performance of a container running in a VM to be 85% * 90% = 76.5%? Fig. 4 exhibits this analysis for a couple of *platform*-benchmark pairs. We see that for HPL on the intel Core i7 hardware (top-left – higher is better), the best combination is XCP-ng + k8s. The predictions are also rather accurate, except may be for Hyper-V & Docker.

For deep learning, again on the Intel Core i7 hardware (top-right – less is better), Hyper-V performance is several degraded, and also more degraded than what one could predict. Finally, for database benchmarks on the two Intel based hardwares (bottom – less is better), we see that the predictor works rather well for k8s but doesn't for Docker. This could indicate that with Docker we are not facing a linear overhead, but rather a sort of impedance mismatch, possibly stemming from a misconfiguration of the engine.

4   Discussion

Within the review process, this paper has received many comments and constructive criticism from the reviewers. Here we discuss some of these points.

One criticism was that our benchmark results, which considered *platforms* as "black-boxes" with default and non-optimized settings, do not provide very useful insights on these products and underlying virtualization technologies. We agree that our results are not insightful if one looks for the *intrinsic* performance of a *platform* for executing a particular task. Yet, one of the biggest advantages of virtualization being to reduce the number of physical servers needed in an IT system, in practice one can hardly optimize a *platform* for a specific type of task. In addition, many SMEs operating a private cloud can hardly afford an expert dedicating his time to fine-tune the hypervisor settings depending on the current workloads. Therefore, we do see value in sticking to default, generic hypervisor configuration as tuned by the vendor.

Other remarks mentioned that we should have disclosed many more settings as the BIOS configuration flags, hypervisors settings, and offered a more in-depth description of the test setups. We can clarify as follows: no particular configurations have been applied to the target BIOSs except disabling the power save modes, which means we sticked to default settings. All the hypervisors have been installed with the default settings as described in the GitHub project [18]. For sure there are many parameters to describe, and to play with, but we believe it is also interesting to report results taken "in the wild". And, again, most users are unaware of all these parameters.

Specifically, we've been asked if direct assignment or paravirtualized I/O were used.

While direct assignment or passthrough works great in a specialized cluster, it is difficult to use in a typical general purpose virtualization cluster, so all our VMs are configured with paravirtualized I/O devices. In each case, the maximum available vCPUs and memory is allocated to the VM. The installation and configuration are described in the Github project [18].

We been rightfully told that both Docker and k0s use containerd and runC. However, there is an added layer, the container runtime interface between k0s and containerd [19].

Finally, a reviewer has been extremely surprised to see notably high overheads from running HPL in a container (Fig. 3a) and hinted a misconfiguration of the container engine. Yet the default configuration has been used. It is possible that the container engine is, by default, optimized not for the performance but to work as good as possible in a maximum of different environment. It could be interesting to conduct a study on how to automatically optimize this configuration or at least notify and expose the problem to the user.

Generally, our study opens the door to many further explorations.

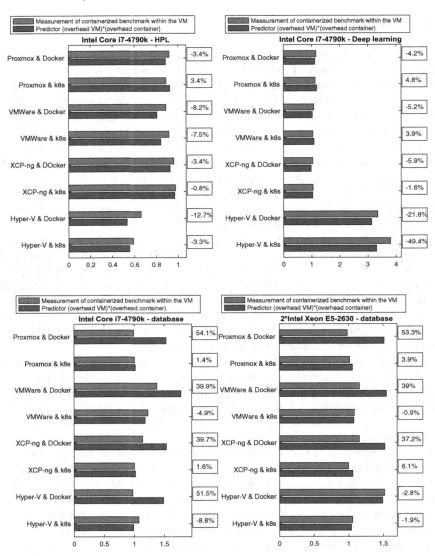

Fig. 4. Comparison of mean performances normalized to the bare-metal case of different VM and container combinations (bar labels), for 4 different *platform*-benchmark pairs. Red bars denote actual performance. Blue bars show a "prediction" obtained by multiplying individual virtualized and containerized performances. Boxes indicate the error of the prediction.

5   Conclusions and Perspectives

The focus of this research was to quantify the performance losses introduced by virtualization to provide valuable information that can help IT departments choose the most efficient technology for their needs: keep using bare-metal machine to guarantee performances, or shift to VMs, containers, or a mix thereof.

A large benchmarking system was created and tested on hardware from different eras and manufacturers, yielding over 15,000 results to compare the performances of bare metal mixed with 4 hypervisors and 2 different container runtimes.

The results showed that by choosing the right virtualization technologies, it is possible to minimize losses to 5% for a container and 10% for a VM. Users should nevertheless be careful to NUMA effects for CPU intensive tasks. Depending on the task, an hypervisor can make a better usage of the available resources. In many cases, VMs outperformed the bare-metal case, even in terms of CPU. This interesting fact deserves further investigation. Both container runtimes and hypervisors offer caching mechanisms that can be interesting to use on storage intensive tasks. Since the performances vary across hypervisors and container runtimes, it might thus be interesting to conduct *in-situ* lab benchmarking to make the right virtualization choices.

Generally we thus conclude that virtualization (VM or OS) does not kills performance, at least when the hardware is not shared among multiple VMs and/or containers. However, our results show that there can be adversarial situations where performance is highly degraded. These situations can potentially be alleviated by changing configuration flags, yet it might be hard to detect these situations. And changing the configuration to solve one situation might affect other situations.

It is also important to note that we *only* considered single workload performance measurements. The performance evaluation when multiple virtualized workloads compete for the resources is kept for future work.

In the future, we also plan to regularly replicate these benchmarks on newer hardware and software systems as it was found that the figures, especially for storage IO, have changed significantly over the years. It would also be interesting to see if and where software developers choose to make improvements and if all the features added each year do not result in increased overhead.

Eventually, we plan to investigate if, when nesting multiple levels of VMs, the losses increase according to the number of added layer or if only the lowest level one matters.

References

1. Gavrilovska, A., et al.: High-performance hypervisor architectures: virtualization in HPC systems. In: HPCVirt 07 (2007)
2. White, J., et al.: A survey of virtualization technologies with performance testing. CoRR, vol. abs/1010.3233. http://arxiv.org/abs/1010.3233 (2010)
3. Padala, P., et al.: Performance evaluation of virtualization for server consolidation. HP Laboratories Report NO. HPL-2007–59R1 (2007)
4. Xavier, M.G., et al.: Performance evaluation of container-based virtualization for high performance computing environments. In: Conference on Parallel, Distributed and Network-Based Proceedings (2013). https://doi.org/10.1109/PDP.2013.41

5. Babu, S.A., et al.: System performance evaluation of para virtualization, container virtualization, and full virtualization using Xen, OpenVZ, and XenServer. In: International Conference on Advances in Computing and Communications (2014). https://doi.org/10.1109/ICACC.201 4.66

6. Arango, C., et al.: Performance evaluation of container-based virtualization for high performance computing environments (2017). https://doi.org/10.48550/arXiv.1709.10140

7. McDougall, R., et al.: Virtualization performance: perspectives and challenges ahead. SIGOPS Oper. Syst. Rev. **44**, 4 (2010)

8. Li, Z., et al.: Performance overhead comparison between hypervisor and container based virtualization. In: IEEE International Conference on Advanced Information Networking and Applications (AINA) (2017). https://doi.org/10.1109/AINA.2017.79

9. Morabito, R., et al.: Hypervisors vs. Lightweight virtualization: a performance comparison. In: IEEE International Conference on Cloud Engineering (2015). https://doi.org/10.1109/IC2E.2015.74

10. Shirinbab, S., et al.: Performance evaluation of container and virtual machine running cassandra workload. In: International Conference of Cloud Computing Technologies and Applications (CloudTech) (2017). https://doi.org/10.1109/CloudTech.2017.8284700

11. Shirinbab, S., et al.: Performance comparison of KVM, VMware and XenServer using a large telecommunication application. CCGrid (2014)

12. https://www.proxmox.com/en/news/press-releases/proxmox-ve-3-4-released

13. https://www.docker.com/blog/speed-boost-achievement-unlocked-on-docker-desktop-4-6-for-mac/

14. https://www.ansible.com

15. http://mass.io

16. Tres, D.: Switchkaas factsheet. https://www.switch.ch/export/sites/default/kubernetes-as-a-service/.galleries/files/SWITCHkaas-Factsheet-EN.pdf

17. Lim, J.T., et al.: NEVE: nested virtualization extensions for ARM. In: Symposium on Operating Systems Principles (2017)

18. Github.com/jojoc4/LSBS

19. https://www.techtarget.com/searchitoperations/tip/A-breakdown-of-container-runtimes-for-Kubernetes-and-Docker#:~:text=The%20container%20runtime%20is%20the,OCI%2Dc ompliant%20runtime%20should%20work

Real-Time Unikernels: A First Look

Luca Abeni$^{(\boxtimes)}$ iD

Scuola Superiore Sant'Anna, Pisa, Italy
luca.abeni@santannapisa.it

Abstract. Real-time virtualization is currently a hot topic, and there is much ongoing research on real-time Virtual Machines and hypervisors. However, most of the previous research focused on the virtualization stack (hypervisor, host Operating System, Virtual Machine scheduling, etc.) and did not investigate the impact of the guest Operating System architecture on real-time performance. This paper is a first step in filling this gap and investigates the suitability of unikernels for serving real-time applications. The most important existing unikernels are investigated, evaluating their usability in the context of real-time virtualization. Finally, the real-time performance of OSv is compared with the ones of the Linux kernel.

Keywords: Real-Time Computing · Virtualization · Operating Systems · Unikernels

1 Introduction

With the ever-growing diffusion of cloud computing, various services or entire OSs can be remotely executed in distributed virtualized environments. This results in an increasing interest in various virtualization technologies, leading people to virtualize even applications that have not traditionally been considered candidates for execution in virtual environments. A typical example is the virtualization of applications characterized by some kinds of temporal constraints, which is challenging because it requires providing *a-priori guarantees* that such temporal constraints are respected. Such guarantees can be provided by using well-known techniques from real-time literature, real-time OSs/hypervisors, and appropriate management software. In particular, it is important to schedule the virtualized real-time applications according to predictable/analyzable algorithms and to introduce *bounded* latencies in their execution.

Analyzable and deterministic scheduling algorithms have been proposed in literature and have already been implemented [1,22,37,38] both in widely used hypervisors [11] or host OSs and in the guest OSs. Moreover, modern hypervisors or host OSs introduce latencies that are low enough for running real-time applications [4,5,23].

Although the usage of Virtual Machines (VMs) is widespread across many different kinds of systems, from cloud/edge servers to low-power embedded devices, real-time virtualization solutions mainly focus on embedded devices or dedicated

A. Bienz et al. (Eds.): ISC High Performance 2023 Workshops, LNCS 13999, pp. 121–133, 2023.
https://doi.org/10.1007/978-3-031-40843-4_10

machines [12,27,33]. In most of these situations, the guest OS can be based on small real-time executives or dedicated kernels. When real-time applications are executed on larger-scale cloud systems, additional issues, such as the applications' start-up times or the guests' resource consumption, must be taken into account. While containers have been traditionally seen as a possible solution to this issue, this paper investigates a possible alternative provided by unikernels (dedicated and/or specialized library OSs that are optimized to execute inside a VM).

Unfortunately, the unikernels' real-time features and performance (in terms of available scheduling algorithms and introduced latencies) have not been previously evaluated. This paper aims to be a first step in the direction of using unikernels to support real-time applications in a cloud environment, presenting an overview of the software projects that can be used for this purpose, analyzing their features, and trying to evaluate their real-time performance.

2   Background and Definitions

Applications running in a cloud are executed using a *guest OS* that runs in some kind of Virtual Machine (VM).

These VMs can be implemented using different technologies; for example, they can be based on *hardware virtualization* or on *OS-level virtualization*. For full hardware virtualization, the VM virtualizes the CPU, the memory, and all the devices of a physical machine. In contrast, for OS-level virtualization, only the OS kernel (and not all the hardware devices) is virtualized.

Using hardware virtualization, the guest OS executes in the VM as if it was on real hardware, and unmodified OSs can easily run in virtualized environments without being aware of the virtualization layer. To improve I/O performance, the VM can implement some "special" paravirtualized devices; in this case, the performance boost is "paid" by the need to modify the guest OS kernel (that must be aware of running inside a VM and must know how to handle the paravirtualized devices). If the CPU's Instruction Set Architecture (ISA) is virtualizable [30], the virtualization performance can be improved by directly executing the guest machine instructions on the host CPU. All the modern CPUs have a virtualizable ISA (or provide some hardware-assisted virtualization features that make the ISA virtualizable). Hence, the most commonly-used hypervisors can take advantage of this technique.

When OS-level virtualization is used, instead, the system runs one single OS kernel (the host kernel), and such a kernel is in charge of virtualizing its services for the guest OSs (and providing isolation between the guests). Hence, all the OSs running on the physical node share the same kernel; this implies that the guests must run the same hardware and software architecture (if the host OS is Linux-based and the physical machine is based on Intel x86_64 CPUs, then the guest OSs must also be based on an x86_64 Linux kernel). In Linux, this form of virtualization is often used to implement the *container* abstraction [10] based on *control groups* to account for the usage of kernel resources and *namespaces* to control their visibility and provide isolation. User space tools such as `docker` or `podman` are used to set up the containers, properly configuring control groups and namespaces to execute the guest OS inside them.

Most of the previous work in real-time literature focused on ensuring that system resources are timely allocated to the virtualized real-time applications so that they can respect their temporal constraints. This mainly requires to:

1. Schedule the applications using a theoretically-sound scheduling algorithm that can be analyzed and allows providing real-time guarantees
2. Implement the scheduling algorithm correctly, limiting the latencies introduced when scheduling each application

The first issue is addressed by building a 2-level hierarchy of schedulers (the host/hypervisor scheduler schedules VMs, and the guest schedulers running inside each VM schedule the applications' tasks when the first scheduler selects the VM) and analyzing its behavior [36]. For example, real-time guarantees can be easily provided if the host kernel/hypervisor provides CPU reservations and the guest scheduler provides fixed priorities [2,8,14,24,28,35].

The second issue is addressed by measuring and analyzing the so-called *kernel latency* (or VM latency, in the case of virtualized environments), which, informally speaking, measures the accuracy of the scheduler's implementation. In fact, it often happens that application tasks are not scheduled at the time when the theoretical scheduling algorithm would schedule them, but their execution is somehow delayed. This latency can be caused by non-preemptable sections in the kernel or in the hypervisor, by the language runtime (think about garbage collection in the JVM), or by similar implementation details. It was originally studied in the context of real-time OSs [6,13], but the definitions and analysis have been extended to VMs, too [4,5] (see the cited papers for more formal definitions).

Since the latency can be accounted for in schedulability analysis as a blocking time, if an upper bound L for the latency is known, then standard real-time analysis can be used to guarantee the respect of the temporal constraints of virtualized applications even if the host kernel or hypervisor introduces some latency. Of course, if this upper bound is too high, then no guarantee can be provided for real-time tasks running inside a VM.

Standard tools such as `cyclictest` are commonly used to measure the worst-case latency introduced by an OS or experienced inside a VM, and previous work already showed that with off-the-shelf hardware and properly tuned hypervisors, it is possible to limit the experienced latency to less than $L = 100$ μs, which is acceptable for many real-time applications.

However, the previous research on real-time VMs focused on scheduling and latency aspects, ignoring other important metrics such as the application's start-up time and the VM's resource consumption. In this regard, OS-level virtualization can help (see the results in Sect. 4). However, containers are generally considered less secure.

To reduce start-up times and resource consumption without renouncing to full hardware virtualization, it is possible to use unikernel architectures for the guest, as discussed in the next section.

3   The Unikernel Approach

Unikernels are a specialized form of library OSs [9,31] in which the OS kernel is designed as a library to be linked to user applications. This allows for reducing the system call overhead and opens the way for kernel customization by removing the subsystems that are not needed/used by the application.

The unikernel approach takes this idea to the limit [26], allowing to build kernels that serve one single application and removing the overhead introduced by memory protection (a unikernel is designed to execute inside a VM, which already implements a protection domain; hence, the kernel does not need to implement any kind of protection). As a result, a unikernel-based system consumes fewer resources and provides better performance.

Although there has not been much previous research on real-time unikernels, it might be conjectured that unikernels also provide better real-time performance (lower latencies). However, this kind of reasoning can sometimes be dangerous and lead to wrong conclusions; for example, since bare-metal hypervisors like Xen [11] are much smaller and simpler than hosted hypervisors (plus the host kernel) such as KVM/Linux [17], many people think that bare-metal hypervisors introduce smaller latencies than hosted hypervisors. This is, however, not the case, as latencies introduced by KVM/Linux actually have a smaller upper bound than the latencies introduced by Xen [5] (probably because Linux and KVM have been fine-tuned for real-time performance for a long time, while support for real-time applications in Xen did not receive as much attention). Hence, it is important to run some systematic sets of experiments to evaluate the suitability of various unikernels for real-time applications. First of all, some candidate unikernels have been identified, analyzing their features.

While some unikernels provide a specialized Application Programming Interface (API) and require developing the guest applications according to such a non-standard API, others try to support some standard API such as POSIX. Other unikernels even try to provide Application Binary Interface (ABI) compatibility with Linux so that native Linux applications can be executed on the unikernel without requiring a recompilation. However, not all the Linux system calls (or the glibc functions) are currently implemented, and some functionalities might be missing. To support the execution of real-time applications, the guest OS must support fixed-priority scheduling [25] so that the compositional scheduling framework analysis [36] can be used. Moreover, real-time applications need high-resolution timers and are often composed of periodic tasks that can be implemented efficiently, accurately, and without race conditions, if the `clock_nanosleep()` call (with the `TIME_ABSTIME` flag) is supported. These are the main features that will be analyzed in the various unikernels.

3.1   RumpRun

Rumprun (https://github.com/rumpkernel/rumprun) is one of the first unikernels, based on the Rump kernel architecture [15,16]. The Rump kernel allows recompiling many subsystems of the NetBSD kernel in different contexts (in the monolithic NetBSD kernel, in user space processes, in different kinds of kernels/microkernels) thanks to some glue code (the "anykernel" code). Rumprun just implements the anykernel code needed to run Rump inside a VM (Xen or KVM) or directly on bare hardware and to link it with some application.

While this idea is interesting and looks suitable for serving real-time applications, Rumprun is unfortunately not developed anymore (the last commit is from May 2020, and just modifies some scripts to support QEMU's hvf; the last real development of the kernel is dated back to 2018). Moreover, Rumprun's scheduler does not seem to support fixed priorities.

3.2   OSv

OSv [18] has been the first project to propose the unikernel architecture as a way to improve the performance of applications running in virtualized environments. It is based on a kernel developed from scratch in C++, which is able to parse dynamic ELF executables and directly link to them. While this approach does not allow discarding the kernel subsystems not used by the application (for example, the virtual filesystem and the ZFS code are used even if the application does not access the filesystem), it greatly improves the applications' performance. While OSv was originally only API compatible with Linux (and required to recompile native Linux applications to link them with the unikernel), ABI compatibility has also been implemented (so OSv can currently execute native Linux applications without requiring to recompile them).

OSv was originally developed by Cloudius Systems[1], which is not involved with OSv anymore. However, this unikernel is still maintained and developed by an active open-source community. While OSv does not support fixed-priority scheduling (and the `sched_setscheduler()` call, for example, is not implemented), there are some out-of-tree patches that implement real-time scheduling and other features needed by real-time applications. Hence, OSv can potentially be used to run real-time applications, and its real-time performance will be evaluated in Sect. 4

3.3   Linux-Based Unikernels

Some recent software projects, such as Unikernel Linux [32] and Lupine Linux [20], aimed at implementing unikernel functionalities based on the Linux codebase. In particular, these projects allow the execution of standard Linux applications in kernel space so that the system call overhead and some part of the context switch overhead can be avoided. While this approach greatly improves the applications' performance (especially in terms of throughput), it does not help reduce boot times or resource usage.

---

[1] https://cloudius-systems.com.

3.4 HermitCore and HermiTux

HermitCore [21] is a research project developed to decrease the so-called "OS noise" (the amount of time stolen by the OS and its kernel) and make the applications' execution times more deterministic and predictable. Unfortunately, it does not support fixed-priority scheduling, and it is hence unsuitable for real-time applications (its focus is on HPC). The HermitCore unikernel was discontinued in 2021 in favor of a re-implementation in Rust, named RustyHermit, which also does not support the features needed to run real-time applications.

HermiTux [29] provides compatibility with the Linux ABI on top of HermitCore, allowing the execution of native Linux applications. It is based on a combination of HermitCore with the musl C library (http://musl.libc.org) and does not support the `sched_setscheduler()` call (which always fails).

3.5 Unikraft

Unikraft [19] is a modern unikernel organized as a set of modular libraries developed from scratch. These libraries can be easily linked with user applications to build small and efficient unikernels; since static linking is used, this approach allows removing all the unused code from the final executable (for example, if the application does not use the network, all the network drivers and stacks are not linked in the final executable).

Although the basic Unikraft libraries are not ABI or API compatible with Linux, an additional module (based on the musl C library) allows linking unmodified Linux applications.

Unikraft is optimized to reduce resource usage, to achieve small boot times, and to provide high performance (in terms of throughput). Unfortunately, support for real-time applications is missing: the scheduler, for example, does not support fixed priorities. However, the development community is very active, and it seems that support for real-time applications can be easily implemented. Hence, Unikraft performance will be evaluated as future work.

3.6 Discussion

None of the considered unikernels supports fixed-priority scheduling, and most of them do not implement `clock_nanosleep()` or similar functions. Even if these functionalities can be easily implemented, their absence seems to indicate that support for real-time applications has never been considered before. For example, most of these projects use the musl C library to provide POSIX functionalities, but musl implements `sched_setscheduler()` by simply returning ENOSYS. While this decision might have some technical value[2], it just shows that running real-time applications on unikernels is not a priority (most of the real-time applications running on Linux actually use `sched_setscheduler()`).

---

[2] It seems that musl developers implemented the function in this way because they think the Linux `sched_setscheduler()` system call is not POSIX compliant.

As a consequence, it is possible that even after implementing fixed-priority scheduling and the appropriate system calls, the latencies introduced by the unikernel will be large (just because no-one ever optimized them).

4   Quantitative Evaluation

This section presents some measurements to evaluate the real-time performance of different guest solutions using the same host kernel and hypervisor. All the experiments have been performed on a system equipped with AMD Ryzen 7 5700U CPU running at 1.4 GHz; the host OS is Ubuntu 23.04, with the 6.2.0-1003-lowlatency Linux kernel, and the VMs are based on QEMU 7.2.0 with KVM. The system has been configured to obtain the most possible deterministic execution times [3].

To have some baseline performance as a reference, the experiments from [4,5] have been repeated using a 5.19.6 Linux kernel as a guest. The worst-case latency experienced by real-time applications running in the QEMU VM (measured with `cyclictest`) $L = 175$ µs, but 99% of the measured latency values are below 10 µs. Using a real-time kernel in the host and in the guest (for example, a Linux kernel with the Preempt-RT patchset [34]), it is possible to reduce the worst-case latency to less than 100 µs [4,5]: for example, using a 6.1.28-rt10 Linux kernel, the worst-case latency measured by `cyclictest` (with a period of 100 µs) running in a QEMU VM resulted in $L = 92$ µs (with 99% of the measured latency values below 15 µs).

These results confirm that using a Linux-based OS as a guest, it is possible to support real-time applications with quite strict temporal requirements. However, the boot times of a Linux-based OS can be too large. This has been verified by starting a VM containing a guest that immediately shuts down and measuring the time QEMU needs to boot and shut down the OS. The worst-case (maximum) boot/shutdown time over 100 runs has been measured as 1180 ms, with an average value of 1108 ms; in some situations, having to wait for more than 1 s to start an application is not acceptable.

Using OS-level virtualization can decrease the boot times; to verify this, the same experiment has been repeated using a container started with `podman`. In this case, the worst-case boot/shutdown time over 100 runs is 440 ms, and the average is 211 ms. It can be noticed that `podman` has been optimized to decrease the average boot time, but it exhibits a large variability in the amount of time needed to start a container.

Unikernels allow decreasing the boot times without renouncing full hardware virtualization. For example, OSv provides a worst-case boot/shutdown time of $390ms$ over 100 runs, with an average time of $323ms$. In this case, it can be noticed that OSv has been optimized to decrease the worst-case boot time and not the average one. As a side note, OSv also measures its own boot time (without considering the time needed to start QEMU and the shutdown time), which has a worst-case of $156ms$ over 100 runs.

Table 1. Boot/Shutdown times for various virtualization solutions.

Virtualization mechanism	Worst-Case	Average
QEMU/Linux	1180 ms	1108 ms
QEMU/Linux with PVH	1060 ms	988 ms
QEMU/Linux microvm with PVH	400 ms	310 ms
QEMU/OSv	390 ms	323 ms
QEMU/OSv with PVH	240 ms	185 ms
QEMU/OSv microvm with PVH	140 ms	102 ms
Podman	440 ms	211 ms

Table 2. Worst-case latencies measured by `cyclictest` with various periods in a VM running OSv.

$P = 50$ μs	$P = 100$ μs	$P = 250$ μs	$P = 500$ μs	$P = 1000$ μs
163 μs	144 μs	134 μs	223 μs	232 μs

When a VM such as QEMU is used, further boot time reductions can be obtained by using a para-virtualized boot protocol[3] and a lighter VM model, such as QEMU's microvm[4], Amazon's Firecracker [7], or Intel's Cloud Hypervisor[5].

Using QEMU's PVH boot method, the worst-case Linux boot/shutdown time decreases to 1060 ms (and the average time decreases to 988 ms). On the other hand, a QEMU microvm can boot/shutdown a Linux kernel with a worst-case of 430 ms and an average time of 323 ms (further optimizing the microvm options, it is possible to reduce the worst-case to 400 ms and the average time to 310 ms). These numbers make QEMU+Linux competitive with containers.

Using the PVH boot protocol for OSv, the worst-case boot/shutdown time decreased to 240 ms, with 185 ms as an average case; with the microvm, the worst-case time further decreased to 140 ms, with an average of 102 ms. For this configuration, the boot time measured by OSv (excluding QEMU and shutdown time) has a worst-case value of 7 ms and an average time of 4.97 ms. Table 1 summarizes these results.

As already mentioned in Sect. 3, OSv does not support fixed-priority scheduling or the `clock_nanosleep()` call needed by `cyclictest`. However, some out-of-tree patches implement the functionalities needed to run `cyclictest` on OSv successfully. After forward-porting these patches to the current OSv version, it has been possible to run some latency-measurement experiments on OSv too, measuring a worst-case latency $L = 2147$ μs for a cyclictest period of 100 μs.

Some investigation on these high latencies revealed that the patched OSv unikernel printed warnings about partially implemented features in a time-critical

---

[3] For example, using PVH https://stefano-garzarella.github.io/posts/2019-08-23-qemu-linux-kernel-pvh.

[4] https://qemu.readthedocs.io/en/latest/system/i386/microvm.html.

[5] https://www.cloudhypervisor.org.

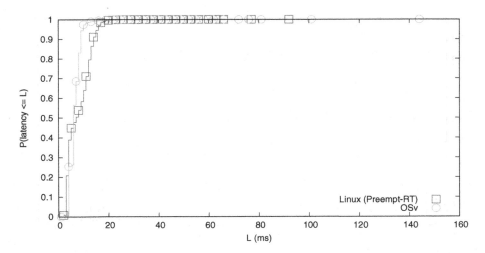

Fig. 1. Experimental CDF of the latencies measured by `cyclictest` with period 100 µs in a VM running Linux and OSv.

path. After moving such warnings out of the latency measurement cycle, the worst-case latency decreased to $L = 144$ µs. Figure 1 reports the experimental Cumulative Distribution Function (CDF) of the latencies experienced using Linux and OSv as guests. As shown in the figure, OSv results in a smaller average latency, although the OSv CDF has a longer tail that is not present in the Linux CDF, when Preempt-RT is used. This probably happens because Preempt-RT kernels have been optimized to reduce the maximum latency at the cost of increasing the average values.

After verifying that the patched OSv unikernel can provide reasonably low latencies and comparing it with Preempt-RT, the next set of experiments investigated the effect of the `cyclictest` period on the experienced latencies. To this purpose, `cyclictest` has been executed on OSv with period 50 µs, 100 µs, 250 µs, 500 µs, and 1 ms. The experimental CDFs of the measured latencies are displayed in Fig. 2. This figure shows that OSv works well even for short periods (50 µs). Hence it is possible to guess that it implements high-resolution timers.

Surprisingly, the latency tends to increase with the `cyclictest` period; this probably happens because, for short periods, QEMU or OSv use active polling. On the other hand, for larger periods the QEMU vCPU threads are actually blocked until the end of the period. Hence, some additional overhead and latency are introduced (this effect is still being investigated).

The worst-case latencies experienced for the various `cyclictest` periods are reported in Table 2. Looking at these values, it is possible to see that the latency decreases when increasing the `cyclictest` period from 50 µs to 250 µs, but then increases for 500 µs and 1 ms; from this observation it can be guessed that the active polling is used for periods smaller than or equal to 250 µs.

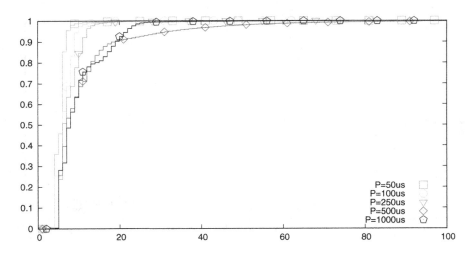

Fig. 2. Experimental CDF of the latencies measured by `cyclictest` with various periods in a VM running OSv.

5 Conclusions

This paper evaluated the suitability of the unikernel architecture for serving guest applications characterized by temporal constraints. While real-time VMs and hypervisors already exist, their boot times and resource consumption can be too high for some applications, and in this case unikernels can help.

At first glance, it might seem that current unikernels are not suitable for executing real-time applications because they do not even support the simplest possible real-time scheduling algorithm (fixed-priority scheduling); however, support for simple real-time applications is available for OSv through some out-of-tree patches (and can probably be implemented easily for Unikraft). Some preliminary experiments showed that the patched OSv can reduce the boot times by a factor of 3, but also ends up introducing a relevant latency.

In future work, the latencies introduced by OSv will be analyzed and reduced, and real-time support will be implemented for Unikraft too.

References

1. Abeni, L., Biondi, A., Bini, E.: Hierarchical scheduling of real-time tasks over Linux-based virtual machines. J. Syst. Softw. **149**, 234–249 (2019)
2. Abeni, L., Biondi, A., Bini, E.: Partitioning real-time workloads on multi-core virtual machines. J. Syst. Archit. **131**, 102733 (2022). https://doi.org/10.1016/j.sysarc.2022.102733, https://www.sciencedirect.com/science/article/pii/S1383762122002181
3. Abeni, L., Cucinotta, T., Pinczel, B., Mátray, P., Srinivasan, M.K., Lindquist, T.: On the use of Linux real-time features for RAN packet processing in cloud environments. In: Anzt, H., Bienz, A., Luszczek, P., Baboulin, M. (eds.) High Performance

Computing. ISC High Performance 2022 International Workshops. ISC High Performance 2022. LNCS, vol. 13387, pp. 371–382. Springer, Cham (2022). https://doi.org/10.1007/978-3-031-23220-6_26

4. Abeni, L., Faggioli, D.: An experimental analysis of the Xen and KVM latencies. In: Proceedings of the IEEE 22nd International Symposium on Real-Time Distributed Computing (ISORC), pp. 18–26, May 2019

5. Abeni, L., Faggioli, D.: Using Xen and KVM as real-time hypervisors. J. Syst. Archit. **106**, 101709 (2020)

6. Abeni, L., Goel, A., Krasic, C., Snow, J., Walpole, J.: A measurement-based analysis of the real-time performance of Linux. In: Proceedings of the 8th IEEE Real-Time and Embedded Technology and Applications Symposium, pp. 133–142. IEEE, San Jose, California, September 2002

7. Agache, A., et al.: Firecracker: lightweight virtualization for serverless applications. In: 17th USENIX Symposium on Networked Systems Design and Implementation (NSDI 20), pp. 419–434. USENIX Association, Santa Clara, CA, February 2020. https://www.usenix.org/conference/nsdi20/presentation/agache

8. Almeida, L., Pedreiras, P.: Scheduling within temporal partitions: response-time analysis and server design. In: Proceedings of the 4th ACM International Conference on Embedded Software, pp. 95–103, September 2004

9. Anderson, T.: The case for application-specific operating systems. In: Proceedings Third Workshop on Workstation Operating Systems, pp. 92,93,94. IEEE Computer Society, Los Alamitos, CA, USA, April 1992. https://doi.org/10.1109/WWOS.1992.275682, https://doi.ieeecomputersociety.org/10.1109/WWOS.1992.275682

10. Banga, G., Druschel, P., Mogul, J.C.: Resource containers: a new facility for resource management in server systems. In: OSDI, vol. 99, pp. 45–58 (1999)

11. Barham, P., et al.: Xen and the art of virtualization. SIGOPS Oper. Syst. Rev. **37**(5), 164–177 (2003)

12. Biondi, A., et al.: Sphere: a multi-SoC architecture for next-generation cyber-physical systems based on heterogeneous platforms. IEEE Access **9**, 75446–75459 (2021). https://doi.org/10.1109/ACCESS.2021.3080842

13. de Oliveira, D.B., Casini, D., de Oliveira, R.S., Cucinotta, T.: Demystifying the real-Time Linux scheduling latency. In: Völp, M. (ed.) 32nd Euromicro Conference on Real-Time Systems (ECRTS 2020). Leibniz International Proceedings in Informatics (LIPIcs), vol. 165, pp. 9:1–9:23. Schloss Dagstuhl-Leibniz-Zentrum für Informatik, Dagstuhl, Germany (2020). https://doi.org/10.4230/LIPIcs.ECRTS.2020.9, https://drops.dagstuhl.de/opus/volltexte/2020/12372

14. Feng, X., Mok, A.K.: A model of hierarchical real-time virtual resources. In: Proceedings of the 23rd IEEE Real-Time Systems Symposium, pp. 26–35 (2002)

15. Kantee, A., Cormack, J.: Rump kernels: no os? No problems!; Login Mag. USENIX SAGE **39**(5), 11–17 (2014)

16. Kantee, A.: Flexible operating system internals: the design and implementation of the anykernel and rump kernels. Ph.D. thesis, Department of Computer Science and Engineering, October 2012

17. Kivity, A., Kamay, Y., Laor, D., Lublin, U., Liguori, A.: KVM: the Linux virtual machine monitor. In: Proceedings of the Linux Symposium, vol. 1, pp. 225–230 (2007)

18. Kivity, A., Laor, D., Costa, G., Enberg, P., Har'El, N., Marti, D., Zolotarov, V.: OSv: optimizing the operating system for virtual machines. In: Proceedings of the 2014 USENIX Conference on USENIX Annual Technical Conference, pp. 61–72. USENIX ATC'14, USENIX Association, USA (2014)

19. Kuenzer, S., et al.: Unikraft: fast, specialized unikernels the easy way. In: Proceedings of the Sixteenth European Conference on Computer Systems, pp. 376–394. EuroSys '21, Association for Computing Machinery, New York, NY, USA (2021). https://doi.org/10.1145/3447786.3456248

20. Kuo, H.C., Williams, D., Koller, R., Mohan, S.: A Linux in unikernel clothing. In: Proceedings of the Fifteenth European Conference on Computer Systems. EuroSys '20, Association for Computing Machinery, New York, NY, USA (2020). https://doi.org/10.1145/3342195.3387526

21. Lankes, S., Pickartz, S., Breitbart, J.: Hermitcore: a unikernel for extreme scale computing. In: Proceedings of the 6th International Workshop on Runtime and Operating Systems for Supercomputers. ROSS '16, Association for Computing Machinery, New York, NY, USA (2016). https://doi.org/10.1145/2931088.2931093

22. Lelli, J., Scordino, C., Abeni, L., Faggioli, D.: Deadline scheduling in the Linux kernel. Softw. Pract. Exp. **46**(6), 821–839 (2016)

23. Li, H., Xu, X., Ren, J., Dong, Y.: ACRN: a big little hypervisor for IoT development. In: Proceedings of the 15th ACM SIGPLAN/SIGOPS International Conference on Virtual Execution Environments. VEE 2019 (2019). https://doi.org/10.1145/3313808.3313816, https://doi.acm.org/10.1145/3313808.3313816

24. Lipari, G., Bini, E.: Resource partitioning among real-time applications. In: Proceedings of the 15th Euromicro Conference on Real-Time Systems, pp. 151–158, July 2003

25. Liu, C.L., Layland, J.W.: Scheduling algorithms for multiprogramming in a hard real-time environment. J. Assoc. Comput. Mach. **20**(1), 46–61 (1973)

26. Madhavapeddy, A., Scott, D.J.: Unikernels: the rise of the virtual library operating system. Commun. ACM **57**(1), 61–69 (2014). https://doi.org/10.1145/2541883.2541895

27. Martins, J., Tavares, A., Solieri, M., Bertogna, M., Pinto, S.: Bao: a lightweight static partitioning hypervisor for modern multi-core embedded systems. In: Bertogna, M., Terraneo, F. (eds.) Workshop on Next Generation Real-Time Embedded Systems (NG-RES 2020). OpenAccess Series in Informatics (OASIcs), vol. 77, pp. 3:1–3:14. Schloss Dagstuhl-Leibniz-Zentrum fuer Informatik, Dagstuhl, Germany (2020). https://doi.org/10.4230/OASIcs.NG-RES.2020.3, https://drops.dagstuhl.de/opus/volltexte/2020/11779

28. Mok, A.K., Feng, X., Chen, D.: Resource partition for real-time systems. In: Proceedings of the 7th IEEE Real-Time Technology and Applications Symposium, pp. 75–84 (2001)

29. Olivier, P., Chiba, D., Lankes, S., Min, C., Ravindran, B.: A binary-compatible unikernel. In: Proceedings of the 15th ACM SIGPLAN/SIGOPS International Conference on Virtual Execution Environments, pp. 59–73. VEE 2019, Association for Computing Machinery, New York, NY, USA (2019). https://doi.org/10.1145/3313808.3313817

30. Popek, G.J., Goldberg, R.P.: Formal requirements for virtualizable third generation architectures. Commun. ACM **17**(7), 412–421 (1974)

31. Porter, D.E., Boyd-Wickizer, S., Howell, J., Olinsky, R., Hunt, G.C.: Rethinking the library OS from the top down. In: Proceedings of the Sixteenth International Conference on Architectural Support for Programming Languages and Operating Systems, pp. 291–304. ASPLOS XVI, Association for Computing Machinery, New York, NY, USA (2011). https://doi.org/10.1145/1950365.1950399

32. Raza, A., et al.: Unikernels: the next stage of Linux's dominance. In: Proceedings of the Workshop on Hot Topics in Operating Systems, pp. 7–13. HotOS '19, Asso-

ciation for Computing Machinery, New York, NY, USA (2019). https://doi.org/10.1145/3317550.3321445

33. Riel, R.V.: Real-time KVM from the ground up. In: KVM Forum 2015 (2015)
34. Rostedt, S.: Internals of the RT patch. In: Proceedings of the Linux Symposium, pp. 161–172. Ottawa, Canada, June 2007
35. Shin, I., Lee, I.: Periodic resource model for compositional real-time guarantees. In: Proceedings of 24th IEEE Real-Time Systems Symposium, pp. 2–13, December 2003
36. Shin, I., Lee, I.: Compositional real-time scheduling framework. In: 25th IEEE International Real-Time Systems Symposium, pp. 57–67, December 2004. https://doi.org/10.1109/REAL.2004.15
37. Xi, S., et al.: Real-time multi-core virtual machine scheduling in Xen. In: Proceedings of the 2014 International Conference on Embedded Software (EMSOFT), pp. 1–10, October 2014
38. Yang, J., Kim, H., Park, S., Hong, C., Shin, I.: Implementation of compositional scheduling framework on virtualization. SIGBED Rev. 8(1), 30–37 (2011)

Accelerating Scientific Applications with the Quantum Edge: A Drug Design Use Case

Vincenzo De Maio$^{(\boxtimes)}$ (ID) and Ivona Brandic (ID)

Vienna University of Technology, Vienna, Austria
vincenzo@ec.tuwien.ac.at, ivona@ec.tuwien.ac.at

Abstract. To address increasing demands of computational resources, scientific applications started to support different type of hardware accelerators, e.g., GPUs, TPUs, ASICs. However, due to the limitation to scalability of hardware resources posed by the Moore Law, a conspicuous amount of research is focusing in integration of Quantum Computers in the overall computing continuum. The high amount of data and the high heterogeneity of quantum architectures necessitate development and integration of additional hardware/software layers to facilitate integration of quantum hardware into the overall computing continuum. In this work, we discuss the possibility of applying edge computing to address this issue, laying the fundamentals to the concept of the Quantum Edge. Further, we present and analyse a drug design use case, identifying challenges and future research directions for Quantum Edge.

Keywords: Scientific computing · Drug design · Quantum computing · High performance computing

1 Introduction

Scientific applications are used by scientists from different domains to simulate complex scientific phenomena and speed up research in different fields. Typical examples of scientific applications are molecular dynamics [14], material science [8], and drug design [4]. Due to their high computational demands, scientific applications rely on HPC resources [15] for their execution.

However, we are currently entering the Post-Moore era, which poses serious limitations to scalability of classic HPC systems. Considering the growing storage and analytics demands, scientific computing recently focused in exploiting different specific-purpose hardware accelerators. Accelerators include devices such as TPU, GPUs, FPGAs and ASICs, each one designed for a very specific problem and with its own specific limitations. To further improve capabilities of future HPC systems, a considerable amount of research is considering the exploitation of so-called Non-Von Neumann architectures, such as Neuromorphic and Quantum Computing [12].

A. Bienz et al. (Eds.): ISC High Performance 2023 Workshops, LNCS 13999, pp. 134–143, 2023.
https://doi.org/10.1007/978-3-031-40843-4_11

Among Non-Von Neumann architectures, quantum computing clearly stands out, due to characteristics such as (1) theoretically proven speedup for many computationally-intensive problems, (2) natural 3D modelling of different scientific problems, and (3) wide availability of different quantum systems and frameworks [24]. At one hand quantum computing can provide significant speedup to many scientific computations, such as computational chemistry, combinatorial optimization and drug design. On the other hand, current state-of-the-art NISQ (Noisy Intermediate Scale Quantum) architectures suffer from drawbacks, such as limited number of qubits and high amount of error, limiting adoption of quantum computing on a larger scale.

Hybrid classic/quantum systems target integration of classic von Neumann hardware with quantum hardware. The main idea of hybrid classic/quantum systems is to use the classic HPC facilities for the preparation of the input data, adaptation of the classic code for the execution on the quantum machine and for the data post processing. The quantum machine is utilized for the execution of very specific program parts that can benefit from the quantum architecture. Once a program is executed on the quantum hardware, classic hardware will perform error correction on its output. However, how to deal with issues such as management of streaming data, privacy and integration between classic and quantum hardware still remains an open challenge.

Edge computing has proven effective in addressing challenges of processing streaming data [11,12], as well as ensuring privacy of geographically distributed systems [20]. Therefore, in this work we investigate the use of Edge computing to address challenges of integrating quantum in the computing continuum.

First, we describe our target use case and identify which components would benefit from quantum execution. Afterwards, we identify challenges of executing target use case on hybrid classic/quantum systems. Finally, we define our concept of Quantum Edge and describe which Edge computing methodologies could be applied to our specific use case. To demonstrate the applicability of Edge Computing in hybrid systems we focus on a computer-assisted drug design use case, which is one of the widely used applications in scientific computing [2].

The paper is organised as follows: First, we introduce background notions in Sect. 2 and our target use case in Sect. 3. In Sect. 4, we identify challenges towards implementation of current use case in hybrid classic/quantum systems. The concept of Quantum Edge is described in Sect. 5. Finally, we describe related work in Sect. 6 and conclude our paper in Sect. 7.

2 Background

2.1 State of the Art in Scientific Computing

Scientific computing is a branch of computer science, spanning different disciplines (i.e., finance, biology, chemistry, engineering) with the goal to develop *standardized, robust* and *accurate* simulations of different phenomena. Simulations can be decomposed in *tasks* (i.e., aggregate data from different sources, average a set of samples). Tasks can be combined into *workflows*, represented as DAGs (Directed Acyclic Graphs) [1] where edges model interdependencies between tasks. Data-intensive workflows are defined as *extreme-data workflows* [11].

Current research trends in scientific computing go towards the convergence of artificial intelligence, data science and physical simulations [5], which rely on HPC systems for their execution. However, given the limitation to hardware scalability posed by the Post-Moore era, together with the increasing data that have to be processed and growing computing demands of scientific applications, scientific community is faced with the challenge of scaling HPC capabilities beyond limitations of Von Neumann's architectures [10].

2.2   Hybrid Classic/Quantum Systems

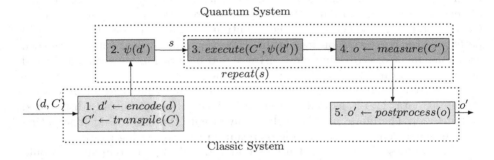

Fig. 1. Hybrid Classic/Quantum Systems.

Hybrid Classic/Quantum Systems define a class of systems that combine classic and quantum computers to solve a problem. The main advantage of this approach is the exploitation of classic computers for specific tasks (e.g., error correction, data encoding) and capabilities provided by quantum machines [24].

Hybrid quantum systems are depicted in Fig. 1: in step 1, data d are encoded on the classic system for execution on the quantum system. At this stage, different data encoding techniques [26] can be applied to transform input in a quantum state. Also, high level circuit description C is transpiled [27]; in step 2, quantum state ψ is prepared based on encoded data d'. In step 3, circuit C' is executed with the given input. Execution and measurement (step 4) are performed s time, due to the intrinsic nondeterminism of quantum computation, in order to create a probabilistic distribution of the output. Finally, in step 5, postprocessing of the output o is applied. Postprocessing can range from error correction [23] to noise mitigation [22], to address limitation of current NISQ (Noisy Intermediate Scale Quantum) machines.

3   Use Case: Computer-Assisted Drug Design (CADD)

Traditional drug design is a long, complex and costly process, with huge impact on pharmaceutical companies profit, as shown by the recent pandemic. Computer-Aided Drug Design (CADD) provides a variety of tools and methods that assist in the various stages of drug design, i.e., (1) discovery of a candidate drug, (2) evaluation of efficacy and safety and (3) drug-target interactions simulations. Recent development of quantum computing affected many branches of scientific computing, including CADD [7].

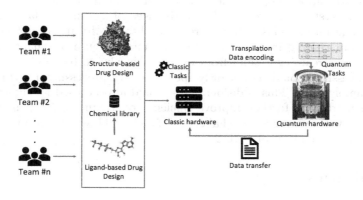

Fig. 2. A Hybrid CADD Workflow.

Figure 2 shows an example CADD hybrid workflow exploiting quantum machines. CADD is a multidisciplinary process, which involves experts from biochemistry, molecular biology, cell biology, bioinformatics and HPC scientists. To this end, typical CADD systems allow collaborations of different teams [18]. Also, CADD involves different families of techniques, namely structure-based drug discovery [3] and ligand-based drug discovery [13]. ML-based techniques are widely applied in both cases [18,19].

All identified CADD techniques require processing of large datasets, such as ChEMBL (https://www.ebi.ac.uk/chembl/) and DrugBank (https://go.drugbank.com/). Also, CADD relies on accurate simulation of target interactions, as well as computation of ground state for weakly-interacting molecules. Such simulation rely on molecular dynamics (MD) simulations and require a huge amount of computational resources, which is provided by remote distributed clusters [15]. However, as proven by [4,10], MD simulations are a very common use case of quantum computing, due to the fact that molecular interactions can be easily modelled by quantum mechanics. Moreover, different computation that are employed by CADD, such as eigenstates calculation, approximate optimization and quantum machine learning, can be easily mapped to Variational Quantum Algorithms, the main candidates to achieve the quantum advantage [8].

3.1 Current Limitations of Hybrid Classic/Quantum CADD

From our analysis, we conclude that executing CADD on hybrid classic/quantum systems can not only allow to overcome the scalability limits of HPC systems, but also to simulate processes that cannot be easily simulated by classic HPC [7]. However, several additional layers between HPC and quantum systems are necessary to enable a seamless integration between classic and quantum nodes, to address challenges arising from their integration.

First of all, current quantum hardware requires very specific facilities, which are not accessible to common data centers. This causes a higher degree of geographical distribution, which hinders latency of communication between classic and quantum systems. Moreover, due to the need of continuous data exchange between quantum and classic hardware, a hardware/software layer focused on encoding data coming from datasets/sensors for their use on quantum hardware, and for streaming results from quantum hardware to HPC systems for further processing, would significantly speed up data processing in hybrid classic/quantum systems. This additional layer could also be used for filtering and preprocessing data to further improve efficiency of streaming data. In the next sections, we will analyze some challenges of hybrid classic/quantum systems, coming from our analysis of CADD.

4 Challenges

4.1 Efficient Data Encoding

CADD requires continuous interaction with different pharmaceutical datasets, in order to evaluate target interactions. Information coming from different databases has to be encoded into a quantum state to enable processing by different quantum algorithms (Sect. 2.2).

Efficiency of data encoding is critical for CADD, since it might constitute a bottleneck in the quantum processing and potentially cancel the effect of a quantum speedup [26]. This is specifically true if we consider the geographical distribution of quantum hardware, which requires very specific facilities to be executed, usually not available in typical HPC infrastructures.

Moreover, considering the limited availability of quantum hardware, data needs to be filtered, aggregated and pre-processed at different system layers, to avoid wasting precious computational resources.

4.2 Security and Privacy

In CADD, privacy is a huge concern, since pharmaceutical companies are usually not willing to share their intellectual property and lose a competitive advantage on their competitors. As a consequence, different privacy-preserving and secure schemes for drug design have been developed to allow pharmaceutical companies to collaborate on the same datasets and or computational clusters without sharing private information [17].

Moreover, execution on quantum nodes requires to (1) encode data coming from different databases, (2) translate high level description of a quantum circuit for the target quantum machine, and (3) send both data and circuit over the network to be executed on the quantum machine. Communication between classic and quantum hardware could be exposed to privacy and security leaks, which might have disastrous effects for the companies involved in CADD.

Considering the huge development of quantum drug design [7], and its importance for pharma industry [2], it is important to guarantee secure and privacy-preserving multi-party interactions between classic and quantum hardware to ensure large-scale adoption of quantum technology.

4.3   Classic/Quantum Integration

As mentioned in [21], simulations of molecular dynamics for CADD processes can be executed on quantum computing, allowing either to speed up specific calculations or even to perform simulations that cannot be executed in classic systems. Also, development of Quantum Machine Learning [6] offers new possibility to ML-based drug discovery methods [9].

However, allowing such hybrid execution requires continuous communication between classic and quantum hardware. To enable such communication, there is a need of an intermediate layer capable to perform the translation between the two types of architectures. Also, considering the high heterogeneity of quantum hardware, each quantum task has to be allocated on the quantum node that guarantees the best performance.

5   The Quantum Edge

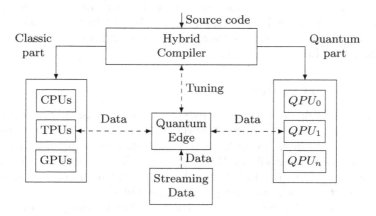

Fig. 3. The Quantum Edge.

We advocate the use of Edge computing to address challenges identified in Sect. 4. Edge computing is a computing model that works by placing processing logic in close proximity to data sources to reduce latency of their processing. The use of Edge nodes allows mitigation of effects of geographic distribution of quantum nodes. Also, it allows preprocessing and filtering of data at different system layers, improving data processing efficiency. In this section, we expand our concept of the Quantum Edge [12] and adapt it to CADD.

Our vision is summarized in Fig. 3. Since only very specific part of computation can be executed on quantum nodes, we employ a hybrid compiler, similar to Qiskit and PennyLane. Hybrid compiler will generate both classic and quantum part, which will be executed respectively in the classic and the quantum hardware. During execution, Edge infrastructure will be responsible for (1) secure and privacy-preserving encoding of streaming input data for the use on classic and quantum part, (2) offload data processing on different classic and quantum hardware, (3) collect data about execution on both classic and quantum hardware to fine-tune execution of both quantum and classic part.

5.1 Efficient Data Encoding

Since quantum machines' availability is limited in comparison to classical machines, allocating fixed resources to data encoding/decoding might result in underutilization of computational resources. Edge computing could be used not only to enable low-latency filtering, aggregation and pre-processing of data, but also to apply data encoding at lower layers of the network allowing their usage at different systems' layers. This model is particularly powerful for the processing of streaming data coming from IoT devices, since it allows developers to not worry about capacity planning, configuration and management of underlying infrastructure. Also, it increases the system elasticity, preventing under/over provisioning of classical infrastructure. Serverless paradigm could be applied to develop data encoding/decoding methods required by different quantum algorithms at the Edge. This choice will allow users to invoke required encoding/decoding methods on-demand, reducing infrastructure overhead and processing latency due to the use of Edge infrastructure.

5.2 Security and Privacy

The efficiency of Edge computing in executing data-intensive workflow computations has been proven by different works. For example, in [11], it is described how executing data-intensive tasks at the Edge allows to significantly speed up execution of scientific workflows. However, in a collaborative environment such as the scenario described in Fig. 2, it is also important to guarantee privacy and security, to protect intellectual property of different teams.

Edge is a natural solution in this context, due to the proximity of edge devices to data sources, which ensures an additional level of data protection by preventing user data to be moved to remote Cloud resources. This guarantees the required level of confidentiality, i.e., the the act of preventing unauthorized entities from reading or accessing sensitive materials [20]. In [25], it is shown how to apply privacy-preserving schemes to Quantum Federated Learning, which can be improved by means of Edge AI.

5.3   Classic/Quantum Integration

Edge nodes could act as intermediate layers in this scenario, either extracting ML-based models from performance data to identify the most suitable node or by performing different data pre-processing and filtering to enable data exchange between the different nodes.

In order to select the most suitable hardware for each quantum algorithm, we need to be able to predict performance of different computations on different quantum hardware. Considering the high variability of performance of quantum hardware, as well as the lack of datasets available, it is important to enable continuous collection of performance data of quantum and automatically tune the model while new performance data arrive. One might use machine learning (ML) on benchmarks suites such as [16] to train a performance model for quantum machines. Data collected can be used by on-line methods, which work by continuous improvement of a model using data coming from measurement, to address the limited amount of data available on quantum execution.

6   Related Work

Computer Assisted Drug Design has a wide application in pharma industry, as discussed in [2]. Most common methods in drug design are structure-based drug design [3] and ligand-based drug design [21]. AI-based methods are instead discussed in [18,19]. Applications of HPC to of drug design, molecular dynamics are described in [15].

Research efforts in the integration of Non-Von Neumann architectures in HPC systems are summarised in works such as [12,24], without considering drug design. Application of quantum computing to scientific applications are discussed in different works, such as [10] in the context of molecular dynamics simulations, [6] in the context of quantum machine learning , showing opportunities and limitation of applying quantum machine learning techniques to different problems, and [25] for federated learning, which is of particular interest for the Edge computing domain. Quantum Drug Design has been extensively discussed by [7], where different technological challenges of the NISQ hardware are described, but challenges related to hybrid classic/quantum systems and integration of classic and quantum hardware are not considered. Different applications of Variational Quantum Algorithms are described in [8], without considering HPC and drug design. Application of quantum computing to structure-based drug design are discussed by [4], while applications of quantum to ligand-based drug design are described in [13], without considering interactions with HPC systems.

7   Conclusion and Future Work

In this work, we lay the foundations for our concept of the Quantum Edge. First, we describe the challenges of executing scientific applications on hybrid classic/quantum systems, focusing on a CADD use case. Based on the specific challenges identified in the analysis, we describe how Edge computing could be applied to address identified challenges. In the future, we plan to investigate similar challenges in different scientific applications.

Acknowledgements. This work has been funded through the FFG Flagship project HPQC (High Performance Integrated Quantum Computing) # 897481.

References

1. Pegasus workflow management system. https://pegasus.isi.edu/
2. Research informatics and in-silico drug discovery. https://www.evotec.com/en/execute/drug-discovery-services/research-informatics-in-silico-drug-discovery. Accessed 04 Mar 2023
3. Anderson, A.C.: The process of structure-based drug design. Chem. Biol. **10**(9), 787–797 (2003)
4. Andersson, M.P., Jones, M.N., Mikkelsen, K.V., You, F., Mansouri, S.S.: Quantum computing for chemical and biomolecular product design. Curr. Opin. Chem. Eng. **36**, 100754 (2022)
5. Ang, J.A., Barker, K.J., Vrabie, D.L., Kestor, G.: Codesign for extreme heterogeneity: integrating custom hardware with commodity computing technology to support next-generation HPC converged workloads. IEEE Internet Comput. **27**(1), 7–14 (2023)
6. Biamonte, J., Wittek, P., Pancotti, N., Rebentrost, P., Wiebe, N., Lloyd, S.: Quantum machine learning. Nature **549**(7671), 195–202 (2017)
7. Blunt, N.S., et al.: Perspective on the current state-of-the-art of quantum computing for drug discovery applications. J. Chem. Theory Comput. **18**(12), 7001–7023 (2022)
8. Cerezo, M., et al.: Variational quantum algorithms. Nat. Rev. Phys. **3**(9), 625–644 (2021)
9. Chan, H.S., Shan, H., Dahoun, T., Vogel, H., Yuan, S.: Advancing drug discovery via artificial intelligence. Trends Pharmacol. Sci. **40**(8), 592–604 (2019)
10. Cranganore, S.S., Maio, V.D., Brandic, I., Do, T.M.A., Deelman, E.: Molecular dynamics workflow decomposition for hybrid classic/quantum systems. In: 18th IEEE International Conference on e-Science, e-Science 2022, Salt Lake City, UT, USA, 11–14 October 2022, pp. 346–356. IEEE (2022)
11. De Maio, V., Kimovski, D.: Multi-objective scheduling of extreme data scientific workflows in fog. Futur. Gener. Comput. Syst. **106**, 171–184 (2020)
12. De Maio, V., Aral, A., Brandic, I.: A roadmap to post-moore era for distributed systems. In: Proceedings of the 2022 Workshop on Advanced Tools, Programming Languages, and PLatforms for Implementing and Evaluating Algorithms for Distributed Systems, pp. 30–34. ApPLIED 2022, Association for Computing Machinery (2022)

13. Ezz Eldin, R.R., et al.: Ligand-based design and synthesis of n'-benzylidene-3, 4-dimethoxybenzohydrazide derivatives as potential antimicrobial agents; evaluation by in vitro, in vivo, and in silico approaches with SAR studies. J. Enzyme Inhib. Med. Chem. **37**(1), 1098–1119 (2022)
14. Hansson, T., Oostenbrink, C., van Gunsteren, W.: Molecular dynamics simulations. Curr. Opin. Struct. Biol. **12**(2), 190–196 (2002)
15. Kutzner, C., et al.: GROMACS in the cloud: a global supercomputer to speed up alchemical drug design. J. Chem. Inf. Model. **62**(7), 1691–1711 (2022)
16. Li, A., Stein, S., Krishnamoorthy, S., Ang, J.: QASMBench: a low-level quantum benchmark suite for NISQ evaluation and simulation. ACM Trans. Quant. Comput. **4**(2), 1–26 (2023)
17. Liu, X., Deng, R.H., Choo, K.K.R., Yang, Y.: Privacy-preserving outsourced support vector machine design for secure drug discovery. IEEE Trans. Cloud Comput. **8**(2), 610–622 (2018)
18. Moingeon, P., Kuenemann, M., Guedj, M.: Artificial intelligence-enhanced drug design and development: toward a computational precision medicine. Drug Discov. Today **27**(1), 215–222 (2022)
19. Palazzesi, F., Pozzan, A.: Deep learning applied to ligand-based. In: Heifetz, A. (ed.) Artificial Intelligence in Drug Design. MMB, vol. 2390, pp. 273–299. Springer, New York (2022). https://doi.org/10.1007/978-1-0716-1787-8_12
20. Ranaweera, P., Jurcut, A.D., Liyanage, M.: Survey on multi-access edge computing security and privacy. IEEE Commun. Surv. Tutorials **23**(2), 1078–1124 (2021)
21. Ryde, U., Soderhjelm, P.: Ligand-binding affinity estimates supported by quantum-mechanical methods. Chem. Rev. **116**(9), 5520–5566 (2016)
22. Shaib, A., Naim, M.H., Fouda, M.E., Kanj, R., Kurdahi, F.: Efficient noise mitigation technique for quantum computing. Sci. Rep. **13**(1), 3912 (2023)
23. Sivak, V.: Real-time quantum error correction beyond break-even. Bull. Am. Phys. Soc. (2023)
24. Stein, S.A., et al.: A hybrid system for learning classical data in quantum states. In: 2021 IEEE International Performance, Computing, and Communications Conference (IPCCC), pp. 1–7. IEEE (2021)
25. Watkins, W.M., Chen, S.Y.C., Yoo, S.: Quantum machine learning with differential privacy. Sci. Rep. **13**(1), 2453 (2023)
26. Weigold, M., Barzen, J., Leymann, F., Salm, M.: Data encoding patterns for quantum computing. In: Proceedings of the 27th Conference on Pattern Languages of Programs, pp. 1–11 (2020)
27. Younis, E., Iancu, C.: Quantum circuit optimization and transpilation via parameterized circuit instantiation. In: 2022 IEEE International Conference on Quantum Computing and Engineering (QCE), pp. 465–475. IEEE (2022)

Event-Driven Chaos Testing
for Containerized Applications

Fotis Nikolaidis[1]([✉]), Antony Chazapis[1], Manolis Marazakis[1],
and Angelos Bilas[1,2]

[1] Institute of Computer Science, FORTH, Heraklion, Greece
{fnikol,chazapis,maraz,bilas}@ics.forth.gr
[2] Computer Science Department, University of Crete, Rethimno, Greece

Abstract. With the dynamicity of emerging systems rapidly multiplying, it is important to evolve our testing infrastructures to better
understand how distributed systems deal with failures. Existing Chaos
tools often lack a comprehensive understanding of the system's runtime
and typically inject faults in a random manner. While random testing
approaches are helpful in uncovering "shallow" bugs, testing deep failure paths requires precise and controlled fault injection at specific runtime conditions in distributed systems. This paper introduces *Frisbee*, an
automated chaos testing platform for distributed applications on Kubernetes. *Frisbee* utilizes both static and dynamic runtime instrumentation
to manage the dependency stack and perform testing actions. It achieves
this by integrating the collection of runtime events from multiple sources
with a scenario modeling language. This approach allows *Frisbee* to inject
realistic software faults in a controlled manner while the target system
runs. Moreover, since our method is based on runtime events, it ensures
deterministic fault injection regardless of the specific system or workload involved. We demonstrate the practicality and relevance of *Frisbee*
across various applications, including Cloud-native databases and Federated learning deployments.

Keywords: Cloud-Native testing · systems benchmarking ·
Event-driven Chaos testing

1 Introduction

Netflix pioneered Chaos Engineering in 2012 as a proactive measure to detect
system failures before outages occur [1]. However, their initial random testing
approach had limitations, only uncovering shallow bugs caused by individual
faults and failing to reveal deep failures stemming from combinations of faults [2,
3]. This posed a problem for the system, as untested code paths remained a
potential risk. As Chaos Engineering advanced, researchers began emulating
worst-case failure scenarios by intentionally driving systems into unlikely but
severe corner cases through surgically injected faults [4].

© The Author(s), under exclusive license to Springer Nature Switzerland AG 2023
A. Bienz et al. (Eds.): ISC High Performance 2023 Workshops, LNCS 13999, pp. 144–157, 2023.
https://doi.org/10.1007/978-3-031-40843-4_12

However, due to complexity and concurrency, injecting faults at precise runtime conditions in distributed systems is challenging. Existing fault injection frameworks are often application agnostic, lacking a deep understanding of the system's runtime context [5]. They cannot access specific system states and consider intricate dependencies between components or services. Coordinating fault injection across multiple nodes or multiple system parts is another hurdle, as most frameworks focus on single faults and do not adequately capture the causality of events that can impact the system's behavior. To address these limitations, companies adopt custom solutions combining fault injection frameworks, advanced monitoring, and custom instrumentation tailored to their specific applications. However, there is no universal solution that remains relevant across different application domains.

This paper introduces *Frisbee*, a Kubernetes-based framework that aims to enhance the precision and control of fault injection at specific runtime conditions in distributed systems. The framework comprises two primary components: the language and the runtime. The language component of the framework empowers users to define declarative testing scenarios, which consist of a sequence of testing actions. By utilizing runtime events, the language component determines the order in which these actions are executed. This functionality facilitates the specification of various aspects, such as dependencies, scheduling conditions for transitioning between fault-free and faulty execution, and programmable assertions for validating transitions related to undesirable states or violations of service level agreements (SLAs). The runtime component offers a scalable Kubernetes environment for executing these testing scenarios. Leveraging containerization, the runtime is application agnostic, enabling the portable execution of scenarios across various environments, from a single laptop to an entire cluster. Additionally, the runtime is designed with observability in mind, providing performance metrics, state changes, and logs. These pieces of information are abstracted as events, which can be utilized within the language component to facilitate precise and controllable experiments.

Our contributions are:

1. A Domain-Specific Language (DSL) to improve the controllability and precision of distributed testing.
2. A event-driven runtime engine that implements the language over Kubernetes.
3. A set of testing patterns for Cloud-native databases and Federated Learning frameworks.

In the rest of this paper, we identify gaps in related works (Sect. 2), present the architecture and key features of the Frisbee framework (Sect. 3), evaluate its relevance in the domains of cloud-native databases and federated learning frameworks (Sect. 4), and conclude the paper (Sect. 5) with key takeaways.

2   Related Work

Testing distributed systems is a well-established field with a variety of existing works. For the purpose of this paper, we exclude works related to formal verification, as they primarily address the correctness of distributed protocols rather than evaluating real implementations in terms of performance and resiliency. When it comes to implementation testing, frameworks like Ginkgo for Go, Robot for Python, and Serenity for Java offer domain-specific languages (DSLs) that enable the creation of expressive test scenarios. While these frameworks are suitable for unit testing, they can also be leveraged to implement scenarios using thin threads [6,7], where each thread represents a single service. Nonetheless, they are not practical for systems composed of components written in different programming languages.

For more realistic testing environments, tools like YCSB [8] and Grafana's k6 [9] are employed to generate distributed workloads, while fault-injection tools such as Chaos-mesh [10] and Gremlin [11] simulate real-world failures. The former allows for the simulation of large-scale workloads to evaluate system performance, while the latter facilitates the assessment of system resiliency. However, both types of tools assume that the system under test is already up and running, which necessitates the use of other tools to handle system's bootstrap. Furthermore, neither workload-generating tools nor fault-injection tools provide means for validating system correctness.

The introduction of Docker has brought about a shift in the testing community towards using containers for deploying systems during testing. Initially, containers were managed manually with scripts, which mixed the test case with the testing mechanism. Subsequently, the Docker-native approach emerged, utilizing the Docker-Compose language for running multi-container tests. This approach has been demonstrated by tools like BenchPilot [12], Fogify [13], and IOTier [14]. However, Docker-Compose lacks language-level assertions and only supports single-node deployments.

The latest trend in end-to-end testing involves creating small multi-node Kubernetes environments to test features beyond a single host. Tools like Cilium [15] and Testground [16] adopt a solution that utilizes unit-testing frameworks to manage test steps, with the logic for managing Kubernetes objects implemented within each step. However, this approach poses significant challenges in state management, as the test suite operates externally to Kubernetes. Consequently, if the suite crashes, it leaves orphaned containers that must be manually removed. Finally, Kubernetes-native testing tools like KUTTL [17] and Iter8 [18] exist, but they do not align with the goals of testing distributed systems. KUTTL is primarily designed for testing Kubernetes controllers, while Iter8 focuses on testing the progressive rollout of microservices.

3   Frisbee Framework Overview

3.1   Architecture of Frisbee

Figure 1 depicts the *Frisbee* architecture. The experiment begins by providing the system templates and the scenario manifest as input. The system template allows the user to define properties of the System Under Testing (SUT), such as listening ports, mounted volumes, and evaluation benchmarks. The scenario

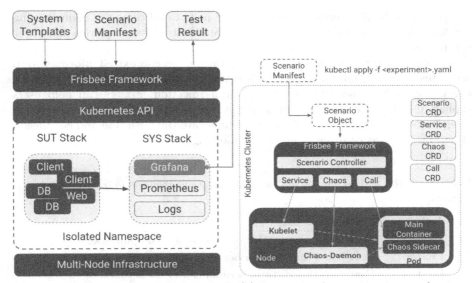

(a) Interaction between *Frisbee* and the user.

(b) Interaction between actions and external subsystems.

Fig. 1. *Frisbee* architecture.

manifest specifies the testing actions and conditions necessary for the test case to succeed. *Frisbee* executes these actions, evaluates the conditions, and provides the test outcome.

Within the experiment, *Frisbee* creates two distinct software stacks: the SUT stack and the SYS stack. The SUT stack consists of containers generated by the testing actions, such as database servers, web interfaces, and workload-generating clients. The SYS stack consists of containers responsible for executing and observing the experiment. This includes *Frisbee* operators, a telemetry stack, log collectors, and other essential components. Importantly, the SYS stack is designed to be immutable to Chaos actions, ensuring critical components like Grafana remain unaffected. This allows for post-execution inspection of the testing environment, auto-generated test result reports, and the ability to download collected runtime metrics for further analysis.

The testing actions in *Frisbee* are developed using the Kubernetes operator pattern [19]. Each action is represented by a Custom Resource Definition (CRD) that exposes the action's parameters in a YAML format and a runtime controller that interacts with the Kubernetes API, or with different subsystems (Fig. 1b). Albeit actions can be used individually, they make more sense when used in conjunction. To do so, the *Scenario* is a special controller that is responsible for scheduling action execution and dispatching requests to the appropriate low-level controller. Testing actions are executed immediately by default unless scheduling constraints or inter-action dependencies are specified. In such cases, execution is postponed until the specified conditions are met. Conditions are defined using *Frisbee* expressions, which can be time-driven, state-driven, metrics-driven, or log-driven.

Finally, *Frisbee* offers enhanced interpretation and contextual information to assist testers in visually connecting observed behavior with underlying events. For instance, by annotating a network fault injection, *Frisbee* can help users explain an otherwise enigmatic drop in the system's throughput. To accomplish this, *Frisbee* collaborates with Grafana to annotate the initiation and conclusion of actions, such as creating a service or injecting a fault.

Table 1. *Frisbee* actions cover a full range of operations required in testing distributed systems.

Action	Description
Service	Standard representation of a containerized application
Cluster	Coordinates multiple services in a shared execution context
Fault	Condition that disturbs a running service, network, or storage
Cascade	Coordinates multiple Faults in a shared execution context
Call	Command executed by the controller to a running service
Checkpoint	Store the status and the metrics of the SUT at the given time
Delete	Cancels and removes one of the previous actions

3.2   Classification of Action

Table 1 summarizes the available actions in *Frisbee*, which cover a full range of operations required to test a distributed system. We categorize these actions into primitives, complex, and virtual.

Primitive actions, such as *Service*, *Chaos*, and *Call* are responsible for interacting with external subsystems. The *Service* action interacts with Kubernetes node agents (Kubelets) to create new pods on the node. The *Chaos* action interacts with a Chaos daemon running on the node to inject faults into a pod. The *Call* action directly communicates with a pod to retrieve logs or execute commands. **Complex actions**, such as *Cluster* and *Cascade*, provide a shared execution context for managing multiple actions as a single entity. For example, the *Cluster* action allows users to automatically create pods by defining a referenced template and specifying the desired number of instances (as shown in Code 1.1). Alternatively, the user could create four *Service* actions explicitly, but that would increase the complexity of the dependency graph exponentially since all interaction among services would have to be accounted for. With the shared context, the context manager (*Cluster* in this case) is responsible for managing the individual *Services* and setting its state to a representative value that provides consistent communication about the lifecycle of the object. The values and their meanings are tightly controlled as defined in Table 2. **Virtual**

actions, such as *Checkpoint* and *Delete*, provide support for managing the state of the experiment at specific times. The *Checkpoint* action is useful for taking take snapshots of the system's state at a certain time and using this information in assertions to compare performance metrics before and after an action (i.e., network partition). Finally, the *Delete* action gracefully shuts down the experiment without leaving any artifacts behind.

Table 2. Lifecycle Semantics used to define inter-action dependencies.

Phase	Description
Uninitialized	the request has been accepted by the Kubernetes API, but it is not yet dispatched to the *Frisbee* controller
Pending	the request has been accepted by a *Frisbee* controller, but at least one of the constituent jobs has not been created
Running	all constituent jobs of the request have been created, and at least one job has not been completed yet
Success	all the constituent jobs of a request have been successfully completed
Failed	at least one job of the request has terminated in a failure

3.3 Scenario Modeling

A *Frisbee* scenario describes a set of dependent actions that collectively describe the testing process. The scenario defines three important properties: 1. a list of actions that drive the testing process, 2. the preconditions of the runtime before each action, and 3. the desired state of the runtime after each action. To achieve these qualities, the actions are formulated using the following format:

- **Action:** the type of the desired action.
- **Name:** action's identifier. Can be referenced by other actions.
- **Depends:** optional field that defined dependencies to other actions.
- **Asserts:** optional field that defines the desired state of the system.
- **ActionSpec:** define the action's parameters.

The Action and ActionSpec represent actions and their corresponding parameters. The scenario controller is agnostic to the ActionSpec, as the low-level action controller handles it. Conversely, the low-level action controllers lack access to high-level fields controlled by the scenario controller. These fields include (i) the action type and name for creating a list of actions to be scheduled; (ii) inter-action dependencies to determine the next action, and (iii) assertions for validating the system's behavior.

It is important to note that assertions are evaluated individually for each action and no global assertion model exists. The hierarchical model offers several benefits. Firstly, it facilitates the decomposition of complex properties into simpler assertions, aligning with the hierarchical nature of testing workflows [20].

For instance, a scenario with hundreds of servers and clients warrants partitioning the large verification problems into a set of properties associated locally with each *Service* or *Cluster*. Secondly, it ensures that assertions are evaluated after an action has been scheduled, reducing the flakiness that could arise from evaluating the impact of an action before it has started. For example, evaluating the throughput of database servers before the workload-generating clients have started would introduce spurious results that may compromise the validity of the tests. Lastly, assertions with local evaluation scope prevent cross-references to pods (or other resources) belonging to different actions, thus avoiding neverending loops (Fig. 2).

```
spec:
# Step 1. Provision 4 individual servers
- action: Cluster
  name: masters
  cluster:
    templateRef: cockroach.cluster.master
    instances: 4
# Step 2. Create a cockroach cluster
- action: Call
  name: boot
  depends: { running: [ masters ] }
  call:
    callable: boot
    services: [ masters-1 ]
    expect: [{ stdout: "Cluster successfully initialized.*" }]
# Step 3. import data to the workload node (node 1)
- action: Service
  name: import-workload
  depends: { success: [ boot ] }
  service:
    templateRef: ycsb.cockroach.loader
    inputs: [{ server: masters-1, recordcount: "100000", threads: "16"}]
# Step 4. Wait for 3x replication
- action: Call
  name: wait-for-3x-replication
  depends: { success: [ import-workload ] }
  call:
    callable: wait-for-3x-replication
    services: [ masters-1 ]
# Step 5. run workload for up to 10 minutes (node 1)
- action: Service
  name: run-workload
  depends: { success: [ wait-for-3x-replication ] }
  service:
    templateRef: ycsb.cockroach.loader
    inputs: [{ server: masters-1, recordcount: "100000", threads: "16"}]
# Step 6. Partition node 1 from the rest of the nodes;
- action: Chaos
```

```
name: partition0
depends: { success: [ wait-for-3x-replication ], after: "3m}
chaos:
  templateRef: system.chaos.network.partition.partial
  inputs:
    - {   source: masters-0, direction: "to", duration: 10m,
          dst: "masters-1, masters-2, masters-3" }
```

Code 1.1: *Frisbee* scenario for injecting network partition fault on a database cluster.

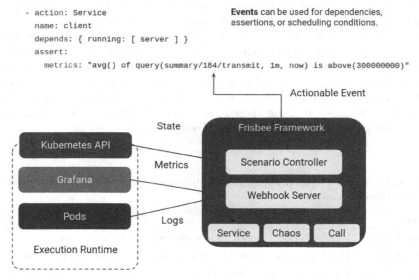

Fig. 2. *Frisbee* runtime collects metrics from multiple sources, and expose them as events to the scenario language.

Actionable Events. To ensure the controllability and precision of experiments, the *Frisbee* language provides direct access to events in the runtime environment. During the scenario execution, *Frisbee* gathers four types of events that are summarized in Table 3

Time-driven events are measured using elapsed time as determined by the scenario controller. The controller also interacts with Kubernetes API to inspect object states. To make these events actionable, *Frisbee* exposes dynamically evaluated expressions that are callable from within the *Scenario*. For example, the user can write the assertion '.*state.failed*() > 4', which will cause the test to fail if more than four services have failed. These expressions can be combined into complex assertions using logical, arithmetic, and string comparators.

Nonetheless, neither time nor state inspection provides any information about the performance of a service's performance. To address performance-related aspects, *Frisbee* interacts with the SYS stack to obtain real-time metrics from pods, such as CPU utilization, available memory, net usage, etc. In the SYS stack, which runs separately from the controllers, Prometheus periodically scrapes the pods for performance metrics, which are then forwarded to Grafana for visualization and inspection. Besides visualization, we also use the analysis and alerting capabilities of Grafana to get notified for important events like throughput dropping below a threshold. To capture these events, *Frisbee* automatically deploys a webhook server and configures Grafana to send events to it. Like in the case of state-driven events, the metrics-driven events are actionable at the level of the *Scenario*. For the programmability of these events, we have adopted the Grafana syntax for writing alerts. For example, '*MAX() QUERY(metric, 1m, now) IS ABOVE(70000)*' roughly translates as 'raise an alert if the max value of the given metric within the last minute has been above 70000'.

Additionally, *Frisbee* offers the ability to deploy a logging sidecar agent within pods. This agent continuously searches the main application's logs and sends events to the webhook server when a match is found. Similar to previous cases, these logging events are actionable and can be defined in the *Scenario* using regular expressions. Importantly, all these expressions are seamlessly integrated into the *Frisbee* language, allowing their reuse across assertions, conditional loops, and the storage of their outputs within *Checkpoints*.

Table 3. Events used to drive assertions, conditional loops, and other places involving execution-driven knowledge.

Event	Description
Time-driven	Fired after an elapsed time measured by the controller
State-driven	Fired by Kubernetes API when managed objects change state
Metrics-driven	Fired by Grafana when the statistical analysis on collected metrics matches a given rule
Log-events	Fired by logging agents where there is a regex match

3.4   Fault-Tolerance and Fault-Aware Semantics

Frisbee is designed to handle failures in a fail-fast manner. When a failure is detected by the *Scenario* controller, the test is immediately aborted and reported as failed. However, this behavior may not always be desirable, particularly in resiliency testing scenarios [21]. For example, it prevents recovery experiments on replicated systems [22], where a service is intentionally terminated to test the resilience of the remaining services.

To address this issue, there is a need to conceal failures from the top-level scenario controller [23,24]. To achieve this, we leverage the hierarchical model of *Frisbee* actions and incorporate failure-tolerance semantics into complex actions, such as the *Cluster*. By doing so, the *Cluster's* controller can identify the failing

Service and ignore it until the number of failing *Services* exceeds the tolerance threshold. At that point, the *Cluster* itself will fail, and the failure will be captured by the *Scenario* controller. However, this mechanism alone cannot differentiate between an unexpected service failure (due to a bug in the application's code) and an expected service failure (as part of a Chaos experiment). We have enhanced our mechanism with "fault-aware" semantics to address this. When the scenario controller encounters a *Chaos* action, it annotates the targeted services with a tag indicating the type of impending fault (e.g., partition, kill) before applying the action. The failure is expected and ignored if the pod crashes and the tag is present. If the crashing pod is no tagged, the fault is unexpected and the test fails immediately.

4   Evaluation

We have chosen applications from the Cloud-native databases and Federated learning worlds to demonstrate the practicality and relevance of *Frisbee* across application domains. In particular, CockroachDB [25] is an emerging database that is designed to run in the cloud and has a high fault tolerance. Flower [26] is a framework for building federated learning systems, typically deployed on constrained devices outside large data centers. The evaluation was conducted on four server-grade nodes with Kubernetes v1.26 installed.

4.1   Detection of Data Corruption

This scenario aims to test the ability of CockroachDB's storage layer (pebble) to successfully detect corruptions in backend data files and trigger panic. The scenario comprises six steps: (i) provisioning three database nodes, (ii) joining the nodes to form a distributed database cluster, (iii) populating the database with entries using YCSB benchmark [8], (iv) corrupting six random backend files on each node, (v) executing queries on the database and (vi) verifying that the corrupted nodes panic within 10 min.

In Fig. 3, we can observe the crashing of the database node after detecting the corrupted files and subsequent termination of the experiment from *Frisbee* after detecting the failing node. The first two vertical lines represent the provisioning and clustering actions. The third vertical line signifies the workload generation phase, where increased activity is seen on the workload-receiving node (masters-1). After the completion of workload generation, data corruption occurs, and queries are initiated (dense lines). The last vertical line indicates that *Frisbee* has detected the crashing node and aborted the experiment. The elapsed time between the file corruption and the detection of the crashing node is divided as follows: 41 s took for the cockroach node to detect the corruption and panic, and less than 1 s it took for *Frisbee* to detect the crashing node and halt the experiment.

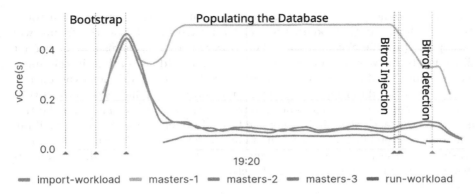

Fig. 3. Timeline of data corruption scenario. It takes 41 s for the Cockroach node to detect the corruption and panic, and less than 1 s for *Frisbee* to detect the failing node and terminate the experiment.

4.2 Goroutine Leak

This scenario aims to test that CockroachDB nodes do not experience goroutine leaks after recovering from a network partition. The scenario is described in Code 1.1 and comprises seven steps: (i) provisioning four database nodes, (ii) joining the nodes to form a distributed database cluster, (iii) running YCSB benchmark on the first node (masters-1) to populate the database cluster, (iv) waiting for the database to replicate data on at least three nodes, (v) start YCSB querying workload for 10 min, (vi) waiting for 3 min and inject a network partition that isolates the first node (masters-1) from the rest of the nodes for 5 min, (vii) verifying that the maximum number of goroutines has not spiked after recovery from the network partition.

In Fig. 4, we observe that the total number of goroutines slightly decreases during the network partition (annotated range) due to the reduced workload reaching the isolated masters-1. Upon recovering the partition, masters-1 resumes receiving workload, leading to increased goroutines. However, this increase remains below the pre-partition level, indicating that there is no goroutine leaking. Thus, the test is considered successful.

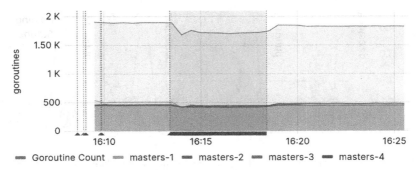

Fig. 4. Evolution of goroutines before and after a network partition. There is no spike in goroutines, indicating that there is no goroutine leaking.

4.3   Tolerating Crashing Nodes

In a federated learning deployment, network fluctuations and resource limitations may prevent all available nodes from actively participating in the training process simultaneously. To enable training despite failures, Flower distinguishes between the minimum number of training nodes (fitting) and the total number of available nodes. The former represents the threshold required to initiate federated learning, while the latter indicates the overall pool of potentially participating nodes.

This experiment aims to validate Flower's behavior when an increasing number of nodes crash. The experiment is conducted as follows: (i) set up an FL server configured to tolerate up to two failures, (ii) create five training nodes, (iii) wait until the second round of training, (iv) gradually terminate two nodes, one every minute, (v) ensure the training can tolerate one failed node but stops after a second failure. Figure 5 demonstrates the observed behavior of Flower during this experiment. The first two vertical lines (blue) represent the initial actions taken. The following two vertical lines (green) mark the completion of each training round. The subsequent two vertical lines (red) indicate the sequential termination of two nodes. The final vertical line (green) signifies the conclusion of the third round, at which point the federated server detects that two clients have failed and terminates the training. It is important to note that the server does not immediately account for failing clients but does so at the end of each round.

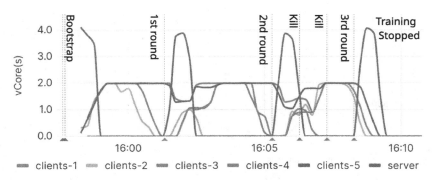

Fig. 5. Evaluation of federated learning training, with tolerated failures. The training stops only after a second node has been removed. (Color figure online)

5   Conclusion

We introduced *Frisbee*, an advanced testing tool designed to facilitate precise, controllable, and observable chaos experiments. Not only does *Frisbee* streamline the identification of deep failures, but it also finds application across a wide range of domains, including Cloud-native databases and federated learning frameworks. Our ultimate objective with *Frisbee* is to promote the development of a universal Cloud-Native Testing Framework for testing distributed systems [27]. The *Frisbee* framework and the experiments are available on GitHub (https://github.com/CARV-ICS-FORTH/frisbee) and through the project's website (https://frisbee.dev).

Acknowledgement. We thankfully acknowledge the support of the European Commission and the Greek General Secretariat for Research and Innovation under the EuroHPC Programme through project EUPEX (GA-101033975). National contributions from the involved state members (including the Greek General Secretariat for Research and Innovation) match the EuroHPC funding.

References

1. Basiri, A., et al.: Chaos engineering. IEEE Softw. **33**(3), 35–41 (2016)
2. Tickets, M.: Recovery problems after network partition (2016). https://jira.mongodb.org/browse/SERVER-23003
3. Schroeder, B., Gibson, G.A.: Understanding disk failure rates: what does an MTTF of 1,000,000 hours mean to you? ACM Trans. Storage (TOS) **3**(3), 8-es (2007)
4. Ford, D., et al.: Availability in globally distributed storage systems (2010)
5. Amaral, M., Pardal, M.L., Mercier, H., Matos, M.: FaultSee: reproducible fault injection in distributed systems. In: 16th European Dependable Computing Conference (EDCC), pp. 25–32. IEEE (2020)
6. Bai, X., Tsai, W.-T., Paul, R., Shen, T., Li, B.: Distributed end-to-end testing management. In: Proceedings of the Fifth IEEE International Enterprise Distributed Object Computing Conference, pp. 140–151. IEEE (2001)

7. Tsai, W.-T., Bai, X., Paul, R., Shao, W., Agarwal, V.: End-to-end integration testing design. In: 25th Annual International Computer Software and Applications Conference. COMPSAC 2001, pp. 166–171. IEEE (2001)
8. Cooper, B.F., Silberstein, A., Tam, E., Ramakrishnan, R., Sears, R.: Benchmarking cloud serving systems with YCSB. In: Proceedings of the 1st ACM Symposium on Cloud Computing, pp. 143–154 (2010)
9. Grafana Labs: Load testing for engineering teams (2023). https://k6.io/
10. PingCAP: A chaos engineering platform for kubernetes (2023). https://github. com/chaos-mesh/chaos-mesh
11. Heorhiadi, V., Rajagopalan, S., Jamjoom, H., Reiter, M.K., Sekar, V.: Gremlin: systematic resilience testing of microservices. In: 2016 IEEE 36th International Conference on Distributed Computing Systems (ICDCS), pp. 57–66. IEEE (2016)
12. Georgiou, J., Symeonides, M., Kasioulis, M., Trihinas, D., Pallis, G., Dikaiakos, M.D.: BenchPilot: repeatable & reproducible benchmarking for edge micro-DCs (2022)
13. Symeonides, M., Georgiou, Z., Trihinas, D., Pallis, G., Dikaiakos, M.D.: Fogify: a fog computing emulation framework. In: IEEE/ACM Symposium on Edge Computing (SEC), pp. 42–54. IEEE (2020)
14. Nikolaidis, F., Marazakis, M., Bilas, A.: IOTier: a virtual testbed to evaluate systems for IoT environments. In: IEEE/ACM 21st International Symposium on Cluster, Cloud and Internet Computing (CCGrid), pp. 676–683. IEEE (2021)
15. Cilium: What is cilium? (2021). https://docs.cilium.io/en/v1.9/contributing/ testing/e2e/
16. Kubernetes: What is testground? (2021). https://docs.testground.ai/
17. KUTTL: What is KUTTL? (2022). Available: The KUbernetes Test TooL
18. Toslali, M., Parthasarathy, S., Oliveira, F., Huang, H., Coskun, A.K.: Iter8: online experimentation in the cloud, pp. 289–304. Association for Computing Machinery, New York (2021). https://doi.org/10.1145/3472883.3486984
19. Kubernetes: Operator best practices (2021). https://sdk.operatorframework.io/ docs/best-practices/best-practices/
20. Kasuya, A., Tesfaye, T.: Verification methodologies in a TLM-to-RTL design flow. In: 44th ACM/IEEE Design Automation Conference, pp. 199–204. IEEE (2007)
21. Tolosana-Calasanz, R., Banares, J.A., Rana, O.F., Álvarez, P., Ezpeleta, J., Hoheisel, A.: Adaptive exception handling for scientific workflows. Concurr. Comput. Pract. Exp. **22**(5), 617–642 (2010)
22. Nikolaidis, F., Chazapis, A., Marazakis, M., Bilas, A.: Frisbee: a suite for benchmarking systems recovery. In: Proceedings of the 1st Workshop on High Availability and Observability of Cloud Systems, HAOC 2021, pp. 18–24. Association for Computing Machinery, New York (2021). https://doi.org/10.1145/3447851.3458738
23. Gupta, R., et al.: CIFTS: a coordinated infrastructure for fault-tolerant systems. In: 2009 International Conference on Parallel Processing, pp. 237–245. IEEE (2009)
24. Di, S., Gupta, R., Snir, M., Pershey, E., Cappello, F.: LogAider: a tool for mining potential correlations of HPC log events. In: 17th IEEE/ACM International Symposium on Cluster, Cloud and Grid Computing (CCGRID), pp. 442–451. IEEE (2017)
25. CockroachDB: CockroachDB - the open source, cloud-native distributed SQL database (2022). https://www.cockroachlabs.com
26. Adap/Flower: A friendly federated learning framework (2023). https://github. com/argoproj/argo
27. Nikolaidis, F., Chazapis, A., Marazakis, M., Bilas, A.: Frisbee: automated testing of Cloud-native applications in Kubernetes. arXiv preprint arXiv:2109.10727 (2021)

HPC I/O in the Data Center (HPC IODC)

Analyzing Parallel Applications for Unnecessary I/O Semantics that Inhibit File System Performance

Sebastian Oeste[1]([ENVELOPE]) [ID], Michael Kluge[1] [ID], Ronny Tschüter[2],
and Wolfgang E. Nagel[1]

[1] Center for Information Services and High Performance Computing (ZIH),
Technische Universität Dresden, Dresden, Germany
{sebastian.oeste,michael.kluge,wolfgang.nagel}@tu-dresden.de
[2] German Aerospace Center (DLR), Dresden, Germany
ronny.tschueter@dlr.de

Abstract. Scalability and performance of I/O intensive parallel applications are major concerns in modern High Performance Computing (HPC) environments. Almost all applications use POSIX I/O explicitly or implicitly through third party libraries like MPI-IO to perform I/O operations on the file system. POSIX I/O is known to be one of the lead causes of poor I/O performance due to its restrictive access semantics and consistency requirements.

Some file systems therefore relax specific POSIX semantics to alleviate I/O performance penalties. In order to make the most effective use of the offered file systems features it is required to know what kind of POSIX semantics an application requires. Existing tools can analyze parallel I/O performance to report type and duration of executed I/O operations. There are even tools that analyse the consistency requirements of data operations, but none that also consider perfromance critical patterns of metadata operations.

In this paper, we present a novel, systematic approach that groups parallel I/O operations and analyzes their I/O semantics with respect to POSIX I/O. We provide the tool *rabbitxx* that identifies concurrent overlapping accesses to the same file but also identifies metadata accesses such as concurrent create operations in the same directory. Our work indicates that POSIX defined I/O access semantics, in its current form, are often not necessary for parallel applications.

Keywords: Performance Analysis · I/O · POSIX · Semantics · File system · HPC

A. Bienz et al. (Eds.): ISC High Performance 2023 Workshops, LNCS 13999, pp. 161–176, 2023.
https://doi.org/10.1007/978-3-031-40843-4_13

1   Introduction

High Performance Computing (HPC) systems use parallel file systems to manage accesses from thousands of compute nodes to the back-end storage system. The file system interface defines available I/O operations along with their semantics. Many common parallel file systems, such as GPFS [21] or Lustre [2], provide a POSIX [19] compliant interface. POSIX was being developed with a strong focus on local file systems. Applied in a parallel distributed file system, its restrictive access semantics can cause considerable performance degradation [10,13,28]. In some cases, like file creations in a directory, POSIX I/O semantics enforce serial processing of operations issued in parallel. The lack of appropriate support of parallel I/O renders POSIX I/O (part of the POSIX standard) a major scalability and performance bottleneck for parallel applications.

Consequently, parallel file system developers have started to discard individual POSIX features or relax their consistency requirements to enable scalability for specific workloads. The NFS [22] file system relaxes the POSIX consistency for parallel accesses to the same file to a *close-to-open* consistency model. The PVFS [5] parallel file system supports non-conflicting write consistency semantics, leaving the results of overlapping writes undefined. Many tools [12,24,32] investigate and characterize parallel I/O performance of HPC applications. A lot of tools [12,24,26,32] provide insight into the usage of programming interfaces, I/O operation types, bandwidth, and files accesses. It has also been shown that strict write consistency is not requried by many HPC applications [31].

In this paper we boarden the view and also examine performance critical pattern of metadata operations. Therefore, we introduce a method that identifies application phases and builds sets of concurrent I/O operations within these steps. We check I/O operation sets for critical I/O access patterns that potentially limit performance and thereby reveal potential for relaxing POSIX I/O semantics of parallel file systems. We provide an exemplary implementation in form of *rabbitxx*[1], an open source, post-mortem analysis tool that identifies parallel I/O operations and investigates their access semantics with regard to POSIX. With this information, developers can optimize their applications, fine-tune I/O consistency requirements of their programs, and choose the most suitable storage infrastructure or file system configuration. Furthermore, parallel file system and I/O middleware engineers can investigate which consistency guarantees today's HPC applications require.

The remainder of this paper is organized as follows. Section 2 highlights performance critical I/O patterns to underline the importance of this work. Section 3 lists related work. Sections 5.1, 5.2, 5.3 present our methodology. First, we introduce an algorithm that creates sets of concurrent I/O operations from an event log of a parallel application. Then, we describe analysis modules that check these sets for different performance critical semantics. Section 6 demonstrates *rabbitxx* by analyzing two real world applications. We conclude and list future work in Sect. 7.

---

[1] https://github.com/blastmaster/rabbitxx.

2   Performance Critical Access Patterns

In this section we highlight three performance critical access patterns. The first two show limitations due to POSIX semantics. POSIX semantics enforce a strict serial processing for these patterns to prevent errors and guarantee data integrity. However, in a parallel use case scenario these semantics are 1) often completely unnecessary as applications can take care of data integrity more efficiently themselves, and 2) induce serious performance penalties. The last example demonstrates so-called anti-patterns that should be avoided in parallel applications.

Concurrent Create Operations within the Same Directory. POSIX requires strict consistency for file metadata and directory structures. Since parallel file creations may access the same directory structure (i.e., directory blocks), file systems have to lock it, see Fig. 1a. This is particularly relevant in parallel file systems where directory structures are globally accessible and all metadata operations have to be immediately visible on all nodes. Among others, this requires a large number of expensive global locking communication and can significantly impact the file system's metadata throughput [28].

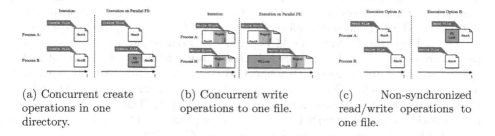

(a) Concurrent create operations in one directory.

(b) Concurrent write operations to one file.

(c)   Non-synchronized read/write operations to one file.

Fig. 1. Illustration of examples of performance critical access patterns.

Concurrent Overlapping File Accesses. The strict write consistency of POSIX requires that writes to the same region of a file are mutually exclusive. Thus, parallel writes appear as a sequential stream of operations, see Fig. 1b. The POSIX I/O semantics further dictate that write operations block until the data has been written to durable storage. Concurrently occurring read operations have to see the new data immediately. Local file systems can utilize the page cache to ensure this semantic restriction. However, parallel file systems need to hold locks and issue additional communication for this purpose.

In practice, the strict consistency semantics of write operations are unnecessary in case of non-overlapping accesses. Moreover, we assume that most HPC applications ensure non-overlapping accesses at a higher application level for scalability reasons.

Concurrent Read-Modify-Write Access to the Same Region of a File. The concurrent Read-Modify-Write access pattern describes the situation where process A reads a region of a file while process B writes to the same region of the file. This pattern indicates a possible data consistency violation. Depending on the runtime scheduling of both operations (process A reads before process B writes, or vice versa) it is undefined which "version" of the file process A reads, see Fig. 1c. In such a case the POSIX semantics only ensure that the read operation is not executed while the write operation is active. Therefore, distributed file systems need to employ global locking communication. We treat this as an anti-pattern for HPC-IO which requires stronger semantics from the underlying file system and poses performance penalties.

3   Related Work

The first paragraph of this section focuses on POSIX I/O semantics, whereas the second paragraph gives an overview on research related to I/O analysis.

POSIX I/O Semantics. The Portable Operating System Interface (POSIX) standard [19] defines portable interfaces between applications and the operating system. Its first formal specification dates back to 1988. The I/O section of the POSIX standard (henceforth referred to as POSIX I/O) comprises two essential parts. First, the POSIX I/O API specifies I/O operations and their syntactic requirements. Second, the POSIX I/O semantics define the behavior of I/O operations, e.g., guarantees with respect to consistency and correctness when using specific POSIX I/O operations. Some of these guarantees are very restrictive and impede efficient parallelization of I/O tasks [14]. The HPC community made efforts to extend POSIX I/O semantics for parallel I/O [30]. In 2006 there was a High End Computing Extensions Working Group [25].

Some parallel file systems discard certain POSIX I/O semantics to circumvent scalability issues. For instance, PVFS [5] supports non-conflicting consistency semantics and leave overlapping access to the same region of a file undefined. GekkoFS [27] is a job-temporal file system that relaxes POSIX I/O semantics for eventual consistency and improves scalability of metadata handling. Current research investigates object stores to explore trade-offs between scalability and flexible semantics [6,15].

I/O Analysis Tools. There is a number of tools to characterize I/O in the past decades [9,16,20]. For instance, Darshan [4] is widely known to characterize application I/O accurately. The Darshan tool is implemented as a set of user-space libraries and records counters for POSIX and MPI-IO operations. It yields statistics, such as MPI-IO adoption rate, number of files opened per job, or the ratio of read and write operations. ScalaIOTrace [29] records event logs including calls to MPI-IO and POSIX I/O. Data compression techniques utilize repetitive event sequences to keep event logs small, but preserve application's communication and I/O structure. Therefore, event logs recorded by ScalaIOTrace are well-suited to replay I/O characteristics of applications. Méndez et al. [17] model I/O phases to estimate the runtime of an application for a certain I/O subsystem. They weight an I/O phase based on their repetitions and request size. Reed published together with different collaborators several papers related to I/O characterization [16,18,23]. The presented characterization is defined by three dimensions: type of operation, spatial and temporal access pattern. Byna et al. [3] present a five-dimensional characterization approach taking even the request size and number of repetition into account. They generate a signature of the I/O behavior to provide online prefetching strategies. The approaches mentioned above record statistics and metrics to describe the I/O behavior of applications or jobs on a cluster. These insights are useful to get an overview of the workload, identify performance critical operations, as well as detecting repetitive patterns.

Wang et al. [31] developed a method for detecting I/O accesses that can cause conflicts under weaker consistency models. Further, they provide a terminology for the categorization of the consistency semantics of parallel file systems. They found out that 16 of 17 applications can utilize file systems with weaker semantics. However, the algorithm to determine consistency semantics needs of an application uses only data operations. In contrast, our work also provides analysis modules for I/O patterns of performance critical metadata operations. Further, we analyze groups of parallel I/O operations, considers all combinations of their concurrent execution. Instead of being focused on the I/O events as they appear in an individual application run.

4   Methodology

This section gives an overview of our approach. The basis of our analysis method is information about I/O operations executed by an application.

Application Instrumentation: To acquire the necessary information from an application, we use the performance measurement infrastructure Score-P[2] [11,26]. Therefore, we intercept application calls to I/O and synchronization routines.

Application Execution and Trace Data Generation: When the instrumented application executes, it generates an OTF2 [7] trace file containing I/O and synchronization operations. A trace file represents an event log. Figure 2a shows information stored within a trace. Each event contains the time when the event occurred, the process that executed the event, and the type of that event. This information enables reconstruction of event sequences and their transformation into a graph structure (Fig. 2b).

Construction of the I/O Graph: We read the event sequences from the trace file and convert them into a *directed acyclic graph* (DAG) data structure.

---

[2] http://www.score-p.org/.

Time	Process	Operation
...		
21	1	open(f1)
42	2	mkdir(d2)
55	1	write(f1)
66	1	close(f1)
...		

(a) Application trace

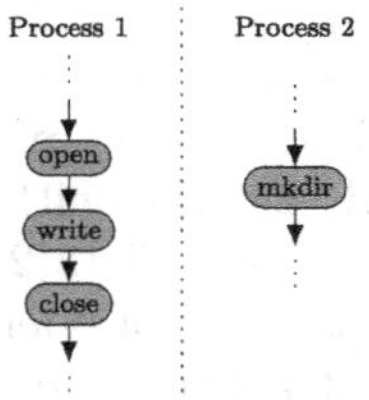

(b) Graph representation

Fig. 2. Example of an application trace along with the corresponding graph representation of the event sequence.

Section 5.1 presents detailed information about the graph construction. Subsequent processing and analysis tasks work on the graph data structure.

Creation of Concurrent I/O Sets: First, we analyze each process individually and identify phases in its event sequence. A *Phase* contains all I/O operations between two synchronization points. Section 5.2 explains the phase identification step in more detail. Then, we expand our analysis over multiple processes. We identify corresponding phases across all processes and define sets of concurrent I/O operations (*CIO-Set*). A *CIO-Set* contains all I/O operations that can be executed concurrently on the participating processes. Consequently, the *CIO-Set* algorithm must not only handle the I/O event sequence as stored in the trace file. Multiple executions of the instrumented application might generate slightly different event sequence orders. Therefore, our creation algorithm also considers event permutations in order to find all possible *CIO-Sets*. We introduce the *CIO-Set* algorithm in Sect. 5.2.

Analysis of I/O Access Patterns and Their Semantics: Our analysis uses the *CIO-Sets* to evaluate whether the I/O access patterns of an application require specific POSIX I/O semantics. Analysis results reveal potential performance bottlenecks as well as options to relax POSIX I/O semantics for HPC applications. Section 5.3 presents currently implemented analysis modules.

5 Implementation

This section describes the implementation of our methodology presented in Sect. 4. We use the example introduced in Fig. 3 throughout this section to explain the construction of the I/O graph and the algorithm identifying the *CIO-Sets*.

5.1 Construction of the I/O Graph

An application trace builds the foundation for the I/O graph construction. We distinguish three kinds of vertices in the I/O graph: *I/O, synchronization* and *synthetic* vertices. An I/O vertex represents an individual I/O event, e.g., a write request, or the creation of a new file. The synchronization vertex represents communication or synchronization between processes. These are either collective operations, e.g., `MPI_Barrier`, or blocking point-to-point operations, e.g., an `MPI_Send`, `MPI_Recv` pair. The synthetic vertices model a dedicated *Program-Start* and *Program-End* vertex. Trace event information (e.g., number of transferred bytes) is stored in the vertex properties.

Each I/O graph starts with a common synthetic *Program-Start* vertex. The *Program-Start* vertex connects to the first non-synthetic vertex of each process. From this point, each branch represents the execution of the respective process including I/O and synchronization events. A common synthetic *Program-End* vertex finalizes the I/O graph. An edge from the last non-synthetic vertex of each process connects to the *Program-End* vertex.

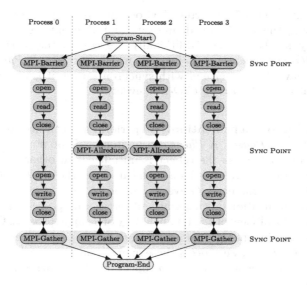

Fig. 3. Example of an I/O graph. The graph consists of synthetic (gray), I/O (red), and synchronization (green) vertices, synchronization points across processes (horizontal green bars), and *Phases* (vertical gray bars). A *Phase* of an individual process is enclosed by a *CIO-Start* (▼) and *CIO-End* (▲) event. (Color figure online)

Figure 3 illustrates the I/O graph constructed from the trace of a program running on four processes. The event sequence starts with an `MPI_Barrier` across all processes. Then, each process reads data, before an `MPI_Allreduce` operation synchronizes process 1 and 2. Subsequently, a second stage of I/O operations starts. The event sequence ends with two `MPI_Gather` operations. Processes 0 and 1 participate in the first operation, processes 2 and 3 in the second operation.

The first part of the I/O graph construction reads the trace data, analyzes the event, and constructs the corresponding vertex. After adding the vertex, the next part creates an edge between the current vertex and the previous one of the process. This reflects the event flow for each process.

Table 1. Summary of notation

Notation	Description
Process-Group	The set of process IDs that participate on a synchronization event
Sync-List	The unique list of *CIO-End* events of the *Phases* in the current *View*
Sync-Pairs	List of all unique combinations of pairs of elements in *Sync-List*

5.2   Identification of Concurrent I/O Sets

In order to identify sets of concurrent I/O operations, we process the I/O graph. While traversing the graph, we define sets of I/O events. Each I/O event is represented by its *Vertex ID*. Additionally, we collect the *Vertex ID*s of the *CIO-Start/CIO-End* synchronization events which start/stop a *Phase*. Since programs do not have to start or end with synchronization, it is also valid to set a synthetic event as *CIO-Start* or *CIO-End* event.

Per-Process Phase Identification. We perform a depth-first-traversal on the graph to identify its *Phases*. A *Phase* can be in one of two states: *open* or *close*. A *Phase* is *open* as soon as the object is initialized. In other words, it has at least a *CIO-Start* event. A closed *Phase* means that the *CIO-End* event of the *Phase* was set and no further I/O events can be added to the *Phase*.

The phase identification finishes when all vertices are processed. The resulting *Phases* provide a local view of the I/O behavior of a single process. Consequently, we store the *Phases* in a per-process queue in the order of their occurrence. While defining global *CIO-Sets*, we process these queues and keep track of the currently active *Phase* in each queue. A *View* is a collection of the currently active *Phases* across all processes.

Global CIO-Sets. The algorithm to identify global *CIO-Sets* consists of four parts. The next paragraphs provide a detailed explanation of each part based on the I/O graph of our example (Fig. 3). Table 1 shows the notation used.

Initialize View. The algorithm starts with a *View* containing the first *Phases* of all processes. In our example, Fig. 4a highlights a *View* containing the first *Phases* of four processes. All I/O events in these *Phases* will be merged into a global *CIO-Set*. To decide how the *View* can be updated, the *CIO-End* event of the *CIO-Set* must be found.

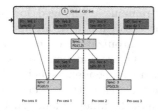

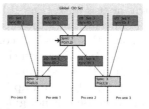

(a) The highlighted fields depict the *Phases* of the current *View*, which will be merged into a new *CIO-Set*.

(b) Identifying the boundaries of the *CIO-Set*. Synchronization 1 becomes the *CIO-End* of the *CIO-Set* of the current *View*.

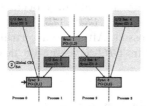

(c) Updated the *View*. The new *View* contains the *Phases* for the next *CIO-Set*, the *CIO-End* is synchronization 2.

(d) Two overlapping *CIO-Sets* resulting from the merge part depicted in Figures 4a to 4c.

Fig. 4. Steps of the CIO-Set algorithm.

Determine Boundaries. The next part analyzes the current *View*, identifies participating *Phases* and inserts all *CIO-End* events contained therein into the *Sync-List*. In our example, this results in *Sync-List* = $\{2, 1, 3\}$ (Fig. 4a). The *CIO-End* events are denoted as *Sync-IDs* in Fig. 4a. Then, all unique combinations of pairs of the elements in *Sync-List* are built. There are $\frac{n(n-1)}{2}$ pairs, where n is the number of *CIO-End* events. In our example, this gives *Sync-Pairs* = $\{\{1, 2\}, \{1, 3\}, \{2, 3\}\}$. Next, for each pair in *Sync-Pairs*, the algorithm checks if the synchronization operations referred in the pair are dependent or independent. Two synchronization operations are called independent if the intersection of their *Process-Group* is empty. Otherwise, synchronization operations with processes participating in both synchronizations of the pair are called dependent. In our example, the synchronizations 2 and 3 depend on synchronization 1. In other words, some processes participating in synchronization 2 or 3 have a *Phase* in their current *View* where the *CIO-End* event refers to another synchronization. In this case, it refers to synchronization 1.

Define Global. CIO-Set Fig. 4b illustrates synchronization 1 as the *CIO-End* event of the first global *CIO-Set*. Therefore, the creation of the global *CIO-Set* is finished and the *CIO-Set* is saved for further analysis.

Update View. Next, all processes in the *Process-Group* of the *CIO-End* event update the *View* to their next *Phase*. In our example, processes 1 and 2 can update to their next *Phase* (Fig. 4b). The *View* remains unchanged for process 0 and 3. Figure 4c shows the next part of the algorithm with an updated *View*. In this part, the *Sync-List* contains the synchronization events 2 and 3 (*Sync-List* $= \{2,3\}$). Both synchronization events are independent, since *Process-Group* (2) $\cap$ *Process-Group* (3) $= \emptyset$. When independent synchronizations are detected, the algorithm updates the *View* for each of them recursively. This is necessary because it is not guaranteed which of the independent synchronization events will occur first. Figure 4d shows both resulting *CIO-Sets* of the parts before. The resulting *CIO-Sets* are overlapping. *Phases* 1 and 4 of the processes 0 and 3 occur in both sets because they are not synchronized with other processes until synchronization 2 and 3. Therefore, they actually may occur in parallel with the *Phases* 2 and 3 but also with 5 and 6.

The algorithm continues until all *Phases* are processed. After the algorithm finished, we start to analyze the I/O behavior within *CIO-Sets*. In the next section, we discuss our analyses.

5.3   Analysis of I/O Access Patterns and Their Semantics

In this section, we describe the design and implementation of our analysis features. The *rabbitxx* design follows a modular approach. Each specific analysis task is implemented in its own analysis module. In a first step, the *rabbitxx* tool reads the event trace and calculates the *CIO-Sets*. In the scope of this work we present three analysis modules covering the three access patterns introduced in Sect. 2. All three modules produce a text-based report as output. The following paragraphs introduce each analysis module. The *rabbitxx* analysis capabilities are easily extendable by adding new analysis modules.

Module A: Concurrent Create Operations within the Same Directory. This analysis module filters `create` operations within a *CIO-Set* and checks if they target the same directory. If it detects such operations, it reports the *CIO-Set* number, the number and the function name of the `create` operations, and the affected directory.

Module B: Concurrent Overlapping File Accesses. This analysis module checks each *CIO-Set* for overlapping accesses. Therefore, it calculates the access intervals of `read` and `write` operations for each process. Then, for each file, it compares the respective intervals between all processes. If the module detects overlaps, it reports the *CIO-Set* number, the file name, the range that overlaps, and all affected processes.

Module C: Concurrent Read-Modify-Write Access to the Same Region of a File. This analysis module checks for all *CIO-Sets* if any read access will be overwritten by another process with a write operation to the same file offset. If the module detects this case, it reports the *CIO-Set* number, the file name, and all affected processes.

6   Experiments and Evaluation

This section presents the results of our analysis modules for two HPC benchmark applications. We choose two benchmarks which utilize I/O kernels from real-world HPC workloads. To verify our approach, we choose the MADbench2 [1] and HACC-IO [8] benchmark applications.

All tests were executed on *Taurus*[3], a generic BULL Linux Cluster at Technische Universität Dresden. Taurus consists of 2189 compute nodes with 43000 cores attached to a 5.1PB disk-based, and a 43TB SSD-based Lustre parallel file system.

6.1   MADbench2

MADbench2 is a benchmark based on the MADspec code, which calculates the maximum likelihood angular power spectrum of the Cosmic Microwave Background radiation. It operates on large floating-point matrices which are too large to hold them completely in main memory. Therefore, data will be written to disk and read back later.

We use MADbench2 in I/O-only mode, which skips calculations. We instrument and run the MADbench2 code on 16 and 64 processes. For the configuration, we choose POSIX as IOMETHOD in synchronous IOMODE. Because we want to investigate overlapping file accesses, we select "shared file access" as FILETYPE. Afterwards, we analyze the resulting trace with our tool *rabbitxx*. Independent of the number of application processes, our analysis identifies six different *CIO-Sets*. The resulting sets are non-overlapping because the MADbench2 code synchronizes with collective MPI synchronization routines encompassing all processes. Except from the number of processes and files accesses, the semantic analysis results are equal for all runs. Thus, we present only analysis results for the runs with 64 processes in the following.

Our first analysis module tests whether concurrent create operations appear in the same directory. The analysis report the application issues 64 create operations in the same directory within *CIO-Set* 2. The affected directory is located on the parallel file system. Consequently, all participating processes open the same file.

The second analysis module tests for overlapping accesses to the same address range within a file. Due to the strong consistency of write operations in POSIX I/O, overlapping writes can significantly impair the scalability of a parallel file system. Overlapping accesses to the same file region could also result in undefined behavior in case of file systems that relax POSIX I/O consistency, such as PVFS [5] or NFS [22]. Our analysis module reports no overlapping accesses for MADbench2. Nevertheless, Table 2 shows that all participating processes access the same file in *CIO-Sets* 2 to 5. Such a non-overlapping access pattern on a shared file is common for HPC applications. Our analysis of MADbench2 provides one example for such applications, that usually coordinate parallel accesses by themselves at a higher level.

Table 2. MADbench2: Concurrent accesses per file.

CIO-Set	File	#processes
2	/lustre/scratch2/.../MADbench2/files/data	64
3	/lustre/scratch2/.../MADbench2/files/data	64
4	/lustre/scratch2/.../MADbench2/files/data	64
5	/lustre/scratch2/.../MADbench2/files/data	64

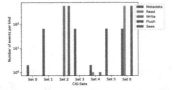

Fig. 5. HACC-IO: The number of operation types per *CIO-Set*.

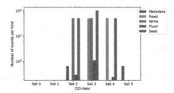

Fig. 6. MADbench2: Number of operation types per *CIO-Set*.

The third analysis module investigates whether concurrent read-modify-write accesses appear to the same region of a file. Our analysis module reports no such accesses for MADbench2. The application coordinates its accesses in a non-contiguous, non-overlapping manner. Figure 6 shows the number of operation types per *CIO-Set* for MADbench2. Concurrent read and write accesses occur only in *CIO-Set* 3. All other *CIO-Sets* perform either read or write or none of both. The results support the assumption that HPC applications typically issue their I/O operations in distinct phases.

6.2   HACC-IO

HACC-IO is an I/O-performance benchmark that computes an n-body simulation of collision-less fluids in space. HACC-IO uses random I/O write operations as well as all-to-all communication patterns. For our analysis we instrument HACC-IO with Score-P and run it with 16, 32, 64, and 128 processes. The *rabbitxx* analysis reports seven non-overlapping *CIO-Sets* for each of these configurations. Again, as all configurations show similar behavior, we present only results for the run with 64 processes here.

The analysis of concurrent creates report *CIO-Set* 1 and 5 issue 64 **open64** operations on the same file. The identified behavior is similar to MADbench2. The POSIX I/O semantics for **open** operations dictate that the file system needs to hold file descriptors for each accessing processes and a corresponding file description entry. If the accessed file does not exist, the file system has to create it and update the metadata entries. This metadata update requires additional locking and communication in distributed environments.

---

[3] https://doc.zih.tu-dresden.de/jobs_and_resources/hardware_overview/.

HACC-IO follows a "shared file access" pattern. Our analysis reports no overlapping accesses to the same address range of a file. However, Table 3 shows that *CIO-Sets* 1, 2, 3, 5, and 6 access the same file concurrently. This result strengthens our assumption that many HPC applications are designed for parallel file systems and avoid accesses to the same file with overlapping offsets.

Table 3. HACC-IO: Concurrent accesses per file.

CIO-Set	File	#processes
0	/lustre/scratch2/.../haccio/haccio-out.data	1
1	/lustre/scratch2/.../haccio/haccio-out.data	64
2	/lustre/scratch2/.../haccio/haccio-out.data	64
3	/lustre/scratch2/.../haccio/haccio-out.data	64
4	/lustre/scratch2/.../haccio/haccio-out.data	1
5	/lustre/scratch2/.../haccio/haccio-out.data	64
6	/lustre/scratch2/.../haccio/haccio-out.data	64

In analogy to MADbench2, our analysis does not report any read-modify-write file access patterns. No *CIO-Set* of HACC-IO contains simultaneous read and write operations. Figure 5 shows that all concurrent write operations are executed in *CIO-Set* 2, while read operations occur in *CIO-Set* 4 and 6.

In summary, our analysis of MADbench2 and HACC-IO shows that both applications concurrently create files in the same directory. Furthermore, they perform non-conflicting, non-overlapping accesses to shared files. Both applications calculate offsets and use seek operations to manage their file accesses. We conclude that these kinds of applications do not require the atomicity and strong consistency for read and write operations defined by POSIX I/O. In addition, the POSIX I/O semantics for metadata consistency and file creation represent a potential performance bottleneck that parallel application cannot circumvent with the current API. HPC applications can benefit from the concept of file descriptors shared across multiple processes or a collective file open operation for multiple processes. Moreover, both applications were only accessing files in a single directory. Consequently, strict consistency of a global namespace as dictated by POSIX I/O seems unnecessary for many HPC applications. Instead, we propose application-private namespaces where consistency requirements hold for participating nodes, not the whole cluster. The analysis of required I/O semantics of HPC applications indeed requires further research.

7   Conclusion and Future Work

This paper presents a systematic approach to analyze parallel applications for understanding the need of specific I/O semantics. Based on the event log of a parallel application, we generate a graph that preserves the happens-before relation of events on individual processes and reflects synchronization points across multiple processes. We present a two-stage algorithm using this information to identify all sets of concurrent I/O events. As a result, we get all sets of I/O events that may occur in parallel within an application – either as observed in the given event log or in any other parallel execution order with the given synchronization operations. Then, we analyze the I/O behavior and determine which POSIX I/O semantics are unnecessary for the application.

Our evaluations indicate that the fundamental semantic restrictions implied by the POSIX I/O standard might not be necessary for many HPC applications. Dropping of unnecessary semantics would remove significant performance bottlenecks from the parallel file system. One example of this is the strict consistency of write operations. The results of our analyses reveal potential for replacing or relaxing POSIX I/O semantics in future storage systems.

In the future, we plan to add more analysis capabilities to *rabbitxx*.

References

1. Borrill, J., Carter, J., Oliker, L., Skinner, D., Biswas, R.: Integrated performance monitoring of a cosmology application on leading HEC platforms. In: 2005 International Conference on Parallel Processing (ICPP 2005), pp. 119–128. IEEE (2005). https://doi.org/10.1109/ICPP.2005.47, https://ieeexplore.ieee.org/document/1488607/
2. Braam, P.J., Zahir, R.: Lustre: a scalable, high performance file system. Clust. File Syst. **8**(11), 3429–3441 (2002). https://cse.buffalo.edu/faculty/tkosar/cse710/papers/lustre-whitepaper.pdf
3. Byna, S., Chen, Y., Sun, X.H., Thakur, R., Gropp, W.: Parallel I/O prefetching using MPI file caching and I/O signatures. In: Proceedings of the 2008 ACM/IEEE Conference on Supercomputing, pp. 1–12. IEEE (2008). https://doi.org/10.1109/SC.2008.5213604
4. Carns, P., Latham, R., Ross, R., Iskra, K., Lang, S., Riley, K.: 24/7 characterization of petascale I/O workloads. In: 2009 IEEE International Conference on Cluster Computing and Workshops, pp. 1–10 (2009)
5. Carns, P., Ligon, W., Ross, R., Thakur, R.: PVFS: a parallel file system for Linux clusters. In: 4th Annual Linux Showcase and Conference, vol. 4, pp. 1–11 (2000)
6. Danilov, N., Rutman, N., Narasimhamurthy, S., Bent, J.: Mero: co-designing an object store for extreme scale (2016). https://www.pdsw.org/pdsw-discs16/wips/danilov-wip-pdsw-discs16.pdf
7. Eschweiler, D., Wagner, M., Geimer, M., Knüpfer, A., Nagel, W.E., Wolf, F.: Open trace format 2: the next generation of scalable trace formats and support libraries. In: De Bosschere, K., D'Hollander, E.H., Joubert, G.R., Padua, D., Peters, F., Sawyer, M. (eds.) Applications, Tools and Techniques on the Road to Exascale Computing. Advances in Parallel Computing, vol. 22, pp. 481–490. IOS Press (2012). https://doi.org/10.3233/978-1-61499-041-3-481
8. Habib, S., et al.: The universe at extreme scale: multi-petaflop sky simulation on the BG/Q. In: SC 2012: Proceedings of the International Conference on High Performance Computing, Networking, Storage and Analysis, pp. 4:1–4:11. IEEE (2012). https://dl.acm.org/citation.cfm?id=2388996.2389002

9. He, J., et al.: Discovering structure in unstructured I/O. In: 2012 SC Companion: High Performance Computing, Networking Storage and Analysis, pp. 1–6. IEEE (2012). https://doi.org/10.1109/SC.Companion.2012.11

10. Hildebrand, D., Nisar, A., Haskin, R.: pNFS, POSIX, and MPI-IO: a tale of three semantics. In: Proceedings of the 4th Annual Workshop on Petascale Data Storage, PDSW 2009, pp. 32–36. ACM (2009). https://doi.org/10.1145/1713072.1713082, https://portal.acm.org/citation.cfm?doid=1713072.1713082

11. Knüpfer, A., et al.: Score-P: a joint performance measurement run-time infrastructure for periscope, Scalasca, TAU, and Vampir. In: Brunst, H., Müller, M.S., Nagel, W.E., Resch, M.M. (eds.) Tools for High Performance Computing 2011, pp. 79–91. Springer, Heidelberg (2012). https://doi.org/10.1007/978-3-642-31476-6_7

12. Kunkel, J.M., et al.: The SIOX architecture – coupling automatic monitoring and optimization of parallel I/O. In: Kunkel, J.M., Ludwig, T., Meuer, H.W. (eds.) ISC 2014. LNCS, vol. 8488, pp. 245–260. Springer, Cham (2014). https://doi.org/10.1007/978-3-319-07518-1_16

13. Latham, R., Ross, R., Thakur, R.: The impact of file systems on MPI-IO scalability. In: Kranzlmüller, D., Kacsuk, P., Dongarra, J. (eds.) EuroPVM/MPI 2004. LNCS, vol. 3241, pp. 87–96. Springer, Heidelberg (2004). https://doi.org/10.1007/978-3-540-30218-6_18

14. Lockwood, G.: What's so bad about Posix I/O (2017). https://www.nextplatform.com/2017/09/11/whats-bad-posix-io/

15. Lofstead, J., Jimenez, I., Maltzahn, C., Koziol, Q., Bent, J., Barton, E.: DAOS and friends: a proposal for an exascale storage system. In: SC 2016: Proceedings of the International Conference for High Performance Computing, Networking, Storage and Analysis, pp. 585–596 (2016). https://doi.org/10.1109/SC.2016.49

16. Madhyastha, T.M., Reed, D.A.: Learning to classify parallel input/output access patterns. IEEE Trans. Parallel Distrib. Syst. **13**(8), 802–813 (2002). https://doi.org/10.1109/TPDS.2002.1028437

17. Méndez, S., Rexachs, D., Luque, E.: Modeling parallel scientific applications through their input/output phases. In: 2012 IEEE International Conference on Cluster Computing Workshops, pp. 7–15. IEEE (2012). https://doi.org/10.1109/ClusterW.2012.37

18. Oly, J., Reed, D.A.: Markov model prediction of I/O requests for scientific applications. In: Proceedings of the 16th international conference on Supercomputing, ICS 2002, pp. 147–155. ACM (2002). https://doi.org/10.1145/514191.514214, https://doi.acm.org/10.1145/514191.514214

19. IEEE Standard for Information Technology-Portable Operating System Interface (POSIX(R)) Base Specifications, Issue 7. IEEE Std 1003.1-2017 (Revision of IEEE Std 1003.1-2008), pp. 1–3951 (2018)

20. Sayed, S.E., Bolten, M., Pleiter, D., Frings, W.: Parallel I/O characterisation based on server-side performance counters. In: Proceedings of the 1st Joint International Workshop on Parallel Data Storage and Data Intensive Scalable Computing Systems (PDSW-DISCS), pp. 7–12. IEEE Press (2016). https://doi.org/10.1109/PDSW-DISCS.2016.006

21. Schmuck, F., Haskin, R.: GPFS: a shared-disk file system for large computing clusters. In: Proceedings of the 1st USENIX Conference on File and Storage Technologies, FAST 2002, pp. 231–244. USENIX Association (2002). https://dl.acm.org/citation.cfm?id=1083323.1083349

22. Shepler, S., et al.: Network file system (NFS) version 4 Protocol. RFC 3530, RFC Editor (2003). https://www.rfc-editor.org/pdfrfc/rfc3530.txt.pdf

23. Smirni, E., Reed, D.A.: Lessons from characterizing the input/output behavior of parallel scientific applications. Perform. Eval. **33**(1), 27–44 (1998). https://doi.org/10.1016/S0166-5316(98)00009-1, http://www.sciencedirect.com/science/article/pii/S0166531698000091
24. Snyder, S., Carns, P., Harms, K., Ross, R., Lockwood, G.K., Wright, N.J.: Modular HPC I/O characterization with darshan. In: Proceedings of the 5th Workshop on Extreme-Scale Programming Tools, ESPT 2016, pp. 9–17. IEEE (2016). https://doi.org/10.1109/ESPT.2016.9
25. The Open Group: High End Computing Extensions Working Group (2006). https://collaboration.opengroup.org/platform/hecewg
26. Tschüter, R., Herold, C., Wesarg, B., Weber, M.: A methodology for performance analysis of applications using multi-layer I/O. In: Aldinucci, M., Padovani, L., Torquati, M. (eds.) Euro-Par 2018. LNCS, vol. 11014, pp. 16–30. Springer, Cham (2018). https://doi.org/10.1007/978-3-319-96983-1_2
27. Vef, M.A., et al.: GekkoFS - a temporary distributed file system for HPC applications. In: 2018 IEEE International Conference on Cluster Computing (CLUSTER), pp. 319–324 (2018). https://doi.org/10.1109/CLUSTER.2018.00049
28. Vef, M.A., Tarasov, V., Hildebrand, D., Brinkmann, A.: Challenges and solutions for tracing storage systems: a case study with spectrum scale. ACM Trans. Storage **14**(2), 18:1–18:24 (2018). https://doi.org/10.1145/3149376, https://doi.acm.org/10.1145/3149376
29. Vijayakumar, K., Mueller, F., Ma, X., Roth, P.C.: Scalable I/O tracing and analysis. In: Proceedings of the 4th Annual Workshop on Petascale Data Storage, PDSW 2009, pp. 26–31. ACM, New York (2009). https://doi.org/10.1145/1713072.1713080, https://doi.acm.org/10.1145/1713072.1713080
30. Vilayannur, M., Lang, S., Ross, R., Klundt, R., Ward, L.: Extending the POSIX I/O interface: a parallel file system. Perspective (2008). https://doi.org/10.2172/946036, http://www.osti.gov/servlets/purl/946036-pnI90N/
31. Wang, C., Mohror, K., Snir, M.: File system semantics requirements of HPC applications. In: Proceedings of the 30th International Symposium on High-Performance Parallel and Distributed Computing, HPDC 2021, pp. 19–30. Association for Computing Machinery, New York (2021). https://doi.org/10.1145/3431379.3460637
32. Wang, C., Sun, J., Snir, M., Mohror, K., Gonsiorowski, E.: Recorder 2.0: efficient parallel I/O tracing and analysis. In: 2020 IEEE International Parallel and Distributed Processing Symposium Workshops (IPDPSW), pp. 1–8. IEEE (2020)

Workshop on Converged Computing of Cloud, HPC, and Edge (WOCC'23)

Preface to the First International Workshop on Converged Computing of Cloud, HPC, and Edge (WOCC'23)

1 Background and Objectives

The landscape of scientific computing is changing rapidly as complex, multi-stage pipelined workflows that combine traditional HPC computations with large-scale data analytics and AI are becoming increasingly common. These next-generation workflows not only seek to improve the efficiency and scale of traditional HPC simulations, but additionally aim to apply large-scale and distributed computing to domains with high societal impact such as autonomous vehicles, precision agriculture, or smart cities. Such complex workflows are expected to require the coordinated use of supercomputers and cloud data centers as well as edge-processing devices, leading to an era of Converged Computing that combines the best of these worlds.

The International Workshop on Converged Computing (WOCC'23) provided the edge, HPC and cloud communities a dedicated venue for discussing challenges and research opportunities, deployment efforts, and best practices in supporting complex workflows on coordinated use of supercomputers and cloud data centers as well as edge-processing devices. The workshop encouraged interaction between participants who are developing applications, algorithms, middleware and infrastructure for converged environments. The workshop was an ideal place for the community to define the current state-of-the-art, and identify fundamental challenges and feasible future technologies and techniques. The workshop aimed to start discussion on questions, including: what changes to architecture, hardware, and middleware designs (including hardware monitoring, operating systems, system software, resource management) are needed? How to monitor and collect system-level metrics for utilization to identify bottlenecks to meet different targets in performance, cost, power budget? How to support different coupling patterns (e.g., loose or tight) between traditional scientific and big-data/AI components? What complex workflows and workloads leverage heterogeneity, elasticity, and dynamic resources provisioning?

2 Workshop Summary

The workshop started with a brief overview by the organizing committee followed by a keynote presentation titled "Minimizing the difference between HPC and cloud: convergence of communities and technologies" delivered by Daniel Milroy. Authors of all five accepted papers were asked to present their presentations in person in Q&A sessions. An invited talk titled "Guaranteeing performance and efficiency on modern Cloud infrastructures" was delivered by Achilleas Tzenetopoulos. Finally, a panel discussion on "Converged computing continuum on the horizon across HPC, Cloud, and Edge: Opportunities and Challenges" was moderated by Stefano Markidis and delivered by

Simon Smart (ECMWF, UK), Utz-Uwe Haus (HPE, CH), Daniel Milory (LLNL, US), Craig Prunty (Sipearl, FR), and Benjamin Czaja (SURF, NL). The workshop ran for four hours for a half-day session.

Organization

Organizers

Ivy Peng	KTH Royal Institute of Technology, Sweden
Daniel Milroy	Lawrence Livermore National Laboratory, USA
Tapasya Patki	Lawrence Livermore National Laboratory, USA

Program Committee

Program Chairs

Tapasya Patki	Lawrence Livermore National Laboratory, USA
Ivy Peng	KTH Royal Institute of Technology, Sweden

Committee Members

Jae-Seung Yeom	Lawrence Livermore National Laboratory, USA
Andrew Younge	Sandia National Laboratory, USA
Jeff Vetter	Oak Ridge National Laboratory, USA
Nathan Tallent	Pacific Northwest National Laboratory, USA
Bill Magro	Google, USA
Martin Schulz	Technische Universität München, Germany
Stefano Marikidis	KTH Royal Institute of Technology, Sweden
Domenico Talia	University of Calabria, Italy
Estela Suarez	Julich Supercomputing Centre, Germany
Erwin Laure	Max Planck Computing and Data Facility, Germany
Jakob Luettgau	University of Tennessee Knoxville, USA
Kento Sato	RIKEN, Japan
Claudia Misale	IBM, USA
Yoonho Park	IBM, USA

Running Kubernetes Workloads on HPC

Antony Chazapis[1(✉)], Fotis Nikolaidis[1], Manolis Marazakis[1],
and Angelos Bilas[1,2]

[1] Institute of Computer Science, FORTH, Heraklion, Greece
{chazapis,fnikol,maraz,bilas}@ics.forth.gr
[2] Computer Science Department, University of Crete, Heraklion, Greece

Abstract. Cloud and HPC increasingly converge in hardware platform
capabilities and specifications, nevertheless still largely differ in the software stack and how it manages available resources. The HPC world typically favors Slurm for job scheduling, whereas Cloud deployments rely
on Kubernetes to orchestrate container instances across nodes. Running
hybrid workloads is possible by using bridging mechanisms that submit
jobs from one environment to the other. However, such solutions require
costly data movements, while operating within the constraints set by
each setup's network and access policies. In this work, we explore a design
that enables running unmodified Kubernetes workloads directly on HPC.
With *High-Performance Kubernetes* (HPK), users deploy their own private Kubernetes "mini Clouds", which internally convert container lifecycle management commands to use the system-level Slurm installation
for scheduling and Singularity/Apptainer as the container runtime. We
consider this approach to be practical for deployment in HPC centers, as
it requires minimal pre-configuration and retains existing resource management and accounting policies. HPK provides users with an effective
way to utilize resources by a combination of well-known tools, APIs,
and more interactive and user-friendly interfaces as is common practice
in the Cloud domain, as well as seamlessly combine Cloud-native tools
with HPC jobs in converged, containerized workflows.

Keywords: Cloud-HPC convergence · Kubernetes · Virtual Kubelet ·
Slurm · Singularity · Apptainer

1 Introduction

Both Cloud and High-Performance Computing (HPC) setups offer developers computing environments to deploy large-scale applications, each with its
unique development tools and supporting utilities. The choice of platform usually depends on the design characteristics and architecture of the application,
or requirements applying to the software frameworks utilized. As an example, it
is common to use HPC for running tightly parallelized codes performing large
simulations, while the Cloud is a better fit for deploying out elastic webs of
microservices or Big Data runtimes. This dichotomy is challenged by the increasing complexity and diversity of large workloads that tend to be composed of

A. Bienz et al. (Eds.): ISC High Performance 2023 Workshops, LNCS 13999, pp. 181–192, 2023.
https://doi.org/10.1007/978-3-031-40843-4_14

multiple processing stages in the form of workflows. *Convergence* is essential for developers of big processing pipelines, as they would like to effortlessly combine Cloud with HPC steps and seamlessly transition between execution environments, using the most effective and efficient solution for each step.

Up to now, Cloud-HPC convergence has generally been realized with interfacing mechanisms for submitting HPC jobs from the Cloud side or vice versa. However, bridging separate Cloud and HPC installations has several disadvantages, as it requires synchronizing data between sites, each with its own storage, data transfer, and authorization restrictions. Having two separate setups also elevates the associated hardware and maintenance costs.

To this end, we explore an HPC-centric solution that accommodates both Cloud and HPC on the same hardware. We focus our work on Kubernetes [9], the most popular distributed container orchestrator in the Cloud [22] and the runtime of choice for supporting the "Cloud-native" ecosystem [4]. We present the design and implementation of *High-Performance Kubernetes* (HPK), an open source integration of unmodified Kubernetes components and custom modules that runs as a user-level service, which in turn acts as a translator from Kubernetes-native descriptions of services and jobs, to Slurm [16] and Singularity/Apptainer [1,17,23] scripts that run on a typical HPC cluster. By delegating execution to Slurm, HPK "mini Clouds" comply with organization policies and established resource accounting mechanisms. HPK requires minimal support from the HPC environment, all being changes to the container runtime configuration, in order to enable private, inter-container communication across cluster nodes and the ability to start containers that internally run commands as arbitrary users.

HPK successfully runs several Cloud-native frameworks without modifications. This includes Argo Workflows [2] with placement of artifacts on MinIO [10] (an S3 service), as well as examples using the Spark operator [8] and TensorFlow Serving [18]. We expect this technology to play a significant role in the world of HPC, as it enables existing HPC users to tap on the vast collection of available Cloud applications and services, as stand-alone solutions or in hybrid computation scenarios combining Cloud frameworks with HPC codes. HPC centers may no longer need to maintain separate hardware partitions for Cloud analytics and HPC, as HPK allows running the Cloud workloads on the main HPC partition. Furthermore, HPK can be used to attract Cloud users to large HPC installations, offering them a familiar interface to seamlessly exploit the raw computing power available.

2 Related Work

We classify work related to Cloud-HPC convergence in two main categories: Systems that maintain the *separation* of Cloud and HPC resources and systems that *embed* one resource management framework into the other. In the former case there are two separate resource managers, while in the latter there is a single authority that controls hardware allocations, shared by both Cloud and HPC deployments; the embedded framework delegates resource management decisions to the overall cluster manager. Works that assume separate clusters can further be divided into *bridging* solutions that operate within the context of the Cloud or HPC runtime, allowing the transparent submission of remote jobs, or *third-party* systems that operate in their own context and are able to administer tasks in both remote Cloud and HPC installations.

Many bridging solutions are available for Kubernetes, enabling Cloud users to integrate the execution of remote HPC jobs into their workflows. In [24], the authors use a utility called *hpc-connector* that acts as an HPC job proxy: Users submit Kubernetes jobs with specific settings, and the hpc-connector forwards them to the HPC cluster, monitors their execution, and collects their results. In [29], a Kubernetes installation is interfaced to a Torque-based HPC cluster, using a custom tool called *Torque-Operator*. The *Bridge Operator* [25] has similar goals and a wider compatibility of remote job execution facilities. All aforementioned projects use language extensions (Kubernetes custom resources) for describing jobs targeted for the HPC cluster. On the other hand, KNoC (Kubernetes Node on HPC Cluster) [26] is a virtual node for Kubernetes that transparently manages the container lifecycle on a remote HPC cluster using Slurm and Singularity. This technique effectively allows users to employ existing Cloud-native tools, such as Argo Workflows to express complex data-processing pipelines for both Cloud and HPC without explicit remote execution steps.

Bridging solutions are especially useful when Cloud and HPC resources are colocated. HPC centers increasingly support on-demand provisioning of Cloud resources—even as partitions of the main HPC machine [14]. However, when the two are remotely situated, bridging suffers from the overhead of maintaining data copies. The user must prepare and send inputs to the remote HPC cluster before issuing any tasks, and then place back outputs in the Kubernetes context. Data synchronization in hybrid workflows is addressed by StreamFlow [21], a third-party system, which extends the workflow language with declarative descriptions of execution sites (either Cloud or HPC) and their relationship to workflow nodes. The runtime automatically infers data dependencies, so to copy required data where needed before running each step.

Embedded convergence solutions avoid data copies and the requirement to manage and maintain two separate setups, as both Cloud and HPC share a common hardware platform. In [28], the authors embed the HPC runtime in Kubernetes, by introducing the concept of the *virtual cluster*, as a group of multiple container instances that function as a private HPC cluster for a user (similar to [11]). Each node in a virtual cluster includes all necessary libraries and utilities, as well as a full Slurm deployment; the user working inside a virtual cluster can only view and manage jobs submitted from within the same context. To coordinate resource allocations between tasks running within virtual clusters and other Kubernetes services, the Slurm controller is extended with a custom protocol that requests resources from the Kubernetes scheduler, effectively placing Kubernetes in charge of resource management for the whole cluster. A custom Kubernetes scheduler is also employed, in order to apply different container placement policies for "HPC" and "data center" services (typical Kubernetes deployments that run in other containers).

From Slurm's perspective, several embedded configurations are presented in [27]: *Over* is defined as the setup where Slurm is in control of the cluster, creating Kubernetes environments ephemerally within batch jobs, *adjancent* when both Slurm and Kubernetes are installed on the same physical nodes but share a common scheduler (i.e., Kubernetes uses Slurm to place jobs [15]), and *under* when Slurm-enabled pods are deployed in Kubernetes (like *virtual clusters*). HPK falls within the *over* class, however it does not create a full Kubernetes environment as a batch job, but rather transforms each Kubernetes-level deployment as an individual Slurm script, allowing for better scheduling flexibility and finer grain resource sharing.

We are not aware of any other system that embeds Kubernetes in HPC. Usernetes [19] is a step in this direction, providing a Kubernetes distribution that can run without root privileges. We did consider extending Usernetes to implement HPK, but quickly realized that the necessity of interfacing with Slurm and Singularity/Apptainer at multiple levels, would require reevaluating the internal structure of Kubernetes leading to reimplementing several subsystems. Interestingly, Usernetes solves the problem of managing the system's routing tables by utilizing a user-level networking stack, although this imposes several requirements to the environment, including availability of specific kernel modules.

3   Design

Our goal is to provide a mechanism for HPC users to run Kubernetes workloads in a typical cluster environment, so they can easily deploy hybrid workflows that combine Cloud-native frameworks with MPI codes. From a design perspective, the requirements for this mechanism are:

- Compatibility: All Kubernetes abstractions should be available and fully functional, except those that directly relate to physical hardware resources (i.e., "NodePort" services that request a specific port number for exposing services at Kubernetes nodes). Higher-level constructs, such as pods (one or more containers that are scheduled and scaled as a group), deployments, services, jobs, and volumes should be applicable with no changes. For supporting microservices, pods should be individually addressable, with inter-container networking and internal service discovery working as expected.
- Compliance: All resource management decisions should be delegated to the cluster manager operating the cluster (i.e., Slurm). Organization policies for resource allocation and accounting should be fully respected. Forwarded workloads should include as much information as possible, so the cluster manager can know at any point what is actually running. Also, minimal (ideally none) configuration changes should be required to be done at the host level by HPC administrators. Reliance on special libraries or binaries that execute with "elevated" permissions should be avoided.

- Usability: Make it easy for end users. Provide one simple command or script to deploy. All binaries should be neatly packaged up with their dependencies into a container, with no host-specific requirements. All relevant configuration and files should reside in the user's home directory.

To this end, we started by envisioning HPK as a user process; a Kubernetes-in-a-box integration, packaging the official Kubernetes binaries in a container that the user would be able to launch using a simple Slurm script. Kubernetes is implemented as a set of communicating subsystems that collectively provide the functionality of distributed container orchestration. A typical Kubernetes deployment constitutes of the following (Fig. 1):

- API server: The "heart" of Kubernetes. The main interface to the cluster and the synchronization point for all controllers.
- etcd: The key-value store holding all state. Always accessed through the API server.
- Controller manager: Watches for configuration changes or failures and performs all necessary actions to reach the desired state set by the user. The controller manager includes the controllers that implement the logic for the base Kubernetes abstractions. As all controllers, it communicates only with the API server.
- Scheduler: A controller that decides which node will be used to run new pods.
- CoreDNS: A controller and DNS server for implementing naming and discovery for pods and internal cluster services.
- Kubelet: An agent running on each worker node, implementing the pod lifecycle using a specific container runtime (i.e., Docker or containerd directly).
- Network plugin: A service supporting the Container Network Interface (CNI) specification that assigns addresses to pods. The network plugin, which—depending on the Kubernetes version—is used by the kubelet or the container runtime directly, implements the Kubernetes network model [7]. In addition to assigning unique, cluster-wide addresses, it makes sure that pods can communicate with each other across hosts. It may also realize traffic shaping policies or other network-level features.
- Proxy: Creates local network routes for virtual IP addresses used by services (i.e., for load balancing). Runs on each worker node, alongside the kubelet.
- Storage controller: A controller that provisions storage of some type that can be attached to pods. Creates physical volumes to match requested persistent volume claims. While this controller is optional, we consider it a core component for a functioning system.

From these, we expected that the *API server, etcd, controller manager*, and *CoreDNS* would require no changes, as they implement specific functions that do not interface with the execution environment. On the other hand, assuming that most HPC centers include Singularity/Apptainer as part of their standard software environment, we would certainly require a custom *kubelet* to interface with the container runtime. We considered several options on how to layout the cross-node Kubernetes components; whether to keep the arrangement of separate

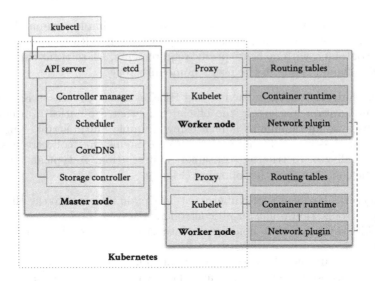

Fig. 1. Components involved in a typical Kubernetes deployment on bare-metal

Kubernetes agents running on every node, or use a single kubelet representing the whole HPC cluster as one execution entity.

The former would require preallocating resources in several machines for a multi-node deployment and then managing them from Kubernetes—essentially running Kubernetes as one large Slurm job, spanning multiple nodes, which would then internally schedule and place its own workloads. This solution, however, had several shortcomings. First, it would result in large, coarse-grain allocations, that would then need to be filled up with jobs, leading to less flexibility (resource allocations in Slurm are static). Second, although not violating the *compliance* requirement, the actual Kubernetes workloads would not show up in Slurm, but remain hidden underneath the overall Kubernetes job. Only Kubernetes would know the actual characteristics of each embedded workload, including its size and duration.

For these reasons, it seemed reasonable to use a single, virtual kubelet in HPK, which instead of interfacing directly with the container runtime, would layer above both *Slurm and Singularity/Apptainer* for execution. In practice, the *hpk-kubelet* is a translator from Kubernetes semantics to Slurm scripts, as shown in Fig. 2. With a single kubelet proxying requests to Slurm, the whole HPK integration can be visualized as a *translation service*: Workloads enter in YAML format through the Kubernetes API endpoint and exit as Slurm scripts from hpk-kubelet. They transparently show up in Slurm queues, and their Kubernetes-level resource requirements end up as allocation requests to Slurm. This architecture has no special requirements for HPK as a whole; it can all run with minimal resources on any cluster node. Additionally, with a single kubelet, the *scheduler* can be greatly simplified. Since cluster-level scheduling is performed by Slurm, the HPK scheduler should always select hpk-kubelet, regardless of actual resource availability.

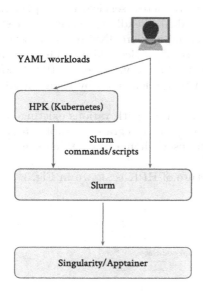

Fig. 2. HPK translates Kubernetes workloads to Slurm and Singularity/Apptainer

The container runtime used also directly influences the mechanisms implementing virtual addresses and networks employed internally by Kubernetes. In a bare-metal Kubernetes setup, there are actually three networks involved: The physical network between hosts, the—typically virtual—network used by pods, and the virtual network used by services. While each uses a different IP address range, the *network plugin* maintains the necessary routes for cross-network communication between pods (and pods with hosts), while the *proxy* manages the respective rules for services. HPK could not include any of these subsystems, as they perform actions at the system level as the root user. Our approach for pod addresses was to require that a corresponding network plugin is configured at the Singularity/Apptainer level by the HPC administrators. Singularity/Apptainer supports CNI plugins and can be easily set up to delegate network addressing to a cluster-wide service (i.e., Flannel [5]). This, in addition to allowing containers to run as *fakeroot* for supporting common Docker images that use the root user, are the only changes HPK requires from the HPC environment; both being configuration options of the container runtime.

The service-level network is used by "ClusterIP" services. When such a service is created, the Kubernetes control plane assigns a new virtual IP and the *proxy* adds respective rules at the host to redirect traffic to a pod that implements the service, or to load-balance between available backend pods. Supporting this functionality without being able to manipulate the routing tables of the host is impossible, so we chose to completely disable "ClusterIP" services, making the proxy obsolete. This would be possible via a Kubernetes admission controller—a hook that monitors API requests and may reject or mutate them before reaching the API server. In Kubernetes, services can explicitly request to not use a virtual service IP (also called "headless" services). In such cases, service discovery continues to function, as CoreDNS maps the service name to the actual pod IPs instead of the virtual service address. Thus, microservice architectures are not affected by the lack of service-specific IPs. If load-balancing between pods is necessary, it can be implemented by using an additional service within a deployment.

For storage, we experimented with various existing offerings and found that it would be straight-forward to integrate a simple *storage controller* for binding directories inside the user's home to containers as volumes (i.e., similar to "HostPath" volumes).

The overall architecture of HPK is shown in Fig. 3.

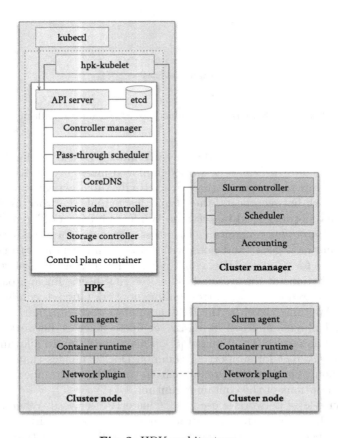

Fig. 3. HPK architecture

4 Implementation

HPK implementation started by integrating most Kubernetes submodules and services into a container. The resulting *Kubernetes-from-scratch* image recipe downloads and builds all relevant binaries. At runtime, necessary keys and certificates are generated, and the control plane is bootstrapped by initializing and starting the executables in order. These include:

- Unmodified versions of the *API server, etcd, controller manager*, and *CoreDNS*. As expected, these required no changes from the official releases.
- A simple *scheduler* that just selects the first available node.
- A simple admission controller that converts all services to "headless", by explicitly setting the "ClusterIP" to "None".

We start this container using Singularity/Apptainer and wait for it to produce the configuration file containing the endpoint and credentials needed to connect to the API server. This "control plane" container uses a virtual, private IP, which is accessible by all hosts in the cluster, as the CNI plugin enabled in Singularity/Apptainer has set up the appropriate network routes. Then, we start *hpk-kubelet*, which uses the configuration file to connect to the API server and announce its availability as a node. Without hpk-kubelet, pods can be created in the API server without ever transitioning to a running state.

Our custom *kubelet* is implemented as a *Virtual Kubelet Provider*. Virtual Kubelet [20] is an open source project that offers an intermediate, simpler API to implement a kubelet; it is mostly used to easily submit containerized jobs for execution on serverless platforms. Providers use Virtual Kubelet as a library which implements the core logic of a node agent, and wire up their specific implementations for supporting the lifecycle of pods and supporting resources on non-standard container execution environments. The hpk-kubelet translates Kubernetes actions into Slurm scripts using Singularity/Apptainer commands.

The main challenge faced when implementing hpk-kubelet, was respecting the network semantics of pods. In Kubernetes, each pod may include multiple containers in the same network namespace. Containers within the same pod share the same external IP address and can use localhost (IP address 127.0.0.1) to communicate with each other internally. As Singularity/Apptainer does not support attaching a container to an existing namespace, we had to produce an embedded container topology: hpk-kubelet starts a "parent" container, which in turn uses Singularity/Apptainer to run each pod container. The pod IP address is assigned to the parent container; "child" containers run within the same network context without extra IP addresses. Synchronization between the hpk-kubelet and parent containers is achieved through files placed under ~/.hpk. The ~/.hpk directory, which is used for holding the state of all running Slurm jobs and respective containers, is mounted by default in all parent containers.

In hpk-kubelet, creating a new pod is implemented as follows:

1. A request for a new pod is received.
2. A pod-specific directory is created and listeners are established to watch for changes in included files.

3. Two scripts are generated: A Slurm script that starts the parent container and a secondary script that runs within the parent and starts all child containers. The secondary script also includes all necessary environment variables expected to be set in the Kubernetes context (mainly information on available services and their respective ports) and volume mounts. The resulting job identifier is recorded in a file within the pod directory.
4. Slurm starts the parent container, which in turn starts its children. The pod directory is used by both scripts to save the generated IP address, as well as exit codes and output of all containers.
5. The listener may react to changes on these files to calculate the new state of the pod (i.e., a change in exit codes may trigger marking the pod as "completed", either with a success or failure).
6. The control plane is informed about the new state.

The hpk-kubelet will convert the requested allocation at the Kubernetes level to corresponding flags specified in the preamble of the Slurm script. Additionally, similar to KNoC [26], it will pass-through specific pod annotations unmodified as additional flags, so that the user may further customize execution. This also allows running a single container as a job in Kubernetes and scaling it up in the HPC environment via MPI-specific Slurm parameters. The usage pattern is unusual for Cloud users, but may prove helpful in HPC, as it allows compiling workflows where each step's scalability is individually controlled using just the annotations. A simple example of an Argo workflow with an HPC running the "embarrassingly parallel" NAS benchmark [12] is shown in Listing 1. We use the language's `withItems` construct to spawn 4 parallel steps, each running another instance of the executable with different parameters. Note the use of a Slurm flag, defined as an annotation on the step template, to control the number of tasks used for each instance. This template showcases a method to run a parallel parameter sweep as part of a larger workflow. The "items" used may be explicitly set or be dynamically generated as the output of a previous step.

```
1   kind: Workflow
2   metadata:
3     ...
4   spec:
5     entrypoint: npb-with-mpi
6     templates:
7     - name: npb-with-mpi
8       dag:
9         tasks:
10          - name: A
11            template: npb
12            arguments:
13              parameters:
14                - {name: cpus, value: "{{item}}"}
15            withItems:
16              - 2
17              - 4
18              - 8
19              - 16
20    - name: npb
21      metadata:
22        annotations:
23          slurm-job.hpk.io/flags: "--ntasks={{inputs.parameters.cpus}}"
24          slurm-job.hpk.io/mpi-flags: "..."
```

```
25        inputs:
26          parameters:
27          - name: cpus
28        container:
29          image: mpi-npb:latest
30          command: ["ep.A.{{inputs.parameters.cpus}}"]
```

Listing 1. A simple Argo workflow executing multiple MPI steps in parallel, each with a different number of Slurm tasks

Deleting a pod results in canceling the respective Slurm job, which in turn updates the exit code of the parent container script that triggers cleanup. The latter requires updating the API server and removing hpk-kubelet state, including the pod directory.

For storage provisioning, we have currently integrated OpenEBS [13] in HPK and configured it to create directories under ∼/.hpk to match volume claims.

HPK is open source and available online [6]. The repository includes documentation and scripts to deploy test environments in AWS ParallelCluster [3]. Most significant open development tasks include mapping GPU/accelerator requests from Kubernetes to Slurm and handling port forwarding from services to the cluster's login node.

5   Conclusion

Kubernetes has become the industry standard runtime in the Cloud, providing the necessary abstractions to embrace the breadth and heterogeneity of available resources. Compatible Cloud-native tools are constantly evolving, covering a wide spectrum of applications, including database and queuing systems, interactive code execution frontends, workflow management utilities, as well as development frameworks that automatically optimize and scale operations. The ability to deploy this software in an HPC cluster via *High-Performance Kubernetes* (HPK) opens up new possibilities for both Cloud and HPC users.

HPK simply runs as a user-triggered service. Container workloads are handled by the hpk-kubelet executable—a virtual Kubernetes node representing the entire HPC cluster as a single entity. The hpk-kubelet translates container lifecycle actions to Slurm scripts and commands that internally use Singularity/Apptainer. HPK also includes several other customized Kubernetes modules to facilitate integration with the HPC environment and simplify adoption by HPC centers.

Acknowledgement. We thankfully acknowledge the support of the European Commission and the Greek General Secretariat for Research and Innovation under the EuroHPC Programme through projects EUPEX (GA-101033975) and DEEP-SEA (GA-955606). National contributions from the involved state members (including the Greek General Secretariat for Research and Innovation) match the EuroHPC funding.

References

1. Apptainer. https://apptainer.org

2. Argo workflows. https://argoproj.github.io/projects/argo
3. AWS ParallelCluster. https://aws.amazon.com/hpc/parallelcluster/
4. Cloud native computing foundation. https://www.cncf.io
5. Flannel. https://github.com/flannel-io/flannel
6. High-performance kubernetes. https://github.com/CARV-ICS-FORTH/HPK
7. The kubernetes network model. https://kubernetes.io/docs/concepts/services-networking/#the-kubernetes-network-model
8. Kubernetes operator for apache spark. https://github.com/GoogleCloudPlatform/spark-on-k8s-operator
9. Kubernetes: Production-grade container orchestration. https://kubernetes.io
10. Minio. https://min.io/
11. MPI operator. https://github.com/kubeflow/mpi-operator
12. NAS parallel benchmarks. https://www.nas.nasa.gov/software/npb.html
13. OpenEBS: Kubernetes storage simplified. https://openebs.io/
14. S8s: Slurmenetes managed kubernetes service on meluxina HPC. https://jpclipffel.s3.lxp.lu/userdoc/cloud/s8s/index.html
15. slurm-k8s-bridge: Experimental slurm scheduling plugin for kubernetes. https://gitlab.com/SchedMD/training/slurm-k8s-bridge
16. Slurm workload manager. https://slurm.schedmd.com/documentation.html
17. Sylabs: Singularity container technology & services. https://sylabs.io
18. TensorFlow serving. https://github.com/tensorflow/serving
19. Usernetes: Kubernetes without the root privileges. https://github.com/rootless-containers/usernetes
20. Virtual-kubelet. https://github.com/virtual-kubelet/virtual-kubelet
21. Colonnelli, I., Cantalupo, B., Merelli, I., Aldinucci, M.: StreamFlow: cross-breeding cloud with HPC. IEEE Trans. Emerg. Top. Comput. **9**(04), 1723–1737 (2021)
22. Coté, M.: Kubernetes is here to stay: this is why (2022). https://tanzu.vmware.com/content/blog/state-of-kubernetes-2022
23. Kurtzer, G.M., Sochat, V., Bauer, M.W.: Singularity: scientific containers for mobility of compute. PLOS ONE **12**(5), 1–20 (2017)
24. López-Huguet, S., Segrelles, J.D., Kasztelnik, M., Bubak, M., Blanquer, I.: Seamlessly managing HPC workloads through kubernetes. In: Jagode, H., Anzt, H., Juckeland, G., Ltaief, H. (eds.) ISC High Performance 2020. LNCS, vol. 12321, pp. 310–320. Springer, Cham (2020). https://doi.org/10.1007/978-3-030-59851-8_20
25. Lublinsky, B., Jennings, E., Spišaková, V.: A kubernetes 'bridge' operator between cloud and external resources (2022). https://arxiv.org/abs/2207.02531v1
26. Maliaroudakis, E., Chazapis, A., Kanterakis, A., Marazakis, M., Bilas, A.: Interactive, cloud-native workflows on HPC using KNoC. In: Anzt, H., Bienz, A., Luszczek, P., Baboulin, M. (eds.) ISC High Performance 2022. LNCS, vol. 13387, pp. 221–232. Springer, Cham (2022). https://doi.org/10.1007/978-3-031-23220-6_15
27. Wickberg, T.: Slurm and/or/vs kubernetes (2022). https://slurm.schedmd.com/SC22/Slurm-and-or-vs-Kubernetes.pdf
28. Zervas, G., Chazapis, A., Sfakianakis, Y., Kozanitis, C., Bilas, A.: Virtual clusters: isolated, containerized HPC environments in kubernetes. In: Anzt, H., Bienz, A., Luszczek, P., Baboulin, M. (eds.) ISC High Performance 2022. Lecture Notes in Computer Science, vol. 13387, pp. 347–357. Springer, Cham (2022). https://doi.org/10.1007/978-3-031-23220-6_24
29. Zhou, N., Georgiou, Y., Zhong, L., Zhou, H., Pospieszny, M.: Container orchestration on HPC systems. In: 2020 IEEE 13th International Conference on Cloud Computing (CLOUD), pp. 34–36 (2020)

A GPU-Accelerated Molecular Docking Workflow with Kubernetes and Apache Airflow

Daniel Medeiros⊕, Gabin Schieffer, Jacob Wahlgren, and Ivy Peng⁽⊠⁾

KTH Royal Institute of Technology, Stockholm, Sweden
{dadm,gabins,jacobwah,ivybopeng}@kth.se

Abstract. Complex workflows play a critical role in accelerating scientific discovery. In many scientific domains, efficient workflow management can lead to faster scientific output and broader user groups. Workflows that can leverage resources across the boundary between cloud and HPC are a strong driver for the convergence of HPC and cloud. This study investigates the transition and deployment of a GPU-accelerated molecular docking workflow that was designed for HPC systems onto a cloud-native environment with Kubernetes and Apache Airflow. The case study focuses on state-of-of-the-art molecular docking software for drug discovery. We provide a DAG-based implementation in Apache Airflow and technical details for GPU-accelerated deployment. We evaluated the workflow using the SWEETLEAD bioinformatics dataset and executed it in a Cloud environment with heterogeneous computing resources. Our workflow can effectively overlap different stages when mapped onto different computing resources.

Keywords: Converged Computing · HPC and Cloud · HPC workflow · Kubernetes · Apache Airflow · Drug Discovery

1 Introduction

The convergence of cloud and high-performance computing (HPC) is emerging to meet the increasing demands of diverse workloads. Major cloud providers, like Amazon Web Services (AWS), now provide on-demand availability to high-end computing capability on HPC hardware. On the other hand, many cloud techniques that have been matured by the community efforts for elastic executions, fault tolerance, virtualization, and isolation, are being explored by HPC users and systems to meet the increasing demands of HPC workloads. Complex workflows are a strong driver that can benefit from efficient management across HPC and cloud boundaries to ease the barrier to reaching wider user communities. For instance, cloud storage is often used for observation data for its high availability, and high computing power from HPC is used for compute-intensive high-fidelity simulations.

A. Bienz et al. (Eds.): ISC High Performance 2023 Workshops, LNCS 13999, pp. 193–206, 2023.
https://doi.org/10.1007/978-3-031-40843-4_15

Workflows are built in many scientific domains to accelerate scientific discovery. Scientific workflows often are built to efficiently connect and coordinate tasks from data generation to pipelined data processing and analysis. For instance, massive data generated from Large Hadron Collider (LHC) experiments in CERN are consumed by numerous scientific analysis procedures built by domain scientists worldwide [6]. In medicine, molecular docking workflows are used for drug discovery [20]. In structural biology, workflows of multi-scale simulations and machine learning methods have furthered the understanding of the structure of viruses [19].

Workflows can be represented as directed-acyclic graphs (DAGs) to capture task dependencies. Depending on the support for different containers and schedulers, we can mainly classify workflow management software as either cloud-native if they support a container-based environment on a Kubernetes cluster or HPC-native if they are designed to be deployed on HPC clusters using Slurm-like schedulers. In this work, we explore using Apache Airflow workflow management software to support a molecular docking workflow that was designed for HPC systems in a container-based cloud-native environment. Our study is based on an important scientific application for drug discovery – virtual screening using molecular docking software on GPU-accelerated compute nodes. For the case study, we use AutoDock-GPU, a state-of-the-art molecular docking software, where previous works have built a workflow for HPC cluster [8] and have been further accelerated with hardware features [18]. Our workflow decouples I/O intensive phases [8,9] from compute-intensive phases and maps them to different hardware resources for improved resource utilization. To our best knowledge, this work is the first study exploring Apache Airflow in supporting such workflow on Cloud.

In summary, we made the following contributions in this work:

- We analyze an HPC-targeted virtual screening workflow and identify opportunities for porting it to a Cloud environment;
- We design our workflow in terms of tasks, dependencies, and resources requirements and provide a DAG-based implementation in Apache Airflow;
- We evaluated our workflow implemented with Kubernetes and Apache Airflow and executed in a Cloud environment with heterogeneous computing resources.

2   HPC and Cloud Workflows

We compare the execution environments, tools and common practices between Cloud and HPC in this section. Table 1 summarizes their main differences. We also describe the Apache Airflow workflow management software.

2.1   Cloud and HPC Environments

The paradigm for resources allocation greatly differs between cloud and HPC infrastructures. HPC systems usually rely on large computing clusters, where users request a particular amount of computing nodes, for a limited amount

Table 1. Comparison of Cloud and HPC, with typical design choices.

	HPC	Cloud
Allocation strategy	static	dynamic/on-demand
Unit for allocation	node-granularity	fine-grained
Execution	bare metal	containerized/virtualized
Scheduler	SLURM	Kubernetes

of time. The characteristics of each node are generally fixed, and cannot be tuned to the application specific requirements – for example CPU type, or presence of hardware accelerators such as GPUs. In addition, infrastructure-related characteristics, such as storage and internode communication, are usually not modifiable by the user. In the cloud, resource allocation is finer, where sub-node allocation is common, and the user can request various types of resources based on their usage.

Opportunity 1: The fine-grained allocation in cloud allows tailoring resource allocation to specific workload needs, and thus improve resource utilization over the entire lifespan of the workload.

HPC users usually execute their workloads on a bare metal environment, with highly-tuned execution environments, specifically tailored to the underlying hardware. This approach allows reaching high efficiency on a given system. However, this comes at the cost of reduced portability, as porting an application to another system may require some adaptation in the code and/or the system. A common solution to this lack of portability, widely used in cloud computing, is using *containers*. A *container* bundles one or more applications with a set of dependencies, and can be executed on various systems. This improves portability and usability of an application, and simplifies the co-location of several workloads on a single system. This technology is particularly used in cloud environments.

Opportunity 2: Containerizing workloads improves portability, and usability, but at the cost of formalizing application requirements.

SLURM, PBS, Torque and Cobalt are popular schedulers in the HPC environment. In this context, any workflow management software targeting HPC environments must integrate with these schedulers in order to execute workflows seamlessly. In a cloud environment, the management of resources can be handled by an orchestrator, which configure and maps computing resources for use by a user workload. Kubernetes is a widely-used open-source orchestrator. It manages containerized workloads, by providing a standardized way of describing workload resources and requirements. Kubernetes provides auto-scaling capabilities, where the amount of computing resources can be automatically adapted as the application is running based on its needs.

Opportunity 3: Using cloud-native orchestration techniques to deploy our workload can improve portability, simplify deployment, and provide elasticity.

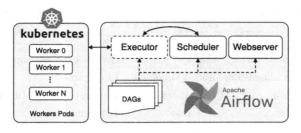

Fig. 1. General architecture of Apache Airflow, and its interaction with a Kubernetes cluster. Arrows represent communication between components.

2.2 Apache Airflow Workflow Management Software

DAG. Workflows can be described as Directed Acyclic Graphs (DAG), where tasks are represented as nodes, and dependencies between tasks are represented as edges. This formal description of a workflow has several advantages. For instance, the DAG describing a workflow being a mathematical object, graph algorithms can be directly used to achieve specific goals without requiring algorithmic adaptation on a per-workflow basis. A relevant example in this work is efficient task scheduling. A DAG-aware task scheduler can be used instead of a customized user-built scheduler to achieve efficient scheduling of tasks, while enforcing requirements such as task dependencies.

Apache Airflow[1] is an open-source workflow management platform, where workflows are described as DAGs using the Python programming language. Airflow provides a simple way of efficiently scheduling and executing tasks from DAG-represented workflows on a Kubernetes cluster, which is leveraged in this work. Figure 1 describes the architecture of Airflow. The user creates a DAG as Python code, which is interpreted by Airflow and presented in a graphical web interface. The user can then interact with Airflow using this interface, for example, to trigger the workflow execution or to check workflow execution state. Once a workflow is triggered by the user, the tasks are automatically scheduled by Airflow, and executed on a Kubernetes cluster as soon as all task dependencies are fulfilled.

The following Airflow features are used in our work:

- Defining a single DAG, along with a Docker image specific for our workflow, which provides the portability of a workflow;
- Delegating task scheduling and execution to Apache Airflow, which results in a concise workflow description, and efficient task scheduling;
- Monitoring tools and visualization, which could be used by domain scientists.

---

[1] https://airflow.apache.org/.

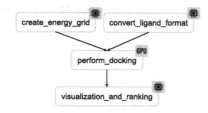

Fig. 2. The DAG of an elementary molecular docking workflow: a single ligand is docked onto a single receptor. Resource requirements for each task is either GPU or CPU.

3   A Virtual Screening Workflow on Apache Airflow

In this section, we detail our design and implementation of a workflow for large-scale GPU-accelerated virtual screening in the Cloud. We first introduce AutoDock-GPU and then present an elementary molecular docking workflow. We then extend this elementary workflow into a large-scale virtual screening workflow on Apache Airflow.

AutoDock-GPU is a state-of-the-art GPU-accelerated molecular docking application. It is a variant of AutoDock [12], one widely used family of software for molecular docking simulations. Molecular docking methods are widely used in the pharmaceutical industry to characterize the ability of candidate drug molecules to bind themselves to identified targets in the human body, and therefore trigger their pharmacological effect. The main challenge in drug discovery is to be able to efficiently evaluate several millions of drug candidates, referred to as *ligands*, against a single identified *protein* target. This large-scale process is called *virtual screening*.

All AutoDock variants use an energy-based scoring function to measure the quality of a given binding pose, i.e. the geometrical conformation of the ligand, this function is evaluated many times for each ligand-protein complex, and incurs high computational cost. Thus, offloading the compute-intensive part onto GPU has achieved orders of magnitude of speedup. A GPU-accelerated version of AutoDock has been developed under the name of AutoDock-GPU [17]. Its CUDA implementation [8] has been successfully used to perform large-scale screening of millions of drug candidates on the Summit supercomputer [8]. In this work, we use the CUDA version of AutoDock-GPU to build a virtual screening workflow. A previous workflow targeting HPC systems using Slurm has been developed [14]. It is worth noting here that since AutoDock variants share similar characteristics, the workflow we describe could be generalized to other AutoDock variants than AutoDock-GPU.

3.1   An Elementary Molecular Docking Workflow

To design our virtual screening workflow, we first studied the data requirements and task dependencies involved in a molecular docking job, between a single

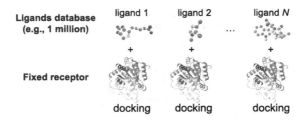

Fig. 3. A virtual screening process, where a single protein receptor is identified beforehand (Fixed receptor), and millions of ligand molecules are evaluated against the receptor using molecular docking methods.

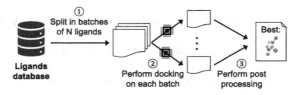

Fig. 4. Virtual screening workflow. The ligand dataset is split in fixed-size batches (①). Then, workers perform docking independently on each batch (②). The results are then gathered for all batches, and post-processed to extract relevant domain-specific information (③).

ligand and a single receptor. This *elementary* workflow is presented in Fig. 2 as a DAG. The first takeaway from this workflow is that we can split the set of tasks into two categories. The first category is I/O-related tasks, where file reading, conversion, and writing are performed. This category of tasks only require limited CPU resources to execute, tasks within this category are depicted with a CPU icon in the DAG. The second category of tasks, which represents the main computational cost of this workflow, is the docking tasks, which require GPU resources atop CPU, to accelerate the process.

3.2   A Large-Scale Virtual Screening Workflow

A key challenge in virtual screening is to evaluate a very large number of drug candidates – on the order of several millions of molecules. A simplified description of a virtual screening job is presented in Fig. 3. The computational cost of this process is linear with the number N of ligands to evaluate. A straightforward approach to perform this large-scale evaluation would be to perform docking as many times as there are ligands. However, this approach would be highly inefficient, since launching AutoDock-GPU comes at a cost, notably induced by the initialization of the CUDA runtime, and by the reading of the receptor file, which is constant across all runs. In addition, the cost of scheduling and starting tasks on any scheduler – be it Kubernetes, Airflow, or Slurm – is generally not negligible.

To solve this issues, a previous work [8] used a batching strategy for large-scale runs of AutoDock-GPU on the Summit supercomputer. This strategy first splits the ligand database into several fixed-size batches. For each batch, an index file contains a reference to the file describing the receptor molecule, and a list of all ligands files, which were obtained from splitting the ligand database. This batching strategy is supported in AutoDock-GPU, and we use it in for our virtual screening workflow. We illustrate this approach in Fig. 4. As their workflow targets HPC environment, they used a custom scheduling mechanism to perform docking on the batches – a fixed amount of workers are launched using a SLURM script, and each idle worker pulls a list of batches to process from a Redis database. Different from the previous workflow [14] on HPC systems, we instead rely on the scheduling capabilities of Airflow to execute docking on all batches. For this purpose, we developed a DAG that fully describes our workflow requirements, including performing docking on multiple batches, where the processing of each batch is independent of other batches.

3.3   Implementation

Our DAG description of the workflow is presented in Fig. 5. Several tasks are defined to achieve our batched approach. First, the `split_sdf` task creates several fixed-size batches from a single input file, which contains all ligand molecules to evaluate, this task returns the number of created batches. This number is then used by the `get_batch_labels` tasks to generate a list of unique batch labels. We then use an Airflow feature, *dynamic task mapping*, to instantiate a group of tasks for each batch in the batch list. This is represented in the blue rectangle on the DAG: for each batch, the task group `docking`, which contains the `prepare_ligands` and `perform_docking` tasks, is instanced. Each task group instance takes a single batch label as parameter, and perform docking for this batch. For each batch, the ligands are first transformed by the `prepare_ligand` task, which converts file formats, and transform ligand molecules. Then, the `perform_docking` task uses AutoDock-GPU to perform the molecular docking job, this is the core computational task in our workflow. The `postprocessing` task is executed when all batches have been processed, and performs gathering of results to provide domain scientist with relevant results, and visualization. In this DAG, parallelism is achieved by running concurrently several instances of the `docking` task group.

We execute the various tasks as Kubernetes pods. For this purpose, we created a single Docker container image that is used for all tasks. This image contains all tools required to run the tasks: AutoDock-GPU, various AutoDock preparation scripts, OpenBabel for molecule file format conversion, and auto-grid4 for receptor pre-processing. The CUDA runtime is also included to enable running AutoDock-GPU on GPU hardware. Finally, we created a shell script for each task. Each script takes runtime parameters – such as batch label and receptor file location – as arguments, reads data from the file system, and writes results to both the file system and the standard output. We use our own file naming convention to ensure consistency between script execution. For example,

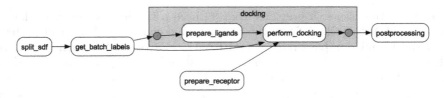

Fig. 5. Our DAG for the AutoDock-GPU workflow on Apache Airflow. The blue rectangle indicates a task group, whose tasks are executed once for each batch. (Color figure online)

`db_batch35_ligand42.pdbqt` is the ligand N°42 of the batch N°35, from the ligand database **db**.

In Airflow, tasks can be defined using *operators*, which are task templates. In our DAG, we define most tasks with the `KubernetesPodOperator`, which allows launching a pod in a Kubernetes cluster. To use this operator, we define the characteristics for the Kubernetes pod, using the standard pod specification format, as defined by the Kubernetes API. For all tasks, our pod specification comprises a reference to our custom Docker image, along with a task-specific shell command. In addition, we attach a persistent volume to each pod, at the `/data` mount point in the containers, which we also use as the working directory for the container definition. This file system is used by our shell scripts to read and write data for the docking workload, and is shared between all pods. As we use the standard Kubernetes approach to attach storage to pods, the underlying storage technology and location are abstracted and can be easily modified to fit specific Cloud provider offers. To enable GPU-acceleration of the `perform_docking` task, we define an additional pod specification for this task, which reuse the generic pod specification, with an added requirement for an NVIDIA GPU.

To enable communication between tasks, we use *XComs* (short for "cross-communication"), which is an Airflow-specific mechanism that allows tasks to communicate with each others. In particular, it can be used to pass parameters to tasks, along with collecting return values, when relevant. For instance, we used XComs in our DAG to collect the result of `split_sdf`, and pass it to `get_batch_labels`, along with passing batch labels to the task instances in the `docking` task group. As a side note, XComs are not represented directly in the DAG, but are explicitly defined in the task definitions, as template strings. The values for XComs are unknown when the python code of the DAG is first parsed by Airflow, but they are populated as the DAG is being executed.

4   Evaluation and Results

In this section, we first study the performance impact of containerized environment on the GPU-accelerated docking. We then evaluate our workflow on a real-world ligands dataset, and study its resource utilization and concurrent task execution abilities.

4.1   Evaluation Setup and Datasets

Our testbed is composed of a single server featuring a consumer-range CPU, along with a single low-end GPU. We deployed a Kubernetes cluster using the lightweight k3d[2] distribution. We performed a full run of our workflow using this setup. We arbitrarily chose to perform docking on the *Carboxypeptidase A* protein as receptor, with ligands from the SWEETLEAD [13] dataset, which contains approximately 10,000 chemical compounds and is widely used in drug discovery works. We used a batch size of 1,000 ligands per batch. This run is not relevant from the perspective of concurrent task execution, as only one GPU is available at a time, and thus only one docking task can be executed at a time. However, it allowed us to assess the correctness of our DAG and obtain some baseline measurements for future larger-scale executions.

The total runtime for this job was ~44 h, that is, on average approximately 17 s to perform docking for one ligand. During this experiment, we observed a strong imbalance in processing time between batches, as some batches were processed in 30 min, while some others required 12 h to finish. We suspect that this imbalance is caused by the distribution of molecule sizes within the original ligand database: as larger ligands may be grouped in specific regions of the file, batches containing those regions may be more computationally expensive to process.

4.2   AutoDock-GPU in Containerized Environment

Fig. 6 reports the distribution of the time measurements for 100 runs of AutoDock-GPU using a single protein-ligand complex, identified by the 7cpa PDBID. Execution time for four phases is measured, including CUDA setup, rest of setup, docking, and shutdown – those phases are reported by the AutoDock-GPU program, and refers to various phases of the program. We compare the execution time on the Kubernetes-Airflow setup with its equivalent bare metal execution. In order to ensure a fair comparison between both configurations, we use the same initialization seed for the pseudo-random number generator between the two methods. As the cloud environment often has other workloads co-running, we present the distribution of the execution time in a whiskers chart showing min, max, median, 25%, and 75% quantiles. The most significant difference lies in the shutdown phase, where the bare metal is much faster than the Airflow mode. However, in the dominant phase – the docking process, both the bare metal and the Airflow execution have similar runtime with the bare metal exhibiting slightly lower time. The results show that for the main GPU-accelerated computation phase, deployment on Airflow/Kubernetes is feasible and performance comparable, likely because the GPU resource is not shared and thus not much influenced by other co-running workloads.

---

[2] https://k3d.io/.

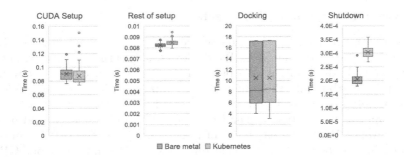

Fig. 6. Performance comparison of AutoDock-GPU on Kubernetes/Airflow with execution on bare metal.

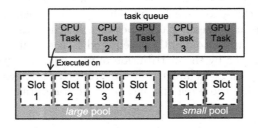

Fig. 7. Tasks execution on Airflow pools. A task is associated to a specific pool, and a limited number of tasks associated with the same pool can run in parallel.

4.3   Task Scheduling and Parallel Execution

To evaluate our workflow from the perspective of parallel task execution, we duplicated our real-world fully-functional DAG into a dummy DAG where the execution time of each task is controlled. In this DAG, no GPU resources are requested in the Kubernetes pod description, so that several docking tasks can be executed in parallel on our single-GPU setup. To ensure that this setup is still realistic, we enforced a limit on the number of concurrently running tasks, to simulate an environment where resources – GPU and CPU – are limited. To achieve this, we used the *pool* feature of Airflow. Pools are used to limit the execution parallelism of a determined set of tasks. Figure 7 shows a diagram to describe this concept. In our setup, we define two pools: a *large* pool, which represents CPU resources, and a *small* pool, which represents more expensive GPU resources. The `perform_docking` task, which is the only task that uses GPU resources, is associated with the small pool, while all other tasks are associated with the large pool. Here, it is important to note that pools do not necessarily represent actual resources, but instead arbitrary limits.

We run this dummy workflow using this two-pool configuration, with 4 slots in the large pool, and 2 slots in the small pools. The duration of each task instance is chosen randomly at runtime, and is on the order of several seconds,

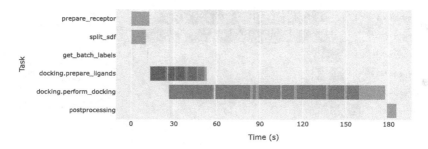

Fig. 8. Gantt chart of the execution of our dummy DAG with 10 batches in Apache Airflow. Task instances are plotted as translucent blue rectangles, darker blue indicate overlap of several rectangles, indicating parallelly executing task instances. (Color figure online)

with the docking tasks set to take significantly longer than the other tasks. We chose to simulate the processing of 10 batches. Figure 8 presents a Gantt chart of this experiment, as found in Airflow's user interface, with improved visualization by using translucent colors. On this plot, each row represents a task, and each rectangle represents a task instance, the width of a rectangle represents the duration of the associated task instance. On this plot, we first observe that two tasks with no interdependence, such as **prepare_receptor** and **split_sdf**, are executed in parallel. The dependencies between tasks also naturally appears on this representation, as all instances of **prepare_ligands** wait for the end of **prepare_receptor** execution before starting. We also observe that some **prepare_ligands** instances overlap with some **perform_docking** instances. This happens naturally, as for a particular batch, the associated **perform_docking** task instance only depends on the **prepare_ligands** instance for this particular batch. These observations show that we achieved parallel task execution, with a simple DAG description of the workflow, and no custom scheduling logic.

To further understand how tasks are mapped to resources, we propose in Fig. 9 a resources-oriented Gantt chart for the same experiment. On this chart, each line represents the utilization of a particular pool slot over time. It is worth noting here that this may not reflect actual resource utilization, as when a task start executing in Airflow, a pod creation request is submitted to Kubernetes, which then handles resources allocation. The execution of a task by Airflow is only conditioned by the availability of a pool slot; a task marked as "running" in Airflow may fail if Kubernetes is not able to meet the resource requirements for this task. On this chart, we visualize overlap in task execution, both between different tasks, such as **split_sdf** and **prepare_receptor**, and also between same-type tasks, but associated with different batches. We also observe that GPU-enabled computing resources are only used to run GPU-accelerated tasks, which was a key motivation in this work, as those resources are quite expensive and should be efficiently utilized. In addition, this Gantt chat highlights that the Airflow scheduler was able to provide with efficient scheduling of our tasks, given

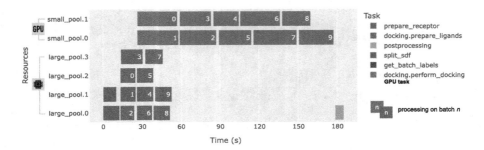

Fig. 9. Resources-oriented Gantt chart of the execution of our dummy DAG with 10 batches, using two pools – *small* with 2 slots, and *large* with 4 slots. Each line in this chart represents the activity for one slot. White numbers refer to the batch number associated with a task instance, when applicable.

the requirements and interdependencies described in the DAG. As the Airflow scheduler is designed to accommodate several parallel DAG executions, other DAG-expressed workflows could easily be executed in this configuration. This would not cause any interference with our workflow execution, and would not require any modification to our DAG.

5   Related Works

Scientific Workflow Platforms. Main frameworks are specifically designed for scientific workflows on HPC systems, including Pegasus [3,4], Taverna [21], FireWorks [7], RADICAL-Pilot [10], Nextflow [5], signac [1], and CRCPs [15]. Additionally, Pegasus and Nextflow can also be deployed in cloud environments; the former can be deployed on the cloud as a HTCondor instance while the latter has support to other platforms such as Kubernetes, Azure Cloud and Google Cloud. Computational Resource and Cost Prediction service [15] allows users to control the financial costs of workflow execution on federated clouds.

HPC Workloads in Cloud Environments. Several previous works have explored executing HPC workloads in cloud environments. Saha, et al. [16] evaluated the Singularity containerization platform and Docker Swarm was used as an orchestrator, focusing on network mapping for MPI. Beltre, et al. [2] run MPI workloads over TCP/IP and InfiniBand (RDMA) communication and measure the overheads between different container orchestrators. Misale, et al. [11] proposes a scheduler for Kubernetes ("KubeFlux") based on the ideas from the Flux scheduler. Our work further expands the scope from a single HPC application but a workflow of multiple tasks on a cloud setting.

6   Conclusions and Future Works

The convergence of HPC and cloud computing is emerging to meet constantly evolving workloads. As a strong driver, complex workflows can benefit from efficient workflow management to ease the barrier to reaching wider user communities. Therefore, in this work, we investigated how a molecular docking workflow that was designed for HPC systems can be deployed on cloud-native infrastructure, represented by Kubernetes and Apache Airflow. We provide a design and implementation of a portable workflow description that supports parallel task execution on heterogeneous computing resources in Cloud environments. Our design batches a fixed number of ligands in one task to amortize overheads associated with Pod creation, termination, and I/O. We evaluated the workflow using a realistic dataset with ligands from the SWEETLEAD dataset. We find that predicting docking time based on ligand structures instead of simply the number of ligands may reduce load imbalance and improve scheduling efficiency. In our future works, we will also evaluate this workflow on a large-scale Kubernetes cluster along with elasticity support in the workflow.

Acknowledgment. This research is supported by the European Commission under the Horizon project OpenCUBE (GA-101092984).

References

1. Adorf, C.S., Dodd, P.M., Ramasubramani, V., Glotzer, S.C.: Simple data and workflow management with the signac framework. Comput. Mater. Sci. **146**, 220–229 (2018)
2. Beltre, A.M., Saha, P., Govindaraju, M., Younge, A., Grant, R.E.: Enabling HPC workloads on cloud infrastructure using Kubernetes container orchestration mechanisms. In: 2019 IEEE/ACM International Workshop on Containers and New Orchestration Paradigms for Isolated Environments in HPC (CANOPIE-HPC), pp. 11–20. IEEE (2019)
3. Deelman, E., et al.: Pegasus: a framework for mapping complex scientific workflows onto distributed systems. Sci. Program. **13**(3), 219–237 (2005)
4. Deelman, E., Vahi, K., Rynge, M., Juve, G., Mayani, R., Da Silva, R.F.: Pegasus in the cloud: science automation through workflow technologies. IEEE Internet Comput. **20**(1), 70–76 (2016)
5. Di Tommaso, P., Chatzou, M., Floden, E.W., Barja, P.P., Palumbo, E., Notredame, C.: Nextflow enables reproducible computational workflows. Nat. Biotechnol. **35**(4), 316–319 (2017)
6. Hasham, K., et al.: CMS workflow execution using intelligent job scheduling and data access strategies. IEEE Trans. Nucl. Sci. **58**(3), 1221–1232 (2011)
7. Jain, A., et al.: Fireworks: a dynamic workflow system designed for high-throughput applications. Concurr. Comput. Pract. Exp. **27**(17), 5037–5059 (2015)
8. LeGrand, S., et al.: GPU-accelerated drug discovery with docking on the summit supercomputer: porting, optimization, and application to COVID-19 research. In: Proceedings of the 11th ACM International Conference on Bioinformatics, Computational Biology and Health Informatics. BCB '20, ACM (2020)
9. Markidis, S., Gadioli, D., Vitali, E., Palermo, G.: Understanding the I/O impact on the performance of high-throughput molecular docking. In: 2021 IEEE/ACM Sixth International Parallel Data Systems Workshop (PDSW), pp. 9–14. IEEE (2021)
10. Merzky, A., Santcroos, M., Turilli, M., Jha, S.: Radical-pilot: scalable execution of heterogeneous and dynamic workloads on supercomputers. CoRR, abs/1512.08194 (2015)

11. Misale, C. et al. Towards Standard Kubernetes Scheduling Interfaces for Converged Computing. In: Nichols, J., et al. (eds.) Driving Scientific and Engineering Discoveries Through the Integration of Experiment, Big Data, and Modeling and Simulation. SMC 2021. CCIS, vol. 1512, pp. 310–326. Springer, Cham (2022). https://doi.org/10.1007/978-3-030-96498-6_18

12. Morris, G.M., et al.: Automated docking using a Lamarckian genetic algorithm and an empirical binding free energy function. J. Comput. Chem. **19**(14), 1639–1662 (1998)

13. Novick, P.A., Ortiz, O.F., Poelman, J., Abdulhay, A.Y., Pande, V.S.: SWEET-LEAD: an in silico database of approved drugs, regulated chemicals, and herbal isolates for computer-aided drug discovery. PLOS ONE **8**(11) (2013)

14. Rogers, D.: ORNL large-scale docking workflow. https://code.ornl.gov/99R/launchad/-/tree/master

15. Rosa, M.J., Ralha, C.G., Holanda, M., Araujo, A.P.: Computational resource and cost prediction service for scientific workflows in federated clouds. Futur. Gener. Comput. Syst. **125**, 844–858 (2021)

16. Saha, P., Beltre, A., Uminski, P., Govindaraju, M.: Evaluation of docker containers for scientific workloads in the cloud. In: Proceedings of the Practice and Experience on Advanced Research Computing, pp. 1–8 (2018)

17. Santos-Martins, D., Solis-Vasquez, L., Tillack, A.F., Sanner, M.F., Koch, A., Forli, S.: Accelerating AutoDock4 with GPUs and gradient-based local search. J. Chem. Theory Comput. **17**(2), 1060–1073 (2021)

18. Schieffer, G., Peng, I.: Accelerating drug discovery in AutoDock-GPU with tensor cores. In: Euro-Par 2023: Parallel Processing: 29th International European Conference on Parallel and Distributed Computing (Euro-Par 2023), Proceedings. LNCS, vol. 14100, pp. 1–15. Springer, Cham (2023). https://doi.org/10.1007/978-3-031-39698-4_41

19. Trifan, A., et al.: Intelligent resolution: integrating Cryo-EM with AI-driven multi-resolution simulations to observe the severe acute respiratory syndrome coronavirus-2 replication-transcription machinery in action. Int. J. High Perform. Comput. Appl. **36**(5–6), 603–623 (2022)

20. Venkatraman, V., et al.: Drugsniffer: an open source workflow for virtually screening billions of molecules for binding affinity to protein targets. Front. Pharmacol. **13** (2022)

21. Wolstencroft, K., et al.: The taverna workflow suite: designing and executing workflows of web services on the desktop, web or in the cloud. Nucleic Acids Res. **41**(W1), W557–W561 (2013)

Cloud-Bursting and Autoscaling for Python-Native Scientific Workflows Using Ray

Tingkai Liu[1], Marquita Ellis[2], Carlos Costa[2], Claudia Misale[2],
Sara Kokkila-Schumacher[2], Jinwook Jung[2], Gi-Joon Nam[2],
and Volodymyr Kindratenko[1]

[1] University of Illinois Urbana-Champaign, 1205 W. Clark St.,
Urbana, IL 61801, USA
{tingkai2,kindrtnk}@illinois.edu
[2] IBM Thomas J. Watson Research Center, 1101 Kitchawan Rd, Yorktown Heights,
NY 10598, USA
{m.ellis,chcost,c.misale,saraks,jinwookjung,gnam}@ibm.com

Abstract. We have extended the Ray framework to enable automatic scaling of workloads on high-performance computing (HPC) clusters managed by SLURM© and bursting to Cloud managed by Kubernetes®. Compared to existing HPC-Cloud convergence solutions, our framework demonstrates advantages in several aspects: users can provide their own Cloud resource, the framework provides the Python-level abstraction that does not require users to interact with job submission systems, and allows a single Python-based parallel workload to be run concurrently across an HPC cluster and a Cloud. Applications in Electronic Design Automation are used to demonstrate the functionality of this solution in scaling the workload on an on-premises HPC system and automatically bursting to a public Cloud when running out of allocated HPC resources. The paper focuses on describing the initial implementation and demonstrating novel functionality of the proposed framework as well as identifying practical considerations and limitations for using Cloud bursting mode. The code of our framework is open-sourced.

Keywords: Cloud bursting · HPC · Kubernetes

1 Introduction

The rapid advancement of scientific computing has led to a significant increase in demand for high performance computing (HPC) resources. However, currently available HPC systems are unable to keep up with this demand, especially when many large-scale jobs are started concurrently. In response, many scientists have turned to the elastic business model of Cloud computing as a potential backup solution for HPC. The ability to easily scale resources up or down as needed makes Cloud computing an attractive option.

© The Author(s), under exclusive license to Springer Nature Switzerland AG 2023
A. Bienz et al. (Eds.): ISC High Performance 2023 Workshops, LNCS 13999, pp. 207–220, 2023.
https://doi.org/10.1007/978-3-031-40843-4_16

Cloud bursting for HPC clusters is an appealing approach for addressing the challenge of meeting fluctuating demand for computing resources. With this strategy, users first run their workload on HPC clusters, and burst some of the workload to the Cloud when the HPC cluster cannot satisfy the demands. However, not all HPC workloads are suited for Cloud bursting, and a general HPC-Cloud bursting framework may be too complex and ineffective.

As such, it is important to carefully consider the suitability of Cloud bursting for a given workload and to carefully design an implementation of an HPC-Cloud bursting system. Meanwhile, Python, with its simplicity and flexibility, became a widely adopted language for scientific computing [7]. As Python continues to grow in popularity within the HPC community, focusing on a Cloud-bursting solution for Python-based workloads on HPC clusters could benefit the entire community by providing a more targeted and effective approach.

Taking into account the above considerations, we present a user-oriented Cloud-bursting framework for Python-based workloads. Specifically, we have extended the Ray framework [5] to enable the automatic scaling of workloads on HPC clusters managed by SLURM© [13] and on Cloud resources managed by Red Hat® OpenShift® [9]. In general, our solution works on Kubernetes® [3] or managed Kubernetes services such as Red Hat OpenShift Kubernetes Service (ROKS) on IBM Cloud.

The main contribution of this work is designing and implementing a novel Cloud-bursting model that addresses several common issues in currently existing HPC-Cloud convergence framework. First, most of the current solutions require the HPC Cluster manager to maintain the Cloud resource, while our framework targets a scenario that users choose and pay for their own Cloud resource, which provides more flexibility and eases the work of cluster admins. Second, unlike some existing solutions that require running a workload exclusively on either the HPC cluster or the Cloud, our solution allows a single parallel workload to be run concurrently on both the HPC cluster and the Cloud. Third, the Python-level abstraction provided by our solution offers a transparent user experience, requiring no direct user interaction with the SLURM batch system or the Kubernetes interface. By leveraging the active development of the open-source Ray framework, our solution also benefits from ongoing improvements and updates.

The remainder of the paper is structured as follows: In Sect. 2, we provide background information relevant to our approach. Section 3 presents a detailed description of our solution. Section 4 presents common use cases and evaluation of our system. Section 5 offers general discussion and potential future work. Finally, we conclude the paper in Sect. 6.

2   Background

2.1   Brief Overview of Existing Solutions

The existing solutions on HPC-Cloud convergence can be classified into two main categories: HPC-centered approaches and Cloud-centered approaches.

HPC-centered approaches keep the HPC management system and use Cloud as supplement resources. This can be achieved by adding the Cloud resource as a separate pool in the HPC-Cloud system. For example, researchers at New York University added the Cloud resource as a distinct partition of SLURM in their Cloud-bursting cluster [6], allowing users to submit to either local or Cloud using the SLURM interface. The other method is to modify HPC network settings so that Cloud resources can be viewed the same as local nodes. Researchers at Purdue university implemented this method by setting up Virtual Private Network (VPN) among their HPC clusters and Cloud resource [12].

For these approaches, Cloud resource is often setup and paid by HPC cluster providers, as the integration of HPC and Cloud resource requires admin level operations. Users of those systems are constrained to use the pre-defined Cloud resource and cluster setup.

Cloud-centered approaches have various designs. The Torque-Operator [14] has been proposed as a bridge between HPC clusters managed by the Torque [11] workload manager and clusters managed by Kubernetes. In this work, the HPC Cluster is treated as a "virtual node" in the Kubernetes cluster, forwarding the container scheduling decisions made by Kubernetes. Liu et al. [4] proposed a system named Balancer to automatically move nodes from an on-premises cluster, managed by Torque, and a Cloud system, managed by OpenStack in order to address resource demands by the users. Piras et al. [8] proposed a method to run HPC-like workloads at larger scale on Kubernetes by deploying more worker nodes as Grid Engine [1] batch jobs. The idea is to accommodate bursting by temporarily dedicating HPC nodes to Kubernetes and releasing them once the job is completed.

Most of the work with Cloud-centered approaches focuses on containerized applications, which is admittedly popular in the Cloud computing community. Our work, on the other hand, focuses on Python-based distributed workloads and we aim to save users from using the job submission interface.

2.2 Ray

Ray [5] is an open-source distributed computing framework initially developed at UC Berkeley. It is designed to scale distributed Python applications, with special support for those related to deep neural networks training. Several components of Ray are relevant to our work and will be helpful for understanding our approach.

The resource management and work scheduling in Ray are based on a virtual "Ray cluster", which is formed by starting a Ray runtime daemon on a group of nodes and connecting them together. The Ray cluster is organized as a centralized system, with a head node that stores the global control storage (GCS) and worker nodes that are primarily responsible for executing tasks. The Ray scheduler, which is aware of the characteristics of each node in the cluster, such as the number of CPUs, GPUs, and memory, is able to assign work to the appropriate nodes based on their capabilities.

To support scalability and elasticity, especially in Cloud environments, Ray includes an autoscaler that allows the size of the Ray cluster to be dynamically adjusted based on demand. The Ray autoscaler is a daemon running on the head node that monitors the resource demand in the scheduling queue and the utilization of each worker node. When starting the Ray cluster, a configuration file specifying the maximum available resources and an idle timeout is provided to the autoscaler. If there are jobs pending in the scheduling queue, the autoscaler attempts to start new nodes and connects them to the existing cluster. When worker nodes are idle for a certain period of time, as determined by the timeout, the autoscaler removes them from the cluster. In order for the autoscaler to function, it requires interfaces to the underlying framework to manage the nodes.

Ray primarily focuses on setting up clusters within a single infrastructure and has limited support for only popular frameworks and Cloud providers. Using Ray with HPC clusters managed by batch systems or across multiple infrastructure requires extending the framework and adding peripheral support.

3   Design and Implementation

In this section, we present our Python-based HPC Cloud bursting solution based on Ray framework extensions. As previously mentioned, Ray is a distributed framework that primarily supports distributing Python-based workloads on a single supported infrastructure. To build our HPC Cloud bursting solution using Ray, we had to address several challenges: enabling the Ray-native infrastructure (including the Ray core and autoscaler) on SLURM-based HPC clusters, supporting Ray on Red Hat OpenShift Cloud resources with the head node hosted on a remote HPC cluster, and combining the support for HPC and Cloud resources with peripheral components to enable HPC Cloud-bursting. We discuss each of these components in detail.

3.1   Ray-SLURM

The first step in implementing our Ray-based HPC Cloud-bursting solution is to enable Ray on SLURM-based HPC clusters.

The integration of Ray cluster and SLURM-based HPC cluster is an integration of two distinct operation models. As Ray mainly focuses on operating on Cloud, it assumes full control of underlying resources. Typically, a Ray worker node refers to a physical node, a virtual machine (VM), or a pod that has Ray runtime started. It is possible to run additional commands or perform updates after the node is allocated, and sometimes necessary to exchange files between the nodes. Its "on-prem" support follows this assumption and uses SSH for starting and updating the Ray runtime on each worker, and uses rsync for file exchanges.

However, a SLURM-based HPC cluster has different operation model. Each user of the cluster does not have a full control over the cluster, and should submit their job via the SLURM interface instead of SSH. Moreover, file exchanges between nodes of the HPC cluster are often not required, as the whole cluster shares a file system.

Our design addresses the mismatch between SLURM and Ray operational requirements. In our implementation, a Ray worker node no longer binds to a physical node, but associates with one SLURM batch job submission. Updating of nodes after creation is disabled, and all the necessary setup operations are done during the node creation, i.e. in the creation batch script. Inter-node file exchange is disabled, too. Those changes don't affect the core functionality of Ray autoscaler, i.e. it can still allocate and delete worker nodes based on demands, as the disabled operations are not required on a SLURM-based cluster during runtime.

Maintaining the status of the Ray nodes requires additional support. Originally, Ray relies on the status queries and tag settings provided by Cloud providers. Those status and tags information are used internally for Ray cluster maintenance, such as indicating the health and types of worker nodes. In our implementation, the state information can be obtained by checking the SLURM job state using the SLURM command (squeue) with the job id. However, SLURM scheduler does not have supports on setting tags on jobs. To save the tag information, we use a lock-protected local file storage, as the file may be accessed by multiple Ray autoscaler threads.

Figure 1 is an illustration of setting up a Ray cluster on top of a SLURM HPC cluster. Each Ray node is a SLURM job that contains Ray runtime. Other traditional HPC workloads running outside of Ray are not affected. Even without the Cloud-bursting part, the Ray-SLURM interface provides new ways for using SLURM-based clusters.

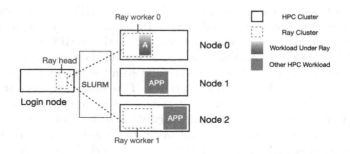

Fig. 1. A Ray cluster on top of an HPC cluster managed by SLURM.

3.2 Ray-Kubernetes

Another major component of our Cloud bursting solution is the connection between Ray and the Cloud resources managed by Kubernetes. While Ray has mature support for setting up a Ray cluster on Kubernetes, our scenario is different. The original support assumes that both the head node and the worker nodes are inside the Kubernetes cluster and can make use of all the inter-pod communication available in Kubernetes. However, in our scenario, the head node of the Ray cluster is located on the HPC cluster, which is outside the Kubernetes network, as the Cloud resources are only accessed when there is a need for bursting. The worker nodes, on the other hand, should be inside Kubernetes. This creates a challenge for maintaining the communication between the Ray head and worker nodes, and requires modification to the original Ray-Kubernetes interface.

To establish communication between the Ray head and worker nodes, it is necessary to expose the Ray worker pods to the external network. Ray uses gRPC for inter-node communication, which requires certain ports to be directly accessible between the head node and worker node for cluster management. Additionally, each worker process on a Ray worker node also requires a worker port to communicate with GCS at the head node. To meet these requirements, our implementation attaches a Kubernetes NodePort Service to each Ray worker node pod, each of which uses a different range of ports to avoid conflicts.

The launch and termination of Ray worker node make use of the Kubernetes Python client. Similar to our Ray-SLURM implementation, we store several YAML templates that specify common worker pods and corresponding NodePort services. When the autoscaler tries to launch a node on the Cloud resource, these templates are loaded, filled with runtime-specific information, and passed to the Kubernetes Python client to launch the job. Kubernetes has built-in support for node status and tags, which can directly handle the requirements of these features for Ray.

3.3   Overall System Design

The Ray head node, located on the login node of the HPC cluster, connects to and controls all the Ray worker nodes using the above two interfaces. The login node of the HPC cluster has control interfaces for both the HPC cluster resources and the Cloud resources, allowing the autoscaler daemon, running on the Ray head node, to start and delete Ray worker nodes on the two platforms using the Ray-SLURM and Ray-Kubernetes interfaces. This design satisfies the goal of HPC Cloud bursting, as workloads that cannot be accommodated by the HPC cluster resources will be automatically scheduled on the Cloud. Since the login node is not intended for computational tasks, the Ray head node only handles cluster management and does not execute any user work. Figure 2 illustrates this setup.

As introduced before, each user on the HPC cluster can start their own Ray cluster with their own Cloud resource at any time. To support customized environments for each user, such as specific versions of Python packages, we added support for using specific Conda environments on the HPC worker nodes or containers on the Kubernetes worker nodes when starting this extended Ray cluster.

Conflict resolutions are implemented for multi-user scenario. The worker nodes started by different users are scheduled and isolated by the SLURM and Kubernetes schedulers. However, multiple Ray head nodes may exist on the login node of the HPC cluster simultaneously without scheduler protection, thus

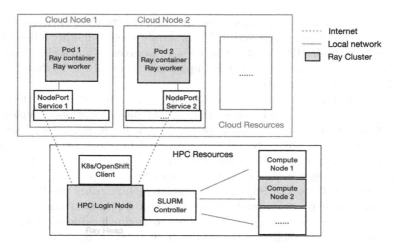

Fig. 2. Illustration of the overall Cloud-bursting system design.

requiring conflict resolution. Each Ray head node is distinguished by its operation ports, primarily the GCS port. By having different users start Ray head nodes with different ports and having the worker nodes communicate with the correct port, multiple Ray head nodes can co-exist on the login node. To achieve this, we implemented automatic port assignment when starting the Ray cluster and store this information as metadata for the cluster in a lock-protected file (the same one used by worker nodes on SLURM). This information is queried every time a worker node needs to be started.

The security of our solution is provided by both Ray and Linux®. For each Ray cluster set up by a different user, a random Redis® password is created at startup and stored as metadata for the cluster. Only with this password can a user connect to the corresponding Ray cluster, including deploying a workload on it or adding a new node to the cluster manually. Additionally, even if multiple Ray head processes are running on the same login node, all of these processes are owned by specific users and Linux prevents other users from accessing them.

In our design, not all worker-to-worker communication is guaranteed, which presents limitations. All worker nodes are connected to the head node, but worker nodes are only guaranteed to be connected to other worker nodes in the same zone (either the HPC cluster or the Cloud), unless all worker nodes are directly reachable from the Internet, which is not usually the case. Enabling all-to-all inter-worker communication in such a setup is still possible by setting additional network rules, and we discusses in Sect. 5 the trade-offs of doing so.

3.4   Deployment and Usage

Deploying our Python-based Cloud-bursting solution requires installing Ray, the Kubernetes Python client, and our extension package. Installing Ray and Kubernetes Python client is straightforward as they are open-source project widely supported by package managers such as pip. For our extension package, we have provided a Python deployment script. Users simply need to modify a few parameters specific to their HPC cluster and Cloud resources in the script. Since the interaction with the Ray framework is implemented entirely in Python, there is no need to recompile the code.

The usage of our solution involves starting a minimal Ray cluster that autoscales based on the workload. After running the above mentioned deployment script, a template Ray cluster configuration YAML file is generated. Users can customize their environment by adding additional initialization commands for the nodes or specifying a custom container in this YAML file. The file is then used to start the Ray cluster using the `ray up` command provided by Ray (the cluster launcher). Once the Ray cluster is started, users only need to work on their Python-based program, and autoscaling and Cloud-bursting are handled automatically by our extensions to Ray. When users finish using the Ray cluster, a single `ray down` command can be used to perform clean-up.

4   Use Cases and Evaluation

In this section, we present two use cases in Electronic Design Automation (EDA) for our Python-based HPC Cloud-bursting model and evaluate their performance and limitations.

The experiments are conducted using a 5-node HPC cluster managed by SLURM and two different public Cloud clusters managed by Red Hat OpenShift. Each HPC cluster's compute node has 40 CPU cores; all nodes share a common file system and are interconnected with EDR InfiniBand network. Two different types of Cloud clusters, 4 CPUs per node and 32 CPUs per node, are used to demonstrate the potential impact of using different types of Cloud resources on the overall application performance. As previously mentioned, the Ray head node is launched on the login node of the HPC cluster, and the Ray worker nodes are distributed across the compute nodes of the HPC cluster and the Red Hat OpenShift Cloud clusters. Initially, there is only one node in the Ray cluster, which is the Ray head node. To simulate a realistic, busy cluster scenario based on resource demand, the Ray cluster could automatically autoscale to up to two worker nodes on the HPC cluster and up to three worker nodes on the Red Hat OpenShift Cloud clusters.

4.1   Analog Circuit Verification

The first use case is transistor-level analog circuit verification. To verify the correctness of the circuit under imperfect manufacturing, Monte-Carlo simulation by repeatedly perturbing device parameters is the most commonly used verification method. In such verification, different trials of verification (with different sets of parameters) can be performed in parallel, and there is no correlation between different trials. The input for each simulation trial is a parameter vector, which can be simply passed as a function argument.

The evaluation is performed on a transistor-level analog circuit verification of under voltage lock-out (UVLO) circuit [2], using 1000 different parameter vectors. Figure 3 shows the total running time for transistor-level analog circuit verification for different Cloud bursting configurations, using the 32-CPU-core Cloud nodes. Since this workload is embarrassingly parallel and does not require large input/output, the overall running time reduces when introducing the Cloud resource, regardless of the number of HPC nodes used. This kind of workload is a good candidate for Cloud bursting.

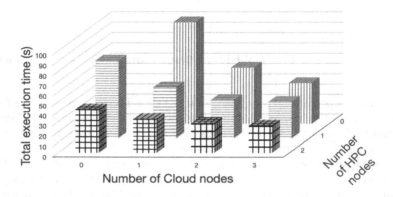

Fig. 3. Overall runtime of transistor-level analog circuit verification as a function of the number of HPC and Cloud nodes.

4.2   Digital Circuit Verification

The second use case is digital circuit verification, such as Register Transfer Level (RTL) or gate-level simulations. For this type of verification, a large variety of input stimuli is run on the device under test to check whether its output signals are as expected. Similar to analog circuit verification, each verification trial is a workload with a different input that can be run in parallel. However, this type of verification requires extra input and output files, since each verification trial takes input of different size and produces output as a file. As a result, running digital circuit verification on a remote Cloud could introduces larger overhead.

For this use case, we run RISC-V CPU core RTL verification with 51 input stimuli [10] under different kind of Cloud-bursting settings. Figure 4 shows the total running time for RISC-V RTL verification for different Cloud bursting configurations. Unlike the analog circuit verification which generally benefits from Cloud bursting, this workload suffers from the overhead introduced due to the need to send data to the Cloud.

When the HPC cluster is busy and user cannot obtain any nodes from it, adding Cloud nodes generally benefits the workload. However, if user can allocate one node on the HPC cluster, adding only one or two Cloud nodes results in

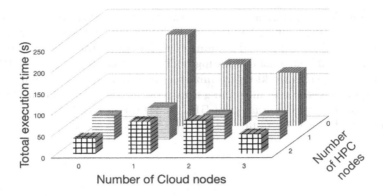

Fig. 4. Overall runtime of RISC-V RTL verification with 32-CPU-core Cloud nodes.

worse overall performance. Only when all three Cloud nodes are used, the Cloud-bursting configuration approaches the performance of a single-node HPC system. When two HPC nodes are available, bursting to the Cloud does not outperform the two-node HPC configuration.

In order to understand the overhead when the job is bursted to the Cloud node, we examine the execution time breakdown for several verification tasks when running on differently sized Cloud nodes. Figure 5 shows the execution time for a small verification task, *rv32ui-p-lui*. This task takes a ≈1.5 kB input file and produces a ≈215 kB output file. Bar chart on the left shows the absolute time spent on various tasks (sending a file to/from the Cloud node and compute) and bar chart on the right shows the relative time for the same tasks. When running this benchmark, the 32-CPU-core Cloud node spends a significant amount of time on I/O, while the 4-CPU-core Cloud node has a significant increase in the time spent on computation in addition to the I/O time.

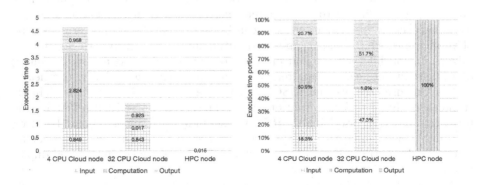

Fig. 5. Execution time profile of rv32ui-p-lui on different nodes.

Bursting overheads show different patterns on larger verification tasks. Figure 6 shows the execution time pattern for *vvadd.riscv*, a much larger verification task. The input file size of this task is ≈41 kB and the output file size is ≈71 MB. Comparing to the smaller task *rv32ui-p-lui*, as the input file sizes are relatively comparable and the actual computation time becomes longer, the proportion of time spent on I/O on a 32-CPU-core Cloud node becomes smaller. However, the output file, which is related to the computation time, takes a bigger proportion of the overall time to transmit the results back to the head node. The execution time of the 4-CPU-core Cloud node is shown with a different scale on the left of the picture, since its actual computation time is much larger than on the other two node types.

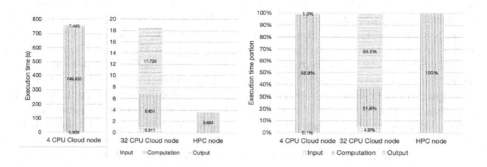

Fig. 6. Execution time profile of vvadd.riscv on different nodes.

The experiments with EDA workloads demonstrate the importance of understanding workload characteristics in order to make an efficient use of the Cloud bursting capability of our proposed framework. Cloud bursting can be advantageous only under the right conditions.

5   Discussion and Future Work

Results presented in prior section demonstrate the baseline functionality of our extensions to Ray framework to enable auto-scaling on an HPC cluster and bursting from the cluster to a Cloud. In this section, we discuss several issues related to our solution and propose several directions for future work. Much remains to be done to address the limitations of this initial baseline implementation.

First, in our system configuration, while the worker nodes on the Cloud are connected to a Kubernetes service which exposes the pods to the Internet, the worker nodes on the HPC cluster do not have similar connectivity, unless the worker nodes on the HPC cluster have a direct connection to the Internet through a public IP address. Exposing the worker nodes on the HPC cluster to the Internet is possible by modifying the network setup. However, whether to provide such capability requires further consideration. In our solution, we target a scenario in which users procure their own Cloud resources. Under this assumption, the networking requirements of the Cloud resources provided by different users may vary greatly, making it challenging to define a universal setup. In addition, modifying the networking configuration on a shared HPC cluster typically requires admin-level privileges and may affect other users, which is not in line with our goal of enabling users to work independently. Exposing the worker nodes of the HPC cluster on the Internet also raises security concerns. On the other hand, workloads requiring frequent inter-worker communication may not be suitable for the Cloud-bursting setup due to the high networking overhead. Even though the workloads requiring only occasional communication may benefit from this setup, it is still worth considering whether the disadvantages outweigh the potential benefits. Our implementation does not yet provide all-to-all inter-worker communication capability; this remains to be a subject of future work.

Second, the current scheduler used is the Ray native scheduler, which prioritizes starting workloads with the "smallest waiting time". However, this scheduler is unaware of the performance differences between HPC and Cloud nodes, which could be leveraged to improve the efficiency of the Cloud-bursting setup. While the bursted tasks are being executed in parallel, once a heavy task is scheduled on the Cloud, it is considered started and will continue running until completion. This can lead to a case in which the HPC cluster finishes all its scheduled tasks and must wait for the heavy task running on the Cloud cluster to complete, resulting in a longer overall completion time. A scheduler that is aware of the overall HPC cluster-Cloud configuration and performance differences may be able to reduce such issues by only scheduling lightweight tasks to the Cloud.

Third, the data movement overhead can be a significant issue when running tasks across different clusters, especially if these are connected over a public Internet. One potential direction for addressing data movement in both cases mentioned is leveraging efficient Cloud-native storage, getting benefits such as data replicas and optimized internal network. For example, utilizing standard S3 storage is a possibility that could be explored in future research. Another direction is to pre-fetch the data prior to starting the computation on either resource. Finding more efficient ways to reduce the overhead due to the data transfers remains to be a subject of our future work.

Fourth, our system has only been tested with a limited number of use cases selected by the authors, and it is assumed that users have a basic understanding of how to use the framework. When introducing our solution to a wider audience, additional concerns may arise, including corner cases and security issues that we have not yet considered. These may include security concerns between different users and potential attacks on the HPC cluster from the Internet in general. We will deploy our framework on public clusters and will collect user feedback.

6   Conclusions

In this paper, we have introduced our HPC Cloud bursting solution, an extension to the Ray framework that enables automatic scaling of workloads across

HPC clusters managed by SLURM and Cloud environments managed by Kubernetes. For customized user experience and easier HPC cluster management, our framework allows users to supply their own Cloud resource without admin-level operations. Our implementation also allows Python-based parallel workloads to be run concurrently on both HPC and Cloud systems, with a minimal learning curve for users thanks to the Python-level abstraction. Overall, our proposed framework offers a convenient and transparent way to scale workloads on on-premises HPC systems and burst to a public Cloud as needed.

We have demonstrated the functionality of our solution using two Electronic Design Automation tasks, and have analyzed the suitability of different workloads for the Cloud bursting solution. Several future directions of this work are proposed, including re-considering HPC-Cloud networking, developing topology awarded schedulers, improving the data movement, and deploying on public clusters to improve the framework based on user feedback. The open source code for this work is available at https://github.com/TingkaiLiu/Ray-SLURM-autoscaler/tree/slurm_k8s.

Acknowledgement. This work is supported by the IBM-Illinois Discovery Accelerator Institute. This work utilizes resources supported by the National Science Foundation's Major Research Instrumentation program, grant #1725729, as well as the University of Illinois Urbana-Champaign.

References

1. Gentzsch, W.: Sun grid engine: towards creating a compute power grid. In: Proceedings First IEEE/ACM International Symposium on Cluster Computing and the Grid, pp. 35–36. IEEE (2001)
2. Hu, H., Li, P., Huang, J.Z.: Enabling high-dimensional Bayesian optimization for efficient failure detection of analog and mixed-signal circuits. In: Proceedings of the DAC, pp. 1–6, June 2019
3. kubernetes: Production-grade container orchestration. https://kubernetes.io
4. Liu, F., Keahey, K., Riteau, P., Weissman, J.: Dynamically negotiating capacity between on-demand and batch clusters. In: SC18: International Conference for High Performance Computing, Networking, Storage and Analysis, pp. 493–503 (2018)
5. Moritz, P., et al.: Ray: a distributed framework for emerging {AI} applications. In: 13th USENIX Symposium on Operating Systems Design and Implementation (OSDI 18), pp. 561–577 (2018)
6. Nyu high performance computing - hpc bursting to cloud. https://sites.google.com/nyu.edu/nyu-hpc/hpc-systems/cloud-computing/hpc-bursting-to-cloudD
7. Oliphant, T.E.: Python for scientific computing. Comput. Sci. Eng. **9**(3), 10–20 (2007). https://doi.org/10.1109/MCSE.2007.58
8. Piras, Marco Enrico, Pireddu, Luca, Moro, Marco, Zanetti, Gianluigi: Container orchestration on HPC clusters. In: Weiland, Michèle, Juckeland, Guido, Alam, Sadaf, Jagode, Heike (eds.) ISC High Performance 2019. LNCS, vol. 11887, pp. 25–35. Springer, Cham (2019). https://doi.org/10.1007/978-3-030-34356-9_3
9. Red hat openshift. https://docs.openshift.com/
10. riscv-mini. https://github.com/ucb-bar/riscv-mini

11. Staples, G.: Torque resource manager. In: Proceedings of the 2006 ACM/IEEE Conference on Supercomputing, p. 8-es. SC '06, Association for Computing Machinery, New York, NY, USA (2006)
12. Weekly, S., Mertes, Z., Gough, E., Smith, P.: Azure-based hybrid cloud extension to campus clusters. In: Practice and Experience in Advanced Research Computing. PEARC '22, ACM, New York, NY, USA (2022)
13. Yoo, Andy B.., Jette, Morris A.., Grondona, Mark: SLURM: simple Linux utility for resource management. In: Feitelson, Dror, Rudolph, Larry, Schwiegelshohn, Uwe (eds.) JSSPP 2003. LNCS, vol. 2862, pp. 44–60. Springer, Heidelberg (2003). https://doi.org/10.1007/10968987_3
14. Zhou, N., Georgiou, Y., Zhong, L., Zhou, H., Pospieszny, M.: Container orchestration on HPC systems. In: 2020 IEEE 13th International Conference on Cloud Computing (CLOUD), pp. 34–36 (2020)

Understanding System Resilience for Converged Computing of Cloud, Edge, and HPC

Luanzheng Guo[1], Jay Lofstead[2], Jie Ren[3], Ignacio Laguna[4], Gokcen Kestor[1,6],
Line Pouchard[5], Dossay Oryspayev[5], and Hyeran Jeon[6(✉)]

[1] Pacific Northwest National Laboratory, Richland, WA, USA
{lenny.guo,gokcen.kestor}@pnnl.gov
[2] Sandia National Laboratories, Albequerque, USA
gflofst@sandia.gov
[3] College of William and Mary, Williamsburg, VA, USA
jren03@wm.edu
[4] CASC, Lawrence Livermore National Laboratory, Livermore, CA, USA
ilaguna@llnl.gov
[5] Brookhaven National Laboratory, Upton, NY, USA
{pouchard,doryspaye}@bnl.gov
[6] EECS, University of California Merced, Merced, CA, USA
hjeon7@ucmerced.edu

Abstract. The emergence of multiple resource management systems, such as SLURM and Kubernetes, for different computational purposes has led to a desire to support a single workflow that spans multiple resource management domains, which can include multiple HPCs, edges, and cloud, over different network domains. Best-of-class tools developed in one domain often do not run well or at all in a different resource management regime demanding these hybrid environments. Understanding the resilience properties and concerns for cross-resource management system workflows is an unexplored area. Further, we lack tools and techniques to test this resilience and to understand how well systems and systems of systems work in the face of faults and failures. We are proposing a Fault Tolerance 500 (FT500) and a related set of benchmarks that test from the hardware layer through the software layers to create resilience scenarios. By making this a scored benchmark set, we offer a public ranking of systems and software and motivation for facilities to allow benchmarking. We also discuss potential approaches to enable fault-tolerant converged computing.

Keywords: fault tolerance · HPC · distributed workflows

1 Introduction

With the looming ends of Moore's law and applications' ever-increasing demands on computing power and big data, HPC clusters adopt diverse hardware

A. Bienz et al. (Eds.): ISC High Performance 2023 Workshops, LNCS 13999, pp. 221–233, 2023.
https://doi.org/10.1007/978-3-031-40843-4_17

resources such as various accelerators (GPUs, FPGAs, and CGRAs) and cache-coherent disaggregated memories (e.g., CXL devices). Furthermore, the degree of heterogeneity is escalated when the workflows are handled across multiple clusters that may reside in different network domains or different geographical locations. For example, an Exascale Computing Project, *Cancer Distributed Learning Environment (CANDLE)* [1] handles a set of collaborative tasks on remotely located distributed systems to utilize the unique computing capabilities of each system, such as clinical scanning instruments (e.g., edges), data storage, simulation infrastructure, and AI analytics engines.

Under this computing environment with extreme diversity and scale, it is challenging to enforce fault tolerance and sustainable performance at the same time. Existing fault tolerance mechanisms that protect individual components (e.g., ECC for memory, CRC for network, dual-modular redundancy for CPU, and Erasure Codes for storage) or small-scale clusters (e.g., checkpoint/restart, MPI daemon recovery, and record/replay) have limitations in 1) tracking fault trajectory to find the root cause of the failures, 2) understanding fault impacts in the organic relations among diverse computing stacks and clusters, and 3) identifying and handling unique (mostly unknown) vulnerabilities of large-scale geographically distributed systems. As the new class of geographically distributed systems becomes the scientific computing paradigm, it is important to understand its vulnerabilities and explore fault tolerance solutions.

To address these limitations, we project the next-generation fault tolerance design to be able to resolve the resilience needs in such an extremely diverse, heterogeneous, and distributed environment. Figure 1 shows our projected next-generation fault tolerance system design process, which runs with two critical parts. First, the *benchmarking performance resilience* provides a comprehensive measurement by using a set of metrics that evaluate resilience of the full system stack (both hardware and software components) and generate a quantitative fault tolerance score. With the fault tolerance score, a new ranking system for fault tolerance, namely *Fault Tolerance 500 (FT500)*, can be designed analogous to the reputed TOP500 [9] and IO500 [18] ranking systems. FT500 emphasizes *performant resilience* rather than *resilience* alone because both performance and resilience are two important pillars in high-performance computing (HPC). By incorporating performance for fault tolerance evaluation, FT500 aims to showcase the resilience and performance impact of various system configurations and combinations of fault tolerance methods such that the community can choose one solution that fits their performance and resilience requirements or revisit the design for better performance and fault tolerance. By designing and testing FT500 on different computing systems, we will be able to identify shortcomings of existing system designs with respect to resilience for performance and find limitations of current fault tolerance techniques, all of which will provide useful insights and guidance to performant resilience optimizations and designs for future computing systems.

Second, the *performant resilience optimization* incorporates insights and findings acquired from the *benchmarking performant resilience* into consideration to improve existing fault tolerance designs or develop new fault tolerance

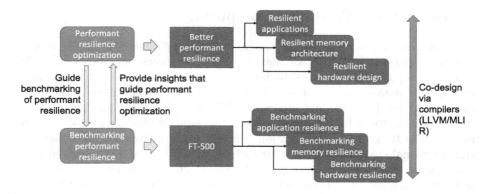

Fig. 1. Projected Next-Generation Fault Tolerant Design Process

techniques that resolve unseen challenges. These new optimizations and techniques will be again fed to the *benchmarking performant resilience* to revisit the FT500 rankings and run further rounds of optimizations.

Another challenge is to offer something system owners are willing to let people run on their systems. By making this into a competitive ranking system through the benchmarks, users can sell their management on the value of comparing qualitatively how their system ranks next to other computing environments. This will give them bragging rights as well as offer motivation and insights on how to improve the science throughput by ensuring faults and failures have smaller impacts than other providers. Secondarily, this will also generate additional data points and system information that can be used for further resilience research both at a component or system level as well as the hybrid, cross-resource systems.

To enable this positive feedback cycle of fault tolerance evaluation and optimization throughout the entire system stack, a *hierarchical inspection model* is needed. The inspection model runs multiple layers of individual component-level inspections each examining individual system components by using fault injection and tracking, which can be implemented with compiler techniques in LLVM or MLIR.

With this projection for the next-generation fault tolerance design process, this paper explores two important components to consider for future fault tolerance system design; 1) the characteristics of distributed workflow computing and 2) the limitations and opportunities of existing fault tolerance methods. Then, we introduce a prototype fault tolerance evaluation framework, FT500, that will be the core component of the future fault tolerance design process, formulated as a multi-level framework, from individual applications to single systems to cross multiple systems, by benchmarking various systems for fault tolerance and performance. We also introduce potential design approaches for next-generation fault tolerance methods.

2   Distributed Workflow Computing

Scientific research and engineering have increasingly relied on workflows executed at scale to perform numerical simulations. Such workflows can be executed with methods ranging from simple submission scripts written ad hoc by researchers, to workflow management systems (WMS) relying for execution on frameworks such as Kepler, Pegasus, and others. WMS's task placement and performance can also be improved by the use of composable building blocks for HPC computing, such as RADICAL[1]. In addition, workflows are being used to orchestrate computational ensemble studies that include simulations and data-driven computing using machine learning, e.g., CANDLE [1] These workflows are referred to as *hybrid workflows*. The complexity of optimizing WMS and building block execution for reliance in traditional simulations and hybrid workflows also increases with geographical distribution, as illustrated in Fig. 2. A detailed provenance trace showing the execution environment, workflow patterns, and I/O can be extracted from WMS. Workflow provenance enables pinpointing latencies and error attribution, however, due to the size of provenance traces, statistical profiles are usually provided.

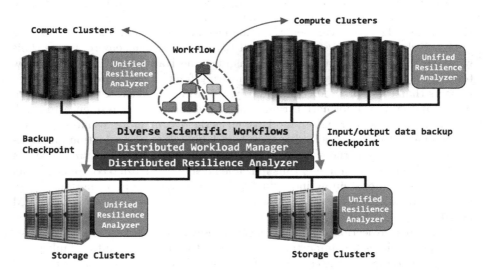

Fig. 2. An Example Distributed Workflow Computing with Resilience in Consideration

For example, CANDLE [1] is a representative distributed workflow computing platform that handles a set of collaborative tasks across a distributed network, including 1) clinical records scanning instrument for data acquisition, 2) a storage system for data collection, and 3) a multi-scale molecular dynamics simulation that starts with 1000 different cancer cell lines and 1000 different drugs, which

---

[1] https://github.com/radical-cybertools.

relies on 4) an in-situ AI analysis with several thousands of supervised and semi-supervised machine learning models to guide the next simulation scope and scale. Each of the four components runs on remotely located systems with different computing power, energy efficiency, reliability, and storage capacity.

Within each HPC cluster, heterogeneity exists to schedule complex workflows on the best-fitting resources. For example, LLNL's AHA MoleS workflow architecture [5] consists of separate Fluence instances for general-purpose workflow steps and domain-specific tasks where domain-specific instance is handled on GPU clusters while the general-purpose instances are operated on CPU clusters. These workflow instances can be scheduled with e.g. Kubernetes (container management), SLURM (scheduling), Merlin (a workflow management system), and RabbitMQ (message routing).

To evaluate fault tolerance for these hybrid and distributed workflows, the future fault tolerance design should have a clear understanding of 1) representative workflow computing flows (reflected as directed acyclic graphs - DAGs), 2) core functions of popular/reliable workflow management and scheduling systems, and 3) interfaces that connects multiple parallel parts of a workflow across networks and systems.

3   Unresolved Challenges

Under HPC and cloud system's increasing scale and heterogeneity, we would like to address the unresolved challenges of existing fault tolerance techniques that focus on single applications or systems with FT500. In this section, we explore a composition of challenges where the existing fault tolerance techniques may fail in our projected hybrid, heterogeneous, and geographically distributed computing environment.

Checkpoint/Restart. Checkpoint/Restart [11,23,30] is an essential fault tolerance technique that periodically saves a system's state to restore it in case of failure, ensuring reliability and availability for various systems, such as cloud and supercomputers. It's implemented at different levels, including the application, compiler, and system levels, to minimize downtime for long-running applications. However, implementing Checkpoint/Restart in a hybrid, heterogeneous computing environment such as HPC and cloud can be challenging. Proper restart requires detecting and restoring the saved state of the affected workflow part(s). MPI-based applications handle failure detection, and users adjust their job execution scripts to restart using the last checkpoint. However, addressing the inconsistent failure awareness between slow processing or a message queue across distributed different systems can be a challenge (also known as Byzantine faults), and state storage for restarts must be determined at a higher control layer. Such fault/intermittent problems are not adequately detected or handled by workflow management systems, such as Pegasus, while crossing domains and systems.

Algorithm-Based Fault Tolerance (ABFT). ABFT [13,14,20] is a generic fault tolerance technique used in large-scale computing systems to ensure data integrity, reliability, and availability of applications. It instruments fault tolerance mechanisms directly into the application source code, uses redundant computations for error detection and correction, and is hardware-independent. An example of ABFT is detecting and correcting bit-flip errors in linear algebra computations with checksums. However, ABFT's redundant computation can cause unacceptable performance overhead, and limit its ability to handle certain types of faults, such as node failures. While ABFT is effective within components, it cannot address inter-component issues or downstream data consumer failures. To restore execution in the event of such failures, it requires many fault tolerance techniques orchestrated together, but it is unclear how to integrate them effectively and efficiently.

Redundancy. Redundancy [6,19,26] duplicates critical components or systems to improve fault tolerance in computing environments, such as Triple Modular Redundancy (TMR) [31] that uses three systems and majority-voting. However, implementing redundancy in heterogeneous, distributed systems presents challenges in ensuring consistent performance and availability across the system, potential variation in output because of distinct computing resources, as well as slow responses that can be interpreted as failures.

Virtualization. Virtualization [16,21,32] is a technology that creates multiple self-contained virtual instances of computer systems on a single physical machine, providing added reliability by enabling rapid migration of virtual systems in case of hardware failure. However, incorporating virtualization into heterogeneous, distributed computing environments can be challenging due to the need to support various hardware and software platforms, leading to complexity in management and potential inconsistency in system performance and availability. More flexible and scalable virtualization solutions are required to adapt to different computing settings. Additionally, virtualization can be used for testing by emulating a hybrid or distributed system in a controlled environment.

Emerging Memory and Storage. The emergence of byte-addressable non-volatile memory (NVM) technologies presents new opportunities for handling HPC under failures [8,24,27]. However, enabling various HPC applications on heterogeneous systems with NVM brings unique challenges, including the need to coordinate multiple system components such as NVM, local SSDs, and remote storage for data object persistence. Additionally, it can be challenging to select efficient fault tolerance strategies while leveraging HPC application semantics and considering the underlying hardware and software architecture. The diversity of NVM, like its non-volatility, requires careful consideration of which data objects to persist and how frequently to persist them to enable efficient fault tolerance.

Job Scheduling. Fault-tolerance approaches [3,25] that rely solely on the resubmission of failed jobs ignore the issue of processor allocation, which can lead to a significant degradation in application response time. Backfill [15,17] is a scheduling technique that maximizes computing resource utilization by filling gaps with short-running jobs. It can reschedule failed short-duration jobs ahead of longer jobs for fault tolerance, improving recovery time and system efficiency. However, applying backfill to large-scale, heterogeneous, geographically distributed systems can be challenging due to varied workloads, network latencies, and resource requirements, making it difficult to accurately predict when a given job will be complete and whether it can be backfilled. Coordinating job scheduling across multiple HPC systems and clouds can also be difficult, further complicating the backfill process. Achieving efficient fault-tolerance in large-scale systems requires considering both job scheduling policy and software and hardware resilience across system stacks.

Fault Emulation and Injection. Fault emulation and injection [7,10,33] test system reliability and resilience by accelerating the rate of real-world faults. This is achieved through simulating faults in a controlled manner using software, data manipulation, or hardware modification. The system's response, with fault tolerance enabled, is observed, and the results are analyzed. For complex and geographically distributed computing systems with new programming models and hardware, existing fault emulators may not work due to new fault types. Developing new fault emulators that offer better portability and adaptability is necessary. Furthermore, coordinating fault injection across multiple nodes and managing the generated data could cause significant performance overhead.

Fault Tolerance & Vulnerability Metrics. Multiple fault tolerance & vulnerability metrics , such as AVF [22] for measuring architecture vulnerability to soft errors and DVF [12,34] for measuring data vulnerability to transient faults are crucial in assessing the reliability of computing systems, especially in HPC systems where transient faults are common. However, fitting these existing fault tolerance metrics in complex, heterogeneous, and geographically distributed computing systems is challenging. These metrics need to be designed separately for individual computer architecture and programming languages, which can result in limited portability, adaptability, and summarization issues. Additionally, there may be unforeseen fault tolerance needs in such environments, requiring the development of new metrics. Our goal is to create a new metrics collection that addresses hybrid and distributed faults and failures unique to these configurations by building upon existing metrics.

4   Fault Tolerance 500 (FT500)

Without a fair evaluation methodology and quantifiable metrics, it is challenging to understand and judge the quality and performance of resilience of various systems that have diverse settings. FT500 tests vulnerabilities of full system stacks from hardware components to applications with 1) a set of benchmarks, 2) a set of mini-app-based unit tests, 3) fault injection modules, 4) fault tracking and storage modules, 5) a set of resilience metrics, and 6) fault tolerance analysis modules.

4.1   Benchmarks

To understand the impact of individual faults and the combination of fault tolerance methods towards the end-to-end workflow execution, we need a set of representative scientific applications. To make FT500 scalable and portable, the applications are selected by considering the following principles: 1) supporting various WMS and scheduling algorithms, 2) operating on single or multiple clusters even across different network domains, 3) utilizing diverse hardware and software components, and 4) having quantifiable output correctness/accuracy.

Because FT500 aims to test virtually any system configuration, we should not use applications that run on a certain environment. Therefore, the benchmark suite includes a balanced number of applications for individual system settings and applications built on LLVM/MLIR or containerized techniques, which are portable and adaptable to various system types.

Also, as the ultimate goal of fault tolerance systems is to guarantee program correctness, the execution correctness of each benchmark application should be clearly judged based on the computation output. Thus, FT500 includes applications that have finite pairs of input and output that are considered correct computation results. For probabilistic applications, such as machine learning-based predictions, a combination of the ground truth and the acceptable accuracy threshold is considered the correct output.

Example applications/workflows include but are not limited to CANDLE (as described in Sect. 2), SOMESPIE [28], and IMPECCABLE [29]. These workflows are used for complex scientific applications such as satellite soil moisture observations and COVID-19 drug discovery by utilizing various WMSes, schedulers, and virtualization engines such as Kubernetes, SLURM, RADICAL, and ParSL on both general-purpose as well as domain-specific computing engines such as CPU and GPUs. Both of them consist of multiple sub-modules which can separately run on distinct clusters that have the required computing capacity, and hence fit well for FT500's goal to test large-scale distributed systems fault tolerance. FT500 starts with highly representative workflows and will evolve and expand periodically.

4.2   Unit Tests with Mini-Apps

The benchmark applications can be used to evaluate end-to-end computation correctness. However, it only shows the final consequence of all faults happening during the application execution. Therefore, it is hard to find the root cause of the incorrect output. To test individual components, FT500 also includes a set of unit tests to narrow down investigation of faults. The tests are implemented with mini-apps where each app consists of up to several hundred lines of code that specifically stress the target component. We extend existing performance unit tests such as Stress-NG [4] for CPU and memory usages and NVIDIA SDK [2] for GPU computing, and design mini-apps that can stress individual system components for fault tolerance. The third and fourth benchmark application selection criteria (Sect. 4.1) are considered when designing the mini-apps, which means that a set of mini-app tests examine all the considered software and hardware components and each of the tests has a clear indicator for correct computation.

4.3   Fault Injection Modules

Though the error occurrence rate is increasing as technology evolves to have billions to trillions of transistors integrated on a processor die and software hierarchy and interfaces become more complex, the error frequency is still rare as counted as the number of failures in a billion device hours (FIT). Also, error occurrence is not predictable except for permanent faults. Thus, FT500 employs fault injection such that all the target systems can be equally evaluated with the same number of injected faults within the limited evaluation time. Fault injection has been extensively studied [7,10,33]. We extend the software-based fault injection technologies to mimic multiple levels of faults, from individual bit flips to HPC node level failures. Different fault levels are mapped to different layers in the computing stack. For example, processor-level faults are typically manifested with bit flips. To mimic various processor errors, we take the application executable and insert bit flips to different parts of instructions such as opcode, operands, and function fields through compiler backend approaches. On the contrary, file system failure is challenging to be designed with bit flips. Instead, we propose to do fault emulation by raising various file system exceptions (e.g., exceeding quota).

The number of faults and the injection timings are pre-determined based on the granularity of tests. The injected faults are recorded in database/files such that the fault tracking module can record the trajectory of the fault throughout the computing stack and the fault tolerance analyzer can calculate the final fault tolerance score by checking how many of them are masked or visible to the computation output. We aim to collaborate with various entities, such as vendors and service providers, in Cloud, Edge, and HPC to ensure comprehensive coverage of fault types in converged computing environments.

4.4   Fault Tracking and Storage Modules

To understand the cross-stack resilience and cascading impact of multiple faults, FT500 employs a novel fault tracking module. Once benchmark applications or mini-app tests begin execution with injected faults, the type and injected timing and locations (e.g., instruction, data, file, etc.) of each fault are recorded in a fault database. Whenever the corresponding fault is reached to an execution/access point, the fault status transition is recorded. For example, if a bit flip is masked without causing any exception or error, the fault is marked as masked in the database and is no longer tracked. If the fault generated incorrect computation output (e.g., incorrect instruction execution result), the fault is marked as unmasked and the incorrect computation output and the information of a following instruction or a memory address that consumes or stores the incorrect output is recorded in the fault database. The consumer instruction and target memory address information are used upon application termination to link between different faults injected in adjacent computing stacks.

Fault recording and replaying may cause unacceptable delay and storage overhead. To avoid that, FT500 identifies only the essential information that can evaluate different aspects of the target system and builds a set of efficient storage mechanisms.

4.5 Resilience Metrics

To summarize and compare the fault tolerance of different systems, we need unified and measurable evaluation metrics. As noted earlier, FT500 considers both performance and fault tolerance. Thus, we design new sets of evaluation metrics, which were not used by earlier fault tolerance methods (e.g., AVF). The most important metrics include, but are not limited to 1) corrected faults over makespan, 2) accuracy over makespan, and 3) the number of recoveries over makespan. All the metrics are normalized to the application makespan to evaluate the performance as well as resilience capability of the fault tolerance methods incorporated in the target system. For the first metric, as FT500 knows how many faults are injected into the target system, the number of corrected faults can be easily measured by checking the fault tracking database. The second metric provides a coarser-grained evaluation by considering only the end-to-end application correctness. The third metric shows the resilience capability of the target system for the coarser-grained faults such as file system failure, node level failures, etc. Besides these, the makespan itself can be also a good indicator of the performance of fault tolerance methods incorporated in the target system. In addition, we incorporate existing resilience metrics in our metric design. For example, to measure silent data corruption (SDC) impact over the makespan, we introduce the data object makespan to DVF [34] and aDVF [12], which originally only measured SDC impact on individual data objects.

4.6 Fault Tolerance Analysis Module

Based on the evaluation metrics, the fault tolerance analysis module finally ranks evaluated systems for various aspects such as fault tolerance, fault tolerance for performance, and performance. By using the fault tracking database, the fault tolerance analysis module of FT500 also provides in-depth analysis such as the influence of faults in different computing stacks towards the application correctness, the cascading impact of multiple faults, the masking impact of faults in multiple layers, the best fault-tolerant solutions (software/hardware configurations) for each layer of the computing stack, etc.

This in-depth analysis will guide researchers and developers to revisit the existing fault tolerance methods, which will lead to a vicious circle of fault tolerance optimization and evaluation, as projected in Sect. 1.

5   Potential Next-Generation Fault Tolerance Methods

So far, we have explored the unresolved challenges to enforce fault tolerance in the converged computing platforms across Cloud, Edge, HPC, and storage systems and proposed a new fault tolerance ranking and evaluation system that uncovers the hidden resilience properties of the new platforms. With better understanding of those properties, the community will be able to revisit or newly design fault tolerance solutions for large-scale computing platforms. We discuss some potential solutions here, especially for tackling the important synchronization issues.

Distributed WMS for Seamless Computing. A WMS can be redesigned to orchestrate seamless computing upon failures. There is not a clear guide for downstream tasks when an upstream task is stuck at a failure. A distributed WMS can be designed to inform the downstream tasks of the failure and force them to stop and run another task rather than pending on the inputs from the failed upstream task. To notify failures or command switching to another task between tasks running on distributed systems, larger-scale workflow graph (DAG) analysis models should be also designed which reinforce reliable and efficient communication channels between tasks that are mapped to distributed systems. Note that the existing job scheduling approaches are designated for single systems, which are not able to synchronize jobs across multiple systems. The workflow DAG analysis models with extended job schedulers could enhance the WMS to more robustly support distributed systems.

Scalable Checkpoint/Restart. Existing checkpoint/restart approaches running on a single system cannot handle synchronization across multiple systems of different settings. To enable scalable checkpoint/restart, a possible solution is to develop a higher-level control system that notifies pause signal and commands rolling back to the latest checkpoint for all the systems upon a participating system's failure. For such a synchronous checkpoint/restart, clock synchronization is essential. But, fine-grained synchronization would be too costly. Considering that failures typically occur with low frequency, the synchronization might be implemented with coarse-grained consistency models, integrated into the distributed WMS, to indicate the global synchronization points. To enable scalable checkpoint/restart on large systems, memory space would be another challenge. For this, we will be able to find new opportunity from the emerging disaggregated memory systems, which can link diverse memory systems to provide a larger aggregated memory space. To utilize this opportunity, the checkpoint/restart control system should employ a decision mechanism to choose the most efficient memory devices to support scalable checkpoint/restart.

6   Conclusion

This paper raises a number of unresolved challenges in enforcing fault tolerance in converged computing platforms. Given the ever-increasing computing demands and diverse computing capabilities of different HPC clusters, various emerging workflows are designed with considerations of distributed computing where data are generated, processed, analyzed, visualized, and stored in different clusters based on their integrated computing resources such as instruments (e.g., edges), domain accelerators (e.g., GPUs and TPUs), and storage capacity. Under this emerging converged computing environment, this paper projects that the next-generation fault-tolerant system design should iterate rounds of benchmarking and optimizations to find hidden vulnerabilities and mitigate those with acceptable performance overhead. To this end, this paper proposes a new benchmarking and ranking framework with an emphasis on fault tolerance, namely FT500. We show the prototype of FT500 with detailed discussions about its essential functions. With the standardized evaluation and ranking system, domain scientists will be able to select the optimal system configurations for their resilience needs and the HPC architects and vendors can showcase their high-performant fault tolerance capability under this new computing environment. Some potential fault tolerance solutions are also discussed in the paper.

Acknowledgment. We thank the anonymous reviewers for their valuable feedbacks. This work was partially supported by the Pacific Northwest National Laboratory (PNNL). operated by Battelle for the U.S. Department of Energy (DOE) under contract DE-AC05-76RL01830. This work was performed under the auspices of the U.S. Department of Energy by Lawrence Livermore National Laboratory under Contract DE-AC52-07NA27344. This work was authored in part by employees of Brookhaven Science Associates, LLC under Contract No. DESC0012704. This work was also supported in part by National Science Foundation (NSF) CCF-2114514.

References

1. Exascale Computing Project CANDLE. https://www.exascaleproject.org/research-group/data-analytics-and-optimization/
2. NVIDIA SDK. https://developer.nvidia.com/hpc-sdk
3. Slurm Fault Tolerant Workload Management. https://ieeexplore.ieee.org/stamp/stamp.jsp?tp=&arnumber=1303290
4. Stress-ng. https://github.com/ColinIanKing/stress-ng
5. Ahn, D.H., et al.: Scalable composition and analysis techniques for massive scientific workflows. In: e-Science (2022)
6. AlZain, M.A., Soh, B., Pardede, E.: A new approach using redundancy technique to improve security in cloud computing. In: CyberSec, pp. 230–235. IEEE (2012)
7. Calhoun, J., Olson, L., Snir, M.: FlipIt: an LLVM based fault injector for HPC. In: Lopes, L., et al. (eds.) Euro-Par 2014. LNCS, vol. 8805, pp. 547–558. Springer, Cham (2014). https://doi.org/10.1007/978-3-319-14325-5_47
8. Chakrabarti, D.R., Boehm, H.J., Bhandari, K.: Atlas: leveraging locks for non-volatile memory consistency. In: ACM OOPSLA (2014)
9. Dongarra, J.J., Meuer, H.W., Strohmaier, E., et al.: Top500 supercomputer sites. Supercomputer **13**, 89–111 (1997)
10. Georgakoudis, G., Laguna, I., Nikolopoulos, D.S., Schulz, M.: REFINE: realistic fault injection via compiler-based instrumentation for accuracy, portability and speed. In: ACM/IEEE SC, pp. 1–14 (2017)
11. Guo, L., Georgakoudis, G., Parasyris, K., Laguna, I., Li, D.: MATCH: an MPI fault tolerance benchmark suite. In: 2020 IEEE International Symposium on Workload Characterization (IISWC), pp. 60–71. IEEE (2020)
12. Guo, L., Li, D.: MOARD: modeling application resilience to transient faults on data objects. In: IPDPS (2019)

13. Guo, L., Li, D., Laguna, I.: Paris: predicting application resilience using machine learning. J. Parallel Distrib. Comput. **152**, 111–124 (2021)
14. Guo, L., Li, D., Laguna, I., Schulz, M.: Fliptracker: understanding natural error resilience in HPC applications. In: SC (2018)
15. Javadi, B., Abawajy, J., Buyya, R.: Failure-aware resource provisioning for hybrid cloud infrastructure. JPDC **72**, 1318–1331 (2012)
16. Jhawar, R., Piuri, V., Santambrogio, M.: A comprehensive conceptual system-level approach to fault tolerance in cloud computing. In: IEEE ISC, pp. 1–5 (2012)
17. Kestor, G., Krishnamoorthy, S., Ma, W.: Localized fault recovery for nested fork-join programs. In: IEEE IPDPS (2017)
18. Kunkel, J., Bent, J., Lofstead, J., Markomanolis, G.S.: Establishing the IO-500 benchmark. White Paper (2016)
19. Laguna, I., Schulz, M., Richards, D.F., Calhoun, J., Olson, L.: IPAS: intelligent protection against silent output corruption in scientific applications. In: IEEE CGO, pp. 227–238 (2016)
20. Li, Z., et al.: A visual comparison of silent error propagation. IEEE TVCG (2022)
21. Mohammed, B., Kiran, M., Maiyama, K.M., Kamala, M.M., Awan, I.U.: Failover strategy for fault tolerance in cloud computing environment. Software (2017)
22. Mukherjee, S., Weaver, C., Emer, J., Reinhardt, S., Austin, T.: A systematic methodology to compute the architectural vulnerability factors for a high-performance microprocessor. In: Proceedings of IEEE/ACM MICRO (2003)
23. Nicolae, B., et al.: VeloC: towards high performance adaptive asynchronous checkpointing at large scale. In: IEEE IPDPS (2019)
24. Oukid, I., et al.: FPTree: a hybrid SCM-DRAM persistent and concurrent B-Tree for storage class memory. In: SIGMOD (2016)
25. Peterson, J.L., et al.: Enabling machine learning-ready HPC ensembles with merlin. FGCS **131**(C), 255–268 (2022)
26. Reis, G.A., Chang, J., Vachharajani, N., Rangan, R., August, D.I.: SWIFT: software implemented fault tolerance. In: IEEE CGO, pp. 243–254 (2005)
27. Ren, J., Wu, K., Li, D.: Exploring non-volatility of non-volatile memory for high performance computing under failures. In: IEEE CLUSTER, pp. 237–247 (2020)
28. Rorabaugh, D., Guevara, M., Llamas, R., Kitson, J., Vargas, R., Taufer, M.: SOMOSPIE: a modular SOil MOisture SPatial inference engine based on data-driven decisions. In: eScience, pp. 1–10 (2019)
29. Saadi, A.A., et al.: Impeccable: integrated modeling pipeline for COVID cure by assessing better leads. In: ICPP, pp. 1–12 (2021)
30. Shahzad, F., Thies, J., Kreutzer, M., Zeiser, T., Hager, G., Wellein, G.: CRAFT: a library for easier application-level checkpoint/restart and automatic fault tolerance. IEEE TPDS (2018)
31. Shin, K.G., Kim, H.: A time redundancy approach to TMR failures using fault-state likelihoods. IEEE Trans. Comput. **43**(10), 1151–1162 (1994)
32. Wang, J., Bao, W., Zhu, X., Yang, L.T., Xiang, Y.: FESTAL: fault-tolerant elastic scheduling algorithm for real-time tasks in virtualized clouds. IEEE TC (2014)
33. Wei, J., Thomas, A., Li, G., Pattabiraman, K.: Quantifying the accuracy of high-level fault injection techniques for hardware faults. In: IEEE/IFIP DSN, pp. 375–382 (2014)
34. Yu, L., Li, D., Mittal, S., Vetter, J.S.: Quantitatively modeling application resiliency with data vulnerability factor. In: SC (2014)

Estimating the Energy Consumption of Applications in the Computing Continuum with *iFogSim*

Saeedeh Baneshi[1]($\boxtimes$), Ana-Lucia Varbanescu[1], Anuj Pathania[1],
Benny Akesson[1,2], and Andy Pimentel[1]

[1] University of Amsterdam, Amsterdam, The Netherlands
`s.baneshi@uva.nl`
[2] TNO-ESI, Eindhoven, The Netherlands

Abstract. Digital services - applications that often span the entire computing continuum - have become an essential part of our daily lives, but they can have a significant energy cost, raising sustainability concerns. The computing continuum features multiple distributed layers (edge, fog, and cloud) with specific computing infrastructure and scheduling decisions at each layer, which impact the overall quality of service and energy consumption of digital services. Measuring the energy consumption of such applications is challenging due to the distributed nature of the system and the application. As such, simulation techniques are promising solutions to estimate energy consumption, and several simulators are available for modeling the cloud and fog computing environment.

In this paper, we investigate *iFogSim*'s effectiveness in analyzing the end-to-end energy consumption of applications in the computing continuum through two case studies. We design different scenarios for each case study to map application modules to devices along the continuum, including the Edge-Cloud collaboration architecture, and compare them with the two placement policies native to *iFogSim*: *Cloud-only* and *Edgeward* policies. We observe *iFogSim*'s limitations in reporting energy consumption, and improve its ability to report energy consumption from an application's perspective; this enables additional insight into an application's energy consumption, thus enhancing the usability of *iFogSim* in evaluating the end-to-end energy consumption of digital services.

Keywords: Digital services · End-to-end energy consumption · Edge computing · Simulation

1 Introduction

Scientific discovery, product development, data science and artificial intelligence, online shopping, and entertainment rely increasingly on digital services. As such, digital services have become a crucial part of our daily life, but they come with a significant, rapidly-increasing energy cost, raising sustainability concerns [20]. Worldwide estimates project the ICT sector to reach 21% of global energy consumption by 2030 [14].

A. Bienz et al. (Eds.): ISC High Performance 2023 Workshops, LNCS 13999, pp. 234–249, 2023.
https://doi.org/10.1007/978-3-031-40843-4_18

Users access digital services through smartphones, laptops, and tablets, triggering the entire continuum from the device to the *edge, fog,* and *cloud* [12]. *Edge* devices are closest to the end-user and improve user experience by reducing latency and providing faster access to data [1]. The *fog,* located closer to the data center, handles data processing, storage, and communication [24]. The *cloud* is a remote location for (large-scale) data storage, management, and processing [18,19]. Each layer has its specific computing infrastructure, and scheduling decisions at each layer impact the overall quality of service (QoS) and energy consumption of digital services [2].

Measuring the energy consumption of digital services spanning the entire computing continuum - from edge to cloud - is a challenging task due to the distributed nature of the system and the application. Simulation techniques can estimate the energy consumption to overcome this challenge [16].

Various simulators are available for modeling the cloud and fog computing environment and estimating the energy consumption and performance of different components of the architectures. For example, *CloudSim* [8] and *GreenCloud* [15] focus on modeling cloud computing, while *EdgeCloudSim* [23] and *iFogSim* [10] model fog computing. We focus on *iFogSim*, a toolkit for modeling and simulating resource management techniques in the IoT (Internet of Things), edge, and fog computing environments.

We explore the effectiveness of *iFogSim* in analyzing the end-to-end energy consumption of applications, aiming to identify its strengths and weaknesses for such an analysis. We find there is a lack of reporting actual energy consumed by the application on the device: in fact, *iFogSim* reports the total energy *consumed by the device*, which is misleading for applications that do not fully utilize all resources available to them (for example, they only use the cloud sporadically). Therefore, we improve iFogSim's energy reporting function to also include energy consumption and performance from the application perspective. We demonstrate the usefulness of such reports using two case studies: the Surveillance application and the Latency-sensitive online VR game.

Specifically, we conduct our investigation using six Edge-Cloud continuum scenarios for the Surveillance application, and four scenarios for the VR game application, and compare the results. We find a significant difference between the energy consumption results of *iFogSim* from the device- and application-perspectives. The results also confirm that running applications on fog devices close to the user can reduce energy consumption and improve performance.

In summary, the main contributions of this paper are as follows:

- We show how to design different Edge-Cloud collaborative scenarios to map application modules to devices along the computing continuum for two applications. These complement the standard Edge-ward and Cloud-only scenarios from *iFogSim*.
- We compare six scenarios for mapping application modules to devices along the continuum in a surveillance application and four mapping scenarios in a VR game application. We demonstrate how to analyze and contrast their energy consumption and performance using *iFogSim*.

The remainder of this article is organized as follows. In Sect. 2, we provide background information on frameworks for modeling cloud and fog computing environments, and we introduce our chosen tool, *iFogSim*. In Sect. 3, we describe the process for modeling the topology architecture and application and configuring them using *iFogSim*. We also present two applications: a surveillance application and a Vr game application used as case-studies in our experiments and explain the scenarios we designed for the mapping of applications modules. Next, in Sect. 4, we discuss our empirical evaluation setup and experiments and analyze our results. Section 5 discusses related work and Sect. 6 concludes the paper and highlights directions for future research.

2   Background

We briefly introduce the setup and technology used in this work: the computing continuum and the *iFogSim* simulation.

2.1   The Computing Continuum

Digital devices can produce massive amounts of (heterogeneous) data that require fast and increasingly complex processing [9,10], using different tools to provide understandable results for users. However, the more complex the analysis is, the more challenging the processing becomes; consequently, resources local to the devices become insufficient, and computation offloading is needed. Offloading *all* data processing to the cloud is not always the most efficient solution due to, for example, the high latency of the centralized computing approach or privacy concerns. Fog computing provides a more effective way for data processing, by offloading the analysis to a combination of different layers of decentralized computing [9,24], and only relying on cloud offloading. In this context, fog and cloud computing form the *computing continuum*. Underlying the compute continuum is a complex infrastructure of devices (i.e., sensors), edge devices (i.e., processing stations between sensors and the cloud), and data centers [12].

Offloading processing to different components of the computing continuum has different impacts on user quality-of-service (QoS) and energy consumption. There is a growing need to quantify these costs and assess the sustainability of digital services [6]. However, measuring the energy consumption of applications across this complex continuum is challenging, because the components are distributed (geographically and in terms of ownership), making uniform measurements virtually impossible [16]. Instead, we rely on *simulators* to help estimate the energy consumption of different applications [7] and different offloading scenarios. The key challenge these simulators face is to provide an accurate system representation.

2.2   Modeling Cloud and Fog Computing

Researchers have developed highly accurate cloud computing simulators to model the complex structure of the data centers, their topology, the resource

managers and schedulers, and the challenges of multi-tenancy. As such, simulators such as *GreenCloud* [15], *CloudSim* [8], or *OpenDC* [17] often provide
a trade-off between very accurate results and the complexity of models, and
the cost of simulation. *GreenCloud* focuses on detailed and expensive energy
consumption simulation, while *CloudSim* and *OpenDC* are cheaper and more
useful for scenario analysis. However, none of them addresses the full computing
continuum.

Expanding towards the computing continuum, there exist several simulators.
For example, *EdgeCloudSim* is an open-source simulator designed to evaluate the
performance of edge computing systems. This tool is based on *CloudSim* and
provides network modeling (WLAN and WAN), a device mobility model, and a
tunable load generator. However, it does not support the energy consumption
model for mobile devices, edge, and cloud data centers. It also does not support
task migration among the Edge or Cloud VMs [23].

iFogSim is a simulator that models IoT and Fog environments, and measures
the impact of resource management techniques in terms of latency, network congestion, energy consumption, and cost. It simulates components of the computing continuum, including edge devices, cloud data centers, and network links, to
measure performance metrics. *iFogSim* uses the *Sense-Process-Actuate* model,
where sensors publish data to IoT networks, and applications running on fog
devices subscribe to and process data from sensors. The insights obtained are
then translated into actions and forwarded to actuators [10].

To study different fog-cloud interactions, *iFogSim* has emerged as a popular
choice for modeling various fog computing scenarios. As *iFogSim* offers a good
trade-off between ease-of-use and ease-of-change (being Java-based), and given
its proven feasibility for many studies, we selected it as the main tool for our own
analysis, where we aim to explore its effectiveness in estimating the energy consumption of digital services using *different mappings* across the entire computing
continuum.

2.3   The *iFogSim* Toolkit

The architecture of *iFogSim* consists of IoT Sensors placed at the bottom-
most layer of the architecture and distributed in different geographical locations, IoT Actuators operating at the same layer, and IoT Data Streams, which
are sequences of immutable values emitted by sensors. Fog devices connect the
sensors to the internet and host application modules; cloud resources are provisioned on-demand from geographically distributed data centers. Developers
model applications developed for fog deployment as a collection of modules comprising data processing elements [10] in a Distributed Data Flow (DDF) model.

Being based on *CloudSim*, *iFogSim* leverages the basic event simulation functionalities of its "ancestor": entities communicate with each other by sending
events, and the core *CloudSim* layer handles events between fog computing
components in *iFogSim*. It models simulated entities and services, including
`FogDevice`, `Sensor`, `Tuple`, `Actuator`, and `Application`, as classes. Each class

has its attributes and methods to specify the characteristics and behavior of the entity it represents [10].

Physical Components. The physical components in *iFogSim* are sensors, fog devices, and actuators. Sensors are the sources of generating data and behave like IoT sensors: they periodically send data to other devices for further processing [16]. In *iFogSim*, there is a class specifically designed for simulating sensors, which includes a reference attribute to its parent - the fog device it connects to - and the latency between them.

Using the `FogDevice` class, *iFogSim* simulates computing resources for performing tasks. This class has specific attributes like instruction processing rate, maximum and idle power, uplink and downlink bandwidths, memory size, and level of fog device. The instruction processing rate reflects the computing capacity of the fog device. The power attributes reflect energy efficiency. Bandwidth defines the communication capacity of Fog devices.

Finally, using the `Actuator` class, *iFogSim* simulates end nodes that are data sinks. Similarly to the sensor, this class also includes a reference attribute to its parent - the fog device it connects to - and the latency between them.

Application Components. *iFogSim* models applications as directed graphs, where vertices represent the modules that execute the processing task on incoming data, and edges show data dependencies between the processing modules. *iFogSim* uses the following classes to model the applications.

AppModule: It defines the processing elements of the application. `AppModules` receive tasks from other `AppModules` (incoming tasks), process them, and produce tasks for further processing by another `AppModule`. For each module, the number of output tasks per incoming task can be defined by a fractional selectivity or a bursty model [10]. It also has attributes like memory size, computational capacity, and bandwidth.

AppEdge: It models the data dependencies between application modules and carries specific tuple types. It also exhibits the computational requirements and data size of the transported tuple. The edges can transport periodic or event-based tuples.

Tuple: It is a task generated by a module for further processing. The tuple is the fundamental unit of communication between entities, characterized by its processing requirements, measured as the number of million instructions needed and the size of encapsulated data.

AppLoop: It is a sequence of modules (and the links between them). This class defines the control loop of the application. By defining this loop from the sensor to the actuator, we can measure the end-to-end latency of the application.

Management Components. The management components in *iFogSim* are the *ModuleMapping* and the *Controller*. The *ModuleMapping* object identifies available resources in fog devices and decides where to map application modules based on their requirements. *iFogSim*'s default placement policy is *Edge-ward* placement, which deploys modules on devices close to the user if they are powerful enough. Otherwise, it forwards modules to higher-level devices toward the cloud. Alternatively, the *Cloud-only* placement policy deploys all modules to the cloud.

The *Controller* launches modules on their target fog devices using information from *ModuleMapping* and collects simulation results upon completion.

3 Scenario Design with Examples

We present the steps needed to design and execute scenario analysis using *iFogSim*.

3.1 Process

To begin the simulation process, we need to perform the following steps.

Define Topology. We must define the continuum's physical topology by adding sensors, actuators, and fog devices such as routers and proxy servers. We then configure their attributes, such as computational capacity and power consumption. Additionally, we need to define the connections between the fog devices and set the latency and bandwidth of the links. Figure 1 shows the physical topologies, which we used for our experiments for two case studies.

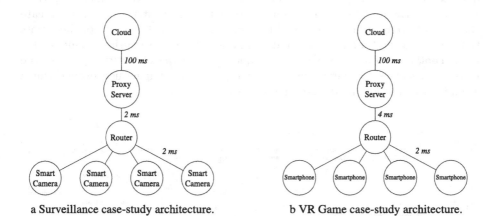

a Surveillance case-study architecture.   b VR Game case-study architecture.

Fig. 1. Case-studies architectures, including link latencies.

Table 1 shows the configuration of the fog devices in our topology for two case studies. Each component is defined by its computational capacity in million instructions per second (MIPS), which reflects its frequency, it's maximum (i.e., when fully utilized) and idle power consumption, and the size of RAM.

Table 1. Configuration of fog devices for two case studies architecture.

(a) Architecture configuration for surveillance application

Device type	Computational Capacity [MIPS]	RAM [GB]	Power [W] Max	Idle
Cloud	44800	40	1648.0	1332.0
Proxy server	2800	4	107.3	83.4
Router	2800	4	107.3	83.4
Smart camera	500	1	87.5	82.4

(b) Architecture configuration for VR Game application

Device type	Computational Capacity [MIPS]	RAM [GB]	Power [W] Max	Idle
Cloud	44800	40	1648.0	1332.0
Proxy server	2800	4	107.3	83.4
Router	2800	4	107.3	83.4
Smartphones	1000	1	87.5	82.4

Define Application. The first step for this purpose is to split the application into interdependent `AppModules` and configure the dependency of these modules by defining `AppEdges`. Next, we must define the input and output `Tuple` types for each `AppModule`, and specify the fractional selectivities. Finally, we can define the control loops of the application by defining `AppLoop`, which we can use to monitor the end-to-end performance or delay of specific parts of the application.

Define the Main Function. In this function, we create instances of the sensors, actuators, and fog device classes to model the physical topology. Additionally, we must create instances of application modules, module mapping objects, and controllers. Finally, we must submit our application to the controller and specify the placement policy.

Start Simulation. Finally, the simulation is initiated using the *CloudSim* core of the simulator. During this stage, the simulator generates the entities and queues for storing the produced events. *iFogSim* saves all events, including their start and estimated finish time, source, target, and event tags, which indicate the type of event, in a queue called `FutureQueue`. At each time step, the events that are scheduled for that particular time are moved to another queue, called `DeferredQueue`, for processing. Subsequently, the target entities process the incoming events according to their respective types and trigger new events, which are added to the `FutureQueue` for processing.

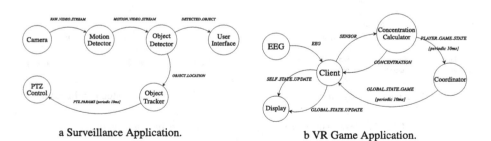

a Surveillance Application.

b VR Game Application.

Fig. 2. Case-study Applications [10].

3.2   Case Studies

In our experiments, we considered two case studies available in *iFogSim*: an area-surveillance application and a latency-sensitive online game. In these applications, a large volume of data is produced by Sensors and sent for further processing to the network [10,16]. The processing can be done in the cloud, which is a centralized approach, or by fog devices closer to the user, which is a decentralized approach. However, the requirement for real-time operation makes a decentralized approach more suitable for efficient processing. Figure 2 depicts these applications and their modules.

Surveillance Application. The function of modules in this application are as follows:

Motion Detector: This module is embedded in smart cameras and detects motion in video streams by continuously analyzing raw video and forwarding it for further processing.

Object Detector: This module receives data from the motion detector, extracts moving objects, calculates their coordinates, and activates tracking for new objects.

Object Tracker: This module receives object coordinates, calculates optimal configuration for Pan-Tilt-Zoom (PTZ) cameras, and sends them to PTZ control periodically.

PTZ Control: This module is embedded in smart cameras and adjusts the physical camera based on PTZ parameters received from the object tracker. It serves as the system's actuator.

User Interface: The application provides a user interface by sending a fraction of video streams with tracked objects to the user's device.

Cameras act as sensors, capturing video feeds every 5 millisecond and sending them for further processing. Each module processes incoming tuples and sends new ones for further processing. Table 2a shows the processing requirements and data size per tuple used for modeling this application.

Table 2. Description of inter-module edges of application case studies [10]

(a) Surveillance application Tuples configurations.

Tuple type	CPU load [MI]	Data Size [B]
RAW_VIDEO_STREAM	1000	20000
MOTION_VIDEO_STREAM	2000	2000
DETECTED_OBJECT	500	2000
OBJECT_LOCATION	1000	100
PTZ_PARAMS	100	28

(b) VR Game application Tuples configurations.

Tuple type	CPU load [MI]	Data Size [B]
EEG	2500	500
SENSOR	3500	500
PLAYER_GAME_STATE	1000	1000
CONCENTRATION	14	500
GLOBAL_GAME_STATE	28	1000
GLOBAL_STATE_UPDATE	1000	500
SELF_STATE_UPDATE	100	500

VR Game Application. The function of modules in this application are as follows:

Client: This module receives EEG signals from the headset and filters them to remove inconsistencies to send for further processing.

Concentration calculator: This module detects the brain state and calculates the concentration level of the user, then updates the player's game state.

Coordinator: This module acts at the global level and updates the state of the game for all connected clients.

In this application, users wear a headset that acts as a sensor for capturing brain signals at a specific rate of 10 ms. Then It sends these signals for further processing in the next modules. Table 2b shows the processing requirements and data size per tuple used for modeling this application.

3.3   Designed Scenarios

In our experiments, we investigate the efficiency of the *iFogSim* simulator in estimating the end-to-end energy consumption of applications. We consider the topologies illustrated in Fig. 1 and the applications illustrated in Fig. 2.

As we assume the device can do some processing, for the surveillance application, we assign the motion detector modules to the smart cameras in all scenarios; we further assign the user interface module to the cloud, as this is the module requiring complex process, without a strict requirement of low latency. For the other processing modules, we designed various mapping scenarios of edge-cloud collaboration. We have listed all six mapping scenarios we considered for the object detector and object tracker modules in Table 3. The Cloud-only and Router-only scenarios are the results of running the application using the two available policies of *iFogSim*: *Cloud-only* and *Edge-ward*.

Table 3. Mapping scenarios of surveillance case study for execution models.

Scenario	Application Module	Target device	Source
Router_only	Object_detector Object_tracker	Router Router	iFogSim
Proxy_only	Object_detector Object_tracker	Proxy server Proxy server	New
Router_Proxy	Object_detector Object_tracker	Router Proxy server	New
Router_Cloud	Object_detector Object_tracker	Router Cloud	New
Proxy_Cloud	Object_detector Object_tracker	Proxy server Cloud	New
Cloud_only	Object_detector Object_tracker	Cloud Cloud	iFogSim

For the VR Game application, by considering the requirements, we assign the client module to smartphones in all scenarios. Additionally, we assign the Coordinator module to the cloud, as this module needs to be globally accessible in order to coordinate users who may not be in the same geographical location.

For the Concentration Calculator module, we designed various mapping scenarios to have insight into the energy consumption on different layers of considered architecture. We have listed all four mapping scenarios we considered for this module in Table 4. The Cloud-only and Edge-only scenarios are the results of running the application using the two available policies of *iFogSim*: *Cloud-only* and *Edge-ward*.

Table 4. Mapping scenarios of VR game case study for execution models.

Scenario	Application Module	Target device	Source
Edge_only	Client Concentration calculator Coordinator	Smartphone Smartphone Cloud	iFogSim
Router_Include	Client Concentration calculator Coordinator	Smartphone Router Cloud	New
Proxy_Include	Client Concentration calculator Coordinator	Smartphone Proxy server Cloud	New
Cloud_Only	Client Concentration calculator Coordinator	Smartphone Cloud Cloud	iFogSim

4 Experimental Analysis and Discussion

Our results have been gathered by simulating the two case studies on their considered architecture for 2000 s seconds per scenario, using *iFogSim*. The simulation output in *iFogSim* includes the execution time, application loop delays, `tuple` execution delays, the energy consumption of each fog device, the cost of execution in the cloud, and the total network usage. We estimate the end-to-end energy consumption by adding the energy of all fog devices in different scenarios.

Figure 3a presents the energy consumption of the surveillance system. We observe no significant difference in the energy consumption of the continuum when running various application scenarios. This lack of difference happens because *iFogSim* reports the energy consumption of devices without considering the application, which is a reasonable approach from the device and overall system energy perspective.

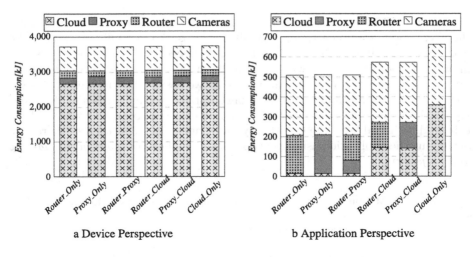

a Device Perspective   b Application Perspective

Fig. 3. Surveillance application energy consumption in different scenarios

However, from the application perspective, this is an unreasonable approach: the idle energy consumption of fog devices *that are not used to run the application* should not be included in the estimation of application energy. Therefore, we revised the energy estimation function of the simulator to report not only total energy, but also active energy consumption, a more accurate estimation of the application's energy consumption. Figure 3b shows the application's energy consumption in different scenarios as a sum of the energy spent only by devices actively participating in the computation.

In the VR Game application, similarly, from the device perspective, we observe no significant difference between the total energy of the continuum and the energy consumed by each device across various scenarios. However, when we change the perspective to the application itself and exclude the idle energy of the devices, notable differences in both the total continuum energy and the energy consumption of each device become apparent. Figure 4 depicts the energy consumption of devices across different scenarios with different perspectives.

For both case studies, we observe that by offloading processing from the device closest to the user to Cloud, the energy consumption of the application increases. To understand the impact of this approach on application performance, we also present the so-called delay of processing for both case studies in Fig. 5. We observe that, as expected, offloading the processing to the cloud leads to a higher average delay in the control loop of the applications.

Our results indicate that offloading the application to devices close to the user is a more effective strategy for performance and energy consumption. However, the computing capacity of fog devices, such as routers and proxy servers, is limited for computationally intensive applications.

In this experimental study, we observed that *iFogSim* is a powerful tool for analyzing performance metrics, such as delay, execution cost, network usage, and

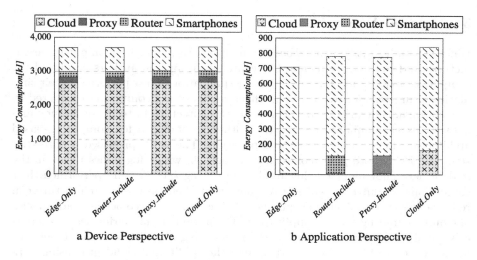

Fig. 4. VR Game application energy consumption in different Scenarios

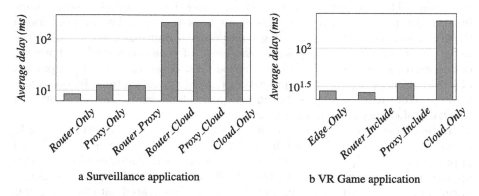

Fig. 5. Average delay of the control loop for different applications.

energy consumption in an IoT, edge, and fog environment. Nevertheless, there exist limitations in its reporting that require further research and improvement. For instance, *iFogSim* reports the energy consumption of individual devices, but it does not provide a realistic estimation of end-to-end energy consumption.

The simple addition of energy from all devices does not accurately represent the end-to-end energy consumption. To obtain a more accurate estimation, we must account for the energy consumed by the links and connections between fog devices. Unfortunately, *iFogSim* does not consider this energy consumption. Additionally, the tool does not account for the application perspective when reporting energy consumption.

5   Related Work

Different studies utilize the *iFogSim* simulator to model fog computing architectures and IoT environments. For example, in [5], the authors employed fog computing architecture for a car parking application. They performed their simulation using *iFogSim* to show the effectiveness of fog computing compared to a traditional, centralized cloud computing architecture in terms of latency and network usage. Similarly, in [11], the authors proposed a fog computing-based architecture for an e-health care application. The work proposed a three-tier structure for remote pain monitoring systems, in which fog nodes reside in the middle tier. They modeled this architecture using *iFogSim* and performed their simulations on different scales to validate that their proposed architecture can reduce execution cost, latency, and network usage, to overcome the inadequacies of cloud computing for this application. The authors of [3] performed a comparative analysis of cloud and fog environments using *iFogSim* to evaluate network usage and cost of execution. Rather than the traditional cloud processing approach, they offloaded the CCTV camera footage analysis to a fog server for processing. The research aimed to decrease execution costs and network usage by introducing a fog setup into the cloud infrastructure. The authors found that offloading computation to a fog server enables multiple users to utilize the same server for different complex tasks. None of these case studies, however, emphasized the process and analysis needed for a detailed, focused comparison of different mappings on the application's energy consumption. In our work, we investigate more scenarios, beyond edge vs. cloud, and showcase a broader spectrum of energy efficiency results.

In two other articles [21, 22], the authors focus on security surveillance applications, which are widely used in our daily lives. They present a fog-based approach for such applications because the traditional cloud-based centralized approach for processing data is likely inefficient due to the latency-sensitive nature of the workload, especially as the amount of generated data from cameras increases. To compare the efficiency of fog-based and cloud-based approaches in various scenarios, including varying numbers of areas and cameras, the authors conducted several experiments using the *iFogSim* framework. They compared different parameters, such as execution cost, latency, network usage, and energy cost of these two approaches to prove the effectiveness of the fog-based approach compared to the cloud-based. However, while these studies used the same application as ours, they did not consider different mapping scenarios beyond edge and cloud devices. Instead, they focused on different topologies, with different numbers of areas and cameras for their comparison.

Research has also focused on module or service mapping within fog computing. For example, in [25], the authors proposed an improved version of the *JAYA* approach for the optimal mapping of application modules to minimize the energy consumption of fog devices. They used *iFogSim* to conduct experiments and analyze performance by varying the load of surveillance applications to demonstrate the effectiveness of their approach in reducing energy consumption. In [4], the authors presented the Heterogeneous Shortest Module First

(*HSMF*) Algorithm for mapping application modules on the heterogeneous fog-cloud computing environment. They also considered surveillance applications for their study and conducted experiments using the *iFogSim* simulator to compare the results of their proposed approach to the available cloud-only and edge-ward placement policies of *iFogSim*. They were able to improve the total execution time and total network usage with their proposed method. By comparison, our work does not focus on proposing new placement algorithms - yet; instead, we study the energy impact of different possible mapping scenarios in detail from the application perspective. This information could be used to determine new placement strategies in future work.

6   Conclusion

In this study, we investigated the effectiveness of *iFogSim*, a popular simulator for modeling and simulating fog computing environments, in analyzing the end-to-end energy consumption of applications. Our investigation includes an assessment of the energy consumption and delays across different scenarios when mapping an application on the Edge-Cloud continuum. Our experiments show that *iFogSim* can estimate the energy consumption of devices along the continuum, but its analysis is presented at device-granularity, and not from the application perspective. To model energy consumption from the application perspective, we propose only considering the energy consumption of fog devices *during their active cycle* within the application's lifetime. We added to *iFogSim* the ability to report the application's energy consumption on each device, in addition to the total energy of the device. Our results indicate the energy consumption difference, with this new analysis mode, can be significant. Furthermore, we found that *iFogSim* does not model the energy consumption of connections and links between the devices in the topology, and we currently work on modeling this energy consumption, aiming to have a more realistic estimation of energy consumption for the computing continuum.

By utilizing *iFogSim*, we have successfully evaluated different mapping scenarios, showing the energy consumption and performance trade-offs, and providing insights for optimizing energy efficiency in digital services. We plan to further work on better calibration of the simulation and validating the results in an emulation environment [13] and in a real computing continuum environment.

References

1. Aghapour, E., Sapra, D., Pimentel, A., Pathania, A.: CPU-GPU layer-switched low latency CNN inference. In: 2022 25th Euromicro Conference on Digital System Design (DSD), pp. 324–331. IEEE (2022)
2. Ahvar, E., Orgerie, A.-C., Lebre, A.: Estimating energy consumption of cloud, fog, and edge computing infrastructures. IEEE Trans. Sustain. Comput. **7**(2), 277–288 (2019)

3. Alam, M.S., Jabin, S.J., Alam, A., Hossain, M.I.: Comparative analysis of cloud and fog environment based on network usage and cost of execution using iFogSim. In: DASA 2021, pp. 132–137. IEEE, (2021)
4. Arora, U., Singh, N.: IoT application modules placement in heterogeneous fog-cloud infrastructure. Int. J. Inf. Technol. **13**(5), 1975–1982 (2021)
5. Awaisi, K.S.: Towards a fog enabled efficient car parking architecture. IEEE Access **7**, 159100–159111 (2019)
6. Brogi, A., Forti, S., Guerrero, C., Lera, I.: How to place your apps in the fog: state of the art and open challenges. Softw. Pract. Experience **50**(5), 719–740 (2020)
7. Byrne, J., et al.: A review of cloud computing simulation platforms and related environments. In: CLOSER, pp. 651–663 (2017)
8. Calheiros, R.N., Ranjan, R., Beloglazov, A., De Rose, C.A., Buyya, R.: CloudSim: a toolkit for modeling and simulation of cloud computing environments and evaluation of resource provisioning algorithms. Softw. Pract. Experience **41**(1), 23–50 (2011)
9. Gubbi, J., Buyya, R., Marusic, S., Palaniswami, M.: Internet of things (IoT): a vision, architectural elements, and future directions. Futur. Gener. Comput. Syst. **29**(7), 1645–1660 (2013)
10. Gupta, H., Vahid Dastjerdi, A., Ghosh, S.K., Buyya, R.: iFogSim: a toolkit for modeling and simulation of resource management techniques in the internet of things, edge and fog computing environments. Softw. Pract. Experience **47**(9), 1275–1296 (2017)
11. Hassan, S.R., Ahmad, I., Ahmad, S., Alfaify, A., Shafiq, M.: Remote pain monitoring using fog computing for e-healthcare: an efficient architecture. Sensors **20**(22), 6574 (2020)
12. Jansen, M., Al-Dulaimy, A., Papadopoulos, A. V., Trivedi, A., Iosup, A.: The SPEC-RG reference architecture for the compute continuum. In: The 23rd IEEE/ACM CCGRID 2023, India, May 1–4, 2023 (2023)
13. Jansen, M., Wagner, L., Trivedi, A., Iosup, A.: Continuum: automate infrastructure deployment and benchmarking in the compute continuum. In: FastContinuum 2023, in conjuncrtion with ICPE, Portugal (2023)
14. Jones, N., et al.: How to stop data centres from gobbling up the world's electricity. Nature **561**(7722), 163–166 (2018)
15. Kliazovich, D., Bouvry, P., Khan, S.U.: GreenCloud: a packet-level simulator of energy-aware cloud computing data centers. J. Supercomput. **62**, 1263–1283 (2012)
16. Mahmud, R., Buyya, R.: Modelling and simulation of fog and edge computing environments using iFogSim toolkit. In: Fog and Edge Computing: Principles and Paradigms, pp. 1–35 (2019)
17. Mastenbroek, F., et al.: OpenDC 2.0: convenient modeling and simulation of emerging technologies in cloud datacenters. In: 2021 IEEE/ACM CCGrid, pp. 455–464, USA, May 2021. IEEE Computer Society (2021)
18. Oma, R., Nakamura, S., Enokido, T., Takizawa, M.: A tree-based model of energy-efficient fog computing systems in IoT. In: Barolli, L., Javaid, N., Ikeda, M., Takizawa, M. (eds.) CISIS 2018. AISC, vol. 772, pp. 991–1001. Springer, Cham (2019). https://doi.org/10.1007/978-3-319-93659-8_92
19. Pan, J., McElhannon, J.: Future edge cloud and edge computing for internet of things applications. IEEE Internet Things J. **5**(1), 439–449 (2017)
20. Preist, C., Schien, D., Shabajee, P., Wood, S., Hodgson, C.: Analyzing end-to-end energy consumption for digital services. Computer **47**(5), 92–95 (2014)

21. Sarkar, I., Kumar, S.: Fog computing based intelligent security surveillance using PTZ controller camera. In: 10th International Conference on ICCCNT, pp. 1–5. IEEE (2019)
22. Shrestha, S., Shakya, S.: A comparative performance analysis of fog-based smart surveillance system. TCSST J. **2**(02), 78–88 (2020)
23. Sonmez, C., Ozgovde, A., Ersoy, C.: EdgeCloudSim: an environment for performance evaluation of edge computing systems. Trans. Emerg. Telecommun. Technol. **29**(11), e3493 (2018)
24. Tang, W., Li, S., Rafique, W., Dou, W., Yu, S.: An offloading approach in fog computing environment. In: 2018 IEEE SmartWorld/SCALCOM/UIC/ATC/CB-DCom/IOP/SCI, pp. 857–864. IEEE (2018)
25. Vadde, U., Kompalli, V.S.: Energy efficient service placement in fog computing. PeerJ Comput. Sci. **8**, e1035 (2022)

7th International Workshop on In Situ Visualization (WOIV'23)

Preface to the 7th International Workshop on In Situ Visualization (WOIV'23)

1 Background and Description

Large-scale HPC simulations with their inherent I/O bottleneck have made in situ an essential approach for data analysis. In situ coupling of analysis and visualization to a live simulation circumvents writing raw data to disk. Instead, data abstracts are generated that capture much more information than otherwise possible.

The "Workshop on In Situ Visualization" series provides a venue for speakers to share practical expertise and experience with in situ visualization approaches. This 7th edition of the workshop, WOIV'23, took place as an on-site half-day workshop on May 25, 2023, co-located with ISC High Performance, after half-day workshops in 2016, 2017, 2021, and 2022, and two full-day workshops in 2018 and 2019. In 2020 we had to cancel the workshop due to the COVID-19 crisis. The goal of the workshop, in general, is to appeal to a wide-ranging audience of visualization scientists, computational scientists, and simulation developers, who have to collaborate to develop, deploy, and maintain in situ visualization approaches on HPC infrastructures.

In addition to two invited talks, presentations at WOIV'23 were selected from submitted papers. These were reviewed by an international program committee comprising diverse members from academia, government, and industry and many nationalities. Each submitted paper received at least three reviews. Accepted papers were invited for presentation at WOIV and are published in this LNCS volume.

2 Workshop Organization

2.1 Keynote

Dave Pugmire gave the keynote speech. He presented insights into how we should think of in situ visualization in the future. Visualization should be able to operate as an as-a-service model, where users can take different visualization "probes" and use them to inspect their data at different points along their data pipeline. An important piece of this puzzle is to have accurate visualization performance models so that the correct visualizations can be done using the right amount of resources for the task. He detailed ongoing research in these areas as well as presenting several technologies that are moving the community towards visualization as-a-service.

Dave Pugmire is a Senior Research Scientist and Visualization Group Lead at Oak Ridge National Laboratory. He is also a Joint Faculty Professor in the Department of Electrical Engineering and Computer Science at the University of Tennessee. His background is in Computer Science, Scientific Visualization and Analysis. His research targets high performance, scalable analysis and visualization. He is particularly interested in in situ analysis, and multi-core and distributed memory scalability.

2.2 Capstone

Barney Maccabe gave the capstone speech. He presented an initiative aimed at building a statewide data commons for the state of Arizona, aimed at providing 'visualization for everyone'. A data commons would be a shared resource for the community at large, allowing for different analysis, visualization, and conclusions to be drawn from various data in a central collection. A challenge with the data commons is how to operate on the data in a "FAIR-Findable, Accessible, Interoperable, and Reusable" and "CARE-Collective benefit, Authority to control, Responsibility, and Ethics" manner. A further challenge is having visualization systems that are intelligent and general purpose enough to operate on many different types of data across various compute platforms, and to transform the data into actionable insights.

Barney Maccabe is the Executive Director of the Institute for Computation and Data-Enabled Insight as well as a Professor in the School of Information at the University of Arizona. This new transdisciplinary institute will bring together student and faculty researchers from colleges across campus, exploring solutions for collecting and making sense of big data.

2.3 Papers

François Mazen et al., in their paper "Catalyst-ADIOS: in-transit analysis for numerical simulations using Catalyst 2 API", present a workflow using Catalyst2 for visualization and analysis of ADIOS data streams. They developed a catalyst implementation with an ADIOS backend, which means that any simulation that has Catalyst built-in can get in-transit data movement with ADIOS with no development required.

Marcel Krüger et al., in their paper "A Case Study on Providing Accessibility-Focused In-Transit Architectures for Neural Network Simulation and Analysis", present Insite, a lightweight in-transit pipeline that provides in-transit visualization and computation capability to various research applications in the neuronal network simulation domain. They describe the development process, including feedback from developers and domain experts, and discuss implications of using this system.

James Kress et al., in their paper "Inshimtu - A Lightweight In Situ Visualization 'Shim'", present a new in situ library aimed at a low-barrier way to demonstrate in situ to visualization stakeholders. In situ visualization adoption by some communities is low, so Inshimtu is designed to give a no-modification pathway for users to try in situ and begin to realize how it could transform their current workflows. The authors demonstrated the package using examples from their publicly accessible repo as well as with the WRF weather simulation.

2.4 Panel Discussion

Matthieu Dorier (Argonne National Laboratory), Jorji Nonaka (RIKEN Advanced Institute for Computational Science), François Mazen (Kitware Europe), and Marcel Krüger (RWTH Aachen University) participated in a panel on "The In Situ Ecosystem: How Evolving Technology and Research Trends are Shaping the Future of In Situ Visualization". In situ visualization is often regarded as a novel visualization technique, yet broad utilization of in situ technologies remains elusive. As technologies evolve and users continue to generate more and more data across HPC, cloud, desktop, sensors and more, in situ visualization must also evolve to meet the changing demand from users. In this panel, we want to discuss some of these changing technologies, approaches, and workloads towards understanding how in situ visualization works today, and where it needs to be positioned in the future.

Organization

Organizing Committee

Workshop Chairs

Peter Messmer   NVIDIA, Switzerland
James Kress   KAUST, Saudi Arabia

Workshop Co-Organizers

Steffen Frey   University of Groningen, The Netherlands
Kenneth Moreland   Oak Ridge National Laboratory, USA
Guido Reina   University of Stuttgart, Germany
Thomas Theussl   KAUST, Saudi Arabia
Tom Vierjahn   Westphalian University of Applied
                             Sciences, Germany

Program Committee

Andy Bauer   US Army Corps of Engineers, USA
E. Wes Bethel   San Francisco State University, USA
Jose Camata   Federal University of Juiz de Fora, Brazil
Berk Geveci   Kitware Inc., USA
Hank Childs   University of Oregon, USA
Ingrid Hotz   Linköping University, Sweden
Shaomeng Li   National Center for Atmospheric Research,
                             USA
Nicole Marsaglia   Lawrence Livermore National Laboratory,
                             USA
Gunther Weber   Lawrence Berkeley National Lab, USA

Inshimtu – A Lightweight In Situ Visualization "Shim"

James Kress[✉️][ID], Glendon Holst, Hari Prasad Dasari[ID], Shehzad Afzal[ID],
Ibrahim Hoteit[ID], and Thomas Theußl[ID]

King Abdullah University of Science and Technology (KAUST),
Thuwal, Saudi Arabia
{james.kress,glendon.holst,hari.dasari,shehzad.afzal,
ibrahim.hoteit,thomas.theussl}@kaust.edu.sa

Abstract. In situ visualization and analysis is a valuable yet under utilized commodity for the simulation community. There is hesitance or even resistance to adopting new methodologies due to the uncertainties that in situ holds for new users. There is a perceived implementation cost, maintenance cost, risk to simulation fault tolerance, potential lack of scalability, a new resource cost for running in situ processes, and more. The list of reasons why in situ is overlooked is long. We are attempting to break down this barrier by introducing Inshimtu. Inshimtu is an in situ "shim" library that enables users to try in situ before they buy into a full implementation. It does this by working with existing simulation output files, requiring no changes to simulation code. The core visualization component of Inshimtu is ParaView Catalyst, allowing it to take advantage of both interactive and non-interactive visualization pipelines that scale. We envision Inshimtu as stepping stone to show users the value of in situ and motivate them to move to one of the many existing fully-featured in situ libraries available in the community. We demonstrate the functionality of Inshimtu with a scientific workflow on the Shaheen II supercomputer.

Inshimtu is available for download at: https://github.com/kaust-vislab/Inshimtu-basic.

1 Introduction

With the launch of the worlds first exascale computer, the benefits that in situ visualization are poised to provide to the community at large are only going to grow. With each new generation of supercomputer the gap between compute and storage capacity continues to grow [2,12]. In order to combat this trend, simulation teams often turn down the frequency of their writes to disk, further opening the possibility of missing important features, while also causing video transitions over time to become jittery. As a whole, the in situ visualization community has created and maintains a number of different in situ visualization packages that are capable of not only speeding up simulations time to solution, but also will allow them to take advantage of higher temporal and spatial resolutions. However, the uptake of in situ technologies by simulation teams is still low, with

A. Bienz et al. (Eds.): ISC High Performance 2023 Workshops, LNCS 13999, pp. 257–268, 2023.
https://doi.org/10.1007/978-3-031-40843-4_19

users concerned over things such as resilience, data integrity, integration time, and code maintenance [20]. The question we must ask then is how aid simulation teams to overcome these issues whether perceived or actual?

In response to this question we present Inshimtu, an in situ shim, that allows simulation codes to experience some of the benefits of in situ with no changes required to their simulations. The idea behind this library is a low barrier try before you buy approach, where simulations can see, strategize about, and understand the different types of in situ and how they could potentially be beneficial, all with very little effort. This ease of use is accomplished through the use of file based in situ, meaning Inshimtu reads directly from the simulation output, and then all of the visualization and analysis is handled by our integration with ParaView Catalyst. The visualization pipelines and scripts used with Inshimtu are exactly the same as those used by the fully simulation-embedded version of Catalyst. So in the end, if Catalyst is chosen as the way forward for a full in situ integration by the simulation team, their existing scripts can be reused. In practice the only modification to existing simulation setup required is one additional line in the batch file to start Inshimtu in the background before the simulation. Inshimtu is thus a stepping stone from basic to complete in-situ visualization, with it's primary goal to be a low barrier to entry teaching tool to educate and inform simulation developers about the benefits they are missing by ignoring in situ techniques.

In this paper we describe Inshimtu and an associated use case on our Shaheen II supercomputer. In Sect. 3 we describe the design and implementation, as well as the underlying technologies used by Inshimtu. In Sect. 4 we present examples of Inshimtu being used for visualization and analysis tasks. We also discuss the easy instrumentation and configuration process which makes Inshimtu have a low barrier to entry. Finally in Sect. 5 we present a summary and provide some thoughts on future directions.

2   Related Work

In situ visualization is a fragmented space, with many different tools and frameworks available, each with their own dedicated use cases and implementation strategies [23]. Generally, a simulation team would need to pick either an inline [7] or in-transit [20,25] visualization tool and then redesign their code and I/O strategy around this new framework. This approach can lead to very powerful and performant visualization [13] that can not only save time vs. pos-hoc visualization but also cost [1,6,21,22,27].

Some of the most current and pervasive tools include: LibSim [30] is a library that allows simulations to use the full set of features of the VisIt [11] visualization tool. ParaView Catalyst [5] offers a similar in situ functionality for the ParaView [3] visualization tool. ADIOS2 [19] is an I/O middleware library that exposes both in-line and in-transit paradigms to a simulation through a POSIX-like API. Its in-transit capabilities are provided by a number of different data transport methods, including DataSpaces [15], DIMES [32], and FlexPath [14]. Damaris/Viz [16] provides both in-line and in-transit visualization using the Damaris I/O middleware. Ascent [24] is a fly-weight in situ infrastructure that supports both distributed-memory and shared-memory parallelism. SENSEI [4,8,9] is a generic data interface that allows transparent use of the LibSim, Catalyst, and ADIOS in situ frameworks. UDJ [17] is a communication library for transporting distributed data between parallel high performance computing applications and has demonstrated a proof of concept using an extension of Inshimtu, which is based on streaming data vs. file synchronization. Freeprocessing [18] is an in situ interposition library that works in either a synchronous or asynchronous mode. Initialize Compute Analyze Render Update Steer (ICARUS) [29] is a ParaView plug-in for in situ visualization and computational steering using a shared memory mapped HDF5 file for data access.

However, the simulation communities uptake of in situ technologies has been slow. There are a long list of reasons typically given why in situ is not used, but it generally boils down to the fact that visualization has traditionally been performed as a post-processing task, where simulation outputs are read from disk by a visualization and analysis tool. This completely un-couples the simulation from the visualization and doesn't distract the simulation team from their true goal, of getting the perfect simulation. As newer and more simulation friendly in situ integration methods are developed (such as visualization as a service [26] and Fides [28]) the resistance for adoption by simulation stake holders will likely decrease.

In the meantime however, to lower the barrier for simulations to experience and benefit from in situ, we present Inshimtu. Inshimtu allows for a low-barrier to entry with no changes needed to existing simulation codes. Simulation codes can try out pseudo-in situ easily, and see the benefits that a full in situ integration could provide. There are numerous flavors of in situ visualization, and Inshimtu falls into one of them, as categorized by an effort led by Childs et al. [10] who created a system by which an in situ systems could be described by six different axes, each with various corresponding sub-categories. Inshimtu is:

- Integration Type: Application Aware (dedicated API)
- Proximity: Off Node, Same Computing Resource
- Access: Indirect
- Division of Execution: Space Division
- Operation Controls: Both - Automatic and Human-in-the-Loop
- Output Type: Varies based on Catalyst script

While Inshimtu isn't, and doesn't purport to be, a long term solution for a simulation codes in situ integration, it can provide a much needed entry point where users can learn about and see the benefits of in situ, and then move on to a full-fledged in situ tool after they have been convinced. This step is something that has been missing in the community up until this point, with the onus of moving to in situ being left to simulation developers, which is one reason why adoption has been so low up until this point.

3   Design and Implementation of Inshimtu

Inshimtu is so named because it is our vision that this code is an in situ shim that can be used to augment existing simulations with in situ capabilities. The goal of Inshimtu is to provide a stepping stone for users coming from a post hoc processing world to try in situ with no development required. A further benefit of Inshimtu to simulation developers is that they do not have to link their codes with any external dependencies in order to test Inshimtu, simplifying the process to try in situ. Inshimtu builds on existing technologies for data visualization and is not designed to replace a full instrumentation of a simulation code with one of the many existing in situ libraries, it is simply a low barrier way for codes that have never tried in situ and don't know what it can offer or where to start, to experience the benefits in situ provides. Simulations write their output to temporary files where Inshimtu reads, processes, visualizes, creates subsets, and can even delete the original output files, saving only what it interesting or useful. The temporary nature of these files means that we can write out higher spatial and/or temporal resolutions than the filesystem might otherwise support; while, the output of the visualization pipelines produce compressed simulation artifacts to save to persistent storage. This process is illustrated in Fig. 1. Of course, the use of Inshimtu comes with a small cost. Inshimtu is not real in-situ, the traditional advantages of in-situ, like speeding up simulation execution time by avoiding costly I/O, can obviously not be exploited. Below, we first describe the existing technologies used in Inshimtu, followed by its overall design and implementation.

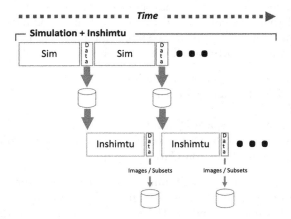

Fig. 1. A simulation plus Inshimtu pipeline over time. This pipeline denotes the simulation outputting data to disk where Inshimtu will then process that simulation output using a ParaView Catalyst pipeline. The output of this processing can be images, summary statistics, or even subsets of the simulation data.

3.1 Existing Technology

Inshimtu uses three primary existing technologies: 1. VTK 2. ParaView and 3. Catalyst.

One of the main design goals was an easy integration into existing visualization tools. We chose the open source ParaView and Catalyst for this task. We leverage the full workflow of these tools for designing in-situ pipelines.

VTK - VTK is used as the underlying data model. A number of different importers have been implemented in Inshimtu that directly make use of existing VTK readers. Using VTK means that the data can be directly passed into Catalyst for processing and visualization.

Catalyst - Catalyst is used for its ability to access the full power of ParaView. By using Catalyst scripts users are able to perform any visualization, subset, or statistics operator that they would be able to use in the full ParaView GUI. Catalyst1 is used in the current implementation of Inshimtu.

ParaView - The main function of ParaView for Inshimtu is to enable live interactive visualization. Inshimtu can connect to ParaView using Catalyst allowing users to interactively explore their data. This is particularly useful for users when they are designing their Catalyst scripts and visualization operations for large runs.

3.2 Inshimtu Design

Inshimtu is composed of four primary components: 1. core 2. sentinels 3. utils and 4. processing.

Core - This component comprises the basic Inshimtu infrastructure (MPI, coordinators, initial argument parsing).

Sentinels - This component is responsible for setting up file system watchers to watch for new files to process, as well as watching for the *done* signal that comes at the end of a batch job.

Utils - This is a helper component that consists of *help* and *logging* classes, allowing for easier debugging when developing new components.

Processing - This component is the main workhorse within Inshimtu. It contains the Catalyst adapter, sets up pipelines, and contains the various importer classes. Currently Inshimtu uses Catalyst1. There are four current implemented importers: 1. RawNetCDF 2. XMLImage 3. XMLPImage and 4. XMLRectilinear. Implementing new importers for different simulation codes is straightforward when making use of existing VTK importers. Thus, Inshimtu can easily be extended to accommodate reading new simulation output.

3.3   Using Inshimtu

Enabling Inshimtu amounts to adding a line to the batch file before running a simulation code. No changes to the simulation code are required. The simulation code is not aware of Inshimtu, and no coupling or synchronization exists between the simulation and Inshimtu. Once the simulation is actively running and saving its outputs to disk, Inshimtu takes those outputs from disk, processes them with a Catalyst script (users can even connect live with ParaView if desired), saves the outputs (images, extracts, summary statistics, etc.), and then watches and waits for new outputs to appear. Once the simulation terminates, the batch script updates a *"*.done"* file which Inshimtu watches in order to know when all processing is complete. One important feature of Inshimtu is that it can be enabled to remove simulation output files after it processes them, thus only keeping its outputs on disk, drastically saving storage space during a long simulation.

There are two ways to launch and configure Inshimtu. First, Inshimtu can parse a JSON file with the necessary arguments (see Fig. 2). This JSON file (see Fig. 3) can either pass a link to a catalyst script, or the script can be embedded into the JSON file. In addition to specific catalyst commands, this JSON file can be used to specify specific pre- or post-processing commands that are run before or after the catalyst functions. The benefit of this is that data can be decompressed by Inshimtu before use if needed, moved, modified, then processed by Catalyst, and then the original data and the output from Catalyst can be manipulated further if needed. Additionally, this script can tell Inshimtu to only process specific variables, which directory to watch for new simulation files, as well as pass control information to tell Inshimtu when to start and stop. Second, all of the required arguments can be specified on the command line (see Fig. 4).

```
1    srun ./Inshimtu -c ../testing/configs/png_watchDir_QVAPOR.json
```

Fig. 2. Launching Inshimtu using the JSON configuration file detailed in Fig. 3.

We believe that the simple interface for using Inshimtu, coupled with the use of well established existing visualization technologies, creates a convenient way to promote in situ to the simulation community. It is our goal that this code be used to educate simulation developers and users to the value of in situ, and guide them in creating true in situ integrations in their codes.

4   Inshimtu Use Cases

In this section we describe two different visualization case studies that demonstrate the functionality of Inshimtu as described in Sect. 3. The first case study in Sect. 4.1 uses Inshimtu to perform basic post processing tasks, demonstrating the Catalyst pipelines and basic Inshimtu functionality. The second case study in

```
 1   { "input": {                              12        "QVAPOR"
 2       "watch": {                            13      ]
 3         "directory_path": "testing",        14    },
 4         "files_regex": "\\w*(.pvti)"        15    "control": {
 5       }                                     16      "done_watchfile": "testing.done",
 6     },                                      17      "initial_connection_wait_secs": 0,
 7     "pipeline": {                           18      "catalyst_importer_nodes": [
 8       "scripts": [                          19        "0"
 9         "../testing/pipelines/pngQVAPOR.py" 20      ],
10       ],                                    21      "delete_processed_input_files": false }}
11       "variables": [
```

Fig. 3. Inshimtu JSON code example that watches a directory for *.pvti files and then processes them with a Catalyst Python script.

```
1   srun ./Inshimtu  -w testing
2                    -d testing.done
3                    -s ../testing/pipelines/pngQVAPOR.py
4                    -f ''\w*(.pvti)''
5                    -v QVAPOR
```

Fig. 4. Launching Inshimtu using explicit command line arguments to match the pipeline described in Fig. 3.

Sect. 4.2 uses WRF, the Weather Research and Forecasting Model [31] run on the Shaheen II supercomputer. Finally, we discuss the results and instrumentation process.

Inshimtu Release. The following two subsections make use of Inshimtu and reference scripts and examples available in our GitHub repository: https://github.com/kaust-vislab/Inshimtu-basic.

4.1   Post Processing with Inshimtu

Inshimtu is designed to be run during an active simulation, but since it is an in situ shim, and designed to work from files, it can easily be used to post process data as well. In fact, this is the perfect way to test catalyst scripts, different Inshimtu settings, and easily process existing simulation output. An example of how to do this is available in our repository, and uses the script shown in Fig. 5

To setup this example, first build Inshimtu according to the *README.md* instructions. Once Inshimtu is built *cd* into the build directory, in order to prepare to run the *png_ enumerated_ QVAPOR.json* example. This example will process all existing files specified in the example script, and exit when all files have been processed. It uses the Catalyst script *pngQVAPOR.py* to transfer data to ParaView, if watching live using ParaView, and creates a **.png* image as output. To run this example use the following steps:

1. Create a directory called *testing* where data files that are to be processed by Inshimtu will be copied
2. Copy the example data files to this directory: *cp -r ../testing/data/wrf/pvti/* testing*

```
 1  { "input": {                                   18        ]
 2       "initial_files": [                        19      },
 3          "testing/dataoutfile_QVAPOR_00.pvti",  20      "pipeline": {
 4          "testing/dataoutfile_QVAPOR_01.pvti",  21        "scripts": [
 5          "testing/dataoutfile_QVAPOR_02.pvti",  22          "../testing/pipelines/pngQVAPOR.py"
 6          "testing/dataoutfile_QVAPOR_03.pvti",  23        ],
 7          "testing/dataoutfile_QVAPOR_04.pvti",  24        "variables": [
 8          "testing/dataoutfile_QVAPOR_05.pvti",  25          "QVAPOR"
 9          "testing/dataoutfile_QVAPOR_06.pvti",  26        ]
10          "testing/dataoutfile_QVAPOR_07.pvti",  27      },
11          "testing/dataoutfile_QVAPOR_08.pvti",  28      "control": {
12          "testing/dataoutfile_QVAPOR_09.pvti",  29        "initial_connection_wait_secs": 10,
13          "testing/dataoutfile_QVAPOR_10.pvti",  30        "catalyst_inporter_nodes": [
14          "testing/dataoutfile_QVAPOR_11.pvti",  31          "0"
15          "testing/dataoutfile_QVAPOR_12.pvti",  32        ]
16          "testing/dataoutfile_QVAPOR_13.pvti",  33      }
17          "testing/dataoutfile_QVAPOR_14.pvti"   34  }
```

Fig. 5. Inshimtu JSON code example that processes an enumerated list of existing data files with a Catalyst Python script.

3. To view the data live in ParaView enable the Catalyst connection in ParaView
    - Select *Catalyst/Connect...* from the ParaView menu
    - Click *OK* in Catalyst Server Port dialog to accept connections from Inshimtu
    - Click *OK* in Ready for Catalyst Connections dialog
    - Select *Catalyst/Pause Simulation* from ParaView menu
4. Run Inshimtu:
    ./Inshimtu -c ../testing/configs/png_ enumerated_ QVAPOR.json
5. View the results in ParaView as well as the images saved to disk

There are several more examples in the *testing/configs* directory that you can try, each one being a derivation of one of Inshimtu's features, or using a different data type. View these files to explore other features of Inshimtu.

4.2   WRF + Inshimtu

For this use case we used the WRF simulation code run on Shaheen II at KAUST. WRF was chosen as an example code as there is a large user community at KAUST and it can produce vast quantities of data when looking at fine temporal resolutions. We ran wrf configured to simulate an area approximately 50 KM in a square centered around Jeddah Saudi Arabia and to create an extreme rain event. The premise behind this visualization is that the scientists were interested in creating a movie of various variables each time the simulation was run, with the catch being, that the phenomena of interest only occurred when simulating at a fine temporal resolution; a great use case for in situ.

Inshimtu was run on a separate compute cluster called Ibex, which is primarily dedicated to running various analysis workflows. Ibex and Shaheen have access to a common filesystem, so Inshimtu was able to read the files as they were produced by WRF. This visualization used a very similar setup to that of the *png_ enumerated_ QVAPOR.json* example and the *pngQVAPOR.py* catalyst script. We just added more complex interactions and more variables. As we were using Catalyst we could also interactively explore the data live in ParaView by having the Ibex Catalyst script connect back to our local desktop. Figure 6 gives an example visualization of the area of interest around Jeddah showing four primary variables.

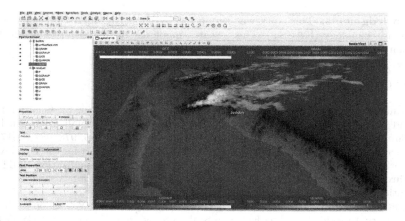

Fig. 6. Example visualization from Catalyst using Inshimtu of one of timesteps in the wrf simulation.

These two use cases are designed to show the functionality of Inshimtu, and the usefulness of being able to enable an in situ shim for simulations that do not yet have built-in in situ capabilities. While Inshimtu will not save time or cost of running a simulation, it allows for repeatable scriptable visualizations that can be interactive and demonstrate the function and power of in situ to a wide audience.

5   Conclusions and Future Work

The visualization community is investing heavily into creating and expanding various in situ visualization libraries and frameworks. These efforts are becoming well established and are ready for integration into simulation codes. However, community adoption of in situ is low, and it is difficult to quickly demonstrate the benefits of in situ for each and every simulation code. Therefore, we presented Inshimtu as a stepping stone towards full in situ visualization workflows. Inshimtu is a low barrier to entry in situ "shim" that works without modifying existing simulation codes, allowing for users to try before they buy into a full in situ integration. We also demonstrated Inshimtu usage on desktop machines as well as a use case on the Shaheen II supercomputer.

In the future, we would like to extend Inshimtu to work with more file types and demonstrate the benefits of using an in situ shim approach vs. a traditional post hoc approach at larger scale. We would also like to update the code base to use the newest iteration of Catalyst. We are also continuing work on integrating a data streaming library into a second version of Inshimtu that will allow simulation codes to bypass the filesystem, which is a current limitation. Finally, we hope to demonstrate the benefits of in situ to other codes run at KAUST and around the world using Inshimtu, helping to promote broader in situ adoption.

Acknowledgments. This work was supported by King Abdullah University of Science and Technology (KAUST). This research made use of the resources of the Visualization and Supercomputing Laboratories at KAUST.

References

1. Adhinarayanan, V., Feng, W., Rogers, D., Ahrens, J., Pakin, S.: Characterizing and modeling power and energy for extreme-scale in-situ visualization. In: IEEE Parallel and Distributed Processing Symposium (IPDPS), pp. 978–987 (2017)
2. Ahern, S., et al.: Scientific discovery at the exascale. In: Report for the DOE ASCR Workshop on Exascale Data Management, Analysis, and Visualization (2011)
3. Ahrens, J., Geveci, B., Law, C.: ParaView: an end-user tool for large-data visualization. In: The Visualization Handbook, pp. 717–731 (2005)
4. Ayachit, U., et al.: The SENSEI generic in situ interface. In: Workshop on In Situ Infrastructures for Enabling Extreme-Scale Analysis and Visualization (ISAV), pp. 40–44 (2016)
5. Ayachit, U., et al.: ParaView catalyst: enabling in situ data analysis and visualization. In: Workshop on In Situ Infrastructures for Enabling Extreme-Scale Analysis and Visualization (ISAV), pp. 25–29 (2015)
6. Ayachit, U., et al.: Performance analysis, design considerations, and applications of extreme-scale in situ infrastructures. In: ACM/IEEE Conference for High Performance Computing, Networking, Storage and Analysis (SC16) (2016)
7. Bauer, A.C., et al.: In situ methods, infrastructures, and applications on high performance computing platforms, a state-of-the-art (STAR) report. In: Computer Graphics Forum, Proceedings of Eurovis 2016, vol. 35, no. 3 (2016)
8. Bethel, E.W., et al.: The sensei generic in situ interface: tool and processing portability at scale. In: Childs, H., Bennett, J.C., Garth, C. (eds.) In Situ Visualization for Computational Science. Mathematics and Visualization, pp. 281–306. Springer, Cham (2022). https://doi.org/10.1007/978-3-030-81627-8_13
9. Bethel, E.W., et al.: Proximity portability and in transit, m-to-n data partitioning and movement in sensei. In: Childs, H., Bennett, J.C., Garth, C. (eds.) In Situ Visualization for Computational Science. Mathematics and Visualization, pp. 439–460. Springer, Cham (2022). https://doi.org/10.1007/978-3-030-81627-8_20
10. Childs, H., et al.: A terminology for in situ visualization and analysis systems. Int. J. High Perform. Comput. Appl. **34**(6), 676–691 (2020)
11. Childs, H., et al.: A contract-based system for large data visualization. In: 2005 Proceedings of IEEE Visualization, pp. 190–198 (2005)
12. Childs, H., et al.: Extreme scaling of production visualization software on diverse architectures. IEEE Comput. Graph. Appl. **30**(3), 22–31 (2010)
13. Childs, H., et al.: Visualization at extreme scale concurrency. In: High Performance Visualization: Enabling Extreme-Scale Scientific Insight. CRC Press, Boca Raton (2012)
14. Dayal, J., et al.: Flexpath: type-based publish/subscribe system for large-scale science analytics. In: IEEE/ACM International Symposium on Cluster, Cloud and Grid Computing (CCGRID) (2014)

15. Docan, C., et al.: Dataspaces: an interaction and coordination framework for coupled simulation workflows. Clust. Comput. **15**(2), 163–181 (2012)
16. Dorier, M., et al.: Damaris/viz: a nonintrusive, adaptable and user-friendly in situ visualization framework. In: IEEE Symposium on Large-Scale Data Analysis and Visualization (LDAV), pp. 67–75 (2013)
17. Esposito, A., Holst, G.: In situ visualization of WRF data using universal data junction. In: Jagode, H., Anzt, H., Ltaief, H., Luszczek, P. (eds.) ISC High Performance 2021. LNCS, vol. 12761, pp. 475–483. Springer, Cham (2021). https://doi.org/10.1007/978-3-030-90539-2_32
18. Fogal, T., Proch, F., Schiewe, A., Hasemann, O., Kempf, A., Krüger, J.: FreeProcessing: transparent in situ visualization via data interception. In: Eurographics Symposium on Parallel Graphics and Visualization: EG PGV: [Proceedings]/Sponsored by Eurographics Association in Cooperation with ACM SIG-GRAPH. Eurographics Symposium on Parallel Graphics and Visualization, vol. 2014, p. 49. NIH Public Access (2014)
19. Godoy, W.F., et al.: ADIOS 2: the adaptable input output system. A framework for high-performance data management. SoftwareX **12**, 100561 (2020)
20. Kress, J., et al.: Loosely coupled in situ visualization: a perspective on why it's here to stay. In: Workshop on In Situ Infrastructures for Enabling Extreme-Scale Analysis and Visualization (ISAV), pp. 1–6 (2015)
21. Kress, J., et al.: Comparing the efficiency of in situ visualization paradigms at scale. In: Weiland, M., Juckeland, G., Trinitis, C., Sadayappan, P. (eds.) ISC High Performance 2019. LNCS, vol. 11501, pp. 99–117. Springer, Cham (2019). https://doi.org/10.1007/978-3-030-20656-7_6
22. Kress, J., et al.: Opportunities for cost savings with in-transit visualization. In: Sadayappan, P., Chamberlain, B.L., Juckeland, G., Ltaief, H. (eds.) ISC High Performance 2020. LNCS, vol. 12151, pp. 146–165. Springer, Cham (2020). https://doi.org/10.1007/978-3-030-50743-5_8
23. Kress, J.M.: In-line vs. in-transit in situ: which technique to use at scale? (2020)
24. Larsen, M., et al.: The ALPINE in situ infrastructure: ascending from the ashes of strawman. In: Workshop on In Situ Infrastructures on Enabling Extreme-Scale Analysis and Visualization (ISAV), pp. 42–46 (2017)
25. Moreland, K., et al.: Examples of in transit visualization. In: Proceedings of the 2nd International Workshop on Petascale Data Analytics: Challenges and Opportunities, pp. 1–6. ACM (2011)
26. Pugmire, D., et al.: Visualization as a service for scientific data. In: Nichols, J., Verastegui, B., Maccabe, A.B., Hernandez, O., Parete-Koon, S., Ahearn, T. (eds.) SMC 2020. CCIS, vol. 1315, pp. 157–174. Springer, Cham (2020). https://doi.org/10.1007/978-3-030-63393-6_11
27. Pugmire, D., et al.: Visualization and analysis for near-real-time decision making in distributed workflows. In: 2016 IEEE International Parallel and Distributed Processing Symposium Workshops, pp. 1007–1013. IEEE (2016)
28. Pugmire, D., et al.: Fides: a general purpose data model library for streaming data. In: Jagode, H., Anzt, H., Ltaief, H., Luszczek, P. (eds.) ISC High Performance 2021. LNCS, vol. 12761, pp. 495–507. Springer, Cham (2021). https://doi.org/10.1007/978-3-030-90539-2_34
29. Rivi, M., Calori, L., Muscianisi, G., Slavnic, V.: In-situ visualization: state-of-the-art and some use cases. PRACE White Paper; PRACE, Brussels, Belgium (2012)
30. Whitlock, B., Favre, J., Meredith, J.: Parallel in situ coupling of simulation with a fully featured visualization system. In: Proceedings of the 11th Eurographics conference on Parallel Graphics and Visualization, pp. 101–109 (2011)

31. WRF – The Weather Research and Forecasting Model, v. 3.7.1 (2015)
32. Zhang, F., et al.: In-memory staging and data-centric task placement for coupled scientific simulation workflows. Concurr. Comput.: Pract. Exp. **29**(12), e4147 (2017). https://doi.org/10.1002/cpe.4147

Catalyst-ADIOS2: In Transit Analysis for Numerical Simulations Using Catalyst 2 API

François Mazen$^{(\boxtimes)}$, Lucas Givord, and Charles Gueunet

Kitware Europe, Villeurbanne, France
`francois.mazen@kitware.com`
`http://www.kitware.eu`

Abstract. In this article, we present a novel approach to bring in transit capabilities to numerical simulations which are already able to do in situ analysis with Catalyst 2. This approach combines the stable ABI of Catalyst 2, to replace the in situ backend at run-time, with a dedicated implementation that pushes data to the ADIOS2 SST Engine. At the end point of this engine, on the visualization nodes, the Catalyst 2 API calls are replayed using the Catalyst-ParaView implementation. This removes most of the blocking calls in the numerical simulation during output and analysis. This approach is released publicly under a permissive license and it opens lots of possibilities to improve performance of large numerical simulations by switching analysis backend without rebuilding the simulation code.

Keywords: In Situ · In Transit · ADIOS2 · Catalyst 2 · I/O · numerical simulation · HPC · ParaView

1 Introduction

Nowadays, some of the most expensive operations of many numerical simulations are input and output (I/O) operations [1]. The time spent reading and writing to the storage system is the most critical part of a process as it may slow down significantly the whole process and reduce the time to result for engineering studies. Another issue is usually the lack of early feedback during a simulation run, especially if advanced rendering like volumetric rendering is required. In situ analysis has been developed to circumvent these two problems. Reducing the amount of time the data is written and doing live data reduction are two separate methods to circumvent the mentioned problem. For early feedback, the live visualization is the de facto solution to inspect the data early. Because the analysis is done with the data loaded from memory of the numerical simulation, in a zero-copy way, the simulation must stop and wait for the analysis to complete. This is a major drawback of in situ analysis, as it wastes useful computation time on analysis time. Many of the current in situ solutions try to minimize these interruptions

© The Author(s), under exclusive license to Springer Nature Switzerland AG 2023
A. Bienz et al. (Eds.): ISC High Performance 2023 Workshops, LNCS 13999, pp. 269–276, 2023.
https://doi.org/10.1007/978-3-031-40843-4_20

by using as many computational resources as possible and return the call to the simulation as early as possible. This is the purpose of VTK-m [2], which leverages data parallelism, including GPU, to do computation for the analysis pipeline.

Another drawback of the in situ approach is that the visualization or analysis is done on the same computation nodes as the simulation. More than anything, the node for simulation may not match requirements for visualization like providing GPU or rendering libraries like OpenGL, OSPRay or NVidia OptiX. Additionally in this setting, the number of visualization processes should match the number of computation processes. As the algorithm for numerical simulations and visual analysis are different, one configuration, tailored for heavy computation, may not match the requirements for analysis.

In transit visualization tries to strike a compromise between a heavy copy on visualization nodes and zero-copy, by having a quick copy on nodes close to the simulations. The idea is to set up dedicated visualization nodes and stream the data to these resources to avoid blocking the simulation, hence speeding up the process. The visualization nodes could have a dedicated hardware and software configuration finely tuned for visualization like dedicated GPUs or optimized libraries, and the number of visualization processes could be different from the number of computation processes. Better overall time to result is expected in the in transit case for most workflows thanks to additional concurrency and better orchestration of computational resources. However some limitations of in transit analysis have been demonstrated by James Kress in [3].

Overall, this short paper proposes the following contributions. First, a new Catalyst 2 implementation named Catalyst-ADIOS2 have been developed in order to switch from in situ analysis to in transit analysis without changing nor rebuilding the simulation code. Second, the in transit capability is highly configurable thanks to ADIOS2 XML configuration file. For example, the user can choose and finely tune the IO engine for a particular case, which is very common in HPC environments. Third, the implementation is publicly available [4] under a permissive license to foster community usage and broader adoption.

2   Related Work

The main challenge of in transit visualization is to copy or stream data in an efficient manner to reduce the interruption of the numerical simulation. The reference library for this usage is ADIOS2: The Adaptable Input/Output System version 2 [5], which acts like a data bus to manage data in an efficient way in an HPC context. An important benefit of ADIOS2 is its ability to deal with various memory backends including GPU specific frameworks like CUDA. Several analysis solutions rely on this backend like Sensei [6] or Ascent [7]. Sensei is an open-source, generic in situ interface that allows parallel simulations or other data producers to code-couple to parallel third-party endpoints. These endpoints may be applications or tools/methods like Catalyst-ParaView, Libsim or ADIOS2. Melissa [8] is also a solution for in transit parameter sensitivity analysis of very large datasets, which avoid intermediate files. It uses a clever Two

Stage Data Transfer in order to limit the number of messages sent to the analysis server. Another interesting application for in transit is the Shared In Situ Visualization Service (SERVIZ) [9] which leverages the power of micro-service architecture to keep the visualization nodes busy. For numerical simulations that already push data to the ADIOS2 framework, the Fides [10] project allows to describe the data for a Catalyst-ParaView interaction. The main drawback of the Fides approach is that your simulation needs to use the ADIOS2 framework as a build-time dependency.

3   Catalyst-ADIOS2

This paper describes an approach to provide in transit capabilities for numerical simulations that already push data to Catalyst 2, with minimal modification of the simulation instrumentation, ideally without modifying the implementation. These advantages, as described in the introduction, are to greatly reduce blocking time of the simulation and to use dedicated computation resources for the live data analysis or data reduction.

Our research showed that ADIOS2 is the current state of the art for efficient data movement in this context. Thanks to the minimal and stable ABI of Catalyst 2, as well as the ability to change the Catalyst 2 implementation at run-time, we propose a new Catalyst 2 implementation that leverages ADIOS2 capabilities.

The process is divided in two parts. The first part is the conversion from Catalyst 2 data to ADIOS2 data and being able to run the Sustainable Staging Transport (SST) engine. This engine allows direct connection of data producers and consumers and it is designed for use in HPC environments. It supports full MxN data distribution, where the number of ranks between the reader and the writer may differ. The second part of this process is being able to replay the Catalyst 2 calls (initialize, execute, finalize) on the visualization nodes using the data streamed by ADIOS2. These two elements are described in what follows.

Figure 1 describes the global process of in transit compared to the in situ equivalent. The Catalyst-ADIOS2 implementation converts the data from the Catalyst 2 format, based on the Conduit library [11], to ADIOS2 format. Then ADIOS2 manages the data streaming to the visualization cluster where the replay runs. The replay process will then convert the ADIOS2 data to Conduit nodes and call the Catalyst-ParaView implementation to do the analysis.

In Catalyst-ADIOS2, the challenge is to convert in an efficient way the data to be streamed via ADIOS2 engine. Catalyst 2 uses Conduit nodes, with the Mesh Blueprint protocol [11] to allow zero-copy of the data, by just describing the memory layout. In Catalyst-ADIOS2 implementation, the meshes from Conduit are mapped to ADIOS2 variables to describe the geometry, the topology and the fields associated with points and cells. This copy mechanism handles all the specific aspects of the zero-copy mapping from Conduit like offsets, strides and multidimensional arrays. Catalyst 2 also uses Conduit nodes to configure the initialization and the finalization of the process. In this case, the nodes contain

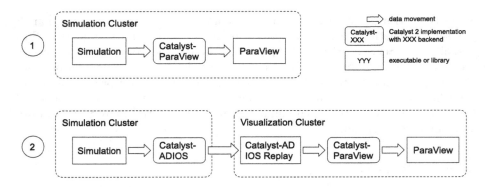

Fig. 1. Comparison of the in situ process with Catalyst-ParaView (1) and the in transit process with Catalyst-ADIOS2 (2).

only small metadata. Converting these small nodes to ADIOS2 variables would introduce overhead for no reason, so the nodes are simply serialized to json and sent through ADIOS2 as string attributes.

For the end points, the visualization nodes, we developed a specific program called Catalyst-ADIOS2 Replay, in order to replay the exact calls to Catalyst 2 API that the simulation performed on the computation nodes. In this case, the mechanism is a mirror of Catalyst-ADIOS2 where initialization and finalization data are converted from json to Conduit node, and execution data are converted back to Conduit nodes with the Mesh Blueprint Protocol. The Replay executable loads the Catalyst-ParaView implementation and it replays the initialize, execute and finalize calls to the Catalyst 2 API. For each of these methods, the associated Conduit node is rebuilt using the metadata and data which have been pushed to the ADIOS2 engine. This mechanism ensures that the analysis will be exactly the same as with in situ analysis. Catalyst 2 API also defines the result method dedicated for steering, which is not supported at the moment.

4   Results

The Catalyst-ADIOS2 approach was successfully used with the Livermore Unstructured Lagrangian Explicit Shock Hydrodynamics (LULESH) simulation code [12] which solves a simple Sedov blast problem. The version used was the Catalyst 2 implementation presented at the ISC22 tutorial about "In Situ Analysis and Visualization with Catalyst-ParaView and" [13]. The tested version of Catalyst-ADIOS2 supports explicit topologies and explicit geometry only because it was initially built for a confidential industrial code that outputs unstructured data. Of course, implicit topology and implicit geometry will be supported at some point, but this limitation forced us to slightly modify the LULESH Catalyst 2 Adaptor to output an unstructured grid instead of a structured grid. The only modifications were to pass the element connectivity in the `catalyst_execute` Conduit node, to change the mesh type accordingly and to provide the correct MPI elements per rank count. Beside these minor modifications which should not be required with future versions of Catalyst-ADIOS2, the rest of the LULESH code remained unchanged, showing that Catalyst 2 stable ABI [14] is promising. The machine used for the experiment was an Intel i9-12900K processor using 24 cores running at 6.500 GHz, 128 GB of memory and a NVidia A6000 graphic card. We use one process for the numerical simulation and one process for the Catalyst-ADIOS2 replay executable. We used ADIOS2 version 2.8.3 and ParaView version 5.11.0.

The LULESH problem size was 128, leading to a cube of $128 \times 128 \times 128$ elements. For the first experiment, we created a visualization pipeline that computes a slice of the data with origin at the center of the volume and plane normal [1.0, 0.0, −1.0], in addition to a 3D surface representation screenshot. Figure 2 displays results at time-step 1000 for in situ and in transit approaches for the 3D screenshot and the slice data reduction. A check with Imagemagick `compare` tool using the PSNR metric showed no difference between the images generated by in situ and in transit approaches.

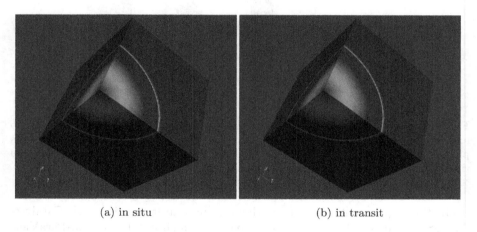

(a) in situ   (b) in transit

Fig. 2. Images generated by the in situ approach Catalyst-ParaView (left) and the in transit approach Catalyst-ADIOS2 (right). Images are identical.

We then checked the performance of numerical simulation using in transit with Catalyst-ADIOS2 compared to the same numerical simulation using in situ with Catalyst-ParaView. We prepared two pipelines. The first one is the previously described one that computes a slice and saves a screenshot of the 3D surface rendering. This pipeline has short execution times. The second pipeline generates a cinema database, which is costly to compute because it takes 1260 screenshots all around of the data at each time step. We also ran the numerical simulation without any analysis as a reference to compare the performance of each approach.

Results are summarized in Fig. 3. The graph depicts the total running time and the performance loss compared to the reference run. The formula to compute the performance loss is:

$$loss = (T_x - T_0)/T_0 \qquad (1)$$

where T_0 is the total running time of the simulation without any analysis, and T_x is the running time of the simulation with in situ or in transit analysis.

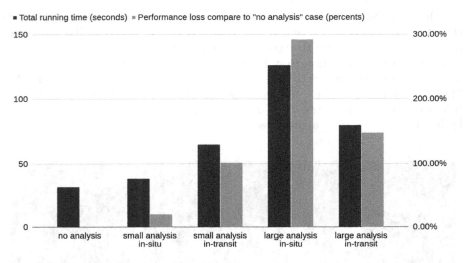

Fig. 3. Performance comparison of in situ and in transit analysis for three use cases: no analysis (left), small analysis pipeline (second and third bar groups) and large analysis pipeline (fourth and fifth bar groups). The left Y-axis is for total running time, the right Y-axis is for performance comparison.

In this experiment, we can see that the in transit pipeline with Catalyst-ADIOS2 speeds up the simulation compared to in situ with Catalyst-ParaView only when the analysis pipeline is significant. The performance loss with the small pipeline is mainly due to the overhead of data transfer with ADIOS2 whereas in situ analysis uses zero-copy mechanism to minimize data copy. Hopefully, similar results have been reported with the CloverLeaf3D application [3]. The experiment ran the ADIOS2 SST engine where several parameters could be tuned to achieve best performance. In addition, our experiment used a single powerful workstation which is not a true HPC, where computation nodes are linked together with dedicated fast network technologies like Infiniband. Hence we hope that the performance bottleneck that we identified, which is the data transfer cost though a shared file system on hard drive, would be mitigated in HPC context with fine tuned SST parameters.

The code of this experiment is publicly available [15].

5   Perspectives and Limitations

This approach opens lots of possibilities about having end-points or doing advanced analysis. In the classic use-case for in situ, we target data reduction and live monitoring, but several new use cases may be imagined like training Deep Learning model live, computing reduced order models (ROM) or steering the simulation from ParaView GUI.

Moving very large amounts of data to the visualization nodes could be very costly and our experiment showed that the overhead should be considered depending on the use case. So a new multi-tier reduction approach could be to set up an hybrid in situ in transit system, where the data are first reduced in situ via Catalyst-ParaView, then the reduced data are sent to the visualization node for analysis via Catalyst-ADIOS2. This approach may be mandatory for very large simulations. As the simulation is not blocked anymore, this approach also emphasized that the analysis pipeline could be more advanced and more time consuming. Some approaches like creating a large cinema database, experimenting with several camera placements, or running costly ParaView filters could be set in a time-effective manner by offloading the work via in transit approach.

Beside the encouraging results of this approach, we noticed several limitations. The first is that by passing data through several technologies (Conduit, ADIOS2, ParaView, VTK), only the smallest common subset of data type would be supported. For instance many advanced data types from VTK like Advanced Mesh Refinement (AMR) or Hyper Tree Grid (HTG) are not compatible with this approach yet. Any new datatype should be added to every pipeline's technologies to be usable in this approach. Another limitation is the idle time of the visualization nodes. In many cases, the analysis time would be small compared to the computation time and the visualization nodes may stay idle for long periods. Some solutions like SERVIZ [9] would circumvent this problem by sharing the rendering node power between several simulations.

6   Conclusion

We presented a new approach to bring in transit capabilities to existing simulation code that are already instrumented with Catalyst 2, with a concrete implementation named Catalyst-ADIOS2, publicly available [4]. Our approach showed that in certain cases we could reduce numerical simulation time by 60% compared to the in situ approach, and use dedicated visualization nodes for live analysis and data reduction, without modifying the numerical simulation code. This approach, where the simulation is not blocked anymore by in situ analysis, opens lots of opportunities for new use cases for live interactions with large simulations, like deep learning model training or larger analysis pipelines which require dedicated resources like powerful GPU or TPU. The capabilities of Catalyst 2 to switch backend at run time should allow quick and easy experimentation to find the best trade-offs between data transfer time and analysis time.

References

1. Bauer, A.C.: In situ methods, infrastructures, and applications on high performance computing platforms. In: Computer Graphics Forum, vol. 35, no. 3, pp. 577–597 (2016)
2. Moreland, K., et al.: VTK-m: accelerating the visualization toolkit for massively threaded architectures. IEEE Comput. Graph. Appl. **36**(3), 48–58 (2016). https://doi.org/10.1109/MCG.2016.48
3. Kress, J., et al.: Opportunities for cost savings with in-transit visualization. In: Sadayappan, P., Chamberlain, B.L., Juckeland, G., Ltaief, H. (eds.) ISC High Performance 2020. LNCS, vol. 12151, pp. 146–165. Springer, Cham (2020). https://doi.org/10.1007/978-3-030-50743-5_8
4. https://gitlab.kitware.com/paraview/adioscatalyst
5. Godoy, W.F., et al.: ADIOS 2: the adaptable input output system. a framework for high-performance data management. In: SoftwareX, vol. 12, p. 100561 (2020). https://doi.org/10.1016/j.softx.2020.100561
6. Loring, B., et al.: Improving performance of M-to-N processing and data redistribution in in transit analysis and visualization. In: Eurographics Symposium on Parallel Graphics and Visualization (2020). https://doi.org/10.2312/pgv.20201073
7. Larsen, M., et al.: The alpine in situ infrastructure: ascending from the ashes of strawman. In: Proceedings of the In Situ Infrastructures on Enabling Extreme-Scale Analysis and Visualization, pp. 42–46 (2017)
8. Terraz, T., Ribes, A., Fournier, Y., Iooss, B., Raffin, B.: Melissa: large scale in transit sensitivity analysis avoiding intermediate files. SC 2017: International Conference for High Performance Computing, pp. 1–14. Storage and Analysis, Denver, CO, USA, Networking (2017)
9. Ramesh, S., Childs, H., Malony, A.: SERVIZ: a shared in situ visualization service. In: SC 2022: International Conference for High Performance Computing, Networking, Storage and Analysis (SC) (SC). Dallas, TX, US 2022, pp. 277–290 (2022)
10. Pugmire, D.: Fides: a general purpose data model library for streaming data. In: Jagode, H., Anzt, H., Ltaief, H., Luszczek, P. (eds.) ISC High Performance 2021. LNCS, vol. 12761, pp. 495–507. Springer, Cham (2021). https://doi.org/10.1007/978-3-030-90539-2_34
11. Conduit: a successful strategy for describing and sharing data in situ. In: Presented at the ISAV 2022 Workshop, held in conjunction with SC 2022, 13th November 2022, Dallas, TX (2022)
12. Karlin, I. et al., LULESH 2.0 updates and changes, pp. 1–9 (2013). LLNL-TR-641973
13. https://github.com/jfavre/InSitu-Vis-Tutorial2022
14. Ayachit, U.: Catalyst revised: rethinking the ParaView in situ analysis and visualization API. In: Jagode, H., Anzt, H., Ltaief, H., Luszczek, P. (eds.) ISC High Performance 2021. LNCS, vol. 12761, pp. 484–494. Springer, Cham (2021). https://doi.org/10.1007/978-3-030-90539-2_33
15. https://gitlab.kitware.com/francois.mazen/lulesh-adios-catalyst

A Case Study on Providing Accessibility-Focused In-Transit Architectures for Neural Network Simulation and Analysis

Marcel Krüger[✉][ID], Simon Oehrl[ID], Torsten Wolfgang Kuhlen[ID], and Tim Gerrits[ID]

Visual Computing Institute, RWTH Aachen University, Aachen, Germany
krueger@vis.rwth-aachen.de

Abstract. Due to the ever-increasing availability of high-performance computing infrastructure, developers can simulate increasingly complex models. However, the increased complexity comes with new challenges regarding data processing and visualization due to the sheer size of simulations. Exploring simulation results needs to be handled efficiently via in-situ/in-transit analysis during run-time. However, most existing in-transit solutions require sophisticated and prior knowledge and significant alteration to existing simulation and visualization code, which produces a high entry barrier for many projects. In this work, we report how Insite, a lightweight in-transit pipeline, provided in-transit visualization and computation capability to various research applications in the neuronal network simulation domain. We describe the development process, including feedback from developers and domain experts, and discuss implications.

Keywords: In-transit visualization · In-transit processing · Neuronal networks · Simulation tools

1 Introduction

Today's wide availability of fast and affordable high-performance computing hardware gave an increasing number of communities access to distributed systems that can simulate large-scale models. However, existing visualizations could not keep up with the scaling that was achieved for simulations. This, in turn, has led to new paradigms and challenges within the visualization and data analysis communities (c.f., [5,16]). While much research has focused on developing solutions that enable large-scale data visualization, the proposed solutions are often application-specific and tailored to specific use cases. Unfortunately, application-specific solutions require a lot of resources to develop and restrict accessibility for new users. However, the advantages of providing in-situ/in-transit capabilities are so predominant that experts call for a new paradigm of "pervasive in-situ visualization (P-ISAV)" [17] to make it available everywhere. There exist solutions that aim toward widespread use of in-situ/in-transit functionality by providing generalized frameworks and tools [2,7,9,15,23]. Many of them, however, introduce new

© The Author(s), under exclusive license to Springer Nature Switzerland AG 2023
A. Bienz et al. (Eds.): ISC High Performance 2023 Workshops, LNCS 13999, pp. 277–287, 2023.
https://doi.org/10.1007/978-3-031-40843-4_21

dependencies for users and are difficult to integrate, especially when retrofitting is needed. This is primarily because the analysis or visualization is coupled with instrumented simulation code. Thus, it often requires the cooperation of end-users, visualization experts, and simulation developers. All this results in the reluctance of developers to introduce in-situ/in-transit functionality to their projects. To reduce this coupling and simplify user integration, approaches such as Insite by Krüger et al. [14] were presented. By decoupling the data gathering and in-situ/in-transit processing of the data from the usage of the data, a trade-off between performance and accessibility, and adaptability can be provided.

In this work, we report and discuss how following such an accessibility-focused approach to in-transit analysis and visualization can affect the development process of respective applications by analyzing examples. First, we briefly introduce existing and well-established in-situ/in-transit solutions. We then give a short revision of the Insite [14] pipeline, which we proposed as a solution for developers of neuronal network simulation analysis software to add in-transit access and processing functionality. We show how a single implementation of a simulation module within the NEST simulator [12] provided easy access to different applications that use the data for visualization. For each of the three use cases, we discuss the tool's functionality, what had to be modified to add in-transit support and present developer feedback. Finally, we summarize and discuss our findings and experiences and present our conclusion.

2 Related Work

The growth of complexity and size of simulations has sparked research and development interest for in-situ/in-transit solutions that span a wide range of domains. Bauer et al. [4], and Childs et al. [6] provide an extensive overview and discussion of applications that use in-situ/in-transit architectures. Besides domain-specific solutions, much effort has been put into creating general-purpose frameworks that connect to well-known visualization software. Prominent in-situ examples are Paraview Catalyst [2], and VisIt Libsim [23]. They can produce synchronous and tightly coupled in-situ visualizations by adding instrumentation to the simulation code. Besides in-situ solutions, there are several other libraries and tools that allow the user to use in-transit workflows [7,9,18] as well as frameworks such as Ascent [15] and SENSEI [3] that combine in-transit and in-situ capabilities. While existing solutions provide efficient implementations, integration is often involved and introduces new dependencies for data consumers. Aside from direct dependencies, they can add indirect dependencies for file formats, such as ADIOS [13], VTK [20], and other libraries.

Pugmire et al. [17] discuss the current state of in-situ visualization and argue that it must become more pervasive. They state the challenges to providing pervasive systems in today's heterogeneous computing infrastructure and propose research directions and requirements to make in-situ available for the general user. Additionally, a survey by Gerrits [11] asked simulation and domain scientists from different fields how they integrate visualization and in-situ/in-transit visualization and analysis into their workflow. When asked for properties encouraging the user to add in-site capabilities, easier integration and more apparent benefits were listed as the primary motivators. Additional motivations were the independence of external tools and having help from external resources for the integration. Furthermore, users reported that the most significant challenges were large file sizes and the need for early feedback in simulations. The results showed that in their existing workflow, most researchers used standardized visualization tools in their community, followed by tools they found the easiest to work with, such as common Python libraries.

In alignment with the goals of accessibility and ease-of-use, Krüger et al. [14] proposed the Insite pipeline. It is an alternative in-transit architecture focused on usability while maintaining a low impact on simulation time at the cost of parts of scalability and performance. To achieve this, Insite requires the simulation code to abstract the internal representation and data acquisition such that it becomes accessible via HTTP REST API. Therefore, raw data from the simulation is collected on the simulation nodes into ring-buffers that can be queried via HTTP endpoints. Data that needs in-transit processing first, is sent to an intermediate processing server, that processes the data based on plugins that are provided by the users. An access node can then be contacted to receive either raw data provided by the simulation nodes or processed data. Bootstrapping of the connections between the components is done via config files or alternatively via environment variables that are provided to the components of the pipeline. This allows to dynamically inject the correct addresses into the pipeline when a static network topology is not given, e.g., when schedulers such as slurm are used to run the simulations. This allows the development of analysis and visualization software independent of the simulation code and the freedom to use any programming language to request data, as long as HTTP REST API calls are supported. As the data is provided via standard data formats, e.g., the well-known JSON format, they are easy to parse via widely available libraries, easy to understand by developers, and require no further knowledge of the simulation code. On the other hand, developers of simulations can choose how and what portion of data to provide and if functionality, such as binning or averaging strategies, should be carried out on the access node or in the simulation module, thus allowing for the transfer of smaller processed data. We want to investigate if these promises hold out against real-world examples.

3   Application Examples

Computational neuroscience relies on large-scale simulations of neuronal networks to investigate complex connections and the development of brain regions. Simulators exist for a variety of models and levels of detail, such as Arbor [1], TVB [19], and NEST [12] to simulate networks. To increase accuracy and functional range, models used on these simulators have grown in size and complexity such that simulation becomes feasible only on high-performance clusters using highly parallel load-sharing infrastructure. The analysis and visualization requirements, however, can be very diverse and difficult to foresee as different users have vastly different requirements and expectations. Therefore, such simulations represent a well-suited example of the need for in-situ/in-transit solutions that adapt to changing needs. In the following, we describe how Insite was used to develop in-transit functionality for different existing applications related to neuronal network simulations. We approached and worked together with the developers of the respective projects and share our experiences and the feedback we received. Applications were provided with an HTTP REST API for the NEST Simulator based on the one described by Krüger et al. [14]. Note, however, that the Insite architecture is not limited to that use case and could also be applied to other domains. The used architecture and data formats can be fitted to apply to various disciplines and do not have any explicit assumptions about the data that is used. Besides the simulator plugin that provides the general mechanism to request data from the simulation, no further modifications had to be made to the simulation to support the described use cases. All applications were intended initially for offline post-hoc analysis of simulated neuron spike data.

In-Transit Enabled VIOLA. VIOLA is a web-based tool developed by Senk et al. [21] that provides visualizations for simulation data from neural simulations. The interface provides different visualization modes that give the user spatial and temporal information regarding the network activity, as shown in Fig. 1. A 3D-Timeline view combines information on the spatial and temporal behavior of the network. Given a planar network layout, the spikes generated by the nodes are binned into spatio-temporal bins laid out on a 3D grid. The network's activity is then visualized by rendering isosurfaces of the binned mean-firing rates.

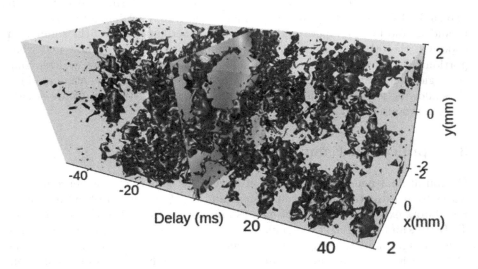

Fig. 1. VIOLA's 3D timeline view. Activity in the network is represented as an iso-surface which is extracted from spatio-temporal binned spike data. The x- and y-axis represent the spatial 2D position of the neurons while the z axis represents the simulation time. Source: [21] (Color figure online)

The original implementation used a classical offline analysis approach. After successful simulation, the raw spike data had to be written to disk first. They were then processed by a Python pre-processing tool before being loaded into the web application for visualization.

Two main components had to be implemented to enable in-transit processing and visualization. First, a Python plugin for Insite was developed that performs the spatio-temporal binning and calculation of mean-firing rate in-transit, thus reducing the amount of data necessary to transfer to the visualization.

Access to the data and changing plugin parameters, e.g., binning sizes, can easily be handled via the REST API requests. This allows different visualizations to process the resulting spatio-temporal binned data individually during the simulation to provide different insights.

Since the reference implementation already assumed pre-processed data, only minimal extensions and modifications had to be made to enable in-transit capabilities. Data is queried periodically via the standard HTTP GET functionality that Javascript provides without the need for external libraries. The JSON-encoded data can be natively consumed in Javascript and are written into the grid presentation.

To represent which part of the data is available to the user, a timeline was added that represents the available timespan as a green area, with a red line indicating the current timestep shown.

The main takeaway from the development was listed as the rather small amount of implementation work, which still resulted in two significant benefits: Users are now able to get early insights into the data, and the pre-processing was shifted from the user side to in-transit processing.

ViSimpl. ViSimpl [10] is one component of a visualization suite developed by the Rey Juan Carlos University Madrid. It visualizes spike activity in a simulation focusing on larger networks and their 3D spatial layout. It provides visual statistics of the network data for different subsets in the simulation and spatial rendering of the network as shown in Fig. 2. Besides basic functionality such as changing the viewport or scale and size of rendered neurons, it allows the user to define transfer functions to visualize spiking behavior and animate the result. Due to the performance requirements for the rendering, ViSimpl is written in C++, which, compared to other languages, is often more cumbersome when integrating external libraries. Here, too, the original implementation required data of the finished simulation to be entirely written to disk before being loaded into the application. As the simulation of especially large neural networks can take a long time and generate a lot of data, integrating in-transit capabilities can significantly benefit the analysis process. ViSimpl was not designed around in-transit capabilities, so such features had to be retrofitted into the existing architecture, which usually requires extensive development effort. However, due to Insite's reliance on standard protocols and data formats, the developers of ViSimpl were free to choose the best-fitting C++ libraries for JSON parsing and HTTP queries. This also allowed the developers to set their own balance between performance and usability regarding library choices, as more performant libraries often use APIs that are more involved to develop against, thus increasing development efforts. A prototypical implementation was done in the context of a two-day hackathon and required very little support due to the simple integration and the provided API documentation. This resulted in an implementation that allowed the in-transit visualization of the network data without major changes in the application's architecture.

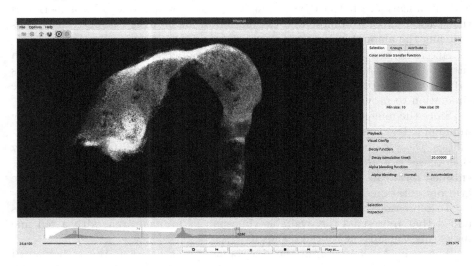

Fig. 2. The user interface of ViSimpl. In the main viewport the spatial arrangement and color-coded activity of neurons can be seen. Below, a timeline shows a timeline with statistics of the network. The user can configure the transfer function and other visualization parameters on the right side. Source: [8] (Color figure online)

Nest Desktop. NEST Desktop [22] is a web-based tool that allows users to design NEST networks via a node-based graphical editor, as shown in Fig. 3. It allows the creation, manipulation, and analysis of network connectivity and is thus valuable for users that want to design networks visually. Once satisfied, a user can generate Python simulation code for the network, which can be directly sent to a simulator instance for simulation. Additionally, NEST Desktop allows to visualize and analyze the result data via various standard visualizations, e.g., raster plots and 3D plots, as shown in Fig. 4. In the first releases, NEST Desktop sent the simulation code to the simulator via REST API and waited until the complete simulated data was returned from the request. This is especially hindering in larger simulations where it is difficult to then determine whether the simulation is still running or if something went wrong. To allow NEST Desktop to provide early feedback on the simulation that the user submitted, Insite was integrated. The interface was slightly extended to provide a simple button that enables the usage of Insite, resulting in two primary effects: First, additional simulation code is generated that instructs NEST to load the Insite NEST module and record the data to the in-transit pipeline. Secondly, it instructs NEST Desktop not to wait for the simulation's end but to periodically request spike data from the simulation and display it to the user. Due to the existing REST API-based architecture, the developers of NEST Desktop only had to make minor modifications to the existing code. Developers described the experience as straightforward and well-documented and deemed Insite a suitable solution, especially when only limited resources are available for implementation time.

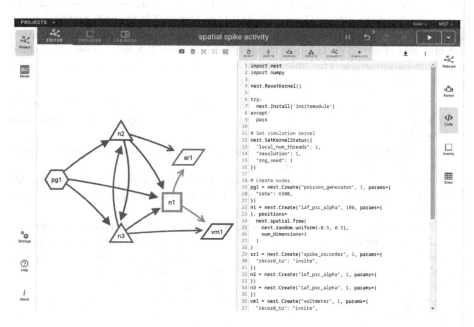

Fig. 3. NEST Desktop user interface. Left: The node-based network editor. Right: The Python simulation code generated for the network. Above the code, the user has buttons to enable in-transit capabilities with a click on "Insite".

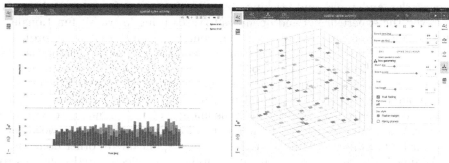

(a) Raster plot visualization of spike train with two populations connected to one spike detector each.

(b) 3D view representing spiking neurons as boxes. Spikes leave a configurable length trail after the spike event.

Fig. 4. NEST Desktop Visualizations.

4   Discussion

While a variety of performance-focused in-situ/in-transit solutions exist, we are interested if an accessibility-based approach, such as Insite, can provide easier access to in-transit functionality and lower the reluctance of developers to add such features to their code. To gain a first idea of possible answers to these questions, we looked at three applications initially limited to post-hoc visualization and analysis of neuronal network simulation data, which have successfully added in-transit capabilities. The following statements can summarize our experience and the feedback provided by developers:

- All developers saw the need and benefits of in-situ/in-transit functionality to their application as it allowed for early feedback, progress monitoring, and potentially reduced data communication.
- Ease-of-use and a low integration time were often listed as necessities to add in-situ/in-transit functionality.
- Developers experienced a low entry barrier due to using standard protocols and data formats in Insite, which allowed easy integration into different programming languages.
- As the simulation code did not have to be altered, no additional developers, such as simulation experts, were needed to integrate in-transit functionality.
- Even though some developers were initially skeptical, the simple data format and transport protocol was reportedly never a limiting factor.
- Once developers saw the benefit of in-situ/in-transit approaches they were more open to discuss the integration of more complex solutions into their application.

We derive that the heightened focus on accessibility is an essential step to make in-situ/in-transit capabilities more practicable. Lowering the number of dependencies provided developers the freedom to choose their programming language, frameworks, and tools, and sticking to well-known data formats significantly improved the experience of and openness towards using in-transit functionality. This becomes even more important in the context of multidisciplinary projects, where a lot of different programming languages, libraries, and technology stacks are used in addition to a variety of hardware architectures but yet, solutions need to be found in limited amounts of time. Based on this, we can also get an idea about how this might be useful in situations where multiple simulations, simulators, or other data sources and consumers need to communicate with one another. While our case study is limited to the domain of neuroscience, we believe that our findings presented in the paper are also applicable to other domains.

Adding Insite to the Nest simulator happened unaffected and oblivious to the visualization and analysis goals pursued by the presented applications. This indicates how such a modular architecture can also benefit simulation developers, as they can integrate the data provider in their code without considering concrete visualization or analysis needs. Further, it enables functionality likely to be used often to be pulled into the access node or simulator nodes. This is especially useful in projects where multiple consumers are interested in the data, e.g., multidisciplinary projects or projects where different conclusions can be drawn from the same data.

While the adaptations to the applications mentioned above indicate the usefulness of lightweight accessibility-based solutions, several questions remain unanswered. Currently, all applications use the same simulation code, and more complex and larger simulations might lead to different experiences. Additionally, the upfront cost of adding the necessary changes to the simulation code must be considered and may vary based on the existing code. Further, the presented approach of using loosely-coupled standard protocols and data formats is not the most efficient solution. However, based on our current experience, this has not been reported to be a limiting factor, and further research is needed to investigate cases where the performance trade-off is no longer capable of meeting application requirements. Due to the freedom provided by the architecture, multiple different data formats and protocols could be added and used to provide more efficient data transfer, thus providing different ease-of-use-to-performance ratios.

5   Conclusion

Simulations are still getting bigger and are producing more and more data. Handling the amount of data is and will become even more challenging and the total amount of resources needed to run complex simulations is likely to keep increasing. Due to this, there is still a high demand for in-situ and in-transit solutions as they alleviate some of these issues. While most in-situ/in-transit solutions are designed to be highly efficient at the cost of involved integration, we investigated if trading efficiency for ease-of-use could be beneficial to the development process. The presented use cases and discussions with developers indicate, that the focus on an easy-to-use and modular architecture as well as the reduction of dependencies can lead to an improved willingness to integrate in-transit capabilities and makes retrofitting solutions easier. While performance has been the main driver behind most solutions, our results indicate, that ease-of-integration and low dependencies are critical factors when adding in-situ/in-transit functionality. This supports the idea, that a shift towards more accessibility-focused paradigms might be able to bridge the gap between the needed in-situ/in-transit capabilities and common practices.

While the presented use cases have similar requirements, we believe that the same paradigm can also be applied to more complex simulations and more complex requirements for visualizations. Due to the positive feedback and headroom for improvements as discussed by Krüger et al. [14] we will continue to evaluate this approach to make in-transit more accessible to users.

Acknowledgments. This project/research has received funding from the European Union's Horizon 2020 Framework Programme for Research and Innovation under the Specific Grant Agreement No. 945539 (Human Brain Project SGA3) and Specific Grant Agreement No. 785907 (Human Brain Project SGA2).

References

1. Akar, N.A., et al.: Arbor – a morphologically-detailed neural network simulation library for contemporary high-performance computing architectures. In: 2019 27th Euromicro International Conference on Parallel, Distributed and Network-Based Processing (PDP), pp. 274–282 (2019)
2. Ayachit, U., et al.: Paraview catalyst: enabling in situ data analysis and visualization. In: ISAV 2015, pp. 25–29. Association for Computing Machinery, New York (2015). https://doi.org/10.1145/2828612.2828624
3. Ayachit, U., et al.: The sensei generic in situ interface. In: 2016 Second Workshop on In Situ Infrastructures for Enabling Extreme-Scale Analysis and Visualization (ISAV), pp. 40–44 (2016). https://doi.org/10.1109/ISAV.2016.013
4. Bauer, A.C., et al.: In situ methods, infrastructures, and applications on high performance computing platforms. In: Computer Graphics Forum, vol. 35, pp. 577–597. Wiley Online Library (2016)
5. Bennett, J.C., Childs, H., Garth, C., Hentschel, B.: In situ visualization for computational science (Dagstuhl Seminar 18271). Dagstuhl Rep. 8(7), 1–43 (2019). https://doi.org/10.4230/DagRep.8.7.1
6. Childs, H., Bennett, J., Garth, C., Hentschel, B.: In situ visualization for computational science. IEEE Comput. Graph. Appl. 39(6), 76–85 (2019)
7. Duque, E.P., et al.: EPIC-an extract plug-in components toolkit for in-situ data extracts architecture. In: 22nd AIAA Computational Fluid Dynamics Conference, p. 3410 (2015)
8. Ebrains: Visimpl (2023). https://ebrains.eu/service/visimpl/
9. Fogal, T., Proch, F., Schiewe, A., Hasemann, O., Kempf, A., Krüger, J.: Freeprocessing: transparent in situ visualization via data interception. In: Eurographics Symposium on Parallel Graphics and Visualization: EG PGV: Proceedings/Sponsored by Eurographics Association in Cooperation with ACM SIGGRAPH. Eurographics Symposium on Parallel Graphics and Visualization, vol. 2014, p. 49. NIH Public Access (2014)
10. Galindo, S.E., Toharia, P., Robles, O.D., Pastor, L.: ViSimpl: multi-view visual analysis of brain simulation data. Front. Neuroinform. 10, 44 (2016)
11. Gerrits, T.: Bringing visualization to national HPC infrastructure: a prologue (2022). https://doi.org/10.5281/zenodo.7715663
12. Gewaltig, M.O., Diesmann, M.: NEST (neural simulation tool). Scholarpedia 2(4), 1430 (2007)
13. Godoy, W.F., et al.: ADIOS 2: the adaptable input output system. A framework for high-performance data management. SoftwareX 12, 100561 (2020)
14. Krüger, M., et al.: Insite: a pipeline enabling in-transit visualization and analysis for neuronal network simulations. In: Anzt, H., Bienz, A., Luszczek, P., Baboulin, M. (eds.) ISC High Performance 2022. LNCS, vol. 13387, pp. 295–305. Springer, Cham (2022). https://doi.org/10.1007/978-3-031-23220-6_20
15. Larsen, M., Brugger, E., Childs, H., Harrison, C.: Ascent: a flyweight in situ library for exascale simulations. In: Childs, H., Bennett, J.C., Garth, C. (eds.) In Situ Visualization For Computational Science. MATHVISUAL, pp. 255–279. Springer, Cham (2022). https://doi.org/10.1007/978-3-030-81627-8_12
16. Ma, K.L.: In situ visualization at extreme scale: challenges and opportunities. IEEE Comput. Graph. Appl. 29(6), 14–19 (2009)
17. Pugmire, D., Huang, J., Moreland, K., Klasky, S.: The need for pervasive in situ analysis and visualization (P-ISAV). In: Anzt, H., Bienz, A., Luszczek, P.,

Baboulin, M. (eds.) ISC High Performance 2022. LNCS, vol. 13387, pp. 306–316. Springer, Cham (2023). https://doi.org/10.1007/978-3-031-23220-6_21

18. Rivi, M., Calori, L., Muscianisi, G., Slavnic, V.: In-situ visualization: state-of-the-art and some use cases. PRACE white paper, pp. 1–18 (2012)

19. Sanz Leon, P., et al.: The virtual brain: a simulator of primate brain network dynamics. Front. Neuroinform. **7**, 10 (2013)

20. Schroeder, W., Martin, K., Lorensen, B.: The Visualization Toolkit, 4th edn. Kitware, New York (2006)

21. Senk, J., Carde, C., Hagen, E., Kuhlen, T.W., Diesmann, M., Weyers, B.: VIOLA-a multi-purpose and web-based visualization tool for neuronal-network simulation output. Front. Neuroinform. **12**, 75 (2018)

22. Spreizer, S., Rotter, S., Weyers, B., Plesser, H.E., Diesmann, M.: NEST desktop: a web-based GUI for NEST simulator (2013). https://github.com/babsey/nest-desktop

23. Whitlock, B., Favre, J.M., Meredith, J.S.: Parallel in situ coupling of simulation with a fully featured visualization system. In: Kuhlen, T., Pajarola, R., Zhou, K. (eds.) Eurographics Symposium on Parallel Graphics and Visualization. The Eurographics Association (2011). https://doi.org/10.2312/EGPGV/EGPGV11/101-109

Workshop on Monitoring
and Operational Data Analytics
(MODA23)

Preface to the Workshop on Monitoring and Operational Data Analytics (MODA23)

1 Objectives and Topics

After three very successful installments of the International Workshop on Monitoring and Operational Data Analytics (MODA), initiated in 2020 at ISC High Performance, we were excited to organize this year its 4th edition – MODA23.

The goal of the MODA workshop series is to provide a venue for sharing insights into current trends in MODA for HPC systems and data centers, identify potential gaps, and offer an outlook into the future of the involved fields of high-performance computing, databases, machine learning, and possible solutions. These insights will contribute to the co-design and procurement of future computing and data processing systems. The workshop is unique to the European HPC arena, being among the few to address the topic of monitoring and operational data analytics for improving HPC operations and research. Keeping with the MODA goal, we solicited contributions presenting novel research ideas that relate to:

- Challenges, solutions, and best practices for monitoring systems at HPC and data centers. Of particular focus are operational data collection mechanisms i) covering different system levels, from building infrastructure sensor data to CPU-core performance metrics, and ii) targeting different end-users, from system administrators to application developers and computational scientists.
- Effective strategies for analyzing and interpreting the collected operational data. Of particular focus are visualization approaches and machine learning-based techniques, potentially inferring knowledge of the system behavior and allowing for the realization of a proactive control loop.

2 Workshop Organization

The workshop organizing and program committees consisted of academics and researchers at leading HPC sites and in industry. The reviewing of the submitted papers was balanced among the program committee members, and each paper received three or more high-quality reviews.

Organization

Organizers

Workshop Chairs

Florina M. Ciorba	University of Basel, Switzerland
Utz-Uwe Haus	HPE HPC/AI EMEA Research Lab, Switzerland
Nicolas Lachiche	University of Strasbourg, France
Martin Schulz	Technische Universität Munich, Germany

Publicity Chair

Thomas Jakobsche	University of Basel, Switzerland

Program Committee

Norm Bourassa	NERSC Lawrence Berkeley National Laboratory, USA
Jim Brandt	Sandia National Labs, USA
Daniele Cesarini	CINECA, Italy
Ann Gentile	Sandia National Laboratories, USA
Thomas Ilsche	Technische Universität Dresden, Germany
Terry Jones	Oak Ridge National Laboratory, USA
Diana Moise	Cray/HPE, Switzerland
Dirk Pleiter	KTH Stockholm, Sweden
Keiji Yamamoto	RIKEN, Japan
Aleš Zamuda	University of Maribor, Slovenia

Technical Program

MODA23 was held as an in-person half-day workshop with a balanced mix between technical paper presentations, keynote and invited talks, and a discussion panel. The full program is available on the MODA23 website
https://moda.dmi.unibas.ch/program/.

- [**Keynote presentation**] *Monitoring and anomaly detection in CINECA's supercomputing facility* by Daniele Cesarini (CINECA, Italy).
- [**Accepted paper**] *Automatic Detection of HPC Job Inefficiencies at TU Dresden's HPC center with PIKA*, by Frank Winkler and Andreas Knüpfer (TU Dresden, Germany)

- **[Accepted paper]** *A Fast Simulator to Enable HPC Scheduling Strategy Comparisons*, by Alex Wilkinson (UCL, UK), Jess Jones, Harvey Richardson, Tim Dykes, and Utz-Uwe Haus (HPE, UK).
- **[Invited talk]** *Current and Future Monitoring at GWDG to Ensure Performant and Secure Operation* by Hendrik Nolte (GWDG Göttingen, Germany)
- **[Accepted paper]** *ML-based methodology for HPC facilities supervision*, by Laetitia Anton, Sophie Willemot, Sebastien Gougeaud (CEA, France), and Soraya Zertal (Univ. of Versailles, France).

MODA23 concluded with a **panel discussion** on *MODA as the foundational component of data center digital twins*, which included workshop speakers and one of the organizers (Utz-Uwe Haus) as moderator. This panel was highly interactive and turned into a discussion with the audience, fast-paced at times, revealing various levels of digital twin design and implementation across institutions.

Workshop Outcome

The MODA23 keynote and invited talks, paper presentations, and panel discussion shows the broad scope of topics addressed, as well as the increasing importance of the MODA topics for the HPC and data analysis communities. At the same time, they documented the progress made since MODA22, showed the current state of the art, and evidenced the missing breadth of solutions as well as their reliability and stability. MODA23 further showed that key challenges still lie ahead and in particular:

- Continuous and holistic monitoring of building infrastructure, large-scale system hardware, system software, and applications are necessary to achieve data center digital twins in order to analyze and understand conditions of interest in relation to the location of objects (e.g. thermal hot spots).
- Availability and open-access of large-scale data sets to foster and advance open, reproducible research on MODA and associated topics. Recent dataset release: M100 Exa-Data: a data collection campaign on the CINECA's Marconi100 Tier-0 supercomputer https://www.nature.com/articles/s41597-023-02174-3.
- HPC job monitoring can reveal jobs with performance issues or inefficiencies with regards to under-utilized resources or uneven distribution of computational workload across processing units to bring efficient HPC within reach.
- HPC job scheduling simulation is growing in importance and necessity for exploration and comparison of scheduling configurations without impacting system efficiency.
- MODA also plays an increasingly crucial role in security-related monitoring and analysis of HPC systems, such as compliance checking and system hardening (prevent a mistake/vulnerability from happening), as well as incident recording and intrusion detection (detect suspicious activities/potential attacks). Security plays an increasingly important role especially in multi-tenant HPC systems and data centers.
- The existence of a wide range of monitoring and analysis tools leads to heterogeneous software stacks that are challenging to integrate.

- Machine learning is driving the analysis of monitoring data. Unsupervised learning techniques such as automatic clustering and outlier detection can be leveraged to detect abnormal behavior even in large unlabeled datasets.

We hope that these and other aspects will figure prominently in submissions to the next edition(s) of the MODA workshop.

Automatic Detection of HPC Job Inefficiencies at TU Dresden's HPC Center with PIKA

Frank Winkler[✉] and Andreas Knüpfer

Center for Information Services and High Performance Computing (ZIH),
Technische Universität Dresden, 01062 Dresden, Germany
{frank.winkler,andreas.knuepfer}@tu-dresden.de

Abstract. The efficient use of High Performance Computing (HPC) resources is essential and requires continuous performance monitoring. The NHR HPC Center at TU Dresden has been using PIKA [5], a continuous job-level performance monitoring system, for more than five years. It is active by default and allows retrospective analysis and comparison with previous jobs. Its results are available to users for their jobs as well as to admins and HPC support for all jobs. It has proven to be very useful for reactive user support on various aspects of efficient use of HPC resources in general as well as on specific performance issues of individual users.

At the same time, the continuously collected data can be scanned proactively, as users may not yet be aware of performance issues. In this article, we report on our methods for scanning for job inefficiencies, and to inspire discussion about appropriate methods. It covers the most useful heuristic checks for a variety of aspects. We focus on meaningful performance criteria and commonly observed performance problems. All parameters and thresholds are derived from experience and tuned to detect the most severe cases in the average job mix. The heuristics range from simple cases that compare against appropriate thresholds to more sophisticated tests with some pre-processing.

Keywords: Job Monitoring · Data Analysis · Performance · Efficiency

1 Introduction

Even when an HPC system is well configured and maintained, HPC jobs can be inefficient due to a variety of factors. Common reasons are poorly optimized codes, incorrect resource allocations, or suboptimal data access. To address these issues, HPC operators need a tool that continuously monitors and analyzes the performance of jobs and classifies them into efficient and inefficient jobs. Criteria for efficient usage are shortest possible runtimes (compared to similar jobs), high utilization of the hardware and an even distribution of computational workloads across processing units.

For early detection and notification of user job inefficiencies, automated heuristics are needed to search jobs for inefficient patterns based on empirical data from the HPC center.

A. Bienz et al. (Eds.): ISC High Performance 2023 Workshops, LNCS 13999, pp. 295–306, 2023.
https://doi.org/10.1007/978-3-031-40843-4_22

PIKA is a performance monitoring stack for HPC clusters to identify potentially inefficient jobs. It consists of several open source components. These include a metric data collector to record runtime performance data on each compute node and a job metadata collector that captures all required job metadata for both exclusive and node-sharing jobs. In order to analyze a job-specific runtime metric, the job metadata must be mapped to it, in particular the node list, the list of physical cores used, and the start and end time of the job. This enables job-specific analysis for performance metrics such as CPU load, instructions per cycle, floating points operations per second or I/O bandwidths. The PIKA web-frontend contains detailed timeline visualizations of each runtime metric and provides correlation analysis between different metrics.

In order to provide HPC operators and users with additional performance feedback, PIKA performs a regular post-processing to prepare the data for further analysis. This includes, for example, the aggregation of all runtime data into so-called performance footprints. Based on the footprint and a corresponding performance model PIKA can for example determine whether a job is memory-bound or compute-bound [5]. However, other performance issues like the overall idle CPU time, load imbalances, periodic blocking I/O phases, or memory leak suspicions require more detailed analysis. For this purpose, a new analysis engine was implemented, which scans jobs for performance issues on a weekly basis. In addition, the PIKA web-frontend has been enhanced with a new feature that allows operators to sort and analyze HPC users by importance whose jobs included performance issues. Those users will be analyzed by the HPC support team and contacted accordingly in order to solve the problem together.

Section 2 describes heuristics for detecting performance issues based on job-specific timeline metrics. A case study of jobs with performance issues on the HPC system at TU Dresden is described in Sect. 3. A review of related work follows in Sect. 4.

2 Job Performance Issues

Job performance issues can be caused by the HPC user due to improper use of the job scheduling system as well as by HPC system problems such as file system overload or poor network configuration. Mostly, however, users are responsible for the efficiency of their jobs. Without knowing the application running in the job, we show that it is possible to capture inefficient jobs by their performance data. Each per-job performance metric captured by PIKA consists of one or more vectors of performance values, depending on the allocated resources and its granularity, e.g. per node, per socket, or per physical core. For example, the CPU/GPU load vectors make it very easy to detect pathological problems, e.g. when more CPUs/GPUs are requested than are used. These types of tests are easy to implement, and it is sufficient to define certain thresholds, such as when a CPU load can be considered idle. For other aspects, e.g. periodic synchronous offloading or the detection of memory leaks, one has to design exactly tailored tests and adjust parameters exactly, sometimes also ensure sufficient data quality.

Table 1. Possible performance issues with the inefficient HPC jobs of a user

Performance Issue	Description
Idle CPU/GPU Time (ICT/IGT)	Summed time intervals of all CPUs/GPUs across all jobs in which the load was close to zero
Idle CPU/GPU Ratio (ICR/IGR)	Quotient of "Idle CPU/GPU Time" and "Total CPU/GPU Time" across all jobs
Maximum Unused CPU/GPU Ratio (Max UCR/UGR)	Maximum ratio of "unused" to "used" CPUs/GPUs across all jobs
Maximum CPU/GPU Load Imbalance (Max CLI/GLI)	Maximum of the average standard deviation of CPU/GPU load across all jobs
Maximum I/O Congestion (Max IOC)	Maximum rate of metadata operations at a measuring point across all jobs. The attribution per job starts with 40 operations
Maximum I/O Blocking Phases (Max IOB)	Maximum periodic number of phases with an inverse correlation between CPU load and I/O metrics across all jobs. The attribution per job starts with 10 periodic phases
Maximum Synchronous Offloading (Max SO)	Maximum periodic number of phases with an inverse correlation between CPU and GPU load across all jobs. The attribution per job starts with 10 periodic phases
Maximum Memory Leak (Max ML)	Maximum of the linear increase of memory usage over time across all jobs

Table 1 lists all HPC job performance issue metrics on a per-user basis that we are able to generate from the job-specific vectors of performance metrics using appropriate heuristics. These have proven very useful to us in identifying users with inefficient jobs. In the following, we present the individual heuristics for each performance issue and go into detail about the threshold values and special features to be considered. It should be mentioned that we currently have chosen the thresholds in a way to provide a manageable set of "worst jobs" in the current job mix. It might be necessary to slightly adjust those thresholds in the future or for other centers.

2.1 Setup and Data Preparation

PIKA stores all metric data in the time series database InfluxDB [1]. This data is available on a long-term basis and is used for visualization and analysis. The metric data used in the following analysis is sampled every 30 s. We analyze the metrics of CPU/GPU load, memory usage, and all recorded metrics of I/O bandwidths and I/O metadata operations. The first step of the analysis is to find eligible jobs. Each of these jobs must have run for at least one hour, have more than one physical core allocated, and terminated with a "completed", "out of memory", or "timeout" Slurm status. Based on the runtime metrics of a job, the performance issues listed in Table 1 are to be checked against the job and attributed to the job if necessary. Performance issues related to the core performance are identified for both exclusive and node-sharing jobs. All other metrics that are recorded on a per-node basis are identified for exclusive jobs.

Regarding node exclusivity and simultaneous multithreading, there are some important remarks. A job is marked as exclusive when either Slurm's exclusive flag has been set or all compute nodes associated with the job have been fully allocated. In terms of simultaneous multithreading (SMT), PIKA only stores the average over the hardware threads per physical core. Therefore, the maximum utilization of a CPU core has the value 1. In the following, we will use the term CPU to refer to a physical core.

2.2 Straightforward Heuristics

In the following, heuristics and their thresholds are presented for CPUs/GPUs that either have long idle phases, are completely unused or have large load imbalances. Idle time of CPUs/GPUs results from unused resources as well as phases in the job where the load is close to zero. These idle phases can also be caused by load imbalances, where some CPUs/GPUs may be overloaded while others remain underutilized respectively idle. For the issue metrics described below, we have defined the following heuristics and thresholds.

1. A measuring point of a CPU is idle, if the usage is below 0.01.
2. A measuring point of a GPU is idle, if the usage has the value 0.
3. A CPU/GPU is unused, if the idle count per measurement point is greater than $(n-2)$ measurement points.
4. A load imbalance is attributed to a job, if the average standard deviation of CPUs/GPUs is greater than 0.2.

Idle CPU/GPU Time is the summed idle time over all CPUs/GPUs across all jobs. Internally, we multiply the idle counts of each CPU/GPU with 30 s and sum them up. Note that the idle time is only an estimation and upper limit as we only measure every 30 s. Nevertheless, this estimation is well suited to capture long idle time phases.

Idle CPU/GPU Ratio is an issue metric that characterises the ratio of idle to total time over all CPUs/GPUs across all jobs. Internally, we compute the quotient of idle time and the sum of CPU/GPU hours per job. A value close to zero means that all CPUs/GPUs were used, while a value close to 1 means, that the user has caused almost no CPU/GPU usage for all jobs.

Maximum Unused CPU/GPU Ratio is an issue metric that characterises the maximum ratio of unused to used CPUs/GPUs across all jobs. Internally, we compute the quotient of unused and used CPUs/GPUs per job and finally provide the maximum quotient of all jobs. A value close to zero means that almost all CPUs/GPUs were used by all jobs, while a value close to 1 means, that almost no CPU/GPU was used by at least one job.

Maximum CPU/GPU Load Imbalance quantifies how the load was distributed over all CPUs/GPUs across all jobs. Internally, we calculate the standard deviation vectors across all CPUs/GPUs for each job and take the average. If the standard deviation is within the range of our defined threshold, the load imbalance issue is attributed to the job. Finally, we provide the maximum average standard deviation of all jobs. A value close to our defined threshold means that the CPUs/GPUs were reasonably evenly distributed in all jobs, while a value close to 1 means that at least one CPU/GPU was almost fully utilized and at least one CPU/GPU was almost idle in at least one job. A value equal to 0 means that no load imbalances could be detected for any of the jobs.

Another heuristic is the detection of inappropriate I/O behavior due to inefficient handling of metadata operations. Using a large number of metadata operations in a very short period of time can overload the file system, which in turn can affect the performance of the job and other jobs. The following performance issue detects jobs with high open/close rates.

Maximum I/O Congestion quantifies the peak rate of I/O metadata operations across all jobs. Internally, for each job, the open/close rate vectors summed over all nodes are queried and added up. Then, the maximum of the summed metadata vector is determined for each job and attributed to the job if the value has at least the threshold we set. Since our cluster has multiple mount points of the Lustre file system, we perform the heuristics described above for each mount point. The mount point that returns the largest value is automatically the mount point used by the job. Finally, we provide the maximum rate of metadata operations of all jobs.

2.3   Periodic Performance Issues

In scientific HPC applications, it is common for the same algorithm to be executed repeatedly for many iterations. One reason for this is that scientific computations often involve solving complex mathematical problems, such as numerical simulations of physical systems. These problems require the repeated execution of the same algorithm on different sets of input data or with different parameter values to obtain accurate results. A common bottleneck in an iteration is the use of synchronous rather than asynchronous large I/O operations at checkpoints for intermediate results, which causes the program to block and wait for the I/O operation to complete. Offloading computation to GPUs can significantly speed up the computation process, if used efficiently. To maximize the performance of those applications, CPU load should overlap GPU load whenever possible.

In the following, we present a heuristic for detecting periodic phases with an inverse correlation between two performance metric vectors. We use this heuristic to detect repetitive I/O blocking phases or synchronous offloading. For the implementation we use the NumPy [2] and SciPy [3] Python packages. Before specifically addressing the corresponding performance issues, we first describe this heuristic in general.

1. Acquire two mean metric vectors (signals) to be analyzed and check whether they are suitable for further analysis.
2. Compute the FFT of both signals using a fast Fourier transform algorithm.
3. Compute the frequency spectrum of both signals from the FFT output.
4. Normalize the amplitudes of each frequency spectrum to 1 and calculate the element-wise sum of both frequency spectra.
5. Find the maximum amplitude of the summed frequency spectrum and check if this is a dominant frequency.
6. If the conditions of a dominant frequency are met, determine the Pearson correlation coefficient between both signals.
7. If the correlation coefficient meets a defined threshold for inverse correlation, attribute the number of periodic phases (dominant frequency multiplied by job duration) to the corresponding job.

In both periodic performance issues described above, we analyze how the CPU load vector correlates with the I/O metrics or the GPU load vector. To avoid having to run the complex heuristic for every eligible job, we first validate whether the metric vectors are useful for our tests. The extensive analysis is **not** executed if the CPU/GPU vector has one of the following properties:

– The mean value of the CPU/GPU load vector is less than 0.1.
– The difference of the maximum and minimum value of the mean CPU/GPU load vector is less than 0.7.

With the second restriction, we want to make sure that there is enough variation of the minimum and maximum CPU/GPU load over time. To include the I/O metrics in the analysis, we have set the following conditions:

– The mean value of an I/O bandwidth vector is at least 1 MB/s.
– The mean value of an I/O metadata vector is at least 1 OPS.

To achieve more precise results for subsequent analysis, we make further adjustments to the appropriate vectors. We round all CPU load values to the first decimal place and set all I/O metric values that are less than the average to zero to avoid capturing very small FFT frequencies and to obtain a better correlation coefficient as we focus only on I/O peak values. To compute the FFT, we must ensure that all vectors are aligned, which means that there must be a value for each timestamp. If a value is missing for a certain time step, it is set with the previous value, if available, or with zero.

In the following, we discuss the term dominant frequency (DF), the threshold for the correlation coefficient (CC) of an inverse correlation as well as other considerations. The DF is located at the maximum amplitude of the normalized summed frequency spectrum (Fig. 1b). It is valid if the maximum amplitude is in the range between 1.8 and 2.0 and the median over all amplitudes does not exceed the value 0.1. If the value is 2.0, both metrics have exactly the same periodic behavior. If it is slightly below 2.0, a metric has one or more stronger subfrequencies unrelated to the metric being compared. If the value is below 1.8, the difference between the maximum amplitudes of both metrics is too large. The

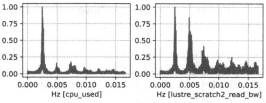

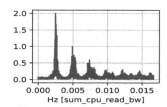

(a) Normalized FFT plots of CPU load and I/O read bandwidth signals. For the original measured signals, the mean value was previously subtracted from each measured signal.

(b) Summed FFT plot of CPU load and read bandwidth. The dominant frequency is 0,0024 Hz with an amplitude of 2.0. The median over all amplitudes is 0.06.

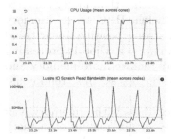

(c) An excerpt from PIKA's timeline visualization showing an inverse correlation between CPU load and I/O read bandwidth. Taking into account that the values of the read bandwidth below the average line were set to zero, the calculated correlation coefficient is −0.46. The number of periods results from the dominant frequency from (b) multiplied by the job duration. Due to a zoomed section, the number of periods is higher than shown on this chart.

Fig. 1. Heuristic for detecting periodic I/O blocking phases

median of 0.1 ensures that there are only a few frequencies with high amplitudes in the entire frequency spectrum. A CC between two metrics ranges from −1 to 1, where a value of −1 indicates a perfect inverse correlation, 0 indicates no correlation, and 1 indicates a perfect correlation. After numerous tests on selected jobs with inverse correlations between CPU load vector and an I/O bandwidth vector, we settled on a CC threshold of −0.4 to identify all these jobs. To obtain an even more accurate CC value, we consider only the phase of the job between 25% and 75% of the runtime, to avoid degrading the value in the initialization and completion of the job.

Maximum I/O Blocking Phases quantifies the periodic number of phases with an inverse correlation between CPU load and I/O metrics across all jobs. Internally we perform the heuristic tests described above for each job. We check the correlation of the CPU load vector with each suitable I/O metric vector. Based on our preconditions, we automatically filter out all I/O metrics that do not belong to the used file system mount point. If we find more valid correlations between CPU load and I/O metric, we select the correlation with the better correlation coefficient. There may be a correlation of CPU Load with I/O bandwidth and I/O metadata. In general, however, read bandwidths, for example, have the same periodic behavior as read requests operations. If a valid frequency and correlation are found, the number of periodic phases is attributed to the job, provided that the value has reached the threshold we have set. Finally, we provide the maximum number of periodic phases of all jobs.

Maximum Synchronous Offloading characterizes the periodic number of phases with an inverse correlation between CPU load and GPU load across all jobs. The entire heuristic is analogous to the I/O blocking tests, except that only one correlation test between two metric vectors is required.

2.4 Memory Leaks

Memory leaks are a recurring and particularly detrimental problem in some HPC applications, occurring when memory is continuously allocated without being released. This is typically caused by code bugs rather than faulty resource allocation. However, it is definitely a problem for efficient HPC usage. Memory leaks of HPC jobs can be detected by observing a strong positive linear trend in memory usage, but it is not a guarantee. For example, if a job is processing increasingly large amounts of data over time, it may require more memory and exhibit a positive linear trend in memory usage. Nevertheless, this trend could be a potential indicator of a memory leak.

We have developed a heuristic (Fig. 2) that checks jobs with a memory leak suspicion based on the memory usage vector. Since a certain amount of memory is allocated during initialization, which is released at the end by the application itself or by the job, we focus our analysis between 25% and 75% of the runtime. After normalizing the timestamp and memory usage values by dividing them by their respective maximum values, we determine the linear trend of the memory usage by assigning the slope m and the y-intercept n of the linear function $f(x) = mx + n$ using NumPy's "polyfit"[1] method. For further memory leak investigation, the linear slope must be between 0.01 and 1. If the slope is less than 0.01, we consider the memory usage to be constant, if it is greater than 1, it is very likely that there is a very high abrupt slope and not a linear one. Note that for long jobs, up to 7 days, a rather small slope is expected, which is why we set the lower limit to $m = 0.01$. High slopes are to be expected for jobs that only have a few hours of runtime or run into "out of memory". Next we calculate the euclidean distance of all measuring points to the linear function. At the last step we determine the maximum of the euclidean distance vector, which must not exceed the maximum value *max_distance*. The *max_distance* value depends on the position of P, which is further to the left at higher slope, see the graphic and formula in Fig. 2. This allows to recognize both steady linear slopes and slopes in the form of stairs or zigzags.

Maximum Memory Leak describes the suspicion of a memory leak on the basis of the linear increase of the memory usage across all jobs. Internally we perform the heuristic tests described above for each job and attribute the slope m of the memory usage vector to the job if a memory leak is suspected. Finally, we provide the maximum slope m of all jobs.

---

[1] https://numpy.org/doc/stable/reference/generated/numpy.polyfit.html

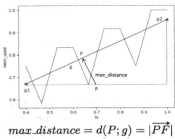

1. Divide each element of ts and mem_used by its maximum value.
2. Determine slope trend via $np.polyfit(ts, mem\_used, 1)$ to get the slope m and the y-intercept n of the linear function $f(x) = mx + n$
3. Determine $p1$ and $p2$ based on linear function for $m \in [0.01; 1]$
4. Calculate euclidean distance dis of each measuring point to the slope line
5. Determine P based on slope m and calculate distance $max\_distance$ for $m \in [0.1; 1]$
6. if $np.max(dis) < max\_distance \rightarrow$ suspected memory leak found

$$max\_distance = d(P; g) = |\overrightarrow{PF}|$$
$$P(ts, mem\_used) = (p1_{ts} +$$
$$((p2_{ts} - p1_{ts}) * \tfrac{1}{m*10}), p1_{mem\_used})$$
$$if \; m < 0.1 \rightarrow P_{ts} = 1$$

Fig. 2. Heuristic to detect a memory leak based on memory usage over time

3   HPC Support Case Studies

Administrators and the HPC support team of TU Dresden's HPC cluster have the possibility to get a weekly overview of HPC users who have sent a large number of inefficient jobs. For this purpose, they can use PIKA's new top-down approach as illustrated in Fig. 3. Starting from the issue table view with the ability to prioritize users by a specific performance issue metric, they can navigate from user issue data, to job issue data, to individual job issue data, and finally to a timeline view that reveals all identified performance issues in timeline charts. Figure 3a shows an interactive table of users with performance issues sorted by the number of I/O blocking phases. The issue data of an individual job run is shown in Fig. 3b. This view lists all job runs with associated job ID that belong to collection of a specific job name. Finally, Fig. 3c shows the job-specific visualization of all recorded performance metrics including the metadata and allows analysts to understand the root cause of the identified issues. At this point, the analyst also has the option to review the user's job submission script.

The following is a brief description of the user support process. Typically, our support team will contact users who have caused the same performance issues on a large number of jobs, or on a highly scalable job with up to 100 nodes. This is done using PIKA's interactive issue table, which is updated weekly by our analysis engine. Once a user with inefficient jobs has been identified, the first step is to create a problem hypothesis. It has proven very useful to provide the Slurm job scripts to the analyst to understand the root cause of performance issues and to derive helpful recommendations for the user. For example, by analyzing the job script and comparing it to the performance data collected by PIKA, analysts can check the job script for misconfigurations that may be causing a job inefficiency. To avoid the perception of spamming, we refrain from sending automated emails to our users. In an initial email, we make the user aware of the performance issue and provide initial instructions on how to resolve the

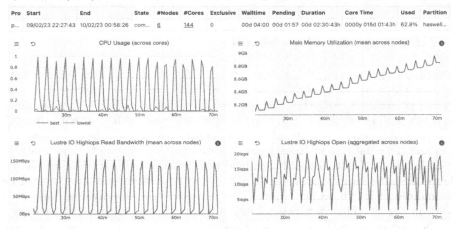

User	Pro	#Runs	ICT ↑↓	ICR	Max UCR	Max CLI	Max IOB ↓F	Max IOC	Max ML	IGT ↑↓	IGR	Max UGR	Max GLI	Max SO
⟩...	p...	14	0000y 095d 21:5...	0.46	0.93	0.43	60	106	0.17	00d 00:00:00h	0	0	0	0
⟩...	p...	183	0001y 210d 00:3...	0.14	0.94	0.68	11	929	0.04	00d 06:22:30h	0.8	0	0	0
⟩...	p...	7355	0157y 005d 10:4...	0.79	1	0.7	0	0	0	101d 10:07:00h	0.54	0	0	0

Total Issue Users: 549

(a) Performance issue table showing HPC users sorted by the number of I/O blocking phases (Max IOB) according to the selected time period (top right). The third column (#Runs) contains the number of the corresponding user's jobs.

Job ID ↑↓	Pro	ICT ↑↓	ICR ↑↓	UCR ↑↓	CLI ↑↓	IOB ↓F	IOC ↑↓	ML ↑↓	IGT ↑↓	IGR ↑↓	UGR ↑↓	GLI ↑↓	SO ↑↓
32966983	p...	0000y 008d ...	0.53	0	0	60	41	0.17	00d 00...	0	0	0	0

(b) Performance issue data of one job run. The ratio of idle and total CPU hours (ICR) is 53%. There are 60 phases with I/O blocking (IOB), a peak rate of 41 open+close operations (IOC), and a suspected memory leak (ML) with a linear slope of 0.17.

(c) A zoomed-in timeline visualization with six fully allocated Haswell nodes. One can see an inverse correlation between the CPU load (top left) and the read bandwidth (bottom left). The high CPU idle time ratio results from the I/O blocking phases as well as from CPUs that are almost idle, as can be seen in the orange graph (lowest). A memory leak can be assumed from the memory usage chart (top right). In addition, one can recognize a high rate of open operations across all nodes (right bottom).

Fig. 3. PIKA's top-down approach to analyze a performance issue job.

issue. Depending on the severity of the problem, we may also offer a face-to-face meeting to resolve the performance issues together.

4   Related Work

We have presented the core architecture of PIKA in [5], which did not deal with detecting inefficiencies as presented here. ClusterCockpit [6] is a web-frontend based on the Likwid Monitoring Stack (LMS) [12] that provides a job issue detection in particular for pathological and inefficient jobs. TACC stats [7] automatically detects underperforming and misconfigured jobs. Julia Roigk describes in her master thesis [13] the determination of periodic resource utilization using FFT analysis. This work involves, among other things, creating a rule set to find HPC jobs that have distinct stages or periodic patterns. Monika Multani shows in her bachelor thesis [10] that system monitoring data, especially from the network area, often have a waveform, which can be determined by means of FFT. Jindal et al. specialize in the aspect of memory leak detection in cloud-based infrastructures based on the system's memory usage using machine learning algorithms [9].

In many publications, the authors have used machine learning techniques to classify jobs on the basis of performance data. Felix Fischer presents in his bachelor thesis [8] an approach for measuring the similarity of HPC jobs based on their hardware performance data using unsupervised clustering methods. Ozer et al. introduce an approach for characterizing performance variation in HPC systems using monitoring and unsupervised learning techniques [11].

5   Conclusion and Future Work

In this paper, we presented heuristics that enable administrators of TU Dresden's HPC cluster to identify users who have submitted a large number of inefficient jobs using the top-down approach in PIKA. A new analysis engine with heuristics and defined thresholds has been implemented to scan jobs for performance issues on a weekly basis. These heuristics can identify jobs that are using excessive idle CPU/GPU hours or have load imbalances, periodic blocking I/O phases, or suspected memory leaks. By detecting such performance issues, administrators can contact and advise HPC users on how to improve the performance of their jobs. By doing so, users can reduce their job runtime, freeing up resources for other users and increasing the overall efficiency of the HPC system. In addition, the assigned jobs with performance issues can be used to investigate former project proposals that have requested very high CPU/GPU hours. Both the allocated and idle CPU/GPU hours of jobs can also be assigned to a project. Taking this information into account, subsequent project proposals with the same request of CPU/GPU hours can be handled accordingly.

Further improvements to the PIKA web front-end are planned to better identify users with major performance issues. We intend to provide an additional severity column in the issue table that better prioritizes problem jobs according to defined characteristics, e.g., highly scalable or very long jobs. In addition, we plan to allow administrators to mark problematic jobs where users have already been contacted to see if future jobs have resolved those issues. Finally, we plan to enrich the recorded jobs with application-specific parameters to be able to classify jobs by application type. One promising tool for this task is XALT [4], which tracks job-specific executable information and the linkage of static shared and dynamically linked libraries.

No Blackbox AI Approach

The heuristics proposed in this paper allow an appropriate classification of inefficient jobs. The computational load is very manageable and the classification criteria are directly comprehensible for human analysts. We refrain from using this classified data set as starting point for machine learning approaches because this offers no additional benefits. The result would be another classification tool, yet our heuristics already provide a suitable tool. It would, however, cost substantial computational effort for training with little hope that inference would provide faster or better answers.

References

1. InfluxDB: Scalable datastore for metrics, events, and real-time analytics. https://github.com/influxdata/influxdb. Accessed February 2023
2. NumPy: The fundamental package for scientific computing with Python. https://numpy.org/. Accessed February 2023
3. SciPy: Fundamental algorithms for scientific computing in Python. https://scipy.org/. Accessed February 2023
4. Agrawal, K., Fahey, M.R., McLay, R., James, D.: User environment tracking and problem detection with XALT. In: 2014 First International Workshop on HPC User Support Tools, pp. 32–40 (2014). https://doi.org/10.1109/HUST.2014.6
5. Dietrich, R., Winkler, F., Knüpfer, A., Nagel, W.: PIKA: center-wide and job-aware cluster monitoring. In: Workshop on Monitoring and Analysis for High Performance Computing Systems Plus Applications. HPCMASPA (2020). https://doi.org/10.1109/CLUSTER49012.2020.00061
6. Eitzinger, J., Gruber, T., Afzal, A., Zeiser, T., Wellein, G.: ClusterCockpit—a web application for job-specific performance monitoring. In: 2019 IEEE International Conference on Cluster Computing (CLUSTER), pp. 1–7 (2019). https://doi.org/10.1109/CLUSTER.2019.8891017
7. Evans, T., et al.: Comprehensive resource use monitoring for HPC systems with TACC stats. In: 2014 First International Workshop on HPC User Support Tools, pp. 13–21 (2014). https://doi.org/10.1109/HUST.2014.7
8. Fischer, F.: Metrics for job similarity based on hardware performance data. Master's thesis, Technische Universität München (2020)
9. Jindal, A., Staab, P., Kulkarni, P., Cardoso, J., Gerndt, M., Podolskiy, V.: Memory leak detection algorithms in the cloud-based infrastructure. CoRR abs/2106.08938 (2021). https://arxiv.org/abs/2106.08938
10. Multani, M.: Statistical characterization of HPC monitoring data (2021)
11. Ozer, G., Netti, A., Tafani, D., Schulz, M.: Characterizing HPC performance variation with monitoring and unsupervised learning. In: Jagode, H., Anzt, H., Juckeland, G., Ltaief, H. (eds.) ISC High Performance 2020. LNCS, vol. 12321, pp. 280–292. Springer, Cham (2020). https://doi.org/10.1007/978-3-030-59851-8_18
12. Röhl, T., Eitzinger, J., Hager, G., Wellein, G.: LIKWID monitoring stack: a flexible framework enabling job specific performance monitoring for the masses. In: 2017 IEEE International Conference on Cluster Computing (CLUSTER), pp. 781–784 (2017). https://doi.org/10.1109/CLUSTER.2017.115
13. Roigk, J.: Feasibility study for detecting different job stages using a system monitoring daemon. Master's thesis (2022)

ML-Based Methodology for HPC Facilities Supervision

Laetitia Anton[1], Sophie Willemot[1], Sebastien Gougeaud[1(✉)],
and Soraya Zertal[1,2]

[1] CEA, Bruyères-le-Châtel, France
{laetitia.anton,sophie.willemot,sebastien.gougeaud}@cea.fr
[2] Li-PaRAD, University of Versailles (UVSQ), Guyancourt, France
soraya.zertal@uvsq.fr

Abstract. Monitoring supercomputing facilities tends to be very time consuming and error-prone as the size of the collected data and the number of supervised devices do not cease to increase. In this paper, we propose a methodology to supervise those facilities based on measurements performed on devices at different levels of the infrastructure. Through its three phases -raw data cleaning, ML-based processing and visualisation using our developed tool- it facilitates the supervision of the computing center facilities and helps detecting irregular behaviours leading to manual correction actions. The case of the energy consumption is considered to illustrate the usefulness of this methodology and highlight its valuable results but it can be applied to any other target metric.

Keywords: Computing center supervision · ML algorithms · Energy consumption

1 Introduction

Applications become both computing and data intensive with increasing demands of computing power and data storage capacity. Consequently, the use of computing centers goes beyond the scope of scientific and strategic applications to include medical, banking, commercial ones, and the advent of Big Data greatly accentuates this phenomenon. HPC is therefore becoming more widespread with more users and computing centers are more in demand to face these applications challenges. To meet these growing and heterogeneous requirements, computing centers gather a huge number of different types of hardware resources as: computing nodes, processors, disks, network switches, cooling fans, converters, power generators, etc. All these resources must be under a continuous supervision to avoid any failure and even anticipate a potential failure or abnormal behaviour.

Energy consumption is a key parameter in the management of these computing centers, particularly their facilities infrastructure. Firstly, energy is essential to the operation of any resource, whatever its role or function, and secondly, economic and environmental concerns cannot be neglected. The energy consumption

A. Bienz et al. (Eds.): ISC High Performance 2023 Workshops, LNCS 13999, pp. 307–319, 2023.
https://doi.org/10.1007/978-3-031-40843-4_23

is even part of the criteria for ranking supercomputers in the Top500 [24]. These facilities infrastructures are monitored via tools to allow administrators to take actions as to adapt some functioning modes or anticipate components replacements. For instance, monitoring energy consumption allows its adjustments to the workload (intensity and allocation pattern) and to weather conditions. Some supervision tools exist in the literature and their use is inevitable to deal with the number of heterogeneous components which can only increase with the transition to exascale [1,2,11,15]. They are based on measurements operated on different components at the computing center that are aggregated in a specific manner and often presented via graphs. Usually, it is up to center administrators to interpret these data and decide what components are involved and what actions to launch. This task has become complex and risky -given the huge number of components- and requires at least partial automation to help administrator decisions and avoid human errors which can be critical. In this paper, we propose a ML-methodology for measurements processing in a computing center and a visualisation and supervision tool to easily detect anomalies from components behaviours. The human action is still needed to decide on the best protocol to gradually achieve the proposed solution.

This paper is organized as follows. Section 2 covers related works and Sect. 3 presents the context of the study. Section 4 describes the methodology followed to conduct this study and Sect. 5 presents the associated experiment plan. The obtained results are detailed are discussed in Sect. 6 before concluding this work and giving some insights for the future in Sect. 7.

2   Related Works

Supervising computing centers have been practiced since their launch and different methods have been applied since then. However, they all have their own specificities and are all "tailored" to the supervised system. They are generally based on simple statistical functions with more or less sophisticated graphic tools. For computing centers dedicated to HPC applications, data is collected and used periodically by administrators to determine if the system is being efficiently used and also to check the operational aspect, identify potential problems and resolve incidents using only visualisation dashboards [4,22]. A fairly large-scale study was conducted to analyse the use of information dashboards for operational facility management in major supercomputing centers [6]. Recently, considerable effort was put on energy consumption and the supervision of devices to reduce it [8,21] and no ML algorithms were used in all these works.

The advent of Artificial Intelligence (AI) and Machine Learning (ML) changed the engineering and high performance computation in all aspects with many contributions and relevant results [19]. However, this is not yet the case of supervising computing centers and only few works can be found in the literature as the exploratory study of Bayesian Gaussian mixture models to characterise the performance of an HPC system's components [14] and the K-means based strategy to build normal and abnormal log classes for anomaly detection [9].

While supervised and semi-supervised approaches have had some success in anomaly detection but remain impractical in production, unsupervised approaches are still in their infancy, and very recent work [13] addresses this need for the monitoring of compute nodes.

Other works deal with energy consumption prediction for jobs [5, 20] or cooling infrastructures [16] and propose guidelines for optimising energy efficiency.

The present work contributes to strengthen the use of unsupervised ML methods for computing centers supervision and shows its usefulness in production.

3   Context

This work was conducted at the CEA[1] for the TGCC computing center [23]. It hosts the 22 Petaflops Joliot-Curie supercomputer part of the european PRACE[2] and since June 2021 Topaze, a petascale class machine which is used by the CEA and its industrial partners. These supercomputers are connected to storage spaces via a very high performance network (Infiniband EDR technology). The whole storage space is more than 120 PB delivering data at a throughput from 60 GB/s to 300 GB/s.

The measurements campaign lasts two years [2020–2022] and the whole extracted data constitute a history of observations injected into our proposed chain of tasks to understand and supervise the different components of the infrastructure.

4   Methodology

We propose a supervision methodology in three phases as depicted by the diagram on Fig. 1. First, raw data is collected and filtered, then processed by the classification and statistical analysis software components. The results feed the visualisation tool that gives guidelines to infrastructure administrators to launch manual actions on the involved devices. The implementation of the automation component that controls some utility devices and makes them auto adaptive is a future project involving hardware, software and admin experts.

4.1   Phase 1: Collecting and Filtering Raw Data

Collecting raw data was carried out at a frequency of one measurement per minute, 7 days a week for two years on different devices and at different levels of the utility infrastructure: the energy consumption of Power Distribution Units (PDU), the temperature along the cooling system, the speed of fans, etc. Raw data come in several files from the measurement probes, gathered according to their timestamp to produce one file per year. As our goal is to ensure the

---

[1] CEA: "Commissariat à l'énergie atomique et aux énergies alternatives" for French Alternative Energies and Atomic Energy Commission.

[2] Partnership for Advanced Computing in Europe.

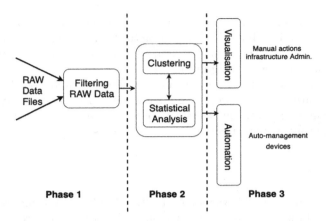

Fig. 1. Data processing diagram

quality and the efficiency of the analysis, we need accurate but reduced-size data. Consequently, this offline phase is essentially dedicated to filtering and reformatting raw data to get rid of:

1. Unreliable data automatically discarded according to infrastructure administrators hints in case a probe was unreliable or even failed during the data collection campaign.
2. Incomplete data where long ranges of measures are missing and cannot be easily approximated. A threshold of 10 minutes is considered here, after which it has been observed that extrapolation recovery is not possible and impactful variations for some data are missed.
3. Data corresponding to highly correlated features as they do not enrich our knowledge of the operating devices and therefore the inference that follows on their behaviour.

4.2   Phase 2: Clustering and Statistical Analysis

The second phase is the core of our methodology. It is in charge of processing the filtered data using statistical and ML-based methods. It characterises typical behaviours by grouping similar events and detects anomalies represented by isolated data. It highlights similar behaviours -if any-, identifies metrics that distinguish them and determines their importance.

The first milestone is to deal with the high randomness of noisy data from a real system. Clustering algorithms based on density as DBSCAN[3] [18] and more precisely HDBSCAN[4] [7] are applied to capture clusters of different shapes without any prior knowledge of their number comparing to other clustering algorithms as K-means [3,17]. Indeed, HDBSCAN is a combination of DBSCAN and

---

[3] Density-Based Spatial Clustering Applications with Noise.
[4] Hierarchical Density-Based Spatial Clustering Applications with Noise.

an HAC algorithm[5] which minimises the clusters internal inertia. To represent this multi-dimensional data in a readable way that facilitates their interpretation, we use a non-linear dimension reduction algorithm. We opted for t-SNE algorithm (t-distributed Stochastic Neighbor Embedding) [12] that identifies the probability of finding two nearby points in the data space and maps this probability to the two-dimensional space it constructs. The result is a 2D representation of clusters corresponding to the initial non-linear separable spaces.

Determining Clusters Which Share the Same Operating Mode
A statistical analysis is performed in parallel with the clustering results (number, properties, etc.) as inputs to evaluate the similarity between pairs of clusters in terms of operating mode to determine the feature that distinguish them and that could be at the origin of abnormal behaviour.

The operating mode is exclusively defined by the admin experts and induces that two clusters C_i and C_j belong to the same operating mode if the following similarity statement is satisfied for each operating metric X:

$$\begin{cases} first\_quartile(X_{C_j}) < median(X_{C_i}) < third\_quartile(X_{C_j}) \\ first\_quartile(X_{C_i}) < median(X_{C_j}) < third\_quartile(X_{C_i}) \end{cases} \tag{1}$$

Figure 2 illustrates this clustering from the operational mode perspective using boxplots. The first row of the figure shows the distribution of three clusters C_1, C_2 and C_3. We observe that all pairs of clusters satisfy (1) for the metric X_1 whilst they do not for metric X_2 and cluster C_2 is discarded. Therefore, we can consider it as a unique operating mode and exclude it from the following comparisons using the other metrics. Thus we continue with clusters C_1 and C_3 which belong to the same operating mode.

Determining the Deviant Metrics and Their Impact
Two clusters belonging to the same operating mode should form a unique cluster. It is assumed that at least one other metric is involved in distinguishing these clusters. As shown in the second row of Fig. 2, metric Y_1 does not differentiate clusters C_1 and C_3 because they satisfy (1). Nevertheless, they are clearly separated by the metric Y_2, which does not satisfy the statement. Then, we can conclude that clusters C_1 and C_3 are differentiated only by the metric Y_2. We determine the impact I of each involved metric Y by measuring the gap between the quartiles of two clusters C_i and C_j:

$$I_Y = \min(\mid first\_quartile(Y_{C_i}) - third\_quartile(Y_{C_j}) \mid, \\ \mid third\_quartile(Y_{C_i}) - first\_quartile(Y_{C_j}) \mid)$$

We estimate the percentage P_Y of importance of metric Y among n ones by:

$$P_Y = \frac{I_Y}{\sum\limits^{n} I_Y} \times 100$$

---

[5] Hierarchical Agglomerative Clustering.

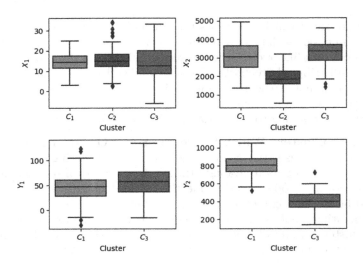

Fig. 2. Operating mode-based clustering

The results must be constantly analysed by the experts. To facilitate this operation, we decided in agreements with them to dismiss insignificant metrics by considering a threshold. Thus all the metrics with $P \geq 10\%$ are monitored.

4.3   Phase 3: Visualisation

To make the results of the processing phase useful for infrastructure administrators, we developed a visualisation tool to provide them with some guidelines to make actions on the different devices of the utility infrastructure. These actions can be of different natures:

- hardware-based actions, such as switching-off or switching-on some devices, repair a failure discovered on a device, upgrade old devices;
- software-based actions, such as updating the parameters settings, adapting configurations of the utility infrastructure to face new workloads or new execution contexts.

This dynamic supervision via a graphical interface helps to highlight and detect the unusual behaviour using contextual interpretations based on the expertise of infrastructure administrators. This is developed in Python 3.8, using Dash library for GUI and Plotly for graph generation [10]. The learning methods are from the HDBSCAN and scikit-learn packages, with pandas and numpy as components for dataframe manipulation and scientific computing.

5   Experimental Design

We expose how the proposed methodology was applied to the TGCC computing center. The goal is to reduce the energy consumption of the utility infrastructure (cooling units, etc.) rather than the computing and storage infrastructures (CPUs, GPUs, Disks, etc.).

5.1 Datasets Description

Our dataset is collected over two whole years at a frequency of one measurement per minute for each of the 93 probes. The probes will collect measurements about power, consumed energy or temperatures, as summarized in Table 1.

Table 1. Collected features

Source	Feature
Facility	External temperature (T)
Utilities: buildings, PDUs	Power, energy
HPC hardware: compute, storage, network, etc.	Power, energy
Cooling units	Power, energy, water flow, fan rotation, input/output temperatures
Other features	Workload intensity (IT) Power Usage Effectiveness (PUE)

Raw data is sparse into multiple files in CSV format for a total size of 1.2 GB. Once the preprocessing phase achieved, data is gathered into a sole file of 264 MB for around 3 million entries or events and 89 features. This step results in a data reduction factor of 4.5.

For the rest of this section, we will focus on the first quarter of the first year because it exhibits behaviours that could be diluted and less visible over a longer period.

5.2 Evaluation Metrics

We selected the main evaluation metrics for the energy consumption effectiveness and those for the most impacting external parameters. First, PUE is the most significant metric in the field and also the one we have to optimise. Let P_{TOT} the total power usage of the HPC facility and P_{IT} the power used for the IT, it is calculated by:

$$PUE = \frac{P_{TOT}}{P_{IT}}$$

In addition, we consider both IT and T features that cannot be controlled but must be taken into account to make adjustments on other parameters to reach a PUE optimisation.

5.3   Experimental Workflow

We selected a subset of 11 features for the clustering based on their high impact on PUE and the admin experts recommendations. Figure 3 represents the evolution of the power used by IT during the first term of the measurements. Five regular clusters are obtained with an extra one gathering all the outliers.

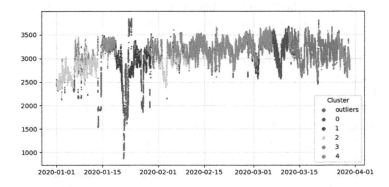

Fig. 3. Clustering power (kW) used by IT, 1st trimester of 2020

To facilitate the interpretation of the clustering, we apply a t-SNE model to our dataset. Figure 4 represents the obtained 2D visualisation. These two dimensions are a linear combination of our input features. All clusters are clearly separated in dense groups and identified by their color.

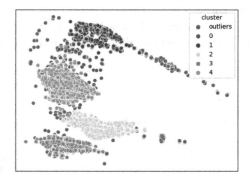

Fig. 4. t-SNE visualisation of the clustered dataset

6   Results and Discussion

In this section, we present our method's capabilities with a focus on PUE and the developed tool to make these capabilities available for administrators.

6.1 Clustering and Anomaly Detection

Clustering does not characterise just similar behaviour, it can lead to possible anomalies detection too. Figure 5 represents the evolution of the power of one PDU during the measurement period according to the clustering. It can be seen that the power is stable for some clusters especially cluster 0 around 60kW, except during some days of March when its power is although still stable but at 80kW. The power of the PDU being proportional to the number of Computer Room Air Conditioner (CRAC) units, this implies that four CRACs are active. Having a different number of working CRACs over time is not an issue, because the operating mode can change and the power to cool the system depends on the external temperature. But in our case, the wiring diagrams show that only three CRACs were bound to that PDU. An anomaly in the wiring scheme of the infrastructure has therefore been detected and corrected.

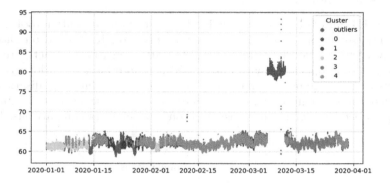

Fig. 5. PDU power (kW), 1st trimester of 2020

6.2 Setting Guidelines for PUE Optimisation

According to statements in Sect. 4.2, two clusters belonging to the same operating mode are represented by the same range of values in terms of external temperature and IT. However, they can have different PUE distributions. The comparison of the mean PUE and the variance for both clusters pointed the best and the most stable PUE. The best PUE corresponds to a lower mean value and a stable PUE is identified by a small variance. Boxplots on Fig. 6 summarise the PUE variation for all clusters. We can notice that both clusters 0 (green) and 4 (blue) are considered belonging to the same operating mode. Nevertheless, even if the cluster 0 has a better median PUE value, it has a spread distribution that stands for an instable PUE. We deduce then that its behaviour is not suitable and recommend to apply the cluster 4 settings when the workload of cluster 0 occurs. A guideline for PUE improvement according to the workload is then suggested to the infrastructure administrator.

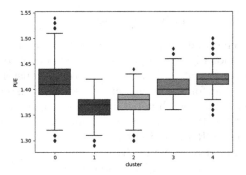

Fig. 6. PUE variation, 1st trimester of 2020 (Color figure online)

6.3 Visualisation Tool

A practical result of our study is the development of a visualisation tool to make our results useful for the infrastructure administrator. It is based on Dash, an open source library available in Python 3, written on top of React.js to build a full-stack web application with customised user interfaces and Plotly.js which supports a full range of scientific charts with interactive data visualisation [10]. The sidebar of its main page gives access to the different treatments to apply on data: preprocessing, clustering, visualisation, and clusters comparisons. In the

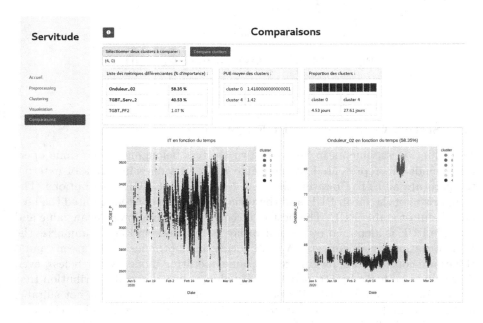

Fig. 7. Screenshot of the visualisation tool – Comparisons page

preprocessing page, raw data file can be uploaded to be filtered. In the clustering page, users can select a time period, the metrics of interest and the density required to apply HDBSCAN clustering. This time period allows a flexible usage, providing the possibility of a long-term study as achieved in this work. A prospect is to provide an online mode to detect outliers and anticipate anomalies detection along with the data collection. The visualisation page offers the choice among 3 types of visualisation: 2D, 3D and t-SNE. Many options to interact with graphs on display are available as zooming in and out, point value display or viewing one or several clusters, display as many and different graphs as needed. A last page offers to users a tool to compare clusters as described in Sect. 4 with the associated stats as shown on the screenshot of Fig. 7.

7 Conclusion and Future Works

In this paper, we propose a supervision methodology that provides a set of ML-based algorithms to be operated on the extracted data from a computing center devices. It allows a clear and dynamic supervision to highlight similar behaviours to apply the same optimised solutions when they occur, and the abnormal ones to solve them. The proposed methodology can be applied to different metrics related to the computing center facilities beyond the PUE example given in this paper. A tool has been developed to expose the several choices of functions to apply to collected data, and to display results in an interactive way. It is available for infrastructure administrators, providing them with guidelines for a secure and efficient supervision of the computing center. Currently, it is successfully used revealing the PDU anomaly which has stayed undetected for about 2 years of service. In the near future, we intend to extend our work to handle the management of trivial anomalies, the implementation of alarms to warn of changes within the same operating mode and anticipate deviant behaviours.

References

1. Agerwala, T.: Challenges on the road to exascale computing. In: 22nd Annual International Conference on Supercomputing (2008)
2. Alvin, K., Barrett, B., Brightwell, R., Dosanjih, S.S.: On the path to exascale. Int. J. Distrib. Syst. Technol. **1**, 1–22 (2011)
3. Bajal, E., Katara, V., Bhatia, M., Hooda, M.: A review of clustering algorithms: comparison of DBSCAN and K-mean with oversampling and t-SNE. J. Recent Patents Eng. **16**(2), 17–31 (2022)
4. Bautista, E., Romanus, M., Davis, T., Whithney, C., Kubaska, T.: Collecting, monitoring, and analyzing facility and systems data at the national energy research scientific computing center. In: 48th International Conference on Parallel Processing (2019)
5. Borghesi, A., Bartolini, A., Lombardi, M., Milano, M., Benini, L.: Predictive modeling for job power consumption in HPC systems. In: Kunkel, J.M., Balaji, P., Dongarra, J. (eds.) ISC High Performance 2016. LNCS, vol. 9697, pp. 181–199. Springer, Cham (2016). https://doi.org/10.1007/978-3-319-41321-1_10

6. Bourassa, N., Johnson, W., Broughton, J., Carter, D.M., Joy, S.: Operational data analytics: Optimizing the national energy research computing center cooling systems. In: 48th International Conference on parallel Processing, pp. 1–7 (2019)
7. Campello, R.J.G.B., Moulavi, D., Sander, J.: Density-based clustering based on hierarchical density estimates. In: Pei, J., Tseng, V.S., Cao, L., Motoda, H., Xu, G. (eds.) PAKDD 2013. LNCS (LNAI), vol. 7819, pp. 160–172. Springer, Heidelberg (2013). https://doi.org/10.1007/978-3-642-37456-2_14
8. Corbalan, J., Alonso, L., Aneas, J., Brochard, L.: Energy optimization and analysis with ear. In: IEEE International Conference on Cluster Computing (2020)
9. Dani, M.C., Doreau, H., Alt, S.: K-means application for anomaly detection and log classification in HPC. In: Benferhat, S., Tabia, K., Ali, M. (eds.) IEA/AIE 2017. LNCS (LNAI), vol. 10351, pp. 201–210. Springer, Cham (2017). https://doi.org/10.1007/978-3-319-60045-1_23
10. Dash website (2023). https://dash.plotly.com/. Accessed 08 Mar 2023
11. Gao, J., Zheng, F., Qi, F.: Sunway supercomputer architecture towards exascale computing: analysis and practice. China Inf. Sci. **64**, 141101 (2021)
12. van der Maaten, L., Hinton, G.: Viualizing data using t-SNE. J. Mach. Learn. Res. **9**, 2579–2605 (2008)
13. Molan, M., Borghesi, A., Cesarini, D., Benini, L., Bartolini, A.: RUAD: unsupervised anomaly detection in HPC systems. Future Gener. Comput. Syst. **141**(C), 542–554 (2023)
14. Ozer, G., Netti, A., Tafani, D., Schulz, M.: Characterizing HPC performance variation with monitoring and unsupervised learning. In: Jagode, H., Anzt, H., Juckeland, G., Ltaief, H. (eds.) ISC High Performance 2020. LNCS, vol. 12321, pp. 280–292. Springer, Cham (2020). https://doi.org/10.1007/978-3-030-59851-8_18
15. Shalf, J., Dosanjh, S., Morrison, J.: Exascale computing technology challenges. In: 9th International Conference on High Performance Computing for Computational Science (2010)
16. Shoukourian, H., Wilde, T., Labrenz, D., Bode, A.: Using machine learning for data center cooling infrastructure efficiency prediction. In: 2017 IEEE International Parallel and Distributed Processing Symposium Workshops (IPDPSW) (2017)
17. Shrikant, K., Gupta, V., Khandare, A., Furia, P.: A comparative study of clustering algorithm. In: Balas, V.E., Semwal, V.B., Khandare, A. (eds.) Intelligent Computing and Networking. Lecture Notes in Networks and Systems, vol. 301, pp. 219–235. Springer, Singapore (2022). https://doi.org/10.1007/978-981-16-4863-2_19
18. Singh, H.V., Girdhar, A., Dahiya, S.: A literature survey based on DBSCAN algorithms. In: 6th International Conference on Intelligent Computing and Control Systems, pp. 751–758 (2022)
19. Su, Y., Zhou, J., Ying, J., Zhou, M., Zhou, B.: Computing infrastructure construction and optimization for high-performance computing and artificial intelligence. CCF Trans. High Perform. Comput. **3**(4), 331–343 (2021). https://doi.org/10.1007/s42514-021-00080-x
20. Tanash, M., Dunn, B., Andresen, D., Hsu, W., Yang, H., Okanlawon, A.: Improving HPC system performance by predicting job resources via supervised machine learning. In: Proceedings of the Practice and Experience in Advanced Research Computing on Rise of the Machines (Learning). PEARC 2019 (2019)
21. Terai, M., Shoji, F., Tsukamoto, T., Yamochi, Y.: A study of operational impact on power usage effectiveness using facility metrics and server operation logs in the k computer. In: IEEE International Conference on Cluster Computing (2020)

22. Terai, M., Yamamoto, K., Miura, S., Shoji, F.: An operational data collecting and monitoring platform for Fugaku: system overviews and case studies in the prelaunch service period. In: Jagode, H., Anzt, H., Ltaief, H., Luszczek, P. (eds.) ISC High Performance 2021. LNCS, vol. 12761, pp. 365–377. Springer, Cham (2021). https://doi.org/10.1007/978-3-030-90539-2_24
23. TGCC-CEA. https://www-hpc.cea.fr/en/TGCC.html
24. Top500 the list (2022). https://www.top500.org/lists/top500/2022/11/

A Fast Simulator to Enable HPC Scheduling Strategy Comparisons

Alex Wilkinson[1,2(✉)], Jess Jones[1], Harvey Richardson[1], Tim Dykes[1], and Utz-Uwe Haus[1]

[1] HPE HPC/AI EMEA Research Lab, Bristol, UK
[2] University College London, London, UK
alexander.wilkinson.20@ucl.ac.uk

Abstract. Accurate and fast simulation of HPC job scheduling is an important tool for exploring the effect of different scheduling strategies on production systems and for providing insight into future HPC design. Current realistic simulations are computationally intensive and cannot provide a rapid feedback loop to facilitate the development of novel scheduling strategies. This work presents a lightweight simulation of the workload manager Slurm that is able to accurately reproduce the performance of the UK's national supercomputer ARCHER2 using historical workload accounting data. The simulation achieves a speed up of ∼400 over a period of full system utilisation, allowing for months of activity to be simulated in hours, while maintaining wait times accurate to 7%. The simulator design supports incorporating external factors into scheduling to enable comparison of power-aware strategies. By using the simulation to evaluate the effect of multiple possible scheduling changes to ARCHER2, focusing on improving power management, the potential to provide insight into configuration changes and extensions to the scheduling logic is demonstrated.

Keywords: HPC Scheduling · Simulation · Slurm

1 Introduction

A well configured workload manager is a critical part of running an efficient HPC system. It is the mechanism through which the system is controlled, allowing for a balance to be struck between maximising utilisation, minimising wait times, ensuring fair allocation among users, and meeting any specific system requirements. Current workload managers, notably the popular open-source workload manager Slurm [2], are capable of striking this balance but have a large configurable parameter space that needs to be tuned and explored to do so. In addition to this, as workloads grow larger and more complex, extensions to current workload managers will be desirable to allow for fine-grained control of system power usage and integration of new advanced scheduling algorithms.

The important work of exploring configurations and new algorithms is difficult on a production system due to the risk of compromising system efficiency.

© The Author(s), under exclusive license to Springer Nature Switzerland AG 2023
A. Bienz et al. (Eds.): ISC High Performance 2023 Workshops, LNCS 13999, pp. 320–333, 2023.
https://doi.org/10.1007/978-3-031-40843-4_24

This can lead to conservative parameter choices and a reluctance to employ new scheduling strategies. Simulation can be used to provide the insight necessary to find more optimal positions in the parameter space. It allows for different combinations of parameters and the integration of novel scheduling algorithms to be evaluated without risk. Although this principle applies to all workload managers, this work attempts to simulate Slurm specifically. Many features of Slurm are common to all workload managers, but focussing on a single piece of software is necessary to ensure a uniform format for job traces and configuration data, and to reproduce any particularities for validation purposes.

There are many grid scheduling simulations that can be used to study scheduling strategies, such as GridSim [3] and SimGrid [4]. Although these frameworks can be configured to study HPC systems, they are not well suited to exploring specific scheduling changes. Simulation of Slurm specifically was initially developed in [9] and has since been iterated on numerous times with attempts to improve accuracy and performance [7,12,13]. Its potential to improve system performance has been demonstrated in [10] and [11] which build frameworks for using the simulation to test configuration changes on production systems. The common approach of these works is to submit jobs to a simulated environment running Slurm code from a job trace. Job allocation and termination messages that would be sent from the daemons running on compute nodes to the controller daemon are emulated. Speed up is achieved by skipping through time between events. These simulators have generally been able to reach high accuracies and successfully scale to large systems and workloads. However, by starting from the Slurm source code they struggle to achieve the speed up necessary for any significant parameter exploration on large systems where they are most needed. In addition, exploration of new functionality requires significant time investment as it requires implementation as a plugin to Slurm. This may be unfeasible if the functionality is not yet proven to be beneficial to a wide number of systems.

Current research into HPC scheduling, especially those taking machine learning approaches, tend to create custom scheduling simulations to evaluate algorithms [5,8]. These often capture some level of job priority calculation and backfilling but do not include many features present in production workloads such as resource limits, node failures, and fair share algorithms. This means that they are not suitable for studying the integration of these new algorithms into production HPC systems. A simulation that can sufficiently model a production system while remaining fast and easily extendable would benefit HPC scheduling research.

This work proposes a fast simulation that includes only the features of Slurm directly relevant to scheduling. Even with Slurm's implementation recreated in full, stochasticity in routine execution guarantees that the precise order of job submission will diverge for a constant stream of job submissions. For this reason, the simulation should be able to accurately reproduce the dynamics of a real system without trying to reproduce the design of Slurm. The simulation is evaluated through how well it can recreate aggregate behaviours and respond to changes in characteristics of the workload over time. The simulation is built

from scratch and validated using a job trace from the production HPC system
ARCHER2. A less thorough validation is performed with other systems. Its use
is then demonstrated by studying the effect of changes to configuration and
scheduling logic on system performance over historical workload data.

2 Simulation

2.1 Overview

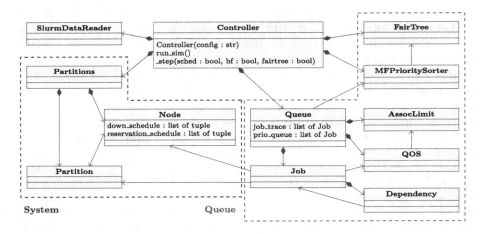

Fig. 1. Class diagram for scheduling simulation. Only a handful of important methods
and attributes are shown for clarity. Classes are grouped into system and queue to
indicate the general scheduling component each collection is responsible for.

The simplified class diagram in Fig. 1 gives an overview of the simulator's design.
The class *Controller* steps through time and controls which operations are executed at each time step. It is also where the main scheduling and backfilling
loops are implemented. The collection of classes labelled queue are responsible
for providing a priority sorted queue of jobs waiting to be scheduled and for
determining which jobs are allowed to be started at any given time. Job submission from the historical data is simulated here. The collection labelled system is
responsible for tracking the current state of the system i.e. the compute nodes.
The controller decides which jobs to schedule based on data from these two col-
lections. The class *SlurmDataReader* is used at the start of the simulation to
parse the Slurm data used to initialise the system and queue.

The simulation is implemented in standard library Python with some use of
libraries for CSV file manipulation. The system is configured using a YAML file
that contains the locations of the Slurm configuration file and Slurm accounting
data dumps for job data, node events, quality of service (QoS), active reservations, and association (4-tuple of user, cluster, partition, and account used

in Slurm accounting) data. Scheduling parameters set by the configuration file can be overridden by explicitly setting them in the YAML file. More substantial changes and extensions to the scheduling can be achieved by directly modifying class methods. This design is intended to be used to realise different scheduling strategies for a production system over part or all of its historical job trace.

2.2 Features

The simulation includes numerous features both general to scheduling and specific to Slurm that are either implemented in their entirety or partially. The three features most relevant to scheduling are discussed in this section.

Backfilling. A conservative backfilling algorithm [6] is implemented to run alongside the main scheduling loop at configured intervals. Backfilling is a computationally expensive operation that can take a long time to complete. Large HPC sites will typically need to configure Slurm's backfilling thread to periodically yield locks so that other operations can be allowed to complete. The backfilling will then continue operation, ignoring any changes to system state that occurred during the lock release interval. To capture this in the simulation, the backfilling executes in steps of the lock yield interval parameter. Between these steps, the main scheduling loop is allowed to run if triggered.

Resource Limits. The *QOS* class is used to track resource use and report if a job should be considered for scheduling at a given time. The hierarchy between limits set in the QoS and limits set at the user association level is also implemented. Slurm has an additional partition level hierarchy which is not implemented at this time. Any resource limits that will prevent a job from running indefinitely e.g. MaxWallDurationPerJob or MaxTRESPerJob, do not need to be implemented since they result in the job being absent from the trace. Of the subset that are relevant for the simulation, the majority are implemented.

Fairshare. A ubiquitous feature of Slurm is its multifactor priority plugin. It is used to sort the queue according to a hierarchy of factors that take into account advanced reservations, partition, and multiple job properties including wait time, size, and a fairshare factor. The fairshare calculation is fully implemented with the fair tree implementation [2]. A rooted ordered tree of associations is constructed and used to sort users by their usage relative to allocated system shares.

2.3 Limitations

A key limitation in any simulation making use of historical Slurm data comes from missing information in the Slurm accounting database. Some job information such as dependencies and requested nodes are not explicitly recorded. They can sometimes be extracted from the submission line but if set inside the submission script or using environment variables it may not be possible to recover them. In addition to this, records of completed reservations are not stored. This means that a reservation history would need to be kept externally or a synthetic set of reservations generated. Lastly, there can be discrepancies coming from human interaction with the system e.g. holding jobs and changing user resource limits, that cannot be replicated.

The simulation was developed by implementing features of Slurm in order of their assumed importance in making scheduling decisions. In this way, the simulation was incremented until the subset of Slurm required to reproduce scheduling behaviour on the HPC systems considered for validation was implemented. This subset encompasses the majority of the desirable features. Many of the missing features are options that slightly alter already implemented parts of the simulation and would require minor changes to incorporate. Notably missing is the ability to specify consumable resources other than compute nodes. The scheduler already chooses nodes from all valid nodes based on the configured node weight, so checking, for example, CPU count would not require much change to the structure of the simulation. Features that are expected to require a more substantial effort to implement are job preemption and heterogeneous job support.

Due to the aforementioned limitations, this work is presented as a demonstration of the ability of a lightweight scheduling simulation to provide useful insight into scheduling strategies. The simulation has the potential to be expanded to be able to produce accurate simulation of any HPC system regardless of its configuration and workload characteristics. At this time however, the simulation does not have sufficient coverage of Slurm's features to guarantee this.

3   Validation

3.1   ARCHER2

ARCHER2 is the UK's national supercomputer consisting of 23 HPE Cray EX cabinets forming a network of 5,860 compute nodes. The workload manager configuration as of the time of writing is described here. The system uses Slurm version 21.08 with a configuration refined from multiple years of operation. Nodes are assigned to overlapping standard and high memory partitions and jobs to a QoS depending on their size, length, and importance. The workload comes from a wide range of academic fields and includes job sizes ranging from a one to a few thousand nodes. System utilisation is consistently over 90% with a queue of at least a few hundred jobs. This means that even minor changes to job scheduling can create significantly different submission orders.

Input to the simulation job data was collected from the Slurm accounting database for four months of operation from October 2022, totalling approximately 600,000 jobs. Where possible, job dependencies and reservations were parsed from the submission line stored in the record. The system state was captured at the end of the four month period and used to configure the simulation.

3.2 Results and Discussion

As discussed previously, the simulation aims to accurately reproduce aggregate features of the scheduling while allowing the precise order of job submission to deviate. To evaluate this, the two week moving average wait time for the results of the simulation and for the true submission times taken from the data are compared. This is shown in Fig. 2 over the four month period. Over this time period the simulation differs from the data by a mean absolute percentage error of 7.3% The simulation closely matches the high frequency trends of the data, suggesting that as groups of jobs enter the moving average they are treated in the same way relative to current jobs in the window for both the simulation and data. Low frequency behaviour is generally captured well but for the wait time it is consistently lower. This is likely due to imperfect historical reservations which were partially recovered for ARCHER2.

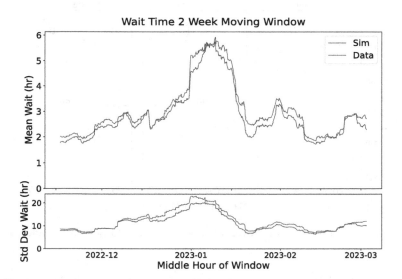

Fig. 2. Moving average wait time and standard deviation for jobs in a two week submission window.

To examine this behaviour over time closer, Fig. 3 shows the two week moving average wait time for jobs from a selection of QoS. Jobs from these QoS differ not only by their resource limits but also by their typical usage, for example *taskfarm* jobs will tend to be from a small group of users submitting a large number of jobs. This means that accurate simulation of their wait times depends on the implementation of many scheduling components in addition to resource limits. The wait times for each QoS are generally well matched between data and simulation. The *lowpriority* jobs are configured to be considered for scheduling only after all jobs from other QoS have been. The resulting long wait times are correctly reproduced in the simulation. Jobs from the *largescale* QoS have significantly shorter simulation wait times. The simulation usually spends much less time attempting to schedule these large jobs, a pronounced example of this is in Fig. 4. The reduced time spent at lower system utilisation is also a factor in the slightly shorter wait times seen in Fig. 2. It is not likely that the shorter *largescale* wait times are caused by the priority calculation or backfilling algorithm as all other metrics suggest these are implemented correctly. The cause may be a constraint, such as a maximum number of leaf switches, set outside the submission line or perhaps more complicated behaviour related to Slurm's design that is not captured by the simulation. Further investigation into the system state during the scheduling of such jobs is required to understand the cause.

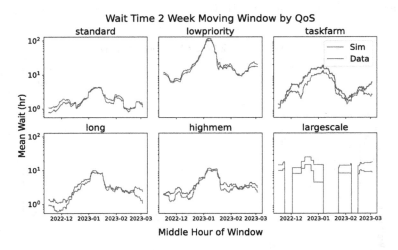

Fig. 3. Moving average wait time over a two week window for jobs from different QoS.

In Fig. 5, the simulated average wait time is compared with the average wait time from data for users with the highest overall system usage over the four month time period. The simulation matches the data reasonably well but has wait times that are generally shorter for most users for the previously stated reasons. This shows that the simulation can be used to provide insight into the effect of scheduling changes down to the user level.

To study the behaviour of the simulator, the relationship between wait time and certain job properties can be examined. Two-dimensional histograms of wait time against both requested nodes and requested time are shown in Fig. 6. Ignoring any correlations between job properties, the distributions are primarily a result of how difficult a job of a given size or length is to backfill. The relationship of wait time to these job properties matches reasonably well between simulation and data, but with wait times for the simulation shifted to earlier times. This suggests that the backfill algorithm is correctly implemented but the simulation operates with a higher throughput.

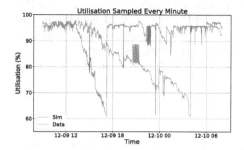

Fig. 4. System utilisation during scheduling of a large scale job.

Fig. 5. Mean wait times for top fifteen users by usage.

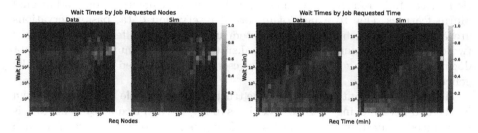

Fig. 6. 2D histograms of job size in nodes (left) and job requested time (right) against wait time. Bin counts in each column, corresponding to a range of job sizes or requested times, are normalised to unity.

Using a single thread on a 64-core AMD EPYC 7742 process at 2.25 GHz, the simulation completes in approximately 7 h and 20 min. This represents a speed up by a factor of 400, meaning 400 simulated hours pass with every 1 h of simulation time. The simulation time is dominated by the backfilling algorithm which requires frequent I/O operations to maintain a map of current and future job placement. For ARCHER2 during the simulated time period, the queue contains 541 jobs on average and the backfilling loop is configured to run for 30 s simulated time over a maximum of 1,000 jobs and then sleep for 30 s simulated time. Simulation time will scale with queue length up to this configured maximum. For larger maxima, the backfill thread will typically need more time to complete and so will run less frequently. This means that simulation times for other systems should not increase significantly. In the current implementation simulation time also scales poorly with queue size due to liberal use of sort operations. Refactoring to use heap data structures would help mitigate this.

Other simulators that modify the Slurm source code typically achieve speed ups between 10 and 25 [10–12] for large HPC systems. An exception to this is in [7] where a speed up of approximately 220 is reached using the CEA Curie log from the Parallel Workloads Archive [1]. However, it is not clear if this job trace can be taken as a good representation of a modern production system. The archive states an average utilisation of 62% compared to over 90% for ARCHER2. This will have a significant impact on the computational cost of backfilling and queue sorting operations which are key drivers in simulation time. In order to gain a better understanding of the differences in performance between simulators, direct comparisons that use the same job traces are required. This is an important direction for future research.

3.3 Other Systems

LUMI. LUMI is a HPE Cray EX system that is currently the third fastest globally. It is made up of 4,096 compute nodes in both GPU and CPU partitions. The component of the system partitions allocatable by node was loaded into the simulator along with a 3 month job trace containing 25,402 jobs. The simulation successfully ran over this time period after implementing some additional Slurm features. Due to a lack of historical reservation data, past reservations are approximated using the total system utilisation at different times. Every two days the maximum utilisation is taken to be the total number of nodes not down or reserved, any jobs specifying a reservation are moved to the front of the general queue.

The simulated wait times match the truth with reasonable accuracy as shown by the two week moving average wait times in Fig. 7. High frequency behaviour is reproduced accurately, but as simulated time progresses discrepancies grow with jobs queueing for approximately 2 h less than in the data at some times. This is at least partially a consequence of the aforementioned approximation used to make up for a lack of historical reservation data. Despite this the simulation achieves a mean absolute percentage error of 10.4%.

The average simulated wait time for users with the greatest system usage is compared with the data in Fig. 8. The agreement between simulation and data is not as close as for ARCHER2 with simulated times being significantly lower for User2 and User4 and slightly lower for other users. This may be caused by job properties not stored in the Slurm accounting database.

While the simulation is not as accurate as for ARCHER2, validation with LUMI shows that it is general enough to be configured for any system running Slurm and at least coarsely reproduce behaviour. This highlights the potential of the simulator to generalise to any HPC system with further development.

Peta4. Peta4 is a 1,468 node supercomputer forming part of the Cambridge Service for Data-Driven Discovery. Anonymised Slurm data was collected over a two month period and the system state and job trace was successfully loaded into the simulator. However, the simulation does not currently have the features necessary to sufficiently reproduce the scheduling behaviour. Extending it with these features is an important direction for future work since its workload has a much higher throughput than ARCHER2 with approximately four million jobs over the two month period. This would make it a valuable test of the simulator's performance.

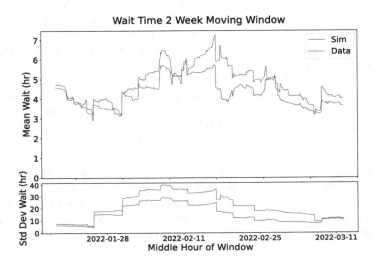

Fig. 7. Moving average wait time and standard deviation for jobs in a two week submission window for LUMI.

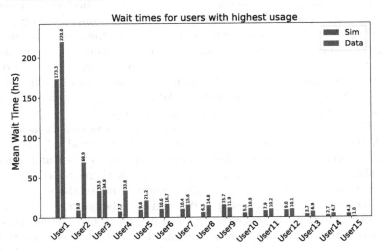

Fig. 8. Mean wait times for top fifteen users by usage for LUMI.

4 Experiments

4.1 High Priority Jobs

It may be desirable for a HPC system to offer a high priority QoS for prioritising time sensitive work. Before implementing this, the simulation can be used to provide insight into its impact on system performance. An example of this with ARCHER2 is shown in Fig. 9, where the effect of putting different proportions of *standard* QoS jobs into a *highpriority* QoS at random is tested. High priority jobs have their wait times reduced by a factor of 8 with little effect on other QoS when 5% of standard jobs are submitted as high priority. As this proportion grows, its impact on other QoS grows also until at 30% they begin to significantly impact scheduling of large jobs and starve high memory jobs of resources. The average system performance across all jobs is negatively impacted when there is a small number of high priority jobs but for larger numbers it is not. This is likely due to reaching a threshold where high priority jobs form a substantial portion of the queue rather than acting as sporadic disruptions to the backfilling. The simulation can be used to study the impact introducing this QoS at different granularities and experiment with the different possible implementations and uses of a high priority QoS, highlighting its value to production HPC systems.

4.2 Large Scale Jobs at Peak Times

Slurm can be configured to associate energy counters collected from compute nodes with running jobs. This is used to provide a consumed energy for each job, allowing for average job power to be inferred from the accounting data. For ARCHER2, energy accounting is configured. To use this data to estimate total system power draw at any given time, the power reported by nodes with running jobs is fitted to power reported at the cabinet level with an occupancy term to account for idle nodes. This allows the simulator to be used to analyse the total power usage over time for different scheduling strategies.

ARCHER2 uses a large scale QoS to manage jobs over one thousand nodes. Although these represent a very small fraction of the workload, they have a significant effect on the system when being scheduled. When being scheduled, the backfilling algorithm will struggle to find jobs with requested times short enough that they will not interfere with the start time of the large job. This results in a significant drop in system utilisation over the hours leading up to the large job being submitted. This effect is inevitable for priority based schedulers. In the context of power management it would be desirable to ensure that this period of low utilisation overlaps with the peak hours of the day when electricity is in high demand and cooling is under the most stress. The simulator can be used to evaluate strategies that attempt to do this.

The *largescale* QoS is adapted to hold all jobs until a specified time the next morning. The simulator determines the time they are allowed to be scheduled from a small set of switch cases dependent on job size and with optimal submit

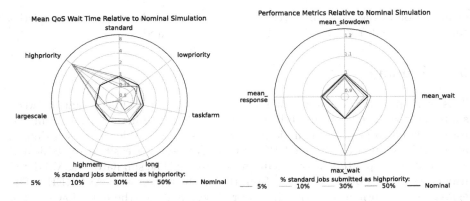

Fig. 9. Effect of different usages of a high priority QoS on wait times by QoS (left) and system-wide performance metrics (right). Nominal refers to the unmodified simulation. Relative metrics are computed such that a larger area enclosed by a line corresponds to better performance over the nominal. For the left, the nominal mean wait time of the *standard* QoS is used in the computation of the relative *highpriority* QoS mean wait time.

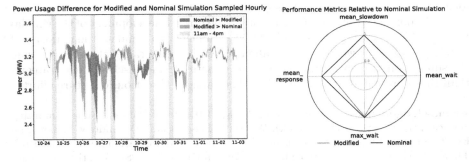

Fig. 10. Effect of holding scheduling of *largescale* jobs until morning on power (left) and system-wide performance metrics (right).

times estimated from average behaviour. The effect of this modification on system power and performance can be seen in Fig. 10. The scheduling of large jobs result in reductions in power usage of up to 0.8 MW depending on their size. Even using the rudimentary method for choosing the release time, the utilisation drops are fairly well aligned with peak times. It would be interesting to explore more advanced algorithms that identify jobs expected to be hard to backfill and hold them until a predicted optimal time, thus trading low utilisation during peak times for higher utilisation at off-peak times. This could be explored by extending the simulator with elements from machine learning libraries. Also shown in the figure is the impact of this scheduling modification on performance metrics. The drop in performance is due to the scheduling of large jobs coinciding with the peak submission time in the day, rather than a drop in throughput. Further examination of the effect on particular users or jobs with certain characteristics can be extracted from the simulation results as required.

5   Summary

This work presents a lightweight scheduling simulator to fill the gap between simple custom schedulers and full simulation of workload managers. The simulator's design incorporates the majority of Slurm's features relevant to scheduling, allowing for simulation of some HPC systems. It's design is easily extendable and well suited for rapid testing of scheduling strategies. The simulator was validated using a recent historical workload from the production system ARCHER2. The aggregated performance of the simulator closely matches the data down to the granularity of a single user despite limitations in recovering complete job properties from Slurm accounting data. Further investigation is required to understand the significantly shorter simulated wait times of a small number of large jobs. The potential of the simulation to provide insight into the effects of scheduling strategies is demonstrated with two experiments. The latter experiment shows how Slurm's energy accounting enables the exploration of scheduling strategies focused on power management using the simulator.

An important avenue for future work is the further development of the simulation to achieve coverage of Slurm's features sufficient to simulate the majority of HPC systems. This would permit validation with a wide range of systems. Using the simulation to demonstrate significantly more advanced scheduling strategies than those presented previously is another valuable direction for future efforts.

Acknowledgements. This work used the ARCHER2 UK National Supercomputing Service (https://www.archer2.ac.uk). We would like to thank Dr Andrew Turner from EPCC for valuable discussions during development and validation with ARCHER2. Thanks to the Cambridge Service for Data Driven Discovery (CSD3) at the University of Cambridge for providing access to workload data. We acknowledge support of CSC who provided access to scheduler data from the LUMI system, owned by the EuroHPC Joint Undertaking.

References

1. Parallel workloads archive. https://www.cs.huji.ac.il/labs/parallel/workload/. Accessed 20 June 2023
2. Slurm workload manager. https://slurm.schedmd.com/documentation.html. Accessed 31 Mar 2023
3. Buyya, R., Murshed, M.: GridSim: a toolkit for the modeling and simulation of distributed resource management and scheduling for grid computing. Concurr. Comput.: Pract. Experience **14**(13–15), 1175–1220 (2002). https://onlinelibrary.wiley.com/doi/abs/10.1002/cpe.710
4. Casanova, H., Giersch, A., Legrand, A., Quinson, M., Suter, F.: Versatile, scalable, and accurate simulation of distributed applications and platforms. J. Parallel Distrib. Comput. **74**(10), 2899–2917 (2014). http://hal.inria.fr/hal-01017319

5. Fan, Y., Lan, Z., Childers, T., Rich, P., Allcock, W., Papka, M.E.: Deep reinforcement agent for scheduling in HPC. In: 2021 IEEE International Parallel and Distributed Processing Symposium (IPDPS), pp. 807–816. IEEE (2021)
6. Feitelson, D., Weil, A.: Utilization and predictability in scheduling the IBM SP2 with backfilling. In: Proceedings of the First Merged International Parallel Processing Symposium and Symposium on Parallel and Distributed Processing, pp. 542–546 (1998)
7. Jokanovic, A., D'Amico, M., Corbalan, J.: Evaluating Slurm simulator with real-machine Slurm and vice versa. In: 2018 IEEE/ACM Performance Modeling, Benchmarking and Simulation of High Performance Computer Systems (PMBS), pp. 72–82 (2018)
8. Kassab, A., Nicod, J.M., Philippe, L., Rehn-Sonigo, V.: Assessing the use of genetic algorithms to schedule independent tasks under power constraints. In: 2018 International Conference on High Performance Computing & Simulation (HPCS), pp. 252–259 (2018)
9. Lucero, A.: Simulation of batch scheduling using real production-ready software tools. In: Proceedings of the 5th IBERGRID (2011)
10. Martinasso, M., Gila, M., Bianco, M., Alam, S.R., McMurtrie, C., Schulthess, T.C.: RM-replay: a high-fidelity tuning, optimization and exploration tool for resource management. In: International Conference for High Performance Computing, Networking, Storage and Analysis, SC 2018, pp. 320–332 (2018)
11. Rodrigo, G.P., Elmroth, E., Östberg, P.-O., Ramakrishnan, L.: ScSF: a scheduling simulation framework. In: Klusáček, D., Cirne, W., Desai, N. (eds.) JSSPP 2017. LNCS, vol. 10773, pp. 152–173. Springer, Cham (2018). https://doi.org/10.1007/978-3-319-77398-8_9
12. Simakov, N.A., et al.: A Slurm simulator: implementation and parametric analysis. In: Jarvis, S., Wright, S., Hammond, S. (eds.) PMBS 2017. LNCS, vol. 10724, pp. 197–217. Springer, Cham (2018). https://doi.org/10.1007/978-3-319-72971-8_10
13. Trofinoff, S., Benini, M.: Using and modifying the BSC Slurm workload simulator. Slurm User Group Meeting 2015 (2015). https://slurm.schedmd.com/SLUG15/BSC_Slurm_Workload_Simulator_Enhancements.pdf

2nd Workshop on Communication, I/O, and Storage at Scale on Next-Generation Platforms: Scalable Infrastructures

Preface to the 2nd Workshop on Communication, I/O, and Storage at Scale on Next-Generation Platforms: Scalable Infrastructures

1 Objectives

Next-generation HPC platforms must deal with increasing heterogeneity in their subsystems, including the following:

- multiple, internal, high-speed fabrics for inter-node communication;
- storage systems integrated with programmable data processing units (DPUs) or infrastructure processing units (IPUs) to support software-defined networks;
- traditional storage infrastructures with global, parallel, POSIX-based filesystems complemented by scalable object stores; and
- heterogeneous compute nodes configured with a diverse spectrum of CPUs and accelerators (e.g., GPU, FPGA, or AI processors) having complex intra-node communication.

To assist the community in planning for and transitioning to such platforms, this workshop pursued the following objectives:

- develop and provide a holistic overview of next-generation platforms with an emphasis on communication, I/O, and storage at scale,
- showcase application-driven performance analysis with various HPC fabrics,
- present early experiences with emerging storage concepts like object stores using next-generation HPC fabrics,
- share experience with performance tuning on heterogeneous platforms from multiple vendors, and
- provide a forum for sharing best practices for performance tuning of communication, I/O, and storage to improve application performance at scale.

2 Workshop Organization

The organization of this workshop was driven by the Intel eXtreme Performance Users Group (IXPUG) with additional support provided by the leaders of the oneAPI Users Group. It was promoted via its own marketing channels: the IXPUG website (www.ixpug.org), IXPUG newsletters, IXPUG member mailing lists, and across IXPUG's social media channels like LinkedIn and Twitter. In addition to the IXPUG channels, the IXPUG members (such as Intel and several high-impact international research centers) announced the event through their own channels. The Program Committee invited three keynote speakers and encouraged participation by several internationally recognized research groups. Eight papers were submitted, which were reviewed using a single-blind review process and accepted by the Program Committee.

Organization

Organizers

Amit Ruhela	Texas Advanced Computing Center, USA
David Martin	Argonne National Laboratory, USA
Nalini Kumar	Intel Corporation, USA
Glenn Brook	Cornelis Networks, USA
Thomas Steinke	Zuse Institute Berlin, Germany

Program Committee

Amit Ruhela	Texas Advanced Computing Center, USA
David Martin	Argonne National Laboratory, USA
Nalini Kumar	Intel Corporation, USA
Glenn Brook	Cornelis Networks, USA
Thomas Steinke	Zuse Institute Berlin, Germany
Clayton Hughes	Sandia National Laboratory, USA
Andrey Kudryavtsev	Intel Corporation, USA
Johann Lombardi	Intel Corporation, USA
Christopher Mauney	Los Alamos National Laboratory, USA
Kelsey Prantis	Intel Corporation, USA

Outcomes

The workshop provided a well-attended forum for the presentation and discussion of next-generation architectures and software approaches to properly leverage them. The keynote presentations focused on the increasing heterogeneity of accelerators within a single system architecture, approaches to rigorously measure performance and portability across the diverse architectures, and software strategies for writing performance portable applications for current and future computing architectures. The keynotes were complemented by presentations that explored the performance and application impact of high-bandwidth memory with Intel CPUs, the use of simulation in the design of next-generation networks and high-performance fabrics, the application performance improvements for a new libfabric provider for Omni-Path fabrics, the extension of the Distributed Asynchronous Object Storage (DAOS) architecture to support configurations without persistent memory, the performance of OpenMP offloading for state-of-the-art accelerators, and the optimization of Apache Spark on a leadership-class high-performance computing system. Collectively, the workshop presentations did an excellent job of highlighting emerging architectures for various subsystems of next-generation computing platforms, along with strategies and approaches to harness their performance potential. The workshop presentations are available on the IXPUG website (https://www.ixpug.org/events/isc23-ixpug-workshop).

Application Performance Analysis: A Report on the Impact of Memory Bandwidth

Yinzhi Wang$^{(\boxtimes)}$ ⓘ, John D. McCalpin ⓘ, Junjie Li, Matthew Cawood, John Cazes, Hanning Chen, Lars Koesterke, Hang Liu, Chun-Yaung Lu, Robert McLay, Kent Milfield, Amit Ruhela, Dave Semeraro, and Wenyang Zhang ⓘ

Texas Advanced Computing Center, The University of Texas at Austin, Austin, TX 78758, USA
iwang@tacc.utexas.edu

Abstract. As High-Performance Computing (HPC) applications involving massive data sets, including large-scale simulations, data analytics, and machine learning, continue to grow in importance, memory bandwidth has emerged as a critical performance factor in contemporary HPC systems. The rapidly escalating memory performance requirements, which traditional DRAM memories often fail to satisfy, necessitate the use of High-Bandwidth Memory (HBM), which offers high bandwidth, low power consumption, and high integration capacity, making it a promising solution for next-generation platforms. However, despite the notable increase in memory bandwidth on modern systems, no prior work has comprehensively assessed the memory bandwidth requirements of a diverse set of HPC applications and provided sufficient justification for the cost of HBM with potential performance gain. This work presents a performance analysis of a diverse range of scientific applications as well as standard benchmarks on platforms with varying memory bandwidth. The study shows that while the performance improvement of scientific applications varies quite a bit, some applications in CFD, Earth Science, and Physics show significant performance gains with HBM. Furthermore, a cost-effectiveness analysis suggests that the applications exhibiting at least a 30% speedup on the HBM platform would justify the additional cost of the HBM.

Keywords: Benchmarking · Performance analysis · Memory bandwidth

1 Introduction

In recent decades, high-performance computing (HPC) has become an indispensable part of numerous scientific and engineering domains, such as molecular

This work is supported by the National Science Foundation through the Frontera award (OAC-1854828) and the CSA award (OAC-2139536).

A. Bienz et al. (Eds.): ISC High Performance 2023 Workshops, LNCS 13999, pp. 339–352, 2023.
https://doi.org/10.1007/978-3-031-40843-4_25

dynamics, computational fluid dynamics, climate modeling, and others. Consequently, the performance of modern computing systems has emerged as a crucial factor in advancing research in these fields. In response to the rising demand for data-intensive applications, memory bandwidth has become a critical consideration in the procurement of large-scale HPC systems, alongside the augmentation of computing capabilities to enhance overall system performance.

The significance of memory bandwidth in HPC systems has resulted in the creation of technologies aimed at enhancing memory bandwidth. Apart from conventional measures such as improving memory channels, clock speed, bus width, etc., novel architectures like High-Bandwidth Memory (HBM) have been developed for parallel computing with efficient power usage. Despite the notable increase in memory bandwidth in contemporary systems, no research has comprehensively assessed the impact of memory bandwidth on a diverse set of HPC applications on HBM systems and justified the extra cost of HBM.

In this study, we aim to explore the impact of memory bandwidth on the performance of a diverse range of HPC applications as part of the planning process for the Leadership-Class Computing Facility (LCCF). Specifically, we investigate the performance improvement of these applications when executed on three different architectures, a compute node on Frontera with two Intel Xeon Platinum 8280 processors (Cascade Lake), a test node with two Intel Xeon Max 9480 processors (Sapphire Rapids) with HBM disabled, and another identical test node with DDR5 disabled but HBM enabled. We then compare the results from the applications with those obtained from standard benchmarks like STREAM, SPEC CPU 2017, and SPEChpc 2021. The objective of this research is to gain insights into the design and evaluation of the memory bandwidth requirement of next-generation HPC systems based on real-world application workloads.

2 Background

2.1 Sapphire Rapids and HBM

Sapphire Rapids is the latest generation of Intel Xeon Scalable processors designed for high-performance computing. It features up to 8-channel DDR5 memory interface with 4 memory controllers, providing up to 300 GB/s of memory bandwidth per socket. HBM is a type of memory technology that offers significantly higher bandwidth than traditional DDR memory [11]. It achieves this by stacking multiple memory dies vertically, and connecting them to the CPU via a high-speed interface. This allows for faster transfer of data between the CPU and memory, which can result in improved performance for memory-intensive applications. The Sapphire Rapids Max processor we are testing supports up to 4 HBM2 stacks onboard to provide a total of 64 GB of memory per socket. It can provide up to 1 TB/s of memory bandwidth per socket.

2.2 Characteristic Science Application

The Characteristic Science Applications (CSAs) are a set of computer codes and challenge problems selected to represent a diverse range of scientific domains and computational approaches. The primary goal of the project is to transform these CSAs to enable next-generation science on the NSF LCCF. The first phase of the CSA has a total of 20 projects covering scientific domains including Astronomy and Astrophysics, Biophysics and Biology, Computational Fluid Dynamics, Earth Science, Materials Science, and Physics. Here, we selected 15 applications from these projects that can well-utilize the performance of the CPU and the WRF benchmark from TACC's internal benchmark applications as our application benchmark to understand how memory bandwidth may further improve the performance on the next-generation CPU platforms.

2.3   Benchmarks and Memory Bandwidth

The STREAM benchmark is the industry standard benchmark designed to measure the sustainable memory bandwidth of a system by testing four basic vector operations: copy, scale, add, and triad [13]. The benchmark reports the bandwidth achieved by each of these operations in MB/s, and it is considered the maximum achievable memory bandwidth of the system. Because the memory bandwidth measurements from STREAM may not be representative of the performance of real-world applications, it is often used in conjunction with other benchmarks, such as the SPEC CPU 2017 [3,15], and SPEChpc 2021 [2,12] benchmarks, to provide a more comprehensive view of the performance of a system.

SPEC CPU 2017 is a set of standardized benchmarks that measure the performance of processors on a variety of tasks, such as integer, floating-point, and memory-intensive workloads. SPEChpc 2021 is a set of benchmarks designed to measure the performance of HPC systems on scientific applications. One limitation of both SPEC CPU 2017 and SPEChpc 2021 is that the selected workloads and applications are mostly memory-bound, especially for SPEChpc 2021, this is partially due to the fact that SPEC benchmarks don't allow strong dependence of external libraries, therefore no math libraries like BLAS or LAPACK are involved [2,15]. Therefore, they will be biased when used alone to evaluate the impact of memory bandwidth on scientific applications.

There are two commonly used application benchmarks: the CORAL-2 and SPP benchmarks. The CORAL-2 (Collaboration of Oak Ridge, Argonne, and Livermore) benchmark was developed to assess the performance of HPC systems for scientific simulations and data analytics commonly supported by the Department of Energy. The SPP (Scalable Parallel Programming) benchmark focuses on the scientific community and includes parallel kernels and full applications that represent typical HPC workloads in academia. Although some applications overlap with the ones in our benchmark, such as AWP-ODC, MILC, and NAMD, the SPP benchmark was last updated in 2017 [1] and may not reflect the latest developments in scientific research. The application benchmark presented in our work serves as an update and expansion, incorporating the most recent scientific test cases and new applications developed by the community.

3   Implementation

3.1   Resources

Three different platforms are used in this work: 1) a compute node on Frontera with two Intel Xeon Platinum 8280 processors (CLX) with 6-channel DDR4 (2933 MT/s) memory per socket, 2) a test node with two Intel Xeon Max 9480 processors (SPR) with 8-channel DDR5 (4800 MT/s) memory per socket and its HBM disabled, and 3) another SPR test node with 4 HBM2 stacks onboard per socket and its DDR5 memory disabled. The CLX node has 28 cores per socket and the SPR node has 56 cores per sockets (Table 1). Both of the SPR nodes are configured to the flat mode in their sub-NUMA clustering configurations.

3.2   Standard Benchmarks

The STREAM benchmark can run with many different configurations. The selected configurations here are aimed to produce consistent and robust results that lie within the 80% to 90% percentile range of tests. It uses all the cores while ensuring that the size of arrays is at least four times larger than the combined sizes of all the L2 and L3 caches. We also tested compiling the benchmark with streaming stores or allocating stores and use the best configuration.

The SPEC CPU 2017 and SPEChpc 2021 runs use binaries compiled from scratch with the icpx, icx, and ifx compilers from Intel oneAPI 2022.1. Compilers flags are chosen from the most recent vendor submissions in order to be comparable. All SPEC runs utilize all physical cores available on the nodes.

3.3   Application Benchmarks

The 16 selected applications include ChaNGa, Enzo-E, Athena++, NAMD, Amber, PSDNS, CHyPS and Plascom, ISSM, SeisSol, CESM, WRF, AWP-ODC, EPW, Parsec, MuST, and MILC. Below, we include a short description of each application as well as its single-node benchmark performed. All the benchmarks were run on all the cores available on the node unless otherwise is documented below. Also, most of the benchmarks were measured by time in seconds, and the exceptions are also described in details below.

ChaNGa. (Charm N-body GrAvity solver) [8] is a cosmological code that performs collisionless N-Body simulations, including optional hydrodynamics using the Smooth Particle Hydrodynamics (SPH) method. A Barnes-Hut tree algorithm is used to structure particles and solve gravity equations within a volume with periodic boundary conditions. ChaNGa uses the Charm++ [9] runtime system for parallelism and relies on its dynamic load-balancing scheme to achieve good parallel efficiency on distributed systems. The 50 million particle zoom-in simulation 'dwf1.6144' case was used as a benchmark with a performance metric obtained by summing the elapsed runtime of 3 'BigSteps'.

Enzo-E. Enzo-E is an extension of the Enzo parallel astrophysics and cosmology application. The Enzo-E application is capable of running numerical simulations to address current scientific questions in astrophysics and cosmology. Enzo-E is a parallel adaptive mesh refinement (AMR) hydrocode. The AMR algorithm leverages the Cello framework. Parallel implementation is achieved through the use of Charm++. Enzo-E consists of roughly 75,000 lines of C++ with a bit of FORTRAN thrown in. The Cello framework consists of about the same number of lines of C++. The benchmark problem consists of a root grid that is 128^3 cells in size with a block decomposition of 8^3 resulting in 16^3 cells per block. The test case was run from scratch without checkpointing enabled to eliminate I/O from the run times. Performance was measured in total elapsed time in seconds.

Athena++. Athena++ is a astrophysical radiation magnetohydrodynamics code. A great strength of the code is the broad range of physics it models, and therefore the wide variety of problems to which it can be applied. The fundamental framework of Athena++ is based on a block-based AMR mesh organized in an oct-tree. A dynamic execution model that implements task-based parallelism is used to improve parallel performance by overlapping communication and computation and simplify the inclusion of a diverse range of physics.

NAMD. NAMD is a massively scaled molecular dynamics simulation package to model the physical movements of atoms and molecules in biological systems and functional materials. [16] Its remarkable parallel performance greatly benefits from Charm++ [9], an adaptive load balancing framework for efficient inter-process communication. In addition, accelerated computing through GPU offloading is now available at NAMD, which can take advantage of the highly optimized NVIDIA cuFFT library for fast Fourier transform when treating the time-consuming electrostatic interactions in an MD simulation. The benchmark case for NAMD is a satellite tobacco mosaic virus (STMV) dissolved in water that entails a total of 1.06 million atoms. Its performance is measured in seconds/step, i.e., seconds of simulation time per MD step.

Amber. Amber is a software suite of molecular simulation programs for biomolecular systems and is most often used with its namesake (amber) force field. Its primary molecular dynamics (MD) engine, PMEMD, is designed for large-scale parallel CPU and GPU computing systems (most of its features support GPU acceleration). The benchmark is the STMV_production_NPT_4fs case from the Amber20 Benchmark Suite (available at https://ambermd.org). In the simulation, the dynamics of a 1.067 million-atom solvated satellite tobacco mosaic virus (STMV) system is propagated under the isothermal-isobaric (NpT-ensemble) condition for 10,000 steps (with 4fs/step). The benchmark ran with 56 (CLX) and 112 (SPR) MPI tasks respectively. For better performance, the I/O was done on the local /tmp directory instead of using a shared filesystem. The performance is evaluated by averaging the timings for all steps and is reported in ns/day.

CHyPS and Plascom. CHyPS and Plascom are multiphysics simulation codes that work together to solve of a full hypersonic vehicle simulation. This including shocks, chemical reaction, radiation, laminar-to-turbulent boundary layer transition, gas-surface interaction, and surface material modeling (degradation, ablation, and oxidization). The benchmark case can only run with 20 MPI tasks, so only 20 cores were used in all the tests.

PSDNS. PSDNS [5] is a software to model large-scale turbulent flow under constant or nearly constant density conditions through the Fourier pseudo-spectral method, which is particularly powerful for investigating nonlinear scale interactions often exhibited by the classical energy cascade. In the case of substantial density fluctuations, PSDNS can still capture the significant departures from classical cascade idealizations in incompressible flows along with the dynamical effect of strong compression and expansion using higher-order compact finite differences for discretization in space. As a result, the parallel performance of PSDNS heavily relies on the efficiency of the large-scale fast Fourier transform library it interfaces with. Our chosen benchmark case for PSDNS consists of $12888 \times 12888 \times 12888$ grid points and 339,738,624 particles, placing an extremely high demand on an HPC system's memory bandwidth. The performance is measured in seconds/step, i.e., seconds of simulation time per propagation step.

ISSM. The Ice-sheet and Sea-level System Model (ISSM) is an open-source software package designed to simulate ice sheet and sea level behavior [10]. It uses a finite element approach to model ice flow and the interactions between ice sheets and the ocean. ISSM can be used to model past, present, and future ice sheet behavior under different climate scenarios, making it a useful tool for studying the impacts of climate change on sea level rise. The code is written in C++, and uses PETSc as the numerical solver. The benchmark case is a medium-sized mesh with 4.7×10^6 elements, and we run it with 5 timesteps. The performance is measured using the total core solution elapsed time reported by the code.

SeisSol. SeisSol is an earthquake simulation software that solves seismic wave propagation in viscoelastic media and dynamic rupture problems on geometrically complex, heterogeneous 3D models using clustered local time stepping on unstructured statically-adaptive tetrahedral meshes [6]. It is a hybrid MPI + OpenMP code. The computational kernels for many CPU architectures are generated via the Yet Another Tensor Toolbox, which uses small-BLAS back-ends such as LIBXSMM or Eigen. The benchmark case is a spontaneous rupture on a vertical strike-slip fault in a homogeneous halfspace. It has $2,051,112$ cells and $346,222$ vertices, and we set the simulation end time to be 2 s. The performance is measured with the elapsed time reported by the code.

CESM. The Community Earth System Model (CESM) [7] is a fully coupled, global climate model that provides state-of-the-art simulations of the Earth's past, present, and future climate states. The EarthWorks Modeling System leverages the CESM, but is especially focused on high-resolution ESM research at Global Storm Resolving (GSR) resolutions. It differs from standard CESM model configurations primarily in the use of the Model for Prediction Across Scales (MPAS) infrastructure for ocean, sea-ice and atmosphere components. The test case is a low-resolution Aqua Planet case (called a QPC6 component set), in which the atmospheric component is run with full physics. The test case makes the simplifying assumption that the entire planetary surface is covered by water. A data ocean component supplies the SST (Sea Surface Temperature) as a lower atmospheric boundary condition. To fit on one node, the resolution is set on a quasi-uniform grid at 120 km (40962 cells) with 32 vertical levels. The model ran for five simulation days. Performance was measured by total elapsed time of the model run.

WRF. The Weather Research and Forecasting(WRF) Model [18] is a widely used numerical weather prediction system used for both research and operational forecasts. WRF has been used as a standard benchmark for HPC procurements for many years. It is primarily a Fortran code implemented using MPI and OpenMP for distributed computing. The benchmark presented here is the standard CONUS 2.5 KM case used to compare the performance of WRF across a variety of architectures. Specifically, it simulates the weather across the continental United States at a horizontal resolution of 2.5 km. The performance is measured from the total elapsed time taken during the domain 1 execution phase with the exception of the first time step. This removes overhead from the initialization steps and the initial I/O.

AWP-ODC. AWP-ODC simulates the propagation of seismic waves. The equations are formulated using a finite difference scheme and a stencil update is used to advance the simulation in time and space (3D). The current production versions of the code are written in C and C/CUDA, respectively. The code base has been under active development for 20+ years. The number of lines of the C code is approximately 6,000 lines. The benchmark case is a dynamic wave propagation study in a homogeneous halfspace. The dimension of the 3D solid is $179.2 \times 102.4 \times 51.2$ (km), with a uniform mesh size of 200 m. The simulation duration and time step are 19.99 sec and 0.01 sec, respectively. The performance is measured with the elapsed time reported by the code.

EPW. The EPW code (https://epw-code.org) is an open-source code released under the GNU GPL consisting of approximately 67K lines of Fortran with MPI/OpenMP. EPW is the most popular code for first-principles calculations of electron-phonon interactions and finite-temperature properties. EPW is highly optimized to compute efficiently and accurately an array of properties and phenomena related to the electron-phonon interaction, e.g. electrical transport, phonon-assisted optical properties, and superconductivity [17]. The benchmark case MgB2 (magnesium diboride) is the phonon-mediated superconductor with the highest superconducting critical temperature (39K) at ambient pressure. This system provides an ideal testbench for developing more accurate and more predictive first-principles theories and algorithms for superconducting materials. The dimensions are nk1=nk2=10, nk3=6, nq1=nq2=10, nq3=6, nkf1=nkf2=nkf3=nqf1=nqf2=nqf3=16. Due to memory size, the benchmark runs with 56 tasks on the SPR nodes.

PARSEC. PARSEC is a versatile Density Functional Theory (DFT) code that solves the Kohn-Sham equations by expressing electron wave-functions directly in real space, without the use of explicit basis sets. It is capable of handling both periodical boundary conditions and confined-system boundary conditions. A finite-difference approach is used for the calculation of spatial derivatives. Pseudopotentials are used to describe the interaction between valence electrons and ionic cores. The code is comprised of approximately 50k lines of Fortran code. Additionally, PARSEC is highly scalable to thousands of nodes, and makes efficient use of AVX512 through ScaLAPACK and BLAS math libraries. The benchmark case is a single-point energy calculation of $Si_{1947}H_{604}$. The grid is set at 0.9Å grid spacing and boundary sphere radius of 50 bohr. Total number of calculated states is 4800.

MuST. MuST is an open-source package designed to perform ab initio electronic structure calculations for the study of quantum phenomena in disordered materials. The code has approximately 250,000 lines, mostly written in FORTRAN-90, and has been under active development for around 25 years. The MuST package is developed based on full-potential multiple scattering theory, also known as the KKR method, with Green's function approach to the Kohn-Sham equation in density functional theory (DFT). It is capable of performing KKR, KKR-CPA, and linear scaling LSMS calculations for materials with complex structures. It also allows for electronic conductivity calculation based on Kubo-Greenwood formula. For details of the LSMS method used in the benchmark case, see [19]. The benchmarking case is a Cantor alloy, CrMnFeCoNi, one of the best-known examples of high entropy alloys (HEAs) with excellent mechanical properties. System size is 56 atoms and 32 energy points. The benchmark runs with 112 tasks on the SPR nodes.

MILC. Lattice QCD is an approach to studying Nature's strong interaction, also called the nuclear force. This force is responsible for holding atomic nuclei together and for binding quarks into the protons and neutrons that comprise the atomic nuclei. Lattice QCD is a nonperturbative technique in which the quantum fluctuations of the quarks and gluons are treated somewhat analogously as in a statistical mechanical system. The MILC collaboration code is one of the community codes that can be used to produce the ensemble of configurations. The code is typically characterized as being memory-bound. It is written in C and contains about 350k lines of code. Libraries being used are QPhiX, QUDA, Grid and FFTW. In this benchmark, we set the lattice grid to be $32 \times 32 \times 32 \times 32$, and the lattice spacing is approximately 0.03 fm. The strange and charm quark masses are set to their physical values, and average values are used for the up and down quarks. The code is run in single precision. The step size is 0.0125 and the total number of steps is 40.

4   Results

The results of the STREAM benchmark are presented in Table 1. The CLX node exhibits a maximum bandwidth of approximately 220 GB/s, while the SPR nodes with DDR5 and HBM demonstrate maximum bandwidths of approximately 399 GB/s and 1400 GB/s, respectively. The outcomes derived from testing the CLX node exhibit negligible fluctuations from one execution to the next. Similarly, the test results for the SPR node with DDR5 indicate minimal variations in performance, although it yields slightly better results without streaming stores. In contrast, the SPR node with HBM demonstrates a significant degree of performance variability, approximately 10%, in relation to the problem size and array alignment. The selected subset in Table 1 is a considerably high Triad result, while the other results are at least 5% lower than the highest across the entire tests.

Table 1. STREAM Benchmark Results

Platform	Sockets	Cores	Copy	Scale	Add	Triad	Size (M)
CLX	2	56	204,396	204,391	220,498	220,219	1600
SPR w/DDR5	2	112	378,852	375,917	397,918	398,578	640
SPR w/HBM	2	112	1,371,992	1,370,889	1,343,482	1,400,131	3200

Table 2 presents the scores obtained from the SPEC benchmark, while Fig. 1 illustrates the speedup achieved by the two SPR nodes over the CLX node. Specifically, the SPECspeed2017_fp_base benchmark demonstrates that the SPR node with DDR5 provides a speedup of 1.66, with an additional 10% improvement achieved through the use of HBM. On the other hand, the SPECrate2017_fp_base metric measures the system's throughput, making higher memory bandwidth more desirable. The SPR node with DDR5 demonstrated a speedup of 2.10, and HBM gave an additional 29% improvement resulting in a speedup of 2.71. The SPEChpc 2021_tny_base benchmark demonstrates an even greater sensitivity to memory bandwidth, with the SPR nodes exhibiting speedups of 2.19 and 3.30, respectively.

Table 3 lists the results from the applications benchmarks, and Fig. 2a displays the speedup of the two SPR nodes relative to the CLX nodes for these

Table 2. SPEC Benchmark Scores

Benchmark	CLX	SPR w/DDR5	SPR w/HBM
SPECspeed2017_fp_base	169	280	308
SPECrate2017_fp_base	350	736	950
SPEChpc 2021_tny_base	3.15	6.89	10.40

Higher score is better.

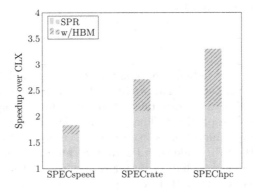

Fig. 1. The performance improvement of the SPEC benchmarks on the two Sapphire Rapids (SPR) nodes compared to the Cascade Lake (CLX) node. The additional performance gained from HBM is shaded in blue in the bar plot. (Color figure online)

Table 3. Application Benchmark Results

Application	Area	CLX	SPR w/DDR5	SPR w/HBM
ChaNGa	Astro	143.70	60.90	60.00
Enzo-E	Astro	763.41	447.76	391.14
Athena++	Astro	243.20	191.30	152.80
NAMD	Bio	0.34	0.21	0.19
Amber	Bio	2.05	3.16	3.92
CHyPS & P	CFD	32.70	20.35	20.02
PSDNS	CFD	916.66	520.83	345.91
ISSM	Earth	162.02	57.79	52.11
SeisSol	Earth	2075.76	1159.84	1006.01
CESM	Earth	1326.00	527.00	407.00
WRF	Earth	1810.74	865.40	509.25
AWP-ODC	Earth	328.00	176.03	87.36
EPW	Materials	137.71	47.17	48.11
Parsec	Materials	574.36	348.25	310.46
MuST	Materials	1631.10	1007.11	872.91
MILC	Physics	2018.30	783.40	520.90

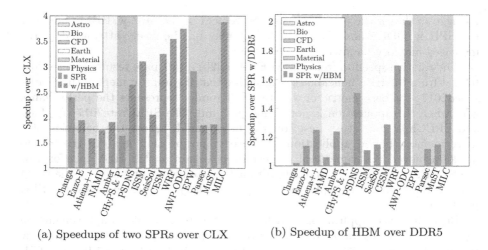

(a) Speedups of two SPRs over CLX   (b) Speedup of HBM over DDR5

Fig. 2. The performance improvement of the application benchmark (a) on the two Sapphire Rapids (SPR) nodes compared to the Cascade Lake (CLX) node, and (b) on the Sapphire Rapids (SPR) node with High Bandwidth Memory (HBM) compared to the one with DDR5. The additional performance gained from HBM is shaded in blue in the bar plot. The applications are classified based on six scientific fields and arranged in increasing order according to the speedup gained from HBM. The red line marks the median of the speedups on the SPR node with DDR5 only. (Color figure online)

benchmarks. The SPR node with DDR5 achieved a speedup ranging from 1.27 to 2.92 with a median of 1.77, while the HBM one achieved a speedup ranging from 1.59 to 3.87 with a median of 2.23. The speedup achieved by utilizing HBM is depicted in Fig. 2b, exhibiting a range of 1 to 2.01, with a median of 1.15.

5   Discussion

The result from the STREAM benchmark indicates that the SPR w/DDR5 has about double the memory bandwidth than the CLX. The improvement is a lot more when moving to the SPR w/HBM node, with an additional 3.5× increase in memory bandwidth. These numbers represent the maximum performance gains that a memory-bound application can achieve.

The results from the SPEC benchmarks require further analysis as the performance improvement is influenced by changes in core count, clock speed, and memory bandwidth. To evaluate a purely compute-bound problem, we used the High-Performance Linpack (HPL) Benchmark [4]. The best HPL results obtained from the CLX, SPR w/DDR5, and SPR w/HBM nodes were 3.25, 5.39, and 5.73 TFLOPS, respectively. These numbers were achieved without fine-tuning but provide insight into the behavior of a compute-bound code. The slightly higher performance of the SPR w/HBM node can be attributed to the higher clock speed of the CPU when using HBM with lower power consumption [14].

It suggests that if the performance improvement of the SPR w/HBM node over the SPR w/DDR5 node is within 6%, it may not be solely attributed to the increased memory bandwidth.

The relative speedup from the SPECspeed2017_fp_base results is very close to that from the HPL benchmark, suggesting that the improvement of the SPEC-speed2017_fp_base metric on the two SPR nodes represents the performance gain when the application is not memory-bound. The SPECrate2017_fp_base and SPEChpc 2021_tny_base, on the other hand, reflect the behavior of a more memory-bound application. It is worth noting that none of the benchmarks achieved the same level of performance gain on the HBM platform as the STREAM benchmark, indicating that the bandwidth provided by the HBM is more than what our applications require with given core count on the SPR platform.

Regarding the application benchmarks, the performance improvement on the two SPR nodes varies depending on the specific application. On average, the speedups of the SPR w/DDR5 and SPR w/HBM nodes are 1.98 and 2.51, respectively. Both of these speedups are lower than the corresponding metrics obtained from the SPEChpc benchmark. These results suggest that the applications selected for our analysis are less memory-bound.

We did not observe any general trends by categorizing the applications into different science domains. However, we did observe that PSDNS, WRF, AWP-ODC, and MILC achieved more than 40% performance gain when moving from DDR5 to HBM. We may also evaluate the cost-effectiveness of HBM based on the application benchmark results. The current "Recommended Customer Price" of the Intel Xeon CPU Max 9480 Processor, which was used in this work, is listed on Intel's website as $12,980. The closest comparable processor without HBM is the Intel Xeon Platinum 8480+ Processor, which is listed as $10,710. Therefore, we may conclude that it is appropriate to acquire the HBM processor if the SPR w/HBM is 21% faster than the SPR w/DDR5. However, this calculation does not take into account other associated costs in a system procurement, and we may need to offset the 6% performance gain from the power consumption. Overall, a more reasonable criteria for cost-effectiveness evaluation would be 30%, and only PSDNS, CESM, WRF, AWP-ODC, and MILC meet this requirement.

6   Conclusion

We compared the performance of three different architectures, the CLX, SPR w/DDR5, and SPR w/HBM, using a suite of benchmarks and application tests. We found that HBM has significantly improved memory bandwidth over DDR5 and results in higher performance gains for memory-bound applications. However, the performance improvement varies depending on the specific application, and on average in our application benchmarks, the speedup of HBM over DDR5 on the SPR nodes is 27%. We observed that PSDNS, WRF, AWP-ODC, and MILC achieved significant performance gain when moving from DDR5 to HBM, and only these applications plus CESM met our criteria for cost-effectiveness evaluation. This suggests that domains such as CFD, Earth Science, and Physics may benefit more from the high memory bandwidth offered by HBM.

References

1. Bauer, G., et al.: Updating the SPP benchmark suite for extreme-scale systems. In: Proceedings of Cry User Group Meeting (CUG-2017) (2017)
2. Brunst, H., et al.: First experiences in performance benchmarking with the new SPEChpc 2021 suites. In: 2022 22nd IEEE International Symposium on Cluster, Cloud and Internet Computing (CCGrid), pp. 675–684 (2022). https://doi.org/10.1109/CCGrid54584.2022.00077
3. Bucek, J., Lange, K.D., v. Kistowski, J.: SPEC CPU2017: next-generation compute benchmark. In: Companion of the 2018 ACM/SPEC International Conference on Performance Engineering, ICPE 2018, pp. 41–42. Association for Computing Machinery, New York (2018). https://doi.org/10.1145/3185768.3185771
4. Dongarra, J.J., Luszczek, P., Petitet, A.: The LINPACK benchmark: past, present and future. Concurr. Comput.: Pract. Experience **15**(9), 803–820 (2003). https://doi.org/10.1002/cpe.728
5. Donzis, D.A., Yeung, P.K., Sreenivasan, K.R.: Dissipation and enstrophy in isotropic turbulence: resolution effects and scaling in direct numerical simulations. Phys. Fluids **20**(4), 045108 (2008). https://doi.org/10.1063/1.2907227
6. Heinecke, A., et al.: Petascale high order dynamic rupture earthquake simulations on heterogeneous supercomputers. In: Proceedings of the International Conference for High Performance Computing, Networking, Storage and Analysis, SC 2014, pp. 3–14 (2014). https://doi.org/10.1109/SC.2014.6. ISSN 2167-4337
7. Hurrell, J.W., et al.: The community earth system model version 2 (CESM2). J. Adv. Model. Earth Syst. **11**(12), 3761–3802 (2019). https://doi.org/10.1029/2019MS001916
8. Jetley, P., Gioachin, F., Mendes, C., Kale, L.V., Quinn, T.: Massively parallel cosmological simulations with ChaNGa. In: 2008 IEEE International Symposium on Parallel and Distributed Processing, pp. 1–12. IEEE (2008). https://doi.org/10.1109/IPDPS.2008.4536319
9. Kale, L.V., Krishnan, S.: CHARM++: a portable concurrent object oriented system based on C++. In: Proceedings of the Eighth Annual Conference on Object-Oriented Programming Systems, Languages, and Applications, OOPSLA 1993, pp. 91–108. Association for Computing Machinery, New York (1993). https://doi.org/10.1145/165854.165874
10. Larour, E., Seroussi, H., Morlighem, M., Rignot, E.: Continental scale, high order, high spatial resolution, ice sheet modeling using the ice sheet system model (ISSM). J. Geophys. Res.: Earth Surface **117** (2012). https://doi.org/10.1029/2011JF002140
11. Lee, D.U., et al.: 25.2 A 1.2V 8Gb 8-channel 128GB/s high-bandwidth memory (HBM) stacked DRAM with effective microbump I/O test methods using 29 nm process and TSV. In: 2014 IEEE International Solid-State Circuits Conference Digest of Technical Papers (ISSCC), pp. 432–433 (2014). https://doi.org/10.1109/ISSCC.2014.6757501. ISSN 2376-8606
12. Li, J., et al.: SPEChpc 2021 benchmark suites for modern HPC systems. In: Companion of the 2022 ACM/SPEC International Conference on Performance Engineering, ICPE 2022, pp. 15–16. Association for Computing Machinery, New York (2022). https://doi.org/10.1145/3491204.3527498

13. McCalpin, J.D.: Memory bandwidth and machine balance in current high performance computers. IEEE Comput. Soc. Tech. Committee Comput. Archit. (TCCA) Newsl. **2**, 19–25 (1995)
14. Nabavi Larimi, S.S., Salami, B., Unsal, O.S., Kestelman, A.C., Sarbazi-Azad, H., Mutlu, O.: Understanding power consumption and reliability of high-bandwidth memory with voltage underscaling. In: 2021 Design, Automation & Test in Europe Conference & Exhibition (DATE), Grenoble, France, pp. 517–522. IEEE (2021). https://doi.org/10.23919/DATE51398.2021.9474024
15. Panda, R., Song, S., Dean, J., John, L.K.: Wait of a decade: did SPEC CPU 2017 broaden the performance horizon? In: 2018 IEEE International Symposium on High Performance Computer Architecture (HPCA), pp. 271–282 (2018). https://doi.org/10.1109/HPCA.2018.00032
16. Phillips, J.C., et al.: Scalable molecular dynamics on CPU and GPU architectures with NAMD. J. Chem. Phys. **153**(4), 044130 (2020). https://doi.org/10.1063/5.0014475
17. Poncé, S., Margine, E.R., Verdi, C., Giustino, F.: EPW: electron-phonon coupling, transport and superconducting properties using maximally localized Wannier functions. Comput. Phys. Commun. **209**, 116–133 (2016). https://doi.org/10.1016/j.cpc.2016.07.028
18. Skamarock, W., et al.: A description of the advanced research WRF version 3. Technical report, University Corporation for Atmospheric Research (2008). https://doi.org/10.5065/D68S4MVH
19. Wang, Y., Stocks, G.M., Shelton, W.A., Nicholson, D.M.C., Szotek, Z., Temmerman, W.M.: Order-N multiple scattering approach to electronic structure calculations. Phys. Rev. Lett. **75**, 2867–2870 (1995). https://doi.org/10.1103/PhysRevLett.75.2867

DAOS Beyond Persistent Memory: Architecture and Initial Performance Results

Michael Hennecke[1]([✉]) [iD], Jeff Olivier[2] [iD], Tom Nabarro[3] [iD], Liang Zhen[4] [iD], Yawei Niu[4] [iD], Shilong Wang[4] [iD], and Xuezhao Liu[4] [iD]

[1] Intel Deutschland GmbH, Am Campeon 10, 85579 Neubiberg, Germany
`michael.hennecke@intel.com`
[2] Intel Corporation, 2200 Mission College Blvd., Santa Clara, CA 95054-1549, USA
`jeffrey.v.olivier@intel.com`
[3] Intel Corporation (UK) Ltd., Pipers Way, Swindon SN3 1RJ, UK
`tom.nabarro@intel.com`
[4] Intel China Ltd., GTC, No. 36 3Rd Ring Road, Beijing, China
`{liang.zhen,yawei.niu,shilong.wang,xuezhao.liu}@intel.com`

Abstract. The Distributed Asynchronous Object Storage (DAOS) is an open source scale-out storage system that is designed from the ground up to support Storage Class Memory (SCM) and NVMe storage in user space. Until now, the DAOS storage stack has been based on Intel Optane Persistent Memory (PMem) and the Persistent Memory Development Kit (PMDK). With the discontinuation of Optane PMem, and no persistent CXL.mem devices in the market yet, DAOS continues to support PMem-based servers but now also supports server configurations where its Versioning Object Store (VOS) is held in DRAM. In this case, the VOS data structures are persisted through a synchronous Write-Ahead-Log (WAL) combined with asynchronous checkpointing to NVMe SSDs. This paper describes the new non-PMem DAOS architecture, and reports first performance results based on a DAOS 2.4 technology preview.

Keyword: DAOS · Storage Class Memory · Optane · CXL.mem · Versioning Object Store · Parallel Filesystem · mdtest

1 Introduction

The Distributed Asynchronous Object Storage (DAOS) [1–3] is an open source software-defined object store designed from the ground up for massively distributed Non-Volatile Memory (NVM) and Storage Class Memory (SCM). It presents a key-value storage interface and provides features such as transactional non-blocking I/O, a versioned data model, and global snapshots – all completely in user space. Its design eliminates many of the bottlenecks of traditional parallel filesystems, as demonstrated by leadership performance rankings in HPC storage benchmarks like the IO500 [4].

As shown in Fig. 1, the DAOS storage engine uses two types of backend storage devices. Storage Class Memory is used to store DAOS internal metadata, application/middleware key/index data, and latency sensitive small I/O. Up until today, DAOS

© The Author(s), under exclusive license to Springer Nature Switzerland AG 2023
A. Bienz et al. (Eds.): ISC High Performance 2023 Workshops, LNCS 13999, pp. 353–365, 2023.
https://doi.org/10.1007/978-3-031-40843-4_26

SCM has been implemented with Intel Optane Persistent Memory (PMem) devices [9] accessed through the Persistent Memory Development Toolkit (PMDK) [5–7]. DAOS creates a *DAX-enabled* ext4 filesystem on the PMem devices (configured in AppDirect mode). Space for the DAOS Versioning Object Store (VOS) is allocated as files in this DAX-enabled filesystem (one file per DAOS pool and per DAOS storage *target*). DAOS memory-maps these files when the engines are up and running, bypassing the Linux page cache. It can then directly access persistent memory in user space by memory instructions like load and store, instead of going through a thick storage stack.

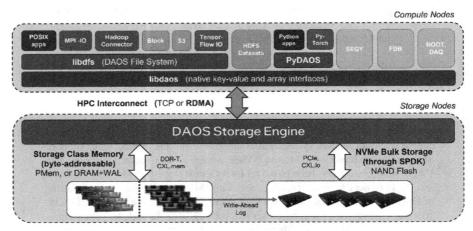

Fig. 1. DAOS Software Architecture.

DAOS uses NVMe SSDs and the Storage Performance Development Kit (SPDK) [8] software to support large storage capacities and large I/O requests. SPDK provides direct, zero-copy data transfer to and from NVMe SSDs. The DAOS engine can submit multiple I/O requests to the NVMe SSDs, using SPDK queue pairs in an asynchronous manner, fully from user space. On completion of the SPDK I/O, DAOS creates indexes in SCM for the data stored on NVMe SSDs.

Intel has discontinued its Optane Persistent Memory product line [9–11]. And while it is possible that future CXL.mem attached storage devices will provide persistent, Byte-addressable storage with performance characteristics that are suitable for DAOS SCM usage, no such devices currently exist in the industry.

DAOS therefore needs an alternative code path for its Storage Class Memory functionality that does not depend on Optane PMem or PMDK. This new functionality has been developed in the DAOS *vos_on_blob* feature branch [12], also known as "*MD-on-SSD*" [13, 14], and is available as a technology preview in the DAOS 2.4 release. This paper explains the new DAOS SCM backend and presents first performance results based on an early *vos_on_blob* development snapshot.

2   DAOS Persistent Memory and Volatile Memory Code Paths

Figure 2 shows the traditional DAOS backend with persistent memory. The DAOS Versioning Object Store (VOS) data structures are stored in memory-mapped files, which reside on Optane PMem devices and are accessed through PMDK. Small (<4kiB) writes are also stored on PMem. Pointers to large *data blobs* that are stored on NVMe SSDs are maintained in the VOS trees.

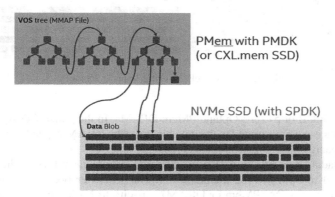

Fig. 2. DAOS Backend using Persistent Memory.

The new DAOS backend is shown in Fig. 3. Here, the VOS data structures are held in DRAM, using VOS files in a *tmpfs* filesystem that is not persistent. Small writes are also stored in DRAM. To persist the data in this volatile tmpfs filesystem, two additional functionalities are added to the code path:

1. A Write-Ahead Log (WAL) [14] performs *synchronous* commits of all write operations to a *WAL blob* that resides on NVMe SSDs. The WAL data structures are very compact to guarantee low latency. Instead of a commit block, the WAL implementation relies on checksums to ensure consistency. Depending on the operation, it is possible to perform parallel commits to the WAL.
2. The complete VOS trees are *asynchronously* checkpointed to a *meta blob* on NVMe SSDs (one per DAOS storage target). The VOS checkpointing is triggered by space pressure in the WAL blob, combined with a timed mechanism that initiates a VOS checkpoint at regular intervals even in the absence of space pressure. The detailed behaviour of the checkpointing mechanism can be fine-tuned through DAOS pool properties.

Compared to the PMem-based DAOS backend, this design has two advantages. Firstly, all reads are served from DRAM, so read performance should be higher compared to reads from Optane PMem. Secondly, by eliminating the Optane PMem hardware dependency it will now be possible to run DAOS servers on additional server hardware platforms, broadening the DAOS ecosystem.

The biggest drawback of the non-PMem design is its limited metadata capacity. The DRAM capacity per DAOS server is significantly smaller than what can be achieved with

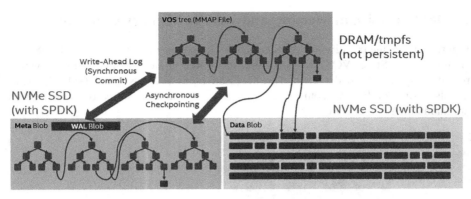

Fig. 3. DAOS Backend using Volatile Memory.

the 128GB, 256GB or 512GB Optane PMem DIMMs. In the *phase 1* design described here, metadata is never migrated to the data blobs, so the DRAM capacity limits the total metadata capacity.

This metadata capacity limitation is addressed in two ways: Firstly, the design has been reviewed to optimize the metadata footprint wherever possible. This allows to reduce the ratio of SCM (PMem or DRAM) capacity to NVMe capacity. Secondly, a *phase 2* roadmap item for the MD-on-SSD feature will implement mechanisms that will allow parts of the metadata to be serialized and migrated to the data blobs. This design will optimize the cost effectiveness of the DAOS servers, at the expense of an increase in latency when sections of the metadata that have been migrated to data blobs need to be loaded back from NVMe SSDs into DRAM. The design of this phase 2 functionality is beyond the scope of this paper.

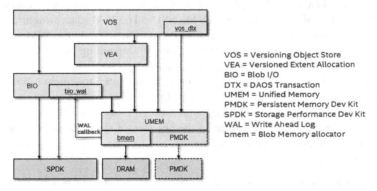

Fig. 4. New DAOS Backend Stack Layering.

It is important to note that the changes to enable DAOS metadata on volatile memory (plus NVMe SSDs) are isolated to a few layers of the DAOS server code stack, with no changes to the DAOS API or client-side software. Figure 4 shows the code paths for the traditional PMem-based DAOS design (in blue), and the added *bmem* blob allocator and *bio_wal* module (in yellow).

3 DAOS Server Design Considerations

In Sect. 2 we have described the DAOS software architecture for DAOS servers with and without Optane Persistent Memory. In this section we are combining that software-centric view with the hardware architecture of the DAOS servers, and we discuss some of the design choices to configure a balanced DAOS server.

The performance evolution of DAOS servers across three hardware generations is described in detail in [15]. DAOS servers with Intel 2nd Gen Intel Xeon SP (formerly codenamed Cascade Lake) and 3rd Gen Intel Xeon SP (formerly codenamed Ice Lake) support Optane Persistent Memory. Configuring these servers is straightforward: DAOS starts one DAOS engine on each CPU socket, there is one SCM tier configured on the Optane PMem DIMMs that are attached to that socket, and one NVMe tier that comprises all the NVMe SSDs that are managed by that engine. Each engine uses a single HPC network port to connect to the DAOS clients.

When configuring DAOS servers with 4th Gen Intel Xeon SP (formerly codenamed Sapphire Rapids), the main design change is the fact that Optane PMem is not available on 4th Gen Intel Xeon SP. The new DAOS code path for volatile memory must be used, and the NVMe SSDs must store the Write-Ahead Log and the asynchronous VOS checkpoints in addition to the end user data.

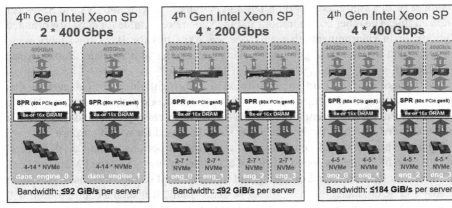

Fig. 5. DAOS Server Design Options for 4th Gen Xeon SP (from [15]).

Figure 5 outlines three typical DAOS server designs with 4th Gen Intel Xeon SP. They differ primarily in the number and speed of HPC network ports, and the corresponding number of DAOS engines. As the bandwidth of an HPC network port needs to be "fed" by a corresponding NVMe SSD bandwidth, these differences also imply a different minimum and maximum number of NVMe SSDs per DAOS engine. These boundaries are relevant for the placement of WAL, VOS checkpoints and user data.

- The continuation of the original DAOS server design of a 2-socket server with one DAOS engine per CPU socket is shown on the left of Fig. 5. To saturate a 400 Gbps HPC network link (e.g., NDR InfiniBand), at least *four* PCIe gen5 NVMe SSDs per DAOS engine are needed. The maximum of 14 NVMe SSDs per DAOS engine shown in the figure is determined by the total number of 80 PCIe gen5 lanes per CPU socket. (Some PCIe lanes are used for other functions, for example a management LAN card, so using 16 NVMe SSDs per DAOS engine is not possible).
- The middle of Fig. 5 shows a server design to support 200 Gbps HPC fabrics, by using PCIe gen5 NICs with two 200 Gbps ports (e.g., dual HDR InfiniBand) instead of a single 400 Gbps port. Because DAOS requires exactly one HPC network port per engine, this configuration requires to run two DAOS engines per CPU socket with 2–7 NVMe SSDs per engine.
- Due to the higher number of PCIe lanes of 4th Gen Intel Xeon SP compared to previous generations, it is now also possible to populate a 2-socket DAOS server with *four* HPC network cards, doubling the peak bandwidth to $\leq$184 GiB/s. This is shown on the right of Fig. 5, together with the resulting 4–5 PCIe gen5 NVMe SSDs per engine to feed those network ports.

The DAOS server configuration with four 400 Gbps network links and 4–5 PCIe gen5 NVMe SSDs provides the best bandwidth. It is the standard configuration for traditional supercomputing environments that use a 400 Gbps HPC fabric. For this reason, the remainder of this study focuses on a DAOS configuration with *four* NVMe SSDs per DAOS engine. The other configurations in Fig. 5 are more suitable for capacity-oriented solutions, or in environments that only operate 200 Gbps (or 100 Gbps) fabrics and cannot fully utilize the PCIe gen5 networking capabilities of a Sapphire Rapids based DAOS server.

The discussion of these different hardware designs highlights a critical question that needs to be answered when using the non-PMem DAOS code path: Because the NVMe SSDs now hold *three* different types of data (WAL, VOS checkpoints, and user data), it must be decided which of the NVMe SSDs should be used for which purpose.

Figure 6 shows the traditional storage configuration options in the DAOS servers' configuration file: There is one SCM tier of class "dcpm" using Optane PMem, and one NVMe tier for the user data. For testing and for ephemeral storage use cases, persistent memory can be emulated by an SCM tier of class "ram". But such a configuration will not survive failures or engine restarts and does *not* use the MD-on-SSD code path.

```
storage:
-
  class: dcpm
  scm_mount: /mnt/pmem1
  scm_list:
  - /dev/pmem1

  class: nvme
  bdev_list:
  - "0000:e3:00.0"
  - "0000:e4:00.0"
  - "0000:e5:00.0"
  - "0000:e6:00.0"
```

```
storage:
-
  class: ram
  scm_mount: /mnt/dram1
  scm_size: 156

  class: nvme
  bdev_list:
  - "0000:e3:00.0"
  - "0000:e4:00.0"
  - "0000:e5:00.0"
  - "0000:e6:00.0"
```

Fig. 6. Traditional Storage Configuration Options in daos_server.yml: Optane PMem-based configuration (left); Ephemeral DRAM-based configuration (right).

In DAOS 2.4, the MD-on-SSD code path will only be used if it is explicitly enabled by specifying the new *bdev_role* property for the NVMe storage tier(s) in the daos_server.yml file. There are three types of *bdev_role: wal, meta,* and *data.* Each role must be assigned to *exactly one* NVMe tier. Depending on the number of NVMe SSDs per DAOS engine there may be one, two or three NVMe tiers with different *bdev_role* assignments.

```
storage:
-
  class: ram
  scm_mount: /mnt/dram1
  scm_size: 156

  class: nvme
  bdev_roles:
  - wal
  - meta
  - data
  bdev_list:
  - "0000:e3:00.0"
  - "0000:e4:00.0"
  - "0000:e5:00.0"
  - "0000:e6:00.0"
```

```
storage:
-
  class: ram
  scm_mount: /mnt/dram1
  scm_size: 156

  class: nvme
  bdev_roles:
  - wal
  bdev_list:
  - "0000:e3:00.0"

  class: nvme
  bdev_roles:
  - meta
  - data
  bdev_list:
  - "0000:e4:00.0"
  - "0000:e5:00.0"
  - "0000:e6:00.0"
```

```
storage:
-
  class: ram
  scm_mount: /mnt/dram1
  scm_size: 156
-
  class: nvme
  bdev_roles:
  - wal
  - meta
  bdev_list:
  - "0000:e3:00.0"
-
  class: nvme
  bdev_roles:
  - data
  bdev_list:
  - "0000:e4:00.0"
  - "0000:e5:00.0"
  - "0000:e6:00.0"
```

Fig. 7. MD-on-SSD Storage Configuration Options in daos_server.yml: Left: One NVMe tier; wal/meta/data shared on four SSDs (*4wmd*). Center: Two NVMe tiers; wal on one SSD, meta/data shared on three SSDs (*1w3md*). Right: Two NVMe tiers; wal/meta shared on one SSD, data on three SSDs (*1wm3d*).

Figure 7 shows three different storage configurations that represent three possible scenarios for a DAOS engine with four NVMe SSDs and MD-on-SSD enabled:

- Figure 7 (left) shows the typical use case for a DAOS server with a small number of NVMe SSDs. With only four or five NVMe SSDs per engine, it is natural to assign all three roles to all NVMe SSDs configured as a *single* NVMe tier.
- Figure 7 (center) presents a configuration where one NVMe SSD is dedicated for the *wal*, while the remaining three NVMe SSDs are assigned to hold the VOS checkpoints (*meta*) and the user *data*. Using two NVMe tiers makes it possible to use a higher endurance and higher performance SSD for the *wal* tier. But note that the performance of a single high-performance SSD may still be lower than the aggregate performance of multiple lower-performance SSDs in the previous scenario.
- Figure 7 (right) also uses two NVMe tiers but co-locates the *wal* and *meta* blobs on the same tier. This may be a better choice than co-locating *meta* and *data* if the endurance of the *data* NVMe SSDs is too low for the relatively frequent VOS checkpointing. But it may also hurt performance by reducing the number of NVMe SSDs available for VOS checkpointing from three to one.

The third option to use two NVMe tiers would be to co-locate *wal* and *data* and dedicate the other tier for *meta*. But the main rationale for a separate *wal* tier is the ability to use a small number of higher-performance SSDs for the synchronous Write-Ahead Log. If *wal* is co-located with *data* then this rationale disappears, and it is better to use a single tier for all three roles. And finally, using three NVMe tiers (one per role) is not reasonable when there are only four NVMe SSDs per engine.

The three MD-on-SSD configurations shown in Fig. 7 will be benchmarked in the next section. They will be compared with the traditional PMem-based configuration shown in Fig. 6 (left), which consist of a single SCM tier and a single NVMe tier with *no* specification of a *bdev_role* for the NVMe tier.

In this study we have fixed the total number of NVMe SSDs per engine to *four* to make performance comparisons easier. But it should be noted that in a production environment the number of NVMe SSDs in the *data* tier should not be reduced below four, because that is typically the minimum number of NVMe SSDs required to saturate the bandwidth of the HPC network link. This implies that for the performance configuration of Fig. 5 (right), a separation into two NVMe tiers is only reasonable if there are *five* NVMe SSDs: Four NVMe SSDs with the *data* role provide sufficient aggregate bandwidth to saturate the engine's HPC network port, and the 5th NVMe SSD can hold the *wal* blobs.

4   Performance Results

To compare the metadata performance of DAOS servers with Optane PMem to the performance of the new DAOS code path, the mdtest [16] benchmark with the DAOS DFS API [17] has been run on a DAOS server with Intel 8352Y CPUs (32 cores, 2.2 GHz). Only a single DAOS engine has been configured on one CPU, to keep the testing setup simple. All tests have used four Intel/Solidigm D7-P5500 3.84 TB PCIe gen4 NVMe SSDs, see [18] for performance specs. The PMem configuration uses 8x 128GB Optane 200 Series PMem DIMMs [9], and DRAM configurations use a tmpfs of size 156GB configured on the 16x 16GB DDR4 DRAM DIMMs of the server.

For DAOS Servers based on Optane PMem, earlier studies have clearly shown that DAOS metadata rates scale with the number of *targets* per engine, where each target runs on a dedicated physical CPU core. Figure 11 of [19] shows this relationship, varying the number of targets per engine from 4 to 32. The current study uses *24 targets* and *six xs_helper* threads for all benchmarks.

The DAOS clients are 2-socket nodes using the same CPUs, connected through a fully non-blocking InfiniBand HDR fabric with NVIDIA QM8790 HDR switches. All mdtest benchmarks have been performed with a stonewall time of 60 s for the write phases. Three sets of benchmarks have been performed, following the setup of the IO500 [4] with one addition:

- *mdtest-easy*: Metadata operations on 0-Byte files, using separate directories for each MPI task. No user data is written to the files.
- *mdtest-hard*: Metadata operations on small (3901 Byte) files in a shared directory. The size of the user data is below the DAOS cut-off limit of 4kiB, so all writes will go to the metadata in PMem or DRAM (plus WAL and metadata/checkpoints).
- *mdtest-hard2*: Same setup as mdtest-hard but using 2x the file size. Here the user data is bigger than 4kiB and will be written to the data blobs on NVMe SSDs.

All benchmarks have been run on one client node and 16 client nodes, and for each node count the number of MPI tasks per node has been varied from 1 to 64, for a total of 1 to 1024 MPI tasks. All performance graphs in this section show the total number of MPI tasks of a benchmark on the x-axis (in log scale), and the different numbers of tasks per node for a given node count are shown as a line-graph of the same color.

For each mdtest benchmark, the following storage configurations (shown in Fig. 6 and Fig. 7) have been measured, with labels in the graphs indicating the engine configuration:

- *PMEM, 4d*: PMem-based configuration with four NVMe SSDs for data;
- *DRAM, 4wmd*: DRAM-based configuration with one NVMe tier, four NVMe SSDs are shared for all three roles (*wal*, *meta* and *data*);
- *DRAM, 1w3md*: DRAM-based configuration with two NVMe tiers, one NVMe SSD dedicated to *wal* and three NVMe SSDs shared for *meta* and *data*;
- *DRAM, 1wm3d*: DRAM-based configuration with two NVMe tiers, one NVMe SSD shared for *wal* and *meta* and three NVMe SSDs dedicated for *data*.

A DAOS pool with an NVMe size of 8 TB and one POSIX container has been used for all mdtest benchmarks. The SCM size was set to 500 GB for the PMem configuration (a ratio of 1:16 = 6.25%), while an SCM size of 125 GB (a ratio of 1:64 = 1.56%) was used for the DRAM configurations.

Figure 8 shows the performance result for the *mdtest-easy* benchmark. Create rates in Fig. 8 (A) are highest when using PMem, indicating that the writing of the WAL and VOS checkpoints to NVMe does slow down the achievable create rate. However, the difference from the DRAM-based configurations using MD-on-SSD is relatively small. Among those, co-locating the WAL and VOS checkpoints on a single NVMe SSD (*1wm3d*) results in the lowest performance. Assigning all roles to a single NVMe tier with four NVMe SSDs (*4wmd*) results in roughly the same performance as sharing three NVMe SSDs for VOS checkpoints and data (*1w3md*), and both are slightly ahead of the *1wm3d* case. This suggests that a higher number of NVMe SSDs is beneficial for the VOS checkpointing. The stat operations in Fig. 8 (B) are read-only operations, so there is no need for *wal* logging and consequently no noticeable performance difference between the four configurations. When deleting the 0-Byte files, Fig. 8 (D) shows a similar behaviour to the create case, which is expected as this operation generates a similar load for the *wal* and *meta* blobs. Overall, the achievable performance is very comparable for all four server configurations. The noticeable degradation at high task counts (particularly for the stat rates) is present for all PMem- and DRAM-based server configurations. This will be subject to further studies.

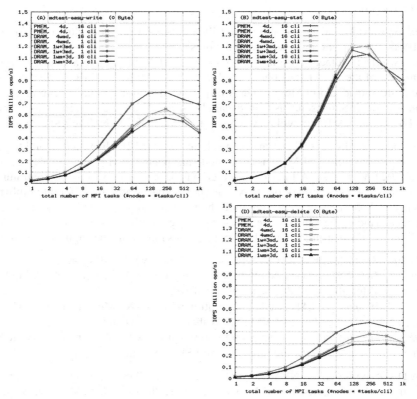

Fig. 8. DAOS Metadata Performance Scaling (mdtest-easy, 0-Byte files): (A) write, (B) stat, no read test (C) for 0-Byte files, (D) delete.

Figure 9 reports the performance for the *mdtest-hard* testcase. Absolute values of the metadata rates are lower because actual data is written and read (instead of just creating empty files). But qualitatively the performance graphs are very similar to Fig. 8, with all three MD-on-SSD configurations showing comparable performance and the PMem-based configuration showing slightly better write and delete rates.

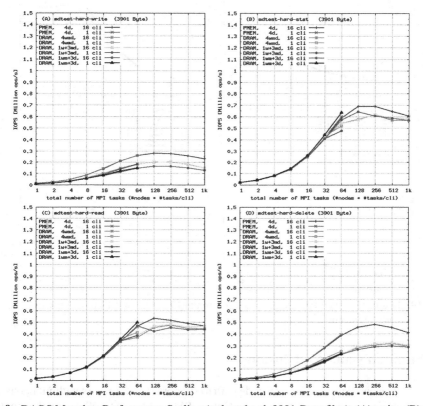

Fig. 9. DAOS Metadata Performance Scaling (mdtest-hard, 3901-Byte files): (A) write, (B) stat, (C) read, (D) delete.

Finally, Fig. 10 repeats the *mdtest-hard* benchmarks but uses an *increased file size* of 7802 Byte to ensure that data is written to the data blobs on NVMe SSDs. The read phase is slower than in Fig. 9, which is expected due to the increased file size. The write, stat and delete performance is almost identical to the performance with the smaller file size. It would be interesting to study this test case with a higher number of NVMe SSDs per engine – four SSDs are probably a too small number to see significant differences between the different configuration options.

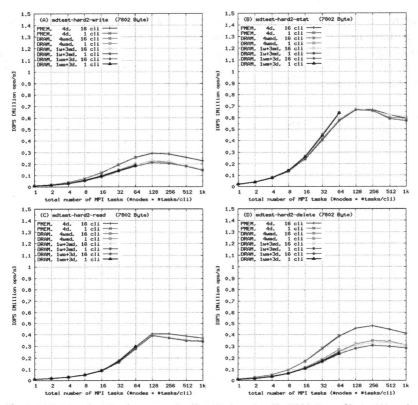

Fig. 10. DAOS Metadata Performance Scaling (mdtest-hard2, 7802-Byte files): (A) write, (B) stat, (C) read, (D) delete.

5 Summary and Conclusions

We have presented the new DAOS code path to support DAOS servers without persistent memory, as an alternative to the existing Optane PMem-based DAOS design that continues to be supported. Code changes are localized to a few code layers on the server side, with no changes to the DAOS APIs or the DAOS clients. Initial studies using a technology preview of the feature are very encouraging. Performance results with an early implementation of the *vos_on_blob* feature show very similar metadata rates across the tested server configurations. Future work will focus on optimizing the implementation for metadata space efficiency, as well as for performance.

The behaviour of VOS checkpointing can be fine-tuned through DAOS pool properties: The *checkpoint* property can be set to either "*timed*" or "*lazy*" mode. The "*timed*" mode is the default and triggers a VOS checkpoint every *checkpoint_freq* seconds – or whenever space pressure in the WAL builds up. In "*lazy*" mode, only space pressure (fill grade of *checkpoint_thresh* percent or higher) will trigger a VOS checkpoint. All benchmarks in this study have been performed with the default ("*timed*" mode with a

5 s interval). More extensive studies are necessary to better understand how to optimize these tunables for specific workloads or NVMe storage media characteristics.

References

1. Liang, Z., Lombardi, J., Chaarawi, M., Hennecke, M.: DAOS: a scale-out high performance storage stack for storage class memory. In: Panda, D.K. (ed.) SCFA 2020. LNCS, vol. 12082, pp. 40–54. Springer, Cham (2020). https://doi.org/10.1007/978-3-030-48842-0_3
2. Liang, Z., Fan, Y., Wang, D., Lombardi, J.: Distributed transaction and self-healing system of DAOS. In: Nichols, J., Verastegui, B., Maccabe, A.', Hernandez, O., Parete-Koon, S., Ahearn, T. (eds.) SMC 2020. CCIS, vol. 1315, pp. 334–348. Springer, Cham (2020). https://doi.org/10.1007/978-3-030-63393-6_22
3. Scot Breitenfeld, M., et al.: DAOS for extreme-scale systems in scientific applications (2017). https://arxiv.org/pdf/1712.00423.pdf
4. IO500. https://io500.org/
5. Rudoff, A.: APIs for persistent memory programming (2018). https://storageconference.us/2018/Presentations/Rudoff.pdf
6. Scargall, S.: Programming Persistent Memory. Apress, Berkeley ISBN 978-1-4842-4931-4 (2020). https://doi.org/10.1007/978-1-4842-4932-1
7. PMDK. https://pmem.io/pmdk/
8. SPDK. https://spdk.io/
9. Intel® Optane™ Persistent Memory 200 Series. https://ark.intel.com/content/www/us/en/ark/products/series/203877/intel-optane-persistent-memory-200-series.html
10. Support for Intel® Optane™ Persistent Memory 200 Series. https://www.intel.com/content/www/us/en/support/products/203877/memory-and-storage/intel-optane-persistent-memory/intel-optane-persistent-memory-200-series.html
11. Customer Support Options for Discontinued Intel Optane Solid-State Drives and Modules. https://www.intel.com/content/www/us/en/support/articles/000024320.html
12. DAOS vos_on_blob Feature Branch (build daos-2.3.106-2.9536.ge3c942ec.el8.x86_64). https://github.com/daos-stack/daos/tree/feature/vos_on_blob
13. Lombardi, J., et al.: Metadata on SSDs design documentation (2022). https://daosio.atlassian.net/wiki/spaces/DC/pages/11196923911/Metadata+on+SSDs
14. Niu, Y.: WAL detailed design (2022). https://daosio.atlassian.net/wiki/spaces/DC/pages/11215339529/WAL+Detailed+Design
15. Hennecke, M.: Performance evolution of DAOS servers (2023). https://www.intel.com/content/www/us/en/high-performance-computing/performance-evolution-of-daos-servers.html
16. IOR and mdtest github repository. https://github.com/hpc/ior
17. The DFS (DAOS File System) driver. https://github.com/hpc/ior/blob/main/README_DAOS
18. Solidigm/Intel SSD D7-P5510 Product Brief. https://www.solidigm.com/content/dam/solidigm/en/site/products/data-center/d7/p5510/documents/d7-p5510-series-product-brief.pdf
19. Hennecke, M.: Understanding DAOS storage performance scalability. In: International Conference on High Performance Computing in Asia-Pacific Region Workshops (HPCASIA-WORKSHOP 2023), 27 February–2 March 2023, Raffles Blvd, Singapore (2023). https://doi.org/10.1145/3581576.3581577
20. Migration from Direct-Attached Intel Optane Persistent Memory to CXL-Attached Memory. https://www.intel.com/content/www/us/en/products/docs/memory-storage/optane-persistent-memory-to-cxl-attached-memory.html

Enabling Multi-level Network Modeling in Structural Simulation Toolkit for Next-Generation HPC Network Design Space Exploration

Sai P. Chenna[1(✉)], Nalini Kumar[1], Leonardo Borges[1], Michael Steyer[2],
Philippe Thierry[3], and Maria Garzaran[1]

[1] Intel Corporation, Santa Clara, USA
{sai.prabhakar.rao.chenna,nalini.kumar,leonardo.borges,
maria.garzaran}@intel.com
[2] Intel Corporation, Munich, Germany
michael.steyer@intel.com
[3] Intel Corporation, Paris, France
philippe.thierry@intel.com

Abstract. The last decade has seen high-performance computing (HPC) systems become denser and denser. Higher node and rack density has led to development of multi-level networks - at socket, node, 'pod', rack, and between nodes. As sockets become more complex with integrated or co-packaged heterogeneous architectures, this network complexity is going to increase. In this paper, we extend Structural Simulation Toolkit (SST) to model these multi-level networks designs. We demonstrate this newly introduced capability by modeling a combination of a few different network topologies at different levels of the system and simulating the performance of collectives and some popular HPC communication patterns.

Keywords: multi-level network modeling · hierarchical network modeling · coarse-grained simulation · design space exploration

1 Introduction

The thin vs fat node debate from a decade ago appears to have been settled with fat nodes ruling the present and the near future systems. The Frontier system at Oak Ridge National Laboratory has one optimized EPYC[TM] processor and four AMD Instinct[TM] accelerators per node [1,4]. The compute nodes of Aurora supercomputer being deployed at Argonne National Laboratory will contain two 4th Gen Intel® Xeon® Max Series CPUs (code-named Sapphire Rapids HBM) and 6 Intel® Data Center GPU Max Series GPUs (code-named Ponte Vecchio) [2]. The Aurora nodes will feature PCIe connectivity between CPU-GPU and Xe link connectivity between GPUs. The nodes themselves will be connected with HPE's Slingshot interconnect in a dragonfly topology with adaptive routing. As is evident from these and other recent HPC procurements [3], network connectivity is becoming more complex. Next generation compute nodes won't just have

© The Author(s), under exclusive license to Springer Nature Switzerland AG 2023
A. Bienz et al. (Eds.): ISC High Performance 2023 Workshops, LNCS 13999, pp. 366–377, 2023.
https://doi.org/10.1007/978-3-031-40843-4_27

more than one socket, but the socket itself will have two or more compute dies co-packaged [5]. In order to understand the performance on these multi-socket nodes with multi-die sockets, we need the ability to model inter-die, inter-socket, inter-node connectivity.

Currently available network modeling tools lack the ability to model such complex systems while simultaneously providing fast turnaround times for design space exploration. Trace-driven simulation tools such as SimGrid [7] are too slow to be productive for investigating a large design space. On the other hand, application pattern driven simulators such as FabSim-X [9], CODES+ROSS [8], and Structural Simulation Toolkit (SST) [6] provide the backbone for coarse-grained simulations but do not have built-in infrastructure for modeling hierarchical networks described earlier.

We solve the problem of fast design-space exploration of multi-level networks by building atop the parallel simulation backend of SST. In this paper, we describe the infrastructure we have created for modeling multi-level network topologies. We demonstrate its use for simulating a big set of system designs driven by communication patterns. Our simulations show that extensive design space exploration can provide deep insight into correlating system designs with application performance. Our contributions described in the paper as follows:

- To the best of our knowledge, this is the first time multi-level network simulation support has been built in any network simulator.
- We present our design for the multi-level network topologies and routing methods. These designs are our contributions to the Structural Simulation Toolkit (SST).
- We evaluate 15 different network configurations for a 128 endpoint system, running 3 HPC communication patterns along with 3 MPI Collectives. These are subset of 720 simulations we ran for different message sizes as part our design space exploration. We observed a simulation throughput of 2 s per simulation, making it feasible to simulate much larger systems in a reasonable amount of time.

Using our multi-level network modeling framework, we quantified the performance improvement of a two-level network over a single network on a test system described in Sect. 4.1. Furthermore, we evaluated the network utilization at each network level with the increase of node size. In the next section, we introduce the simulation infrastructure on which we built the support for multi-level network modeling.

2   SST Infrastructure for Network Modeling

Structural Simulation Toolkit (SST) [6] is a scalable, parallel discrete event simulator developed by researchers at Sandia National Laboratories to explore hardware innovations and how they interact with programming models and communication systems. The SST simulator has a modular design that enables extensive exploration of individual system features and parameters without the need for intrusive changes to the simulator. SST provides both simple and detailed models for processor, network and memory, to enable system-level simulations.

Simulating large-scale systems generates prohibitively large simulation graphs which consume huge amounts of memory and time to perform the simulations. To alleviate this bottleneck, SST provides an MPI backend which partitions the simulation graph onto multiple MPI processes, performing the discrete event simulation in parallel. This provides a high level of performance and the ability to simulate large systems. In addition, SST provides interoperability with other cycle-accurate simulators for memory [13–16], GPU [17] and AI accelerators [18], thereby providing a large design space for architecture evaluation.

There are three primary components in SST that can be used to model networks.

Ember provides a collection of scalable, light-weight, endpoint models for generating network traffic. Due to the light-weight nature of these endpoint models, we can simulate a large-scale system scaling upto a million of nodes. Ember generates the network traffic based on the application communication patterns, known as *motifs*. Ember provides a diverse motif library capturing communication patterns of various HPC applications and MPI Collectives, with an easy interface to create custom motifs.

Firefly acts an interface between the network driver (Ember) and the router models(Merlin). It provides the packetization and byte movement engine that generates the packets and coordinated with the Merlin network layer. In addition, Firefly provides the implementation of various MPI Collectives which can be configured to include additional collective algorithms.

Merlin provides a low-level, flexible networking components that can be used to simulate high-speed networks (machine level). It provides a high-radix router component that models flit-level moment, physical routing and delivery of packets.

We are currently working on extending the capability of these SST elements in order to enable a much wider HPC network design space exploration. Examples include adding the support for trace-driven simulation in Ember, incorporating additional MPI collective algorithms in Firefly. In the next section, we present our design and implementation of modeling multi-level networks in SST.

3   Modeling Multi-level Networks in SST

Unlike traditional system level topologies, multi-level network provides a higher path diversity in order to provide low-latency high bandwidth communication for endpoints which maintain spatial locality. Nvidia's recent "Super-Pod" [3] configuration, which claims 1 ExaFLOP of AI compute, comprises of 32 DGX H100 nodes connected over NVLink interconnect. Each DGX H100 node, in turn consists of 8 H100 GPUs which are connected to each other using multiple NVLinks and NVSwitches, in addition to the 900G/B coherent CPU-GPU

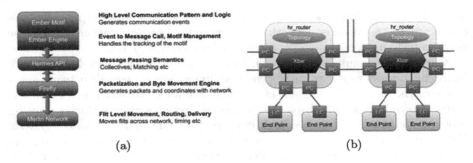

Fig. 1. (a): SST network modeling library stack. (b): A High-radix router model in Merlin which performs flit-level network modeling. Image courtesy: Sandia National Laboratories https://www.osti.gov/servlets/purl/1513506

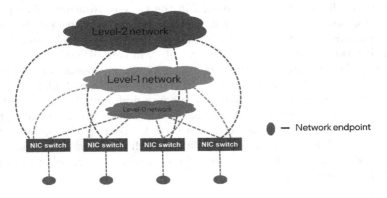

Fig. 2. A Multi-level network system.

interconnect. Finally, multiple of such *SuperPods* can be connected with a high-level interconnect to form a GPU supercomputer. Simulating such large scale systems would require multi-level network modeling.

In order to model the multi-level network topologies, we make use of the several high-level communication patterns and network libraries (known as simulation components) available in SST, shown in Fig. 1. Building support for multi-level network topologies in SST consists of two key phases, building the topology and implementing the routing policy.

Building the Topology. We build the network using a high-radix router component available in SST's Merlin library(Figure 1(b)). In SST, a system is built by instantiating multiple system sub-components and connecting them through SST links. Our system under study comprises of endpoints connected to multiple network levels. Figure 2 shows our approach for building multi-level networks in SST. In order to connect each endpoint to different network hierarchies, we connect each endpoint to a router component we refer to as *NIC switch*. Each network endpoint is connected to its own NIC switch whose output ports are connected to the various networks. Our modular implementation enables the users to pick different topologies for each of the network levels.

Currently our multi-level network topology supports three levels of network hierarchy. Level-0 topology, more commonly refered as *intra-node* network specifies how the endpoints are connected within the node. Level-1 topology (*inter-node*) determines how multiple nodes are connected within a cluster. Level-2 topology defines how multiple such clusters are connected in a larger system. We are currently working on adding more topologies at each level of the hierarchy to increase the architectural design space and enable users to perform an extensive network co-design.

Routing. Once the system construction has been complete, we specify the routing policy for all the router components in the system. Routing policy provides the logic for determining the output port for an incoming packet in a router. SST design makes it flexible to include different routing policies for routers based on their location in the hierarchy. For example, in case of NIC switch, for each incoming packet arriving from the network endpoint, we forward to the packet to the corresponding network level based on the destination endpoint, i.e., packet whose destination endpoint is within the same node will be forwarded to an intra-node network. Currently our routing policy takes a deterministic approach in selecting the network hierarchy to be used for routing the packets. Future work includes adding more adaptive policies which considers additional metrics such as link load, congestion into consideration while determining the optimal network for transmission.

4   Simulation Results

We evaluate our multi-level network modeling framework by simulating a two-level network system containing 128 endpoints. Endpoints in a node are connected in a fully connected fashion using a single switch. We use two-dimensional HyperX as our Level-1 (inter-node) topology to connect multiple nodes. As part of our evaluation, we vary the node size and the shape of our HyperX topology to identify the best possible configuration for a given communication pattern (*motif*). In order to drive the network, we use the HPC communication patterns and MPI collective *motifs* provided in the Ember module of SST.

In the following section, we specify the experimental setup used for our simulations, followed by a detailed performance analysis for various topology configurations.

4.1   Experimental Setup

Table 1 shows the design space of our simulation experiments. As mentioned above, we are using a fully connected network as our intra-node topology to connect all the endpoints of a node. Further, we vary the node size from a thin node

Table 1. System configuration for SST simulation of a two-level network.

Level-0 (intra-node) Topology	
Topology	Fully Connected (single switch)
Node size	2, 4, 8, 16, 32
Link Bandwidth	256 GB/s
Link Latency	1ns
Level-1 (inter-node) topology	
Topology	2-D HyperX
Shape	(2, 2), (2, 4), (2, 8), (2, 16), (2, 32), (4, 2), (4, 4), (4, 8), (4, 16), (8, 2), (8, 4), (8, 8), (16, 2), (16, 4), (32, 2)
Width	1×1
Routing	Dimension Order Routing (DOR)
Link Bandwidth	128 GB/s
Link Latency	11ns
Communication Pattern	
Motifs	Halo2D, Halo3D, Sweep3D
Collectives	Allreduce, Allgather, Alltoall

having 2 endpoints per node, all the way to a much fatter node comprising of 32 endpoints per node. We would like to study the performance impact of fatter nodes on application's communication performance. We would also like to quantitatively evaluate the reduction in traffic on inter-node network by the addition of a low-level intra-node network. Our multi-level network modeling framework makes it possible to perform a detailed analysis of network performance.

We assigned higher link bandwidth for our intra-node network, a factor of 2 over the inter-node network bandwidth. In general, lower level networks benefit from higher link bandwidths and lower link latencies in order to accelerate near neighbor communication. Coming to our inter-node network, we employed a two-dimensional HyperX topology. HyperX is a diameter-2 direct network, where each switch in the network is connected to all it's neighbors along the X, Y, and Z (in case of 3-D HyperX) dimensions. For a given number of system endpoints and node size, there are different shapes in which a 2-D HyperX network can be built. In our evaluation, we built systems with various shapes as mentioned in Table 1. Figure 3 shows one of our simulated systems which contain four endpoints per node which are fully connected using a single switch. All the 32 nodes are connected in a two-dimensional HyperX fashion with the shape of (8,4). The shape of the HyperX network can have a significant performance impact for certain communication patterns, as we demonstrate in Sect. 4.2.

To drive the multi-level network, we used three HPC communication patterns, Halo2D, Halo3D and Sweep3D, and three MPI Collectives, Allreduce, Allgather, and Alltoall.

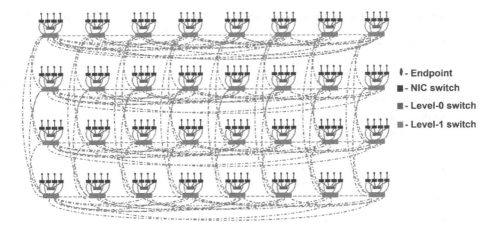

Fig. 3. A Two-level network of a system with 128 endpoints comprising of 32 nodes. Each node has four endpoints connected using a single switch. 32 nodes are connected using a 2-D HyperX topology with a shape of 8 × 4.

Halo2D/3D. In most scientific HPC applications, the computational domain is decomposed into MPI ranks based on the cartesian grid. Each MPI rank communicates with it's cartesian neighbor to exchange the data on each face. In Halo2D, each MPI rank has pairwise exchange of face data to four of it's neighbors along X and Y dimension. In case of Halo3D, each MPI rank performs a pairwise exchanges with 6 neighbors along X, Y, and Z dimensions. The Ember implementation of Halo2D uses Blocking Send-Receive where as Halo3D uses a Non-Blocking Send-Receive.

Sweep3D. In case of Sweep3D motif, the 3-D computational domain is decomposed onto a 2-D processor grid. As a result each MPI rank has a stencil of data across the Z-dimension. During the communication phase, the processor which holds the data of one corner of the 3-D computation grid sends a slice of stencil data to it's immediate neighbors. Once the neighbors received the data, they compute on the data and forward it to their neighbors, creating a wavefront type of communication. We replicate the behavior from the next corner, creating a total of 8 sweeps. Sweep3D stresses the network latency as at any given time the message sizes are small and network bandwidth is rarely stressed. In addition, majority of processors have to wait for a large amount of time to receive the stencil data, thereby resulting in high communication times.

Collectives. In terms of MPI collectives, we evaluate our multi-level topologies using Allreduce, Allgather and Alltoall collectives.

4.2   Analysis

Figure 4 shows the communication time for the six communication motifs mentioned above. We ran all the motifs for 10 iterations and reported the total simulated time in microseconds. As shown in the figure, two-level network had better performance than a single network system. The magnitude of performance improvement is more prominent in the motifs that exhibit near neighbor communication such as Halo2D, Halo3D and Allreduce. Note that the amount speedup in communication time performance for a two-level system observed in Fig. 4 are mainly driven by the latency and bandwidth of the intra-node network in relation with the inter-node network. Additionally, as the nodes get fatter (i.e., more endpoints per node) the performance benefits of a two-level network seem more prominent as shown on the right side of the plots in Fig. 4. This is due to the fact that when we increase the number of endpoints per node, more and more of the MPI communication drops from inter-node level to intra-node level.

Figure 5 quantifies the network utilization at inter-node level for our two system topologies. The network utilization is calculated by the number of packets utilizing the inter-node network, normalized to the total number of packets communicated in the system. For example, the value of 0.2 means that only 20% of the total network packets are utilizing the inter-node network, while the rest 80% of the packets are utilizing the intra-node network. Halo2D, Halo3D and Sweep3D benefit greatly from a lower level network as they exhibit a great degree of locality due to the cartesian neighbor communication.

In case of MPI Collectives, we do not observe much locality in communication as is evident in Fig. 5. Increasing the node size from 2 to 32, by a factor of 16, only reduced the inter-node network traffic by a factor of 1.33 in case of Allreduce and Alltoall, and by a factor of 1.21 in case of Allgather. Note that the amount of reduction in network traffic at inter-node level is determined completely the routing policy at the NIC switch.

5   Related Research

Various network simulators have been proposed to study the performance of large-scale system networks. In our paper, we are not proposing a new simulator tool but rather extending support for an existing network simulator, SST, to model multi-level networks. To the best of our knowledge, this is the first time multi-level network simulation support has been built in any network simulator. Owing to the page limit constraint, we would briefly discuss the characteristics and limitations of some of the prominent network simulators used for network evaluation. Readers are encouraged to peruse the related work mentioned in [8] for a detailed overview of some of the widely used simulators for network design.

NS-3 [10] is a popular discrete event network simulator developed for network research. It provides detailed models for the network subcomponents, which are closer to the real software and hardware implementations. Additionally, NS-3 provides a high-level APIs for easier debugging and network visualization.

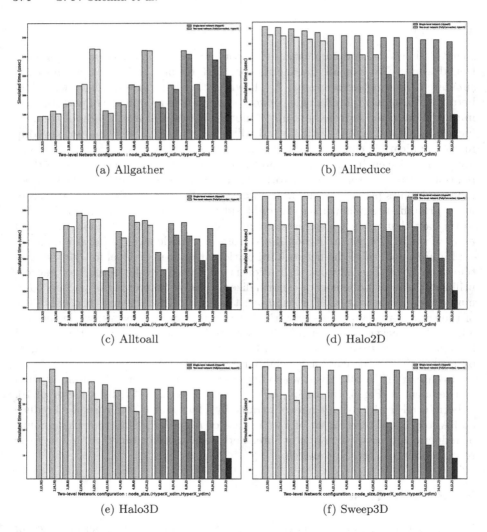

Fig. 4. Performance comparision of simulated time for various communication pattern on a 128 endpoint system built using single-level (HyperX) vs two-level (HyperX-FullyConnected) network. Note: The shades of the color in the plot are used to distinguish the node size. Also, the message size is fixed to 16 kB for all the motifs mentioned above.

OMNet++ [11] is a modular, component-based C++ library designed to simulate both wireless and wired networks. OMNet++ simulates network protocol layers (IPv4,Ethernet,UDP, etc.) which is out of scope for SST. BookSim [12] is a cycle-accurate interconnect network simulator developed for network research and education purposes. Most of the BookSim's capabilities intersect with that of SST. BookSim and SST contain detailed high radix router models with support

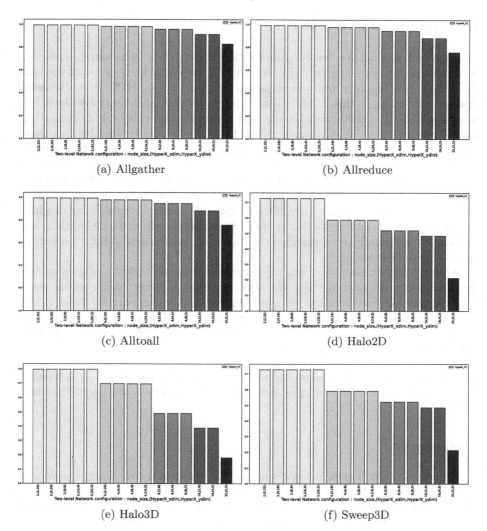

(a) Allgather

(b) Allreduce

(c) Alltoall

(d) Halo2D

(e) Halo3D

(f) Sweep3D

Fig. 5. A comparision of inter-node network traffic between single-level and two-level network. The vertical axis shows the number of packets entering the inter-node network, normalized to a single-level network. Note: The shades of the color in the plot are used to distinguish the node size. Also, the message size is fixed to 16 kB for all the motifs mentioned above.

for various system topologies and adaptive routing policies. BookSim's *Traffic Manager* module provides various synthetic traffic patterns to study network latency and bandwidth. However, BookSim does not support motif or trace-driven network simulation. Finally, NS-3, OMNet++, and BookSim have limited scalability making it infeasible to simulate the networks at HPC level.

6   Conclusions and Future Work

The current and future system topologies are becoming increasingly complex, with the nodes getting much denser, leading to hierarchical network designs. Modeling such complex multi-level networks is crucial for HPC network design space exploration. In this paper, we include support for modeling multi-level networks in SST, a scalable parallel discrete event simulator capable of simulating large-scale systems. We evaluated our modeling framework by simulating various topology configurations of a two-level network system containing 128 network endpoints. We studied how node size and application's communication pattern can have significant impact of both intra-node and inter-node network performance. We assessed the communication performance on different node sizes for three HPC motifs, Halo2D, Halo3D, and Sweep3D which exhibit near neighbor communication behavior and three MPI Collectives, Allreduce, Allgather, and Alltoall. Additionally, we quantified the reduction in inter-node traffic for various topology configurations.

Going forward, we would like to add support for multiple topologies at each level of network hierarchy. We are also currently working on including adaptive routing policies. Finally, we are planning to add support for trace-driven simulations in SST which would help us study a wide variety of application communication patterns, those which cannot be captured in the current set of motifs provided in the Ember module of SST.

Acknowledgements. We would like to thank Scott Hemmert from Sandia National Laboratories for answering our questions and helping us understand the SST backend better.

References

1. Frontier: ORNL's exascale supercomputer designed to deliver world-leading performance in 2021. https://www.olcf.ornl.gov/frontier/
2. Stevens, R., Ramprakash, J., Messina, P., Papka, M., Riley, K.: Aurora: argonne's next-generation exascale supercomputer. United States (2019)
3. Choquette, J.: NVIDIA hopper H100 GPU: scaling performance. IEEE Micro (2023). https://doi.org/10.1109/MM.2023.3256796
4. Smith, A., Norman, J.: AMD Instinct™ MI200 series accelerator and node architectures. In: 2022 IEEE Hot Chips 34 Symposium (HCS). IEEE Computer Society (2022)
5. https://www.intel.com/content/www/us/en/newsroom/news/intel-technology-roadmaps-milestones.html
6. Rodrigues, A.F., et al.: The structural simulation toolkit. ACM SIGMETRICS Perform. Eval. Rev. 38(4), 37–42 (2011)
7. Casanova, H., Legrand, A., Quinson, M.: SimGrid: a generic framework for large-scale distributed experiments. In: Tenth International Conference on Computer Modeling and Simulation (uksim 2008), pp. 126–131. IEEE (2008)
8. Mubarak, M., et al.: Enabling parallel simulation of large-scale HPC network systems. IEEE Trans. Parallel Distrib. Syst. 28(1), 87–100 (2016)

9. Musleh, M., et al.: Fabsim-X: a simulation framework for the analysis of large-scale topologies and congestion control protocols in data center networks. In: 2020 28th International Symposium on Modeling, Analysis, and Simulation of Computer and Telecommunication Systems (MASCOTS). IEEE (2020)

10. Riley, G.F., Henderson, T.R.: The ns-3 network simulator. In: Wehrle, K., Günes, M., Gross, J. (eds.) Modeling and Tools for Network Simulation, pp. 15–34. Springer, Heidelberg (2010). https://doi.org/10.1007/978-3-642-12331-3_2

11. Varga, A., Rudolf, H.: An overview of the OMNeT++ simulation environment. In: 1st International ICST Conference on Simulation Tools and Techniques for Communications, Networks and Systems (2010)

12. Jiang, N., et al.: A detailed and flexible cycle-accurate network-on-chip simulator. In: 2013 IEEE International Symposium on Performance Analysis of Systems and Software (ISPASS). IEEE (2013)

13. Li, S., et al.: DRAMsim3: a cycle-accurate, thermal-capable DRAM simulator. IEEE Comput. Archit. Lett. **19**(2), 106–109 (2020)

14. Stevens, J., et al.: An integrated simulation infrastructure for the entire memory hierarchy: cache, dram, nonvolatile memory, and disk. Intel Technol. J. **17**(1), 184–200 (2013)

15. Leidel, J.D., Yong, C.: HMC-sim-2.0: a simulation platform for exploring custom memory cube operations. In: 2016 IEEE International Parallel and Distributed Processing Symposium Workshops (IPDPSW). IEEE (2016)

16. Kim, Y., Yang, W., Mutlu, O.: Ramulator: a fast and extensible DRAM simulator. IEEE Comput. Archit. Lett. **15**(1), 45–49 (2015)

17. Bakhoda, A., et al.: Analyzing CUDA workloads using a detailed GPU simulator. In: 2009 IEEE International Symposium on Performance Analysis of Systems and Software. IEEE (2009)

18. Muñoz-Martínez, F., et al.: STONNE: enabling cycle-level microarchitectural simulation for DNN inference accelerators. In: 2021 IEEE International Symposium on Workload Characterization (IISWC). IEEE (2021)

Portability and Scalability of OpenMP Offloading on State-of-the-Art Accelerators

Yehonatan Fridman[1,2,3], Guy Tamir[4], and Gal Oren[3,5(✉)]

[1] Department of Computer Science, Ben-Gurion University of the Negev,
Be'er Sheva, Israel
fridyeh@post.bgu.ac.il
[2] Department of Physics, Nuclear Research Center - Negev, Be'er Sheva, Israel
[3] Scientific Computing Center, Nuclear Research Center - Negev, Be'er Sheva, Israel
[4] Intel Corporation, Santa Clara, USA
guy.tamir@intel.com
[5] Department of Computer Science, Technion - Israel Institute of Technology,
Haifa, Israel
galoren@cs.technion.ac.il

Abstract. Over the last decade, most of the increase in computing power has been gained by advances in accelerated many-core architectures, mainly in the form of GPGPUs. While accelerators achieve phenomenal performances in various computing tasks, their utilization requires code adaptations and transformations. Thus, OpenMP, the most common standard for multi-threading in scientific computing applications, introduced offloading capabilities between host (CPUs) and accelerators since v4.0, with increasing support in the successive v4.5, v5.0, v5.1, and the latest v5.2 versions. Recently, two state-of-the-art GPUs – the Intel Ponte Vecchio Max 1100 and the NVIDIA A100 GPUs – were released to the market, with the oneAPI and NVHPC compilers for offloading, correspondingly. In this work, we present early performance results of OpenMP offloading capabilities to these devices while specifically analyzing the portability of advanced directives (using SOLLVE's OMPVV test suite) and the scalability of the hardware in representative scientific mini-app (the LULESH benchmark). Our results show that the coverage for version 4.5 is nearly complete in both latest NVHPC and oneAPI tools. However, we observed a lack of support in versions 5.0, 5.1, and 5.2, which is particularly noticeable when using NVHPC. From the performance perspective, we found that the PVC1100 and A100 are relatively comparable on the LULESH benchmark. While the A100 is slightly better due to faster memory bandwidth, the PVC1100 reaches the next problem size (400^3) scalably due to the larger memory size.

The results are available at: https://github.com/Scientific-Comp uting-Lab-NRCN/Accel-OpenMP-Portability-Scalability.

© The Author(s), under exclusive license to Springer Nature Switzerland AG 2023
A. Bienz et al. (Eds.): ISC High Performance 2023 Workshops, LNCS 13999, pp. 378–390, 2023.
https://doi.org/10.1007/978-3-031-40843-4_28

1 Introduction

1.1 Opportunities and Challenges of GPUs

Supercomputers provide essential infrastructure for groundbreaking research, simulation modeling, and data analysis in various scientific domains [1]. High-performance computing and storage are critical for achieving high resolution and fidelity and analyzing large outputs. As the demand for performance enhancement of algorithmic classes and associated scientific applications constantly increases, new hardware architectures and designs have been developed [2]. Specifically, General-Purpose GPUs (GPGPUs) [3] have emerged to reduce the execution time of dense linear algebra and Fast Fourier Transform (FFT) calculations [4] that are common in material science, chemistry, astrophysics, and deep learning applications.

GPUs are highly parallel and can perform thousands of computations simultaneously [5]. This makes GPUs particularly useful for scientific applications that require massive parallelism, such as simulations, modeling, and data analysis. However, programming GPUs can be challenging. GPUs have complex architectures that require a deep understanding of the hardware and the underlying software stack [6–8]. This complexity can make it challenging for developers to optimize their code for performance. Furthermore, different vendors have their own specific GPU architectures and programming models, and different compilers may have varying levels of support for those architectures and models [8]. For example, NVIDIA's CUDA programming model is specific to NVIDIA GPUs, and the NVIDIA HPC compilers (such as *nvcc*) are specifically designed to work with CUDA.

Additional challenges for programming GPUs are related to memory [9]. GPUs are typically used to accelerate compute-intensive tasks that involve large amounts of data. However, transferring data to and from the GPU can be time-consuming, and developers need to optimize their code to minimize data transfer overhead. Also, GPUs have limited memory compared to traditional CPUs, which can be a bottleneck for certain types of applications [9]. Developers need to carefully manage memory usage to avoid performance issues. In addition, debugging GPU code can be more challenging than debugging CPU code due to the complex interactions between the hardware and software stack [10]. Developers need to use specialized tools and techniques to debug GPU code effectively.

1.2 OpenMP for Heterogenous CPU-GPU Computing

As stated, in recent decades, computing architecture has shifted towards multi-core and many-core shared memory architectures to meet the increasing demand for improved performance. To accommodate these architectures, computational paradigms have been adapted by introducing shared memory parallelism.

The OpenMP API [11] is the most comprehensive API that implements the shared memory model. It includes a set of compiler directives (*pragmas*), library routines, and environment variables that allow a program to be executed in parallel within a shared memory environment. One of the reasons for the popularity of the OpenMP API is its flexible and straightforward interface that is readable and easily interpreted [12].

Originally, OpenMP was designed for shared-memory parallel architectures such as multicore CPUs [12]. However, with the advent of accelerator devices such as GPUs, there has been a growing demand for OpenMP to support offloading computations to these devices [13]. OpenMP first introduced support for offloading computations to accelerators in its version 4.0, which was released in 2013 [14]. The OpenMP 4.0 specification added a set of directives for offloading computations to accelerator devices, including the *target* directive and the *map* clause. These directives allow OpenMP programs to offload computations to an accelerator device, such as a GPU, while still maintaining a single codebase for both the host CPU and the accelerator.

Initially, the support for offloading computations to GPUs in OpenMP was experimental and dependent on the specific compiler and runtime library being used. However, support for offloading computations to GPUs in OpenMP has become more widespread in recent years, with many compilers and runtime libraries adding support for OpenMP offloading to GPUs [15].

In 2018, the OpenMP Architecture Review Board (ARB) released the OpenMP 5.0 specification, which included several new features and enhancements for offloading computations to accelerators, including GPUs [16]. The OpenMP 5.0 specification includes new directives for managing data transfers between the host and the accelerator, as well as new constructs for managing task dependencies in offloaded computations. The current version is 5.2, released in November 2021 [17].

Today, many widely-used compilers and runtime libraries, including GNU Compiler Collection (GCC) [18], Intel oneAPI [19], NVIDIA HPC SDK [20], and Clang [21], provide support for OpenMP offloading to GPUs. In addition, many GPU vendors, including NVIDIA, Intel, and AMD, have developed tools and libraries that integrate with OpenMP to provide optimized support for offloading computations to their GPUs [22]. Other hardware enhancements also improve efficiency, such as the introduction of high bandwidth memory (HBM) [23] and DDR5 for memory-bound kernels.

1.3   Contribution

The support of various compilers in the latest OpenMP specifications is crucial to utilize GPUs in many systems effectively. Moreover, the hardware design also plays a critical role in the success of the kernels' scalability. In this work, we present a comprehensive portability and performance scalability evaluation of OpenMP offloading directives on two state-of-the-art comparable accelerators (Intel PVC1100 and NVIDIA A100, described at Sect. 2) using the latest oneAPI [24] and NVHPC compilers [25], respectively. In order to test the portability of OpenMP for said accelerators, we use the state-of-the-art SOLLVE OMPVV test suite (Sect. 3.1), while for the scalability testing, we use the LULESH benchmark (Sect. 3.2) varient [26,27], which supports OpenMP offloading.

The findings of our study demonstrate that the latest oneAPI and NVHPC compilers provide support for most of the offloading directives included in

OpenMP v4.5. However, support for these directives in OpenMP versions 5.0, 5.1 and 5.2 is currently insufficient, specifically in the NVHPC compiler, while their importance is immense. In terms of performance, we noticed that both PVC1100 and A100 accelerators produced similar results for the LULESH benchmark but with a slight advantage for A100, which was around 34% better. Nevertheless, the PVC100 was capable of running a larger problem (400^3), while the A100 experienced memory exhaustion. We also suggest further specific needed support, which can dramatically affect said results.

2   State-of-the-Art Examined HPC Accelerators

2.1   Intel Data Center Max 1100 GPU (Ponte Vecchio, PVC)

Intel Data Center Max GPU (also known as Ponte Vecchio, in short PVC) [28] is a new high-performance computing GPU architecture that is being developed specifically for exascale computing and artificial intelligence workloads. One of the main advantages of Ponte Vecchio is its use of Intel's advanced packaging technology, known as Foveros [29]. This allows multiple chips to be stacked on top of each other in a 3D configuration, which can lead to significant improvements in performance and power efficiency. Another key feature of Ponte Vecchio is its use of Intel's Xe architecture [30], which is designed specifically for high-performance computing and AI workloads. Xe includes specialized hardware for tasks like matrix multiplication, which are common in AI training and inference. Ponte Vecchio is also designed to work with Intel's oneAPI software stack [31], which is an open, unified programming model that allows developers to write code that can run on a wide variety of processors, including CPUs, GPUs, and FPGAs. This can make it easier for developers to optimize their code for Ponte Vecchio and other Intel processors. While the PVC is available in three versions (1100, 1350, and 1550), we consider the 1100 version relatively comparable to NVIDIA's A100 GPU [32].

2.2   NVIDIA A100 GPU

The NVIDIA A100 GPU [33] is a flagship GPU from NVIDIA designed for high-performance computing, data analytics, and artificial intelligence workloads. It features a 3rd-Generation Tensor Core that provides significant improvements in deep learning performance, as well as an enhanced L2 cache and HBM2 DRAM for faster memory access. The A100 GPU also includes a new asynchronous data movement and programming model, which improves efficiency, and 3rd-generation NVIDIA NVLink I/O, which enables fast and efficient interconnectivity between multiple GPUs [34]. The A100 GPU is optimized to function with the NVHPC [25] compilers and libraries suite, which is specifically designed for NVIDIA GPU architectures. Overall, the NVIDIA A100 GPU is a highly powerful and versatile solution for demanding computing workloads across various industries and applications.

3   OpenMP Offloading Port' and Scal' Benchmarks

3.1   SOLLVE OpenMP Validation and Verification (OMPVV)

The OpenMP language is continuously developing with the release of each new specification, resulting in the need to validate and verify the new features implemented by different vendors. The latest versions of OpenMP, 5.0, 5.1, and 5.2, have introduced many new target offload and host-based features to the programming model, indicating the growing maturity of OpenMP and the increasing number of compiler and hardware vendors that support it [15]. The SOLLVE Validation and Verification test suite [35] was built to provide open-source vendor-agnostic feature tests for the latest OpenMP specifications with a focus on features of interest to applications. The SOLLVE OMPVV project [35] focuses on evaluating the implementation progress and conformity of various compiler vendors, such as Intel, NVIDIA, Clang/LLVM, IBM, GNU, and Cray, for the 4.5, 5.0, 5.1, and 5.2 versions of the specification. The effort of fault-finding in these implementations is particularly valuable for application developers using new OpenMP features to speed up their scientific codes. Huber et al. [36] provide insights into the current implementation status of different vendors, the progression of specific compilers' OpenMP support over time, and examples of how the test suite has influenced discussions regarding the correct interpretation of the OpenMP specification. However, this work does not show results for the state-of-the-art GPUs.

3.2   OpenMP Offloading LULESH

LULESH is a well-known mini-application that simplifies the simulation of the Sedov-Taylor problem [37] using unstructured Lagrangian rezoning to solve hydrodynamic equations (Navier-Stokes) explicitly on an unstructured grid. This makes it latency and bandwidth-bound [38]. LULESH supports various parallelization schemes and programming paradigms such as MPI, OpenMP, CUDA, OpenACC, and OpenCL [39]. It was developed as part of one of the five challenge problems defined by the DARPA UHPC program [39,40] and aims to simulate a small portion of various multi-physics applications (specifically, ALE3D [41]) that consume up to 30% of the computing resources of the DoD and DoE [26,42,43]. Due to its popularity, LULESH is widely used for testing new hardware, applying optimizations, parallelization schemes, APIs, and more [26,44]. For instance, Laney et al. [45] used LULESH and several other benchmarks to assess the effects of data compression on performance, as they are representative of real scientific applications. Bercea et al. [26] evaluated the effectiveness of the OpenMP offloading capabilities on NVIDIA Kepler GPUs K40m (2015), and it is the latest known version of its kind, using OpenMP version 4.0 [26].

4   Results and Analysis

4.1   Settings and Hardware

Both NVIDIA A100 and Intel Ponte Vecchio MAX are designed for high-performance computing and AI workloads. The A100 is based on NVIDIA's Ampere architecture, while the Ponte Vecchio MAX is based on Intel's Xe architecture [46]. These two accelerators are considered comparable (in the PVC1100 version), and their specifications are listed in Table 1. In this work, we compare OpenMP portability and performance scalability on two systems, as Table 2 presents. To compile OpenMP pragmas we use the latest Intel oneAPI DPC++/C++ Compiler (2023) for system #1 and the latest NVHPC 23.3 for system #2. To compile LULESH and SOLLVE OMPVV tests with OpenMP offloading, we use supportive flags, as presented in Table 3.

Table 1. Intel Data Center GPU Max 1100 (PVC) specifications [47] v.s. NVIDIA A100 Tensor Core PCIe [48].

	Intel PVC1100	NVIDIA A100
GPU Architecture	Xe-HPC	NVIDIA Ampere
Memory	48 GB HBM2e	40 GB HBM2e
Memory Bandwidth	1228.8 GB/s	1555 GB/s
Compute Cores	7168	6912

Table 2. Compared systems in this work and the compilers used in each system.

System	CPU (host)	GPU (device)	Compiler
#1	×2 Intel 4th Gen Xeon (Sapphire Rapids) processors [49]	Intel Data Center GPU Max 1100 [47]	oneAPI 2023.1.0 ifx/icpx/icx
#2	×2 Intel Xeon Gold 6338 processors [50]	NVIDIA A100 Tensor Core GPU [33]	NVHPC 23.3 nvfortran/nvc++/nvc

Table 3. Compilation flags in each system listed in Table 2.

System	Compilation flags
#1	`-O3 -qopenmp -fopenmp-targets=spir64` `-fiopenmp` `-fopenmp-version={50,51,52}`
#2	`-O3 -mp=gpu -gpu=cc80`

4.2 OpenMP Portability Evaluation with **SOLLVE OMPVV**

The results of SOLLVE OMPVV are presented in Figs. 1, 2, 3 and 4 for OpenMP v4.5, v5.0, v5.1 and v5.2 respectively[1]. The total number of tests is 603 (230 for v4.5, 281 for v5.0, 80 for v5.1, and 12 for v5.2). The tests cover OpenMP pragmas for C, C++, and Fortran programs, although the coverage for C++ and Fortran is lacking. The test outcomes are labeled as "PASS" for those that successfully pass compilation and execution, and "FAIL" for those that fail during compilation or execution. The results show that both oneAPI 2023 and NVHPC 23.3 compilers provide almost complete coverage for v4.5 directives on the corresponding systems. While oneAPI provides relatively good support for OpenMP v5.0 and v5.1 directives (yet still far from completion), the support for v5.0 and v5.1 by NVHPC is lacking. In addition, both compilers provide lacking support for v5.2 directives. Our analysis reveals limited progress in support

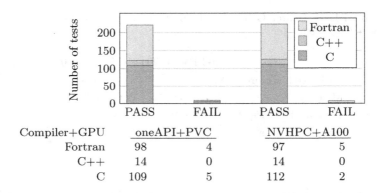

Compiler+GPU	oneAPI+PVC		NVHPC+A100	
Fortran	98	4	97	5
C++	14	0	14	0
C	109	5	112	2

Fig. 1. OpenMP 4.5 tests with oneAPI & NVHPC for PVC1100 & A100, respectively.

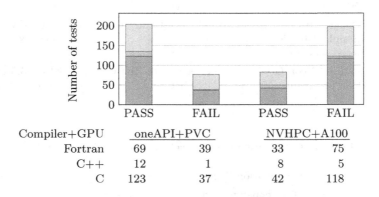

Compiler+GPU	oneAPI+PVC		NVHPC+A100	
Fortran	69	39	33	75
C++	12	1	8	5
C	123	37	42	118

Fig. 2. OpenMP 5.0 tests with oneAPI & NVHPC for PVC1100 & A100, respectively.

---

[1] The results are fully listed in https://github.com/Scientific-Computing-Lab-NRCN/Accel-OpenMP-Portability-Scalability/tree/main/Sollve_vv.

of NVHPC for OpenMP directives since 2021, as similar results were reported
in [36] for NVHPC in version 21 on Summit [51], and have not been improved
upon since. Table 4 lists some inconsistencies in the results between oneAPI 2023
and NVHPC 23.3. However, there are directives with immense importance that
are not supported by both compilers. For example, both systems do not support
reverse offloading and unified memory capabilities introduced in OpenMP v5.0
and later (Table 5 lists noticeable ones). The reverse offloading directive allows
for seamless offloading of work to accelerators, while shared and unified memory
directives simplify the memory management between the CPU and accelerator. With strong compiler support, these OpenMP directives become accessible
and widely used, resulting in improved performance and productivity in parallel
computing applications.

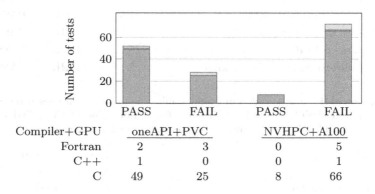

Fig. 3. OpenMP 5.1 tests with oneAPI & NVHPC for PVC1100 & A100, respectively.

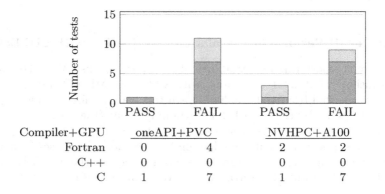

Fig. 4. OpenMP 5.2 tests with oneAPI & NVHPC for PVC1100 & A100, respectively.

Table 4. Inconsistencies of SOLLVE OMPVV tests passing and failing on oneAPI+PVC1100 v.s. NVHPC+A100. While some of the failed tests are managed to compile, the others compile successfully but fail to execute.

Test Name	OMP Version	oneAPI 2023	NVHPC 23.3
test_declare_target_device_type_nohost.c	5.0	PASS	FAIL
test_requires_unified_shared_memory _omp_target_alloc.c	5.0	PASS	FAIL
test_requires_unified_shared_memory _omp_target_alloc_is_device_ptr.c	5.0	PASS	FAIL
test_target_defaultmap_present.c	5.1	PASS	FAIL
test_target_is_accessible.c	5.1	PASS	FAIL
test_target_update_devices.F90	4.5	FAIL	PASS
test_declare_target_parallel_for.F90	5.0	FAIL	PASS
test_requires_unified_shared_memory_static.F90	5.0	FAIL	PASS
test_metadirective_target_device_kind.c	5.1	FAIL	PASS

Table 5. OpenMP reverse offloading and unified memory\ addresses directives fail both on oneAPI+PVC1100 and NVHPC+A100. While some of the failed tests are managed to compile, the others compile successfully but fail to execute.

Test Name	OMP Version	oneAPI 2023	NVHPC 23.3
test_requires_reverse_offload.c	5.0	FAIL	FAIL
test_requires_unified_address.c	5.0	FAIL	FAIL
test_requires_unified_shared_memory_static.c	5.0	FAIL	FAIL
test_requires_unified_shared_memory _heap_is_device_ptr.F90	5.1	FAIL	FAIL
test_requires_unified_shared_memory _stack_is_device_ptr.F90	5.1	FAIL	FAIL

4.3   OpenMP Performance Scalability Evaluation with LULESH

To evaluate the performance scalability of PVC1100 against A100, compilation and execution of LULESH were done with v4.0 OpenMP offloading [52]. The grid size was scaled from 100^3 to 400^3. Each test was run for 20-time steps. We analyze the results by the total LULESH running time[2] (Fig. 5a).

In an effort to amplify the outcomes, we made initial endeavors to incorporate support for cutting-edge unified memory\addresses capabilities of PVC1100 using the latest directives obtainable on the v5, 5.1, and 5.2 OpenMP specifications. Regrettably, we were unsuccessful in executing the

---

[2] The LULESH benchmark output results are fully presented in https://github.com/ Scientific-Computing-Lab-NRCN/Accel-OpenMP-Portability-Scalability/tree/ main/LULESH_Results.

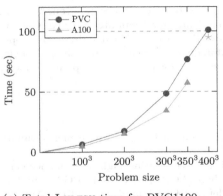
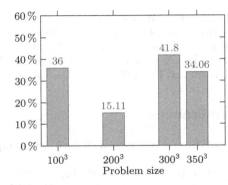

(a) Total LULESH time for PVC1100 and A100 (lower is better).

(b) Improvement percentage of A100 over PVC1100 on total LULESH time (see Figure 5a) (higher is better).

Fig. 5. Comparison of LULESH timings on PVC1100 and A100 (for 20 iterations).

majority of the directives, as shown in Table 5. Furthermore, the directives that we were able to execute yielded unsatisfactory outcomes or terminated with *ZE_RESULT_ERROR_OUT_OF_DEVICE_MEMORY*.

5   Conclusions and Future Work

This work comprehensively evaluates the performance scalability and portability of OpenMP offloading on modern compilers and state-of-the-art GPUs. The findings indicate that the latest oneAPI compiler mostly complies with the latest OpenMP specifications, while NVHPC's support is still lacking. In both compilers, support is particularly lacking in the area of unified and shared memory/address directives. Our research shows that the NVIDIA A100 outperforms the Intel PVC1100 (up to %34 better performance on LULESH with OpenMP 4.0). To further optimize hardware capabilities, we recommend thoroughly exploring integrating the latest OpenMP directives, which can greatly enhance LULESH performance. Specifically, we suggest utilizing *requires unified memory*, and *unified addresses* and *reverse offload* directives to optimize results.

For future work, we propose examining additional proxy apps like XSBench, SNAP, HPGMG, CoMD [53,54], and ScalSALE [55,56] with OpenMP offloading. Due to improvements in compilers support for the newest OpenMP offloading directives that we expect, our goal is to create an enhanced version of LULESH that utilizes these directives to optimize data movements and minimize computational overheads. We further recommend a deeper examination of the portability and scalability of OpenMP offloading in real-world applications using the latest OpenMP directives. Additionally, we propose assessing the scalability of OpenMP in the aforementioned applications across several devices within a single node.

Acknowledgments. This research was supported by Intel Corporation (oneAPI CoE program) and the Lynn and William Frankel Center for Computer Science. Computational support was provided by the NegevHPC project [57] and Intel Developer Cloud [58]. The authors want to thank Jay Mahalingam, Omar Toral, Oshana Douglas of Intel, and Israel Hen, Gabi Dadush of NegevHPC for their great help and support.

References

1. Wilson, K.G.: Grand challenges to computational science. Future Gener. Comput. Syst. **5**(2–3), 171–189 (1989)
2. Liu, B., Zydek, D., Selvaraj, H., Gewali, L.: Accelerating high performance computing applications: using CPUs, GPUs, hybrid CPU/GPU, and FPGAs. In: 2012 13th International Conference on Parallel and Distributed Computing, Applications and Technologies, pp. 337–342. IEEE (2012)
3. Aamodt, T.M., et al.: General-purpose graphics processor architectures. Synthesis Lect. Comput. Archit. **13**(2), 1–140 (2018)
4. Chen, Y., Cui, X., Mei, H.: Large-scale fast Fourier transform. In: GPU Computing Gems Emerald Edition, pp. 629–642. Elsevier (2011)
5. Bridges, R.A., Imam, N., Mintz, T.M.: Understanding GPU power: a survey of profiling, modeling, and simulation methods. ACM Comput. Surv. (CSUR) **49**(3), 1–27 (2016)
6. Niemeyer, K.E., Sung, C.-J.: Recent progress and challenges in exploiting graphics processors in computational fluid dynamics. J. Supercomput. **67**, 528–564 (2014)
7. Pallipuram, V.K., Bhuiyan, M., Smith, M.C.: A comparative study of GPU programming models and architectures using neural networks. J. Supercomput. **61**, 673–718 (2012)
8. Lee, S., Vetter, J.S.: Early evaluation of directive-based GPU programming models for productive exascale computing. In: SC 2012: Proceedings of the International Conference on High Performance Computing, Networking, Storage and Analysis, pp. 1–11. IEEE (2012)
9. Qureshi, Z., et al.: Tearing down the memory wall. arXiv preprint arXiv:2008.10169 (2020)
10. Knobloch, M., Mohr, B.: Tools for GPU computing-debugging and performance analysis of heterogenous HPC applications. Supercomput. Front. Innov. **7**(1), 91–111 (2020)
11. Dagum, L., Menon, R.: OpenMP: an industry standard API for shared-memory programming. IEEE Comput. Sci. Eng. **5**(1), 46–55 (1998)
12. Mattson, T.G., He, Y.H., Koniges, A.E.: The OpenMP Common Core: Making OpenMP Simple Again. MIT Press, Cambridge (2019)
13. Van der Pas, R., et al.: Using OpenMP-the Next Step: Affinity, Accelerators, Tasking, and SIMD. MIT Press, Cambridge (2017)
14. OpenMP Architecture Review Board. OpenMP application program interface, version 4.0 (2013)
15. OpenMP Architecture Review Board. OpenMP offload in applications of the exascale computing project (2022)
16. OpenMP Architecture Review Board. OpenMP application program interface version 5.0 (2018)
17. OpenMP Architecture Review Board. OpenMP application program interface version 5.2 (2021)

18. GNU Project. GNU offloading and multi-processing project (GOMP) (2023)
19. Intel. oneAPI GPU optimization guide (2023)
20. Hammond, J.: OpenMP in NVIDIA's HPC compilers (2021)
21. The Clang Team. Clang 17.0.0git documentation (2023)
22. Mehta, N.A., Gayatri, R., Ghadar, Y., Knight, C., Deslippe, J.: Evaluating performance portability of OpenMP for SNAP on NVIDIA, Intel, and AMD GPUs using the roofline methodology. In: Bhalachandra, S., Wienke, S., Chandrasekaran, S., Juckeland, G. (eds.) WACCPD 2020. LNCS, vol. 12655, pp. 3–24. Springer, Cham (2021). https://doi.org/10.1007/978-3-030-74224-9_1
23. Jun, H., et al.: HBM (high bandwidth memory) dram technology and architecture. In: 2017 IEEE International Memory Workshop (IMW), pp. 1–4. IEEE (2017)
24. Intel. oneAPI DPC++ compiler (2023)
25. NVIDIA. Nvidia HPC SDK (2023)
26. Bercea, G.T., et al.: Performance analysis of OpenMP on a GPU using a coral proxy application. In: Proceedings of the 6th International Workshop on Performance Modeling, Benchmarking, and Simulation of High Performance Computing Systems, pp. 1–11 (2015)
27. AMD. Lulesh 2.0 using OpenMP 4.0 (2015)
28. Intel. Intel®Data Center GPU Max Series (2023). https://www.intel.com/content/www/us/en/products/details/discrete-gpus/data-center-gpu-max-series.html
29. Intel. A new era of chipmaking to meet the world's demand for compute (2023)
30. Intel. Intel iris Xe GPU architecture (2023)
31. Intel oneAPI. A new era of accelerated computing (2023)
32. Intel. Intel data center GPU max series (2023)
33. NVIDIA. NVIDIA A100 GPU (2020). https://www.nvidia.com/en-us/data-center/a100/
34. Choquette, J., Gandhi, W., Giroux, O., Stam, N., Krashinsky, R.: NVIDIA A100 tensor core GPU: performance and innovation. IEEE Micro 41(2), 29–35 (2021)
35. ECP (Exascale Computing Project. OPENMP VALIDATION AND VERIFICATION TESTSUITE (2023). https://crpl.cis.udel.edu/ompvvsollve/
36. Huber, T., et al.: ECP SOLLVE: validation and verification testsuite status update and compiler insight for openMP. arXiv preprint arXiv:2208.13301, 2022
37. Kamm, J.R.: Evaluation of the Sedov-von Neumann-Taylor blast wave solution. Astrophys. J. Suppl. 46 (2000, submitted)
38. Wen, S., et al.: ProfDP: a lightweight profiler to guide data placement in heterogeneous memory systems. In: Proceedings of the 2018 International Conference on Supercomputing, pp. 263–273 (2018)
39. LLNL. LULESH webpage (2012). https://asc.llnl.gov/codes/proxy-apps/lulesh
40. Feldman, M.: DARPA sets ubiquitous HPC program in motion (2010). https://www.hpcwire.com/2010/08/10/darpa_sets_ubiquitous_hpc_program_in_motion/
41. Noble, C.R., et al.: ALE3D: an arbitrary Lagrangian-Eulerian multi-physics code. Technical report, Lawrence Livermore National Lab. (LLNL), Livermore, CA, USA (2017)
42. Karlin, I., et al.: Tuning the Lulesh mini-app for current and future hardware. Technical report, Lawrence Livermore National Lab. (LLNL), Livermore, CA, USA (2013)
43. Hornung, R.D., et al.: Hydrodynamics challenge problem. Technical report, Lawrence Livermore National Lab. (LLNL), Livermore, CA, USA (2011)

44. Vergara Larrea, V.G., et al.: Scaling the summit: deploying the world's fastest supercomputer. In: Weiland, M., Juckeland, G., Alam, S., Jagode, H. (eds.) ISC High Performance 2019. LNCS, vol. 11887, pp. 330–351. Springer, Cham (2019). https://doi.org/10.1007/978-3-030-34356-9_26
45. Laney, D., et al.: Assessing the effects of data compression in simulations using physically motivated metrics. In: SC 2013: Proceedings of the International Conference on High Performance Computing, Networking, Storage and Analysis, pp. 1–12. IEEE (2013)
46. technical.city. Intel®Data Center GPU Max 1100 v.s. NVIDIA A100 PCIe (2023). https://technical.city/en/video/A100-PCIe-vs-Data-Center-GPU-Max-1100
47. Intel. Intel Data Center GPU Max 1100 (2023). https://ark.intel.com/content/www/us/en/ark/products/232876/intel-data-center-gpu-max-1100.html
48. NVIDIA. NVIDIA Ampere Architecture In-Depth (2015). https://developer.nvidia.com/blog/nvidia-ampere-architecture-in-depth/
49. Intel. Intel 4th Gen Xeon Scalable Processors (2023). https://www.intel.com/content/www/us/en/newsroom/news/4th-gen-xeon-scalable-processors-max-series-cpus-gpus.html#gs.ti3gm6
50. Intel. Intel Xeon Gold Processors (2023). https://www.intel.com/content/www/us/en/products/sku/212285/intel-xeon-gold-6338-processor-48m-cache-2-00-ghz/specifications.html
51. Wells, J., et al.: Announcing supercomputer summit. Technical report, Oak Ridge National Lab. (ORNL), Oak Ridge, TN, USA (2016)
52. Github, LULESH OpenMP v4 Offloading GitHub Page (2015). https://github.com/AMDComputeLibraries/OpenMPApps/tree/master/lulesh-mp4
53. LLNL. CORAL Benchmark Codes (2014). https://asc.llnl.gov/coral-benchmarks
54. Github. OpenMPApps mini-apps GitHub Page (2015). https://github.com/AMDComputeLibraries/OpenMPApps
55. Harel, R., et al.: ScalSALE: Scalable sale benchmark framework for supercomputers. arXiv preprint arXiv:2209.01983 (2022)
56. Rusanovsky, M., et al.: Backus: comprehensive high-performance research software engineering approach for simulations in supercomputing systems. arXiv preprint arXiv:1910.06415 (2019)
57. NegevHPC Project. https://www.negevhpc.com
58. Intel. Intel Developer Cloud (2023). https://www.intel.com/content/www/us/en/developer/tools/devcloud/overview.html

An Earlier Experiences Towards Optimizing Apache Spark Over Frontera Supercomputer

Samuel Bernardo[2(✉)] [iD], Amit Ruhela[1] [iD], John Cazes[1] [iD],
Stephen Lien Harrell[1] [iD], and Jorge Gomes[2] [iD]

[1] Texas Advanced Computing Center Austin, Austin, TX, USA
`{aruhela,cazes,sharrell}@tacc.utexas.edu`
[2] LIP - Laboratório de Instrumentação e Física Experimental de Partículas,
Lisbon, Portugal
`{samuel,jorge}@lip.pt`

Abstract. Apache Spark has become a very popular computing engine that allows distributing computing tasks on a compute cluster. However, the current approaches lack necessary optimizations and often lead to non-optimal resource usage. This paper briefly describes our earlier experiences on the Frontera supercomputer towards deployment and optimizing the Apache Spark components and presents our approach to running Apache Spark jobs efficiently. We ran the simulation at different scales to understand the performance trend of the proposed implementation.

Keywords: HPC · Apache Spark · Parallel computing and distributed computing · Optimization and scalability · Monte Carlo

1 Introduction

Fault-tolerant Optimized processing engines are nowadays extremely popular in the Scientific Community. HPC infrastructures are extremely tailed and specialized to specific software, such as MPI implementations. Adding newer engines to Supercomputers carries numerous integration and scalability challenges to obtain the expected performance. Apache Spark is one of the most used processing engines for large-scale data processing. This research work focuses on deploying and optimizing the Apache Spark engine experiment over the Frontera Supercomputer.

Apache Spark engine is a distributed computing solution that allows scaling an application to use the resources of multiple nodes. It provides distributed task dispatching, scheduling and communication over a computer cluster. Apache Spark setup usually uses Spark Cluster Managers such as Hadoop YARN, Apache MESOS or Kubernetes. There are standard solutions to deploy it over Cloud

Supported by BigHPC consortium (https://bighpc.wavecom.pt/), TACC and LIP.

environments or dedicated computer endpoints. Nevertheless, when facing existing HPC clusters, it is required to pursue approaches that meet the requirements of a given computation environment.

The process execution over HPC clusters is confined to the rootless execution context. The available software suite on a given supercomputer is managed independently by the system administrators. It's not required that the same set of software will be available over other compute clusters. Considering the management policies, the required software dependencies for Apache Spark are hard to keep for this specific purpose. Apache Spark engine architecture also requires optimization over the HPC clusters to achieve the best performance and minimize computational costs. The most acceptable parameterization between Apache Spark and Frontera supercomputer needs to be reviewed in more detail.

In order to allow a better reference for this work, we select a widespread and fundamental benchmark: performing pi estimation using the Monte Carlo methodology and applying the rejection sampling methodology. This application is available on the official Apache Spark website and configured for our optimization tests using Python language.

The Apache Spark engine is setup in standalone deploy mode. The master and worker components are launched manually using launch scripts provided by Apache Spark. Using the standalone deploy mode makes it possible to develop our own cluster management solution and accomplish the integration task with the HPC cluster environment. The implemented wrapper for job submission is tailed to the Slurm workload manager. Apptainer, an open-source container platform, loads the Spark image into the execution environment. Apptainer supports container images prepared via docker format. We selected the spark-py image sponsored by Apache Software Foundation. All tests are orchestrated using the latest software version available: v3.3.2.

1.1 Contributions

This paper presents the implemented wrapper to launch Apache Spark cluster engine dynamically taking into account the available resources gathered by the Slurm job context. Then the Spark job submission using the pi estimation script, applying the required optimizations. We compare the cost efficiency when scaling the number of nodes. The study starts with a single-node execution analysis, understanding the parallel execution optimizations. We, then scale the application to multiple nodes and evaluate the performance trend.

2   Background

2.1   Frontera

Frontera is a Texas Advanced Computing Center (TACC) petascale computing system [12]. The primary compute system was provided by Dell EMC with 8008 nodes powered by Intel Xeon Platinum 8280 ("Cascade Lake") processors with 28 cores and base frequency 2.7 GHz. Each compute node is composed of two CPUs providing a total of 56 available cores, 192 GB DDR-4 memory, 480 GB SSD drive and Mellanox InfiniBand HDR-100 network capable of 200Gbps. In 2019, Frontera earned the 5th spot on the twince-annual Top500 list and achieved 23.5 PetaFLOPS on the high-performance LINPACK benchmark, with the main system's theoretical peak performance as 38.7 PetaFLOPS. Frontera storage system is composed of a Lustre-based storage of 60 PB with a 3 PB flash storage for data-driven science applications that depend upon fast access to large amounts of data. Over this storage pool three Lustre file systems are shared across all nodes: home, work and scratch. There is also a fourth file system, flash, for the flash storage pool mentioned before. The computing jobs mentioned in this paper are using the home file system to keep the code and collected logs and the scratch file system for the process workspace. As we will explain in more detail later, the Pi estimation with Apache Spark generates the samples during runtime, so this minimizes the file system I/O and allows us to focus on communication and computation performances.

2.2 Apache Spark

Apache Spark is an unified analytics engine for large-scale data processing. It provides a high level API in multiple languages that includes Python, besides higher-level tools for machine learning with MLlib [11], among others. The architectural foundation for this engine provides a working set for distributed programs over distributed shared memory with the resilient distributed dataset (RDD) [17]. This implementation was a response to limitations in the MapReduce cluster computing paradigm. One of the most popular MapReduce solutions is Apache Hadoop where it can be observed that a particular linear dataflow structure is forced on distributed programs [18]. The processing workflow inside Apache Spark is managed as a directed acyclic graph (DAG). Looking into the DAG representation, the nodes are the RDDs while edges are the applied operations over the RDDs. Apache Spark can handle acyclic and cyclic graphs allowing efficient representation of iterative methods. This ability to express iterative algorithms behind the traditional MapReduce framework limitation [5], makes Apache Spark one of the most popular processing engines nowadays. The engine deployment requires a cluster manager and a distributed storage system. As cluster manager we adopted the standalone native Spark cluster solution. This allows better control over the cluster operation as necessary for the limitations in rootless HPC environments. The cluster manager is responsible to allocate resources across applications and send the application code to the executors. From the application side (client) it is launched the SparkContext that corresponds to the Apache Spark driver program. The driver is then responsible to send application code and the corresponding tasks to the available executors. The executors are acquired on the nodes during Apache Spark job initialization, which are processes that run the computations and manage the application data. The application data is cached by Block Manager, a key-value store for data blocks in Apache Spark. Block Manager acts as a local cache that runs on every node in the context of the Apache Spark driver and executors. It also provides an interface for uploading and fetching blocks both locally and remotely using memory, disk and off-heap (external block) stores. The interaction between all mentioned components of Apache Spark are represented in Fig. 1. Apache Spark allows launching the client application in three different modes of execution. The execution model helps determine where the resources are physically located when the application is run. Cluster mode depends on the selected cluster manager support and the driver implementation language. With this mode the driver process is launched on a worker node inside the cluster by the cluster manager, in addition to the executor processes. This way the cluster manager is in charge of all Spark processes. Since we are using *py-spark* for our implementation, we cannot use this mode because it is not supported. Anyway this is not an issue as we are going to show next. Client mode is almost the same as cluster mode except that Spark driver remains on the client machine that submitted the application. Since the client machine is always a node of Apache Spark cluster within our implementation, this has the same result as using cluster mode. In the local mode all processes of Spark application run on a single machine. Even though it provides parallelism through threads on that single machine. This mode is used in our base tests using a single node.

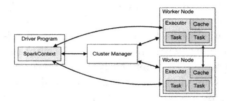

Fig. 1. Apache Spark engine architecture (image retrieved from "cluster-overview" in the Apache Spark documentation)

2.3   Monte Carlo Method with Rejection Sample Approach

Monte Carlo methods belong to the class of computational algorithms that rely on repeated random sampling to obtain numerical results. In principle, Monte Carlo methods can be used to solve any problem that could have a probabilistic interpretation. It can be also used for numerical integration using random numbers, particularly useful for higher-dimensional integrals. In practice there are many different methods for the different purposes where it can be applied, but here we focus on sampling methods to do the numerical estimation. As some examples of Monte Carlo sampling methods we have direct sampling, importance sampling and rejection sampling. To do the Pi value estimation the best fit method is rejection sampling, that allows to select samples within a region of the sampled distribution. To estimate the value of Pi, the idea is to simulate random (x, y) points in a 2-D plane with domain as a square around a circle, with square size equal to the diameter of the circle. Then a number of random generated points inside the square are generated. Finally the estimation is accomplished by doing the ratio between the number of points that lie inside the circle and total number of generated points as referred in Fig. 2.

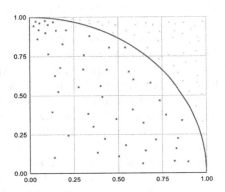

Fig. 2. Representation of Pi estimation using Monte Carlo rejection sample method

Looking to the model we can formulate the equation that will allow to use Monte Carlo rejection sample methodology. With this representation we are comparing the area of the square with the area of the circle. The ratio between this two areas can be translated to:

$$\frac{\pi}{4} = \frac{number\ of\ points\ generated\ inside\ the\ circle}{total\ number\ of\ points\ generated} \Leftrightarrow$$
$$\Leftrightarrow \pi = 4 * \frac{number\ of\ points\ generated\ inside\ the\ circle}{total\ number\ of\ points\ generated} \tag{1}$$

The algorithm implementation turns very simple, since we can generate the random (x,y) pairs and then check:

$$x^2 + y^2 \leqslant 1 \tag{2}$$

This algorithm was implemented using python language and the application *pi_estimation.py* is at a private repository in Gitlab [2]. The repository is still private at the time of writing this paper because we haven't yet decided about a license for the code.

3   Performance Optimization over Frontera

3.1   Single Node Performance

Even though Pi calculation can be considered a solved problem, estimating the value of Pi using Monte Carlo methodology is a popular solution to benchmark hardware. The code implementation of Monte Carlo method to estimate Pi value can be used to get the computer floating point operations per second (FLOPS) performance. But in this experiment we are using it for parallelization and communication performance optimization towards minimization of execution cost over HPC infrastructure when using Apache Spark engine. The base test for Pi estimation is set to 10^{10} samples, since this sample size uses all resources of a Frontera single node. During almost the execution time, the node was with all available cores working and about 50% of node memory was used. The algorithm tends to be more CPU intensive, which is important to answer the main purpose of this experiment. We start to test the application using Apache Spark in local mode execution. Our first step is to run with only a single RDD partition that is transformed in a single threaded execution of Pi estimation. The CPU real time to compute all samples with a single thread was 1 m 56.985 s. The estimated value of Pi was roughly well precise (3.141594), but the result precision can vary since we are generating new samples for each run. So we don't rely on the Pi result to check the efficiency of the computation. The estimated value of Pi just allows us to check that the code worked and the result is an acceptable estimation. The next step is to test the same application but varying the number of partitions. We get the highest speedup when using 55 cores of the 56 cores available in a node (Fig. 3). Leaving one core available for the operating system and driver proved to be sufficient in this computing environment.

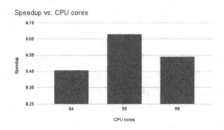

Fig. 3. Representation of Pi estimation using Monte Carlo rejection sample method

3.2 Executors Multi-node Scaling with Spark Cluster

Analyzing the results of single node execution, we start to do the parameterization for the number of partitions and executors to be created by the Spark driver. Those will be part of the formulated equations that provide the dynamic adjustment of the optimal configurations. The sbatch job script *job_submit.sh* receives as parameters the number of executors and the number of samples. The number of partitions and the Spark processes distribution between nodes is done automatically using the Slurm environment variables with the equations described below.

Equation 3 gives the condition to check the maximum number of cores a driver could get. One core is always subtracted because the result of the single node simulation shows that the best performance is achieved when leaving a spare core, as explained before. The driver cores number is set as default to 1 and can be parameterized using the environment variable NUMBER_DRIVER_CORES. For all tests we only set one core for the driver since the profiled workload is low on this process during all parallel execution processes.

$$driver\_cores < node\_cpus - master\_cores(job\_node\_number) - 1 \atop , \forall driver\_cores \in \mathbb{N}} \tag{3}$$

Equation 4 and Eq. 5 delivers the optimal number of cores to the Spark controller that runs on the so-called Spark Master that works as the workload scheduler for all workers and handles all the initial setup and negotiation inside the spawned Spark cluster. As a best rule of thumb, the core number required to the Master node is proportional to the number of nodes, until there are no more cores available.

$$master\_cores(job\_node\_number) = job\_node\_number - 1,$$
$$if \ master\_cores(job\_node\_number) < node\_cpus - driver\_cores \tag{4}$$
$$, \forall job\_node\_number, node\_cpus \in \mathbb{N}$$

$$master\_cores(job\_node\_number) = node\_cpus - driver\_cores - 1,$$
$$if \ master\_cores(job\_node\_number) >= node\_cpus - driver\_cores \tag{5}$$
$$, \forall job\_node\_number, node\_cpus \in \mathbb{N}$$

Spark Worker nodes are responsible to compute the tasks within the application. They will do the majority of the computation and because of that we maximize the cores number taking into account the previous conditions. In this regard, there is a node with both Spark Controller and Worker processes using the remaining available cores as expressed by the Eq. 6. This equation sets the number of executors for the Worker node.

$$executors(slurm\_node\_cpus) = slurm\_node\_cpus-$$
$$master\_cores(job\_node\_number) - driver\_cores - 1,$$
$$if \ node = \text{``sparkmasternode''} \tag{6}$$
$$, \forall slurm\_node\_cpus \in \mathbb{N}$$

For the remaining nodes the number of executors for Spark Workers are expressed by Eq. 7.

$$executors(slurm\_node\_cpus) = slurm\_node\_cpus - 1,$$
$$if \ node! = \text{``sparkmasternode''} \tag{7}$$
$$, \forall slurm\_node\_cpus \in \mathbb{N}$$

The number of partitions for the RDD is equal to the total number of execu-tors launched in all Spark Worker nodes as in Eq. 8. This parameter is retrieved during the Spark cluster setup and used in the *job_submit.sh* when launching the Spark driver.

$$rdd\_partitions = \sum_{1}^{job\_node\_number} executors(slurm\_node\_cpus) \qquad (8)$$

For each node we only use 140G ram, since we optimize the memory to be equal on all nodes, regarding the limitation of the node that runs the Spark Controller. We also checked that during the single node execution with the 55 cores the allocated memory was below that value. With 140 GB ram per node we assure at least 2.5 GB memory for each task processed by each executor. The memory size for each executor is a weighted average between the number of nodes, the number of executors and the maximum memory size available in the node. For the distributed computing model we started with the combination of 4, 8, 10, 12, 14, 16 and 32 nodes to run a sample with 10^{10} points (Fig. 4).

To understand better the speedup acceleration in relation to the superscalar efficiency regarding the distributed cache effect and the parallel slowdown caused by the communication bottleneck between nodes and processes, there are repre-sented two series: speedup relative to one node and speedup normalized to the four nodes simulation. Comparing the speedup for one node we can understand that for the data input the best result would be around 12 nodes. The cost of computation measured in service units (SUs) only has a bad ratio between per-formance and cost starting from 16 nodes. With the normalized value of 4 nodes turn clear the bottleneck as a result from parallel slowdown being higher then the superscalar acceleration from Intel processors and its cache. We don't reduce the number of executors for cluster size above 12 since that will lead to lesser cores being used which results in a big penalty in the end for the execution time and service cost.

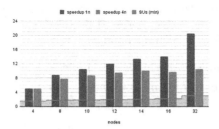

Fig. 4. Sample with 10^{10} points

Next step we just scaled up the size of the sample ten times (Fig. 5). This could still run in the four node Spark cluster but the performance improvement is now much evident for the clusters bigger than 12 nodes, where in the previous case was below that size. This result allows demonstrating that the communication bottleneck depends on the dataset size and the memory usage in the node. The number of tasks to run are 10 times more and the RDD partitioning is exactly the same as in the previous case. This makes more evident the efficiency improvement since tasks are losing less time in communication and achieving better acceleration, taking advantage of the CPU cache when executor memory is almost filled.

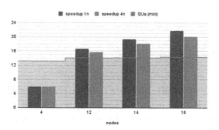

Fig. 5. Sample with 10^{11} points

Scaling to 10^{13} points (Fig. 6) allows us to understand the dataset size's relevance to the computation efficiency relative to the communication overhead. This sample size is above 17.4TB (128 nodes workers available memory). So it is only possible to run the simulation with at least 256 nodes. We present as a reference the time of running the simulation for 10^{11} one hundred times. The acceleration on this case overwhelms any of the previous simulations because it evidences the optimization we did to take advantage of the superscalar capability of Intel CPU's, its cache and the communication between nodes. Since the number of nodes is bigger than the number of cores of a single machine, there is one less Spark Worker. The Spark Controller takes all available cores from the node as explained before and it is only running along the driver. The cost of execution is almost linear and shows that we could scale the number of nodes even further and take advantage of the distributed computing efficiency of the Frontera Supercomputer.

There are also references [13] about issues with latency and loss of efficiency that required to tune Apache Spark parameters related to network timeout. With the Frontera supercomputer that is not the case, since we could optimize the communication in both ways. The tasks that do the data mapping over the RDD and the counter in the end are at most possible confined to each node with the application to minimize communication between nodes *pi_estimation.py*, even though Frontera as a great efficiency on that regard.

As a final remark for all the experiment, we can now provide an easy to use wrapper script for the users to submit jobs using Apache Spark. This implementation is optimized for the Frontera cluster, but is possible to tune it for additional Supercomputer environments.

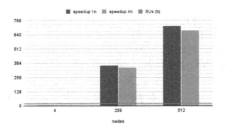

Fig. 6. Sample with 10^{13} points

4   Related Work

Compute nodes communication has been optimized to run over RDMA-based mechanisms [9]. Network communication improvement over shuffle phase and workloads can take advantage of Apache Spark architecture, exploring the low-latency and high-bandwidth [10].

Spark Cluster Managers provides the Apache Spark implementation to manage resources such as CPU, memory, storage, ports and other resources available on a cluster of nodes [6]. Apache Spark was developed targeting multi-tenant cloud-based environments, but results of existing experiments show that data analysis tasks over traditional supercomputing environments could be applicable to HPC architectures [13]. Usual implementations of Spark Cluster Managers, such as Hadoop YARN [14], Apache Mesos [8] or Kubernetes [15], require dedicated clusters to work on.

The speedup evaluation of pilot jobs over traditional batch scheduling is moderate to non-existent for Apache Spark over HPC clusters [7]. The integration with HPC clusters would be better with traditional batch scheduling since pilot jobs provide additional overhead. SLURM [16] workload manager provides the batch scheduling over Frontera HPC cluster.

On this study we select Apache Spark because it is one of the most popular in research and business environments [4]. The application developed in this work can also be extended to other engines such as Apache Flink [3].

MPI4Spark [1] launch Apache Spark ecosystem using MPI launchers to utilize MPI communication inside the Big Data framework. This framework bridges semantic differences between the event-driven communication in Apache Spark compared to the application-driven communication engine in MPI. The tests were also conducted in Frontera and other clusters from TACC.

5   Discussion and Future Work

This experiment is a first exercise to understand the deployment of Apache Spark over HPC environment, more specifically with the Frontera supercomputer. We provide an improved code to deploy Apache Spark and run the user scripts in a confined context using apptainer to get all required software in the Frontera nodes. The implemented scripts can also run in any cluster since they only depend on *bash* (command interpreter) and *sed*. It also takes advantage of bash capability of running multiple bash jobs.

We also get an optimized configuration to use the resources as efficiently as possible. The user only needs to care about doing the required Spark API code integration into their python application. In the end, the users only need to set a script path with its arguments to run the work in a distributed computing environment.

This way we could overcome many challenges, adapting the Apache Spark cluster manager to be implemented by the provided scripts and optimized to run in the Frontera supercomputer. There were collected some results that allowed us to understand the scalability dependencies, the computation cost and the communication parameterization to achieve better performance.

As future work, we pretend to run the test with a larger number of nodes (above 1000) to ascertain the communication required for fine tuning when reaching the limit of network capacity. There is also the next step of start testing this work with real use cases and compare the performance of the original implementation and afterwards using the proposed solution presented in this paper.

References

1. Al-Attar, K., Shafi, A., Abduljabbar, M., Subramoni, H., Panda, D.K.: Spark meets MPI: towards high-performance communication framework for spark using MPI. In: 2022 IEEE International Conference on Cluster Computing (CLUSTER), pp. 71–81. IEEE (2022)
2. Bernardo, S.: Distributed computing toolkit for machine learning operations/workshops/isc 2023 ixpug/pi calculus · gitlab, March 2023. https://gitlab.com/distributed-computing-toolkit/workshops/isc-2023-ixpug/pi-calculus. Accessed on 03 Mar 2023
3. Carbone, P., Katsifodimos, A., Ewen, S., Markl, V., Haridi, S., Tzoumas, K.: Apache flink: stream and batch processing in a single engine. Bull. Tech. Comm. Data Eng. **38**(4) (2015). https://asterios.katsifodimos.com/assets/publications/flink-deb.pdf
4. Conejero, J., Corella, S., Badia, R.M., Labarta, J.: Task-based programming in COMPSs to converge from HPC to big data. Int. J. High Perform. Comput. Appl. **32**(1), 45–60 (2018)
5. Dean, J., Ghemawat, S.: Mapreduce: simplified data processing on large clusters (2004)
6. Guller, M., Guller, M.: Cluster managers. Big Data Analytics with Spark: A Practitioner's Guide to Using Spark for Large-Scale Data Processing, Machine Learning, and Graph Analytics, and High-Velocity Data Stream Processing, pp. 231–242 (2015)
7. Hayot-Sasson, V., Glatard, T.: Evaluation of pilot jobs for apache spark applications on HPC clusters. In: 2019 15th International Conference on eScience (eScience), pp. 146–155. IEEE (2019)
8. Hindman, B., et al.: Mesos: a platform for fine-grained resource sharing in the data center. In: NSDI, vol. 11, p. 22 (2011)

9. Lu, X., Rahman, M.W.U., Islam, N., Shankar, D., Panda, D.K.: Accelerating spark with RDMA for big data processing: early experiences. In: 2014 IEEE 22nd Annual Symposium on High-Performance Interconnects, pp. 9–16. IEEE (2014)

10. Lu, X., Shankar, D., Gugnani, S., Panda, D.K.: High-performance design of apache spark with RDMA and its benefits on various workloads. In: 2016 IEEE International Conference on Big Data (Big Data), pp. 253–262. IEEE (2016)

11. Meng, X., et al.: Mllib: machine learning in apache spark. J. Mach. Learn. Res. **17**(1), 1235–1241 (2016)

12. Stanzione, D., West, J., Evans, R.T., Minyard, T., Ghattas, O., Panda, D.K.: Frontera: the evolution of leadership computing at the national science foundation. In: Practice and Experience in Advanced Research Computing, pp. 106–111 (2020)

13. Thiruvathukal, G.K., Christensen, C., Jin, X., Tessier, F., Vishwanath, V.: A benchmarking study to evaluate apache spark on large-scale supercomputers. arXiv preprint arXiv:1904.11812 (2019)

14. Vavilapalli, V.K., et al.: Apache Hadoop YARN: yet another resource negotiator. In: Proceedings of the 4th Annual Symposium on Cloud Computing, pp. 1–16 (2013)

15. Verma, A., Pedrosa, L., Korupolu, M.R., Oppenheimer, D., Tune, E., Wilkes, J.: Large-scale cluster management at Google with Borg. In: Proceedings of the European Conference on Computer Systems (EuroSys). Bordeaux, France (2015)

16. Yoo, A.B., Jette, M.A., Grondona, M.: SLURM: simple Linux utility for resource management. In: Feitelson, D., Rudolph, L., Schwiegelshohn, U. (eds.) JSSPP 2003. LNCS, vol. 2862, pp. 44–60. Springer, Heidelberg (2003). https://doi.org/10.1007/10968987_3

17. Zaharia, M., et al.: Resilient distributed datasets: a fault-tolerant abstraction for in-memory cluster computing. In: Presented as part of the 9th {USENIX} Symposium on Networked Systems Design and Implementation ({NSDI} 12), pp. 15–28 (2012)

18. Zaharia, M., Chowdhury, M., Franklin, M.J., Shenker, S., Stoica, I., et al.: Spark: cluster computing with working sets. HotCloud **10**(10–10), 95 (2010)

Bandwidth Limits in the Intel Xeon Max (Sapphire Rapids with HBM) Processors

John D. McCalpin[✉] [ID]

Texas Advanced Computing Center, University of Texas at Austin, Austin, TX 78712, USA
mccalpin@tacc.utexas.edu

Abstract. The HBM memory of Intel Xeon Max processors provides significantly higher sustained memory bandwidth than their DDR5 memory, with corresponding increases in the performance of bandwidth-sensitive applications. However, the increase in sustained memory bandwidth is much smaller than the increase in peak memory bandwidth. Using custom microbenchmarks (instrumented with hardware performance counters) and analytical modeling, the primary bandwidth limiter is shown to be insufficient memory concurrency. Secondary bandwidth limitations due to non-uniform loading of the two-dimensional on-chip mesh interconnect are shown to arise not far behind the primary limiters.

Keywords: Memory Bandwidth · Concurrency · HBM · Sapphire Rapids

1 Introduction

Sustained memory bandwidth has been recognized as a fundamental component of application performance in a large subset of high performance computing applications for about 30 years [1, 2]. High Bandwidth Memory (HBM) is a technology that provides significantly higher memory bandwidth per DRAM chip, using stacked DRAM die (connected by through-silicon vias), and a very wide (1024 bit) interface running at essentially the same transfer rate per pin as would be available in DIMM-based DRAM configurations providing only 64 bits of data per cycle.

The Intel Xeon Max processor family is a variant of the 4th-generation Xeon Scalable Processor Family ("Sapphire Rapids") that adds supports for four HBM2e stacks, which collectively provide 5.33x higher peak memory bandwidth than the DDR5 interfaces (Table 1).

Many examples of increased application performance using Xeon Max with HBM have been demonstrated. The current work asks a more theoretical question: Why is the maximum sustainable memory bandwidth on the HBM-equipped processors a much smaller fraction of peak than is seen with DDR5 memory, or on other architectures that use HBM2 memory?

© The Author(s), under exclusive license to Springer Nature Switzerland AG 2023
A. Bienz et al. (Eds.): ISC High Performance 2023 Workshops, LNCS 13999, pp. 403–413, 2023.
https://doi.org/10.1007/978-3-031-40843-4_30

2 Test Systems and Bandwidth Measurements

The results presented here were obtained from a pair of 2-socket test systems equipped with Xeon Max 9480 processors. These systems have identical processors and motherboards, with one system configured to use only DDR5 memory (HBM disabled by BIOS) and the other configured to use only HBM memory (DDR5 DIMMs physically removed). Both systems were configured with Rocky Linux 8.6. Applications were compiled with the Intel compiler identifying itself as version 19.1.1.217 (20200306), and the same binaries and libraries were used on both systems. Unless otherwise specified, the systems were tested in "flat" memory mode, with one NUMA node per processor (socket) and memory interleaved across all memory controllers in each socket. Some additional testing was performed on a similar system equipped with two Xeon Platinum 8480 + processors. Peak memory bandwidths of the systems are provided in Table 1.

Table 1. Comparison of peak DRAM bandwidth between the 4th-generation Xeon Scalable Processor Family and the two configurations of the Xeon Max Processor Family tested here.

Processor	DDR5 interfaces	HBM interfaces
4th-gen Xeon Scalable Processor Xeon Platinum 8480+ (56 cores, 2.0 GHz)	8x 64-bit @ 4.8 GT/s 307.2 GB/s (peak)	N/A
Xeon Max 9480/DDR5 (56 cores, 1.9 GHz)	8x 64-bit @ 4.8 GT/s 307.2 GB/s (peak)	(disabled)
Xeon Max 9480/HBM (56 cores, 1.9 GHz)	(Not installed)	4x 1024-bit @ 3.2 GT/s 1638.4 GB/s

For all systems, memory bandwidth was measured using the STREAM benchmark (using the compilers listed above) and the Intel Memory Latency Checker (version 3.10). Most testing was done on a single socket – this reduces the occurrence of thermal throttling on these air-cooled systems as well as providing better control over the system. Results are presented in Table 2, both as absolute bandwidth values in GB/s and as a fraction of the corresponding peak bandwidth. The Xeon Platinum 8480+ and Xeon Max 9480/DDR5 showed highly repeatable performance (e.g., ~1% variation across 150 runs with varying array size and alignment) and showed minimal cross-platform performance differences. Bandwidth on the Xeon Max 9480/HBM server showed much larger run-to-run variability (>10%) and strong sensitivity to the combination of array size and array alignment (up to ~2x bandwidth drops in the worst cases).

Table 2. Peak and Sustained memory bandwidth for a single socket in the three test systems.

Single-Socket Memory Bandwidth	Peak BW GB/s	STREAM Triad GB/s (%Peak)	ReadOnly GB/s (%Peak)
Xeon Platinum 8480+	307.2	200 (65.1%)	240 (78.1%)
Xeon Max 9480/DDR5	307.2	201 (65.4%)	237 (77.1%)
Xeon Max 9480/HBM	1638.4	700 (42.7%)	590 (36.0%)

3   Concurrency-Limited Bandwidth

Performing a parallel scaling analysis quickly showed that not even perfect parallel scaling would allow the platform to approach the HBM bandwidth limits. STREAM benchmark results using a single core are in the range of 19–20 GB/s, limiting bandwidth to approximately 68% of peak (~1120 GB/s) even with perfect scaling across the 56 cores. The underlying problem is therefore a single-core performance limitation.

In multicore server processors with multiple memory channels, single-core bandwidth is almost always limited by inadequate concurrency (outstanding cache misses) to tolerate the memory latency, rather than by the aggregate peak memory bandwidth.

Memory latency was measured using the using the Intel Memory Latency Checker (v3.10) using the "*—idle_latency*" option and again using the "*—loaded_latency*" option (using the default "ALL Reads" workload). Table 3 provides numerical values for the idle latency and for the loaded latency with the lowest and highest loads, averaged over a dozen or more run, while Fig. 1 shows the dependence of latency on bandwidth.

Table 3. Idle and Loaded latency ranges for a read-only workload in 1 socket with HBM memory.

	Load Bandwidth range (GB/s)	Latency range (ns)
No load	N/A	130.2
Minimum load	2.25–2.29	138–139
Maximum load	500–565	177–194

Modeling sustained memory bandwidth for a stationary system in the concurrency-limited regime is based on Little's Law:

$$\text{Concurrency} = \text{Bandwidth} \times \text{Latency} \tag{1}$$

where "Bandwidth" is the average rate at which data arrives from memory, "Latency" (often called "occupancy") is the average amount of time that each buffer handling a memory request (cache miss or prefetch) is occupied, and "Concurrency" is the average number of buffers that are occupied handling memory requests.

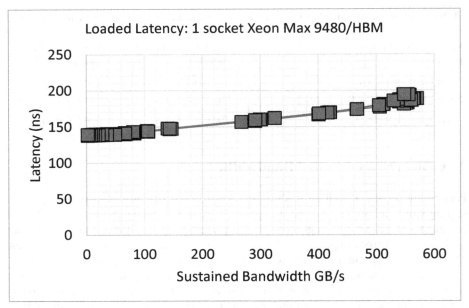

Fig. 1. Latency under load for one socket of Xeon Max 9480/HBM with read-only workload. Results from 9 runs of the Intel Memory Latency Checker (version 3.10) are shown.

For a multi-level cache hierarchy, Little's Law must be obeyed at each level of the cache. In the Xeon Max processor, each core supports a maximum of 16 outstanding L1 Data Cache misses. If these buffers are occupied for the full 130 ns memory latency, they will limit the maximum sustainable bandwidth to 16*64 Bytes / 130 ns = 7.9 GB/s. Fortunately, the L2 hardware prefetchers are often able to initiate the memory requests early, reducing the average occupancy required at the L1 miss buffers. Each L2 cache supports a maximum of 48 outstanding memory requests – referred to as "offcore requests". A maximum of 16 of these can be L1 Data Cache misses that also miss in the L2 cache – occupying more L2 miss buffers requires the use of L2 hardware prefetches.

At low levels of utilization, we can assume that the memory access latency is equal to the idle latency of 130 ns, and that the L2 memory request buffers will be occupied for approximately that same amount of time. Assuming all 48 offcore request buffers are in use, the single-core bandwidth will be limited by concurrency to 48*64 Bytes / 130 ns = 23.6 GB/s. This is consistent with single-core STREAM benchmark performance of ~20 GB/s and single-core ReadOnly benchmark performance of ~22 GB/s.

Recent Intel processors provide hardware performance counter events in each core that measure occupancy and concurrency for either the L1D cache miss buffers or the L2 offcore request buffers. For this study a microbenchmark code was produced that binds to a single core, flushes the target data range from the caches, reads the core performance counters, reads 2 MiB of contiguous data, then reads the performance counters again. For the L1 Data Cache, the events are:

- L1D_PEND_MISS.PENDING

  – Accumulates the number of active miss buffers each cycle.

- L1D_PEND_MISS.PENDING_CYCLES_GE_ <threshold>

  – Accumulates the number of cycles that at least <threshold> L1 miss buffers were occupied. Thresholds used were 1 to 17.

For the offcore requests from the L2, the primary event is OFFCORE_REQUESTS_OUTSTANDING, with modifiers of:

- DATA_READS

  – Accumulates the number of active offcore memory request buffers each cycle.
  – Counts buffers used for both demand cache misses and hardware prefetches.

- CYCLES_WITH_DATA_READS_GE_ < threshold>

  – Accumulates the number of cycles that at least <threshold> offcore request buffers were occupied by misses or prefetches. Thresholds used were 1 to 49.

- DEMAND_DATA_READS

  – Accumulates the number of active offcore memory request buffers each cycle.
  – Only counts buffers allocated by demand reads, or buffers allocated by hardware prefetches after arrival of the corresponding demand read upgrades the buffer request type from "prefetch" to "demand".

- CYCLES_WITH_DEMAND_DATA_READS_GE_ < threshold>

  – Accumulates the number of cycles that at least <threshold> offcore request buffers were occupied by demand read requests.

Dividing the accumulated number of active buffers by the number of cycles with at least one active buffer gives the average number of buffers occupied. Dividing the accumulated number of active buffers by the number of requests gives the average duration of occupancy (in core cycles) for the buffers. Repeating the experiments with different "threshold" values in the cycle counter allows one to compute the number of cycles with each degree of concurrency. Increasing the threshold until the "CYCLES_WITH" count is never incremented confirms the maximum number of L1 Data Cache misses as 16 and the maximum number of L2 offcore requests as 48.

For the single core 2MiB ReadOnly test case, the fraction of cycles with each degree of L2 offcore request concurrency is shown in Fig. 2.

Important notes from Fig. 2:

- The maximum number of outstanding requests is 48, but this only occurs in about 10% of cycles.

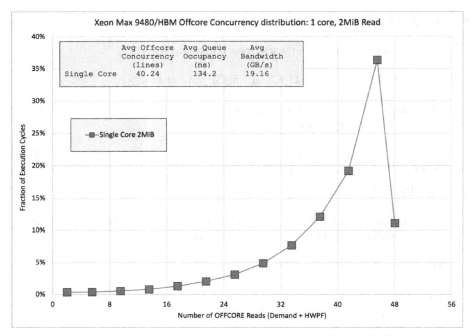

Fig. 2. Average fraction of kernel execution cycles associated with each level of concurrency of offcore (L2 miss) read transactions (demand plus prefetch) over an ensemble of 1000 trials.

- The measured average buffer occupancy is a close match to the idle memory latency.
- Combining the measured concurrency with the measured occupancy predicts a bandwidth of 19.19 GB/s, while the direct measurement of execution time shows 19.16 GB/s. This provides strong confirmation of the reliability of these performance counter events.

Of the 38 offcore requests outstanding in this case, about 10–11 were L1 Data Cache demand misses that also missed in the L2 cache, with the remaining offcore requests being L2 hardware prefetches. Detailed analysis is challenging because a buffer allocated for an L2 hardware prefetch request is counted as an offcore "DATA_READ" event for its duration but is only counted as a DEMAND_DATA_READ event after the corresponding demand miss arrives at the L2 and causes the buffer's transaction type to be upgraded to "demand read". It is not clear that it is possible to determine how many cycles a buffer is in the "hardware prefetch" request state before being upgraded to the "demand read" request state.

Perfect linear scaling of the single-core ReadOnly performance of 19.8 GB/s would result in just over 1100 GB/s foe one socket, while the highest value measured is under 600 MB/s. An important correction in the multiprocessor case is to adjust the occupancy to match the measured latency under load from Fig. 1 and Table 3. At 38 offcore requests per core, 56 cores, and a latency of 190 ns, the concurrency-limited bandwidth bound is 717 GB/s – still significantly higher than the best observed values.

It is known that the L2 hardware prefetch engines are dynamically adaptive, but neither the input parameters nor the heuristics are documented. It therefore makes sense to measure the average number of offcore requests. Repeating the measurements reported in Fig. 2 but with all cores active shows that the average number of offcore requests decreases significantly under load as illustrated in Table 4 and Fig. 3. The concurrency-based model matches the observed performance in all cases and allows us to separate out the latency and concurrency contributions to the bandwidth comparison.

Table 4. Breakdown of factors in concurrency model leading to decreased performance per core for an all read workload on a single socket of Xeon Max/HBM.

	Average concurrency (cache lines per core)	Average offcore buffer occupancy (ns)	Average bandwidth (GB/s)
Single Core	40.2	134.2	19.2
All Cores	31.8	198.6	574.8
Per-core performance decrease ratio	1.26x	1.48x	1.87x

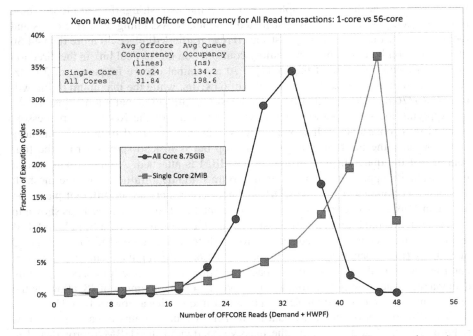

Fig. 3. Distribution of offcore concurrency levels for the single-core and all-core read test. Average concurrency when using all cores is reduced to under 32 lines per core and average occupancy increases to almost 199 ns.

4 Mesh-Limited Bandwidth

Concurrency provides the primary limiter to sustained bandwidth in the Xeon Max processors, but the >5x increase in bandwidth provided by HBM2e also places great demands on the bandwidth of the mesh interconnect. To evaluate and model these effects, it is first necessary to understand the layout of the various units in the processor, along with any details of the data traffic routing on the mesh.

To infer the layout of the chips, mesh traffic was measured using the methodology described in [3–5]. The earlier microbenchmarks were ported to the Xeon Platinum 8480+ processor and run on a quiet system. Using the schematic layout provided in https://www.intel.com/content/www/us/en/developer/articles/technical/fourth-generation-xeon-scalable-family-overview.html, the methodology of [4] and [5] was used to determine a mapping of core numbers and CHA/SF/LLC numbers to die locations that would be consistent with the known Y-X routing and the measured performance counter data. The mesh traffic results showed the same patterns as seen in earlier Intel processors, particularly with the alternating meaning of "Left" and "Right" mesh traffic in alternating columns. In addition, the four dies in the package are also mirror images of each other, with reflections in the left-right direction, the up-down direction, or both.

Each memory controller manages two DDR5/4800 memory interfaces, providing an aggregate bandwidth of 76.8 GB/s. Assuming that memory is interleaved across all four memory controllers, the simple Y-X routing makes it straightforward to compute traffic distribution for uniformly distributed workloads. Assuming 56 active cores and the topology of Fig. 4, uniformly distributed read traffic will place no more than 44/56 of the traffic outbound from each memory controller on the vertical link in the direction of the horizontal mid-line of the package. At a nominal uncore frequency of 2 GHz, each mesh link has a peak data bandwidth of 64 GB/s, while the maximum traffic will be (44/56)*76.8 GB/s = 60.3 GB/s – a high level of utilization, but not overloaded.

Applying the same methodology to infer the layout of the Xeon Max processors resulted in inconsistencies. It was quickly evident that data read from HBM memory does not enter the mesh at a single mesh stop but is instead spread across the four columns of the quadrant (die) to which the HBM is attached. A more vexing set of inconsistencies appeared when attempting to trace the data traffic across the mesh. It eventually became clear that the DDR5 memory controllers are in different places on the Xeon Max die – one row closer to the horizontal mid-line of the mesh, as shown in Fig. 5. With this modification in the assumptions, the mesh traffic data from both HBM and DDR5 matched the expected patterns for reads from each core. One core is disabled in each die (lower panel) for these 56-core processors. Moving the memory controllers one row closer to the mid-line of the package reduces the number of cores requesting data via the busiest mesh link from a maximum of 44 to a maximum of 38, allowing the mesh to handle the required DDR5 data traffic at frequencies as low as 1.6 GHz.

The distribution of the HBM data traffic across four columns in each quadrant is required to get close to handling the massive bandwidth that HBM2e provides. The maximum uncore frequency of this Xeon Max 9480 processor is 2.5 GHz, but under

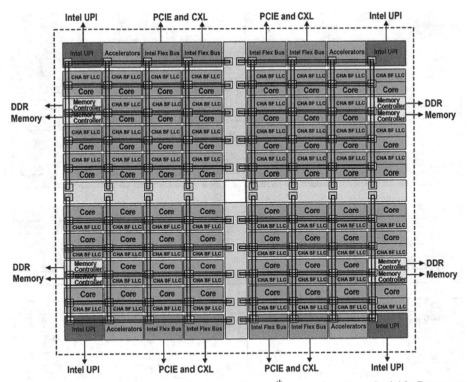

Fig. 4. Block diagram of largest configuration of the 4th-generation Xeon Scalable Processor, showing the layout of the cores, CHA/SF/LLC slices, DDR memory controllers, and die-to-die connections. Image from https://www.intel.com/content/www/us/en/developer/articles/technical/fourth-generation-xeon-scalable-family-overview.html

high bandwidth loads it drops to 1.6 GHz[1]. At 1.6 GHz, each mesh link has a peak unidirectional bandwidth of 51.2 GB/s, giving each HBM controller access to 204.8 GB/s of mesh bandwidth per direction, exactly ½ of the peak HBM bandwidth of 409.6 GB/s per stack. This limits the peak HBM read bandwidth per socket to 819.2 GB/s, independent of the concurrency available. Note that this limit applies equally to both "flat" mode (one NUMA node per socket) and "SNC" mode (4 NUMA nodes per socket). In practice, the reduced memory latency seen in SNC4 mode does result in an increase in the single-socket read bandwidth, from ~575–590 GB/s to slightly over 700 GB/s.

Finally, we consider the impact of the HBM data traffic routing on single-core bandwidth. Although each core is attached to four mesh links (up/down/left/right), the traffic from the memory controllers is distributed non-uniformly across those links. For reads from HBM, the most uneven distribution occurs for cores in the left and right columns of the package. For each of these cores, 1/16 of the requested data comes "down" from the

---

[1] Unlike other processor models (including the Xeon Platinum 8480+), on the Xeon Max 9480 processor setting minimum and maximum uncore frequencies in MSR 0x620 only seems to control the uncore frequency while the processor is mostly idle.

HBM 1				HBM 3			
IO	IO	IO	IO	IO	IO	IO	IO
26	27	28	29	56	57	58	59
22	23	24	25	52	53	54	55
IMC 1	19	20	21	49	50	51	IMC 3
15	16	17	18	45	46	47	48
11	12	13	14	41	42	43	44
IMC 0	8	9	10	38	39	40	IMC 2
4	5	6	7	34	35	36	37
0	1	2	3	30	31	32	33
IO	IO	IO	IO	IO	IO	IO	IO
HBM 0				HBM 2			

HBM 1				HBM 3			
IO	IO	IO	IO	IO	IO	IO	IO
24	25	26	27	52	53	54	55
21	<disabled>	22	23	49	50	<disabled>	51
IMC 1	18	19	20	46	47	48	IMC 3
14	15	16	17	42	43	44	45
10	11	12	13	38	39	40	41
IMC 0	7	8	9	35	36	37	IMC 2
4	<disabled>	5	6	32	33	<disabled>	34
0	1	2	3	28	29	30	31
IO	IO	IO	IO	IO	IO	IO	IO
HBM 0				HBM 2			

Fig. 5. Upper panel: Layout of the Xeon Max 9480 multi-die package with numbering of all CHA/SF/LLC units. Lower Panel: As above but showing enabled Core numbers for core enable mask 0x0FBF FFEF FF7F FFDF. Note that the memory controller units (IMC) are located one row closer to the horizontal mid-line than in the 4th-generation Xeon Scalable Processor version.

HBM controller at the top, 1/16 comes "up" from the HBM controller at the bottom, and the remaining 14/16 is delivered on the horizontal link coming from the middle of the package. Each core can only receive data on each mesh link every other cycle, with half of the cores receiving data on odd cycles and half on even cycles. This allows the core to receive at full bandwidth if the data is uniformly distributed across two mesh links, as occurs for data from the DDR5 controllers for all cores that are not in the left or right columns of the package. For the cores in the left or right columns the peak bandwidth at a 1.6 GHz uncore clock is $(51.2/2)*(16/14) = 29.3$ GB/s – only modestly higher than current sustainable values. For the cores near the center of the die, the distribution of HBM read traffic is 1/16 "down", 1/16 "up", with the remaining 14/16's of the traffic split with a modest imbalance (6/16 vs 8/16) between the "left" and "right" mesh link links. At a 1.6 GHz uncore frequency, this results in a peak HBM read bandwidth of 51.2 GB/s per core for these centrally located cores (since the busiest link for each core carries exactly ½ of the total traffic).

In SNC4 mode, the distribution for local HBM accesses is slightly less uneven than in "flat" mode, with ¼ of the traffic arriving vertically from the local HBM and up to

¾ of the data arriving on the horizontal link from the middle of the die. This is more uneven than the best case in "flat" mode and is due to local HBM read traffic arriving at the core from only two directions in SNC4 mode.

5 Summary

The Xeon Max processors obtain a large increase in sustainable memory bandwidth from their HBM memory subsystem, with STREAM Triad performance increasing by a factor of almost 3.5. The peak bandwidth ratio is even higher (5.33x), so it is not unreasonably to ask "why?". Using performance counter measurements and analytical models, this report has shown that the maximum sustainable bandwidth on the Xeon Max with HBM is limited by memory concurrency. As the number of cores used is scaled up, the L2 hardware prefetchers appear to become less aggressive (reducing average concurrency) and the memory latency increases. The combination of these factors is consistent with observed all-core read bandwidth limited to under 40% of peak. Either substantially more cores or substantially more outstanding misses per core will be necessary to overcome this limitation. (Lower latency would help, but it cannot plausibly be lowered enough to overcome the deficit in concurrency.)

Further analysis shows that, despite modifications to spread HBM traffic over multiple columns, the peak bandwidth of the on-chip mesh links will provide a global bandwidth limiter if the available concurrency is increased. The single-core bandwidth is also approaching mesh limits for cores in the left and right columns of the chip. Significant increases in concurrency would likely expose significant variations in maximum sustainable memory bandwidth between cores in the center columns and cores in the left and right columns of the package.

References

1. McCalpin, J.D.: Memory bandwidth and machine balance in current high performance computers. IEEE TCCA Newsl. **2**, 19–25 (1995)
2. McCalpin, J.D.: Memory bandwidth and system balance in HPC systems. In: Invited talk at the International Conference for High Performance Computing, Networking, Storage and Analysis (2016). https://doi.org/10.26153/tsw/13794
3. McCalpin, J.D.: Observations on core numbering and "core ID's" in intel processors. Technical Report TR-2020-01, 30 November 2020. https://doi.org/10.26153/tsw/10858
4. McCalpin, J.D.: Mapping core and L3 slice numbering to die locations in intel xeon scalable processors. Technical Report TR-2021-01b, 28 February 2021. https://doi.org/10.26153/tsw/13119
5. McCalpin, J.D.: Mapping, core, CHA, and memory controller numbers to die locations in intel xeon phi x200 ("Knights Landing", "KNL") Processors. Technical Report TR-2021-02, 20 May 2021. https://doi.org/10.26153/tsw/13120

First International Workshop
on RISC-V for HPC

Preface to First International Workshop on RISC-V for HPC

1 Objectives

RISC-V is an open standard Instruction Set Architecture (ISA) which enables the royalty free development of CPUs and a common software ecosystem to be shared across them. Following this community-driven ISA standard, a very diverse set of CPUs have been, and continue to be, developed which are suited to a range of workloads. Whilst RISC-V has become very popular already in some fields, and in 2022 the ten-billionth RISC-V core was shipped, to date it has yet to gain traction in HPC.

However, there are numerous potential advantages that RISC-V can provide to HPC and, assuming the significant rate of growth of this technology to date continues, as we progress further into the decade it is highly likely that RISC-V will become more relevant and widespread for high-performance workloads. Furthermore, recent advances in RISC-V are making it a more realistic proposition for these workloads and an example of this is the vectorisation extension, which provides important performance advantages but was only standardised in early 2022, so we are only now seeing mature CPUs that fully implement this.

The open and standardised nature of RISC-V means that the large and growing community can be involved in shaping the standard and tooling. This is important from two perspectives. Firstly it is an opportunity for the HPC community to help shape the future of RISC-V to ensure that it is suitable for the next generation of supercomputers. Secondly, whilst there are a wide variety of RISC-V CPUs currently available, the standard nature of the tooling means that very often the same software ecosystem comprising the compiler, operating system, and libraries will run across these whilst requiring few changes.

The objective of this workshop was to bring together those already looking to popularise RISC-V in the field of HPC with the supercomputing community at large. By sharing benefits of the architecture, success stories, and techniques we aimed to further popularise the technology and increase involvement of the HPC community in RISC-V.

2 Workshop organization

In total, there were 16 research papers submitted to the workshop, with 11 accepted. All papers underwent single-blind review and received at least three reviews from the programme committee. Following these reviews papers were accepted in two categories; full papers, which were granted a 20-minute speaking slot, and short papers, which were given a 10-minute slot during the session. In addition to the research paper presentations, the workshop began with an invited talk by Luca Benini who described the work of his group in developing high-performance open hardware based upon RISC-V that can be used by the HPC and ML communities for their high-performance workloads.

Organization

Organizers

Nick Brown	EPCC at the University of Edinburgh, UK
John Davis	Barcelona Supercomputing Centre, Spain
John Leidel	Tactical Computing Labs, USA
Andy Gothard	Siemens, UK
Michael Wong	Codeplay, Canada

Program Committee

Oliver Perks	Rivos, UK
Unsal Osman	Barcelona Supercomputing Centre, Spain
Maurice Jamieson	EPCC at the University of Edinburgh, UK
Ruyman Reyes	Codeplay, UK
Luis Plana	Barcelona Supercomputing Centre, Spain
Joseph Lee	EPCC at the University of Edinburgh, UK
Luc Berger-Vergiat	Sandia National Laboratories, USA
Teresa Cervero	Barcelona Supercomputing Centre, Spain
Chris Taylor	Tactical Computing Labs, USA

Outcome of the workshop

The papers presented in these proceedings represent the state of the art in the role of RISC-V for HPC and ML workloads as of June 2023. Whilst these papers report a wide range of work in the field, there are several higher-level themes that can be observed. Firstly, RISC-V is moving very rapidly and progress in a few years matches that made by other technologies over decades. Whilst high-performance RISC-V hardware availability has been a challenge, it is highly likely that there will be greater availability of high-peformance RISC-V CPUs in the near term. Secondly, that the greatest threat to a new technology is an existing solution which is *good enough*. Consequently, whilst there are specific examples of benefits that RISC-V can provide to the HPC community, for RISC-V to be adopted by HPC centres wholesale a clear and strong case must be made around how RISC-V can provide a step change in HPC capability. Thirdly, that there is still work to be done in the software ecosystem to provide a complete and mature set of tooling that HPC developers would expect to have available on supercomputing systems. Nevertheless, given the popularity of the workshop it is clear that HPC is a critically important area for RISC-V and there is the potential for this rapidly growing area of technology to revolutionise the field of supercomputing in the coming decade.

Quantum Thermodynamics

Test-Driving RISC-V Vector Hardware for HPC

Joseph K. L. Lee[(⊠)] [iD], Maurice Jamieson[iD], Nick Brown[iD],
and Ricardo Jesus[iD]

EPCC, University of Edinburgh, Bayes Centre, 47 Potterrow, Edinburgh, UK
{j.lee,m.jamieson,n.brown}@epcc.ed.ac.uk, rjj@ed.ac.uk

Abstract. Whilst the RISC-V Vector extension (RVV) has been ratified, at the time of writing both hardware implementations and open source software support are still limited for vectorisation on RISC-V. This is important because vectorisation is crucial to obtaining good performance for High Performance Computing (HPC) workloads and, as of April 2023, the Allwinner D1 SoC, containing the XuanTie C906 processor, is the only mass-produced and commercially available hardware supporting RVV. This paper surveys the current state of RISC-V vectorisation as of 2023, reporting the landscape of both the hardware and software ecosystem. Driving our discussion from experiences in setting up the Allwinner D1 as part of the EPCC RISC-V testbed, we report the results of benchmarking the Allwinner D1 using the RAJA Performance Suite, which demonstrated reasonable vectorisation speedup using vendor-provided compiler, as well as favourable performance compared to the StarFive VisionFive V2 with SiFive's U74 processor.

1 Introduction

Vector instructions bring many benefits to an Instruction Set Architecture (ISA), for instance they enable applications to exploit data parallelism, reduce code size, increase instruction bandwidth and improve energy efficiency. Many modern applications including machine learning, graphics, digital signal processing, and cryptography are built around algorithms that are designed to heavily take advantage of vector instructions. Indeed vectorisation was a traditional way in which HPC was undertaken on the likes of the Cray-1 and Thinking Machines' CM series before distributed memory parallelism became widespread. Modern day variants of these ideas, such as AVX-512, the NEC SX-Aurora Vector Engine and the flexibility provided by Arm SVE in the A64FX, are highly successful.

Over the past years RISC-V has become a well-established open ISA standard, where RISC-V is the fifth major RISC ISA design from the Univerity of California Berkeley, preceded by RISC-I, RISC-II, SOAR, and SPUR. The most powerful feature of RISC-V in comparison to other RISC designs, such as the SPARC, PowerPC, MIPS and Arm, is its modular design. In practice this means that a small base integer ISA is specified and then ISA extensions, such as floating-point and vector support, can be chosen and added to the CPU

© The Author(s), under exclusive license to Springer Nature Switzerland AG 2023
A. Bienz et al. (Eds.): ISC High Performance 2023 Workshops, LNCS 13999, pp. 419–432, 2023.
https://doi.org/10.1007/978-3-031-40843-4_31

implementation. Vector support has been a key extension for RISC-V since its inception, *We also pun on the use of the Roman numeral "V" to signify "variations" and "vectors", as support for a range of architecture research, including various data-parallel accelerators, is an explicit goal of the ISA design.* [23]

Version 1.0 [13] of the RISC-V vector extension (RVV) was ratified in late 2021. Similarly to Arm SVE, it is inherently vector length agnostic (VLA) and the same code can be executed on implementations with different vector lengths, and the element size and vector length can also be reconfigured at run time. Whereas the x86 AVX and Arm NEON use the vector length specific (VLS) approach of packed SIMD and the code will need to be re-optimised and re-compiled for each vector processor, VLA code remains portable across different vector processor design and generations.

RVV has already been used in production for physical RISC-V hardware, for example T-Head's XuanTie C906 core provides RVV v0.7.1 and has made a submission for MLPerf Tiny Inference [16], a benchmark designed to measure trained neural network performance for low power devices. However, as an emerging standard it is not entirely straightforward to utilise and test the RISC-V vector extension. This paper aims to evaluate the current landscape when it comes to RISC-V vectorisation and assess the potential gain from utilising RISC-V vectors for HPC applications. Ultimately our objective is to provide guidance for users interested in testing or adopting available vector hardware using experiences we have gained from setting up the EPCC RISC-V testbed [4]. The key contributions of this paper are:

1. We review the state of play of the RISC-V vector extension and available processor implementations
2. We evaluate the availability of open source software such as compiler toolchains and Linux kernels to support running vectorised code on available hardware
3. We perform benchmarks and evaluate vectorisation efficiency using a currently available compiler and commercially available RISC-V vector processor.

2   Background and Related Work

2.1   V Extension

The RISC-V 'V' standard extension introduces 32 new vector registers, and requires a minimum vector register length (VLEN) of 128 bits up to a maximum 65,536 bits.[1] This can be compared to SVE, which also has a minimum vector length of 128 bits, but only a maximum of 2048 bits. Another feature of the vector instruction set is that multiple vector registers can be grouped together as a single combined vector and this is known as *LMUL*. Whilst previously one could only group 2, 4 or 8 registers, in RVV v1.0 fractional groupings of $\frac{1}{2}$,

---

[1] The Zvl32b and Zvl64b extensions allow for a smaller minimum VLEN of 32 and 64 bits respectively.

$\frac{1}{4}$ and $\frac{1}{8}$ are also allowed where part of a single vector register will be used. These features of the instruction set provide great flexibility because, within a single code, the vector length can be varied by different groupings of vector registers dynamically, and is therefore particularly useful when operating on mixed-width values. Combined with the fact that the same compiled code can run on hardware implementations with significantly different vector width and automatically exploit the widest vector lengths, RVV encourages portable code with greater utilisation of vector register resources without the need for platform-specific optimisation.

Prior to the ratification of v1.0 of the V extension, the beta version of RVV, v0.7.1, was adopted in production for example by the XuanTie C906 processor and BSC's Vitruvius+ [27] which is part of the European Processor Initiative (EPI) project. Even though the difference between the v1.0 and v0.7.1 is fairly minimal, the two versions are incompatible in terms of source code or binary. One major difference is the lack of support for fractional LMUL in version 0.7.1.

2.2 Intrinsics

At the time of writing, the official RISC-V task group is converging towards v1.0 of the C intrinsics API [20], which is expected to be released later in 2023. Currently, LLVM supports v0.10 of the intrinsics specification and mainline GCC provides no support at all. It is in the roadmap of both compilers to support v1.0 in the future once it is ratified. However the XuanTie 900 series toolchain, which is a modified version of the GCC 8.4 compiler targeting the C906 and C910 supports a custom set of intrinsics for v0.7.1 and v1.0. As does the LLVM compiler from BSC for the EPI project's RISC-V Toolchain [15] providing their set of v0.7.1 and v1.0 intrinsics. These bespoke compiler versions can be useful when developing for vectorisation due to limitations in the mainline compilers.

2.3 P Extension

It should also be noted that there is packed a SIMD 'P' extension to the base ISA which uses the floating point registers and is aimed at embedded cores and low-power digital signal processing (DSP) applications, such as audio and video encoding/decoding, image interpretation and computer vision. The extension has not yet been ratified, the latest version is v0.9.11 [8], and provides a large number of SIMD and partial-SIMD instructions, such as 8/16-bit minimum and maximum instructions (including SMIN8, UMIN8, SMAX16 and UMAX16), and 16/32-bit multiply with 64-bit add/subtract instructions (including SMAL, SMALBB and SMAR64).

2.4 Related Work

Even though RVV has been ratified relatively recently, studies focusing on other (scalable) vector ISAs can be applicable when wishing to improve vector performance for RISC-V. For example, there has been studies comparing the performance of Arm SVE against NEON [31] and AVX [35], and evaluating the vectorisation efficiency and usage on mini-apps for available SVE compilers [30]. Another parameter which has significant impact on performance with the VLA programming model is the implementation vector length, where [28] and [32] study the performance of a variety of vectorised applications with different vector lengths using the gem5 simulator for Arm SVE and RVV respectively.

There is currently a rapid development of research-based RVV enabled hardware underway, for example ETH Zurich have introduced *Ara* [22] and its upgrade [29], and BSC introduced *Vitruvius+* [27]. Whilst none are yet mass-produced or widely available, these RISC-V vector accelerator designs have been taped-out and their performance compared in [27].

3   RVV CPU Implementations

There is a broad selection of IP cores which have implemented RVV and this is summarised in Table 1. RISC-V cores on this list target a wide range of applications, including edge artificial intelligence/machine learning (SiFive X280), general high-performance application (SiFive P series), and decoupled vector accelerator (Ara/Vitruvius+). The decoupled accelerator approach is especially interesting because this allows vector instructions to be offloaded from the scalar pipeline, and paired with support for long vectors, for instance 256 double precision elements per vector register are supported by the Vitruvius+, these present high performance RISC-V vector accelerators for HPC workloads. In taped-out implementations the New Ara core reports achieving 37.1 GFLOPS per Watt [29] and Vitruvius+ reports 47.3 GFLOPS per Watt [27] on matrix multiplication benchmarks.

Table 1. List of available RVV processors. The last three entries are open source.

Processor	Vector Length	RVV version
SiFive P270/P470/P670 [10]	256-bit/128-bit/dual 128-bit	1.0
SiFive X280 [9]	512-bit	1.0
Andes NX27V [7]	Configurable from 128 to 512-bit	1.0
Andes AX45MPV [6]	Configurable from 128 to 1024-bit	1.0
Vitruvius+ [27]	16384-bit	0.7.1 (update to 1.0 in future)
Hwacha [34] (V4 [33])	512-bit	custom
New Ara [29]	Configurable e.g. 4096-bit	1.0
Tenstorrent BOOM-ocelot [17]	Configurable from 128-bit	1.0
T-Head XuanTie C906 [18]	128-bit	0.7.1

These energy efficiency numbers delivered by the New Ara and Vitruvius+ cores are impressive, especially considering that they are still research prototypes rather than production parts. For comparison, whilst the Green 500 reports whole systems rather than the individual machine components, based on the November 2022 list those HPC machines that are able to achieve greater than

50 GFLOPS per Watt are based around either the AMD Instinct or Nvidia Grace Hopper GPUs. These represent mature technologies with a rich lineage, whereas by comparison the New Ara and Vitruvius+ are the first generation of RISC-V vector accelerators and therefore as time progresses are likely to significantly increase their performance and energy efficiency.

Physical Cores. At the time of writing, the only mass-produced and commercially available physical RISC-V vector core is the XuanTie C906 from T-Head, which is the chip division of Alibaba. This contains 128-bit wide vector registers, and supports vector element sizes of 8, 16, and 32 bits. Noticeable by its absence however is support for elements of size 64 bits, meaning that the XuanTie C906 does not support 64 bit double precision floating point. This is a major disadvantage for HPC, where the vast majority of our workloads are in double precision. Nevertheless it is still interesting to benchmark with single precision workloads as understanding the performance and software ecosystem can provide insights around RVV, albeit at single precision. The XuanTie C906 core is available as part of the Allwinner D1 SoC, part of the EPCC RISC-V testbed and the main system on which we perform our vector benchmarks in Sect. 5.

4   Toolchain and Software Support

In this section we review the current status of the RISC-V open source software ecosystem which supports compiling and running vectorised code on RVV processors.

4.1   Compiler Toolchain

GNU. At the time of writing, the upstream GNU compiler toolchain does not support the vector extension. There is a branch, *rvv-next* [24], which provides limited support for RVV v1.0 and an older deleted branch *rvv-0.7.1* which targeted RVV v0.7.1. T-head provides a modified GNU toolchain which targets their C906 CPU [11], and contains optimised vectorisation for v0.7.1. This is the compiler used in this paper to benchmark the C906 CPU. Since the compiler is optimised for the C906, it generates code specifically for 128-bit vector width.

However, it should be noted that in recent weeks the T-Head GNU compiler has been removed from their download page and-so is no longer available. Because the compiler is under the GNU licence, it has been mirrored at [4].

LLVM. LLVM 15 and 16 support RVV v1.0, and several of the auto-vectorisation characteristics have been studied in [21]. LLVM supports compiling vector length agnostic RVV code via the *scalable-vectorization=on* flag, as well as vector length specific via the *riscv-v-vector-bits-min=N* flag (where N is the fixed vector width in bits). LLVM also supports standard extensions with minimum vector length *Zvl** and its counterpart for embedded processors *Zve**.

Since LLVM only targets RVV v1.0 and cannot run natively on the physical hardware available, it is not tested in this paper. A rollback tool that translates generated RVV v1.0 to v0.7.1 has been developed and is reported, along with a performance comparison against GCC, in [26] for both VLS and VLA modes.

4.2   Linux Kernel

Whilst there is now general availability of common Linux distributions for RISC-V boards, including Debian, Ubuntu and Fedora [2], many are early developer variants [3] or unsupported releases [1]. The Sipeed Linux image for the Allwinner D1, is easy to deploy using the proprietary tools and supports vectorisation out of the box. However, due to the proprietary, protected format of the bootloader, Linux images must be built using cross-compilation tools on another host and vendor-specific patches must be applied to *buildroot*. Furthermore, the T-Head specific GCC compiler version must also be used for this to ensure that the resulting image is RVV compatible.

This requirement to rebuild the bootloader and apply vendor patches is not only time consuming but also requires considerable knowledge and expertise to achieve. This is definitely an area in which the vendors of these boards could improve upon to open up their systems further and lower the barrier to entry.

4.3   Performance Analysis Tooling and Instrumentation

The RISC-V hardware ecosystem is moving very quickly and the HiFive Unmatched, released in late May 2021, and Allwinner Nezha D1, released in April 2021, are an example of where the software support sometimes struggles to keep up, especially when board and/or CPU specific support is required by tooling. Profiling tools are an example of this problem, where support for tools such as *perf* has lagged the hardware.

For instance, with the HiFive Unmatched, the Linux kernel version 5.18 only supports instruction and cycle count hardware events for *perf*, and in order to obtain further events then one must patch the kernel and OpenSBI [5]. With the Allwinner D1, containing the XuanTie C906 core, official support for *perf* was only released in the Linux kernel version 6.2 on February 19th, 2023, almost two years after the hardware was made available.

This lack of performance analysis tooling is a major drawback for HPC workloads, where it is imperative that programmers can gain insights around performance bottlenecks in codes and use this feedback to then optimise their applications.

4.4   Emulation

Given the limited physical hardware currently available that supports RVV, and none that supports v1.0, an obvious alternative is to run RVV-based codes under emulation. There are two main emulators for RISC-V, QEMU and Spike.

Current upstream QEMU supports RVV v1.0 along with the *zve32f* and *zve64f* standards which provide 32-bit and 64-bit vectorisation floating point support for embedded RISC-V CPUs respectively. Versions of QEMU prior to December 20th, 2021 supported RVV v0.7.1 only.

Likewise, Spike also supports RVV v1.0 and releases prior to November 12th, 2019 support v0.7.1. However, whilst emulation might appear to be a good choice for those wishing to experiment with RISC-V vectorisation in their applications, in absolute terms the application will run far slower than on physical hardware. Even for exploratory purposes this could be an issue as it will potentially limit the scale of testcases that can be executed.

Vehave. Developed by Barcelona Supercomputing Center (BSC), Vehave [14] is a functional emulator based on QEMU which is able to dynamically handle and emulate vector instructions when running vectorised binaries on hardware that does not support the vector extension. There are separate versions supporting RVV v1.0 and v0.7. Whilst this provides a convenient way of supporting RVV on hardware that is not equipped with this RISC-V extension, it is far slower than the performance that would be provided by a physical CPU.

4.5   Softcores

Whilst the C906 is the only RVV hard CPU core readily available, there are a number of RVV softcores, such as the Andes NX27V [7], Andes AX45MPV [6] and Tenstorrent BOOM-ocelot [17] that can be included in field-programmable gate array (FPGA) designs to test RISC-V vectorisation codes. However, creating soft-core FPGA designs requires comprehensive knowledge of the FPGA tooling and logic circuit design, such as *negative slack* [12].

4.6   Libraries

Most HPC libraries can be cross-compiled for RISC-V, but there tend to be limited vectorisation optimisation applied within these. One library which already includes vector optmisation is OpenBLAS, which has been optimised for RVV v0.7.1 (specifically for XuanTie C906/C910) [36]. At the time of writing there are numerous efforts on-going across the community to optimise HPC libraries for RVV, and within the next year we will likely see significantly increased support in this regard.

5   Benchmarks

5.1   System

The main RISC-V system that we benchmark in this paper is the Allwinner D1, which contains a C906 processor and supports RVV v0.7.1 with 128-bit vector registers. For comparison against a scalar-only RISC-V CPU, we use the StarFive

VisionFive V2 board (VF2), which contains a StarFive JH7110 processor (quad core SiFive U74). In order to provide some context with similar vector designs already in use for HPC, we also performed runs on a Fujitsu A64FX system (Armv8), which supports fixed length SIMD (NEON), as well as vector length agnostic (SVE), instruction sets.

Because the C906 only contains a single core, all benchmarks are run on a single core to enable direct comparison across CPUs, and only NEON with 128-bit vector width is used on A64FX for an objective evaluation (the XuanTie GCC compiler only generates fixed 128-bit vector instructions). These systems are summarised in Table 2. It should be noted that we recognise the A64FX processor is designed for HPC applications and completely different in nature to the RISC-V cores, which are designed for embedded and single-board computers (SBC). However, a comparison against the A64FX is still valuable as it can highlight important differences and potential design improvements for an HPC-class RISC-V processor in the future.

Table 2. Compute system specifications

	Allwinner D1	StarFive JH7110 (VF2)	A64FX
Processor	XuanTie C906	SiFive U74	Fujitsu A64FX
Clock speed	1.0 GHz	1.5 GHz	1.8 GHz
Cores	1	4	48
Cache	32 KB I-cache + 32 KB D-cache	32 KB I-cache + 32 KB D-cache + 2 MB L2	64 KB I-cache + 64KB D-cache, 8 MB shared L2 cache per 12 cores (core memory group)
Memory	512 MB DDR3	8 GB DDR4	32 GB HBM2
ISA	RV64GC+V0.7	RV64GC	ARMv8.2 with SVE
Vector width	128bit	N/A	dual 128-bit (NEON)/dual 512-bit (SVE)

5.2   Methodology

To evaluate the vectorisation performance we use the RAJA Performance Suite (RAJAPerf) [19], which comprises the following sets of benchmarks: ALGO-RITHM, APPS, BASIC, LCALS (Livermore Compiler Analysis Loop Suite), POLYBENCH, and STREAM (Babel Stream). Since the C906 only supports vector element sizes up to 32-bit, we configure the benchmark to use the single-precision floating point data type. The compilers and respective compiler flags for RISC-V and Arm systems are specified in Table 3. The benchmark timings are averaged over three runs.

Table 3. Compiler specifications

Name	Compiler	Vector width	Compiler flags
RV-GCC8.4-scalar	XuanTie GCC 8.4	N/A	-O3 -march=rv64gc -ffast-math
RV-GCC8.4-vector	XuanTie GCC 8.4	128-bit	-O3 -march=rv64gcv0p7 -ffast-math
ARM-GCC11.2-scalar	GCC 11.2	N/A	-O3 -ffast-math -mcpu=a64fx -march=armv8.2-a+nosimd+nosve
ARM-GCC11.2-vector	GCC 11.2	128-bit	-O3 -ffast-math -mcpu=a64fx -march=armv8.2-a+simd+nosve

5.3   Results

Table 4 summarises the list of kernels which are vectorised by the XuanTie GCC 8.4 compiler. It can be seen that 30 of the 64 kernels are successfully vectorised by the compiler, but for 7 of these only the scalar code and no vector instructions were executed at runtime. This is due to the compiler's oversensitivity to loop ranges, and the scalar branch is preferred and executed even when a vectorised branch is available. Clang 15.0, which generates RVV v1.0 assembly, is capable of vectorising more kernels than GCC 8.4; for a full comparison, see [26].

Figure 1 reports runtimes for the RAJAPerf kernel normalised against the kernel's scalar runtime. For the A64FX, normalisation is against running in scalar mode on the A64FX, whereas for the Allwinner D1 and StarFive JH7110 it is normalised against running scalar on the D1. The orange and purple bars show the vectorisation performance difference on the A64FX and D1 respectively, and the green bars show a comparison of the scalar performance between the JH7110 (VF2) and the D1.

It can be observed from these plots that for most linear algebra kernels, the vectorised code on the RISC-V D1 is faster compared to its scalar counterpart, at around 84% faster for AXPY, 53% for GEMM, 45% for GEMVER, 40% for ATAX, and 46% for MVT. Vectorised code also sustain much higher bandwidth for streaming kernels such as Stream ADD, COPY, DOT, MUL, and TRIAD. In only one case, the FIR kernel, is the vectorised code slower than its scalar counterpart. Whilst in most cases the speedup from RVV on the D1 is not as significant as from NEON on A64FX, there are some exceptions; for example, matrix multiplication kernels on the A64FX compiled with ARM-GCC11.2-vector did not execute the vector instructions. Therefore, the runtime performance was the same as the scalar executable. Furthermore, the vectorised A64FX PRESSURE kernel was almost three times slower than the scalar version.

When comparing the RISC-V processors AllWinner D1 and StarFive JH7110, it can be observed that for high arithmetic intensity kernels the JH7110 (VF2), which has a higher clock frequency, significantly outperforms the D1. For example, GEMM is six times faster on the VF2 compared to running scalar on D1, and four times faster than the vectorised version of this benchmark on the D1. However, even though the theoretic memory bandwidth for the VF2 is higher than the D1, these benchmarking results demonstrate that with vectorisation the D1

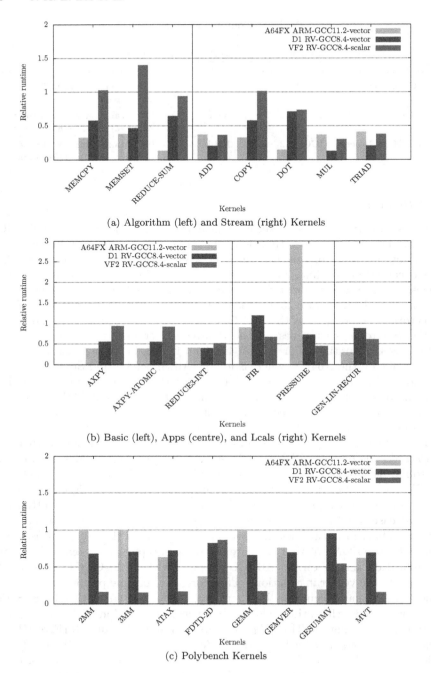

Fig. 1. Normalised runtime for RAJA Performance Suite kernels. ARM-GCC11.2-vector result (orange bars) are normalised against ARM-GCC11.2-scalar on A64FX, and both D1-RV-GCC8.4-vector (purple bars) and VF2-RV-GCC8.4-scalar (green bars) are normalised against D1-RV-GCC8.4-scalar. (Color figure online)

Table 4. RAJA Performance Suite Kernels vectorised by RV-GCC8.4-vector

Kernels		
Vectorised and executed		**Total: 23**
Algorithm	MEMCPY, MEMSET, REDUCE_SUM	
Apps	ENERGY, FIR, PRESSURE	
Basic	AXPY, AXPY_ATOMIC, REDUCE3_INT	
Lcals	GEN_LIN_RECUR	
Polybench	2MM, 3MM, ATAX, FDTD_2D, GEMM, GEMVER, GESUMMV, MVT	
Stream	ADD, COPY, DOT, MUL, TRIAD	
Vectorised		**Total: 7**
Lcals	FIRST_SUM, FIRST_DIFF, HYDRO_1D, HYDRO_2D, TRIDIAG_ELIM	
Polybench	JACOBI_1D, JACOBI_2D	
Scalar		**Total: 34**
Algorithm	SCAN, SORT, SORTPAIRS	
Apps	CONVECTION3DPA, DEL_DOT_VEC_2D, DIFFUSION3DPA, HALOEXCHANGE, HALOEXCHANGE_FUSED, LTIMES, LTIMES_NOVIEW, MASS3DPA, NODAL_ACCUMULATION_3D, VOL3D	
Basic	IF_QUAD, INDEXLIST, INDEXLIST_3LOOP, INIT_VIEW1D, INIT_VIEW1D_OFFSET, INIT3, MAT_MAT_SHARED, MULADDSUB, NESTED_INIT, PI_ATOMIC, PI_REDUCE, REDUCE_STRUCT, TRAP_INT	
Lcals	DIFF_PREDICT, EOS, FIRST_MIN, INT_PREDICT, PLANCKIAN	
Polybench	ADI, FLOYD_WARSHALL, HEAT_3D	

executes the streaming kernels faster than the VF2. For example, Stream ADD is 82% faster and COPY is 77% faster on the D1. This is the reason why we observe that the D1 can perform low arithmetic intensity operations faster than VF2, for example AXPY on D1 with vectorisation enabled is 71% faster than the VF2 which is running in scalar mode.

6 Conclusions and Recommendations

At the time of writing, generating and testing RVV codes on the currently available physical CPUs is problematic due to the mismatch between the available tooling, such as GCC and Clang, and the RVV version (v0.7.1) implemented in hardware. However, as demonstrated in Sect. 5.3, compiling for RVV on the D1 can result in codes being up to 80% faster than the scalar alternative (RAJAPerf AXPY and Stream ADD). The standardisation of tooling with v1.0 RVV and intrinsics will greatly simplify the development of vectorised codes in the future, running on RVV v1.0 compliant CPUs. Therefore our view is that, whilst at the time of writing there are challenges around developing and running vectorised code on RISC-V due to the immaturity of tooling and hardware, in the medium term these challenges will be solved and RVV provides a strong foundation for leveraging RISC-V for high performance workloads. Furthermore, the improved auto-vectorisation of LLVM, coupled with increased VLEN in future CPUs, is expected to increase kernel runtime performance even further.

Although the later versions of the T-Head GCC toolchain supports both RVV v0.7 and v1.0, neither the mainstream GCC or LLVM toolchains support v0.7. Whilst it is understandable that the toolchain development teams only want to support the ratified version of RVV, the currently available RVV hard CPU cores only support v0.7 and the runtime performance benefits of leveraging RVV on the C906-based devices are tangible, as shown in Sect. 5.3. Furthermore, T-Head have proven that it is possible to provide RVV v0.7 and RVV v1.0 support within the GCC toolchain, providing the -march=rv64gcv0p7 and -march=rv64gcv1p0 compiler options. With the large volume of RVV v0.7 devices in circulation we would like to see support for both v0.7 and v1.0 RVV in mainstream GCC and Clang/LLVM toolchains.

6.1   Recommendations

In order to leverage the runtime performance benefits of vectorisation on current RISC-V hardware and to minimise the impact of the code incompatibilities between RVV v0.7 and v1.0 [25], we recommend the use of the T-Head GCC 8.4 auto-vectorisation and not using the T-Head RVV v0.7 intrinsic API. This will ensure that codes can simply be recompiled, without modification, to target RVV v1.0 compatible hardware. Another option, is to generate code for RVV v1.0 using GCC or Clang/LLVM auto-vectorisation or the v1.0 intrinsics API, and utilise a conversion tool such as [26] to create binaries for RVV v0.7 hardware.

We would also recommend building RVV-enabled Linux images with a patched mainstream *buildroot* using the T-Head GCC 8.4 compiler, as support for the Allwinner D1 has recently been added.

Acknowledgement. The authors would like to thank the ExCALIBUR H&ES RISC-V testbed for access to compute resource used in this work.

References

1. Architectures/RISC-v/allwinner - fedora project wiki. https://fedoraproject.org/wiki/Architectures/RISC-V/Allwinner
2. Architectures/RISC-v/installing - fedora project wiki. https://fedoraproject.org/wiki/Architectures/RISC-V/Installing
3. Download ubuntu for RISC-v platforms. https://ubuntu.com/download/risc-v

4. ExCALIBUR H&ES RISC-V testbed. http://riscv.epcc.ed.ac.uk/
5. How to setup additional 'perf' events on the HiFive unmatched. https://arch.cs. ucdavis.edu/blog/2022-09-15-perf-hifive
6. RISC-V: AX45MPV.   https://www.andestech.com/en/products-solutions/ andescore-processors/riscv-ax45mpv/
7. RISC-V:NX27V. https://www.andestech.com/en/products-solutions/andescore-processors/riscv-nx27v/
8. riscv-p-spec/P-ext-proposal.pdf at master · riscv/riscv-p-spec · GitHub. https:// github.com/riscv/riscv-p-spec/blob/master/P-ext-proposal.pdf
9. SiFive Intelligence X280. https://www.sifive.com/cores/intelligence-x280
10. SiFive Performance. https://www.sifive.com/cores/performance
11. T-Head Open Chip Community Download. https://occ.t-head.cn/community/ download
12. Timing analyzer clock analysis. https://www.intel.com/content/www/us/en/ programmable/support/support-resources/design-examples/design-software/ timinganalyzer/clocking/tq-clock.html
13. RISC-V "V" Vector Extension 1.0 (2021). https://github.com/riscv/riscv-v-spec/ releases/tag/v1.0
14. Vehave User Guide · Wiki · EPI-public/RISC-V Vector Environment · Git-Lab (2021). https://repo.hca.bsc.es/gitlab/epi-public/risc-v-vector-simulation-environment/-/wikis/Vehave-User-Guide
15. BSC Risc-V Vector Toolchain · Wiki · EPI-public/RISC-V Vector Environ-ment · GitLab (2022). https://repo.hca.bsc.es/gitlab/epi-public/risc-v-vector-simulation-environment/-/wikis/BSC-RISC%E2%80%90V-Vector-Toolchain
16. MLCommons MLPerf Inference Tiny v0.7 Results (2022). https://mlcommons. org/
17. Ocelot: The Berkeley Out-of-Order RISC-V Processor with Vector Support (2023). https://github.com/tenstorrent/riscv-ocelot
18. OpenC906 (2023). https://github.com/T-head-Semi/openc906
19. RAJA Performance Suite (2023). https://github.com/LLNL/RAJAPerf
20. RISC-V Vector Extension Intrinsic Document (2023). https://github.com/riscv-non-isa/rvv-intrinsic-doc
21. Adit, N., Sampson, A.: Performance left on the table: an evaluation of compiler autovectorization for RISC-V. IEEE Micro **42**(5), 41–48 (2022). https://doi.org/ 10.1109/MM.2022.3184867
22. Cavalcante, M., Schuiki, F., Zaruba, F., Schaffner, M., Benini, L.: Ara: A 1-GHz+ scalable and energy-efficient RISC-V vector processor with multiprecision floating-point support in 22-nm FD-SOI. IEEE Trans. Very Large Scale Integr. (VLSI) Syst. **28**(2), 530–543 (2020). https://doi.org/10.1109/TVLSI.2019.2950087
23. Waterman, A., Asanovic̀, K. (eds.): The RISC-V Instruction Set Manual, Volume I: User-Level ISA, Document Version 20191213. RISC-V FOUNDATION (2019)
24. GNU, International, R.V.: RISC-V GNU compiler toolchain (RVV-next branch). https://github.com/riscv-collab/riscv-gnu-toolchain/tree/rvv-next
25. Wang, H., et al.: RISC-V vector extension intrinsic API reference manual. https://occ-oss-prod.oss-cn-hangzhou.aliyuncs.com/resource//1663142187133/ Xuantie+900+Series+RVV-0.7.1+Intrinsic+Manual.pdf#section*.243
26. Lee, J.K.L., Jamieson, M., Brown, N.: Backporting RISC-V vector assembly. In: Bienz, A., Weiland, M., Baboulin, M., Kruse, C. (eds.) ISC High Performance 2023 International Workshops. LNCS, vol. 13999, pp. 433–443. Springer, Cham (2023). https://doi.org/10.1007/978-3-031-40843-4_32

27. Minervini, F., et al.: Vitruvius+: an area-efficient RISC-V decoupled vector coprocessor for high performance computing applications. ACM Trans. Archit. Code Optim. **20**, 1–25 (2022). https://doi.org/10.1145/3575861
28. Odajima, T., Kodama, Y., Sato, M.: Performance and power consumption analysis of arm scalable vector extension. J. Supercomput. **77**(6), 5757–5778 (2020). https://doi.org/10.1007/s11227-020-03495-5
29. Perotti, M., Cavalcante, M., Wistoff, N., Andri, R., Cavigelli, L., Benini, L.: A "New Ara" for vector computing: an open source highly efficient RISC-V V 1.0 vector processor design. In: 2022 IEEE 33rd International Conference on Application-specific Systems, Architectures and Processors (ASAP), pp. 43–51 (2022). https://doi.org/10.1109/ASAP54787.2022.00017. iSSN: 2160-052X
30. Poenaru, A., McIntosh-Smith, S.: Evaluating the effectiveness of a vector-length-agnostic instruction set. In: Malawski, M., Rzadca, K. (eds.) Euro-Par 2020. LNCS, vol. 12247, pp. 98–114. Springer, Cham (2020). https://doi.org/10.1007/978-3-030-57675-2_7
31. Pohl, A., Greese, M., Cosenza, B., Juurlink, B.: A performance analysis of vector length agnostic code. In: 2019 International Conference on High Performance Computing & Simulation (HPCS), pp. 159–164. IEEE, Dublin (2019). https://doi.org/10.1109/HPCS48598.2019.9188238. ISBN: 9781728144849
32. Ramírez, C., Hernández, C.A., Palomar, O., Unsal, O., Ramírez, M.A., Cristal, A.: A RISC-V simulator and benchmark suite for designing and evaluating vector architectures. ACM Trans. Archit. Code Optim. **17**(4), 1–30 (2020). https://doi.org/10.1145/3422667
33. Schmidt, C., Ou, A., Asanović, K.: Hwacha V4: decoupled data parallel custom extension. https://riscv.org/wp-content/uploads/2018/12/Hwacha-A-Data-Parallel-RISC-V-Extension-and-Implementation-Schmidt-Ou-.pdf
34. Schmidt, C., et al.: An eight-core 1.44-GHz RISC-V vector processor in 16-nm FinFET. IEEE J. Solid-State Circ. **57**(1), 140–152 (2022). https://doi.org/10.1109/JSSC.2021.3118046
35. Soria-Pardos, V., Armejach, A., Suárez, D., Moretó, M.: On the use of many-core Marvell ThunderX2 processor for HPC workloads. J. Supercomput. **77**(4), 3315–3338 (2020). https://doi.org/10.1007/s11227-020-03397-6
36. Xianyi, Z.: OpenBLAS (2023). https://github.com/xianyi/OpenBLAS

Backporting RISC-V Vector Assembly

Joseph K. L. Lee$^{(\boxtimes)}$ (iD), Maurice Jamieson (iD), and Nick Brown (iD)

EPCC, University of Edinburgh, Bayes Centre, 47 Potterrow, Edinburgh, UK
{j.lee,m.jamieson,n.brown}@epcc.ed.ac.uk

Abstract. Leveraging vectorisation, the ability for a CPU to apply operations to multiple elements of data concurrently, is critical for high performance workloads. However, at the time of writing, commercially available physical RISC-V hardware that provides the RISC-V vector extension (RVV) only supports version 0.7.1, which is incompatible with the latest ratified version 1.0. The challenge is that upstream compiler toolchains, such as Clang, only target the ratified v1.0 and do not support the older v0.7.1. Because v1.0 is not compatible with v0.7.1, the only way to program vectorised code is to use a vendor-provided, older compiler. In this paper we introduce the rvv-rollback tool which translates assembly code generated by the compiler using vector extension v1.0 instructions to v0.7.1. We utilise this tool to compare vectorisation performance of the vendor-provided GNU 8.4 compiler (supports v0.7.1) against LLVM 15.0 (supports only v1.0), where we found that the LLVM compiler is capable of auto-vectorising more computational kernels, and delivers greater performance than GNU in most, but not all, cases. We also tested LLVM vectorisation with vector length agnostic and specific settings, and observed cases with significant difference in performance.

Keywords: RISC-V vector extension · HPC · Clang · RVV Rollback

1 Introduction

Whilst the first proposal of the RISC-V vector extension (RVV) was introduced in June 2015, this was only ratified in late 2021. The goal of the vector extension is to be efficient and scalable, and the result is a Cray-style, variable sized vector model. RVV can reconfigure element size and vector length at run time, and is flexible so that it works on different data types such as integer, fixed-point and floating-point, and microarchitectures such as in-order, out-of-order and decoupled. When combined with the base ISA the total instruction count is around 300 instructions which is far fewer than typical packed-SIMD alternative, and fits into a standard fixed 32-bit encoded space [9]. RVV also forms the foundation for other vector extensions, such as the vector cryptographic extension.

Prior to ratification at version 1.0, a draft version 0.7.1 was released in 2019. According to this release: *version 0.7 is intended to be stable enough to begin developing toolchains, functional simulators, and initial implementations, though will continue to evolve with minor changes and updates* [4]. With the

© The Author(s), under exclusive license to Springer Nature Switzerland AG 2023
A. Bienz et al. (Eds.): ISC High Performance 2023 Workshops, LNCS 13999, pp. 433–443, 2023.
https://doi.org/10.1007/978-3-031-40843-4_32

warning that *backwards-incompatible changes will be made prior to ratification*, toolchains, simulators, and hardware implementations were developed.

The first, and currently only, mass-produced hardware implementation of the vector extension v0.7.1 is the T-Head XuanTie C906 [3], which contains 128-bit wide vector registers and supports up to 32-bit vector elements. This is used in the low-cost, widely available Allwinner D1 SoC, which reuses their existing Arm SoC peripheral IP. As of yet, no commercially available hardware cores implementing v1.0 have been announced, only IP cores are available for soft-core designs. Since v0.7.1 was not ratified, upstream compilers and software do not, and will not, target this RVV version.

The aim of this paper is to address the gap between v1.0, the target for current and future tool development, and v0.7.1, the version supported by available hardware. This paper is structured as follows, in Sect. 2 we describe the background to this work by exploring the differences between v1.0 and v0.7.1 of RVV before surveying support in different toolchains and highlighting related work. Our *rvv-rollback* tool is then presented in Sect. 3 where we describe both the design and how this is to be leveraged within the compiler flow. Section 4 then undertakes benchmarking comparisons between different compilers using our tool to better understand the performance properties of common toolchains and setting, before drawing conclusions and discussing further work in Sect. 5.

The key contributions of this paper are:

1. We review the main differences between the ratified RVV v1.0 and implemented v0.7.1 by currently available hardware
2. We present our *rvv-rollback* tool designed for translating RVV v1.0 assembly code into v0.7.1
3. We utilise our *rvv-rollback* tool to test the auto-vectorisation of available compilers using the RAJA Performance Suite [6] and explore the impact that settings and compilers have on the overarching performance obtained.

2   Background and Related Work

2.1   RVV Version 1.0 vs Version 0.7.1

The RISC-V vector extension (RVV) adds 32 vector registers which are specified by two implementation-defined parameters, the maximum size in bits of a vector element, $ELEN \geq 8$, and the number of bits in a single vector register, $VLEN \leq 2^{16}$. RVV v0.7.1 adds five unprivileged Control and Status Registers (CSRs) *vstart*, *vxsat*, *vxrm*, *vl* and *vtype*, whereas v1.0 extends this list with two additional registers, *vcsr* (a vector control and status register) and *vlenb* (vector register length in bytes). Among other information, these CSRs contain settings about the selected element width *SEW*, vector register group multiplier *LMUL* (the number of vector registers grouped together), and operational vector length *vl* (the number of elements to be updated from a vector instruction).

Other important differences between RVV v1.0 and v0.7.1 include:

- **Configuration-setting instructions:** To update the vector type settings, configuration-setting instructions *vsetvl* and *vsetvli* have to be used, where the application specifies the element type and total number of elements to be processed. The hardware then configures the *vl* and *vtype* CSRs to match what is required by the application. RVV v1.0 introduced an extra instruction *vsetivli*, where the application can provide an immediate value directly as the application vector length, enabling more compact code to be generated by the compiler.
- **Fractional LMUL:** RVV allows multiple vector registers to be grouped together so that a single vector instruction can operate on multiple vector registers concurrently. This allows double-width, or larger, elements to be operated on with the same vector length as single-width elements. It is also possible for instructions to accept source and destination vector operands with differing element widths but the same number of elements, thus increasing flexibility. Vector register grouping can also improve the execution efficiency for longer application vectors because the hardware is then flexible enough to enable these to run concurrently.
The grouping is defined by the vector length multiplier *LMUL* which represents the default number of vector registers that are combined together to form a vector register group. Implementations must support *LMUL* of integer values 1, 2, 4, and 8. For v1.0, *LMUL* can also accept the fractional values $\frac{1}{2}$, $\frac{1}{4}$ and $\frac{1}{8}$, which reduces the number of bits used in a single vector register. This is particularly useful when operating on mixed-width values, enabling the compiler to effectively increase the number of usable vector register groups.
- **Tail/mask agnostic policy:** Tail elements are those which lie past the current vector length, *vl*, setting. By contrast, inactive elements are those within the current vector length but are disabled by the current mask because they do not receive new results during a vector operation. For v0.7.1, all regular vector instructions place zeros in the tail elements of the destination vector register group, and inactive elements are undisturbed. For v1.0, these elements can be independently marked either undisturbed or agnostic. The agnostic setting allows for the corresponding destination elements to either retain their values or be overwritten with 1s, the pattern of which is not required to be deterministic when the instruction is executed with the same inputs. The agnostic policy was added in RVV v1.0 to increase efficiency when the inactive or tail values are not required for subsequent calculations. For v1.0 all configuration-setting instructions, *vsetvl*, *vsetvli* and *vsetivli* must include the flags for whether it is following the tail and mask agnostic (*ta* and *ma*) or undisturbed policies (*tu* and *mu*).
- **Other changes:** RVV v1.0 simplifies the mask register layout by mapping the mask bit for element *i* to bit *i* of the mask register. Furthermore, v1.0 also introduces several new instructions, such as *vl1r* which is a whole register load instruction, and also renames some instructions for example the *vfredsum.vs* has become *vfredusum.vs*. It should also be noted that because instruction encodings are different between v1.0 and v0.7.1 they are not binary compatible.

2.2   Toolchain Support

The current upstream RISC-V GNU compiler toolchain does not provide support for any version of the vector extension. Whilst the GNU repository does contain an *rvv-next* branch [8] which aims to support v1.0, at the time of writing this is not actively maintained. There is also a previous, and now deleted, *rvv-0.7.1* branch which targeted v0.7.1. Because of this lack of GCC support, T-Head, who are the chip division of Alibaba, provides their own modified GNU compiler toolchain (XuanTie GCC) which has been optimised for their C906 processor. This bespoke compiler supports both RVV v0.7.1 and also their own custom extensions. Several versions of this compiler have been provided, and through experimentation we found that GCC8.4 as found in their 20210618 release (a mirror is available at the EPCC RISC-V testbed website [1]) provides the best auto-vectorisation capability and-so is used for benchmark comparisons in Sect. 4 because this version generates code specifically targeting 128-bit vector lengths.

By comparison, Clang 15, provided as part of LLVM supports RVV v1.0. Furthermore, programmers are able to target RVV assembly which is vector length agnostic via the flag *scalable-vectorization=on* or vector length specific via the flag *riscv-v-vector-bits-min=N* (where N is the fixed vector width in bits). Therefore it can be stated that, at the time of writing, Clang provides greater support for RVV than vanilla GCC.

In this paper, we use the RAJA Performance Suite [6] to test the auto-vectorisation performance across compilers for a range of loop-based computational kernels. We observed that T-Head's XuanTie GCC 8.4 is capable of vectorising fewer kernels than Clang 15 with either vector length agnostic (VLA) or vector length specific (VLS) settings. This can be seen in Table 3, which lists the kernels which are able to be auto-vectorised by the different compilers at different settings. This demonstrates the benefit of being able to leverage Clang on existing RISC-V hardware, and furthermore as further developments to main branch versions of these compilers will only support RVV v1.0, in future vectorisation will only be usable on existing vector hardware if the code are translated to RVV v0.7.1. This is the aim of the *rvv-rollback* tool we have developed and describe in this paper.

2.3   Related Work

This paper aims to bridge the gap between compilers that are targeting RVV v1.0 and mass-produced physical hardware available for consumer purchase which only supports v0.7.1. [11] presents an upgrade of Ara, a vector co-processor design, and reviewed the differences between RVV v0.5 and v1.0 to study the design changes required for updating to v1.0. [7] studied the auto-vectorisation capability of Clang 15 for RVV via dynamic instruction counting, and identified areas of improvements including the requirement to undertake improved shuffle pattern analysis and outer-loop vectorisation.

The RISC-V vector landscape and software ecosystem was surveyed in [10], exploring results from benchmarks running on T-Head's C906 using the XuanTie

GCC 8.4 compiler. However, the authors were unable to include Clang in their benchmarking because of the RVV version issues that we are looking to address in this paper.

Vehave [5] developed by BSC is a runtime library that enables the execution of vector instructions conforming to RVV v0.7.1 on RISC-V CPUs which do not support the vector extension, effectively trapping the unknown instructions and emulating them in software. Whilst this approach provides the ability to simulate vector instructions, the trapping and execution in software is far slower than execution over hardware. By contrast, in our approach we directly modify the assembly code generated by the compiler to *roll back* the vectorisation to the v0.7.1 standard, thus enabling the code to run on the hardware directly and not requiring any runtime support.

3   The RVV Rollback Tool

We have developed *rvv-rollback*, a Python based tool that backports RVV v1.0 assembly code to v0.7.1 assembly, and this is available at [2]. Whilst this tool is capable of translating most v1.0 instructions into version v0.7.1, some lesser used features of v1.0 such as fractional LMUL are not yet supported.

RVV v1.0 introduced instructions which are immediate value versions of those found in v0.7.1. This is where the RVV instruction being issued contains part of the data being operated upon, such as a constant, rather than loading this from a register. Examples are the configuration set instruction *vsetivli*, and the whole register load/store *vl1r* and *vs1r*. By default, our tool will convert these instructions to first store the current vector configuration in memory, then reconfigure the vector settings, followed by performing the instruction itself, and finally restoring the setting from memory. However, this process adds some overhead and furthermore is often unnecessary because a temporary register can be used instead or the reconfigurations being issued by the compiler are simply redundant. In verbose mode, the tool will print out these instances and recommend alternative optimised configuration options, with the user then able to manually determine the appropriate translation.

It should be noted that this tool is aimed primarily to aid benchmarking applications, and whilst we have tested it extensively we make no guarantee as to bit reproducibility between the Clang generated RVV v1.0 assembly and our translated v0.7.1 code.

3.1   RVV Rollback Compiler Workflow

In order to use our tool and generate RVV v0.7 executables using Clang, the user follows the following steps:

1. Compile with Clang to obtain RVV v1.0 assembly code with the appropriate vector flags, for instance *-march=rv64gcv -O3 -mllvm -riscv-v-vector-bits-min=128* for VLS or *-scalable-vectorization=on* for VLA. The *-no-integrate-*

as flag is also necessary as it directs the compiler to generate assembly which can be assembled by the GNU assembler in the third step.[1]
2. Translate the assembly code to RVV v0.7.1 using our *rvv-rollback.py* Python tool
3. Assemble the generated assembly code using T-Head's XuanTie GCC assembler, provided as part of v2.6.1 of the Xuantie-900-gcc-linux toolchain (also available at [1]). This is required because a RVV v0.7.1 conforming compiler is needed to translate the v0.7.1 assembly into machine code.

It should be highlighted that those RAJA kernels which failed to automatically vectorise with T-Head's XuanTie GCC compiler detailed in Table 3 are due to limitations in the front-end of the GCC compiler, where automatic vectorisation opportunities are identified and applied, rather than the assembler. Consequently, whilst we leverage the GNU assembler as our third step it does not reduce opportunities for automatic vectorisation that have been identified by Clang higher up in the compilation process.

4   Benchmarking and Comparison

To demonstrate the use of our RVV rollback tool and the compilation workflow described in Sect. 3, we utilise the RAJA Performance Suite compiled using Clang 15 (generating RVV v1.0 assembly and backported to v0.7.1 using *rvv-rollback*) and XuanTie GCC 8.4 which natively generates an RVV v0.7.1 executable. The suite is compiled with single-precision floating point numbers (some double precision constants found within the code were manually converted to single precision). The compiler and relevant flags are listed in Table 1.

Table 1. Compiler specifications

Name	Compiler	RVV Version	Compiler flags
GCC8.4-scalar	XuanTie GCC 8.4	N/A	-O3 -march=rv64gc -ffast-math
GCC8.4-vector	XuanTie GCC 8.4	0.7	-O3 -march=rv64gcv0p7 -ffast-math
Clang15-scalar	Clang 15.0	N/A	--march=rv64gc -O3 -ffast-math
Clang15-vector-vls	Clang 15.0	1.0	-march=rv64gcv -O3 -mllvm --riscv-v-vector-bits-min=128 -ffast-math
Clang15-vector-vla	Clang 15.0	1.0	-march=rv64gcv -O3 -mllvm -scalable-vectorization=on -ffast-math

In this section we compare vectorisation performance of these benchmarks across the compilers on the Allwinnner D1. For reference, we also include result

---

[1] the -save-temps flag can be useful for saving all intermediate assembly files if this is desired by the programmer.

from the popular StarFive VisionFive V2 board (VF2), which contains a non-vectorised StarFive JH7110 processor (quad core SiFive U74). For these results benchmarks are run on a single core to provide a like-for-like comparison. The details of the systems we use in our experiments are reported in Table 2.

Table 2. Compute system specifications

	Allwinner D1	StarFive JH7110 (VF2)
Processor	XuanTie C906	SiFive U74
Processor clock speed	1.0 GHz	1.5 GHz
Cores	1	4
Cache	32 KB I-cache + 32 KB D-cache	32KB I-cache + 32 KB D-cache + 2MB L2
Memory	512MB DDR3	8 GB DDR4
ISA	RV64GC+V0.7	RV64GC
Vector width	128bit	N/A

4.1 Performance Results

Table 3 lists the kernels which are able to be auto-vectorised by the different compilers at different settings. As mentioned, T-Head's XuanTie GCC 8.4 is capable of vectorising fewer kernels than Clang 15 with either vector length agnostic (VLA) or vector length specific (VLS) settings. Out of the kernels listed in Table 3, 22 were translated using the compiler workflow described in Sect. 3. For reporting performance comparisons in Figs. 1a, 1b and 1c, we group kernels into three separate categories:

1. Those kernels not vectorised by T-Head's XuanTie GCC 8.4 compiler
2. Kernels vectorised by XuanTie GCC 8.4, but the kernel executed scalar code instead of vectorised code
3. Kernels vectorised by XuanTie GCC 8.4, and the vectorised code was executed

Figures 1a, 1b and 1c report the runtime for each kernel compiled using GCC 8.4 and Clang 15.0 with scalar and vector for the Allwinner D1, and scalar for VF2. All runtimes are averaged across three runs and normalised against scalar code compiled with GCC8.4 on the Allwinner D1.

There are a number of noticeable features and behaviours that can be highlighted in these figures. Firstly it can be seen that Clang is capable of vectorising more kernels than GCC, especially for the LCALS routines, and this provides a significant speedup as seen when comparing Clang and GCC results

Table 3. List of RAJA Performance Suite kernels auto-vectorised by XuanTie GCC 8.4 and Clang 15.0 compilers. * denotes kernels vectorised by GCC 8.4 but only scalar code was executed during runtime, and † denotes kernels vectorised by Clang (VLS and VLA) but only scalar code was executed during runtime.

Kernels	XuanTie GCC8.4 vector	Clang15 vector VLA	Clang15 vector VLS
Algorithm: MEMCPY, MEMSET, REDUCE_SUM	X	X	X
Apps: ENERGY, FIR, PRESSURE			
Basic: SAXPY, SAXPY_ATOMIC, REDUCE3_INT			
Lcals: FIRST_DIFF*, FIRST_SUM*, GEN_LIN_RECUR, HYDRO_1D*, HYDRO_2D*, TRIDIAG_ELIM*			
Polybench: 2MM†, 3MM†, ATAX, FDTD_2D, GEMM†, GEMVER, GESUMMV, JACOBI_1D*, JACOBI_2D*, MVT			
Stream: ADD, COPY, DOT, MUL, TRIAD			
Total: 30			
Apps: LTIMES, LTIMES_NOVIEW, VOL3D		X	X
Basic: IF_QUAD, INDEXLIST_3LOOP, INIT_INIT_VIEW1D, INIT_VIEW1D_OFFSET, INIT3, MAT_MAT_SHARED, MULADDSUB, NESTED_INIT, PI_ATOMIC, PI_REDUCE, REDUCE_STRUCT, TRAP_INT			
Lcals: DIFF_PREDICT, EOS, INT_PREDICT			
Polybench: FLOYD_WARSHALL, HEAT_3D			
Total: 21			
Algorithm: SORT			X
Apps CONVECTION3DPA, DEL_DOT_VEC_2D, DIFFUSION3DPA, HALOEXCHANGE_FUSED, MASS3DPA, NODAL_ACCUMULATION_3D			
Lcals: PLANCKIAN			
Total: 8			
Algorithm: SCAN			
Apps: HALOEXCHANGE			
Basic: INDEXLIST			
Lcals: FIRST_MIN			
Polybench: ADI			
Total: 5			

in Figs. 1a and 1b. However, for some kernels such as INIT3, TRIDIAG_ELIM, and GESUMMV Clang's vectorised code is slower than its scalar counterpart.

For the 2MM, 3MM and GEMM matrix multiplication kernels whose performance is reported in Fig. 1c it can be seen that Clang's vectorised performance exactly matches that of its scalar performance. This is because, whilst Clang was able to auto-vectorise the routines, the scalar code was executed, whereas by contrast for these benchmarks GCC executed its vectorised code and produces significantly faster runtimes. It can be seen therefore that whilst the

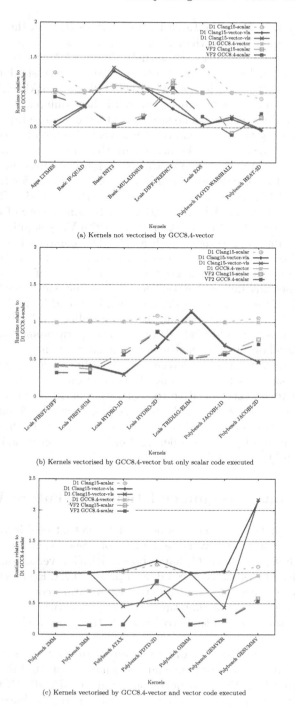

(a) Kernels not vectorised by GCC8.4-vector

(b) Kernels vectorised by GCC8.4-vector but only scalar code executed

(c) Kernels vectorised by GCC8.4-vector and vector code executed

Fig. 1. Runtime for RAJA Performance Suite kernels normalised against Allwinner D1 with GCC8.4 scalar

auto-vectorisation reported in Table 3 demonstrates that on the whole Clang is able to vectorise more kernels than GCC, there are some exceptions to this rule.

Across most of the benchmark kernels Clang VLA (vector length agnostic) and VLS (vector length specific) settings provide very similar performance, except for specific kernels such as ATAX, FDTD_2D and GEMVER. This demonstrates that it is important to experiment with these different compiler settings as it can make a difference in some situations to the achieved performance.

When comparing the performance of non-vectorised, scalar, code execution, it can be seen that for almost all kernels Clang 15 and GCC8.4 provide very similar performance, often within around 10% of each other. However several kernels are an exception to this rule, for instance GCC is 52% faster for the EOS kernel, 29% faster for FIRST_DIFF and 15% faster for FIRST_SUM. When comparing scalar performance on the Allwinner D1 against a single core of the U74 which is in the VisionFive V2, it can be observed that the V2 is significantly faster for high arithmetic intensity kernels, such as GEMM, compared to the Allwinner D1 running either vector or scalar code. However, for most kernels the vectorised kernels running on the Allwinner D1 is comparable with, if not faster than, the U74. This is especially impressive considering that the Allwinner D1 is considerably cheaper than the VisionFive V2, although it should be highlighted that we are comparing single-core performance here and unlike the D1 the U74 contains four compute cores so would likely deliver greater performance in practice.

A more general observation across our benchmark kernels was that we found when it comes to the compiler determining whether to generate vectorised or scalar instructions for execution depends heavily on loop ranges, which both compilers tend to be very sensitive to. For example, for some kernels the vectorised code is run only when the loop range is divisible by 8, and this demonstrates that it is therefore crucial that users manually check whether vectorised code is being emitted by the compiler, and executed, after compilation in order to obtain best performance.

5   Conclusions, Recommendations and Future Work

In this paper we have explored compiler toolchains that enable vectorisation on mass-produced, commodity available RISC-V physical hardware. Whilst there is no main branch version of GCC that supports RISC-V vectorisation, a bespoke version by T-Head based on GCC 8.4 does support v0.7.1. However, as illustrated in Table 3, it is less capable of automatic vectorisation compared to Clang 15. The challenge with Clang is that this only supports RVV v1.0 and-so we have introduced our tool, *rvv-rollback*, to backport the generated v1.0 assembly to v0.7.1

We have demonstrated that our tool runs across a wide set of benchmark codes, and the gathered performance numbers have illustrated that, in the main, vectorisation via Clang 15 is beneficial compared to T-Head's GCC 8.4 although there are always exceptions to this rule. Furthermore, we have demonstrated that whilst for most of our benchmark kernels the performance difference when compiling using VLA or VLS via Clang is narrow, for some codes it can make a more significant difference and-so it is important for programmers to experiment with these compiler flags.

One of the surprising aspects for us was that whilst the compiler will report that it has auto-vectorised code, it can sometimes revert to executing scalar-only code without the programmer knowing. Therefore it is crucial that programmers are aware of this and manually check what has been generated. One of our recommendations is that Clang should be clearer on this and also improve range checking to reduce the sensitivity around whether it picks one path or the other. Furthermore, effort should be invested into investigating why Clang is currently unable to execute auto-vectorised matrix multiplication operations.

In terms of future work, at the time of writing Clang 16 was released just a couple of days ago. Whilst we do not anticipate that this will have any impact on our *rvv-rollback* tool, it will be interesting to explore whether the performance insights reported in Sect. 4 have changed at all due to this latest version.

Acknowledgement. The authors would like to thank the ExCALIBUR H&ES RISC-V testbed for access to compute resource and for funding this work.

References

1. ExCALIBUR H&ES RISC-V testbed. http://riscv.epcc.ed.ac.uk/
2. RISCVtestbed/rvv-rollback: Translate RISC-V Vector Assembly from v1.0 to v0.7. https://github.com/RISCVtestbed/rvv-rollback
3. T-Head C906. https://www.t-head.cn/product/c906?lang=en
4. RISC-V "V" Vector Extension 0.7.1 (2019). https://github.com/riscv/riscv-v-spec/releases/tag/0.7.1
5. Vehave User Guide · Wiki · EPI-public/RISC-V Vector Environment · GitLab, November 2021. https://repo.hca.bsc.es/gitlab/epi-public/risc-v-vector-simulation-environment/-/wikis/Vehave-User-Guide
6. Raja performance suite, February 2023. https://github.com/LLNL/RAJAPerf
7. Adit, N., Sampson, A.: Performance left on the table: an evaluation of compiler autovectorization for RISC-V. IEEE Micro **42**(5), 41–48 (2022). https://doi.org/10.1109/MM.2022.3184867, conference Name: IEEE Micro
8. GNU, International, R.V.: Risc-v gnu compiler toolchain (rvv-next branch). https://github.com/riscv-collab/riscv-gnu-toolchain/tree/rvv-next
9. International, R.V.: Risc-v "v" extension 1.0. https://github.com/riscv/riscv-v-spec/releases/download/v1.0/riscv-v-spec-1.0.pdf
10. Lee, J.K.L., Jamieson, M., Brown, N., Jesus, R.: Test-driving RISC-V vector hardware for HPC. In: Bienz, A., Weiland, M., Baboulin, M., Kruse, C. (eds.) ISC High Performance 2023 International Workshops. LNCS, vol. 13999, pp. 419–432. Springer, Cham (2023). https://doi.org/10.1007/978-3-031-40843-4_31
11. Perotti, M., Cavalcante, M., Wistoff, N., Andri, R., Cavigelli, L., Benini, L.: A New Ara for vector computing: an open source highly efficient RISC-V V 1.0 vector processor design. In: 2022 IEEE 33rd International Conference on Application-specific Systems, Architectures and Processors (ASAP), pp. 43–51, July 2022. iSSN: 2160-052X, https://doi.org/10.1109/ASAP54787.2022.00017

Functional Testing with STLs: A Step Towards Reliable RISC-V-based HPC Commodity Clusters

Josie E. Rodriguez Condia$^{(\boxtimes)}$ [ID], Nikolaos I. Deligiannis[ID], Jacopo Sini[ID],
Riccardo Cantoro[ID], and Matteo Sonza Reorda[ID]

Department of Control and Computer Engineering (DAUIN),
Politecnico di Torino, Turin, Italy
{josie.rodriguez,nikolaos.deligiannis,jacopo.sini,
riccardo.cantoro,matteo.sonzareorda}@polito.it

Abstract. The reliability of High-Performance Computing (HPC) systems is an essential concern due to their massive size and the complexity of their operation. Thus, functional tests have been extensively used to monitor HPC systems and use software routines to verify the software stack's operation, mainly focusing on high-level abstraction features. However, the miniaturization of transistor technologies and the increment of computational resources (to face the performance and computation capabilities of HPC systems for the exascale generation) impose new reliability challenges that involve the development of clever testing strategies considering the underlying hardware characteristics. Interestingly, resorting to open-hardware architectures (such as RISC-V-based platforms) in the HPC domain offers a unique opportunity to effectively combine traditional HPC functional testing techniques with the adoption of effective fine-grain hardware testing solutions, such as those based on the Software-Based Self-Test (SBST) strategy.

This work proposes the SBST strategy as an enhanced and complementary technique for functional testing of RISC-V platforms for HPC systems. The method provides fine-grain evaluations of the CPU cores, including quantitative information on the state of the CPU cores and the presence of faults. For the experiments, we resort to two RISC-V cores (`RI5CY` and `ibex`) to develop and verify the effectiveness of the SBST strategy. In total, we developed 11 STLs (SBST routines) showing that a considerable percentage of hardware faults (from about 82% and up to 90%) can be detected with minimal overhead, thus, allowing their use during empty time intervals or in combination with other in-field functional testing approaches for HPC clusters.

Keywords: High-Performance Computing · Open-hardware ·
Reliability · RISC-V architecture · Software-Based Self-Test (SBST)

This work has been supported by the National Resilience and Recovery Plan (PNRR) through the National Center for HPC, Big Data and Quantum Computing.

A. Bienz et al. (Eds.): ISC High Performance 2023 Workshops, LNCS 13999, pp. 444–457, 2023.
https://doi.org/10.1007/978-3-031-40843-4_33

1   Introduction

Current High-Performance Computing (HPC) systems exploit parallelism to handle massive data and application complexity by distributing tasks among the available commodity clusters. This distribution provides very high levels of performance and throughput in the system. Moreover, the current demand for exascale computing capabilities involves scaling the size of HPC machines and exploiting the latest technology node approaches to increase performance and computational power, meanwhile reducing power and energy budgets. Unfortunately, new integration technologies are highly prone to system failures due to hardware faults in the components (e.g., permanent faults produced by premature aging), so imposing new reliability challenges [21,23]. Thus, the development of effective testing mechanisms for the in-field operation of HPC machines and their internal components are of major importance for an HPC system to achieve required reliability thresholds [18], as well as to reduce possible economic impacts by ineffective uses of HPCs due to system anomalies.

Traditional testing strategies to verify the correct operation of HPC's commodity clusters usually consists of several (hundreds) software procedures intended to identify possible software errors and hardware faults affecting the system. These routines are applied to determine the current operative state of commodity clusters and their interconnections, as well as to support the subsequent correction stages of the system. Most testing procedures focus on the high-level abstraction of the HPC and mainly target the software stack (e.g., *scheduler, compilers*, and *libraries*). However, the current reliability challenges (e.g., the premature rising of permanent hardware faults) exacerbate the need for clever, focused, extensive, and exhaustive test routines considering the underlying hardware architecture in the system (e.g., in CPUs and hardware accelerators) to guarantee sufficiently low error rates [11,14,22].

Current techniques include profiling and *regression testing* [24] as essential steps for the integration of software/application into HPCs. Other test approaches involve several stages and some of these consider the underlying hardware as part of their test objectives. In [27], the authors describe an HPC *acceptance* software test comprising two stages: *i) Hardware Acceptance Testing* (HAT) and *ii) Final Integration Testing* (FI). HAT consists of hardware diagnostics (usually performed by manufacturers or integrator companies) to ensure that each component (e.g., processors, memory, interconnect) meets the required operational specifications for the HPC system. FI includes *Functionality Testing* to ensure the correct operation of the software stack, *Performance Testing* that checks the achievement of the nominal performance and the execution and scale of applications, and *Stability Testing* focused on verifying the status of the software layers and the execution of diverse workloads continuously and for an extended period on top of the system. Other typical testing approaches (e.g., sanity checks, such as Node Health Check (NHC) [38], Nagios [4], Ganglia [30], and benchmarks [29]) target functional and operational features in the HPC machine, such as the performance or the variation in precision in the components (e.g.,

Variety [26]). Unfortunately, all the previous approaches neglect the exhaustive evaluation and test of the hardware in HPC commodity clusters.

In contrast, HAT tests focus on the functionality of the system's components, and are mainly used during HPC setup, configuration steps, or after major changes in their compositions (e.g., hardware updates). However, these tests require structure information of the hardware, which is usually protected and only available to the HPC manufacturer or system integrator (e.g., *Intel*, *Nvidia*, or *AMD*). Moreover, the quantitative HAT test's fault coverage is **barely** specified, possibly limiting their effectiveness for all components. It is worth noting that hardware-focused tests are not usually used for the production stage of HPCs.

Modern exascale HPC design strategies are based on co-design schemes to optimize performance and power consumption by the direct collaboration between hardware designer and system integrator companies, which can also support the development of more effective reliability mechanisms. Given the importance of the underlying hardware in HPC commodity clusters, effective alternatives of hardware-oriented and in-field tests, such as the Software-Based Self-Test (SBST) strategy [32], might contribute to increasing the detection of failures caused by faulty hardware. The SBST is a non-intrusive and effective near-structure strategy for the test of processor-based systems since it exploits their on-chip resources to run (at speed) and self-test the correct operation of their components (e.g., peripherals, hardware accelerators, and memories) [2,10,25,32,34]. Moreover, the SBST strategy can focus on the unit's structure and identify low-level hardware faults. The strategy focuses on the development of compacted software Test Programs (TPs) to compose libraries (*Self-Test Libraries* or STLs) using the native instruction sets of a target processor [16,17]. Furthermore, the SBST strategy has been successfully used as a complementary in-field testing mechanism for safety-critical applications [5].

This work proposes the use of the SBST strategy to develop efficient STLs for the test of permanent (stuck-at) faults in RISC-V-based cores used in the HPC domain. The proposed method focuses on the main CPU core of an HPC cluster. For this purpose, we considered two RISC-V processors as a case study (RI5CY and ibex), and we developed 11 STLs (one per targeted sub-unit). All test routines for the cores were implemented using RISC-V assembly instructions according to their base-ISA implementation and extensions. The current adoption of open hardware into HPC systems, such as the RISC-V architecture, offers an excellent opportunity for adopting the SBST strategy and developing efficient and effective STLs considering the available access to the underlying architecture of the components in RISC-V-based HPC clusters, which can then be combined with other tests for the in-field (production) test of the system. These additional detection capabilities can support fine-grain anomaly detection on commodity clusters and reduce impacts in terms of job failures and their associated economical costs for the HPC system operators.

The paper is organized as follows. Section 2 overviews the main functional testing strategies for HPCs and introduces the SBST strategy. Section 3 describes the proposed methods and algorithms to adapt the SBST strategy to the functional test of RISC-V CPU cores. Section 4 presents the experimental results and the effectiveness of the developed algorithms for functional testing. Finally, Sect. 5 provides the main conclusions and outlines some future works.

2   Related Works of Software-Based Testing Strategies

2.1   Related Works

In the HPC domain, several functional testing techniques have been developed to monitor the component's operation in commodity clusters. Most of them are based on the smart deployment of software programs to identify failures and check the system's operation, collect information, and determine system features, such as power consumption, performance, occupancy, and usage at any layer of an HPC. Most of them focus on the software stack using conventional testing approaches (e.g., regression testing) [15,24] that are customized (ad-hoc) to support the identification of functional and non-functional failures, especially when performing system's enhancements or configuration changes. Other tests resort to machine learning approaches and autoencoders [6]. Similarly, software approaches (e.g., *Functionality, Performance* and *Stability Testing*) check the performance achievement of applications in terms of scale [36,39], and the stable execution of several applications into the HPC resources [31]. Similarly, sanity checks [4,30,38], and benchmarks [29] are complementary tests and mainly target operational and functional features in the system [26].

Unfortunately, most works focused on software infrastructures to test the system and neglected the underlying hardware features of the clusters. Interestingly, analyses on real HPCs revealed that a major percentage (from 53% to 64%) of anomalies are directly associated with malfunctions in the hardware of HPCs [35], so exacerbating the need for testing mechanisms using the underlying hardware architecture to achieve low error rates [11].

Some functional tests, such as the *Hardware Acceptance Test* [27,37], already consider the underlying hardware features as part of the tests. This test targets the hardware diagnostics to ensure that each cluster component (e.g., processors, accelerators, memory, and interconnect) meets the operational specifications. Unfortunately, these procedures are usually performed by manufacturers of system integrator companies, which possess or have access to detailed information from the hardware structures (usually protected or unavailable). Moreover, these tests are applied before the production state of the HPC system (i.e., during the configuration and setup steps) without clear information regarding their test coverage, possibly limiting their effectiveness in some machine components. In addition, such tests are barely deployed during the production stages of the HPC by restrictions on their time execution or the availability of effective and compacted hardware tests.

Hybrid mechanisms consider the smart combination of field sensors and hardware controllers (e.g., *Baseboard Management Controller* or BMC) with software infrastructures to monitor and test the in-field system's state by resorting to the definition of *healthy* and *unhealthy* states from the collected in-field parameters. The authors in [3] resorted to compacted embedded systems devoted to monitoring and testing tasks. In addition, in [28], the authors proposed a structure to monitor HPC equipment based on the clever combination of BMCs and control software. In both cases, the need of additional hardware structures is required to collect the in-field parameters and identify any anomaly in the system.

To solve the previous issues, we propose the adaptation of functional testing solutions based on the SBST strategy to exploit its flexibility to extract and detect faults in the underlying hardware, while reducing the cost in terms of performance. The TPs and STLs developed using the SBST strategy have been proven in several domains that were effectively adapted and deployed. Moreover, the TPs using the SBST strategy can be ported and combined to other testing mechanisms, such as stability or performance testing that are normally employed during the in-field state of HPCs. It must be noted that TPs and STLs crucially target faults that cannot be detected nor identified by workloads or other high-level functional test strategies, but which can potentially affect or produce erroneous results.

2.2   The Software-Based Self-Test Strategy

The SBST strategy is a non-intrusive and flexible approach for functional hardware testing in processor-based systems [9]. Indeed, the SBST strategy has been successfully adapted to the safety-critical domain as a vital and complementary strategy to monitor and evaluate fault effects (i.e., permanent faults) arising in hardware components [5]. This approach allows the functional test of the hardware components by developing compacted and efficient special TPs and building STLs. These STLs are deployed at speed on a target unit and are able to verify and identify a considerable amount of hardware faults. The STLs are composed of routines developed using purely machine instructions, high-level languages, or a clever combination of both. In particular, three approaches (*i*) automatic, *ii*) deterministic, and *iii*) custom) are mainly used for the development of TPs. The automatic approach resorts to special algorithms to analyze the structure of a target hardware unit and identifies the possible patterns activating most faults. Then, the patterns are converted into equivalent instructions to build routines and programs [12,13]. A variation might include the use of random and pseudo-random patterns to increase hardware fault detection. Both techniques can be complemented by software compacting algorithms to reduce the size and improve execution performance while providing acceptable fault coverage [19,33]. The deterministic approaches exploit well-known algorithms to generate TPs and address specific structures (e.g., controllers, schedulers, or the register file). In contrast, custom approaches use structural details of the underlying hardware to determine the most efficient combination of instructions for the functional test of a unit (e.g., ALU).

The SBST strategy resorts to software-signature mechanisms, that propagate through software, to one or more structural observable points (e.g., *memory results*). The accumulative use of TPs allows the identification and coverage of most structures from a system. Interestingly, the adoption of the SBST strategy into the HPC domain requires access to the structural features of the underlying hardware that is not typically available for HPC machines. In the case of an open-source RISC-V-based cluster node, the internal structural details are available, so providing an opportunity to effectively adapt the SBST approach in HPC machines. As can be depicted in Fig. 1, the SBST strategy is closer to hardware than other typical functional test strategies.

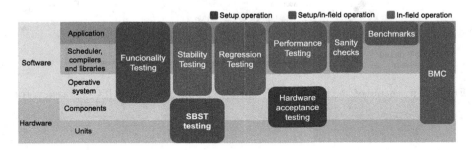

Fig. 1. A general scheme of the different functional testing strategies for HPC machines.

3   Testing RISC-V-based Cores with STLs

The method uses a clever combination of several strategies to develop software test routines and allow the development of STLs to support the functional test of permanent faults (*Stuck-at*) affecting structures in RISC-V cores. The proposed approach is divided into five steps: *i)* Structural analysis of the core and definition of the main test targets, *ii)* Selection of test strategies, *iii)* Development and implementation of test programs, *iv)* Evaluation, and *v)* Validation and fitting of test programs, as depicted in Fig. 2.

3.1   General Idea

Our approach exploits a bottom-up scheme to analyze the available open structure/descriptions of RISC-V-based cores (e.g., core/cluster of cores) and then focus on each component for the development of test routines resorting to the SBST strategy. The method is applied to every unit to cover the complete system by accumulating TPs among the units of the system. For this purpose, the strategy divides the target units (e.g., functional units, logic units, and controllers), considering the main functional operation and the availability of machine instructions, routines, or functions to address them. Considering the type of units, we select one or more SBST strategies to develop feasible TPs. The TPs provide effective test patterns and propagate any effect in case of faults in the hardware. Finally, a development-flow framework supports the evaluation and validation of

TPs on the gate-level implementations of the units, and quantifies the effectiveness of test coverage for each TP on the target structures. The next subsections describe the steps of the proposed approach of testing.

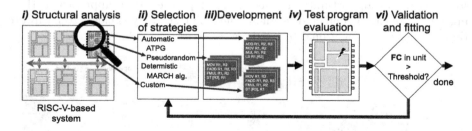

Fig. 2. An scheme of the method to adopt SBST strategies into RISC-V-based cores.

3.2 Structural Analysis

First, we analyze the target unit's structure and its operational features (functionality and interaction with the system) to identify feasible strategies using machine instructions and possible routines to excite hardware faults inside the unit and propagate their effects (e.g., a fault in the ALU might be activated and propagated by one or a set of logic instructions). This step provides, as the main outcome, the sub-units identification.

3.3 Selection of Test Strategies

Table 1. SBST types and candidate units for the development of TPs.

SBST	Type	Unit							
		Functional units	Fetch unit	Decode unit	Controllers	Schedulers	Local memories	Register files	Interconnections
Automatic	ATPG-based	✓							
	Pseudorandom		✓	✓	✓	✓			
Deterministic	March algorithms						✓	✓	✓
	Others				✓	✓			
Custom		✓	✓	✓	✓	✓	✓	✓	✓

This step correlates the hardware sub-units with the feasible functional test strategies. We analyze the sub-units to determine which test strategy might offer better coverage under reasonable efforts. The test strategies can be divided into *i)* automatic, *ii)* deterministic, and *iii)* custom, as previously introduced in Sect. 2.2. Table 1 shows the relation between the strategies and different sub-units from a processor-based system.

In particular, automatic methods are effective on testing *functional*, *Fetch*, *Decode*, and *controller* units. The ATPG-based approaches usually resort to testing routines created using commercial Automatic-Test Pattern Generators (ATPG) tools and post-processing wrappers that are mainly employed to analyze the structure of a sub-unit and determine feasible test patterns to map as equivalent instructions or values (i.e., to support the fault activation and propagation). This approach is effective when the complexity of the unit limits the use of deterministic approaches. Other approaches consist of pseudo-random testing algorithms (e.g., based on *Linear-feedback shift registers* or *LFSRs*) that produce pseudo-random patterns that can be used as values and operands on data-path sub-units, such as functional units. Similarly, the pseudo-random technique can generate random instructions for the later building of TPs. On the other hand, deterministic approaches employ well-defined algorithms to address regular hardware structures (e.g., register file and memories), and units following deterministic operations, such as embedded controllers. Among the deterministic approaches, MARCH algorithms [20] focus on the execution of well-defined operations (e.g., sequence of *writings* and *readings*) for the functional test of memories. Another approach focuses on the custom development of one or more specific routines targeting the functional testing of the sub-units of a system. This approach directly employs the functional operation and their constraints to select the best instructions able to provide effective fault detection. Moreover, this method can be applied to any sub-unit but it is used to require considerable timing efforts in their development. Moreover, custom approaches provide lower scalability (these can hardly be reused into similar structures on different cores). Interestingly, most custom approaches are hybrid combinations of manual, automatic, and deterministic procedures.

Each developed TP integrates a software signature (e.g., one or more characteristic values produced by the correct operation of the test program) to indicate when a given hardware unit has correctly executed a routine and no faults were detected. A mismatch in the signature after the execution of the test programs usually indicates the propagation of a hardware fault that allows its detection from the software. For each unit, one or more software strategies are defined as candidates for developing the test procedures. The main idea is to identify at least one strategy to apply to each target system sub-unit.

3.4   Development and Implementation of Test Programs

We use a development-flow framework to support the TP generation and develop one or more routines for functional testing on each targeted sub-unit. Cross-compilation schemes support the translation from algorithms into valid machine instructions for a target RISC-V core processor. Then, a golden and fault-free micro-architectural logic simulation is performed with the purpose of collecting the signals and the TP's behavior when running on hardware. This information is employed in the next step to support the evaluation and validation of TPs.

3.5 Evaluation

The third step targets the evaluation of TPs resorting to an automatic framework that injects and evaluates the fault detection features of each TP through a sequence of fault injection campaigns (i.e., a procedure to inject one hardware fault per sub-unit and then evaluate the TP's behavior). For this purpose, we resort to one commercial grade parallel logic simulator tool to inject permanent (stuck-at) faults and identify propagation and detection effects on every targeted sub-unit of a RISC-V core. In the simulation process, the framework evaluates the complete processor core and employs the interconnections with the main memory to determine the propagation and detection of faults. It must be noted that for the evaluation, we inject only one permanent fault per simulation to the gate-level description of the sub-unit under test.

3.6 Validation and Fitting of Test Programs

In this case, the complete set of TPs is executed in the target hardware unit. the automatic framework determines the TP fault coverage and evaluates a quality threshold (e.g., a percentage of fault identified as detected). When the threshold is achieved, a new TP is targeted for development and evaluation. Otherwise, improvement and changes on TPs are performed for new evaluations. It must be noted that the fourth step is optional, but it is common that several iteration steps are required to describe an efficient and effective TP for a given sub-unit.

4 Experimental Results

To evaluate and validate the proposed approach, we target the functional testing of permanent hardware stuck-at faults in the internal structures of the individual cores inside the commodity clusters. We consider that memories (e.g., cache or main RAM) and the interconnect infrastructures are protected by one or several levels of fault detection and mitigation mechanisms (e.g., Error-Correcting Codes or ECCs) and are not of direct interest to the functional testing targets.

For the evaluation of the SBST strategy, we employ two representative implementations of RISC-V architectures (*IBEX* and the *RI5CY*). *RI5CY* uses 4 in-order pipeline stages at 32-bit. The ISA of RI5CY was extended to support multiple additional instructions including hardware loops, post-increment load and store instructions and additional ALU instructions that are not part of the standard RV ISA. RI5CY has become a popular core for a huge variety of applications, especially for IoT designs. Similarly, the *Ibex* is a production-quality open source 32 bit RISC-V CPU core written in SystemVerilog. The CPU core is heavily parametrizable and well suited for embedded control applications. *Ibex* is being extensively verified and has seen multiple tape-outs. For the experiments, the processors' RTL `SystemVerilog` description was synthesized using the *Silvaco* 45nm Open Cell Library [1] using `Design Compiler` by Synopsys. All the experiments were performed on a server with 12 Intel Xeon CPUs running at 2.5 GHz and 256 GB of RAM.

4.1 Adapting the SBST Strategy

For both RISC-V cores, we divide their internal organizations to use a bottom-up approach and develop independent and focused TPs for each sub-unit. It must be noted that similar sub-units might reuse a given SBST strategy, but it must be adapted to the specific underlying architecture of the targeted RISC-V core.

The *IBEX* core was divided into five main targets for testing (*Fetch, Decode, Execution, Load-store,* and local memories (register file and control status registers). Similarly, the *RI5CY* core is divided into six testing targets (*Fetch, Decode,* local memory hierarchy or register file, *Execution* that is internally divided as ALU and multiplier unit, *Load-store* unit, and *control-flow* controller).

4.2 Development Flow

We use an incremental approach to tune the best trade-off of fault coverage for each sub-unit. For some units, we combine more than one test strategy and obtain acceptable fault coverage.

As depicted in Table 1, some test strategies can be used to test internal units in processors. In the proposed approach, we identify that pseudo-random strategies are simple and effective, hence we employ a software-based LFSR approach to target the *Fetch* and *Decode* units. Moreover, we use a MARCH algorithm (MATS+) to target the local memory units. MATS+ $(\uparrow\downarrow (w_0); (\uparrow (r_0), \downarrow (w_1)); \downarrow (r_1, w_0))$ provides effective test coverage when applied into all registers/cells of a memory. For other units, we include pseudo-random and custom strategies to allow the execution of the instructions and propagate fault effects by resorting to software signatures.

In the evaluation experiments, each developed TP is evaluated through a fault injection campaign aiming to evaluate and verify the effectiveness of the implemented test strategies on both RISC-V cores. A total of 11 fault injection campaigns evaluate 125,196 and 162,146 permanent faults in the IBEX and RI5CY cores, respectively.

For the experiments, we resort to one commercial fault simulator tool (in our case *Z01X* by *Synopsys*) to perform the incremental evaluation and verify the operation of each developed TP on each RISC-V core implemented at gate-level. Table 2 summarizes the main features of the targeted RISC-V cores and their sub-units. Regarding the STL testing effectiveness, Fig. 3 depicts the coverage of permanent faults on each sub-unit and the overall for both cores.

Table 2. Number of hardware faults per sub-unit in the evaluated RISC-V cores.

	Units	Fetch	Decode	Execute	LS	Mem.	CF	Overall
Number of Faults	*IBEX*	12,278	12,616	45,832	4,420	50,050	–	125,196
	RI5CY	12,024	65,582	37,838	5,608	39,590	1,504	162,146

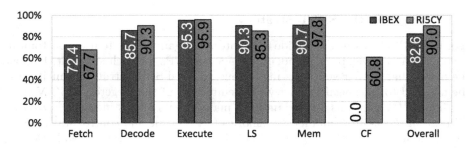

Fig. 3. Fault Coverage (FC) results for the sub-units (*Fetch, Decode, Execute, Load-Store* or 'LS', *Register File* or 'Mem', and *Control-Flow* 'CF') in both RISC-V cores.

Some of the developed TPs perform better for some sub-units (e.g., *Execute*, *Load-Store* 'LS', and the register file *'MEM'*). Interestingly, all previous units are mainly part of the data-path of the processor cores and directly interact with the machine instructions, so an extensive coverage is expected. In contrast, other units, such as the *Fetch* and the *Decode* obtained a slightly lower fault coverage. Unfortunately, since these units directly interact with the main memories (the *Fetch* case) and with any possible instruction format (*Decode* case), the requirements of the test program require of manual support for their development. i.e., in the case of the *Fetch* unit, several faults remain untested due to the limit to address high sectors of the memory resources. Similarly, for the *Decode* unit, the implemented strategies do not include all possible instructions, so some faults associated with those instructions are not identified.

The execution times, in terms of clock cycles, of the set of TPs per RISC-V core (109,194 and 80,455 for the IBEX and RI5SCY, respectively) denote the different operative times required to test faults in the cores. In principle, complete in-field testing sequences might be deployed periodically in available time slots. In the results, we focused on the sub-units of one processor core. However, the same strategies can be scaled from one up to several core units in cluster configurations. Thus, an equivalent percentage of faults covered is expected in homogeneous clusters.

The observed results only consider the internal logic of the cores. Interestingly, the results show that independently of the organization of the RISC-V core, the selected and implemented SBST techniques and test programs can effectively detect (around 82% in *IBEX* and about 90% in *RI5CY*) of the possible permanent hardware faults arising inside the sub-units. Moreover, as observed for most sub-units in both RISC-V core processors, equivalent TPs provide acceptable and similar levels of fault coverage in the *Fetch, Decode, Execute, LS*, and *Mem* (from about 0.6% up to 6.9% of difference).

The reported fault coverage results focused on permanent stuck-at faults and do not consider possible functionally untestable (or *safe*) faults in the sub-units, which by definition cannot produce any failure in the considered operational scenario. Thus, the percentage of fault coverage per sub-unit can significantly increase after identifying the untestable set of faults in the core by resorting to structural analysis and automatized methods [7,16]. Interestingly, for some units, the proposed STLs are effective even when considering different organizations in the target processors. In the case of the *Decode* unit, the implemented test programs were effective to reduce the difference between the fault coverage percentages on both processor cores (lower than 5%), even considering that the *RI5CY* implementation includes ISA extensions.

The flexibility of the SBST technique supported and allowed the adaptation and development of Testing mechanisms for different structural organizations of RISC-V cores. In particular, in case of the RISC-V cores, the standard ISA for both cores contributes to identify and implement common software routines considering the underlying structures for each sub-unit. This means that similar approaches can be used to target more complex RISC-V-based core processors specially conceived for the HPC domain (e.g., including SIMD or Vector extensions). It must be noted that additional effort is expected to extend a test strategy for the additional features of a processor core.

Finally, the results support the claim that SBST strategies can be used as complementary mechanism for the in-field testing of the elements in a HPC system and deploy them in combination with other tests (e.g., functionality, or performance testing). Similarly, we are already working on extending the same strategy to support the testing of other fault phenomena arising in the hardware components of processor-based systems, such as path delay faults [8].

5   Conclusions and Future Work

In this work, we elaborate on the use of the SBST strategy to perform fine-grain functional testing of the internal units of RISC-V-based processors. The flexibility of the SBST strategy allows the development of compact and effective test programs to address the permanent hardware faults possibly affecting the units of processors used in HPCs. The reported results prove that these special testing programs can be effectively used as complementary mechanisms to those already used in HPC systems during the setup/configuration and during in-field operation. Moreover, the experimental results demonstrate that a combination of different testing strategies can provide acceptable levels of stuck-at-fault coverage (from around 82% to 90%) for the internal units of RISC-V-based processors. These figures are in line with those required for highly safety-critical applications in other domains (e.g., automotive), taking into account that a significant percentage of the remaining faults are likely to belong to the class of *safe faults* (i.e., cannot produce any failure).

In the future, we plan to adapt SBST strategies into shared resources in commodity clusters, such as hardware accelerators, memory resources, arbiter controllers, and on-chip and off-chip interconnect infrastructures. We are also working on STL extensions on fault models describing delay defects, which are known to be produced by semiconductor aging phenomena.

References

1. Silvaco 45nm Open Cell Library. https://si2.org/open-cell-library. Accessed 17 Mar 2022
2. Apostolakis, A., et al.: Software-based self-testing of symmetric shared-memory multiprocessors. IEEE Trans. Comput. **58**(12), 1682–1694 (2009)
3. Baghyalakshmi, D., et al.: WSN based temperature monitoring for high performance computing cluster. In: 2011 International Conference on Recent Trends in Information Technology (ICRTIT), pp. 1105–1110 (2011)
4. Barth, W.: Nagios: system and Network Monitoring. No Starch Press, San Francisco (2008)
5. Bernardi, P., et al.: Development flow for on-line core self-test of automotive microcontrollers. IEEE Trans. Comput. **65**(3), 744–754 (2016)
6. Borghesi, A., et al.: Anomaly detection using autoencoders in high performance computing systems. In: Proceedings of the AAAI Conference on Artificial Intelligence, vol. 33, no. 01, pp. 9428–9433 (2019)
7. Cantoro, R., et al.: An analysis of test solutions for cots-based systems in space applications. In: 2018 IFIP/IEEE International Conference on Very Large Scale Integration (VLSI-SoC), pp. 59–64 (2018)
8. Cantoro, R., et al.: New perspectives on core in-field path delay test. In: 2020 IEEE International Test Conference (ITC), pp. 1–5 (2020)
9. Chen, L., Dey, S.: Software-based self-testing methodology for processor cores. IEEE Trans. Comput. Aided Des. Integr. Circuits Syst. **20**(3), 369–380 (2001)
10. Condia, J.E.R., et al.: Using STLs for effective in-field test of GPUs. IEEE Des. Test **40**(2), 109–117 (2023)
11. DeBardeleben, N., et al.: GPU behavior on a large HPC cluster. In: Euro-Par 2013: Parallel Processing Workshops, pp. 680–689 (2014)
12. Deligiannis, N.I., et al.: Automating the generation of programs maximizing the repeatable constant switching activity in microprocessor units via MaxSAT. IEEE Trans. Comput.-Aided Des. Integr. Circuits Syst. (2023)
13. Deligiannis, N.I., et al.: Automating the generation of programs maximizing the sustained switching activity in microprocessor units via evolutionary techniques. Microprocess. Microsyst. **98** (2023)
14. Dixit, H.D., et al.: Silent data corruptions at scale. CoRR abs/2102.11245 (2021). https://arxiv.org/abs/2102.11245
15. Evans, T., et al.: Comprehensive resource use monitoring for HPC systems with TACC stats. In: 2014 First International Workshop on HPC User Support Tools, pp. 13–21 (2014)
16. Faller, T., et al.: Constraint-based automatic SBST generation for RISC-V processor families. In: 28th IEEE European Test Symposium (ETS2023), to be apear, pp. 1–6 (2023)
17. Faller, T., et al.: Towards SAT-based SBST generation for RISC-V cores. In: 2021 IEEE 22nd Latin American Test Symposium (LATS) (2021)
18. Gomez, L.B., et al.: GPGPUs: how to combine high computational power with high reliability. In: 2014 Design, Automation & Test in Europe Conference & Exhibition (DATE), pp. 1–9 (2014)
19. Guerrero-Balaguera, J.D., et al.: A novel compaction approach for SBST test programs. In: 2021 IEEE 30th Asian Test Symposium (ATS), pp. 67–72 (2021)
20. Hamdioui, S., et al.: March SS: a test for all static simple ram faults. In: Proceedings of the 2002 IEEE International Workshop on Memory Technology, Design and Testing (MTDT2002), pp. 95–100 (2002)

21. Hamdioui, S., et al.: Reliability challenges of real-time systems in forthcoming technology nodes. In: 2013 Design, Automation & Test in Europe Conference & Exhibition (DATE), pp. 129–134 (2013)

22. Hochschild, P.H., et al.: Cores that don't count. In: Proceedings of the 18th Workshop on Hot Topics in Operating Systems (HotOS 2021) (2021)

23. IEEE: The international roadmap for devices and systems: 2022. In: Institute of Electrical and Electronics Engineers (IEEE) (2022)

24. Karakasis, V., et al.: Enabling continuous testing of HPC systems using reframe. In: Juckeland, G., Chandrasekaran, S. (eds.) HUST/SE-HER/WIHPC -2019. CCIS, vol. 1190, pp. 49–68. Springer, Cham (2020). https://doi.org/10.1007/978-3-030-44728-1_3

25. Kranitis, N., et al.: Software-based self-testing of embedded processors. IEEE Trans. Comput. **54**(4), 461–475 (2005)

26. Laguna, I.: Varity: quantifying floating-point variations in HPC systems through randomized testing. In: 2020 IEEE International Parallel and Distributed Processing Symposium (IPDPS), pp. 622–633 (2020)

27. Larrea, V.G.V., et al.: Towards acceptance testing at the exascale frontier. In: Proceedings of the Cray User Group 2020 Conference (2020)

28. Li, J., et al.: Monster: an out-of-the-box monitoring tool for high performance computing systems. In: 2020 IEEE International Conference on Cluster Computing (CLUSTER), pp. 119–129 (2020)

29. Luszczek, P., et al.: Introduction to the HPC challenge benchmark suite, April 2005

30. Massie, M.L., et al.: The ganglia distributed monitoring system: design, implementation, and experience. Parallel Comput. **30**(7), 817–840 (2004)

31. Pedicini, G., Green, J.: Spotlight on testing: stability, performance and operational testing of LANL HPC clusters. In: State of the Practice Reports. SC '11 (2011)

32. Psarakis, M., et al.: Microprocessor software-based self-testing. IEEE Des. Test Comput. **27**(3), 4–19 (2010)

33. Riefert, A., et al.: A flexible framework for the automatic generation of SBST programs. IEEE Trans. Very Large Scale Integr. (VLSI) Syst. **24**(10), 3055–3066 (2016)

34. Sabena, D., et al.: On the automatic generation of optimized software-based self-test programs for VLIW processors. IEEE Trans. Very Large Scale Integr. (VLSI) Syst. **22**(4), 813–823 (2014)

35. Schroeder, B., Gibson, G.A.: A large-scale study of failures in high-performance computing systems. IEEE Trans. Dependable Secure Comput. **7**(4), 337–350 (2010)

36. Sickinger, D., et al.: Energy performance testing of Asetek's RackCDU system at NREL's high performance computing data center, November 2014

37. Smara, M., et al.: Acceptance test for fault detection in component-based cloud computing and systems. Futur. Gener. Comput. Syst. **70**, 74–93 (2017)

38. Sollom, J.: Cray's node health checker: an overview. In: Proceedings of the Annual Meeting of the Cray Users Group-CUG-2011, Fairbanks, Alaska, USA (2011)

39. Tronge, J., et al.: BeeSwarm: enabling parallel scaling performance measurement in continuous integration for HPC applications. In: 2021 36th IEEE/ACM International Conference on Automated Software Engineering (ASE), pp. 1136–1140 (2021)

Challenges and Opportunities for RISC-V Architectures Towards Genomics-Based Workloads

Gonzalo Gómez-Sánchez[2]([✉]), Aaron Call[1]([✉]), Xavier Teruel[1], Lorena Alonso[1], Ignasi Moran[1], Miguel Ángel Pérez[1], David Torrents[1,3], and Josep Ll. Berral[1,2]

[1] Barcelona Supercomputing Center (BSC), Barcelona, Spain
{aaron.call,xavier.teruel,lorena.alonso,ignasi.moran,miguel.perez,
david.torrents}@bsc.es
[2] Universitat Politècnica de Catalunya - BarcelonaTECH, Barcelona, Spain
{gonzalo.gomez,josep.ll.berral}@upc.edu
[3] Institut Català de Recerca i Estudis Avançats, Barcelona, Spain

Abstract. The use of large-scale supercomputing architectures is a hard requirement for scientific computing Big-Data applications. An example is genomics analytics, where millions of data transformations and tests per patient need to be done to find relevant clinical indicators. Therefore, to ensure open and broad access to high-performance technologies, governments, and academia are pushing toward the introduction of novel computing architectures in large-scale scientific environments. This is the case of RISC-V, an open-source and royalty-free instruction-set architecture. To evaluate such technologies, here we present the Variant-Interaction Analytics use case benchmarking suite and datasets. Through this use case, we search for possible genetic interactions using computational and statistical methods, providing a representative case for heavy ETL (Extract, Transform, Load) data processing. Current implementations are implemented in x86-based supercomputers (e.g. MareNostrum-IV at the Barcelona Supercomputing Center (BSC)), and future steps propose RISC-V as part of the next MareNostrum generations. Here we describe the Variant Interaction Use Case, highlighting the characteristics leveraging high-performance computing, indicating the caveats and challenges towards the next RISC-V developments and designs to come from a first comparison between x86 and RISC-V architectures on real Variant Interaction executions over real hardware implementations.

Keywords: RISC-V · Scientific Computing · HPC applications · Epistasis · Genomics · EPI

1 Introduction

Scientific applications depending on Big-Data processing rely on large-scale supercomputers to ingest large amounts of data towards the discovery of relevant clinical, environmental, social, or economics indicators at large and small

A. Bienz et al. (Eds.): ISC High Performance 2023 Workshops, LNCS 13999, pp. 458–471, 2023.
https://doi.org/10.1007/978-3-031-40843-4_34

scales (e.g. 1 PetaByte on genomics datasets [13]). This evidences the need for governments and research institutions' investment in supercomputing infrastructures to provide high-performance computing on efficiently managed resources. Current computing architectures are based on x86 and ARM, both proprietary and closed-source technologies. The limited access to such technologies for open research and hardware development generates a lack of trustworthiness regarding both privacy and security. To solve the mentioned issues, here we propose using RISC-V, an open-source and royalty-free instruction-set architecture. During the last few years, there has been an increased interest in industry and academia to adopt RISC-V, mostly incentivized by strategic national/international benefits. As an example, the European Commission is pushing towards a mature RISC-V development, building an entire ecosystem around the European Processor Initiative [17] (EPI), seeking technological sovereignty over the reduced group of non-European designers and manufacturers. The EPI project intends to design and manufacture the first entirely European chip based on an open standard, in collaboration with the local and international industry as well (i.e., Intel). The software industry has already started to support RISC-V architectures, like Red Hat providing support for Linux Fedora distributions [3,15] or Google announcing Android support for such [2]. Meanwhile, the hardware industry is moving towards adopting the RISC-V standard, collaborating with the design and manufacturing of newly RISC-V-based chips [8]. At the current time, functional prototypes are already on the market: for instance, HiFive [5] is a manufacturer of commercially available implementations of chip + board based on RISC-V, among others.

RISC-V is becoming a natural alternative and a de facto standard for a new era of hardware, replacing current commodity chips. However, there is not yet a manufactured chip with equivalent characteristics to x86. Current RISC-V implementations lack fundamental extensions, and many applications lack support for specific hardware-depending features. Furthermore, other languages only support a subset of the RISC-V extensions, lacking vectorization or floating-point operations, for example. Therefore, benchmarking the proposed implementations requires new benchmarks focusing on the current state-of-art, which on one hand, are able to compare the existing capabilities and to point out the open challenges towards non-implemented ones, and on the other hand, are realistic towards their applicability in both academia and industry. The lack of standardization regarding how to benchmark workloads under this new architecture opens a new field of research in high-performance computing. As existing benchmarks on classic x86 architectures would not be fair for comparison against RISC-V in their state of implementation, here we propose a standard benchmark reaching the current capabilities of the architecture based on the real genomic analyses performed in supercomputing infrastructures for research. The goal is to be able to fairly compare the progress of the RISC-V development, identify the challenges and possibilities of improvement, and extract conclusions on the progress toward a complete and fully comparable RISC-V implementation. In this paper, we present the Variant Interaction Analysis workload, proposed as

a performance benchmark to explore the differences between the x86 and currently implemented RISC-V architecture, identifying the areas of improvement
for the latter one regarding our scientific-based real HPC workload. We analyze
the challenges RISC-V has to solve to perform as well as x86, also highlighting the principal *to-do's*. Such analysis has not been done so far, and gathering
this knowledge is crucial for the ongoing design of RISC-V prototypes as scientific HPC bound applications are one of the main targets that will benefit
from such novel architectures. The Variant-Interaction Analytics (VIA) workload, proposed here as a benchmark suite, is a genomics use case where a large
number of pairwise combinations of genomic variants need to be analyzed to find
its association with the disease [26], one of the goals of human computational
genomics. Typically, the effect of each variant with the complex disease is studied
one at a time. In variant interaction studies, the focus is on variants that interact
with the complex disease depending on at least a second variant (see Fig. 1).
Methodologies such as Multifactor Dimensionality Reduction (MDR) combined
with HPC technologies allow us to study the effect of pairwise combinations
in large genomic datasets, helping us understand these diseases. The number of
combinations in this type of study can ascend to more than 10^{12}. Due to the high
number of tests to perform and the requirements in terms of resources consumption, performance, and volume of data (from storage to in-memory processing),
we can consider that such an analytics application is HPC-oriented, along with
a genomics background and a sensitive use case to analyze as a reference for
Key performance Indicators (KPIs) evaluating real HPC workloads on RISC-V
architectures. The main contributions of this presented work are:

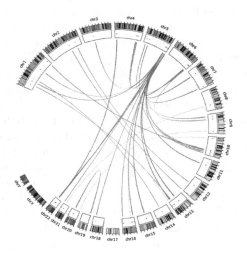

Fig. 1. An example representation using CIRCOS [18] of different pairwise variant
combinations.

- Contribution 1: A Benchmark for Scientific HPC-based Analytics Application for RISC-V, adapted to the capabilities of current RISC-V implementations and designs, towards comparing with other established architectures and tracking its progress.
- Contribution 2: The identification of the challenges explaining the performance differences between RISC-V implementations and x86 on real HPC applications.
- Contribution 3: A discussion and recommendations on the progress and improvement in RISC-V towards next step designs.
- Contribution 4: The creation of a publicly available open-data repository of benchmarks to run on RISC-V platforms [4].

The rest of the paper is structured as follows: Sect. 2 introduces the state of the art, Sect. 3 discusses the standard datasets and benchmarking methodology, Sect. 4 shows the performed evaluation. Finally, Sect. 5 concludes with a discussion and recommendations of challenges found and the next steps.

2   Related Work

In the context of European sovereignty, the EU built an ecosystem around designing and manufacturing its chips. For this, they elected RISC-V as it is an open-source ISA. The cornerstone element is the European Processor Initiative (EPI) [17]. Around it, the MareNostrum Experimental Exascale Platform (MEEP) [14] project proposes an open-source platform based on RISC-V to experiment on a RISC-V-based HPC ecosystem. MEEP is an open-source digital laboratory providing an ideal experimentation platform for RISC-V-based workloads. It integrates an accelerator that allows disaggregate computation from memory operations, optimizing the accelerator for dense (compute-bound) and sparse (memory-bound) workloads. MEEP invites software and hardware engineers to solve future challenges in the HPC, AI, ML, and DL domains.

In the context of the "Designing RISC-V-based Acccelerators for next generation Computers" (DRAC) [11] project, authors on [23] implement a RISC-V vector instructions pipeline on the gem5 processor. Then they run a standard benchmark suite for HPC applications [19] and adapt it to benchmark performance of vector instructions on RISC-V with a vector-length agnostic mechanism so that it is easily comparable with any other SIMD-compatible ISA (e.g., x86, ARM).

RISER [9], OpenCUBE [6], Vitamin-V [7], and AERO [1] are four new EU-HORIZON projects that, combined together will provide a mature cloud environment for RISC-V. RISER will integrate low-power components and build an accelerator platform that includes the Arm-based Rhea processor from EPI and a PCIe acceleration board. OpenCUBE will provide a full-stack solution of a cloud computing blueprint deployed on European infrastructure, whereas Vitamin-V will deploy a complete hardware-software stack for cloud services based on cutting-edge and cloud open-source technologies for RISC-V and particularly focusing on EPI. Finally, the AERO project aims to bring and optimize the open-source software ecosystem to compile, runtimes, and auxiliary software deployment services on the cloud. Vitamin-V will as well port a relevant benchmark suite for Big Data applications developed by the industry under the umbrella of the TPC council [10] and their Big Data Analytics TPC-H benchmark.

Furthermore, RISC-V is also starting to be used for genomics. Wu et al. [27], implement a RISC-V-based design on an FPGA that is later used for base-calling in DNA sequencing. DNA sequencing is the base method to obtain the genome sequence of an individual, thus making it fundamental for many bioinformatic applications, such as genomics. In this paper, they analyze using RISC-V as a better energy-efficient platform to sequence DNA. They achieve a 1.95x energy efficiency ratio compared to x86 architectures while being 38% more energy-efficient than ARM architectures.

In the genomics field, the search for significant associations between genomic variants and complex diseases has been primarily studied using Genome-Wide Association Studies (GWAS) [25]. These studies focus on the discovery of variants associated with the risk of developing the disease. This implies the use of a wide variety of methods including the logistic regression [16], Bayesian partitioning [29], and other statistical methods [12].

While GWAS focuses on the detection of disease-susceptibility loci in a single independent manner, in variant interaction studies, the search is broadened to inspect the effects from the interaction of variants, which can be both additive or epistatic [20]. To tackle variant interactions, different methods, tools, and strategies have then arisen, focusing mainly on pairwise interactions [21]. Importantly, Multifactor Dimensionality Reduction (MDR) [24] is a supervised classification approach based on contingency tables that has become a reference in the field to reduce the dimension of the problem and to identify variant combinations associated with complex diseases.

3   Benchmarking Methods

3.1   Variant Interaction Analytics (VIA) Workload

The method we are applying in the Variant-Interaction Analytics (VIA) Workload is the MDR: a statistical method that, based on contingency tables, reduces the dimension of the problem. The variant-variant analysis, converts the counts obtained for the cases and controls into a simple binary variable by classifying all the possible allelic combinations for each pair in high-risk/low-risk, therefore, reducing the analysis to only one dimension. It follows a naive Bayes approach, building a probabilistic classifier from every variant-variant interaction and summarizing the best combinations for prediction. Figure 2 shows the 5 steps of the algorithm. The process of computing a pair of variants does not imply a lot of memory or computational power. However, the high volume of pairs of variant combinations that we need to process demands the use of High-Performing Computing (HPC) technologies to make it feasible (see the description of the data at the end of this section). Since processing a pairwise combination of variants is

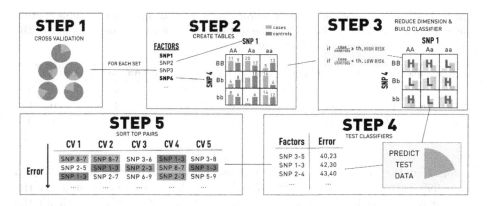

Fig. 2. Multifactor Dimensionality Reduction algorithm steps. Step 1 is the cross-validation division. Step 2 is the building of contingency tables. In step 3, the dimension of the contingency tables is reduced to 1. In step 4, each multifactor is tested. Steps 2–4 are repeated for each cross-validation set and in Step 5, the top pairs are selected.

computationally independent of the rest of the combinations, we can leverage the use of parallel computation frameworks. Furthermore, due to this independence of the combinations, we can also scale it down to test it in different architectures and extrapolate the results to real-case scenarios.

3.2   Framework

The method has been developed using Python and leveraging Apache Spark framework for parallel computation [28]. Apache Spark is an open-source distributed processing system for high-volume workloads. Thanks to its in-memory caching and a system of optimized queries, it can be used against data of any size. It has a master-slave architecture, combining a single master with multiple slaves.

3.3   Dataset

The dataset used for the benchmarking experiments is a synthetic dataset based on the Northwestern NuGENE project cohort [22]. Maintaining the structure and the number of patients we have recreated a single part of a chromosome using randomized values for the new synthetic patients. The data is stored in compressed CSV format, following the structure in Table 1.

The labels of the data are saved in a different file, including the patient ID and a binary marker that indicates if the patient is a case or a control. A cohort such as NuGENE is composed of 11,297,253 variants, forming a dataset of 11,297,253 rows × 3,389 columns. In a variant interaction analysis, we are studying the association between each pairwise interaction with the disease, which means that in the most simple case, we are going to process every possible pair. This

Table 1. First three rows of synthetic chromosome 22. The first four columns contain the identification of the variant while the rest of the columns contain the value of the variant per each patient of the 1,128 patients.

chromosome	variant pos	Ref hom	Alt hom	AA	Aa	aa	AA	Aa	aa	...	AA	Aa	aa
22	16231367	A	G	1	0	0	1	0	0		0	1	0
22	17052123	G	A	0	1	0	0	0	1		0	0	1
22	17055458	G	A	0	1	0	1	0	0		0	1	0

means that the number of combinations ascends approximately to $(11{,}297{,}253 \times 11{,}297{,}252)/2 = 63{,}813{,}957{,}024{,}378$. The synthetic dataset created for the benchmark is a reduced version, generating 10 files of 50 SNPs with all the patients. We have not decreased the number of patients because maintaining the same structure allows us to easily extrapolate the computation time just by multiplying the number of combinations that need to be processed.

4   Experiments

4.1   Evaluation Infrastructure

To perform the evaluation, we have deployed a cluster of up to four HiFive Unmatched development boards (Fig. 3a), comprising a quad-core RISC-V chipset operating at 1.2 GHz. The chip supports extensions IMAFDC, thus not including vectorial extensions. Each board has 16 GB of DDR4 and is interconnected with a 1Gbps ethernet network.

On the other hand, our x86 cluster was composed of an OpenStack environment with four virtual machines with the following characteristics: 8 cores, 16 GB of DDR3, and interconnected using an OpenStack Neutron network. Unlike the development boards, the actual hardware on the OpenStack is much more mature and is a production environment. The infrastructure (Fig. 3b) consists of SandyBridge-EP E5-2670, with eight cores at 2.6 GHz and 64 GB DDR3 memory. The interconnection between nodes is comprised of an FDR10 InfiniBand network at 40Gbps. This has a relevant impact on understanding the performance divergences discussed in the next section. Notice that this is an outdated platform. However, we are comparing with a low-performance RISC-V infrastructure. Consequently, the comparison still allows us to understand the challenges that we need to solve to bring RISC-V to become commodity hardware.

We built a Java Zero VM 11 into RISC-V to support Apache Spark. When developing this work, no Java was fully ported to RISC-V. This was the reason for choosing Zero VM as the only feasible option. On the other hand, version 11 was chosen as it was the version some other workloads in the context of our project depended upon. Moreover, support for Python runtime was enabled in RISC-V. This allowed us to run PySpark, a Python library to call Spark runtime (based on Java), on which the workload depends.

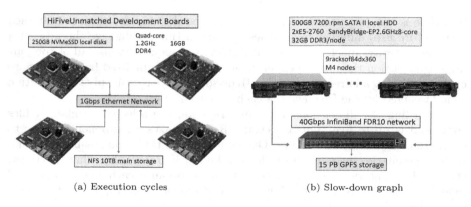

(a) Execution cycles   (b) Slow-down graph

Fig. 3. Figure (a) shows Unmatched development architectures. While Fig. (b) shows Nord3 architecture, managed by OpenStack.

4.2   Scalability Analysis

To study the scalability of the workload in terms of data volume, we have performed experiments varying the Snumber of files. We have performed the expected 1, 3, and 5 files. Since we perform a pairwise combination of every file, each increment of files is more than a linear increment of the number of combinations processed, resulting in 2,500, 22,500, and 37,500 combinations respectively per case.

To study the behavior in different environments, experiments have also been performed varying the number of nodes and cores available, simulating up to twelve different combinations.

We scale per node and per core.

– Per cores scalability: we scale up to four cores, as the RISC-V Unmatched boards only have up to four cores available.
– Per nodes scalability: we scale up to three nodes as worker nodes (under Spark point of view). That is because we had up to four RISC-V development boards. We could not test it using four nodes as workers because that would imply one node would need to share its resources with the master node. Doing so did not allow the experiments to run because of a lack of resources due to Spark runtime being a memory-intensive and compute-intensive runtime. It is designed for Big Data, but on RISC-V we have a more limited platform. Thus, we must adapt the execution tests to our platform's capabilities without sacrificing the process of the experiments.

Consequently, multiplying three combinations to scale nodes and up to four cores to scale production up to twelve simulations. Those simulations have been run on all the experiments described below (when relevant).

We have compared the performance of both architectures in terms of time consumption using similar resources. Given the goal of the workload is to compute as many variant combinations as possible in the lesser time possible, execution time is an appropriate KPI. However, since the chipsets operating at each architecture uses different frequencies, execution time might give the false idea that x86 is always much better than RISC-V. Consequently, instead of comparing the execution time in the experiments, we have normalized from seconds to cycles, achieving a fairer comparison. To do so, we have to multiply the execution time (seconds) by the frequency of each processor (Hertzs).

Regarding the dimension of the experiments, the selected number of files computed is up to five. This is because RISC-V takes an exponential time to compute a bigger amount of files. One could believe this is not realistic as, in a real-case scenario, the number of files will be much greater than that. However, the obtained metrics are valid and reasonable because each file is computed independently. Therefore, the times obtained are easily extrapolated to a real-case dataset.

The experiments performed are explained below.

4.3   Vectorial vs Non-vectorial

Initially, we run different experiments on both x86 and RISC-V platforms. In Fig. 4 can be seen the comparison between the performance using two different versions for x86:

- Vectorial: the original implementation for x86 architecture using vectorial operations leveraging numpy libraries. All the experiments performed in the 12 environments show that x86 performs at least more than 5 times faster than RISC-V.
- Non-vectorial: since RISC-V chipset is not supporting vectorial operations yet, we have tested and implemented a non-vectorial version of the workload for x86 to make a more fair comparison. The results show that the gap in cycles between both architectures gets smaller using this version. However, x86 is still at least three times faster than RISC-V. Most of the workload computational part relies on numpy to do the operations. Our non-vectorial x86 version disables it and attempts to use as many scalar operations as possible, achieving a suboptimal performance.

In both cases, the difference increase when the number of files is smaller. The reasons for this are, on one hand, because in RISC-V the time needed to load Spark and deploy the nodes is about $535\,s$ (2.6×10^{10} cycles), 25 times slower in terms of cycles than in x86, which is less than $10\,s$ (6.4×11^{11} cycles). On the other hand, we have disabled the vectorization on x86 via disabling numpy. However, this does not prevent the Python just-in-time (JIT) compiler from doing some optimizations of its own and using some vector instructions. Moreover, the Apache Spark runtime was not re-compiled without vector instructions, therefore, on the context initialization and some internal calls to it, there will be the presence of vector instructions as well. The reason for not to re-compile the Spark runtime is its complex build system, added to the complexity of disabling vector instructions on Java, having to do so both in the compiler and the JIT compiler.

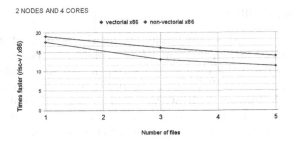

Fig. 4. Slow-down graph of x86 using vector operations against RISC-V and x86 without vector operations against RISC-V. This example has been done using four cores and 2 workers, performing the runs for 1,3, and 5 files.

4.4   Cores Scalability

Based on our prior results, we set the non-vectorial x86 version as the fairer comparison version with our RISC-V boards. Looking into the performance as we increase the number of cores, it can be seen in Fig. 5a how the cycles needed decrease as the cores do for both x86 and RISC-V. However, the gap between x86 and RISC-V is maintained and increased: x86 scales better in cores than RISC-V, as depicted in Fig. 5b. The reasons for this gap increase are yet to be determined. To find out the reason one would need to examine the chip designs of both the x86 chipset and the RISC-V one. We know they are different, as one is a production chipset while the other is a development and rather immature. Their purposes are different. Hence would expect different capabilities in terms of cores-to-memory communication as well as cores-to-cache, and many other design elements. This exploration is left as future work, given this paper wants to focus more on the software side.

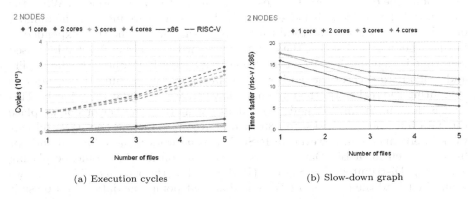

(a) Execution cycles

(b) Slow-down graph

Fig. 5. Runtime (in cycles) comparison between non-vectorial x86 and RISC-V using different amounts of cores using 1,3 and 5 files.

4.5 Nodes Scalability

In Figs. 6a and 6b, we show the scalability on the number of nodes (i.e., the number of worker nodes) on x86 and RISC-V platforms respectively. It is seen that when we increase the number of nodes, in x86 the number of cycles is decreased, scaling in nodes. This increase in performance is more notable as more files are processed. However, in RISC-V, we do not see any notable improvement in using more nodes. There is a slight decrease in cycles using more than one node processing five files, but no improvement at all when we go from 2 to 3. In fact, in most of the tests performed, going from two to three nodes produces a performance degradation on RISC-V.

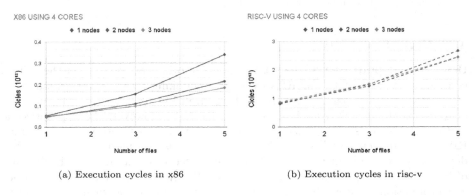

(a) Execution cycles in x86   (b) Execution cycles in risc-v

Fig. 6. Execution cycles using a different number of nodes in x86 and RISC-V.

To make a deeper analysis of what is happening in RISC-V, we have measured the execution time of the different steps of the algorithm. Figure 7 depicts the execution time of the different stages when running the VIA workload. While the run time of the workload is indeed slightly decreasing as we increase the number of nodes (i.e., workers), the total time is increasing due to the time expended in loading the data and saving the results. One potential reason for this increased load time is that, in the current implementation, Spark produces the data splits and sends it to each of the worker nodes during execution time. Thus, prior to computing the real work, the node must have received the data previously. This split is done in the master node, so it does not matter whether or not we place the data into the local disks. In x86 we do have a production and powerful network interconnection, however, in RISC-V this network is more limited and not fitting so well for a Big Data use case. One solution for this would be placing a Hadoop Distributed File System (HDFS) below the runtime. This way, we would first load the data into HDFS, and at that point, the data would be split between the worker nodes. This would achieve the effect that when running the workload, the data would be already split and in place onto the worker nodes. So the time spent on the data loading stage would be minimal, and not have the impact we are currently experiencing. Finally, we have included all the results of the aforementioned experiments in an open-data repository, provisionally available at [4]. In the near future, we plan to move it into a proper website with visualization of the different charts and metrics online. Moreover, the repository includes access to download the VIA workload as well as descriptions on how to reproduce it on your own platforms, either x86 or RISC-V. The repository and the workload are published under Apache License 2.0.

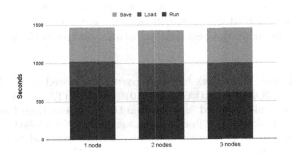

Fig. 7. RISC-V Execution time for the different steps of the algorithm. For this experiment, 5 files were processed using 4 cores for each worker.

5   Recommendations and Discussion

From the conducted benchmarking experiments, RISC-V still presents an expected significant gap in terms of performance compared to x86 architectures. The principal challenge comes from the lack of vectorial extensions to be yet introduced or properly enabled on the RISC-V development boards. When disabling such extensions up to the feasible extent, the performance gap narrows. The remaining gap, below an order of magnitude, relies on the fact that available RISC-V platforms are in the research and development stages while x86 is already a trustworthy production environment. Thus, becoming the immediate next step to close the gap.

When benchmarking node scalability, we observe that data loading becomes a bottleneck for the tested RISC-V boards. Performed experiments show that RISC-V implementations scale properly as expected, but time improvement is eclipsed by the overhead of data loading. The proposed benchmark runs on Spark, which leverages in-memory data distribution, so when the blocking logic of data distribution is available, e.g., by using HDFS, worker nodes can quickly fetch data blocks concurrently. However, if such blocking logic is not available, e.g., reading a file in a regular File System, data must be fetched by the master node (first I/O bottleneck) and then shuffled across working nodes (second I/O bottleneck). The next step would be to port and enable HDFS or an equivalent format or DFS to allow us to observe the node scalability regardless of current differences in I/O performance between architectures. This includes as well network communication.

Summarizing, at this time the main challenge in comparing architectures is that there is no one-to-one match between instructions in x86 and the instructions available on currently implemented RISC-V chips. Moreover, other differences in design between chipsets challenge performing absolutely fair comparisons between platforms. For this reason, we are forced to use different metrics focusing more on metrics related to cycles/operation-per-analytics/data.

The next steps towards refining the benchmarking process are, first, to isolate the data load time from the execution itself of the workload. And second, to have a compiled runtime and workload with equivalent instructions on both architectures, comparing the best implementation of the workload for both architectures.

Acknowledgements. This work has been partially financed by the European Commission (EU-HORIZON NEARDATA GA.101092644, VITAMIN-V GA.101093062), the MEEP Project whichreceived funding from the European High-Performance Computing Joint Undertaking (JU) under grant agreement No 946002. The JU receives support from the European Union's Horizon 2020 research and innovation program and Spain, Croatia and Turkey. Also by the Spanish Ministry of Science (MICINN) under scholarship BES-2017-081635, the Research State Agency (AEI) and European Regional Development Funds (ERDF/FEDER) under DALEST grant agreement PID2021-126248OB-I00, MCIN/AEI/10.13039/ 501100011033/FEDER and PID GA PID2019-107255GB-C21, and the Generalitat de Catalunya (AGAUR) under grant agreements 2021-SGR-00478, 2021-SGR-01626 and "FSE Invertint en el teu futur".

References

1. Accelerated European cloud. https://aero-project.eu. Accessed 16 Mar 2023
2. Android open source project ports to RISC-V. https://www.eenewseurope.com/en/android-open-source-project-ports-to-risc-v/. Accessed 06 Mar 2023
3. Fedora/RISC-V project homepage. https://fedoraproject.org/wiki/Architectures/RISC-V. Accessed 23 Mar 2023
4. Genomics RISC-V open-data repository. https://github.com/MortI2C/genomics_riscv_openrepo/. Accessed 23 Mar 2023
5. Hifive unmatched RISC-V board. https://www.sifive.com/boards/hifive-unmatched. Accessed 23 Mar 2023
6. OpenCube open-source cloud-based services on epi systems. https://cordis.europa.eu/project/id/101092984. Accessed 16 Mar 2023
7. Project vitamin-v virtual environment and tool-boxing for trustworthy development of RISC-V based cloud services. https://vitamin-v.upc.edu. Accessed 16 Mar 2023
8. RISC-V shines at embedded world with new specs and processors. https://www.allaboutcircuits.com/news/risc-v-shines-at-embedded-world-with-new-specs-and-processors/. Accessed 23 Mar 2023
9. Riser RISC-V for cloud services. https://www.riser-project.eu. Accessed 16 Mar 2023
10. Transaction processing performance council. https://www.tpc.org/. Accessed 16 Mar 2023

11. Abella, J., et al.: An academic RISC-V silicon implementation based on open-source components. In: 2020 XXXV Conference on Design of Circuits and Integrated Systems (DCIS), pp. 1–6 (2020)
12. Cantor, R.M., et al.: Prioritizing GWAS results: a review of statistical methods and recommendations for their application. Am. J. Hum. Genet. **86**(1), 6–22 (2010)
13. Eisenstein, M.: Big data: the power of petabytes. Nature **527**(7576), S2–S4 (2015). https://doi.org/10.1038/527S2a
14. Fell, A., et al.: The marenostrum experimental exascale platform (MEEP). Supercomput. Front. Innov. **8**(1), 62–81 (2021). https://superfri.org/index.php/superfri/article/view/369
15. Ince, M.N., Ledet, J., Gunay, M.: Building an open source Linux computing system on RISC-V, pp. 1–4 (2019)
16. Kooperberg, C., Ruczinski, I.: Identifying interacting SNPS using Monte Carlo logic regression. Genet. Epidemiol.: Off. Publ. Int. Genet. Epidemiol. Soc. **28**(2), 157–170 (2005)
17. Kovač, M.: European processor initiative: the industrial cornerstone of EuroHPC for exascale era. In: Proceedings of the 16th ACM International Conference on Computing Frontiers, CF 2019, p. 319. Association for Computing Machinery, New York (2019). https://doi.org/10.1145/3310273.3323432
18. Krzywinski, M., et al.: Circos: an information aesthetic for comparative genomics. Genome Res. **19**(9), 1639–1645 (2009)
19. Luszczek, P., et al.: Introduction to the HPC Challenge Benchmark Suite (2005). https://www.osti.gov/biblio/860347
20. Moore, J.H.: A global view of epistasis. Nat. Genet. **37**(1), 13–14 (2005)
21. Niel, C., Sinoquet, C., Dina, C., Rocheleau, G.: A survey about methods dedicated to epistasis detection. Front. Genet. **6**, 285 (2015)
22. Gottesman, O., et al.: The electronic medical records and genomics (emerge) network: past, present, and future. Genet. Med. **15**, 761–771 (2013)
23. Ramírez, C., Hernández, C.A., Palomar, O., Unsal, O., Ramírez, M.A., Cristal, A.: A RISC-V simulator and benchmark suite for designing and evaluating vector architectures. ACM Trans. Archit. Code Optim. **17**(4) (2020). https://doi.org/10.1145/3422667
24. Ritchie, M.D., et al.: Multifactor-dimensionality reduction reveals high-order interactions among estrogen-metabolism genes in sporadic breast cancer. Am. J. Hum. Genet. **69**(1), 138–147 (2001)
25. Uffelmann, E., et al.: Genome-wide association studies. Nat. Rev. Methods Primers **1**(1), 59 (2021)
26. Wood, A.R., et al.: Another explanation for apparent epistasis. Nature **514**, E3–E5 (2014)
27. Wu, Z., Hammad, K., Beyene, A., Dawji, Y., Ghafar-Zadeh, E., Magierowski, S.: An FPGA implementation of a portable DNA sequencing device based on RISC-V. In: 2022 20th IEEE Interregional NEWCAS Conference (NEWCAS), pp. 417–420 (2022)
28. Zaharia, M., et al.: Apache spark: a unified engine for big data processing. Commun. ACM **59**(11), 56–65 (2016)
29. Zhang, Y., Liu, J.S.: Bayesian inference of epistatic interactions in case-control studies. Nat. Genet. **39**(9), 1167–1173 (2007)

Optimizations for Very Long and Sparse Vector Operations on a RISC-V VPU: A Work-in-Progress

Gopinath Mahale$^{(\boxtimes)}$ ⓘ, Tejas Limbasiya ⓘ, Muhammad Asad Aleem ⓘ,
Luis Plana ⓘ, Aleksandar Duricic ⓘ, Alireza Monemi ⓘ, Xabier Abancens ⓘ,
Teresa Cervero ⓘ, and John D. Davis ⓘ

Barcelona Supercomputing Center, Barcelona, Spain
{gopinath.mahale,tejas.limbasiya,muhammad.aleem,luis.plana,
aleksandar.duricic,alireza.monemi,xabier.abancens,teresa.cervero,
john.davis}@bsc.es

Abstract. A substantial scope to vectorize the present-day workloads in scientific computations and machine learning have highlighted Vector Processing Unit (VPU) as a target accelerator in high performance computing systems. The performance of sparse vector operations in these systems is generally limited by memory throughput due to a small fraction of non-zeros in the operand vectors. Beyond the conventional methods used to improve the memory throughput, this work considers an approach of supporting sparse very long vector operations to improve memory-level parallelism. This comes with a need to efficiently handle these sparse long vector operations on vector engines, to improve performance as well as to save energy. This paper presents enhancements to a RISC-V VPU to achieve this and a supporting infrastructure around the VPU in a manycore system. This work-in-progress paper discusses the current results on the enhanced VPU with pointers to the planned modifications.

Keywords: Vector Processing Unit · vector arithmetic · sparse vectors · long vectors · RISC-V · OpenPiton · FPGA · MLP

1 Introduction

The ever-increasing performance gap between processor and memory [11] has been a limiting factor for performance in high performance computing (HPC) systems. This gap is noticeable in sparse applications where the sparse data [9] is characterized by a small fraction of non-zeros. The sparse matrix vector multiplication, which is a common operation in the sparse applications, involves a

The work has received funding from the European High-Performance Computing Joint Undertaking (JU) under grant agreement No. 946002. The JU receives support from the European Union's Horizon 2020 research and innovation programme and Spain, Croatia, Turkey.

sparse matrix A in a compressed form (e.g. compressed sparse row) and a vector b in dense form as operands. Here, the memory throughput is majorly affected while accessing elements of b based on the indices of non-zeros in rows of matrix A when the non-zeros are farther apart. Moreover, due to the sparse nature of matrix A it is hard to achieve spatial reuse in cache on vector b since the indexed elements are farther in space. Temporal reuse is possible only when the vector b can fit in the cache. Therefore it is beneficial to selectively bypass the conventional power-expensive caches for such vector memory accesses. This scenario is often found in HPC systems since the practical workloads in domains such as scientific computations and machine learning are dominated by sparse data of density often less than 1%. A similar memory behaviour is observed for dense vector load/stores with large strides.

A well-known approach to improve memory throughput in general is by maintaining outstanding memory requests [7] to exploit Memory-Level parallelism (MLP). In a cache subsystem this is achieved by maintaining *Miss Status Handling Registers* (MSHRs). However, it is not feasible to increase the number of MSHRs beyond a certain point [6] due to timing and hardware resource constraints. This work attempts to extend the dynamic memory window further through a support for sparse long vector operations with a provision to bypass the cache. With multiple outstanding vector load/store requests at the memory controller or a supporting module close to the memory there is a larger scope to improve MLP.

Vector Processing Unit (VPU) [4] has been one of the target accelerators for applications with vector operations. Operations on VPU have the advantages of reduced instruction memory, reduced address translations and scope for deeper pipelines leading to an overall improvement in compute performance, in contrast to execution on scalar processors. Features such as predicated execution, chaining, etc. make VPU very suitable for workloads with predominant vector operations. Execution of a RISC-V vector instruction [2] on a VPU involves, first, the application querying the VPU with *vsetvl* instruction with an *Application Vector Length* (AVL). This is followed by the VPU responding with a *Granted Vector Length* (GVL). Vector length (vl) and standard element width ($vsew$) are set and the instruction is executed for a vector of this length from the operands. This is followed by the next query with the remaining vector length, which continues for the entire length of the operand vector. GVL is determined by the micro-architecture of the accelerator, e.g., the size of vector registers on a VPU.

The advantages of a VPU are hard to extend to support very long vector operations since the GVL on VPUs are limited by register space provided by the Vector Register File (VRF). The VRF space is difficult to be scaled indefinitely owing to energy constraints. This work focuses on the ever-increasing high-performance requirements in practical workloads, and provides a solution to optimize very long sparse vector operations on a VPU. The contributions of the work are as follows:

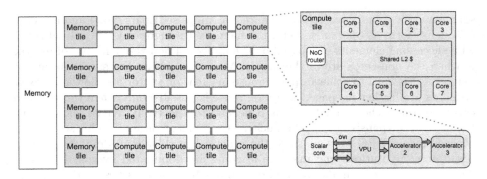

Fig. 1. High-level block diagram of the ACME Architecture

- The work proposes micro-architectural changes on a RISC-V VPU to improve performance of very long and sparse vector operations.
- Infrastructure in the form of Network-on-Chip (NoC), data read/write and transfer management is implemented to facilitate efficient execution of instructions accessing the main memory.
- This work-in-progress paper presents preliminary results that include RISC-V vector instruction simulation and resource utilization on an FPGA.

The rest of the paper is structured as follows. Section 2 gives a brief introduction to the ACME architecture along with descriptions of relevant components, and an introduction to the baseline VPU. Section 3 describes enhancements to the baseline VPU to support very long and sparse vector arithmetic. Section 4 describes support for different RISC-V instruction categories. The related simulation and synthesis results are presented in Sect. 5. Section 6 concludes the paper.

2   The ACME Architecture

The *Accelerated Compute and Memory Engine* (ACME) [8] accelerator is designed to meet the requirement of mixed practical workloads involving both cache-friendly dense-vector operations, and very long sparse vector operations which do not gain much benefits from caching. The architecture of ACME, shown in Fig. 1, comprises multiple compute tiles and *memory tiles* connected over a Network on Chip (NoC). A baseline implementation of ACME is built upon the OpenPiton [5], an open-source manycore framework, by substituting the core, cache memory, etc. in the framework with matching components. A description of OpenPiton and interfaces is provided in Sect. 3.2. Each compute tile consists of 8 compute cores that share an L2 cache. Every compute core hosts a scalar core with multiple domain-specific accelerators, VPU being one of them, connected over an Open Vector Interfaces v1.0 (OVI) [1]. The compute tiles offload memory access operations to the memory tile, thus implementing decoupled memory access and execution. More information about memory tile and its operation are described in Sect. 2.1.

2.1 Memory Tile

Memory tiles provide a path to main memory that bypasses L1 and L2 caches. This path is used to transfer vector data between the memory and the VPU. These tiles service primarily three types of requests: L2 cache misses, L1 TLB misses, and VPU vector loads/stores. A memory tile is organized as three parallel elastic pipelines that handle cache, TLB and vector requests, respectively. Cache requests are essentially transferred transparently to memory and the result is sent back to the requesting compute node. TLB requests cause a TLB lookup to translate a virtual address to a physical address, which is sent back to the requesting core. On a miss, a page table walk is executed and the TLB is updated. Memory tiles are most effective with vector requests.

RISC-V vector operations support three different addressing modes: unit stride, strided and indexed. Unit stride requests are managed as dense memory accesses while in strided and indexed requests, which are the major latency-inducing steps in sparse operations, memory transfers contain few vector elements. These sparse elements are collected locally and transferred to the VPU as a dense vector representation, saving power by bypassing the cache hierarchy and also reducing NoC traffic.

In addition, the tile can non-speculatively prefetch vector data based on the difference between the requested (AVL) and granted (GVL) vector lengths. Once an initial vector request has been made, the tile can prefetch the next GVL worth of vector elements knowing that the request will eventually arrive.

2.2 The Baseline VPU

The proposed VPU is built upon a baseline VPU [12] with enhancements and infrastructure to support very long and sparse vector operations. The baseline VPU has an in-order issue and out-of-order completion instruction execution pipeline. It is connected with a scalar core over OVI. After vector instructions are issued over the OVI, they go through a pre-issue queue, unpacker (decoder), vector register renaming, and instruction issue queue before executing on the vector lanes. The VPU consists of two instruction issue queues namely memory and arithmetic queues to stage the respective instructions. Each vector lane consists of a VRF, functional unit and modules to support loads and stores of vector data to the VRF. The VRFs are single ported register banks and maintain 32 vector registers as per the specifications of RISC-V ISA [2]. Additional vector registers are included to enable vector register renaming.

Memory instructions are dequeued in-order from the memory queue when source or destination registers are available in the VRF. During execution of memory instructions the memory hierarchy is accessed by the scalar core for loads/stores and the vector data is transferred on the OVI. In the case of vector loads, the OVI loads a cache line of data to the vector lanes which gets interleaved across the vector lanes, thus realizing a slice of VRF under every lane. Instructions in the arithmetic queue are dequeued based on the validity of operand vector registers in the VRF, and executed on the vector lanes. The 64-bit functional unit has a 5-stage compute pipeline that can perform integer arithmetic with data widths of 8, 16, 32 and 64, and floating point arithmetic with single and double precision operands. The lane-interconnect moves vector elements between the lanes which is necessary in instructions such as reduction, slide, etc.

3   Enhancements to the Baseline VPU

The enhancements to the baseline VPU are introduced in such a way that they retain the baseline functionality under the *classic-mode* and support a special mode of operation termed *acme-mode*. In ACME, the classic-mode is intended to be used for dense vector operations and sparse short vector operations. This is because in the classic-mode memory access for vector loads and stores are done through a conventional cache hierarchy (through the L2 cache), and the dense vector operands can fully take advantage of cacheability through spatial locality. In addition, the short vectors can fit in the VRF of the VPU and therefore both dense and sparse operations may gain through temporal reuse. On the other hand, for sparse long vector operations and dense long vector operations with strided load/stores there are not many gains achieved from the cache, and therefore the vector loads/stores in acme-mode make use of a memory path that bypasses the L2 cache and connects to the memory tile. Thus, unlike in

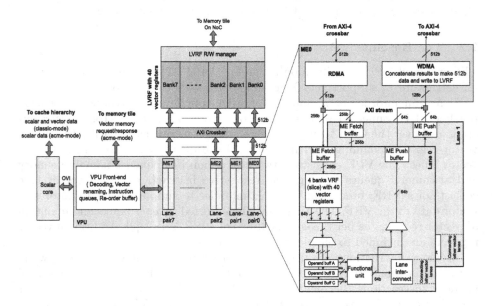

Fig. 2. The proposed enhanced VPU

classic-mode where the memory accesses are done in the form of cache misses, in acme-mode the VPU and other accelerators send vector load/store requests explicitly, during the execution of vector memory instructions, to the memory tile and get responses from it about the completion.

To gain the benefits of long vector operations in acme-mode, it is hard to increase the limit on GVL since it is hard to scale the VRF for this large dimension. Therefore a large scratchpad memory, termed Long Vector Register File (LVRF), is included in the compute core that acts as an extension of the VRF in ACME mode. In addition, the size of the VRF is reduced so that it is sufficient to hold short vectors. Vectors larger than this size are categorized as long vectors and stored in LVRF. DMA engines, termed Microengines (ME) perform read and writes to the LVRF as per the needs of the instruction under execution on the VPU. Details of the LVRF and its data layout, and ME are described in Sect. 3.1. Memory tile is responsible for loads and stores of vector data to the LVRF in response to the load/store memory requests from the accelerators. LVRF read/write manager handles read/write requests from the memory tile to store/load vector data to LVRF.

Vector lanes on VPU are grouped into vector-lane-pairs. Each vector-lane-pair is associated with an ME, and receives cache line worth of data and writes back results independent of other vector-lane-pairs. An AXI-4 crossbar [10] enables multiple MEs to access banks of LVRF, in parallel. Thus, the VPU is able to receive data at a high bandwidth from the LVRF. The vector lane-pairs can individually work on threads of execution, thus opening scope for multi-threaded execution (yet to be supported). In addition, the number of active lane-pairs are made configurable as 2, 4, 8 or 16 lanes for memory bound applications to save power by switching off unused lanes.

3.1   LVRF, Microengine and Instruction Execution

The LVRF scratchpad memory is implemented using SRAM banks with size sufficient to maintain vector registers to hold long vectors up to 2048 elements of 64b width each. The LVRF space is divided into 32 vector registers, similar to the VRF on the VPU, as per the specifications of RISC-V ISA. LVRF holds additional vector registers to enable vector register renaming. MEs are configured at the beginning of a non-memory instruction execution in acme-mode, and MEs read from or write to LVRF based on the number of valid sources. For example, read-DMA (RDMA) of ME reads a fragment of the operand vector data from LVRF every cycle and provides the data to the vector lanes. The processing of those elements in the vector lanes will be overlapped in time with the supply of the next fragment of the operand vector. This process, termed hardware data strip-mining, continues until the entire operand vector length is covered. Similarly, the generated output vector fragments are written to the LVRF by write-DMA (WDMA) of ME.

Each ME accesses a single bank of LVRF in most of the vector operations. Figure 3 shows the data layout of vector elements interleaved across banks of

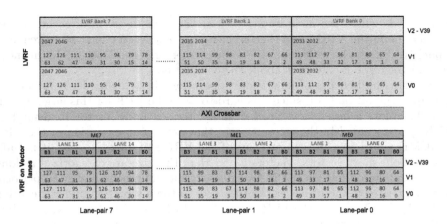

Fig. 3. Vector data interleaving on LVRF and VRF

LVRF and across lanes upon read by MEs. The indices in LVRF banks represent vector elements with element width equal to 64. Thus, the vector data is interleaved in banks of LVRF in the form of data chunks of 128 bits. When an ME reads from a bank of LVRF, the 128 bit vector data is interleaved between the lane pairs, and hence the overall vector elements are interleaved across the vector lane as shown in Fig. 3.

MEs are configured by the VPU on the fly over an APB interface during an instruction execution in acme-mode. During the configuration for a non-memory instruction, details such as source register address, destination register address and valid bits for the source registers are written to the ME configuration registers. The RDMA starts reading 512-bit vector data fragment from each of the valid source registers in sequence. The 512 bit vector data fragment is interleaved in the form of 64bit data across the vector lanes in the associated vector lane-pair. The 256 bit vector data is buffered in the ME fetch buffer and then stored in the VRF in respective vector registers, which is depicted in Fig. 2. 256b of each operand in the VRF are read in sequence into the operand buffer. The next vector fragments read by the MEs are stored in the VRF, thus implementing double buffering. Once all the number of operands expected by the instructions are available in the operand buffers the 64b from each buffer are fed to the functional unit every cycle, in parallel. The generated 64-bit result in the functional unit is written to the ME push buffer, and then to the WDMA after concatenating with the output of the adjacent lane in the lane-pair. The WDMA collects 512 bits of results in 4 such cycles and writes it to the LVRF.

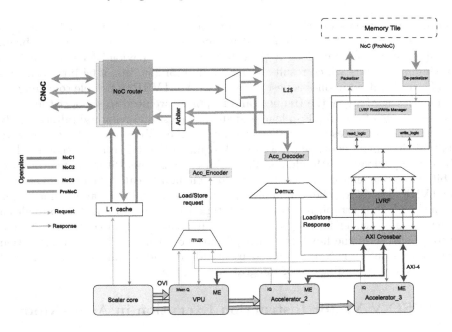

Fig. 4. Interface with OpenPiton and ProNoC

3.2 OpenPiton Framework, ProNoC, and Integration

OpenPiton is a tiled manycore framework designed to be scalable in terms of inter-chip and intra-chip [5] communication. The intra-chip connectivity in OpenPiton is provided by three different NoCs, which connect the tiles in 2-D mesh topology. Conventional OpenPiton tile comprises OpenSPARC T1 core, an L1.5 cache and an L2 cache along with a few other compute units and network bridges. The framework is modified in ACME by replacing each component with its analogous one and trying to scale the architecture for FPGA synthesis and simulation.

In the OpenPiton framework, the requests and responses are represented by messages. There is a different message type for either load from memory, store to memory etc. Thus a similar mechanism is adopted to integrate with Open-Piton, a few custom message types are defined to entertain requests generated by the VPU and get the response back from the memory tile to the VPU. The custom message types are used to generate requests on NoC2 while responses are received at NoC3. They require custom encoders and decoders (*acc_ encoder*, *acc_ decoder*) to decode the newly created message types and to encode these in a fashion similar to OpenPiton requests yet bypassing the conventional route from scalar core to L2 cache. NoCs 1, 2 and 3 are collectively termed as CNoC.

OpenPiton makes use of 192-bit header information to decode, and route messages correctly. These 192 bits are subdivided into a few fields namely, source and destination node coordinates, message type, message length, etc. While establishing a communication channel between the memory tile and LVRF, this pre-defined header structure with a fixed number of bits ends up being a problem. In OpenPiton, message_length (length of header + payload length) can be a maximum of 8 bits which results in a maximum of 256 flits of 64 bits each that can be transmitted in one request or response. For LVRF to be able to communicate with the Memory tile (request and response) we need to support the entire address range of the LVRF in load and store request and response (alternatively as read and write responses). For example, if the LVRF supports vl equal to 4096, with element width of 64, we would require at least 16 bits to accommodate the entire payload length while available bits as per OpenPiton configuration is 8 bits (message length); which clearly is not enough to cater the entire length of the LVRF. Therefore, the communication route between LVRF and Memory tile, termed VNoC, is established using Prototype NoC (ProNoC) [13]. It provides a much simpler header format, and greater data bandwidth in contrast to Open-Piton, because of the flexibility through parameterization. The communication between modules on NoC is guided by standard ready-valid protocol. Figure 4 shows a block-level diagram of integration.

4   RISC-V Vector Instruction Execution in Acme-Mode

The proposed VPU supports RISC-V ISA Vector extension v0.7.1, in which the supported vector instructions can be grouped into the following categories: vector memory instructions, non-memory vector instructions, and masked instructions.

4.1   Vector Memory Instructions

Vector load and store instructions issued on VPU are decoded into a load/store operation with values for source and destination register indices (both original and renamed), vector length, element width (vsew), *vlmul*, width encoding, stride, a flag for masked operation, *vstart* [2], and the virtual memory address. Multiple such issued memory instructions are queued in the memory queue. In acme-mode, the memory queue is de-queued when the source/destination register is marked as available in the LVRF register scoreboard. The instruction is sent to the memory tile on CNoC as a load/store memory request. Based on the request, upon a TLB lookup (and a memory read in case of a load request), the memory tile generates a write/read request message to the LVRF r/w manager on VNoC. The LVRF r/w manager performs the write/read operation on LVRF and returns a response message to the memory tile. This is followed by memory tile sending a response to the VPU in order to notify the completion of the operation. The bit corresponding to the destination register is updated in the LVRF register scoreboard upon receipt of the response. The flow for a vector load instruction is shown in Fig. 5.

Indexed Loads. Sparse matrix multiplication, which involves multiplication of a sparse matrix with a dense vector, is a common operation in the context

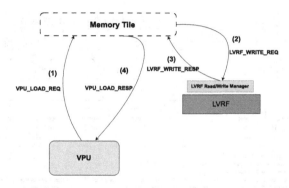

Fig. 5. Message transactions during a vector load instruction

of high-performance computing. Due to a small fraction of non-zero elements, sparse matrices are generally stored in a compressed format such as Compressed Sparse Row (CSR) format. Column indices of rows in the matrix in CSR format are readily available with the corresponding non-zero vector data, also available in a dense form. In order to multiply a row of the sparse matrix with a dense vector, it is required to read elements from the dense vector with column indices of every row of the sparse matrix as indices, resulting in multiple indexed load (vlx*.v) operations. In acme-mode the indexed load is handled by the memory tile, and involves two requests to the LVRF r/w manager. First, a read request to read the index vector. The memory tile collects elements of the vector from memory as per the indices, and the resulting packed dense vector is loaded on to the LVRF with a write request. A similar procedure is followed for indexed store (vsx*.v) operation.

4.2 Non-memory Vector Instructions

This category of instructions include arithmetic instructions (element wise operations, reduction), register move instructions, slide instructions (position-shift of vector elements) and gather instructions. These instructions are decoded and queued in the arithmetic queue. Instructions are de-queued when the source registers of an instruction are marked as valid in the LVRF register scoreboard, as a result of a vector load or a prior arithmetic instruction. The de-queued instruction is executed on the vector lanes and the bit for the destination register in the LVRF scoreboard is set upon completion of the execution, to mark the register as available for the subsequent instructions.

Scatter-Gather, Slide Instructions. Vector register gather (*vrgather.vv*) instruction gathers vector elements from a source vector according to indices in an index vector. Vector slide instructions (*vslideup, vslide1up, vslidedown, vslide1down*) shift vector elements in either direction. During execution of these instructions, in classic-mode, the vector elements are transferred between the

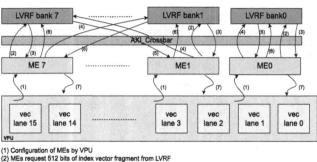

(1) Configuration of MEs by VPU
(2) MEs request 512 bits of index vector fragment from LVRF
(3) MEs receive the index vector fragment
(4) A new request for every index is generated (for example element width of 64 generates 8 reads from LVRF)
(5) Receive 512 bit vector data containing indexed value data from LVRF. Separate the indexed value.
   Repeat step 4 and step 5 multiple times based on element width
(6) Write the read indexed vector elements packed as a cache line to LVRF
   Go to step 2 until the vector length is covered
(7) VPU is notified about the instruction completion, and the instruction is committed

Fig. 6. The scheme for vrgather instruction in the acme-mode

VRF of lanes via the lane-interconnect. In acme-mode, since the entire source vectors are not available in VRF at any point of time, these instructions need to be handled specially. Moreover, since scatter-gather and slide instructions are not arithmetic instructions, performing these operations on MEs instead of vector lanes is an optimal approach. In order to do this, MEs are enabled to perform these operations and the logic in vector lanes is bypassed. Figure 6 lists the steps in the *vrgather* instruction. After RDMA of ME reads 512b from the index vector it generates read requests based on the indices until all the elements are read. This triggers the WDMA of ME to write back the result to the destination register. This continues for the entire source vector length. A similar approach is followed for *vslide* instructions. Since MEs do not have access to mask registers on vector lanes, it needs to read register *V0* (renamed) from LVRF to get mask bits in the case of masked *vrgather* and *vslide* instructions.

4.3 Masked Instruction Execution

RISC-V masked instructions enable predicated execution of vector instructions with mask bits stored in register *V0*. In the baseline VPU upon a load to *V0* (renamed to another vector register address) the instruction is followed by a micro instruction that copies, in a compressed form, contents of the register to small *mask registers* provided in the vector lanes. This makes the mask bits available during masked instruction execution. Similarly, in acme-mode, the same micro-instruction is used to configure MEs to load the contents of *V0* (renamed) to the mask registers. To implement this, the size of mask registers are increased to match the size of long vector masks. A similar process to load the mask registers is followed when result of an arithmetic instruction is written to *V0* (renamed). The masked loads are implemented as the memory tile sending a write request to the LVRF r/w manager with *masked* flag in the message

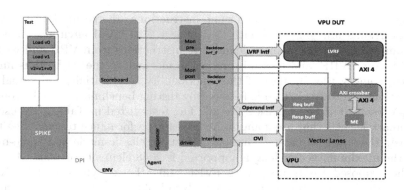

Fig. 7. The UVM testbench for VPU

Table 1. Results on bench kernels from RISC-V vectorized benchmark suite

# Kernel	Characteristics	classic-mode	acme-mode
MatMul	Dense matrix multiplication	PASS	PASS
SpMV	Sparse matrix vector multiplication	PASS	PASS
Somier	Dense linear algebra kernel	PASS	PASS
Axpy	Dense Axpy	PASS	PASS
FFTW	Dense Fast Fourier transform	PASS	PASS

Table 2. Resource utilization for an integration of VPU, ME and LVRF on Xilinx Alveo U55C.

# lanes	Total LUTs	Logic LUTs	LUTRAMs	SRLs	FFs	RAMB36	RAMB18	URAM	DSP Blocks
2 lanes	100412	99208	1204	0	89881	112	16	0	22
4 lanes	194604	192366	2236	2	173484	128	0	0	44
8 lanes	385882	381574	4304	4	340782	128	0	0	88
16 lanes	768877	760429	8440	8	679515	128	0	0	176
Available	1303680	1303680	19934		868528	2016	4032	960	9024

asserted. The LVRF r/w manager reads the vector register containing mask bits (*V0* renamed) and writes the input data according to the mask bits. In the case of masked stores, the memory tile sends a read request to read the mask register, which is followed by another read request to read the vector data. Memory tile writes the data to memory as per the mask information.

5   Verification and Synthesis Results

To verify functional correctness at module-level, the proposed VPU is tested with instructions from RISC-V ISA in both classic-mode and acme-mode by using the UVM verification environment shown in Fig. 7. The environment generates vector instructions using an Instruction Set Simulator (ISS, Spike) that mimics a specific scalar core. The same instructions are executed on the VPU, and the results are compared with that of ISS. The UVM environment is also programmed to receive memory load/store instructions from VPU and write to or read from LVRF, and to send a response message to the VPU, thus imitating the memory tile. As part of the functionality test, initially individual ISA instructions are tested, which is followed by testing benchmark kernels from the RISC-V vectorized benchmark suite [3]. The tests listed in Table 1 are used as benchmark kernels that are going to be used for performance testing. The table also lists the status of passing simulation tests in classic-mode and acme-mode. Here the maximum vector length supported is 2048 elements of *vsew* 64.

The proposed VPU, along with LVRF and MEs, is synthesized for Xilinx xcu55c FPGA, which is a part of Xilinx Alveo U55C high-performance compute card. Synthesis reports for four configurations with an increasing number of lanes is listed in Table 2. The VPU and LVRF are clocked at 50 MHz. Since vector lanes consume most of the resources in VPU, and the number of MEs are included based on the number of lanes, we see an approximately linear increase in utilization with the number of lanes. The size of LVRF (4 MB) is fixed in all the configurations, which is visible in the block RAM utilization.

6   Conclusion

The modifications to a RISC-V VPU to optimize very long and sparse vector operations are presented. Using a per-tile scratchpad memory (which maintains vector registers) and DMA engines to load/store data, the VPU is integrated into a manycore system. The integration involves definition of new message types in OpenPiton, and introduction of a dedicated NoC (ProNoC) for vector data. The work proposes methods to execute different categories of RISC-V vector instructions on the VPU. This work-in-progress paper described preliminary simulation results and FPGA synthesis results to present the status of the work.

References

1. open vector interface spec. https://github.com/semidynamics/OpenVectorInterface/blob/master/open_vector_interface_spec.pdf. Accessed 19 June 2023
2. Risc-v "v" vector extension. https://github.com/riscv/riscv-v-spec/blob/0.7.1/v-spec.adoc. Accessed 19 June 2023
3. Risc-v vectorized benchmark suite. https://github.com/RALC88/riscv-vectorized-benchmark-suite. Accessed 19 June 2023
4. Asanovic, K., Wawrzynek, J.: Vector microprocessors. Ph.D. thesis (1998). aAI9901978
5. Balkind, J., et al.: OpenPiton: an open source manycore research framework. In: Proceedings of the Twenty-First International Conference on Architectural Support for Programming Languages and Operating Systems (2016)
6. Ceze, L., Tuck, J., Torrellas, J.: Are we ready for high memory-level parallelism (2006)

7. Cristal, A., Ortega, D., Llosa, J., Valero, M.: Kilo-instruction processors. In: Veidenbaum, A., Joe, K., Amano, H., Aiso, H. (eds.) ISHPC 2003. LNCS, vol. 2858, pp. 10–25. Springer, Heidelberg (2003). https://doi.org/10.1007/978-3-540-39707-6_2

8. Fell, A., et al.: The Marenostrum experimental exascale platform (MEEP). Supercomput. Front. Innov. **8**(1), 62–81 (2021). https://doi.org/10.14529/jsfi210105. https://superfri.org/index.php/superfri/article/view/369

9. Gale, T.: The future of sparsity in deep neural networks (2020). https://www.sigarch.org/the-future-of-sparsity-in-deep-neural-networks/

10. Kurth, A., et al.: An open-source platform for high-performance non-coherent onchip communication. CoRR abs/2009.05334 (2020). https://arxiv.org/abs/2009.05334

11. McKee, S.A., Wisniewski, R.W.: Memory wall. In: Padua, D. (ed.) Encyclopedia of Parallel Computing, pp. 1110–1116. Springer, Boston (2011). https://doi.org/10.1007/978-0-387-09766-4_234

12. Minervini, F., et al.: Vitruvius+: an area-efficient RISC-V decoupled vector coprocessor for high performance computing applications. ACM Trans. Archit. Code Optim. **20**, 1–25 (2022). https://doi.org/10.1145/3575861

13. Monemi, A., Tang, J., Palesi, M., Marsono, M.N.: ProNoC: a low latency network-on-chip based many-core system-on-chip prototyping platform. Microprocess. Microsyst. **54**, 60–74 (2017). https://doi.org/10.1016/j.micpro.2017.08.007

Performance Modelling-Driven Optimization of RISC-V Hardware for Efficient SpMV

Alexandre Rodrigues[✉] , Leonel Sousa , and Aleksandar Ilic

INESC-ID, Instituto Superior Tecnico, Universidade de Lisboa, Rua Alves Redol, 9,
1000-029 Lisbon, Portugal
{alexandre.d.rodrigues,leonel.sousa,aleksandar.ilic}@inesc-id.pt

Abstract. The growing need for inference on edge devices brings with it a necessity for efficient hardware, optimized for particular computational kernels, such as Sparse Matrix-Vector Multiplication (SpMV). With the RISC-V Instruction Set Architecture (ISA) providing unprecedented freedom to hardware designers, there is now a greater opportunity to tailor these microarchitectures to both the application requirements and the data it is expected to process. In this paper, we demonstrate the use of the insights provided by the Cache-Aware Roofline Model (CARM) in the hardware design process, optimizing a RISC-V architecture for efficient and performant execution of SpMV. Specifically, we assess the effect architectural parameters associated with the processor's cache and floating-point unit have on the architecture and SpMV performance. Following a reparameterization closely guided by the CARM, we demonstrate a 2.04× improvement in performance and a significant decrease in underused computational resources.

Keywords: RISC-V · Performance modelling (CARM) · SpMV

1 Introduction

Sparse Matrix-Vector Multiplication (SpMV) is a widely used computational kernel that plays a critical role in numerous scientific, engineering, and industrial fields, ranging from physics simulations to optimization problems. In recent years, SpMV and other sparse computational kernels have gained significant importance in the field of machine learning, where they are used to reduce the storage requirements and improve performance of both training and inference algorithms. Furthermore, the demand for efficient neural network inference on edge devices has grown substantially [11], for which hardware designs based on RISC-V represent one of the most promising solutions. However, designing and tailoring the capabilities of hardware resources for efficient SpMV processing is not a trivial task, for which efficient solutions are yet to be proposed. This is a specific gap that this paper intends to close.

ⓒ The Author(s), under exclusive license to Springer Nature Switzerland AG 2023
A. Bienz et al. (Eds.): ISC High Performance 2023 Workshops, LNCS 13999, pp. 486–499, 2023.
https://doi.org/10.1007/978-3-031-40843-4_36

As with other sparse computations, efficiently processing SpMV is essential to fully exploit the benefits of the reduced memory footprint and performance increase offered by the sparse data representation. However, due to its deeply memory-bound nature and irregular memory access patterns, optimizing SpMV on general-purpose processors with a multi-level memory hierarchy can be quite challenging. As such, most state-of-the-art approaches focus on software optimizations and data transformations [1,4,6,15], typically aiming at exploiting the features of a specific class of sparse matrices and/or hardware capabilities of specific devices and systems. Recent studies also focus on designing new fixed-function hardware accelerators specialized for sparse data processing [7].

To demonstrate efficiency of the proposed software or hardware solutions, the state-of-the-art works typically rely on insightful modeling of computer architectures, such as the Original [12] or Cache-Aware Roofline Model [5]. These performance models may provide an intuitive understanding into which optimization techniques allow to better exploit the capabilities of the available compute and memory resources, or they aid in the evaluation of the performance upper-bounds of novel hardware by visual means. To this respect, a common denominator between all the above-mentioned approaches lies in their predominant focus on improving the SpMV efficiency on fixed hardware resources. However, the sheer variability of the sparsity patterns may result in highly irregular memory accesses in SpMV, leading to limited applicability of traditional optimization techniques, such as vectorization. When coupled with its deeply memory-bound nature, these aspects contribute to much of the hardware's computational resources being unused, especially if the architecture has wide SIMD capabilities.

To tackle this issue, in this paper, we propose a methodology, orthogonal to the existing literature, which exploits the insights of the [5] to tailor the capabilities of a general-purpose processor to the requirements of SpMV, enabling its execution to be performant and efficient. The specific contributions of this work can summarized as follows:

- In-depth exploration of the effects that architectural parameters pertaining to the processor's cache and floating-point unit have on the performance of SpMV and the overall system;
- Derivation of the range of attainable Arithmetic Intensities (AIs) for an SpMV kernel, which is used in conjunction with the CARM to determine the performance upper bounds, applicable to all sparse matrices;
- CARM-driven system reparameterization for efficient use of hardware resources, while guaranteeing no performance degradation.

The proposed methodology exploits the CARM's insights to determine the attainable performance given the architecture's performance upper-bounds and the application requirements, which are used to scale the latency of a floating-point unit and the size of the caches to improve SpMV performance and efficiency, thus reducing wasted computational power. These concepts were experimentally verified on a RISC-V CPU in gem5 [8], with the results showing the methodology proposed in this work can achieve a 2.04× performance increase, along with a 14.5× improvement to the efficiency in the usage of computational resources.

2   Background and Related Work

The state-of-the-art approaches tackling the SpMV optimization usually center around the preprocessing of the input dataset, involving the blocking and reordering of matrix elements, in order to improve cache locality or mitigate branch mispredictions. A method for identifying conflict-free execution phases to partition an SpMV dataset and improve its performance is elaborated in [4], while the work proposed in [1] makes use of a coloring engine to perform blocking of a sparse matrix to improve its spatial and temporal locality. Regarding the sparse matrix preprocessing, the study in [6] aims at identifying the types of vertices in the graph it represents, adapting the SpMV kernel to each vertex in order to improve temporal locality, while the work in [15] explores the penalties of incorrect speculation in SpMV execution, thus proposing a preprocessing method that divides the sparse matrix according to the submatrices' non-zero distribution characteristics. Additionally, each submatrix sees its rows reordered to further improve performance.

Several research works focus on development of an entirely new sparse matrix formats for efficient SpMV processing. A novel compressed format optimized for FPGAs that reorders the sparse matrix is proposed in [7], which improves data reuse and requires less fetches from the main memory. A hardware accelerator is designed to process this format, showing overall performance improvements. The work proposed in [10] derives an analytical model for determining effective matrix block size, developing a new column-based blocked SpMV format to exploit the improved memory locality.

A number of studies aim to model the SpMV performance on general-purpose hardware with specialized tools, in order to derive insights that may help in the software optimization process. The work in [13] proposes a comprehensive performance model specific to SpMV, taking into account factors such as the compute pipeline and memory throughput. The insights provided by the model are then used to develop a novel SpMV kernel, demonstrating improved performance. In contrast, a machine learning method for predicting the performance of a sparse matrix across different formats and SpMV kernels was proposed in [14], enabling the selection of the most efficient algorithm for a given matrix.

In terms of more general-purpose performance models, the use of Roofline Modelling has become increasingly popular in recent years, mainly for software optimization and performance evaluation of novel hardware [2]. The CARM [5] stands out in this class of models, by introducing a distinct approach to modelling multiple levels of memory hierarchy in a single plot, thereby providing more detailed and accurate performance characterization, while still retaining the intuitive nature of the original roofline plot [12]. It takes into account the performance limits of a processor's floating-point functional units (F_p, FLOP/s) and the realistically attainable bandwidth of each level of the memory subsystem (Byte/s). By correlating an application's AI (its ratio between FLOPs and bytes) with the attainable performance (F_a, FLOP/s), this modeling approach serves as an intuitive and powerful tool for identifying the architectural limits and application performance. Equation 1 describes this relationship, also dependent on the bandwidth of the memory level in question, B:

$$F_a(AI) = \min\{B \cdot AI, F_p\} \tag{1}$$

The model is well established, seeing use in the Intel® Advisor [9] as a tool for software optimization for both Intel® CPU and GPU devices. In a nutshell, this model facilities the identification of performance bottlenecks and provides valuable insights towards the improvements areas a software or hardware engineer should focus on during the optimization process. Although it is widely used for application characterization and optimization on general-purpose computing platforms, the research on the use of roofline principles for performance evaluation and design of novel hardware is in its very early days [2].

To the best of our knowledge, the work proposed herein is the first study that explores the potential of the CARM for domain-specific hardware design, using its insights to drive the scaling of hardware resources according to application characteristics. For this purpose, we specifically focus on SpMV, where the existing state-of-the-art approaches rely on Roofline Modelling for software optimization, mainly to identify capabilities of hardware resources for the software to exploit. In contrast, we aim to exploit these same insights to identify the application requirements and its realistically attainable performance upperbounds, scaling the capabilities of the underlying hardware to meet them. The proposed methodology can be a valuable tool for RISC-V hardware design space exploration, especially when considering the current trends towards specialized hardware accelerators.

3   Performance Modelling-Driven Hardware Optimization

Our proposed optimization methodology involves the analysis of the arithmetic intensity and size of the matrix in study, applying a reduction to the system's peak performance according to the former and, according to the latter, evaluating the feasibility of scaling one of the cache levels. By applying both of these procedures it is possible to obtain significant improvements in terms of performance, by streaming the data from a memory level with a higher bandwidth, and in terms of efficiency, by lowering the compute roof and reducing the wasted arithmetic performance.

In this section, we detail our proposal and the core concepts it is based on. We begin with a description of the developed SpMV kernel, followed by an analysis of the range of arithmetic intensities it can cover. Then the architectural parameters the methodology focuses on are discussed, along with the methodology itself.

3.1   SpMV Kernel Implementation

SpMV can be written as $A \cdot x = y$, where x and y are dense vectors, and A is a sparse matrix, usually with a low density of non-zero values. In order to represent and process SpMV data efficiently, a number of specialized formats for

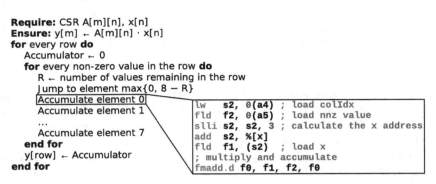

Fig. 1. Pseudo-code and snippet from the optimized SpMV algorithm

sparse matrices exist, one of the most popular of which is Compressed Sparse Rows (CSR), which uses three arrays to encode a sparse matrix: *val* contains the non-zero values, *colIdx* their column indexes, and *rowPtr* the index of each row's first non-zero element within the other two arrays. The format is parsed by first traversing through the rows, which determine the index of the y vector to calculate. Following this, the row's non-zero elements are traversed, using *colIdx* to index the x vector, with which they are multiplied and accumulated. At the end of the row, the accumulated value is stored in the respective index of the y vector.

In this work, we have developed a hand-optimized version of the SpMV kernel for the CSR format written in RISC-V assembly. *rowPtr* and *colIdx* are comprised of 32-bit integers, while the *val* and x arrays use doubles, 64-bit floating-point numbers. Pseudo-code for this implementation is presented in Fig. 1.

This kernel was optimized with a focus on unrolling the inner loop, which iterates over the non-zero elements of each row. This loop is unrolled by a factor of eight, producing eight similar code blocks, each responsible for fetching one non-zero value, its column index and respective element of the x vector, multiplying the two and accumulating the result in a temporary register, like the code snippet in Fig. 1 shows. Our approach is based on dynamically calculating a target jump address within the unrolled portion based on the number of non-zero values remaining in the row, so that no more than that many elements are processed. A more naive translation of the base algorithm would result in an inner loop with one conditional branch per non-zero value, which would cause a significant drop in performance, especially given the unpredictable nature of the matrix's sparsity and the resulting branch mispredictions.

The specific unroll factor of eight was chosen as it can perform a single iteration per row for the vast majority of our dataset, which is obtained from *SuiteSparse* [3] and detailed in the following Section. This unroll factor is flexible and may be adapted depending on the characteristics of the dataset and code size concerns, but is limited to 256 elements per iteration due to the immediate offset associated with the instruction loading the non-zero values (the second instruction in the snippet seen in Fig. 1), which increases by 8 bytes between each unrolled block.

3.2   Arithmetic Intensity Analysis

Through an analysis of the developed SpMV algorithm, it is possible to determine the number of floating-point operations performed and bytes transferred during execution analytically, from the characteristics of the sparse matrix. With these, it is possible to calculate the Arithmetic Intensity of the workload as (2):

$$AI = \frac{FLOPs}{Bytes} = \frac{m + 2 \cdot nnz}{4 + 20 \cdot nnz + 12m} \tag{2}$$

where m is the number of rows and nnz the number of non-zero values of the matrix. By manipulating and simplifying the expression, we can determine the arithmetic intensity exclusively using the ratio between non-zero values and rows, as demonstrated by Eq. 3:

$$AI = \frac{2\frac{nnz}{m} + 1}{\frac{4}{m} + 20\frac{nnz}{m} + 12} \approx \frac{2\frac{nnz}{m} + 1}{20\frac{nnz}{m} + 12}, \text{ if } m \gg 1 \tag{3}$$

By defining the limits of the aforementioned ratio, we can determine the range of arithmetic intensities attainable by the kernel. Excluding matrices with empty rows from this analysis, the minimum ratio is limited to 1 (a minimum of one non-zero value per row). Since there is no upper limit to the ratio of non-zeros and rows, given that rows can be arbitrarily long and dense, it can be concluded that the range of arithmetic intensities covered by the adopted SpMV kernel is $\left[\frac{3}{32}, \frac{1}{10}\right]$. By using the CARM and the determined AI range, it is possible to predict the performance upper bound of any sparse matrix on a particular architecture. To this end, the initial CPU parameterization is benchmarked in order to build its CARM, where the AI range is highlighted, shown in Fig. 2a.

3.3   Arithmetic Performance Analysis

Through the use of the CARM it becomes evident that the maximum attainable performance, limited by the L1 roofline within the AI range and shaded in red in Fig. 2a, is significantly distant from the architecture's peak floating-point performance, which is illustrated by the compute roof. As such, it might be pertinent to evaluate ways in which the architecture's peak performance can be lowered, reducing the wasted compute power. Equation 4 establishes the relationship between the architecture's peak performance (F_p) following a reparameterization with the original peak performance (F_{po}) and a scaling factor, k.

$$F_p = \frac{F_{po}}{k} \tag{4}$$

By using a scaling factor that moves the compute roof to just above the maximum attainable performance (1) at the upper limit of the AI range ($\frac{1}{10}$),

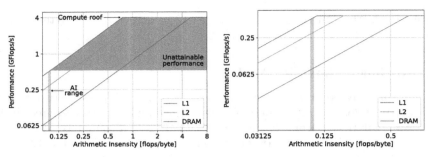

(a) CARM for the original architecture (b) CARM for the scaled architecture,
with the reparameterized FP unit

Fig. 2. The system's CARM before and after reparameterization of the floating-point unit

we guarantee the SpMV performance will not decrease, which is equivalent to (5):

$$k \cdot F_{po} \geq B_{\text{L1} \rightarrow \text{C}} \cdot \frac{1}{10} \tag{5}$$

where $B_{\text{L1} \rightarrow \text{C}}$ is the effective bandwidth from the L1 cache. In other words, and in the context of Eq. 1, this means the memory-bound term of the attainable performance $(B \cdot AI)$ remains the smaller, limiting factor.

This scaling may be achieved in a number of ways which reduce the throughput, such as reducing the core frequency, the issue-width to the floating-point units, or replacing them with a non-pipelined version.

Figure 2 shows an example of the application of these principles, demonstrating how the compute roof approximates itself much closer to the AI range while not impacting its performance roof. This reduction results in a much more efficient use of compute resources, removing much of the unattainable portion of the performance roof.

3.4   Cache Dynamics Analysis

Given the memory-bound nature of SpMV, one obvious method to improve its performance is to raise the memory bandwidth of the system, usually by increasing the cache frequency. However, this is usually tied to the core frequency, also leading to an increase in peak performance, which cannot be exploited. As a result, we instead explore the size of the SpMV dataset and of the caches. If a sparse matrix is large enough to not fit the L1 cache, its SpMV performance will decrease substantially, as it becomes limited by the L2 bandwidth and the associated roofline, which is visibly below the L1 roofline. As such, it could be relevant to increase the size of the L1 cache to fit the set of data. Note that the same logic applies to scaling the L2 cache, which may be more adequate with a large enough sparse matrix that resides in the DRAM.

The size required to house and process a set of CSR data (S, Bytes) can be determined analytically from the properties of the sparse matrix, shown in Eq. 6, where m and n represent the number of rows and columns of the matrix, respectively, and nnz the number of non-zero values. This size includes the y vector to account for caches with a write-back policy, which is the case in our particular setup. Recall that the *rowPtr* and *colIdx* arrays use 32-bit integers, while *val*, x and y use 64-bit floats.

$$S = 12\,m + 8n + 12nnz \tag{6}$$

4   Experimental Results

The tests and design space exploration performed in this work use gem5 [8], a computer architecture simulator with a number of parameterizable CPU models. The ability to expediately modify the architecture through a configuration file aids in the process of characterizing the relationship between the hardware parameters in study and the performance. The Minor CPU, an in-order RISC-V CPU with a four-stage pipeline is used, initially parameterized with a 32 kB L1 cache, a 128 kB L2 cache, 64 byte cache lines, a pipelined FPU and a frequency of 2 GHz. In our experiments, we modify this architecture in two ways: We explore the use of a non-pipelined FPU, configuring its latency and thereby controlling the architecture's compute roof, and modify the size of the caches, increasing their size as necessary to fit particular sparse matrices.

We first explore the performance along the algorithm's AI range, generating synthetic matrices designed to target specific points on that spectrum, thereby evaluating the accuracy applicability of the CARM to SpMV. Following this, the effect of the non-pipelined FPU's latency on the SpMV performance is evaluated, exploring how this affects the compute roof and the efficiency in the use of architectural resources. The size of the L1 cache is then studied, determining the effect it has on matrices of different sizes. Finally, the complete optimization methodology is applied to a particular matrix, scaling the cache and the FPU's latency guided by the insights of the CARM.

4.1   Arithmetic Intensity Exploration

In order to explore the performance within the AI range, two sets of matrices are created, the *L1 set* and *L2 set*, named after the cache level they target and aim to characterize. The matrices within each set are generated to achieve different AIs, sweeping through the range of possible values. This is achieved by keeping the number of non-zero values and columns constant between matrices, varying instead their number of rows. The non-zero elements are evenly distributed through each row, each one having identical and contiguous column indexes, so as to obtain the best possible performance, with maximal cache line reuse. This results in matrices with varying ratios between the number of non-zero elements and number of rows, thereby attaining differing AIs and characterizing

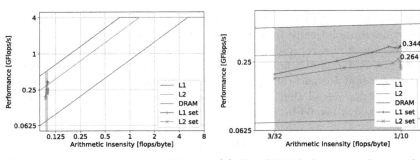

(a) Full view of the system's CARM   (b) The CARM plot zoomed in on the relevant arithmetic intensity range

Fig. 3. Performance of the two matrix sets plotted on the system's CARM

the performance across its range. The first set, characterizing the L1 performance, targets a matrix size of 24 kB, each having 1228 non-zero values and 614 columns. The L2 set targets a size of 64 kB, with 3276 non-zero elements and 1638 columns.

The system is first benchmarked in order to build its CARM, after which the sets of matrices are processed. Each matrix is processed a number of times in order to level the cache data and obtain the median performance figures, which more closely match the CARM's performance rooflines. Figure 3 shows the architecture's CARM with the AI range shaded in red, along with the performance of both sets plotted onto it.

The results of both sets show an increase in performance as the AI increases, consistent with what is expected due to the memory-bound nature of the range in study. The set targeting the L1 cache is capable of delivering a higher performance than the one targeting the L2 cache, as expected due to the higher L1 bandwidth, and resulting higher roofline. However, it is clear both performance curves are positioned significantly below their theoretical maximums, i.e. their respective rooflines. One of the reasons for this behaviour lies in the algorithm's significant complexity compared to the synthetic benchmarks with which the CARM is built, with other dynamics at play such as frequent conditional branching and data dependency. This is expected, as the model represents the performance roof, which is only attainable in ideal conditions. Additionally, the execution paradigm of the in-order, single-issue processor differs from CARM's assumption that memory and floating-point operations execute in parallel, more in-line with superscalar processors. This results in an true performance roof slightly below what the plot illustrates, particularly near the ridge point, where both instruction types would see significant overlap. Despite this, the observed performance still correlates strongly with the visual representation provided by the CARM, which can be used to expeditely determine the performance upper limits of the arithmetic intensity range being operated in.

4.2   Arithmetic Performance Exploration

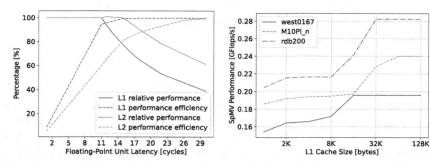

(a) SpMV performance vs floating-point unit latency

(b) SpMV performance vs L1 cache size for three SuiteSparse matrices (see Table 1)

Fig. 4. Design space exploration of the SpMV performance

In this section, the use of the non-pipelined floating-point unit is explored, evaluating the system's peak performance and the SpMV performance for a range of latencies. The aforementioned scaling factor (4) can be substituted directly with the latency, as they have the same relationship with performance – while a pipelined unit can be issued to every cycle, a non-pipelined unit with a latency of k cycles may only be issued to every k cycles, meaning its throughput is scaled down by that same factor. As such, we may calculate the maximum latency that satisfies the condition set by Eq. 5 as Eq. 7 describes, which results in a latency of 7 cycles for this architecture, when considering the L1 cache bandwidth.

$$L = \text{floor} \left(\frac{F_{po}}{B_{\text{L1} \rightarrow \text{C}} \cdot \frac{1}{10}} \right) \tag{7}$$

While evaluating performance improvements is trivial, we propose the use of the *performance efficiency* metric in order to evaluate the benefits of lowering the system's compute roof. This metric measures the ratio between the attained SpMV performance and the system's peak performance, relaying the proximity between the application and the compute roof.

The SpMV performance is evaluated for the two matrices at the upper limit of the AI range, one from each set. These are the closest to the compute roof, where the arithmetic performance has a more significant impact. Figure 4a shows the relative performance compared to the pipelined implementation, and our performance efficiency metric.

The results show that for a small enough latency, the SpMV performance remains unchanged, that is, the performance relative to the pipelined implementation (the solid lines) is 100%. The increase in latency naturally results in an

Table 1. Properties of the three matrices from *SuiteSparse*

Name	west0167	rdb200	M10PI_n
SuiteSparse ID	265	1630	2361
Dimensions	(167, 167)	(200, 200)	(682, 682)
Non-zero elements	507	1120	1633
Size (Bytes)	9436	17452	33248

decrease of the peak performance, which lowers the compute roof and consequently improves the performance efficiency. At 11 cycles, further increases in latency results in a gradual degradation of performance for the L1 matrix, while the performance efficiency begins to slow in growth. This represents the point at which the compute roof meets the original performance figures, meaning the workload now becomes compute-bound and suffers a loss in performance. Note that this is higher than the 7-cycle latency we determined analytically through the performance model, as the SpMV performance does not reach the theoretical roofline, like Fig. 3b shows, for the reasons discussed in the exploration of the AI range. This means there is more room for the compute roof to descend to without reaching the attained performance, and proves the latency determined through our methodology does not impact the performance, like expected.

Note also that the L2 matrix only suffers performance losses at a higher latency, or lower peak-performance. This is expected as it is mostly bound by the lower bandwidth of the L2 roofline, and its original performance was lower than the L1 matrix.

4.3   Cache Size Exploration

The impact of cache size on performance was evaluated by analyzing SpMV performance across a range of L1 cache sizes. For this purpose, three sparse matrices of different sizes were sourced from the *SuiteSparse* [3] matrix collection, the properties of which are shown in Table 1. The resulting performance presented in Fig. 4b.

The results show a clear performance improvement with the increase of the L1 cache size, up to a point. As the cache becomes sizeable enough to contain the entirety of the dataset, further increases to the cache size provide no benefit, as expected. Looking at the *west0167* matrix in particular, whose size is approximately 9 kB, we observe that the performance plateaus when the cache size reaches 16 kB, the smallest size able to fully contain it. The performance then remains constant for any further size increases, as the data is already fully cached and there are no more gains to be had.

4.4   Hardware Optimization

In order to demonstrate the effectiveness of the proposed performance modelling-driven optimization methodology, it is applied to a sparse matrix, again sourced

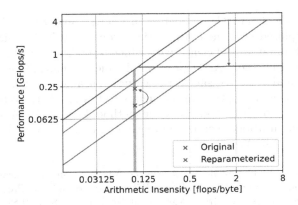

Fig. 5. CARM plot and SpMV performance before and after reparameterization

from the *SuiteSparse* collection. The matrix for which the architecture is optimized is *cryg2500*, possessing 2500 rows and columns, and 12349 non-zero values, equating to an approximate size of 194 kB.

The total size is slightly above the L2 cache's original size of 128 kB, and so the L2 cache is scaled to 256 kB in order to fit the entire dataset. Furthermore, the matrix's AI is calculated through Eq. 3, and used to determine the maximum latency that preserves the attainable performance at that AI, through Eq. 7. This results in an AI of approximately 0.0982 and a latency of 7 cycles, using the bandwidth of the L1 cache. While it might seem logical to use the L2 bandwidth, given that the matrix is too large to fit L1, it should be noted that there is often reuse of the x vector's data from L1. SpMV produces non-linear and unpredictable memory accesses, and certain portions of the x vector may be loaded multiple times per execution, depending on the distribution of the non-zeros across the columns. In this case, these elements will be cached in the L1, despite the majority of the data originating from the L2 cache. If the peak performance were brought down to the L2 roofline, the sections of the kernel that make use of the higher L1 bandwidth would become compute-bound, and the overall performance would decrease slightly. Figure 5 shows the system's CARM plot and SpMV performance before and after the system's reparameterization.

The plot evidences the significant improvement of the SpMV performance resulting from the cache scaling, as well as the improvement to performance efficiency, which results from both changes to the architecture. The SpMV performance goes from 0.111 to 0.226 GFLOP/s following the hardware optimization, an improvement of 2.04×, while the performance efficiency increases from 2.76% to 40%, a substantial reduction in the wasted computational power.

5   Conclusions

We proposed a hardware optimization methodology guided by the lCARM, applied to a RISC-V CPU in order to accelerate and improve the efficiency of SpMV. The architectural parameters in analysis and their effect on performance were explored, and the optimization process resulted in significant gains in performance and in the efficiency with which available resources are used. The insights provided by the CARM proved valuable in determining the optimization approach and the necessary architectural parameters, while also visually and intuitively showcasing the improvements to both metrics. While SpMV was chosen as the focus of this work, this same methodology can be applied to a number of other computational kernels, potentially paving the way for the future of domain-specific RISC-V processors.

Acknowledgement. This project has received funding from the European High Performance Computing Joint Undertaking (JU) under Framework Partnership Agreement No 800928 and Specific Grant Agreement No 101036168 (EPI SGA2) and Grant agreement No 956213 (SparCity). The JU receives support from the European Union's Horizon 2020 research and innovation programme and from Croatia, France, Germany, Greece, Italy, Netherlands, Norway, Portugal, Spain, Sweden, Switzerland and Turkey. It also received funding from FCT (Fundação para a Ciência e a Tecnologia, Portugal), through the UIDB/50021/2020 project.

References

1. Alappat, C., et al.: Level-based blocking for sparse matrices: sparse matrix-power-vector multiplication. IEEE Trans. Parallel Distrib. Syst. **34**(2), 581–597 (2023)
2. Chen, X., Chen, Y., et al.: ReGraph: scaling graph processing on HBM-enabled FPGAs with heterogeneous pipelines. Technical report (2022). arXiv:2203.02676 [cs] type: article
3. Davis, T.A., Hu, Y.: The university of Florida sparse matrix collection. ACM Trans. Math. Softw. **38**(1), 1–25 (2011)
4. Elafrou, A., Goumas, G., Koziris, N.: Conflict-free symmetric sparse matrix-vector multiplication on multicore architectures. In: International Conference for High Performance Computing. Networking, Storage and Analysis, Denver, Colorado, pp. 1–15. ACM (2019)
5. Ilic, A., Pratas, F., Sousa, L.: Cache-aware roofline model: upgrading the loft. IEEE Comput. Archit. Lett. **13**(1), 21–24 (2014)
6. Koohi Esfahani, M., Kilpatrick, P., Vandierendonck, H.: Exploiting in-hub temporal locality in SpMV-based graph processing. In: International Conference on Parallel Processing, Lemont, IL, USA, pp. 1–10. ACM (2021)
7. Li, S., Liu, D., Liu, W.: Optimized data reuse via reordering for sparse matrix-vector multiplication on FPGAs. In: IEEE/ACM International Conference On Computer Aided Design (ICCAD), Munich, Germany, pp. 1–9. IEEE (2021)
8. Lowe-Power, J., et al.: The gem5 Simulator: Version 20.0+. arXiv:2007.03152 [cs] (2020)
9. Marques, D., Duarte, H., et al.: Performance analysis with cache-aware roofline model in intel advisor. In: 2017 International Conference on High Performance Computing & Simulation (HPCS), pp. 898–907 (2017)
10. Namashivavam, N., Mehta, S., Yew, P.C.: Variable-sized blocks for locality-aware SpMV. In: IEEE/ACM International Symposium on Code Generation and Optimization (CGO), Seoul, South Korea, pp. 211–221. IEEE (2021)

11. Shuvo, M.M.H., et al.: Efficient acceleration of deep learning inference on resource-constrained edge devices: a review. Proc. IEEE **111**(1), 42–91 (2023)

12. Williams, S., Waterman, A., Patterson, D.: Roofline: an insightful visual performance model for floating-point programs and multicore architectures. Technical report 1407078 (2009)

13. Xia, T., et al.: A comprehensive performance model of sparse matrix-vector multiplication to guide kernel optimization. IEEE Trans. Parallel Distrib. Syst. **34**(2), 519–534 (2023)

14. Yesil, S., et al.: WISE: predicting the performance of sparse matrix vector multiplication with machine learning. In: ACM Symposium on Principles and Practice of Parallel Programming, Montreal, Canada, pp. 329–341. ACM (2023)

15. Zhao, H., et al.: Exploring better speculation and data locality in sparse matrix-vector multiplication on Intel Xeon. In: IEEE International Conference on Computer Design (ICCD), Hartford, CT, USA, pp. 601–609. IEEE (2020)

Prototyping Reconfigurable RRAM-Based AI Accelerators Using the RISC-V Ecosystem and Digital Twins

Markus Fritscher[1,2]([✉]) [ID], Alessandro Veronesi[1] [ID], Andrea Baroni[1] [ID],
Jianan Wen[1], Thorsten Spätling[4], Mamathamba Kalishettyhalli Mahadevaiah[1],
Norbert Herfurth[1] [ID], Eduardo Perez[1,2] [ID], Markus Ulbricht[1] [ID],
Marc Reichenbach[2] [ID], Amelie Hagelauer[3,4] [ID], and Milos Krstic[1,5] [ID]

[1] IHP - Leibniz Institut für Innovative Mikroelektronik, Frankfurt (Oder), Germany
{fritscher,veronesi,baroni,wen,mahadevaiah,herfurth,perez,ulbricht,
krstic}@ihp-microelectronics.com
[2] BTU Cottbus-Senftenberg, Senftenberg, Germany
marc.reichenbach@b-tu.de
[3] Fraunhofer EMFT Research Institute for Electronic Microsystems and Solid State
Technologies, Munich, Germany
[4] Chair of Micro- and Nanosystems Technology, Technical University of Munich,
Munich, Germany
{amelie.hagelauer,thorsten.spaetling}@tum.de
[5] Institute for Informatics and Computational Science, University of Potsdam,
Potsdam, Germany

Abstract. The recent decades have given advent to the rise of sophisticated High Performance Computing (HPC) accelerators, vastly speeding up calculations. In the last years dedicated AI accelerators, meant for the evaluation of Artificial Neural Networks, have gathered traction. Resistive Random Access Memory (RRAM) devices are a possible future candidate for these accelerators since crossbar implementations allow for the evaluation of matrix vector multiplications in $\mathcal{O}(1)$. Unfortunately integrating these novel devices into accelerators challenges since they still suffer from device variations and require sophisticated peripheral circuitry. Additionally, suitable design flows are missing since these cells are difficult to integrate into the traditional digital flow. While multiple foundries are able to fabricate promising RRAM prototypes suffering less from device variations, full system integration tends to be lacking. Fortunately the rise of the RISC-V ecosystem has enabled eased access to a fully customizable ISA. We propose to exploit the advantages of the RRAM devices combined with the flexibility of RISC-V cores by integrating multiple RRAM-based blocks into a RISC-V core via Memory Mapped I/O (MMIO), resulting in an architecture which can be reconfigured in software. Additionally, we propose a possible approach for the design, simulation and verification of large RRAM systems, namely setting up three closely intertwined simulation environments and illustrate its applicability by integrating, characterizing and validating a RRAM-based MVM block fabricated in 130 nm technology. Finally, we demonstrate that RRAM technologies might be ready for HPC.

© The Author(s), under exclusive license to Springer Nature Switzerland AG 2023
A. Bienz et al. (Eds.): ISC High Performance 2023 Workshops, LNCS 13999, pp. 500–514, 2023.
https://doi.org/10.1007/978-3-031-40843-4_37

Keywords: RRAM · HPC · RISC-V · ANN · System integration · ASIC · EDA

1   Introduction

In 2002 most entries of the famous Top500 list of the fastest supercomputers [12] relied on CPUs for the computations. In the following decades dedicated accelerator cards, such as the Xeon Phi and Nvidia Tesla GPGPUs, have emerged, taking over an ever-increasing fraction of total systems within the list. In November 2022 80% of the Top10 systems within the list use kinds of dedicated accelerators to achieve their performance. Apparently, general purpose architectures, such as CPUs, struggle to provide adequate performance, which has supported the rise of these accelerators. In recent years more specialized accelerators, for example made specifically for artificial neural networks (ANN) like the Google TPU, have been proposed and evaluated [16]. While they are not as flexible as GPGPUs they yield advantages regarding both ANN performance and performance per watt.

Resistive Random Access Memory (RRAM) is a promising technology for future accelerators since it can serve as storage as well as computing, providing a solution for the von-Neumann bottleneck [20]. However, since RRAM is a rather new technology, researchers still struggle to mitigate device-to-device (DTD) and cycle-to-cycle (CTC) variations [18]. Fortunately ANNs have proven to be partially tolerant towards these errors [4], which enables the adoption of this novel technology.

Various cores have been implemented using RRAM technology; Truong et al. were able to demonstrate that their RRAM-based design implementing bit-pipelined processing units can outperform both a recent GPU and a recent CPU by one and two orders of magnitude respectively [13]. Zhu et al. have implemented STT-MRAM blocks within a RISC-V system using a 28 nm node [19]. Peters et. al. have recently integrated 800 kB of RRAM cells with an ARM Cortex M0 core within 28 nm technology and were able to conclude that "overall, 28 nm RRAM is an adequate successor of embedded flash" [10].

Crossbar implementations provide a very efficient basic computing element, performing matrix vector multiplications in $\mathcal{O}(1)$ [6,11]. Additionally, the same crossbar can be used both for data storage and computation, breaching the boundaries of von-Neumann architectures. Xia et al. have provided a detailed

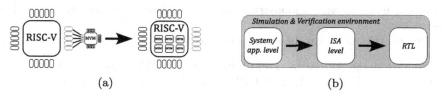

(a)   (b)

Fig. 1. Proposed concept (a) and required simulation & verification environment (b).

introduction to RRAM crossbar MVM implementations and a thorough investigation how RRAM device variations could be mitigated by using appropriate mapping algorithms [17]. They were able to demonstrate that a 4-bit RRAM ANN implementation allows for sufficient accuracy within a benchmark dataset by performing inference with hand-written digits. Unfortunately their work lacks a full-system integration.

The logical next step lies within adapting these novel accelerators for the needs of HPC, using larger crossbars and higher bit-widths. Unfortunately, while researchers have built efficient RRAM-based implementations, these designs typically use embedded interfaces such as SPI. As a consequence integrating these blocks into larger systems is difficult both for architectural and tooling reasons. Furthermore, the traditional mixed signal simulation and verification environments struggle with the computational complexity and inaccuracies of RRAM models, leading to long simulation times and incomplete verification. Within this work we propose to move away from this traditional approach in favor of a three-step design and verification approach, each addressing a separate challenge of RRAM integration. However, this involves setting up a sophisticated tool flow.

Directly integrating these prototypes into dedicated cores such as RISC-V CPUs might be a possible mitigation to overcome both these challenges. RISC-V is an open, extensible Instruction Set Architecture (ISA) [2,5], unlike other architectures such as x86 or ARM the designer can easily both adapt and extend the core. This flexibility has lead to the development of core and SoC generators such as Vexriscv and LiteX [7]. A sophisticated set of tools and simulators has been developed, assisting with the design and simulation on different levels. Cores such as the Rocketchip [1] provide an interface for the implementation of accelerators called RoCC. Damian et al. have proposed an interface for ISA extensions named *SCAIE-V* [3]. Unfortunately, these extensions might not be flexible enough for a set of reconfigurable RRAM crossbars since the RRAM blocks can not only be utilized both for storage and computations but also combined to perform operations collaboratively. We propose to use MMIO instead as a means of integration.

Within this paper we propose to extend on this ecosystem to elevate a RRAM-based vector-matrix multiplication block from an SPI-based prototyping block to a fully integrated reconfigurable RISC-V based AI accelerator (see Fig. 1). Additionally, we demonstrate how the overall design efforts can be reduced significantly by reusing and adapting parts of the RISC-V ecosystem. As an example for the flexibility of this approach we will compare the effect of choosing two different RRAM programming algorithms for initializing the devices. Finally, we will demonstrate the performance of the integrated architecture.

Our contributions can be summarized as follows:

– We have designed, layouted and fabricated a RRAM-based MVM accelerator block and a Vexriscv RISC-V CPU in IHP[1] 130 nm SG13S technology.

---

[1] Leibniz-Institut für innovative Mikroelektronik.

- We evaluated a RRAM based non-von-Neumann CPU architecture
- We demonstrate a concept for the simulation and validation of large systems embedding RRAM, namely integrating Digital Twins of RRAM blocks into three different simulation environments, each covering different aspects:
    - System/Application level (building on Python) covering individual blocks
    - ISA level (built on Spike) [14] covering the MVM block interactions
    - Register Transfer Level (RTL) (built on the LiteX SoC generator [7]) validating the digital implementation and interfaces
- We demonstrate that RRAM technologies are suitable for future RISC-V based HPC accelerators.

2   Methodology

Integrating novel RRAM-based accelerator cores into large systems is challenging since the intrinsic variability, the computational complexity of the utilized models and the differences to classical von-Neumann architectures render them difficult to integrate into the classical chip design flow. Within this section we propose a methodology to address both design and simulating problems. We propose to simulate and prototype on three different levels of abstraction, starting from application level and ending in the RTL, ultimately creating multiple digital twins of the to-be fabricated chip. We will firstly introduce the implemented hardware blocks and subsequently illustrate our concept for system integration and simulation.

2.1   MVM Block

We have designed a RRAM-based matrix-vector multiplication block in IHP's 130 nm CMOS technology node. This block multiplies a vector of 16 2-bit inputs with a matrix of 16×16 2-bit weights by employing a 16×16 1T-1R RRAM-crossbar. The RRAM device is made using a $TiN/HfO_2/Ti/TiN$ Metal-Insulator-Metal (MIM) structure using a 8 nm HfO_2 layer deposited with ALD. The embedded transistor uses a W/L ratio of 15/13. The prototype chip, entailing the MVM block as well as a SPI controller block, is illustrated in Fig. 2.

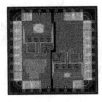
(a) Design

(b) Microscope image

Fig. 2. Design (a) and microscope image (b) of the fabricated MVM prototype chip.

Due to the analog nature of in-crossbar multiplications the output needs to be digitized in order to be usable for subsequent calculations. Shafiee et al. have devised an equation to determine the required ADC resolution when performing in-crossbar-multiplications (Eq. 1), where R depicts the rows, v depicts the input bitwidth while w depicts the weight bitwidth [11]. Subsequently, this mandates the usage of an 8-bit ADC to properly represent the outputs of this operation.

$$A = log(R) + v + w - 1 \tag{1}$$

While the multiplication itself (within the RRAM crossbar) happens in negligible time [17] each ADC bit requires about 100 ns for proper digitization. Subsequently, each multiplication takes about 1 μs. Given that each vector-matrix multiplication entails 256 operations this leads to an overall performance per block of

$$\frac{256Op}{1\mu s} = \frac{256\text{Mega}Op}{s} \tag{2}$$

Additionally, each reprogramming of weights takes further time and might entail using sophisticated algorithms [9]. We ignore this overhead for our investigations since we assume that the same weights are being reused often.

2.2 Combining Multiple MVM Blocks

There are three fundamental ways to configure multiple MVM blocks (depicted in Fig. 3): They can either perform individual multiplications (left), be combined to allow for high-precision multiplications (middle) or serve as mere memory blocks (right). Since this is only defined by providing appropriate controls via the memory bus this can easily be reconfigured at runtime.

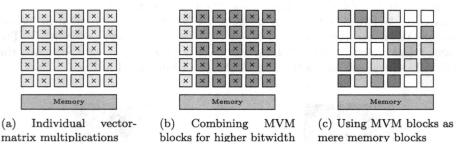

(a) Individual vector-matrix multiplications

(b) Combining MVM blocks for higher bitwidth

(c) Using MVM blocks as mere memory blocks

Fig. 3. Fundamental ways to utilize MVM blocks.

In our proposed design the main memory serves as an interface to both provide input and control data to the individual blocks and to retrieve the multiplication results. Utilizing n of the individual MVM blocks leads to a combined performance of

$$n \times \frac{256 Op}{1\mu s} = n \times \frac{256 \mathrm{Mega} Op}{s} \tag{3}$$

Subsequently, plugging in e.g. 100 blocks leads to a combined performance of 25.6GigaOp/s while requiring a chip area of about 100 mm^2 in 130 nm technology. While this cannot (yet) compete with the computational density of e.g. a recent HPC GPU the power efficiency greatly benefits from the nonvolatile nature of the RRAM devices - the weights stay within the MVM blocks when the chip (or parts thereof) is powered down. The evaluation section will provide insights into how the performance scales for larger crossbars.

Multiple blocks can be combined into a single high-precision block by combining them as depicted in Fig. 4. The inputs vector bits are split up upon MVM blocks by applying shift operations. Similarly, the final result vector can be put together by applying shift and add operations to the individual MVM block outputs. Higher bit accuracies can be achieved in a similar fashion.

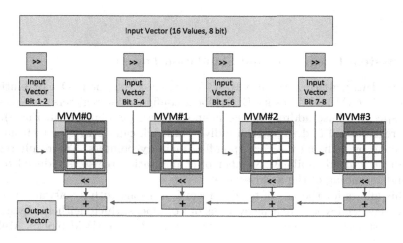

Fig. 4. Concept: This schematic depicts how multiple MVM block can be combined into one high-accuracy MVM block.

Lastly, the embedded crossbars can be used as mere storage elements, providing nonvolatility. This emphasizes that this approach breaches the boundaries of von-Neumann architectures - the same blocks can be used both for computation *and* storage. In the following we will evaluate solutions to the inevitable challenges for the design and verification environment.

2.3 RISC-V Core

We use the VexRiscv core [15], since it is highly configurable using a plugin system; Available configurations span from a tiny core utilizing about 500 LUTs and Flipflops within an FPGA implementation to sophisticated SoC designs. It can be configured to support a multitude of RISC-V instruction set variants and provides interfaces to established on-chip interfaces. Its integration with various debugging frameworks significantly eases handling multi-level simulations (see next Section). We have designed and taped out a Vexriscv by using the OpenLane flow and the IHP 130 nm PDK; The design is depicted in Fig. 5.

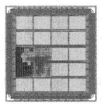

Fig. 5. The Vexriscv RV32IM core taped out using IHP 130 nm technology.

2.4   System Integration and Simulation Layers

System Integration. We use RISC-V's memory-mapped IO capabilities to integrate RRAM-based blocks. Each blocks configuration registers are accessible via a specified base address in the memory space (as depicted in Fig. 6). The input registers r0 and r1 of each individual block can be written to from arbitrary code by utilizing the corresponding memory pointers. The result register r2 can be fetched similarly. Number of configuration registers reduced to ease the understanding of the architecture.

This allows for the use of flexible reconfigurations within software, which is highly beneficial when creating systems out of blocks which neither fully categorize into storage nor compute elements such as RRAM-MVM-blocks. Multiple

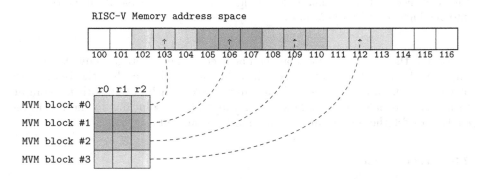

Fig. 6. Concept: Serial mapping of MVM blocks in RISC-V memory address space.

blocks can easily be added to a simulation environment and subsequently to the actual implementation. This enables the efficient exploitation of this non von-Neumann architecture.

Simulation/Synthesis. We propose to introduce three levels of abstraction (Fig. 7) before putting a RRAM-based design to silicon:

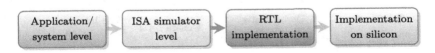

Fig. 7. Three levels of simulation environments entailing different levels of abstraction need to be implemented before moving a complex RRAM-based-design to silicon.

Any RRAM-based simulation or model needs to be fundamentally based on raw device measurement data in order to be true to actual implementations. Subsequently, we propose an (automated) process to generate *Digital Twins* (DT) of actual hardware which are fast to simulate and true to actual devices (Fig. 8). Raw measurements of a large number of devices (This work: 4096 devices per digital twin) serve as the ground truth. We take measurements after each individual step and each individual target state of a given programming algorithm (see Fig. 10). Subsequently, we fit 100 different statistical distributions per dataset, select the distribution yielding the lowest RMSE for each and combine that with parametrizations of ADC circuits to form a DT which is representative of actual device behaviour. This is fully automated, comparing different wafers, devices or programming algorithms merely entails doing appropriate measurements and rerunning our DT creation framework.

The first simulation environment simulates on the application/system level, determining whether a given application can cope with the errors caused by the inherent variability of RRAM blocks. While this is not true to the hardware implementation this provides high accuracy regarding RRAM variabilities. This simulation level does not yet include the mapping of inputs and weights to individual crossbars.

The next step is a significant step towards being true to the hardware; We have written a simulation model of our platform (in C++) and have introduced it to the Spike instruction level simulator [14]. This includes the mapping of multiplications to crossbars and the implemented DAC/ADC resolution while still being true to device variations. This is significantly slower than the previous evaluation, but still fast enough to run simulations to evaluate whether a given crossbar mapping and implementation can deal with RRAM variations. Arbitrary code utilizing an arbitrary number of MVM blocks can be evaluated.

Lastly, the required interfaces to the configuration registers and the specifics of the implementation need to be evaluated. We use Verilator to co-simulate our VexRiscv RISC-V implementation with our simulation model of the MVM block.

The LiteX environment [7] vastly eases this simulation. The RRAM variation simulation is simplistic since the focus lies on validating the system design itself. This is closely related to the implementation on silicon since a) the digital RTL can directly be synthesized and b) the synthesized netlist can be plugged into the simulation. Additionally, digitally characterized versions of the MVM design can be integrated as macrocells. A detailed description and evaluation of this environment will be part of a later publication.

Fig. 8. Steps required for Digital Twins for RRAM-based blocks. We create many individual DT in order to evaluate the RRAM block at different phases of multiple algorithms.

3   Evaluation

Within this section we will demonstrate the applicability of our approach by creating three individual sets of DTs of the MVM block and demonstrating how this helps the design process. Firstly, we will describe the measurement data and model creation. Subsequently, we will run an application level simulation in order to determine which out of two RRAM device programming algorithms is better suited for tasks at the application level. We proceed to fully integrate the block into the Spike ISA simulator, evaluating the correct implementation of the algorithm depicted in Fig. 4. Subsequently, we will discuss the achievable performance and the suitability of current RRAM technology for HPC.

3.1   Creating Models from Raw Measurement Data

Albeit RRAM is a promising technology it still suffers from process variations, which means that individual devices might store incorrect values. We have measured raw data on 1T1R 64 × 64 crossbars of memristors fabricated using IHP 130 nm SG13S technology (as also used for the MVM blocks) to investigate these variations. We have defined four different states LRS1, LRS2, LRS3 and HRS at certain resistance values. We applied two different writing algorithms, namely the ISPVA-100 and the IGVVA-100 algorithm (as described in [8]) to achieve programming the devices to these states. The results after completing the algorithms are depicted in Fig. 9. The results after each individual programming step are depicted in Fig. 10.

Since this involves 20 individual programming pulses per algorithm we generate 40 Digital Twins from this raw data in order to fully represent the device variation. Ultimately an individual Digital Twin per crossbar size, writing algorithm and pulse count is constructed, leading to high simulation accuracy. These serve as the fundamental basis for the following simulations.

One can see that it is not possible to accurately write a given resistance, each state actually yields a distribution of resistances. These distributions overlap, resulting in errors on the system level even when doing digital calculations. Unfortunately the effect on analog calculations might be stronger since even slight variations affect computation results. This ultimately creates the need for the following simulations and evaluations.

3.2 Application Level

Figure 9 depicts the device variation after completing the last cycle. This poses two questions on the application level: a) Can a given algorithm cope with the resulting errors? b) Running a complete writing algorithm entails applying about 20 programming pulses which takes significant time. Will the computation still yield acceptably accurate results when only the first x programming pulses are completed? In the following we describe the impact on both multiplication and storage operations. We simulated 10^5 individual calculations for each individual programming pulse, algorithm and approach.

We use our DT approach to simulate analog multiplications on individual MVM blocks with an increasing number of completed programming cycles for setting the weights. The inputs were scaled between 0V and 1V when doing the multiplication simulations. Subsequently, a relative error of 0.3 is unacceptable while an error of 0.05 is reasonable. The results are depicted in Fig. 11a. The error is quite severe when only a few pulses have been applied to program the weights. Fortunately, the error becomes much smaller for relatively small number of programming pulses, five pulses seem to be enough when using the *ISPVA* algorithm. Surprisingly, for this specific implementation, the more sophisticated *IGVVA* algorithm gets outperformed by the *ISPVA* algorithm on system level.

Using the MVM blocks as mere digital storage leads to an error distribution as depicted in Fig. 11b. A higher number of pulses, namely seven, is required

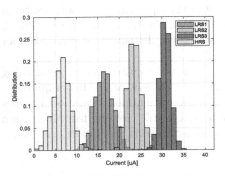

(a) Results: ISPVA-100 algorithm.

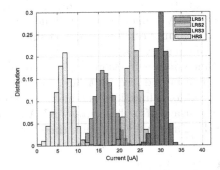

(b) Results: IGVVA-100 algorithm.

Fig. 9. Histogram of resistances when using two different writing algorithms to program a total of 4096 RRAM devices fabricated using the IHP 130 nm node.

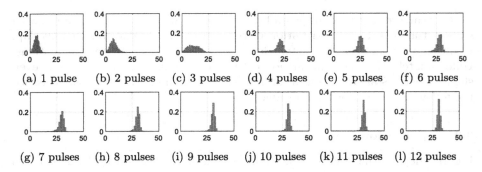

(a) 1 pulse   (b) 2 pulses   (c) 3 pulses   (d) 4 pulses   (e) 5 pulses   (f) 6 pulses

(g) 7 pulses   (h) 8 pulses   (i) 9 pulses   (j) 10 pulses   (k) 11 pulses   (l) 12 pulses

Fig. 10. Histogram of resistances after having applied an increasing number of ISPVA-100 programming pulses to 4096 RRAM devices. The current target has been set to 30 uA which is defined as the LRS3 state. The x axis depicts the current (in uA) while the y axis depicts the distribution. We ommited the last 10 programming pulses. The histogram derived after the very last programming pulse is part of Fig. 9.

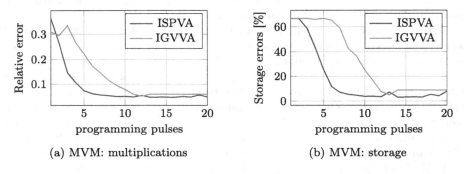

(a) MVM: multiplications   (b) MVM: storage

Fig. 11. Simulation results: Using the MVM blocks for multiplication (left) and storage (right) leads to the depicted corresponding relative errors and erroneously stored values.

to adequately reduce the error. Again, the IGVVA algorithm gets outperformed by the ISPVA algorithm. Subsequently, the ISPVA algorithm should be utilized. The remaining error is expected since the statistical distributions shown earlier show a small overlap.

Since only a fraction of programming pulses are required the programming time can be reduced by a factor of 75% and 65% respectively. This emphasizes the need for a high level simulation - having a separate application model allows for the usage of high-accuracy RRAM model while still yielding fast simulation speeds. The total simulation time for these investigations was below one hour.

3.3   ISA Level

Within the previous section we have shown that the MVM block yields an acceptable error both for multiplications and storage. However, as mentioned in Sect. 2.2, one of the great benefits of this approach lies within the flexibility,

MVM blocks can not only be used individually, they can also be combined in order to achieve higher accuracy.

Since we proposed a memory mapped I/O approach this entails the need for evaluating both the simulated MVM block and the environment running it together. The Spike ISA simulator provides a great starting point since it allows both for the execution of individual instructions and the modification of involved memory addresses while being true to actually run instructions. Subsequently, we have created and integrated a suitable simulation model for the MVM block.

We have introduced a model of our block into Spike in order to validate the correct implementation of the concept depicted in Fig. 4. We have run 10^4 individual simulations within our DT containing different counts of MVM blocks embedding different crossbar sizes and deducted the number of simulated matrix operations per second. The performance numbers relevant for our implemented block are the numbers given for a crossbar size of 16. The results are depicted in Fig. 12. The left image depicts the DT running as pure x86 code (serving as a baseline) while the right image depicts the DTs performance when integrated within Spike. Benchmarks run on a single Intel i9-12900K CPU core. The difference in performance is to-be expected since the Spike simulation entails emulating a RISC-V CPU running arbitrary code interacting with the DT instead of merely simulating the DT. While this simulation takes a significant performance hit from the Spike integration it is still fast enough to validate the involved concepts while taking device variations into account.

3.4   Overall System Performance and Suitability for HPC

The overall system performance when placing differently sized crossbars is depicted in Fig. 13a (numbers derived analytically). It becomes apparent that future work should introduce larger crossbars since the total number of op/s

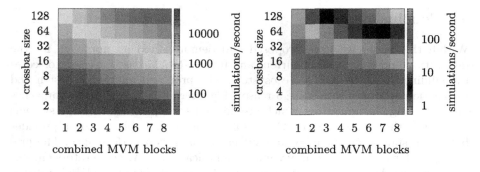

(a) Pure x86 implementation   (b) MVM block integrated within Spike

Fig. 12. Running 10^4 individual simulations using Digital Twins both when running as pure x86 code (a) and integrated within the Spike ISA simulator (b) yields these performance metrics.

increases strongly with crossbar size while the ADC conversion time increases rather slowly. Subsequently, placing multiple large crossbars within a design is likely to be competitive with recent CPUs and GPUs. According to our simulation results (Fig. 13b) current RRAM technology can achieve a weight storage error of 5–10% and a relative multiplication error of 0.05, even when placed within large crossbars. Each data point represents an individual DT running a set of individual simulations. We have demonstrated in an earlier publication that ANNs can cope with this kind of error [4]. Subsequently, this technology might be a possible candidate for future ANN accelerators. Using the RISC-V platform in combination with MMIO significantly eases the prototyping process and might provide a stepping stone for future integrations. However, larger crossbars implementations than 16×16 seem required for real performance benefits.

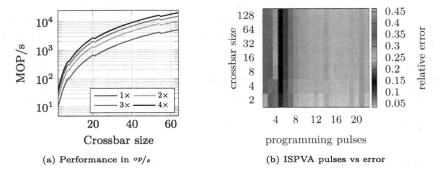

(a) Performance in op/s (b) ISPVA pulses vs error

Fig. 13. Achieved performance (a) and the required number of programming pulses to reach a given multiplication accuracy (b) for different crossbar sizes and counts.

4   Conclusion

Within this paper we have proposed and demonstrated an approach for the integration and validation of current and future RRAM-based accelerator cores by building upon the RISC-V ecosystem. The proposed multi-step design and verification approach seems like a reasonable alternative to classical approaches like mixed-signal simulations which are difficult to implement for large systems embedding these novel devices. Our results indicate that this approach provides both high simulation accuracy and sufficient simulation performance. The presented performance and accuracy numbers indicate that AI accelerators embedding large RRAM crossbars might be a good candidate for future HPC systems.

Acknowledgement. This work was supported in parts by the BMBF by the Federal Ministry of Education and Research (BMBF, Germany) in the Projects iCampus II (Project No. 16ES1128K), KI-PRO (Project No. 16ES1002), KI-IoT (Project No. 16ME0092), HEP (Project No. 16KIS1339K) and 6G-RIC (Project No. 16KISK026).

The authors gratefully acknowledge the scientific support and HPC resources provided by the Erlangen National High Performance Computing Center (NHR@FAU) of the Friedrich-Alexander-Universität Erlangen-Nürnberg (FAU). The hardware is funded by the German Research Foundation (DFG). The authors would also like to thank Tim Henkes (Hochschule RheinMain) for creating the Vexriscv layout and Frank Vater (IHP) for continuous support.

References

1. Asanovic, K., et al.: The rocket chip generator. EECS Department, University of California, Berkeley, Technical report UCB/EECS-2016-17 4 (2016)
2. Asanović, K., Patterson, D.A.: Instruction sets should be free: the case for RISC-V. EECS Department, University of California, Berkeley, Technical report UCB/EECS-2014-146 (2014)
3. Damian, M., Oppermann, J., Spang, C., Koch, A.: SCAIE-V: an open-source scalable interface for ISA extensions for RISC-V processors. In: Proceedings of the 59th ACM/IEEE Design Automation Conference, pp. 169–174 (2022)
4. Fritscher, M., et al.: Mitigating the effects of RRAM process variation on the accuracy of artificial neural networks. In: Orailoglu, A., Jung, M., Reichenbach, M. (eds.) SAMOS 2021. LNCS, vol. 13227, pp. 401–417. Springer, Cham (2022). https://doi.org/10.1007/978-3-031-04580-6_27
5. Greengard, S.: Will RISC-V revolutionize computing? Commun. ACM **63**(5), 30–32 (2020)
6. Hu, M., Li, H., Chen, Y., Wu, Q., Rose, G.S., Linderman, R.W.: Memristor crossbar-based neuromorphic computing system: a case study. IEEE Trans. Neural Netw. Learn. Syst. **25**(10), 1864–1878 (2014)
7. Kermarrec, F., Bourdeauducq, S., Badier, H., Le Lann, J.C.: LiteX: an open-source SoC builder and library based on Migen Python DSL. In: OSDA 2019, Colocated with DATE 2019 Design Automation and Test in Europe (2019)
8. Milo, V., et al.: Accurate program/verify schemes of resistive switching memory (RRAM) for in-memory neural network circuits. IEEE Trans. Electron Devices **68**(8), 3832–3837 (2021)
9. Perez, E., Zambelli, C., Mahadevaiah, M.K., Olivo, P., Wenger, C.: Toward reliable multi-level operation in RRAM arrays: improving post-algorithm stability and assessing endurance/data retention. IEEE J. Electron Devices Soc. **7**, 740–747 (2019)
10. Peters, C., Adler, F., Hofmann, K., Otterstedt, J.: Reliability of 28nm embedded RRAM for consumer and industrial products. In: 2022 IEEE International Memory Workshop (IMW), pp. 1–3. IEEE (2022)
11. Shafiee, A., et al.: ISAAC: a convolutional neural network accelerator with in-situ analog arithmetic in crossbars. ACM SIGARCH Comput. Archit. News **44**(3), 14–26 (2016)
12. Strohmaier, E., Meuer, H.W., Dongarra, J., Simon, H.D.: The TOP500 list and progress in high-performance computing. Computer **48**(11), 42–49 (2015)
13. Truong, M.S., et al.: RACER: bit-pipelined processing using resistive memory. In: MICRO-54: 54th Annual IEEE/ACM International Symposium on Microarchitecture, pp. 100–116 (2021)
14. Various: Spike RISC-V isa simulator. https://github.com/riscv-software-src/riscv-isa-sim (2023)

15. Various: VexRiscv RISC-V implementation. https://github.com/SpinalHDL/VexRiscv (2023)
16. Wang, Y.E., Wei, G.Y., Brooks, D.: Benchmarking TPU, GPU, and CPU platforms for deep learning. arXiv preprint arXiv:1907.10701 (2019)
17. Xia, L., Gu, P., Li, B., Tang, T., Yin, X., Huangfu, W., Yu, S., Cao, Y., Wang, Y., Yang, H.: Technological exploration of RRAM crossbar array for matrix-vector multiplication. J. Comput. Sci. Technol. **31**(1), 3–19 (2016)
18. Yu, S., Guan, X., Wong, H.S.P.: On the switching parameter variation of metal oxide RRAM-part II: model corroboration and device design strategy. IEEE Trans. Electron Devices **59**(4), 1183–1188 (2012)
19. Zhu, L., et al.: Heterogeneous 3D integration for a RISC-V system with STT-MRAM. IEEE Comput. Archit. Lett. **19**(1), 51–54 (2020)
20. Zou, X., Xu, S., Chen, X., Yan, L., Han, Y.: Breaking the von Neumann bottleneck: architecture-level processing-in-memory technology. Sci. China Inf. Sci. **64**(6), 160404 (2021)

Optimization of the FFT Algorithm
on RISC-V CPUs

Xiang Zhao[1,2], Xianyi Zhang[3](✉), and Yiwei Zhang[2]

[1] Ocean University of China, Qingdao, China
[2] Institute of Computing Technology, Chinese Academy of Sciences, Beijing, China
[3] PerfXLab (Beijing) Technologies Co., Ltd., Beijing, China
`xianyi@perfxlab.com`

Abstract. The emergence of RISC-V as a reduced instruction set architecture has brought several advantages such as openness, flexibility, scalability, and efficiency compared to other commercial ISAs. It has gained significant popularity, especially in the field of high-performance computing. However, there is a lack of high-performance implementations of numerical algorithms, including the Fast Fourier Transform (FFT) algorithm. To address this issue, the paper focuses on optimizing the butterfly network, butterfly kernel, and single instruction multiple data (SIMD) operations to achieve efficient calculations for FFT with a computation scale of 2^n on a RISC-V architecture CPUs. The experimental results demonstrate a significant improvement in the performance of the FFT algorithm library implemented using the proposed optimizations compared to existing implementations like FFTW on RISC-V CPUs.

Keywords: FFT · RISC-V · SIMD · Cooley-Tukey

1 Introduction and Motivation

RISC-V [1] is an emerging open-source instruction set architecture, which was designed and proposed by the University of California, Berkeley, in 2010. Because of its openness, accessibility, and user-customizable characteristics, scientific and industrial communities have widely supported and used it. But because it was proposed late, its software ecology is not perfect compared to the x86 and Arm instruction set architecture. To establish a complete, stable, and efficient RISC-V software ecosystem, community workers need to make continuous efforts in RISC-V software development and architecture promotion.

FFT [2,3] is a fast algorithm for calculating discrete Fourier transform or inverse transform. It is one of the thirteen "dwarfs" [4] in science and engineering. It has outstanding achievements in partial differential solutions, signal processing, image processing, and bioengineering. With the advent of the era of big data and artificial intelligence to meet real-time requirements, the requirements

X. Zhang—This work is partly supported by Beijing Municipal Science and Technology Program under Grant No. Z211100004421002.

A. Bienz et al. (Eds.): ISC High Performance 2023 Workshops, LNCS 13999, pp. 515–525, 2023.
https://doi.org/10.1007/978-3-031-40843-4_38

for the efficiency of FFT algorithms in various fields are also increasing. In the RISC-V software ecological environment, there is no FFT algorithm optimization for the RISC-V architecture. Therefore, the FFT algorithm on the RISC-V platform is of great value.

In this paper, we proposed a series of optimization methods combined with the characteristic of RISC-V for FFT. We implemented a high-performance FFT Library called PerfMPL-FFT on RISC-V CPUs. First, we discuss the optimization and realization of the principle of the FFT algorithm. Since the twiddle factor in the discrete Fourier transform has three properties: periodicity, symmetry, and reducibility, we can use these three properties to optimize its Cooley-Tukey FFT algorithm further so that it can be realized in the mathematical calculation—the most simplified [6]. In terms of algorithm implementation, we used the SIMD vectorization, and vector features of the RISC-V instruction set architecture to assemble and implement the optimized FFT algorithm manually and optimized the selection and sequencing of instructions to maximize and improve the performance of the FFT algorithm library based on the RISC-V architecture, and finally realize a high-performance algorithm library based on the RISC-V CPUs. The experimental results show that: on the RISC-V platform, the PerfMPL-FFT algorithm library implemented in this paper has a better performance improvement for DFT processing of single-precision and double-precision data compared with the open-source FFTW library.

The key contributions of this paper are summarized as follows:

- We propose a set of optimization strategies and methods for the butterfly kernel in the Cooley-Tukey FFT algorithm.
- According to the characteristics of the RISC-V architecture system, we designed an optimization technology system for the FFT algorithm, which improves the performance of the FFT algorithm on the RISC-V platform.
- We implemented an FFT algorithm library on the RISC-V platform, which has a good performance advantage.

The remainder of this paper is organized as follows. Section 2 introduces the essential background of the Cookey Tuky FFT algorithm. Section 3 first introduces the optimization of the FFT algorithm and then introduces the assembly optimization and algorithm implementation for the characteristics of the RISC-V instruction set architecture. Section 4 presents the experimental results and analyzes them. Finally, Sect. 5 concludes the paper.

2   Background

Discrete Fourier transform is an essential algorithm in high-performance computing, and its basic definition is shown in Eq. (1) [7].

$$Y(k) = \sum_{n=0}^{N-1} x(n)W_N^{nk} = \sum_{n=0}^{N-1} x(n)e^{\frac{-2\pi i}{N}nk} \tag{1}$$

where $x(n)$ is the input sequence and $Y(k)$ is the output sequence ($n, k \in [0, N-1]$). $W_N^{nk} = e^{\frac{-2\pi i}{N} nk}$ is called the twiddle factor, and $i = \sqrt{-1}$ is the imaginary unit.

When N is large enough, the computational efficiency of DFT becomes very low. To meet high-performance requirements, researchers use the periodicity $\left(W_N^{k+N} = W_N^k\right)$, reducibility $\left(W_N^{mnk} = W_{N/m}^{nk}\right)$, and symmetry $\left(W_N^{\frac{N}{2}+k} = -W_N^k\right)$ simplifies the discrete Fourier transform in different forms. The Cookey-Tukey FFT algorithm [8] is one of the most widely used implementation methods. It uses the characteristics of the rotation factor, adopts the strategy of divide and conquers, and recursively resolves a large-scale DFT into multiple small-scale DFTs, reducing the algorithm complexity from $O(n^2)$ to $O(nlogn)$. Taking the input scale of DFT as an even number as an example, the decomposition method of the Cookey-Tukey algorithm is shown in Eq. (2).

$$
\begin{aligned}
Y(k) &= \sum_{n=0}^{N-1} x(n) W_N^{nk} \\
&= \sum_{n=0}^{\frac{N}{2}-1} x(2n) W_N^{2nk} + \sum_{n=0}^{\frac{N}{2}-1} x(2n+1) W_N^{(2n+1)k} \qquad (2) \\
&= \sum_{n=0}^{\frac{N}{2}-1} f(n) W_{N/2}^{nk} + \sum_{n=0}^{\frac{N}{2}-1} g(n) W_{N/2}^{nk}
\end{aligned}
$$

Among them, $f(n)$ and $g(n)$ are a complex sequence of length $N/2$. This way, the original DFT calculation of length N is converted into two DFT calculations of length $N/2$. Similarly, the two DFT calculations after decomposition can be further decomposed by the same method until they cannot be decomposed.

3 FFT Implementation and Optimization

3.1 Choice of Butterfly Networks

According to the traditional butterfly network formed by the decomposition method of the FFT algorithm, its data input and output are discontinuous. So, the conventional butterfly network makes the data read-and-write operations more complicated and unsuitable for using SIMD vectorization technology. Therefore, this paper uses a new type of butterfly network (Stockham butterfly network, such as Fig. 1) for implementation, which will not change the generation method of the butterfly network, and only needs to be realized by recalculating the address [9, 10]. However, the Stockham butterfly network has several advantages: 1. The input and output are all natural sequences, which can better perform memory access operations. 2. SIMD optimization. Continuous input and output enable parallel processing of multiple butterfly calculations. 3. Perfect support for mixed bases. We can combine butterflies with different bases to handle DFTs of any size.

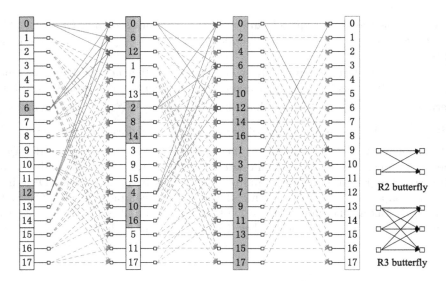

Fig. 1. The Stockham butterfly network diagram for the FFT of size eighteen. The red line represents a butterfly of the current stage. (Color figure online)

3.2   Computational Optimization of Butterfly Kernel

When the large-scale DFT is decomposed, several smaller-scale DFT calculations are formed, which we call the FFT butterfly kernel. The twiddle factor $(W_N^n k)$ in the FFT butterfly kernel can be expressed separately as a twiddle factor matrix, such as Eq. (3).

$$\begin{bmatrix} W_N^0 & W_N^0 & W_N^0 & \cdots & W_N^0 \\ W_N^0 & W_N^1 & W_N^2 & \cdots & W_N^{N-1} \\ W_N^0 & W_N^2 & W_N^4 & \cdots & W_N^{2(N-1)} \\ \vdots & \vdots & \vdots & \cdots & \vdots \\ W_N^0 & W_N^k & W_N^{2k} & \cdots & W_N^{k(N-1)} \\ \vdots & \vdots & \vdots & \cdots & \vdots \\ W_N^0 & W_N^{(N-1)} & W_N^{2(N-1)} & \cdots & W_N^{(N-1)(N-1)} \end{bmatrix} \tag{3}$$

In implementing the butterfly calculation, we will use the three characteristics of the twiddle factor to resolve the twiddle factor matrix first, and the even base twiddle factor matrix will show specific symmetric features after being determined. Then we use the characteristics of the simplified twiddle factor matrix to merge similar items for the butterfly calculation kernel to simplify the kernel calculation formula.

Taking the FFT butterfly kernel with size eight as an example (R8), we can simplify its rotation factor matrix into Eq. (4).

$$
DFT_8 =
\begin{bmatrix}
1 & 1 & 1 & 1 & 1 & 1 & 1 & 1 \\
1 & W_8^1 & -i & W_8^3 & -1 & W_8^{-3} & i & W_8^{-1} \\
1 & -i & -1 & i & 1 & -i & -1 & i \\
1 & W_8^3 & i & W_8^1 & -1 & W_8^{-1} & -i & W_8^{-3} \\
1 & -1 & 1 & -1 & 1 & -1 & 1 & -1 \\
1 & W_8^{-3} & -i & W_8^{-1} & -1 & W_8^1 & i & W_8^3 \\
1 & i & -1 & -i & 1 & i & -1 & -i \\
1 & W_8^{-1} & i & W_8^{-3} & -1 & W_8^3 & -i & W_8^1
\end{bmatrix}
\tag{4}
$$

Therefore, according to the rotation factor matrix (4), the butterfly calculation formula of R8 can be expressed as Eq. (5).

$$
\begin{aligned}
Y(0) =& x(0) + x(1) + x(2) + x(3) + x(4) + x(5) + x(6) + x(7) \\
Y(1) =& x(0) + W_8^1 \cdot x(1) - i \cdot x(2) + W_8^3 \cdot x(3) - x(4) + W_8^{-3} \cdot x(5) + i \cdot x(6) \\
& + W_8^{-1} \cdot x(7) \\
Y(2) =& x(0) - i \cdot x(1) - x(2) + i \cdot x(3) + x(4) - i \cdot x(5) - x(6) + i \cdot x(7) \\
Y(3) =& x(0) + W_8^3 \cdot x(1) + i \cdot x(2) + W_8^1 \cdot x(3) - x(4) + W_8^{-1} \cdot x(5) - i \cdot x(6) \\
& + W_8^{-3} \cdot x(7) \\
Y(4) =& x(0) - x(1) + x(2) - x(3) + x(4) - x(5) + x(6) - x(7) \\
Y(5) =& x(0) + W_8^{-3} \cdot x(1) - i \cdot x(2) + W_8^{-1} \cdot x(3) - x(4) + W_8^1 \cdot x(5) + i \cdot x(6) \\
& + W_8^3 \cdot x(7) \\
Y(6) =& x(0) + i \cdot x(1) - x(2) - i \cdot x(3) + x(4) + i \cdot x(5) - x(6) - i \cdot x(7) \\
Y(7) =& x(0) + W_8^{-1} \cdot x(1) + i \cdot x(2) + W_8^{-3} \cdot x(3) - x(4) + W_8^3 \cdot x(5) - i \cdot x(6) \\
& + W_8^1 \cdot x(7)
\end{aligned}
\tag{5}
$$

It can be seen from matrix Eq. (4) that the rotation factor matrix has good symmetry up and down and left and right, so we can further simplify Eq. (5) by merging similar items. In the twiddle factor of R8, the real parts of W_8^1 and W_8^3 are opposite numbers, and the imaginary parts are equal. The real parts of W_N^k and $W_N^{-}k$ are identical, and the imaginary parts are opposite numbers. Therefore, the above properties are used to finally resolve Eq. (5) into Eq. (6).

In Eq. (7), $W_8^1 \cdot r$ and $W_8^1 \cdot i$ represent the real part and imaginary part of the rotation factor W_8^1, respectively. $W_8^1 \cdot r$ is $\cos\left(-\frac{\pi}{4}\right) = \frac{\sqrt{2}}{2}$, and $W_8^1 \cdot i$ is $\cos\left(-\frac{\pi}{4}\right) = -\frac{\sqrt{2}}{2}$.

When calculating, proceed from the inside to the outside according to the order of the brackets. That is, first calculate the values such as $(x(0) + x(4))$, $(x(2) + x(6))$, and then calculate $s(0)$ $s(7)$, and finally calculate $Y(0)$ $Y(k)$. This can minimize the number of multiplication, addition, and subtraction operations and improve computational efficiency. Butterfly calculation kernels of other even bases can also be simplified similarly.

$$
\begin{cases}
Y(0) = s(0) + s(4) \\
Y(1) = s(1) - i \cdot s(7) \\
Y(2) = s(2) - i \cdot s(6) \\
Y(3) = s(3) + i \cdot s(5) \\
Y(4) = s(0) - s(4) \\
Y(5) = s(3) - i \cdot s(5) \\
Y(6) = s(2) + i \cdot s(6) \\
Y(7) = s(1) + i \cdot s(7)
\end{cases}
\tag{6}
$$

let

$$
\begin{cases}
s(0) = (x(0) + x(4)) + (x(2) + x(6)) \\
s(2) = (x(0) + x(4)) - (x(2) + x(6)) \\
s(4) = (x(1) + x(5)) + (x(3) + x(7)) \\
s(6) = (x(1) + x(5)) - (x(3) + x(7)) \\
s(1) = (x(0) - x(4)) + W_8^1 \cdot r \cdot [(x(1) - x(5)) - (x(3) - x(7))] \\
s(3) = (x(0) - x(4)) - W_8^1 \cdot r \cdot [(x(1) - x(5)) - (x(3) - x(7))] \\
s(5) = (x(2) - x(6)) + W_8^1 \cdot i \cdot [(x(1) - x(5)) + (x(3) - x(7))] \\
s(7) = (x(2) - x(6)) - W_8^1 \cdot i \cdot [(x(1) - x(5)) + (x(3) - x(7))]
\end{cases}
\tag{7}
$$

3.3 RISC-V Assembly Optimization

SIMD Vectorization. The RISC-V instruction set architecture supports RISC-V vector extension (RVV) instructions, which can process multiple sets of data with different bit widths or types in parallel to improve computing efficiency [11]. As shown in Fig. 2, four R2 butterfly calculations require four scalar calculations in total, while SIMD vectorization requires only one SIMD vector calculation [10]. In this paper's implementation process of the FFT algorithm, except for the input and output data, the number and order of vectorized instructions executed by each butterfly kernel are consistent. Therefore, in terms of single-precision data processing, this paper expands the butterfly kernel loop at each level four times and implements it with vectorized instructions. Regarding double-precision data processing, the butterfly kernel loop of each level is expanded twice. In this way, when the number of loops of the butterfly kernel is greater than 4 or 2 during execution, vectorized instructions will be executed, and 4 or 2 butterfly calculations will be processed simultaneously to improve calculation efficiency.

Vector Properties. During the butterfly calculation, we usually do loop unrolling four times for SIMD vectorization, but when the base is small, many vector registers will be free. For example, if the R2 butterfly loop is expanded four times, we only need four vector registers to complete it, and the remaining 28 are idle. The RISC-V architecture has the feature of dynamically distributing

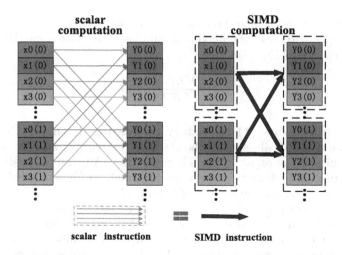

Fig. 2. R2 butterfly vectorization calculation with parallelism 4.

vector registers, so when the registers are sufficient, the parallelism can reach eight or even 16 [12]. Taking R2 as an example, the R2 butterfly kernel uses very few registers, so when expanding the butterfly kernel loop eight times, the following instructions can be used:

vsetvli rd, rs1, vtypei
rd = new vl, rs1 = AVL, vtypei = new vtype setting

Among them, rd is the target register, and the default value is zero; rs1 is the length of the vector register to be enabled; vtype is the vector data type register.

In RISC-V, the implementation of register sets is supported, and multiple vector registers can piece together a vector register set. A vector instruction can act on all registers in the vector register bank at the same time. In the C910 CPU used in this article, the number of registers (LMUL) in a vector register group can be 1, 2, 4, or 8, and its assembly parameters correspond to Table 1 [13].

Table 1. Vsetvli assembly parameters.

Assembly Name	SEW	Assembly Name	LMUL
e8	8b	m1	1
e16	16b	m2	2
e32	32b	m4	4
e64	64b	m8	8

Given the current element precision and the size of the vector register group, the calculation method of the maximum number of data that can be controlled by one instruction is Eq. (8).

$$N_{\max} = \frac{VLEN}{SEW} \cdot LMUL \tag{8}$$

Other Optimizations (1) Boundary processing. In the RISC-V architecture, we can dynamically specify the state of the register and set the number of enabled bits of the register [13]. Therefore, the AVL can be modified by the vsetvli instruction to dynamically control the number of bits enabled by the register. In the implementation process of this article, when the number of cycles is greater than or equal to 4, the number of enabled bits of the register will remain at the value of 4. When it is less than or equal to 4, the value of the enable bit of the register will be set to a state equivalent to the number of cycles.

(2) **Data access optimization and instruction selection.** In this article, complex numbers are stored in memory as a whole. That is the values of the real and imaginary parts alternate in storage. However, during calculation, the real and imaginary parts of the same complex number are calculated separately in different registers. Therefore, directly fetching numbers will cause redundant operations and reduce computing efficiency. The RISC-V instruction set provides load instructions such as VLSEG<NF>E.V. During the single-precision data load process, the offset is set to 4, and each fetch can read across a single-precision element. Currently, the fetched result can meet the computing requirements of the butterfly kernel.

At the same time, in this paper, we selected efficient instructions for implementation. Such as: using the vfmacc.vv instruction to replace the vfmul.vv and vfadd.vv instructions; using the vfnmsac.vv instruction to replace the vfmul.vv and vfadd.vv instructions, etc.

(3) **Register allocation.** Since only 32 vectorization registers exist in a RISC-V CPU, reasonable use of vectorization registers can improve computing efficiency. In this paper, the vectorized registers of the RISC-V CPUs are classified into four categories (twiddle factor registers, input registers, calculation registers, and output registers). The value in the twiddle factor register will be reused, so it will not be allocated to other alias registers after allocation. The vector registers represented by the input registers, calculation registers, and output registers all have a period of idle time. Therefore, a vector register may play multiple roles, such as input registers and calculation registers. This approach can maximize the use of vectorized registers in the RISC-V CPUs to ensure maximum computing efficiency. In addition, when R is large, there may be insufficient vectorization registers. At this time, this article will use stack technology to alleviate the problem of an insufficient number of vectorization registers.

4   Performance Evaluation

We have completed the high-performance implementation of the FFT algorithm (PerfMPL-FFT) for the RISC-V architecture scale of 2^n in the PerfMPL high-performance mathematical algorithm library on the C910MP CPU. PerfMPL is a high-performance mathematical algorithm library of PerfXLab (Beijing) Technologies Co., Ltd., and the FFT algorithm library is one of the modules. In addition, PerfMPL also includes BLAS, Sparse, and VML modules. CPU parameters are shown in Table 2. FFTW is a widely used and mature open-source FFT algorithm library that can support RISC-V architecture friendly. Therefore, this paper adopts FFTW as a performance comparison object. The performance measurement unit is the general performance unit (GFlops) in the industry [14], which can intuitively reflect the performance difference.

Table 2. Experimental Environment

CPU	C910MP	Register Number	32
Architecture	RISC-V	Register Length	128
Vector Extension	Version 0.7.1	GCC Version	5.5.0
Frequency	30 MHz	FFTW	3.3.10

This article currently only implements 2^n scale DFT high-performance computing, so this article only tests the performance of the 2^n scale FFT algorithm on the C910MP CPU. Note that the C910MP CPU has not yet been fabricated, so the experiments are currently only conducted on the C910MP simulator. As shown in Table 2, the frequency of the simulator is only 30 MHz, but in the performance graph, we benchmarked it to 2.1 GHz. That is, we multiplied the original GFlops value by 70.

In Fig. 3, the broken black line, broken yellow line, and broken green line represent the processing capabilities of PerfMPL-FFT SIMD code, FFTW algorithm library, and PerfMPL-FFT C code for different scales of DFT, where Fig. 3(a) represents the data when the data is single-precision floating-point Processing capacity, Fig. 3(b) represents the processing capacity when the data is a double-precision floating-point number.

In the algorithm performance analysis, we provide the C code of PerfMPL-FFT and the SIMD code of PerfMPL-FFT. Using the C code as a benchmark, it can intuitively reflect the performance after SIMD vectorization. From (a) and (b) of Fig. 3, we can observe that the average performance of the PerfMPL-FFT C code in this paper is comparable to the average performance of the FFTW algorithm library, whether it is DFT processing of single-precision data or DFT processing of double-precision data. The performance is the same. Therefore, this result illustrates that our algorithm optimization is effective. Compared with the performance of the FFTW algorithm library, the SIMD code of PerfMPL-FFT has reached 3.67 and 3.60 in terms of single-precision data and double-precision

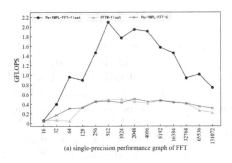
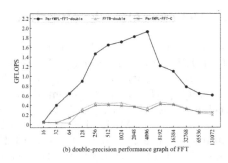

(a) single-precision performance graph of FFT   (b) double-precision performance graph of FFT

Fig. 3. (a) and (b) are the DFT processing performance of PerfMPL-FFT SIMD code, PerfMPL-FFT C code, and FFTW algorithm library on C910MP CPU for single-precision and double-precision data, respectively. (Color figure online)

data processing, respectively, indicating that SIMD vectorization is feasible and effective. Finally, the experimental results show that in the RISC-V architecture, a series of methods, such as algorithm optimization, SIMD vectorization, and memory access optimization proposed in this paper for the Cooley-Tukey FFT algorithm, are implementable and effective.

5   Conclusion

In this paper, we optimize and implement the Cooley-Tukey FFT algorithm by using a series of features such as the vectorization feature and Vector feature of the RISC-V instruction set architecture and the symmetry of the FFT butterfly kernel twiddle factor. In our performance evaluation study, compared with the FFTW algorithm library, the performance of our algorithm achieves a speedup of 3.67 and 3.60 in single precision and double precision, respectively, when dealing with DFTs of size 2^n. Through performance optimization experiments, we realized that the basic mathematical algorithm libraries still have a lot of room for improvement in the field of RISC-V for HPC.

References

1. Asanovic, K., Patterson, D.A.: Instruction sets should be free: the case for RISC-V. https://people.eecs.berkeley.edu/krste/papers/EECS-2014-146.pdf. Accessed 23 Mar 2023
2. Cooley, J.W., Tukey, J.W.: An algorithm for the machine calculation of complex Fourier series. Math. Comput. **19**(90), 297–301 (1965)
3. Chen, T., Jia, H., Li, Z., Li, C., Zhang, Y.: A transpose-free three-dimensional FFT algorithm on ARM CPUs. In: 2021 IEEE 23rd International Conference on High Performance Computing & Communications; 7th International Conference on Data Science & Systems; 19th International Conference on Smart City; 7th International Conference on Dependability in Sensor, Cloud & Big Data Systems & Application (HPCC/DSS/SmartCity/DependSys), pp. 1–8. IEEE (2021)

4. Asanovic, K., Bodik, R., Catanzaro, B.C., et al.: The landscape of parallel computing research: a view from Berkeley (2006)
5. Frigo, M., Johnson, S.G.: The design and implementation of FFTW3. Proc. IEEE **93**(2), 216–231 (2005)
6. Li, Z., et al.: AutoFFT: a template-based FFT codes auto-generation framework for ARM and X86 CPUs. In: Proceedings of the International Conference for High Performance Computing, Networking, Storage and Analysis, pp. 1–15 (2019)
7. Rao, K.R., Kim, D.N., Hwang, J.J.: Fast Fourier Transform: Algorithms and Applications, vol. 32. Springer, Dordrecht (2010). https://doi.org/10.1007/978-1-4020-6629-0
8. Cooley, J.W., Lewis, P.A., Welch, P.D.: The fast Fourier transform and its applications. IEEE Trans. Educ. **12**(1), 27–34 (1969)
9. Swarztrauber, P.N.: FFT algorithms for vector computers. Parallel Comput. **1**(1), 45–63 (1984)
10. Li, Z., Jia, H., Zhang, Y., Chen, T., Yuan, L., Vuduc, R.: Automatic generation of high-performance FFT kernels on arm and x86 CPUs. IEEE Trans. Parallel Distrib. Syst. **31**(8), 1925–1941 (2020)
11. Patterson, D., Waterman, A.: The RISC-V Reader: An Open Architecture Atlas. Strawberry Canyon (2017)
12. Patsidis, K., Nicopoulos, C., Sirakoulis, G.C., Dimitrakopoulos, G.: RISC-V 2: a scalable RISC-V vector processor. In: 2020 IEEE International Symposium on Circuits and Systems (ISCAS), pp. 1–5. IEEE (2020)
13. Waterman, A.S.: Design of the RISC-V Instruction Set Architecture. University of California, Berkeley (2016)
14. Frigo, M., Johnson, S.G.: The benchmarking methodology of benchFFT (2020)

Software Development Vehicles to Enable Extended and Early Co-design: A RISC-V and HPC Case of Study

Filippo Mantovani[1]([✉]), Pablo Vizcaino[1], Fabio Banchelli[1],
Marta Garcia-Gasulla[1], Roger Ferrer[1], Georgios Ieronymakis[2],
Nikolaos Dimou[2], Vassilis Papaefstathiou[2], and Jesus Labarta[1]

[1] Barcelona Supercomputing Center, Plaça Eusebi Güell, 1-3, 08034 Barcelona, Spain
{filippo.mantovani,pablo.vizcaino,fabio.banchelli,marta.garcia,
roger.ferrer,jesus.labarta}@bsc.es
[2] FORTH-ICS, N. Plastira 100, Vassilika Vouton, 70013 Heraklion, Crete, Greece
{ieronym,ndimou,papaef}@ics.forth.gr

Abstract. Prototyping HPC systems with low-to-mid technology readiness level (TRL) systems is critical for providing feedback to hardware designers, the system software team (e.g., compiler developers), and early adopters from the scientific community. The typical approach to hardware design and HPC system prototyping often limits feedback or only allows it at a late stage. In this paper, we present a set of tools for co-designing HPC systems, called software development vehicles (SDV). We use an innovative RISC-V design as a demonstrator, which includes a scalar CPU and a vector processing unit capable of operating large vectors up to 16 kbits. We provide an incremental methodology and early tangible evidence of the co-design process that provide feedback to improve both architecture and system software at a very early stage of system development.

Keywords: RISC-V · HPC prototypes · co-design methodology

1 Introduction and Related Work

The typical high-level approach to hardware design foresees to develop a new design, implementing it at Register Transfer Level (RTL) using Hardware Description Language (HDL), and finally maps the implementation on a given technology using Computer-Aided Design (CAD) tools for post-design validation. This flow is represented on the right part of Fig. 1A.

The software development for new hardware designs relies on a microarchitectural simulator which collects the inputs from the hardware design and its implementation to mimic the behaviour of the proposed new hardware. Software developers can therefore test their codes and analyze their performance thanks to the simulator. This flow is represented on the left part of Fig. 1A.

Besides the fact that booting an operating system and running complex codes through a simulator can be extremely time consuming (or even impossible), from

A. Bienz et al. (Eds.): ISC High Performance 2023 Workshops, LNCS 13999, pp. 526–537, 2023.
https://doi.org/10.1007/978-3-031-40843-4_39

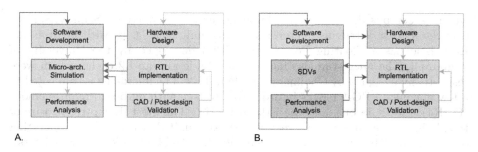

Fig. 1. Co-design flow for hardware (green) and software (blue) (Color figure online)

Fig. 1A it is clear that the software development (blue) can not influence much the hardware flow (green).

In this paper, we propose a methodology that allows software developers to provide feedback both to the architects designing the architecture and to the engineers implementing the RTL. Moreover, our infrastructure guarantees the possibility of porting, testing, benchmarking, and optimizing software on the new proposed hardware as early as possible. The proposed method is depicted in Fig. 1B. Instead of a software simulator, it leverages a collection of hardware platforms (mostly FPGAs) and software tools called Software Development Vehicles (SDVs). The SDV allows software developers to test and analyze their codes on an environment using software tools for collecting insights from the executions while running on the latest RTL implementation of the proposed architecture. Thanks to this infrastructure, software developers can therefore provide valuable feedback to the hardware team as represented by the red arrows of Fig. 1B. Also, the SDV reduces the dependencies from the hardware design flow (green arrows), since it only depends on the RTL implementation of the new proposed architecture.

The method is conceptually similar to the one enabled with tools such as e.g., Siemens Veloce[1]. However, it is more lean, since it is working on a single FPGA (at the additional price of not having visibility on all signals of the system). The method does not require software simulators, such as riscvOVPsim[2] and FireSim [1] nor meta-hardware description languages, such as Chisel or SystemC [3]: on the positive side the whole SDV infrastructure is faster and allows to run OS, libraries and applications as in high TRL system. On the negative side, some modifications can require more time to be implemented, since they can involve RTL development.

For our evaluation, we have chosen to focus on the hardware development of a RISC-V-based design that targets the HPC domain and is developed within the European Processor Initiative project[3]. This design includes a RISC-V micro-tile,

---

[1] https://eda.sw.siemens.com/en-US/ic/veloce/.

[2] https://github.com/riscv-ovpsim/imperas-riscv-tests.

[3] https://www.european-processor-initiative.eu/.

which is composed of an Avispado scalar core developed by Semidynamics[4], connected to a Vitruvius vector processing unit (VPU) [6] with eight lanes. Each lane has a Floating Point Unit (FPU) developed by the University of Zagreb [4]. The micro-tile also has a Home Node and an L2 cache, which were respectively designed by Chalmers[5] and FORTH[6]. The micro-tile is connected to a few ancillary FPGA blocks in order to interface with on-board main memory (DDR4), the PCIe bus, and the Ethernet PHY. The most disruptive feature of this design is the presence of a vector processing unit that is capable of operating on vectors of 256 double-precision elements (i.e., 16 kbits-wide vector registers).

The design point of such a RISC-V system is rather extreme, as it can operate on vectors that are up to 32 times larger than current SIMD architectures used in HPC[7]. Therefore, it is crucial for the software community to have an environment where to test the behavior of current scientific applications and the readiness of system software to exploit such a design. At the same time, it is important for RTL designers and system software developers to receive feedback from application developers so that they can improve the efficiency of their implementation while still keeping it as general-purpose as possible. We consider this paper a contribution to the HPC community and an example of co-design since the Software Development Vehicles tools introduced improve the design cycle of HPC hardware and software.

The main contributions of this paper are: i) the methodology for building a stronger connection between software and hardware during its design phase; ii) the tools and the infrastructure needed to run a complex software stack on top of implementation of early hardware designs; iii) the evaluation of the proposed methodology with a library used for the computation of the Fast Fourier Transform running on an emerging design that includes a RISC-V core and a vector processing unit (VPU).

The rest of this paper is structured as follows: Sect. 2 lists the hardware and components of the SDV environment. Section 3 explains the steps that compose the proposed methodology. In Sect. 4 we provide evidences of the methodology, applying it to a code for computing Fast Fourier Transform on a RISC-V vector architecture. We conclude the paper with Sect. 5 where we summarize some conclusions remarks.

2   Components of the Software Development Vehicles (SDVs)

2.1   RISC-V Commercial Platforms

There are several RISC-V based commercial platforms on the market. The compute node of our cluster is powered by a RISC-V-based SoC by SiFive (Freedom

---

[4] Semidynamics. https://semidynamics.com/.

[5] Chalmers University of Technology. https://www.chalmers.se.

[6] FORTH Institute of Computer Sciences. https://www.ics.forth.gr/carv.

[7] Intel x86 AVX512 operates SIMD vectors of 8 double-precision elements.

U740 SoC). Each SoC houses four 64-bit RISC-V cores running at up to 1.2 GHz. Each core supports the I, M, A, F, D, and C extensions of the RISC-V Instruction Set Architecture (ISA). The SiFive SoC is mounted on a miniITX PCB with 4 GB of RAM, a slot for a micro-SD for the boot of the OS and an m.2 connector for SSD where we store the filesystem. We assembled two motherboards in a 1U chassis, so to have a higher density, similar to the system described in [2]. Nodes of the cluster are connected using the on-board 1 GbE Ethernet link. The board is known on the market as HiFive Unmatched and more details can be found on the provider web site: https://www.sifive.com/boards/hifive-unmatched. The nodes of the cluster are operated with a standard Linux distribution (Ubuntu 20.04 at the moment of the writing of this document). A standard GNU Compiler Suite is available on those platforms. However, BSC developed an LLVM-based compiler toolchain which supports vector specifications v0.7.1 and v1.0. Vectorization can be achieved *i)* enabling compiler auto-vectorization capabilities, *ii)* adding vector pragmas, or *ii)* manually using intrinsics.

2.2   Software Emulation: Vehave

Vehave is a user-space emulator for the vector extension of the RISC-V ISA (RVV) that runs on RISC-V Linux. It allows a functional verification of a program that uses RVV instructions or a code generator, such as a compiler, that emits RVV instructions. It runs on top of the RISC-V commercial platforms described in Sect. 2.1 (configured by the user running the `module` environment) and it is distributed as binary here https://ssh.hca.bsc.es/epi/ftp/vehave-EPI-development-latest.tar.bz2.

Vehave emulates instructions by intercepting the illegal instruction exception that a CPU emits when it encounters an unknown/invalid instruction. Once an illegal instruction is found, Vehave decodes it and if it is a valid RVV instruction it emulates it, else an error is propagated back. The program resumes once the emulation of the vector instruction is complete. Vehave relies on the LLVM libraries of the compiler which already supports the RVV for the process of decoding the instructions. The output of Vehave is collected in a `.trace` file which stores in plain text extensive details about each vector instruction emulated and some quantitative figure of the scalar code executed before each vector instruction. The `.trace` file generated by Vehave is parsed and converted to `.prv` format which can be visualized with Paraver [8]. These traces may not include cycle accurate data, but include detailed data on the vector instructions executed that are valuable to study regions of code with potential for vectorization.

2.3   FPGA-Based Emulation

The FPGA-based emulation platform comprises of an FPGA evaluation board and a host x86 server. The server is a commodity server housing an AMD Ryzen 5 5600 CPU with 32 GB of DDR4-3200 memory, both mounted on a Mini-ITX motherboard. It runs a regular Ubuntu Server 20.04 with local storage and a mounted Network Filesystem.

The FPGA board is the Virtex UltraScale+ HBM VCU128 FPGA Evaluation Kit[8], commonly referred to in the rest of the document as *VCU128*. The board includes a VU37P FPGA[9], with 8 GB of integrated HBM memory. There are also five on-board DDR4 memory modules, adding up to a total of 4.5 GB of memory.

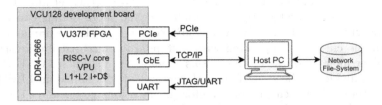

Fig. 2. Connection between host server and VCU128 board: schematic view

Figure 2 shows the connection scheme between the host server and the VCU128 device. The host and the VCU128 are connected through three different interfaces. The first one being the UART/JTAG interface, used to program the FPGA and also to access a UART terminal once a Linux image is running on the VCU128. The Ethernet PHY connector establishes a point-to-point TCP/IP network between host and device that is used to access the RISC-V SoC running on the FPGA via SSH and give access to a network filesystem (NFS) to the RISC-V SoC once booted Linux. Lastly, the VCU128 is configured to operate its PCIe interface using 16 lanes of Gen 3 PCIe. The PCIe link is used to pre-load the on-board DDR4 memory with the Linux image and configure the VCU128 board to autonomously boot Linux. The RISC-V SoC runs the same Linux distribution that is deployed on the RISC-V commercial platforms described in Sect. 2.1, so that binaries (both statically or dynamically generated) are compatible on the two platforms. A compute node is composed of the host server and the VCU128 board. There are several compute nodes available via a job scheduler (SLURM) for users of the SDV platform.

Hardware Counters. When running on native SoC, even on FPGA, hardware counters provide information about the micro-architecture. These counters are available through CSR read instructions. Since counters are protected and can only be read in machine mode, the SBI interface bridges between machine mode and system calls. We implement a custom system call that bridges between user code and kernel space.

Tracing Executions. The PAPI library [7] offers a standard interface for users to read hardware counters. Our current implementation allows reading

---

[8] https://www.xilinx.com/products/boards-and-kits/vcu128.html.
[9] Complete device name: XCVU37P-2FSVH2892E.

`hpmcounter0-4` and other contextual information (e.g., current vector-length). Users can manually instrument their code with calls to PAPI or use Extrae [5]. Extrae is a tracing tool that polls hardware counters via manual instrumentation or with automatic hooks of supported libraries such as MPI and OpenMP. We leverage the Integrated Logic Analyzer (ILA)[10], a signal-level monitor of Xilinx-based FPGAs, to record the values of selected signals during each clock from a given time window. The start time of the monitoring is triggered upon a user-defined condition (e.g., a signal value must be zero).

Visualization. Paraver [8] is a trace visualization tool developed at BSC. In-house tools convert Vehave, Extrae, and ILA traces to a format that can be understood by Paraver. Using the same visualization tool to analyze experiments in different platforms of the SDV ecosystem and with different levels of detail is key to *i)* achieve wide adoption across users and *ii)* accelerating the feedback loop between software and hardware teams.

3   Co-design Methodology

In this section we present the methodology that creates a feedback loop between hardware and software teams thanks to the SDV approach. We propose an evaluation workflow with three steps as depicted in Fig. 3.

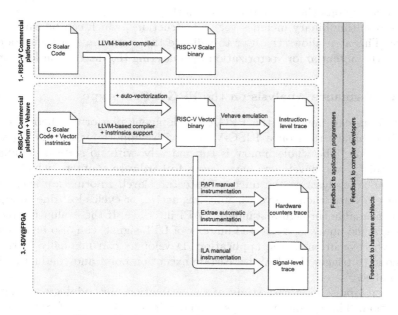

Fig. 3. Performance analysis workflow in SDV

---

[10] https://www.xilinx.com/products/intellectual-property/ila.html.

3.1   Porting to Scalar RISC-V Commercial Platforms

First, users port their application to the RISC-V architecture. The LLVM-based compiler generates binaries compatible with the `rv64gc` architecture. At this stage, the generated binary is RISC-V compatible but it contains only scalar instructions. The application can run natively, using the commercial RISC-V platforms. This step is useful *i)* to verify the compatibility of the code under study with the RISC-V architecture (e.g., no intrinsics or inline assembly of other architectures); *ii)* to verify that the compiler supports all data structures and code features required by the code under study; *iii)* to benchmark the code on a commercial scalar RISC-V.

3.2   Vectorization and Software Emulation

The next step is to vectorize the code, leveraging compiler auto-vectorization, using pragmas or adding vector intrinsics. The resulting binary includes vector instructions. When this binary runs on the RISC-V commercial platforms together with Vehave, the vector instructions will be emulated and details about their execution stored in a trace file that can be analyzed post mortem. In this step we can gather information about *i)* potential of the code to be vectorized or patterns that can prevent its vectorization, *ii)* ability and limitations of the compiler to auto-vectorize code, *iii)* efficiency of the vectorization, e.g., checking if the code exploits the optimal vector length.

The resulting binary includes vector instructions, which can be run through Vehave. This step allows the user to validate the correctness of their code and discover the potential for vectorization by analyzing the instruction-level traces.

3.3   Performance Analysis on the FPGA Prototype

Lastly, users can now use the FPGA development platform, where the same vectorized binary runs on a RISC-V core with support for the RVV (vector) ISA extension. The whole binary is run natively, with no software emulation. During this phase, developers have access to hardware counters, which enables performance analysis at the micro-architecture level. Information such as the number of cycles when the vector unit was active, or cycles lost due to pipeline stalls is available through a standard PAPI interface. If the evaluation requires a finer grained analysis, a selected number of RTL signals can also be monitored during the execution of the application. Developers can manually instrument their code to trigger the ILA at a certain execution point and conduct a signal-level analysis.

Section 4 presents a case study of the evaluation methodology presented in this section. Throughout the steps depicted in Fig. 3, users of SDV can provide feedback to other teams: *i)* Instruction-level traces to study the algorithm implementation and give feedback to both the application programmers and the compiler developers. *ii)* Hardware counters and signal-level traces to study the effects of micro-architectural features to give feedback to hardware architects.

4   Evaluation

To showcase the potential and benefits of the SDV, we use our proposed methodology to evaluate a vectorized Fast Fourier Transform (FFT) implementation for RISC-V [9].

4.1   Step 1: Porting to RISC-V Scalar Commercial Platforms

As presented in Sect. 3, the first step proposed in the SDV methodology is running the application on a scalar RISC-V platform. Firstly we compiled the FFTW[11] using the LLVM-based compiler, confirming that although the library could be run on RISC-V, it did not include vector instructions. Our next step was to code an FFT algorithm with the potential for long-vector vectorization, and again try it on the scalar platforms for verification purposes. After this was done, we started vectorizing and analyzing the implementation.

4.2   Step 2: Vectorization and Software Emulation

Once the vectorized implementation is ready, we instrumented the code to identify the different code phases. This step is optional, but it helps identifying the different phases later on when analyzing the trace generated when running with the Vehave emulator. After opening the resulting trace in Paraver, we can look at the different code phases by either using the event we added in our instrumentation or looking at the Program Counter (PC). Figure 4 shows on the x-axis the sequence of the 4821 vector instruction executed. The color code of the top timeline identifies the phases that we marked with the manual instrumentation. We find the highest amount of vector instructions in the code phase 2 (i.e., the pink phase has the highest number of vector instruction). The bottom plot of Fig. 4 reports on the y-axis the value of the PC. We can observe the saw-toothed shape of the PC, typical of an iterative execution.

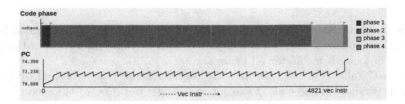

Fig. 4. Vehave trace with Code phase (top) and Program Counter (bottom) of the FFT vector implementation. (Color figure online)

---

[11] https://www.fftw.org.

Since Vehave emulates each instruction individually, we also have detailed information about them, such as the number of elements used by vector instructions, the so called *vector length*. With these values, we can compute the average vector length per each user-defined phase, as seen in Fig. 5. Phase 2, where we find most instructions, also has the lowest vector-length. Ideally, we want to use the maximum vector length of the machine (256 double precision elements) for all phases.

Fig. 5. Vehave trace with the Vector Length per FFT phase.

Since we developed this first version of the vectorized FFT library, we can learn from this first observations and improve it to take advantage of the maximum vector length. Figure 6 shows the Vehave trace of this improved implementation.

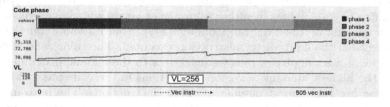

Fig. 6. Vehave trace with Code phase, PC and Vector Length for the improved FFT implementation. (Color figure online)

As it can be seen, all four phases have approximately the same number of instructions, phase 2 and 3 are completed with a single internal iteration, and the Vector Length is 256 for all phases.

Figure 7 takes a closer look into the vector instructions emulated by Vehave for both versions of the code, focusing on a single iteration of the second phase. We see that in order to increase the vector length, the implementation now contains indexed memory operations, which have a much lower bandwidth than their unit-strided counterparts.

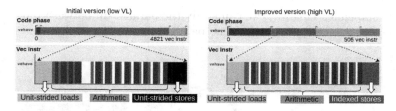

Fig. 7. Vehave trace with Vector instructions in the second phase of the FFT for both implementations. (Color figure online)

4.3 Step 3: Performance Analysis on FPGA Prototype

After this initial evaluation using Vehave, we can jump to the FPGA system and get actual timing measurements and traces. Figure 8 shows three views from Extrae traces of both implementations, obtained in the FPGA. The duration of the pink region (phase 2) decreased when the VL changed from 8 to 256 elements. At the same time, the yellow region (phase 3) worsened when changing from 64 to 256, most likely due to the inefficient memory operations presented in Fig. 7 outweighing the gains of a larger vector length.

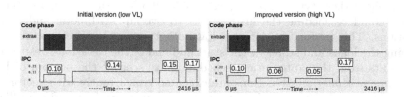

Fig. 8. Extrae timelines with Phase time (top) and Instructions per Cycle (bottom) of both FFT implementations. (Color figure online)

Figure 8 shows on the x-axis the execution time and on the y-axis the value of the Instructions per Cycle (IPC) in each of the phases with vector instructions for two versions of the code. On the left we show an execution that uses small vector lengths and on the right an execution with larger vector length. When we change our implementation to take advantage of a larger vector length, we obtain a code that uses less instructions to process the same amount of data, reducing the overall IPC. As a consequence, the phases affected by our optimization (pink and orange) show a reduction of IPC and the ratio of vector instructions to total instructions also decreased.

Finally, we can use the ILA in the FPGA to perform a fine-grain analysis of the vector instructions (similar to Vehave but with cycle-accurate data).

At the top of Fig. 9 we show a Vehave timeline, and below it a ILA timeline of the same region of code. The vector instructions in the ILA timeline vary in length depending on their actual duration, and we present a different row for each hardware pipeline. This way, we can study the parallelism between pipelines. In this case, we detected that little to no parallelism is being exploited.

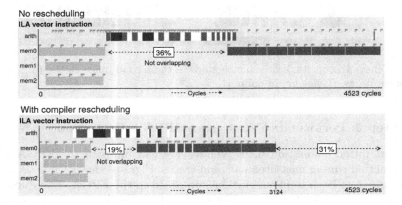

Fig. 9. Vector Instructions reported in Vehave (top), in the ILA (mid), and after implementing and applying compiler rescheduling (bottom).

Looking at these types of traces, we gave feedback to the compiler developers so they could reschedule the instructions to overlap arithmetic and memory operations. This is done by interleaving both types of instructions instead of grouping the loads and stores at the start and end of the iterations, respectively. The results from this automatic rescheduling are seen at the bottom of Fig. 9. Now, some arithmetic instructions are executed concurrently with vector loads or stores, reducing the time where there is not a memory instruction in flight.

5   Conclusions

We present an incremental methodology, starting from less detailed to more detailed, which is applied to a RISC-V architecture with large vectors targeting HPC. This methodology enables the early adoption and tuning of software when developing new hardware platforms. It has the great advantage of allowing the system software to be ready before the hardware is ready. In addition, this tool allows the preparation of all layers of software required for an efficient HPC execution, such as compilers, libraries, and scientific applications.

This method enables running the same binary on commercial platforms and on the FPGA emulator. It also allows any kind of system calls, making it highly flexible for software developers. The tool infrastructure includes the ability to spy on the values of signals that are internal to the implementation, providing valuable insights. Furthermore, this methodology is cheaper than a full system simulator and runs faster than a simulator, even though it requires an RTL implementation.

The approach taken by Vehave results in a fast execution for scalar code but slow for vector instructions and it only allows to study post-mortem trace of vector instructions. QEMU could be faster than Vehave and could allow us to gather traces of all kind of instructions, both vector and scalar. It is slower than native execution but it can run on fast x86 hosts. Indeed, we are considering it as an extension of the SDV tool-chain. The FPGA implementation of the RTL runs at lower frequency than any ASIC, but still order of magnitude faster than any software simulator. The study using the logic analyzer signals has great potential but it is limited by the number of instructions/signals that can be monitored.

As a future work, we plan to extend the monitored observables to include power drain and expand the toolchain to include QEMU and a multi-FPGA infrastructure.

Acknowledgments. This research received funding from the EU-HPC-JU under FPA N. 800928 (EPI) and SGA N. 101036168 (EPI-SGA2). The JU receives support from some member countries. The EPI-SGA2 project, PCI2022-132935 is also co-funded by MCIN/AEI/10.13039/501100011033 and by the UE NextGenerationEU/PRTR.

References

1. Farshchi, F., et al.: Integrating NVIDIA deep learning accelerator (NVDLA) with RISC-V SoC on FireSim. In: Workshop on Energy Efficient Machine Learning and Cognitive Computing for Embedded Applications (EMC2), pp. 21–25. IEEE (2019)
2. Ficarelli, F., et al.: Meet monte cimone: exploring RISC-V high performance compute clusters. In: Proceedings of the 19th ACM International Conference on Computing Frontiers, pp. 207–208 (2022)
3. Kim, D.: FPGA-Accelerated Evaluation and Verification of RTL Designs. University of California, Berkeley (2019)
4. Kovač, M., et al.: FAUST: design and implementation of a pipelined RISC-V vector floating-point unit. Microprocess. Microsyst. **97**, 104762 (2023)
5. Llort, G., et al.: On the usefulness of object tracking techniques in performance analysis. In: SC 2013: Proceedings of the International Conference on High Performance Computing, Networking, Storage and Analysis (2013)
6. Minervini, F., et al.: Vitruvius+: an area-efficient RISC-V decoupled vector coprocessor for high performance computing applications. ACM Trans. Archit. Code Optim. **20**(2), 1–25 (2023)
7. Mucci, P.J., Browne, S., Deane, C., Ho, G.: PAPI: a portable interface to hardware performance counters. In: Proceedings of the Department of Defense HPCMP Users Group Conference, vol. 710 (1999)
8. Pillet, V., Labarta, J., Cortes, T., Girona, S.: Paraver: a tool to visualize and analyze parallel code. In: Proceedings of WoTUG-2018: Transputer and Occam Developments, vol. 44, pp. 17–31. Citeseer (1995)
9. Vizcaino, P., Mantovani, F., Ferrer, R., Labarta, J.: Acceleration with long vector architectures: implementation and evaluation of the FFT kernel on NEC SX-Aurora and RISC-V vector extension. Concurr. Comput. Pract. Exp. e7424 (2022)

Evaluation of HPC Workloads Running on Open-Source RISC-V Hardware

Luc Berger-Vergiat, Suma G. Cardwell, Ben Feinberg, Simon D. Hammond,
Clayton Hughes, Michael Levenhagen, and Kevin Pedretti[✉]

Center for Computing Research, Sandia National Laboratories,
Albuquerque, NM 87185, USA
{lberge,sgcardw,bfeinbe,chughes,mjleven,ktpedre}@sandia.gov
https://www.sandia.gov/ccr

Abstract. The emerging RISC-V ecosystem has the potential to improve
the speed, fidelity, and quality of hardware/software co-design R&D
activities. However, the suitability of the RISC-V ecosystem for co-design
targeting HPC use cases is not yet well understood. In this paper, we
examine the performance of several HPC benchmark workloads running
on simulated open-source hardware RISC-V cores running under the
FireSim FPGA-accelerated simulation tool. To provide a realistic and
reproducible HPC software stack, we port the Spack package manager
to RISC-V and use it to build our workloads. Our key finding is that
each of the RISC-V cores evaluated is capable of running complex HPC
workloads executing for long durations under simulation, with simulation
rates of approximately 1/50th real-time. Additionally we provide a baseline set of performance results that can be compared against in future
studies. Our results highlight the readiness of the RISC-V ecosystem for
performing open co-design activities for HPC. We expect performance
to improve as co-design activities targeting RISC-V ramp up and the
RISC-V community makes further contributions to this space.

Keywords: RISC-V · HPC · Benchmarking · Open-Source
Hardware · Simulation

1 Introduction

The emerging RISC-V ecosystem has the potential to improve the speed, fidelity,
and quality of hardware/software co-design. In the research space, a growing
menu of open-source RISC-V hardware designs and high-productivity hardware
design tools enable increased agility and the ability to develop hardware more
like software. In the commercial space, technologies such as chiplets and standardized die-to-die interconnects and protocols enable RISC-V commercial IP to
be more easily mixed and matched with IP from multiple vendors and combined
with customer-provided IP. While not specific to RISC-V, these capabilities are
benefiting from the rapidly growing community around RISC-V and a renewed
interest in developing customized hardware designs targeting specific workloads.

A. Bienz et al. (Eds.): ISC High Performance 2023 Workshops, LNCS 13999, pp. 538–551, 2023.
https://doi.org/10.1007/978-3-031-40843-4_40

It is still an open question, however, whether the RISC-V software stack and hardware simulation ecosystem are sufficiently mature to support configuring, building, and running complex HPC workloads on open-source RISC-V hardware.

In this paper, we measure the performance of several common HPC benchmarks running on open-source RISC-V processor designs. Specifically, we run the STREAM, HPCG, HPL, and Kokkos Kernels Sparse-Matrix-Vector (SpMV) benchmarks on the CVA6 (Ariane), Rocket, and BOOM cores in several different configurations. We use the FireSim FPGA-accelerated cycle-accurate simulation tool to carry out these experiments. Our motivation for conducting this study was first to see whether it was even feasible to run these fairly complex HPC benchmarks on simulated RISC-V cores, and second to gain a better understanding of the relative performance levels of these cores for HPC workloads. Our specific contributions include:

1. We port the Spack package manager to RISC-V and use it to build our workloads and their dependencies, providing a set of reusable build recipes.
2. We demonstrate that the simulated hardware and software environment provided by FireSim is able to successfully run our target HPC benchmarks.
3. We provide guidance on the relative simulation rates achieved for FPGA-accelerated simulation vs. software-based simulation.
4. We provide performance measurements of several common HPC benchmarks running on current RISC-V designs, providing a baseline for tracking performance improvements over time.

While we find the absolute performance of open-source RISC-V core designs running HPC workloads is still relatively low, we anticipate this will rapidly improve as co-design activities targeting RISC-V ramp up and the RISC-V community makes further contributions to this space.

The remainder of this paper is organized as follows. In Sect. 2, we describe our RISC-V HPC software stack bring-up activities. In Sect. 3, we describe the simulated RISC-V environments used for our experiments, followed by a description of the open-source RISC-V cores evaluated in Sect. 4. In Sect. 5, we describe our test HPC workloads and testing methodology. Section 6 presents our results followed by discussion in Sect. 7. Section 8 presents related work and conclusions are stated in Sect. 9.

2   RISC-V HPC Software Stack

Efforts are underway within the RISC-V community to build an integrated and optimized software stack for supporting HPC workloads. Key ingredients of this stack include low-level system software support such as optimized Linux distributions, network stacks, filesystems, and container runtime support, as well as a productive application development environment that includes robust and performant compilers, math libraries, tools, MPI implementations, and programming model support (e.g., OpenMP, Kokkos, Raja). While RISC-V is at the beginning of the journey to build a mature HPC software stack, a solid foundation is now in place with RISC-V support available in the GCC and LLVM compiler toolchains and Fedora, Ubuntu, and Debian Linux OS distributions.

A challenge that remains, however, is building and optimizing the many software packages and third-party libraries that are required by modern HPC applications. To help ease this process, we have ported the Spack [12] package manager to RISC-V. Spack includes build recipes for most HPC packages and uses a SAT-solver based concretization process to find and install all of their downstream dependencies. For example, the "spack install trilinos" command will install the Trilinos framework by first building a directed acyclic graph of all its software dependencies, including OpenMPI, NUMACTL, HWLOC, OpenBLAS, and then build them in the order required followed by building the Trilinos package itself. Spack facilitates creating reproducible HPC software stacks and normally builds packages from source, which is particularly appropriate for RISC-V because binary repositories of HPC packages are not yet readily available and even if they were, compilers and RISC-V package ports are rapidly evolving and often require recompiling to obtain the latest optimizations.

The port of Spack to RISC-V was relatively straightforward due to efforts within the Spack community to support multiple architectures and microarchitecture optimizations as a core capability. The pull requests we contributed to Spack and the Archspec library that Spack uses for managing microarchitecture detection are summarized in Table 1. With these changes, we were able to use Spack to build all of the benchmark workloads used in this paper. We have tested Spack natively on a HiFive Unmatched board running Ubuntu and on Fedora running under Qemu emulation. Builds can be quite slow, requiring roughly a day to build our software stack in either environment. An area for future work is speeding up the Spack first-time use bootstrap for RISC-V, which currently requires several hours to build the required Clingo SAT solver from source. Other architectures, such as x86_64 and aarch64, provide pre-built binaries and complete bootstrap in a matter of seconds.

Table 1. Pull Requests Contributed for porting Spack to RISC-V

Package	Pull Request	Description
Archspec	PR #35	Add riscv64 arch and u74mc uarch
Archspec	PR #58	Detection code for generic riscv and u74mc uarch
Spack	PR #26364	Use gnuconfig package for config file replacement for RISC-V
Spack	PR #26541	Patch from upstream needed to build numactl on riscv64
Spack	PR #26565	openblas: fix build on riscv64

3   Simulated RISC-V Environment

Figure 1 shows a high-level view of the full-stack co-design framework that we used to simulate the open-source RISC-V cores evaluated in this paper. Conceptually, this involves a researcher selecting from a menu of parameterized open-source hardware register-transfer level (RTL) components on the left-hand side of the figure, combining and configuring them with the assistance of an open-source system-on-chip (SoC) design tool, and outputting a hypothetical SoC design that is ready for simulation. The SoC design is then combined with a complete software environment that includes a full Linux operating system, HPC programming environment, and the target benchmark workload, shown on the right-hand side of the figure. The full stack, consisting of a high-fidelity RTL hardware design and fully-functioning software stack, is then simulated to measure the performance of the target benchmark running in the simulated hardware and software environment. Ideally this end-to-end flow can be carried out quickly to enable rapid co-design – where a researcher is able to iterate over the design space, modifying both the hardware components and software stack, including the low-level OS system software and the application, to see how performance is affected.

In the past, this workflow has been hard to achieve due to the slow-speed of software-based simulation, however recent advances in the RISC-V community have dramatically improved simulation speed by making use of FPGAs. Specifically, we make use of the Chipyard [2] and FireSim [14] platforms developed by the Berkeley Architecture Research Group, together with our HPC software stack, to form the core of our full-stack co-design framework. FireSim makes use of cloud-hosted FPGAs or local FPGA resources to perform cycle-accurate simulation of SoC designs and datacenter networks. It uses a decoupled architecture, where simulated time advances independently of wall-clock time, to maintain accurate memory and device timings. This is in contrast FPGA emulation approaches that expose the SoC design under test directly to native hardware latencies, producing unrealistic performance projections. FireSim is able to perform cycle-accurate simulation of complex SoC RTL designs at approximately 1/50 of real time, which is orders of magnitude faster than software-based simulation.

Fig. 1. Full-stack Co-design Framework

4   Open-Source RISC-V Cores

We focus on evaluating three open-source application-class RISC-V cores in this study, specifically CVA6 [27], Rocket Core [4], and BOOM [30]. Each of these cores is a RV64GC architecture core that includes virtual memory support needed to run a full Linux operating system and 64-bit floating point capabilities needed by most HPC workloads. We focus on evaluating single core instantiations of these cores running at comparable clock frequencies in order to be able to make cross-core comparisons. However, we note that the clock frequencies tested may not reflect what is physically realizable when a given design is taped out and manufactured.

Each core is instantiated as the processor component in a Rocket Chip SoC instance generated by the Rocket Chip Generator [4] in Chipyard. The Rocket Core and BOOM core are implemented in the Chisel [5] hardware description language and are designed to directly integrate with the other Chisel-based hardware components available within Chipyard. The CVA6 core is implemented in SystemVerilog and must be wrapped in a Chisel adapter shell in order for it to be integratable into Rocket Chip. A compilation process is used to convert the high-level SoC design created by Chipyard into an intermediate representation and ultimately to Verilog RTL that can be simulated by Verilator, FireSim, or taken to an ASIC tape out process.

In terms of micro-architecture, CVA6 and Rocket Core are single-issue, in-order designs, while BOOM is an out-of-order design with a 3-wide issue width and 10-stage pipeline in the configuration we evaluated. CVA6 and Rocket Core use 6-stage and 5-stage pipelines, respectively. All three cores are instantiated with a 32 KB L1 data cache. At the SoC level, the Rocket Chip SoC was instantiated with a 4 MB last level cache with 4096 sets and 8-ways each. The DDR3 main memory subsystem models a 16 GB memory split across 4 ranks of 8 banks each. The memory access scheduler has a window size of 8 and transaction queue depth of 8. This is a sampling of the key configuration parameters used for these designs. The reader is referred to the Chipyard source code for more details on the default CVA6, Rocket Core, and BOOM Large configurations used in this study. An area for future work is generating human readable descriptions of the parameters used for SoC generation, so that different configurations can be more easily compared to one another.

5 Approach

In this section we describe the HPC benchmark workloads and testing procedure used to gather our results.

5.1 Benchmark Workloads

We used two micro-benchmarks, STREAM and the Kokkos Kernels SpMV Performance Test, along with the two Top500 benchmarks, HPL and HPCG, in order to assess the performance of our target RISC-V cores. Historically, these have been common benchmarks used to evaluate the performance limits of processors for HPC workloads. While not representative of real HPC application behavior, results from these benchmarks can help identify potential performance bottlenecks and project performance for a range of application domains.

STREAM [17] measures memory subsystem performance using four kernels (COPY, SCALE, ADD, and TRIAD) that operate on arrays of 64-bit floating point values with unit stride. We focus on the TRIAD operation since it is the most complex of the kernels and is frequently used to measure the memory bandwidth of new HPC systems. The TRIAD kernel performs the operation $A[i] = B[i] + s * C[i]$, which involves multiplying a vector by a scalar value, adding it to another vector element-wise, and storing the result in an output vector. We used the default input configuration, which resulted in each of the arrays being 76 MB in size and a total memory footprint of 229 MB.

The Kokkos Kernels SpMV Performance Test measures the performance of sparse matrix-vector multiplications (SpMV). SpMV is required in all iterative solvers for residual calculation as well as for various preconditioning techniques. It often dominates the so called "solve phase" of numerical simulations that rely on discrete PDE representations of a problem. Kokkos Kernels implements multiple versions of the matrix-vector product for matrices stored in compressed row sparse (CRS) format as presented in [21]. These implementations target the serial, OpenMP and GPU backends of the Kokkos Core library and have been optimized and tested on numerous HPC platforms (e.g., Intel, IBM, Fujitsu-ARM, NVIDIA, and AMD). Kokkos Kernels also offers the option to use alternative implementations through its third-party library layer that interfaces with MKL, cuSPARSE and rocSPARSE. These implementations are used by Trilinos and PETSc for their local SpMV, which are used by numerous applications developed at Sandia, Argonne, and other institutions.

For our experiments we focus on the serial implementation of SpMV, $y = A \times x$. Its main computational features are the streaming of matrix A row by row and the reduction of the row-vector product to compute the entries of y. As the entries in the rows of A correspond to discontinuous entries in x, the memory access pattern for values of x is not optimal. For small matrices this issue is mitigated since x might fit in cache, however at larger sizes this is no longer the case and performance is reduced. To ensure a large enough problem to exercise main memory performance, we configure the Kokkos Kernels SpMV Performance test to operate on a 1 million row matrix with an average of 10 non-zero entries per row.

The High Performance LINPACK (HPL) benchmark has been used for several decades to determine the rankings of the world's top 500 supercomputers. It measures the performance of a dense LU factorization with $O(n^3)$ compute operations for $O(n^2)$ data movement, enabling it to achieve a high fraction of peak on most modern microprocessor architectures. We configured HPL for a single core run (P = 1 and Q = 1) with an input problem size of N = 4000.

The High Performance Conjugate Gradient (HPCG) [7,8] benchmark has recently been developed to complement HPL. HPCG was designed to address concerns that HPL no longer serves as an accurate predictor of application performance in supercomputing installations. As new algorithms have emerged, there has been increasing focus on memory subsystem performance rather than pure computational power. HPCG is comprised primarily of low computational intensity operations like SpMV and places considerable stress on memory bandwidth. We configure HPCG for a $104 \times 104 \times 104$ problem, which results in a memory footprint of about 950 GB.

5.2 Testing Procedure

FireSim release 1.12.1 was used to perform experiments. To prepare for testing, the Firemarshal tool was used to build a Fedora 32 (Rawhide) base OS image. The "marshal launch" command was then used to create an interactive shell running inside the base OS image via Qemu, which was used to build the benchmarks via Spack. Firemarshal configures the emulated RISC-V environment with support for internet connectivity, which made it straightforward to use the standard Spack workflow where source code is downloaded from the upstream projects and built locally. The version of Spack used was commit hash 10d10b61 and it was configured to use the GCC 12.1.1 compiler provided by Fedora. No changes were required to the benchmark source code or their dependencies in order to build with GCC 12.1.1. Listing 1.1 shows the main Spack commands that were used to build the benchmarks.

Listing 1.1. Spack commands used to build benchmark workloads.

```
git  clone  -c  feature.manyFiles=true
        https://github.com/spack/spack.git
.  spack/share/spack/setup-env.sh
spack  compiler  find
spack  install  stream@5.10%gcc  +openmp
spack  install  hpcg@3.1%gcc
spack  install  hpl@2.3%gcc
spack  install  --test=root
                kokkos@3.7.00%gcc  +openmp  +tests
spack  install  --test=root
                kokkos-kernels@3.7.00%gcc  +openmp
                ^kokkos@3.7.00%gcc  +openmp  +tests
```

After this one-time setup was performed, the same OS image and benchmark binaries were used in all subsequent FireSim experiments. Each core was "booted" in a FireSim simulation running on an Amazon F1 FPGA instance, we interactively logged into the simulated node, and proceeded to run each benchmark in sequence. Benchmark results were copied out at the end of the simulation run.

6   Results

Figure 2 shows the performance of STREAM running on the three cores under evaluation. There are two sets of results included in this figure and in Fig. 5. The blue bars represent standard configurations that were run using our current FireSim 1.12.1 simulation framework described in this paper. The red bars were previously run under FireSim 1.11.1 in a configuration that set the DRAM clock frequency to the core clock frequency, which, while not within DDR3 spec, may provide some insight into the maximum achievable performance for the core.

In the standard configurations, we see that CVA6 and Rocket have similar performance while BOOM has noticeably higher performance for STREAM. This trend holds for most of our benchmark workloads and is expected due to the more advanced microarchitecture and out-of-order execution used in BOOM. We note that with BOOM, there is negligible performance improvement provided by doubling the core clock frequency from 1.6 GHz to 3.2 GHz while holding the memory subsystem constant at 1.0 GHz, indicating the memory subsystem, is likely saturated.

For STREAM, the BOOM Max configuration peaks out at about 7 GB/s. This is comparable to the ThunderX2 Arm processor core used in the Astra [18] supercomputer, which achieves 9.5 GB/s for a single core running the same benchmark.

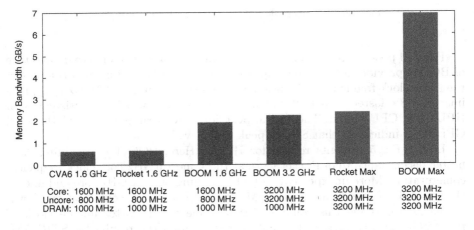

Fig. 2. STREAM TRIAD Performance (Color figure online)

Figure 3 presents results for the Kokkos Kernels SpMV Performance test. Performance trends are similar to results for STREAM. Here, BOOM is approximately 3.2× faster than Rocket Core when running at the same 1.6 GHz core frequency, compared to 2.95× faster for STREAM. We speculate the improved speedup is due to BOOM's out-of-order execution engine benefiting the more complex memory access patterns of the Kokkos Kernels SpMV test compared to STREAM's simple unit-stride memory accesses.

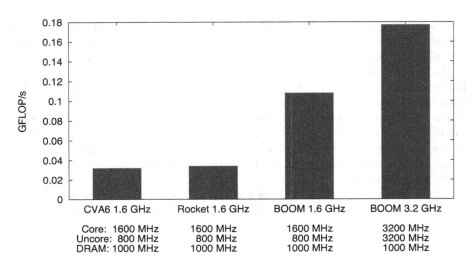

Fig. 3. Kokkos Kernels Sparse-MatVec Performance Test

Figure 4 presents results for HPL. Here, the more advanced microarchitecture of BOOM provides a 2.4× speedup compared to Rocket Core when running at the same clock frequencies. Additionally, BOOM running at 3.2 GHz is approximately 1.8× faster than BOOM running at 1.6 GHz, which is consistent with HPL being CPU bound. Theoretical peak for BOOM running at 3.2 GHz is 3.2 GFLOP/s, indicating that 82% of peak is achieved for HPL.

Lastly, Fig. 5 presents results for HPCG. Here, BOOM is providing 2.3× better performance than Rocket Core at the same 1.6 GHz core clock frequency configuration. More unexpectedly, BOOM running at a 3.2 GHz core and uncore clock is 1.6× faster than the BOOM 1.6 GHz core clock configuration shown in the figure. While this could be attributable to the faster uncore clock of the 3.2 GHz configuration, it is not consistent with the results for STREAM, where memory bandwidth was not improved much by increasing clock rates. This suggests that HPCG has both memory-bound and compute-bound behavior when running on this BOOM configuration. This may be an artifact of the relatively low peak compute rate of 1 FLOP/clock. Cores that can execute more FLOPs per clock may be able to overlap more of the compute done by HPCG with memory accesses. We plan to investigate this phenomena in future work.

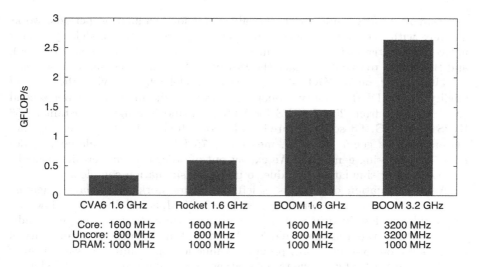

Fig. 4. HPL Performance

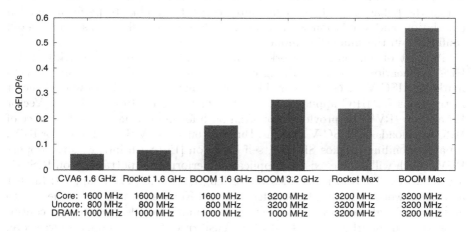

Fig. 5. HPCG Performance (Color figure online)

7   Discussion

In addition to our analysis of open source and commercial RISC-V cores on HPC workloads, we have developed Vanadis, a cycle-level MIPS and RISC-V out-of-order CPU model for the Structural Simulation Toolkit (SST) [19]. Although the widely-used gem5 simulator [6,13,16] can be integrated with SST, Vanadis provides a native cycle-level CPU simulator to reduce the reliance on external simulators. Native integration provides the ability to leverage the parallelization available in SST's parallel event engine with MPI and C++ threads, leading to scalable simulations that have multi/many-core processors with >1,000 processing elements. Native integration also allows for long simulation periods, works natively with the SST memory subsystem and accelerator models, produces native SST statistics for feedback modeling (e.g. energy, DVFS, resilience etc.), and the ability to extend/replace the ISA using SST modules/sub-components.

Throughput on a BOOM-like processor model when varying the level of fidelity in the DDR memory model, measured in kilo-instructions per second (KIPS), varies from 25–52 KIPS for STREAM and is roughly constant at 56 KIPS for HPCG. These results are broadly consistent with other cycle-level simulators such as gem5. Ta *et al.* measured 175 KIPS for a simulated in-order RISC-V core using gem5 [24]. We expect out-of-order core models like Vanadis to have a lower simulation rate due to increased simulation complexity.

A full evaluation of Vanadis is left for future work as validation against known open-source processor models, such as BOOM, is still underway. However, the workloads described in Sect. 5 have all been successfully run using Vanadis and SST's integrated memory and NOC models. Importantly, the availability of open source out-of-order cores provides a unique opportunity for validation of simulators against fully-known targets rather than attempting to match behavior suggested by microbenchmarks. Although commercial RISC-V cores will not match the behavior of these open source cores, the ability to perform detailed correlation and validation against open-source cores will increase our overall confidence in the simulation model.

As part of our on-going work to understand the potential of RISC-V for HPC applications, we are working on improving software support and benchmarking RISC-V cores. Systems like Fugaku have shown the power of vector instructions for HPC applications [22,23]. The recently frozen RISC-V Vector Extensions (RVV) [1] provide a potential path for improving the performance of HPC workloads on RISC-V systems. Building on the LLVM 15 support for RVV, we are extending Kokkos SIMD (itself based on [15]) with intrinsics to support RVV, which will enable existing application performance portability on RISC-V architectures. This work provides vector length specific (VLS) support; further additional work on linear algebra algorithms in Kokkos Kernels will be needed to add vector length agnostic (VLA) support in math kernels. We are also continuing our benchmarking efforts with the Tenstorrent Ocelot [3] open-source core, which adds RVV support to the BOOMv3 core discussed previously. Together this should help develop the software ecosystem for RVV and demonstrate a path toward greater RISC-V performance on HPC applications.

Lastly, we are beginning to leverage our framework to explore novel neuromorphic accelerator architectures inspired by our understanding of how computation is done in the brain, which can be 100–1000× more efficient than traditional computing approaches. Tightly integrating RISC-V with neuromorphic accelerators is already an active area of research [20,26,28] and open-source neuromorphic architectures such as Wenquxing 22A [25], ODIN [11] and ReckOn [10] make RTL code available that can be integrated into RISC-V systems and evaluated in simulation platforms such as FireSim. We plan to leverage our framework to develop and evaluate neuromorphic architectures such as these in the context of HPC workloads.

8   Related Work

Several other papers have evaluated the performance of open-source RISC-V processors. Dörflinger et al. compared Rocket, BOOM, CVA6, and SHAKTI C on SPECintrate 2017, as well as evaluating area, energy consumption, and frequency for both FPGA and ASIC implementations [9]. This comparison found significant performance advantages for BOOM, as expected for an out-of-order core compared to in-order cores. However, Rocket was significantly more area and energy efficient. Consistent with our results, Rocket showed a moderate performance advantage over the other in-order cores.

Zhang et al. evaluated the Riscy-OO out-or-order core against BOOM and Rocket on SPEC CINT 2006 [29]. Zhang et al. found that Riscy-OO performed similarly to BOOM when the core structures were similarly sized. Importantly however, this analysis predates BOOMv3 which resulted in an approximately $2\times$ improvement in IPC [30].

To the best of our knowledge, our work is the first to evaluate open-source RISC-V cores running the Top500 HPL and HPCG benchmarks, as well as demonstrating Kokkos Kernels on RISC-V. These are fairly complex workloads that we configured for non-trivial input configurations, which required several days of simulation time to perform. Additionally, we are the first to port Spack to RISC-V and use it in a simulation methodology.

9   Conclusions

In this paper we have demonstrated that our full-stack co-design framework, built from tools developed by the RISC-V community, is capable of executing complex HPC workloads running for long time scales via FPGA-accelerated simulation. To facilitate a feature-full and reproducible HPC software stack, we have ported the Spack package manager to RISC-V and integrated it with our framework. We have used our framework to evaluate several open-source RISC-V cores and collect a baseline set of performance results that can be compared against in future studies.

In future work we plan to evaluate additional RISC-V cores and associated accelerator hardware. Additionally, we plan to use our framework to validate the SST Vanadis RISC-V model against open-source RISC-V cores and real RISC-V hardware.

Acknowledgments. This paper describes objective technical results and analysis. Any subjective views or opinions that might be expressed in the paper do not necessarily represent the views of the U.S. Department of Energy or the United States Government.

This article has been authored by an employee of National Technology & Engineering Solutions of Sandia, LLC under Contract No. DE-NA0003525 with the U.S. Department of Energy (DOE). The employee owns all right, title and interest in and to the article and is solely responsible for its contents. The United States Government retains and the publisher, by accepting the article for publication, acknowledges that the United States Government retains a non-exclusive, paid-up, irrevocable, world-wide license to publish or reproduce the published form of this article or allow others to do so, for United States Government purposes. The DOE will provide public access to these results of federally sponsored research in accordance with the DOE Public Access Plan https://www.energy.gov/downloads/doe-public-access-plan.

References

1. Amid, A., Asanovic, K., Baum, A., Bradbury, A., Brewer, T., et al.: RISC-V 'V' Vector Extension (2021). https://github.com/riscv/riscv-v-spec/releases/download/v1.0/riscv-v-spec-1.0.pdf

2. Amid, A., et al.: Chipyard: integrated design, simulation, and implementation framework for custom SoCs. IEEE Micro **40**(4), 10–21 (2020). https://doi.org/10.1109/MM.2020.2996616

3. Arekapudi, S., Xie, D.: Ocelot: open source vector unit. In: RISC-V Summit 2022, San Jose, California (2022)

4. Asanović, K., et al.: The rocket chip generator. Technical report UCB/EECS-2016-17, EECS Department, University of California, Berkeley (2016). http://www2.eecs.berkeley.edu/Pubs/TechRpts/2016/EECS-2016-17.html

5. Bachrach, J., et al.: Chisel: constructing hardware in a scala embedded language. In: Proceedings of the 49th Annual Design Automation Conference, DAC 2012, pp. 1216–1225. Association for Computing Machinery, New York (2012). https://doi.org/10.1145/2228360.2228584

6. Binkert, N., et al.: The gem5 simulator. SIGARCH Comput. Archit. News **39**(2), 1–7 (2011). https://doi.org/10.1145/2024716.2024718

7. Dongarra, J., Heroux, M.: Toward a new metric for ranking high performance computing systems. Technical report SAND2013-4744, Sandia National Laboratories, NM, USA (2013)

8. Dongarra, J., Luszczek, P., Heroux, M.: HPCG technical specification. Technical report SAND2013-8752, Sandia National Laboratories, NM, USA (2013)

9. Dörflinger, A., et al.: A comparative survey of open-source application-class RISC-V processor implementations. In: Proceedings of the 18th ACM International Conference on Computing Frontiers, CF 2021, pp. 12–20. Association for Computing Machinery, New York (2021). https://doi.org/10.1145/3457388.3458657

10. Frenkel, C., Indiveri, G.: ReckOn: a 28nm sub-mm2 task-agnostic spiking recurrent neural network processor enabling on-chip learning over second-long timescales. In: 2022 IEEE International Solid-State Circuits Conference (ISSCC), vol. 65, pp. 1–3. IEEE (2022)

11. Frenkel, C., Lefebvre, M., Legat, J.D., Bol, D.: A 0.086-mm^2 12.7-pJ/SOP 64k-synapse 256-neuron online-learning digital spiking neuromorphic processor in 28-nm CMOS. IEEE Trans. Biomed. Circ. Syst. **13**(1), 145–158 (2018)

12. Gamblin, T., et al.: The Spack package manager: bringing order to HPC software chaos. In: Proceedings of the International Conference for High Performance Computing, Networking, Storage and Analysis, SC 2015 (2015). https://doi.org/10.1145/2807591.2807623

13. Hsieh, M., Pedretti, K., Meng, J., Coskun, A., Levenhagen, M., Rodrigues, A.: SST + gem5 = a scalable simulation infrastructure for high performance computing. In: Proceedings of the 5th International ICST Conference on Simulation Tools and Techniques, pp. 196–201 (2012)

14. Karandikar, S., et al.: FireSim: FPGA-accelerated cycle-exact scale-out system simulation in the public cloud. In: Proceedings of the 45th Annual International Symposium on Computer Architecture, ISCA 2018, Piscataway, NJ, USA, pp. 29–42. IEEE Press (2018). https://doi.org/10.1109/ISCA.2018.00014

15. Kretz, M.: Extending C++ for explicit data-parallel programming via SIMD vector types. Doctoral thesis, Universitätsbibliothek Johann Christian Senckenberg (2015). https://doi.org/10.13140/RG.2.1.2355.4323

16. Lowe-Power, J., et al.: The gem5 simulator: version 20.0+ (2020). https://doi.org/10.48550/arXiv.2007.03152

17. McCalpin, J.D.: Memory bandwidth and machine balance in current high performance computers. IEEE Comput. Soc. Tech. Comm. Comput. Archit. (TCCA) Newsl. **2**, 19–25 (1995). https://www.cs.virginia.edu/mccalpin/papers/balance/

18. Pedretti, K., et al.: Chronicles of Astra: challenges and lessons from the first petascale arm supercomputer. In: SC 2020: International Conference for High Performance Computing, Networking, Storage and Analysis, pp. 1–14. IEEE (2020)

19. Rodrigues, A.F., et al.: The structural simulation toolkit. SIGMETRICS Perform. Eval. Rev. **38**(4), 37–42 (2011). https://doi.org/10.1145/1964218.1964225

20. Rutishauser, G., Hunziker, R., Di Mauro, A., Bian, S., Benini, L., Magno, M.: ColibriES: a milliwatts RISC-V based embedded system leveraging neuromorphic and neural networks hardware accelerators for low-latency closed-loop control applications. arXiv preprint arXiv:2302.07957 (2023)

21. Saad, Y.: Iterative Methods for Sparse Linear Systems. SIAM (2003)

22. Sato, M., Kodama, Y., Tsuji, M., Odajima, T.: Co-design and system for the supercomputer "Fugaku". IEEE Micro **42**(2), 26–34 (2022). https://doi.org/10.1109/MM.2021.3136882

23. Stephens, N., et al.: The ARM scalable vector extension. IEEE Micro **37**(2), 26–39 (2017). https://doi.org/10.1109/MM.2017.35

24. Ta, T., Cheng, L., Batten, C.: Simulating multi-core RISC-V systems in gem5. In: Workshop on Computer Architecture Research with RISC-V (2018)

25. Wang, J., et al.: RISC-V toolchain and agile development based open-source neuromorphic processor. arXiv preprint arXiv:2210.00562 (2022)

26. Yousefzadeh, A., et al.: SENeCA: scalable energy-efficient neuromorphic computer architecture. In: 2022 IEEE 4th International Conference on Artificial Intelligence Circuits and Systems (AICAS), pp. 371–374. IEEE (2022)

27. Zaruba, F., Benini, L.: The cost of application-class processing: energy and performance analysis of a Linux-ready 1.7-GHz 64-bit RISC-V core in 22-nm FDSOI technology. IEEE Trans. Very Large Scale Integr. (VLSI) Syst. **27**(11), 2629–2640 (2019). https://doi.org/10.1109/TVLSI.2019.2926114

28. Zelensky, A., Alepko, A., Dubovskov, V., Kuptsov, V.: Heterogeneous neuromorphic processor based on RISC-V architecture for real-time robotics tasks. In: Artificial Intelligence and Machine Learning in Defense Applications II, vol. 11543, pp. 94–101. SPIE (2020)

29. Zhang, S., Wright, A., Bourgeat, T., Arvind, A.: Composable building blocks to open up processor design. In: 2018 51st Annual IEEE/ACM International Symposium on Microarchitecture (MICRO), pp. 68–81 (2018). https://doi.org/10.1109/MICRO.2018.00015

30. Zhao, J., Korpan, B., Gonzalez, A., Asanovic, K.: SonicBOOM: the 3rd generation Berkeley out-of-order machine. In: Fourth Workshop on Computer Architecture Research with RISC-V (2020). https://carrv.github.io/2020/papers/CARRV2020_paper_15_Zhao.pdf

Accelerating Neural Networks Using Open Standard Software on RISC-V

Kumudha Narasimhan[ID] and Mehdi Goli[(✉)][ID]

Codeplay Software Ltd., Edinburgh, Scotland, UK
{kumudha.narasimhan,mehdi.goli}@codeplay.com

Abstract. Deep neural networks have the ability to learn patterns from huge amounts of data and hence have been adopted in many high performance computing and scientific applications. To achieve cost effective performance on such applications, vendors and chip designers are increasingly looking at domain-specific accelerators. To facilitate adapting the design to the needs of the workload, we need a generic open standard solution all through the stack - software to hardware. This paper explores one such approach.

On the hardware side, RISC-V ISA has a minimal base integer set and provides custom extensions which works as a good starting point for designing these special accelerators. This design can further benefit from the RISC-V vector extensions which help achieving high compute density leading to performance improvement for user applications.

On the software side, SYCL provides a C++-based portable parallel programming model to target various devices. Thus, enabling SYCL applications to run on RISC-V accelerators provides an open standard way of accelerating neural networks.

This paper elaborates the usage of open standards and open source technology to run complex SYCL applications on RISC-V vector processors.

Keywords: SYCL · RISC-V · Deep neural networks

1 Introduction

Deep neural network models are becoming more and more prevalent due to their ability to learn patterns from huge amounts of data. They are increasingly being adopted by high-performance computing and scientific applications. Processing massive amounts of data efficiently requires exploiting the parallelism inherently available in neural network models. With advancements in hardware architectures, there are many accelerators available for AI and high-performance computing domains from high-end GPUs such as A100 and H100, TPU [26] to embedded system-on-chip such as NVIDIA Jetson and ASICs. While all these accelerators serve the same purpose, they differ in architecture, ISA design, and programming languages supported. These differences can propagate to the

A. Bienz et al. (Eds.): ISC High Performance 2023 Workshops, LNCS 13999, pp. 552–564, 2023.
https://doi.org/10.1007/978-3-031-40843-4_41

entire software stack run on such architectures, affecting the end-user programmers, compilers, and driver developers. Several domain-specific languages and frameworks such as Raja [7], Kokkos [25], Tensorflow [16], ONNX Runtime [6], PyTorch [24], etc. have been proposed to alleviate the burden of rewriting the same code for end-user. However, it is at the cost of massively inflating the framework/DSL with several library or vendor-specific code. Thus, one of the viable solutions to tackle the software divergence is to adopt an open standard open source solution across the entire. RISC-V and SYCL is one such open standard option available.

RISC-V [8] provides an open standard minimal base integer set. It also provides custom extensions that act as a good starting point for designing custom accelerators for neural network models. RISC-V also allows vector extensions for achieving high-compute density in the accelerators, thereby improving the performance of applications.

Introduced by Khronos [3], SYCL [13] is an open-standard, C++-based portable parallel programming model to target heterogeneous devices. SYCL is a single-source programming model supporting advanced memory management and scheduling policies. Moreover, SYCL provides a rich ecosystem of open-source, portable software stack including frameworks and libraries that can run across various SYCL-enabled devices with comparable performance with vendor-optimized equivalents.

In this paper, we aim to tackle the entire software stack portability problem through an open-standard approach by enabling neural network models provided by high-level frameworks such as ONNX Runtime to be lowered down to RISC-V ISA through SYCL programming model. In particular, we:

- explain the process of mapping the neural network models to RISC-V ISA.
- discuss the support for RISC-V accelerators in the SYCL compilations flows.
- discuss the support for RISC-V CPUs in the SYCL compilation flow.
- integrate our framework with the RISC-V simulator [11] and present the results on two neural network models.

The rest of the paper is organized as follows: We provide a brief background about SYCL in the rest of this section. Section 2 discusses the support required to run neural network models on RISC-V accelerators. Section 3 discusses the support required to run neural network models on RISC-V CPUs. Section 4 presents some initial results and Sect. 5 concludes the paper.

1.1   Background on SYCL

SYCL [14] is an industry-driven Khronos open standard that adds data parallelism to C++ for heterogeneous systems [13]. It's a single-source programming model and a cross-platform abstraction layer originally built on top of runtime APIs which can offload the kernel code on to appropriate devices. SYCL promises improved maintainability, productivity, and ease of use while offering the same degree of low-level control and optimization through its underlying backends. It uses dedicated backends to target specific hardware accelerators, such as OpenCL, HIP, and CUDA using adequate IRs (SPIR/SPIR-V, PTX etc.).

SYCL applications consist of host code (required to orchestrate and offload the kernel) and device code(compute-intensive kernel). The device code generally consists of kernel functions that get compiled separately into device kernels/binaries before getting combined with the host binaries generated by a common C++ compiler. The resulting single executable is then orchestrated by the SYCL runtime library, the device offloaded kernels being executed asynchronously relative to the host code.

One core construct of any SYCL code is the *Queue* object. *Actions* (kernels and memory operations) are submitted to the queue. A SYCL queue then sequentially incorporates a task graph that wraps actions within its node and expresses events and data dependencies through its edges. The SYCL runtime schedules these actions without breaking any dependencies from producer-consumer relationship.

2   DNN and RISC-V Accelerators

In this section we describe how we can use RISC-V as a custom accelerator to run DNN models written in SYCL. We first look at high level architecture and the various open source, open standard applications and frameworks needed to achieve this. Next, we look at the compilation flow which allows the generation of RISC-V ISA from SYCL kernels. Finally, we discuss how the memory is transferred between the host and the accelerator.

2.1   High Level Architecture

Figure 1 represents the high-level architecture for running deep neural network applications using SYCL programming model. The oneAPI [4] ecosystem provides all the supporting open source libraries and frameworks needed to build the neural network models. Firstly, we use ONNX [5] which defines an interoperable open standard format of DNN models representation. This model is usually stored in an ONNX file format. This model is then consumed by an open source framework called ONNX Runtime [6].

ONNX Runtime (ORT) is open source project [6] that aims to accelerate Neural Network (NN) inference across different operating systems and hardware platforms. ORT was extended to add a SYCL backend [23] in order to support a wider variety of platforms without having to re-write kernels each time. This was added by introducing a sycl queue and submitting all the operations in a network to this queue. Further, the operator implementations in the SYCL backend are library calls to open source optimized kernels in the oneAPI ecosystem libraries - SYCL-DNN [15] and SYCL-BLAS [12]. SYCL-DNN is an open source library which has optimized implementations for the common neural network operations like convolution, pooling etc. It has only SYCL kernels and

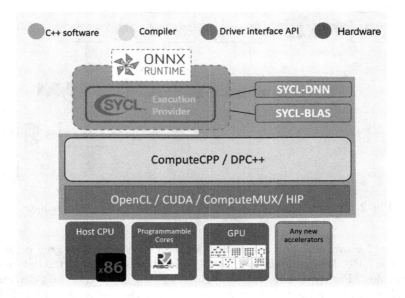

Fig. 1. Overall architecture of DNN models running on RISC-V chips

does not depend on any vendor-specific implementation. SYCL-BLAS is a similar library for linear algebra operations. The optimized SYCL kernels from the libraries are then compiled by a SYCL compiler like ComputeCPP or DPC++ and a single executable is created. Finally, SYCL uses a runtime like OpenCL, CUDA or ComputeMUX to target different devices. Any device with OpenCL support allows running SYCL kernels with the help of a SYCL compiler. CUDA is primarily used to support NVIDIA devices. ComputeMUX provides driver APIs which can be implemented by any hardware drivers to enable SYCL support. This makes it easier for newer hardware to make use of the SYCL ecosystem and then run neural network models and in general any SYCL kernel. We exploit this feature of CompuetMUX to consume the SPIR-V code generated and further lower it to generate custom RISC-V ISA, which is then either run on the hardware or a simulator. The next section describes the compilation flow in more detail.

2.2 Compilation Flow

SYCL [14] is a single source programming model, which means, both the host and the device code reside in the same file. The same file is compiled twice, once to compile the host code (can be done by any C++ compiler) and a second time to compile the device code (Requires a SYCL compiler).

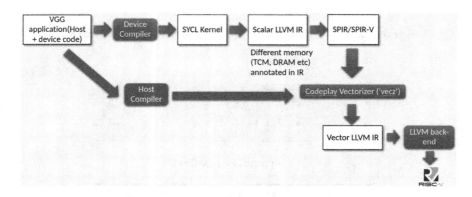

Fig. 2. Compilation flow for RISC-V accelerators with vector support

Figure 2 shows the compilation flow for a SYCL kernel. The grey boxes represent the CPU/host compilation flow. The red boxes represent the device compilation flow. Firstly, the device compiler scans the C++ code and detects the SYCL kernels. From the SYCL kernel, it generates the scalar LLVM IR (Fig. 3a) based on the type of memory being used. This LLVM IR is then translated into a portable format like SPIR/SPIR-V [10] (Fig. 3b). Finally, this code needs to be vectorized. For this we use the *vecz* from ComputeAorta [22]. This consumes the SPIR/SPIR-V and generates a vectorized LLVM-IR (Fig. 4a). The vectorized LLVM-IR is then lowered using the RISC-V LLVM backend to generate RISC-V ISA(Figure 4b). Since the LLVM-IR is vectorized, it generates RVV instructions. Apart from vectorizing the code, ComputeMux or ComputeAorta also performs optimizations like unrolling inorder to improve the performance of the code.

Figure 4 shows the vectorized LLVM IR and the RVV instructions generated for a fully connected operator which is commonly used as the last layer in image classification models. Notice the *fmul* $<4 \times float>$ and *fadd* $<4 \times float>$ operations in the LLVM IR. These show that a vector width of 4 was used to generate the LLVM IR. Thus, the multiplication or addition operations are performed on a vector of 4 floats simultaneously. Similarly the *vfmul* and *vfadd* represent the generated vectorized multiplication and addition instructions on floating point operands. Next we look at how the offloading the kernel to the device is achieved.

2.3 Offloading and Memory Movement

Figure 5 shows a schematic of a CPU and a RISC-V accelerator. It consists of 2 cores, each consisting of 6 compute units (simd or vector width of 6), a small tightly coupled memory and a connection to a higher capacity DRAM memory. The accelerator DRAM memory accepts DMA commands from the host CPU memory. SYCL memory model uses buffers. Buffers can either be mapped to the host(CPU) memory or the accelerator memory. Inorder to access this memory, SYCL kernels need to create accessors. This represents what memory needs to be available on the accelerator before the kernel execution can begin. Hence, the

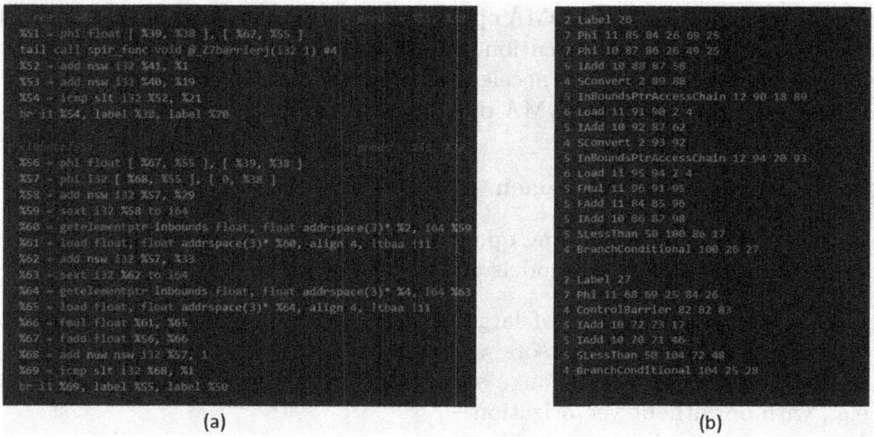

Fig. 3. Snippet of (a)Scalar LLVM IR generated (b) SPIR generated from SYCL kernel for fully connected operator

Fig. 4. Snippet of (a)vector LLVM IR generated (b) RISC-V RVV instructions generated from SYCL kernel for fully connected operator

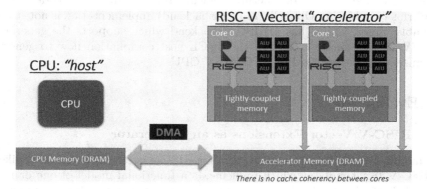

Fig. 5. Offloading to a vector RISC-V accelerator

accessors are used to perform DMA operations to ensure that the data is available before the kernel can start execution. Once the DMA operation is complete, the kernel code is launched on the accelerator. Any data created is then transferred back to the host via another DMA operation.

2.4 Benefits of this Approach

There are many benefits to using open standard and open source frameworks in order to run neural network models on RISC-V accelerators:

- It allows for easy porting of large scale SYCL applications from GPUs to custom cost effective processors with no re-write of any code.
- It allows to choose from a range of features when designing new processors - e.g., with or without vectorization.
- It reuses the scheduling and offloading mechanism provided by SYCL.

3   DNN and RISC-V CPUs

In this section we discuss running SYCL applications on RISC-V CPUs. There has been on-going work to support *SYCL host compilation* [19] which provides a CPU-directed compilation flow for SYCL applications. This compilation flow is beneficial for CPUs since the host and the device code is run on the same hardware. This creates a new opportunity where the vectorization and other optimizations can be done on the entire code and not only the kernel. The compilation pass shown in Fig. 2 is slightly modified to make sure that the host and the device IRs are combined and optimized before generating the vectorized IR.

The SYCL host compilation allows to exploit any backend available in the Clang/LLVM compiler infrastructure, allowing us to execute SYCL code on CPU platforms for which an OpenCL (or other backend) implementation is not readily available. Since, LLVM has a RISC-V backend which supports the generation of RVV instructions, we can use the SYCL host compilation flow to generate optimized and vectorized ISA for RISC-V CPUs.

4   Evaluation

4.1 RISC-V Vector Extensions as an Accelerator

We modified Spike [11], to add support for RISC-v vector instructions. Spike is a RISC-V ISA simulator which implements a functional model of one or more RISC-V harts. We used Spike for functional verification and for benchmarking. It is then integrated with a SYCL compiler (ComputeCPP [1] - CE 2.11.0 Device Compiler (Experimental) - clang version 15.0.0) and ComputeAorta [22] with RISC-V offload support. All of this was packaged for ease of use and is available as Acoran for Process Developer [2]. The system configuration used to report the results is described in Table 1. We report the executed instruction count and total DMA access where applicable.[1,2]

Table 1. System configuration details

Host CPU	Intel(R) Core(TM) i7-9700K CPU @ 3.60 GHz, 32 GB memory
Host OS	Ubuntu 18.04.3
Acoran for Process Developers [2]	0.9.0 (Pre-Alpha)
Docker version	20.10.7
Date tested	27 March 2023

Table 2. Numbers of executed RISC-V instructions when running Vector addition of size 128000

Vector width	Num instructions	Speedup w.r.t no vectorize
1	36312000	1
2	26488000	1.370885
4	25724000	1.4116
8	25340000	1.432991
16	25148000	1.443932
32	25064000	1.448771
64	37388000	0.971221

We first run a simple vector addition example with different vector widths as shown in Table 2. The size chosen for vector addition is 128000. A single vector register is 128 bits length. The Vector width represented in the table is the vectorization factor. We see that increasing the vector width gives consistently better speedup until vector width 32. We see a negative impact in number of instructions for vector width of 64. Hence, this setup can be used to ascertain correct vector width parameters based on the type of computation being performed.

Further, the vector add example does not scale with vector width as it is not computationally intensive. Since, most of the compute intensive neural network operations (convolutions, fully connected layer) use matrix multiplication as their building block. We run a matrix multiplication example for square matrices of size 128 as shown in Table 3. We notice that vector width 16 gives the best

---

[1] See Table 1 for system configurations. Results may vary. This notice applies to all reported performance results in this Section.

[2] All performance measures were collected by the paper authors in the period between 01/01/2023 and 27/03/2023.

Table 3. Numbers of executed RISC-V instructions when running Matrix multiplication of size 128

Vector width	Num instructions	Speedup w.r.t no vectorize
1	31248448	1
2	19762368	1.58121
4	9972800	3.133368
8	5074880	6.157475
16	2630784	11.878
32	31968576	0.977474

performance. Also the reduction in number of instructions scales well with the increasing vector width.

Neural Network Models: We use two well known models for our evaluation. We run them in inference model. VGG-16 [21] is a very common network used for image classification. It consists of 16 layers of 3×3 convolutions interleaved with max pool layers.

ResNet-50 [20] is a 50-layer network. It consists of number of blocks each having: 1×1 convolution, 3×3 convolution and 1×1 convolution, in that order. We use a batch size of 1 when running both the networks

Table 4. Neural network model results with vector size 8 and memory read/written in MB

Model	Num instructions	DMA write into accelerator (input data in MB)	DMA read from accelerator (output data in MB)
VGG-16	12314401560	534	3
RESNET-50	7551505532	100	3

Table 4 shows the results for these two models. We report the number of instructions as well as the number of direct memory writes written to the accelerator. The DMA read is the output classification of the network and hence is constant in both the cases. Thus, we see that using an open standard and open source stack, allowed us to run complex SYCL application easily on the RISC-V spike simulator.

4.2   RISC-V Vector Extension on CPUs

The *SYCL host compilation* as described in Sect. 3 allows to exploit any backend available in the Clang/LLVM compiler infrastructure, to execute SYCL code on CPU. To demonstrate this, we have successfully run matrix multiplication example on QEMU's RISC-V target [9]. We use the QEMU [17] emulator, version 7.2.50 and ComputeCPP version 2.8. The details of the system configuration is described in Table 5.

Table 5. System configuration details

Host CPU	Intel SkyLake (i7-6700), 4.20 GHz, 32 GB DDR4
OS	Ubuntu 18.04.3
QEMU version	7.2.50
ComputeCPP version	2.8
Date tested	27 March 2023

Listing 4: RISC-V instructions for the scalar simple vector add sample

```
000300000014774 <SYCL_class_SimpleVadd_int_>:
  14774:  fd010113            addi    sp,sp,-48
  14778:  02113423            sd    ra,40(sp)
  1477c:  00d13423            sd    a3,8(sp)
  14780:  02c13023            sd    a2,32(sp)
  14784:  00058613            mv    a2,a1
  14788:  00813583            ld    a1,8(sp)
  1478c:  00c13823            sd    a2,16(sp)
  14790:  00a13c23            sd    a0,24(sp)
  14794:  00000613            li    a0,0
  14798:  110000ef            jal    ra,148a8 <_Z13get_global_idj>
  1479c:  01013683            ld    a3,16(sp)
  147a0:  01813683            ld    a1,24(sp)
  147a4:  00050613            mv    a2,a0
  147a8:  02013503            ld    a0,32(sp)
  147ac:  00261613            slli    a2,a2,0x2
  147b0:  00c686b3            add    a3,a3,a2
  147b4:  0006a683            lw    a3,0(a3)
  147b8:  00c50533            add    a0,a0,a2
  147bc:  00052603            lw    a0,0(a0)
  147c0:  00d6053b            addw    a0,a0,a3
  147c4:  00c585b3            add    a1,a1,a2
  147c8:  00a5a023            sw    a0,0(a1)
  147cc:  02813083            ld    ra,40(sp)
  147d0:  03010113            addi    sp,sp,48
  147d4:  00008067            ret
```

Listing 5: RVV instructions for the simple vector add sample

```
0000000000124dbc <__vecz_v16_SYCL_class_SimpleVadd_int_>:
  12dbc:  fd010113            addi    sp,sp,-48
  12dc0:  02113423            sd    ra,40(sp)
  12dc4:  00d13423            sd    a3,8(sp)
  12dc8:  00c13c23            sd    a2,24(sp)
  12dcc:  00058613            mv    a2,a1
  12dd0:  00813583            ld    a1,8(sp)
  12dd4:  00c13823            sd    a2,16(sp)
  12dd8:  02a13023            sd    a0,32(sp)
  12ddc:  00000613            li    a0,0
  12de0:  221000ef            jal    ra,13800 <_Z13get_global_idj>
  12de4:  01013683            ld    a3,16(sp)
  12de8:  01813603            ld    a2,24(sp)
  12dec:  00050593            mv    a1,a0
  12df0:  02013503            ld    a0,32(sp)
  12df4:  00259593            slli    a1,a1,0x2
  12df8:  00b686b3            add    a3,a3,a1
  12dfc:  c5287057            vsetivli    zero,16,e32,m4,ta,mu
  12e00:  0206a607            vle32.v    v12,(a3)
  12e04:  00b60633            add    a2,a2,a1
  12e08:  02066407            vle32.v    v8,(a2)
  12e0c:  02860487            vadd.vv    v8,v8,v12
  12e10:  00b50533            add    a0,a0,a1
  12e14:  02056427            vse32.v    v8,(a0)
  12e18:  02813083            ld    ra,40(sp)
  12e1c:  03010113            addi    sp,sp,48
  12e20:  00008067            ret
```

The latest Clang backend allows to emit RISC-V vector instructions (RVV) (enabled by specifying -*march* = "*rv64iv*"). We have tested that the backend correctly emits vector instructions. Code listings 4 and 5 shows a side by side view of the scalar and vectorized RISC-V ISA instructions, with vector instructions correctly emitted for the vectorized sample.

Table 6 shows the number of instructions executed on the CPU for the vector vs the scalar version of the matrix multiply operation. We notice that overall there is a 3.4× reduction in the number of instructions executed for the vector version of the generated code. Even though lower instruction count does not directly lead to lower execution time, it is a good indicator of the positive impact of vectorization on architectures that support the RISC-V Vector Extension.

Table 6. Numbers of executed RISC-V instructions (vector instruction vs scalar instruction) when running GEMM operation with vector width 8.

Instruction	Vector I.C	Scalar I.C	Ratio
fmad	37664248	278830430	7.4×
add	25009180	134658739	5.38×
branch	35259781	126322089	3.58×
load	51288413	301149676	5.87×
total	330626967	1140008455	3.44×

5 Conclusion and Future Work

This paper focused on the benefits of the portability of open standard software stack across different architectures. We have demonstrated that existing applications written in SYCL, can be lowered down to RISC-V/RVV ISA and further executed on the Spike simulator or RISC-V core emulator. The SYCL open standard-based software stack not only helps end-user programmers to reuse existing code across different architectures, but also helps framework developer to minimize code duplication to exploit different vendor-specific architectures, leading to better framework maintainability.

The experiments have been executed on the RISC-V/RVV Spike simulator. To generate RISC-V/RVV ISA and offload the SYCL code on Spike Simulator we used ComputeAorta. We have demonstrated how ComputeAorta can generate RISC-V vector extension ISA, from the same SPIR-V generated from the SYCL application by using its whole function vectorizer module. Our results indicate that using vector extension in RISC-V increases the computational intensity leading to better performance. We have demonstrated how ComputeAorta can seamlessly leverage the DMA memory operation provided in the Spike simulator to improve memory movement and leverage the DMA support when available. We have demonstrated that automatic exploitation of DMA memory operation and RISC-V vector extension through ComputeAorta led to performance improvements in SYCL application by using our proposed compilation workflow.

Using ComputeAorta enables the future chip provider to design a processor that uses vectorization and is easily programmable using SYCL. This will help the providers to work on the next generation of AI applications using neural networks.

The Two supported AI models in this paper have demonstrated a successful proof of concept SYCL-based support for RISC-V architecture. As future work, we are planning to support the full AI framework model such as PyTorch by using oneAPI DPC++ compiler by lowering it to RISC-V/RVV ISA via the ComputeAorta toolkit.

Moreover, we plan to expand RISC-V/RVV support via SYCL for other domain through ComputeAorta such as big data and cloud-based applications.

ComputeAorta can consume SPIR-V/LLVM-IR and lower to different vendor-specified ISA. Hence it is possible to accelerate non-SYCL Frameworks/APIs that generates SPIR-V/LLVM-IR on RISC-V/RVV architectures via ComputeAorta. An example of such architecture is TornadoVM [18] - a Java-based open source framework that accelerates Java applications by lowering it to SPIR-V/PTX. As a future work, we are planning to enable RISC-V support for TornadoVM via ComputeAorta.

Acknowledgments. This project has received funding from the European Union HE research and innovation programme under grant agreement No 101092877 and grant 101092850 (project AERO).

References

1. Acoran for process developers. https://developer.codeplay.com/products/acoran/processor-developers/home/. Accessed 31 Mar 2023
2. Computecpp compiler. https://developer.codeplay.com/products/computecpp/ce/home. Accessed 08 Mar 2022
3. Khronos group. https://www.khronos.org/. Accessed 31 Mar 2023
4. The oneAPI specification. https://www.oneapi.com/. Accessed 08 Mar 2022
5. ONNX github repo. https://github.com/onnx/onnx. Accessed 08 Mar 2022
6. ONNX runtime github repo. https://github.com/microsoft/onnxruntime. Accessed 08 Mar 2022
7. Raja. https://github.com/LLNL/RAJA. Accessed 31 Mar 2023
8. Reduced instruction set arcitecture. https://riscv.org/. Accessed 08 Mar 2023
9. RISC-V system emulator. https://www.qemu.org/docs/master/system/target-riscv.html. Accessed 31 May 2022
10. Simple binary intermediate language for graphical shaders and compute kernels. https://registry.khronos.org/SPIR-V/specs/unified1/SPIRV.html. Accessed 08 Mar 2023
11. Spike RISC-V ISA simulator. https://github.com/riscv-software-src/riscv-isa-sim. Accessed 08 Mar 2023
12. SYCL-BLAS: An implementation of BLAS using the SYCL open standard. https://github.com/CodeplaySoftware/SYCL-BLAS. Accessed 08 Mar 2022
13. SYCL: C++ single-source heterogeneous programming for OpenCL. https://www.khronos.org/sycl/. Accessed 08 Mar 2022
14. SYCL: C++ single-source heterogeneous programming for OpenCL. https://www.khronos.org/registry/SYCL/specs/sycl-2020-provisional.pdf. Accessed 08 Mar 2022
15. The SYCL-DNN neural network acceleration library. https://github.com/CodeplaySoftware/SYCL-DNN. Accessed 08 Mar 2022
16. Abadi, M., et al.: TensorFlow: a system for large-scale machine learning. In: 12th USENIX Symposium on Operating Systems Design and Implementation (OSDI 2016), pp. 265–283. USENIX Association, Savannah (2016). https://www.usenix.org/conference/osdi16/technical-sessions/presentation/abadi
17. Bellard, F.: Qemu, a fast and portable dynamic translator. In: USENIX annual technical conference, FREENIX Track, California, USA, vol. 41, pp. 10–5555 (2005)

18. Fumero, J., Papadimitriou, M., Zakkak, F.S., Xekalaki, M., Clarkson, J., Kotselidis, C.: Dynamic application reconfiguration on heterogeneous hardware. In: Proceedings of the 15th ACM SIGPLAN/SIGOPS International Conference on Virtual Execution Environments, VEE 2019. Association for Computing Machinery (2019). https://doi.org/10.1145/3313808.3313819

19. Ghiglio, P., Dolinsky, U., Goli, M., Narasimhan, K.: Improving performance of SYCL applications on CPU architectures using LLVM-directed compilation flow, PMAM 2022, pp. 1–10. Association for Computing Machinery, New York (2022). https://doi.org/10.1145/3528425.3529099

20. He, K., Zhang, X., Ren, S., Sun, J.: Deep residual learning for image recognition. In: 2016 IEEE Conference on Computer Vision and Pattern Recognition (CVPR), pp. 770–778 (2016)

21. Karen Simonyan, A.Z.: Very deep convolutional networks for large-scale image recognition (2014). https://arxiv.org/abs/1409.1556

22. Murray, A., Crawford, E.: Compute aorta: a toolkit for implementing heterogeneous programming models. In: IWOCL 2020. Association for Computing Machinery, New York (2020). https://doi.org/10.1145/3388333.3388652

23. Narasimhan, K., Farouki, O.E., Goli, M., Tanvir, M., Georgiev, S., Ault, I.: Towards performance portability of AI graphs using SYCL. In: 2022 IEEE/ACM International Workshop on Performance, Portability and Productivity in HPC (P3HPC), pp. 111–122 (2022). https://doi.org/10.1109/P3HPC56579.2022.00016

24. Paszke, A., et al.: PyTorch: an imperative style, high-performance deep learning library. In: Wallach, H., Larochelle, H., Beygelzimer, A., d Alch-Buc, F., Fox, E., Garnett, R. (eds.) Advances in Neural Information Processing Systems, vol. 32, pp. 8026–8037. Curran Associates, Inc. (2019). http://papers.nips.cc/paper/9015-pytorch-an-imperative-style-high-performance-deep-learning-library.pdf

25. Trott, C.R., et al.: Kokkos 3: programming model extensions for the exascale era. IEEE Trans. Parallel Distrib. Syst. **33**(4), 805–817 (2022). https://doi.org/10.1109/TPDS.2021.3097283

26. Yazdanbakhsh, A., Seshadri, K., Akin, B., Laudon, J., Narayanaswami, R.: An evaluation of edge TPU accelerators for convolutional neural networks. CoRR abs/2102.10423 (2021). https://arxiv.org/abs/2102.10423

Second Combined Workshop on Interactive and Urgent Supercomputing (CWIUS)

From Desktop to Supercomputer: Computational Fluid Dynamics Augmented by Molecular Dynamics Using MaMiCo and preCICE

Louis Viot(✉), Yannick Piel, and Philipp Neumann

Helmut-Schmidt-Universität Hamburg, Holstenhofweg 85, 22043 Hamburg, Germany
{viotl,yannick.piel,philipp.neumann}@hsu-hh.de

Abstract. Molecular-continuum flow simulations apply computationally intensive molecular dynamics (MD) simulations in localized regions of a geometry under consideration whereas classical, computationally cheaper computational fluid dynamics (CFD) solvers are employed for the vast amount of the rest of the computational domain. This approach to micro- and nanofluid dynamics already reduces computational efforts tremendously while still considering molecular effects in the flow solution. Yet, MD still dominates costs by far and demands for supercomputing capacities, and researchers and engineers who strive to have rather rapid (but at the cost of limited accuracy) feedback on their simulation results could in principle rely on CFD, even at workstation level.

In this contribution, we propose to extend our molecular-continuum coupling tool MaMiCo towards a desktop-to-supercomputer architecture. By connecting MaMiCo with the multi-physics coupling library preCICE, TCP/IP socket-based data streaming and partitioned molecular-continuum coupling are enabled which allows to run the CFD simulation on a desktop computer while an ensemble of MD simulations is executed on a supercomputer. The latter is coupled strongly to the CFD solver.

We discuss implementational aspects, point out further features of our approach and present performance results of the desktop-to-supercomputer approach, which is validated in differently sized Couette flow scenarios.

Keywords: Molecular-continuum · Multiscale · Software coupling

1 Introduction

The simulation of micro- and nanoflows often faces a scale-bridging challenge. State-of-the-art computational fluid dynamics (CFD) solvers [1], used to model

This project has been supported by dtec.bw – Digitalization and Technology Research Center of the Bundeswehr (projects hpc.bw and MaST). dtec.bw is funded by the European Union – NextGenerationEU. The authors further thank HLRS for the provision of computational resources (project GCS-MDDC).

A. Bienz et al. (Eds.): ISC High Performance 2023 Workshops, LNCS 13999, pp. 567–576, 2023.
https://doi.org/10.1007/978-3-031-40843-4_42

fluids at the continuum scale, are not necessarily accurate enough. This particularly holds when modeling the fluid behavior in nanochannels [20] or, in general, close to surfaces which imply inter-molecular surface-fluid interactions that need to be resolved [12]. Molecular dynamics (MD) simulations [18] are in these cases a good method of choice. MD models molecular behavior bottom-up in the sense that molecular interactions are prescribed and then allow to model fluid phase separation or fluid-surface interactions, resolving aforementioned challenging situations. However, since typically millions of molecules (or even more) are required, computing all their trajectories is—compared to continuum-based CFD solvers—inherently computationally intensive and often results in the use of supercomputers [22,23].

In these cases, molecular-continuum methods [11,13] represent one way to solve this conundrum. Molecular-continuum methods have been, amongst others, developed to spatially couple computationally affordable, (at the nanoscale) inaccurate CFD methods with computationally intensive, yet molecular interaction-resolving MD. This allows to invest into MD only for localized spots of the computational domain and to rely on CFD methods everywhere else.

Nevertheless, MD still typically dominates computational cost by far, see for example [2]. Besides, sampling and averaging MD quantities (such as flow velocities) is required to provide smooth quantities to the CFD solver due to molecular Brownian motion (i.e., thermal noise). For the latter reasons, molecular-continuum and related simulation approaches still often rely on the use of HPC systems [8,14].

In this contribution, we present our work towards interactive computing to assess nanoflows using the molecular-continuum approach. The main idea is to execute the CFD-based portion of the simulation on the engineer's desktop computer, while executing the computationally intensive MD portion on a supercomputer. To couple MD and CFD, we rely on two well-established pieces of software: the macro-micro-coupling tool (MaMiCo) for molecular-continuum algorithmics [15] and preCICE [3] for the partitioned coupling from desktop to supercomputer. This approach is expected to enable engineers in the future to obtain first insights into the overall flow problems via CFD and refining their views by MD and respective supercomputing usage. We will particularly focus on the implementational aspects for this endeavor. While in a traditional approach, one would run the entire coupled simulation, i.e. MD *and* CFD, on a supercomputer and send back the results for interactive visualization and analysis to a desktop, our approach to strictly separate CFD/desktop and MD/supercomputer execution provides some advantages. First, instead of transferring the entire flow field data from the supercomputer to the desktop, only small portions of it, corresponding to the size of the embedded MD domain, need to be communicated. Second, the use of engineering software typically comes with licensing costs and restrictions of their use to (sub-)networks or single hardware devices. Our approach will allow in the future to use standard preCICE-supporting CFD software, such as the widely spread packages Ansys Fluent or COMSOL, on stand-alone desktops, without the need to migrate this software to supercomputing environments.

After discussing related work in Sect. 2, we describe the pieces of software that our implementation for multiscale flow simulation leverages in Sect. 3. Their integration and performance results are presented in Sect. 4, followed by a short summary and outlook to future work, cf. Sect. 5.

2   Related Work

Only few software packages are available that enable molecular-continuum coupling such that arbitrary MD and CFD solvers can be plugged together [15,19, 21]. To couple arbitrary mesh-based CFD and particle-based (e.g., MD) solvers on supercomputers, MaMiCo [15] has evolved over the last years. MaMiCo supports ensemble averaging of MD systems, i.e. coupling one CFD solver instance to an entire ensemble of quasi-identical randomized MD simulations. The software further incorporates noise filters, enables automated dynamic error control via on-the-fly adaption of the MD ensemble size and has recently been extended by a fault tolerance mechanism; see [9,10] for details on all these features.

Distributed compute resources for (ensembles of) computationally intensive MD simulations have been established for various MD packages, such as for the MD software GROMACS [5] or the MD software NAMD [16] on grid environments. An interactive approach to MD simulations has been reported in [17]. For GROMACS, interactive MD simulations using HPC resources have been reported in [6].

An approach to execute molecular-continuum fluid flow solvers in a partitioned way has been reported in [4]. Using the Bespoke Framework Generator (BFG), a grid-deployable concept was developed for such simulations.

In our work, we present in the following a fully operable implementation of a HPC-aware molecular-continuum simulation which can execute CFD and MD parts in a partitioned setting, enabling the execution of the CFD solver on one's personal desktop computer while the expensive MD simulations are executed on a supercomputer.

3   Coupling Software

3.1   MaMiCo

The macro-micro-coupling tool (MaMiCo)[1] [9,10,14,15] strives to couple arbitrary MD and CFD solvers. It is implemented in C++, supports MPI and uses a Cartesian grid structure to exchange hydrodynamic quantities such as mass or momentum between the solvers. The original implementation of MaMiCo is monolithic in the sense that both MD and CFD solver are, together with MaMiCo, compiled into one executable which can be run on a supercomputer. Simulations on up to 65.536 compute cores have already been reported in [14]. Currently, MaMiCo interfaces on MD side, amongst others, the community MD

---

[1] https://github.com/HSU-HPC/MaMiCo.

software LAMMPS as well as the MD software ls1 mardyn [23], a massively parallel molecular simulation software for process engineering applications. On CFD side, various Lattice Boltzmann solvers as well as more simplistic test solvers are supported [15].

While the monolithic approach taken by MaMiCo is sufficient for pure use on supercomputers or workstations, it forbids a partitioned execution on both at the same time.

3.2 preCICE

preCICE [3] is a coupling library for partitioned multiphysics simulations. Written in C++ and supporting both TCP/IP socket-based and MPI communication, preCICE is shipped with a variety of explicit and implicit time coupling schemes and surface and volumetric data interpolation methods. To leverage the coupling methodology, *adapters* are required to connect one's favorite solver with preCICE. Currently, 9 official adapters, including an adapter to the widespread CFD community code OpenFOAM [7] as well as 15 community-developed adapters are available for preCICE[2].

4   Integration of preCICE and MaMiCo to Enable Desktop-to-Supercomputer Molecular-Continuum Simulation

4.1   Computing Platform: HSUper

In the following, we detail how we realized a desktop-to-supercomputer molecular-continuum flow simulation. We leveraged for this purpose the supercomputer HSUper, hosted at Helmut-Schmidt-Universität. HSUper consists of three compute partitions; we will only focus on its biggest partition, which consists of 571 dual-socket Intel Icelake compute nodes. Each socket holds an Intel Xeon Scalable Platinum 8360Y processor with 36 cores. Every node is equipped with 256 GB RAM. All nodes are connected by a non-blocking fat-tree NVIDIA InfiniBand HDR100 network. HSUper uses SLURM for batch-based compute job execution.

4.2   Technical Integration

To overcome the aforementioned restriction of MaMiCo to monolithic execution, a new class has been created to call the preCICE library from the MaMiCo framework, cf. Fig. 1.

On the one hand, this class acts as a CFD-like component to MaMiCo in the sense that it is used to retrieve (resp. send) data from (resp. to) the CFD solver that is coupled through preCICE. preCICE handles data interpolation in case

---

[2] see https://precice.org/adapters-overview.html, as of 02 March 2023.

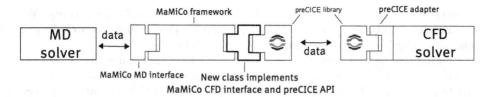

Fig. 1. preCICE integration within MaMiCo. The new MaMiCo adapter class acts as a CFD interface on MaMiCo side and as coupling adapter on preCICE side.

of non-matching grids between the CFD and MD solvers. On the other hand, this class is used to steer the solving between the two solvers so that the time coupling schemes of preCICE can be fully leveraged and the legacy MaMiCo time-loop and hard coded coupling scheme is no longer used. As a result, a coupled molecular-continuum simulation can now be run in a truly partitioned way with two different executables both calling the preCICE library.

To connect the CFD solver, executed on one's personal computer, with the MD simulations, executed on a supercomputer, we used the socket implementation of preCICE together with ssh port forwarding. A typical workflow we used on HSUper to connect all the components and run the coupled simulation is as follows:

1. All connections through port N_{port} from the local computer are forwarded to port N_{port} on the login node through local ssh port forwarding.
2. The CFD + preCICE executable is executed.
3. On the login node, a job containing the next steps (4+5) is submitted to slurm for the respective allocation of nodes.
4. When the job starts on each compute node, ssh remote port forwarding allows to redirect all connections from port N_{port} on the login node to port N_{port} on the current compute node.
5. Finally, on each compute node, the MD+MaMiCo+preCICE executable is run and connects to the local computer.

4.3   Performance Results

We investigated the desktop-to-supercomputer coupling in molecular-continuum Couette flow scenarios. In these scenarios, the MD domain is embedded in the CFD domain and both domains are overlapping. In the overlap, data transfer takes place to establish two-way coupling between the solvers. The outermost three cell layers of the overlap region are required to impose CFD data to the MD system whereas MD data are sampled in the forth layer to provide boundary conditions to the CFD solver. The scenario is highly transient, i.e. every coupled CFD time step is also fully resolved in time by MD. In our setting, this translates into 50 MD time steps covering one CFD time step, and into the CFD flow field being strongly coupled to the MD trajectories over the entire course of a coupled simulation. Data exchange is required in each CFD time step. See [14] for details on the parametrization and more details on the Couette setup. We use the community code OpenFOAM v2112 on CFD side and, without loss of generality, the MD test code SimpleMD [15] on MD side.

Simulations were executed over a total of 3000 CFD time steps. The CFD solver was executed sequentially, whereas an ensemble of 50 MD simulations was simulated. Domain decomposition was employed for each MD simulation, so that $3 \times 4 \times 6$ sub-domains were created. The evolving 72 sub-domains were solved on one entire compute node (i.e., one compute node was, in terms of compute cores, fully saturated by a single MD simulation), so that in total 50 compute nodes were used for the entire coupled simulation.

We considered two different scenarios named MD-30 and MD-60, corresponding to two sizes for the embedded MD domain. MD-30 consists of a MD region of size $30 \times 30 \times 30$ (MD units), covered by $12 \times 12 \times 12$ cells of size 2.5. For MD-30, the embedded CFD domain is of size $50 \times 50 \times 50$ with a moving wall and fixed wall boundary conditions for the bottom and top boundaries and periodic boundary conditions for the remaining boundaries, representing the channel for the Couette channel. Scenario MD-60 arises from MD-30 by doubling the domain sizes and, thus, the number of grid cells along each of the three spatial dimensions. Figure 2 shows the profile of the velocity in x-direction, computed along the cross-section of the channel, over time considering the CFD and MD solver as well as the analytical solution for the MD-60 Couette flow scenario.

We particularly evaluated the impact of the amount of data transferred through the network; for each grid cell, one density and three velocity values (all values are stored in double-precision) are transferred between CFD and MD solver.

To evaluate the deterioration of performance that occurs once the CFD solver is executed remotely on the personal computer, we considered three lines of experiments for each scenario MD-30 and MD-60. In the first line, the coupling was executed entirely on HSUper. This line corresponds to the performance baseline. In the second line, the personal computer was hosted on university campus, which features a GBit-capable network connection to HSUper. In the third line, the personal computer was hosted off-campus with regular internet connectivity. For both on-campus and off-campus, the personal computer is using an ethernet connection. Table 1 lists the respective time measurements.

The runtime results show that an increase of the reference HSUper runtime of 31 % (resp. 23 %) was observed for MD-30 (resp. MD-60) when run on-campus. When running off-campus, an increase of 94 % (resp. 49 %) was observed for MD-30 (resp. MD-60).

With the explicit time coupling scheme used for these simulations, a coupling cycle consists of the following steps:

1. CFD is solved and CFD data are sent to MD
2. MD is solved and MD data are sent back to CFD

In addition to communication, preCICE also performs other operations during each coupling cycle such as data mapping (interpolation) between meshes. Hence, for all simulations, the runtime can be roughly decomposed into three

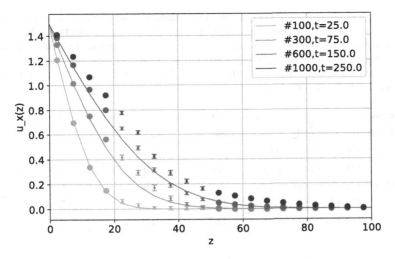

Fig. 2. Visualization of the velocity (x component) along the z-axis for the MD-60 molecular-continuum Couette flow simulation. Continuous lines are analytical solutions, big dots are solutions from the CFD solver and small dots with error bars are MD solutions.

parts: solving the CFD solver, solving the MD solver and receiving data (MD and CFD). From HSUper to on-campus, communications increase significantly by a factor of 8 for MD-30 and by a factor of 15 for MD-60. This could be explained by going from a low latency Infiniband network to an Ethernet/GBit network with TCP/IP sockets with ssh port forwarding. From On-Campus to Off-campus, the jump in communication times is approximately of a factor of 2 for both scenarios.

Adding both the MD solving time and the communication time, 'augmenting' the CFD solver with data from MD does come at a certain cost. Note that in the given examples, the time-to-solution of MD cannot be significantly reduced further by strong scaling: one molecular simulation of MD-30 comprises approx. 21 000 molecules, one MPI rank thus handles solely approx. 300 of these which is a very small amount of work already. However, the considered Couette flow has a relatively small CFD domain compared to MD. In both cases MD-30 and MD-60, the MD region covered ca. 22% over the entire domain. This is in contrast to actual CFD applications, which are expected to have a ratio that tends towards more cost on CFD side.

To further investigate the data transfer times, a test on integral software- and network-sided latency was performed. A coupled simulation between two dummy solvers[3] was created. Both dummy solvers actually do not compute anything and exchange fixed double values on two different meshes, each composed of only three 3D vertices. Both solvers are coupled via preCICE. One solver is executed

---

[3] https://github.com/precice/precice/blob/develop/examples/solverdummies/cpp/
  solverdummy.cpp.

Table 1. Time measurements (s) of coupled molecular-continuum simulations. Receiving Data corresponds the communication in both directions for the two solvers and do not include initialization nor data projection. HSUper only: entire molecular-continuum simulation executed on HSUper. On-campus: CFD solver was executed on personal computer within campus network. Off-campus: CFD solver was executed on personal computer, hosted outside of campus.

Scenario		Runtime	Solving MD	Receiving Data	Solving CFD
MD-30	HSUper only	366	293	17	56
	On-Campus	483	290	135	57
	Off-Campus	715	292	295	54
MD-60	HSUper only	2122	1350	48	523
	On-Campus	2602	1359	700	538
	Off-Campus	3195	1373	1188	541

on HSUper, while the other one is executed on HSUper or the personal computer (on-Campus or off-Campus). Table 2 lists the respective time measurements.

Table 2. Time measurements (s) with a coupled simulation between two dummy solvers exchanging three 3D vertices for 3000 coupling cycles.

Scenario		Runtime	Solver 1	Receiving Data	Solver 2
Dummy solver	HSUper only	5.5	0.7	4	0.7
	On-Campus	264	0.9	262	0.8
	Off-Campus	365	0.9	361	0.9

Despite the small amount of data exchanged, the communication time from HSUper only to on-campus (resp. off-campus) is multiplied by almost a factor of 70 (resp. 90). This allows us to conclude that the communication overhead already observed in Table 1 does not come from MaMiCo, but from the TCP/IP connection, the ssh port forwarding or additional overheads induced by preCICE.

5   Summary and Outlook

In this contribution, we have detailed our approach to establish a new feature of MaMiCo, that is to run coupled molecular-continuum flow simulations interactively, using a personal computer for the computationally affordable CFD solver and a supercomputer as backend for the computationally intensive MD ensemble simulations.

Although the TCP/IP-based communication (time) requires more in-depth investigation, we believe that this approach can open up the possibility to augment CFD simulations—if required—by dynamically triggered MD systems in a computational steering approach in the future: once an engineer encounters potential inconsistencies in stand-alone CFD simulations—e.g. by checking local Knudsen numbers in the flow field, which is subject to current work in an interdisciplinary project of computer scientists, physicists and engineers—, MD simulations can be triggered by the engineer and become executed on a supercomputer. This, however, requires more work. Amongst others, automated job script submissions need to be incorporated and interactive visualization has to be provided. Besides, security plays a crucial role and will require further considerations to avoid cyber-attacks on both personal computer and, in particular, the supercomputing environment.

Coupling MaMiCo and preCICE opens up various more perspectives: the volumetric interpolation provided by preCICE can now be used to couple unstructured-mesh-based CFD solvers with MaMiCo. The domain decomposition coupling algorithms of preCICE can be investigated for their application in molecular-continuum settings. MaMiCo can be executed with all CFD solvers in the future for which a preCICE adapter is already available. Investigation of these points is subject to current work.

References

1. Anderson, J.: Computational Fluid Dynamics: The Basics with Applications. McGraw-Hill Education, New York (2005)
2. Barsky, S., Delgado-Buscalioni, R., Coveney, P.: Comparison of molecular dynamics with hybrid continuum-molecular dynamics for a single tethered polymer in a solvent. J. Chem. Phys. **121**(5), 2403–2411 (2004)
3. Chourdakis, G., et al.: preCICE v2: a sustainable and user-friendly coupling library [version 2; peer review: 2 approved]. Open Res. Eur. **2**(51) (2022)
4. Delgado-Buscalioni, R., Coveney, P., Riley, G., Ford, R.: Hybrid molecular-continuum fluid models: implementation within a general coupling framework. Philos. Trans. Roy. Soc. A: Math. Phys. Eng. Sci. **363**(1833), 1975–1985 (2005)
5. van Dijk, M., Wassenaar, T., Bonvin, A.: A flexible, grid-enabled web portal for GROMACS molecular dynamics simulations. J. Chem. Theory Comput. **8**(10), 3463–3472 (2012)
6. Dreher, M., et al.: Interactive molecular dynamics: scaling up to large systems. Procedia Comput. Sci. **18**, 20–29 (2013)
7. The OpenFOAM Foundation: OpenFOAM (2023). www.openfoam.org. Accessed 02 Mar 2023
8. Grinberg, L., Insley, J., Fedosov, D., Morozov, V., Papka, M., Karniadakis, G.: Tightly coupled atomistic-continuum simulations of brain blood flow on petaflop supercomputers. Comput. Sci. Eng. **14**(6), 58–67 (2012)
9. Jafari, V., Neumann, P.: Fault tolerance for ensemble-based molecular-continuum flow simulations. In: HPC Asia 2023: Proceedings of the International Conference on High Performance Computing in Asia-Pacific Region, pp. 35–45 (2023)
10. Jarmatz, P., et al.: MaMiCo 2.0: an enhanced open-source framework for high-performance molecular-continuum flow simulation. SoftwareX **20**, 101251 (2022)
11. Kalweit, M., Drikakis, D.: Coupling strategies for hybrid molecular-continuum simulation methods. Proc. Inst. Mech. Eng. C J. Mech. Eng. Sci. **222**(5), 797–806 (2008)

12. Karniadakis, G., Beskok, A., Aluru, N.: Microflows and Nanoflows - Fundamentals and Simulation. Springer, Heidelberg (2005). https://doi.org/10.1007/0-387-28676-4

13. Mohamed, K., Mohamad, A.: A review of the development of hybrid atomistic-continuum methods for dense fluids. Microfluid. Nanofluid. **8**, 283–302 (2009)

14. Neumann, P., Bian, X.: MaMiCo: transient multi-instance molecular-continuum flow simulation on supercomputers. Comput. Phys. Commun. **220**, 390–402 (2017)

15. Neumann, P., Flohr, H., Jarmatz, P., Tchipev, N., Bungartz, H.J.: MaMiCo: software design for parallel molecular-continuum flow simulations. Comput. Phys. Commun. **200**, 324–335 (2016)

16. Phillips, J., et al.: Scalable molecular dynamics with NAMD. J. Comput. Chem. **26**(16), 1781–1802 (2005)

17. Rapaport, D.: Interactive molecular dynamics. Phys. A **240**(1), 246–254 (1997)

18. Rapaport, D.: The Art of Molecular Dynamics Simulation. Cambridge University Press, Cambridge (2004)

19. Ren, X.G., Wang, Q., Xu, L.Y., Yang, W.J., Xu, X.H.: HACPar: an efficient parallel multiscale framework for hybrid atomistic-continuum simulation at the micro- and nanoscale. Adv. Mech. Eng. **9**(8), 168781401771473 (2017)

20. Ritos, K., Borg, M.K., Lockerby, D.A., Emerson, D.R., Reese, J.M.: Hybrid molecular-continuum simulations of water flow through carbon nanotube membranes of realistic thickness. Microfluid. Nanofluid. **19**(5), 997–1010 (2015). https://doi.org/10.1007/s10404-015-1617-x

21. Tang, Y.H., Kudo, S., Bian, X., Li, Z., Karniadakis, G.E.: Multiscale universal interface: a concurrent framework for coupling heterogeneous solvers. J. Comput. Phys. **297**, 13–31 (2015)

22. Germann, T.C., Kadau, K.: Trillion-atom molecular dynamics becomes a reality. Int. J. Mod. Phys. C **19**(09), 1315–1319 (2008)

23. Tchipev, N., et al.: TweTriS: twenty trillion-atom simulation. Int. J. High Perform. Comput. Appl. **33**(5), 838–854 (2019)

Open OnDemand Connector for Amazon Elastic Kubernetes Service (EKS)

Faras Sadek[1] (ID), Milson Munakami[2] (ID), Arthur Barrett[3] (ID), Vesna Tan[3] (ID), Jeremy Guillette[3], Robert M. Freeman Jr.[4] (ID), and Raminder Singh[5]([✉]) (ID)

[1] Harvard University School of Engineering (SEAS Computing), Cambridge, USA
[2] Harvard University Research Computing (URC), Cambridge, USA
[3] Harvard University Academic Technology (ATG), Cambridge, USA
[4] Harvard Business School Research Computing Services, Cambridge, USA
[5] Faculty of Arts and Sciences Research Computing (FASRC) at Harvard University, Cambridge, USA
r_singh@g.harvard.edu

Abstract. Demand for computational resources is increasing in the classroom, and instructors want to train users on real-world problems by providing access to the latest resources. The Open OnDemand Connector for Amazon Elastic Kubernetes Service (EKS) is built on top of Open OnDemand (OOD), a web-based platform for accessing and managing Cluster and Cloud resources. In this paper, we have discussed how to leverage the power of Kubernetes and the flexibility of Open OnDemand to deploy a complex cloud-native solution using containerized applications, such as Jupyter, in a secure, scalable, and efficient manner.

Keywords: Open OnDemand (OOD) · Amazon Elastic Kubernetes Service (EKS) · High-Performance Computing (HPC) · AWS Cloud

1 Introduction

In modern learning environments, courses have increased their use of computational resources in the classroom. At the same time more courses are adding increasingly intensive analytical and quantitative elements to their curriculum. Faculty who use tools like Jupyter notebooks and services such as high-performance computing in their research, also desire to teach with these same tools; however, using the traditional HPC resource manager like Simple Linux Utility for Resource Management (SLURM) [4] does not enable Research Computing groups to support the needs of courses specifically, nor the large influx of users at the start of each semester.

At Harvard, in partnership with Academic Technology (ATG) and School of Engineering (SEAS), University research computing (URC) and Faculty of Arts and Sciences research computing (FASRC), we set up an interactive computation platform using Open OnDemand [5]. Open OnDemand is an open-source project designed to lower the barrier to HPC use across many diverse disciplines [1]. In our data center, this web-based platform fronts an Academic Cluster with 50 nodes. This solution supports 30+ courses each term, providing access to Jupyter, RStudio, Stata, Matlab etc. software and statistical tools, and has 1000+ unique users every semester.

A. Bienz et al. (Eds.): ISC High Performance 2023 Workshops, LNCS 13999, pp. 577–586, 2023.
https://doi.org/10.1007/978-3-031-40843-4_43

2   Problem Statement

A few of the courses require access to GPUs to teach machine learning and deep learning for half a term in a year, which presents a challenge as service providers to provide on-premises support for such expensive resources. This effort aims to build a scalable, cost-effective, and easy-to-use computation environment by integrating and extending the on-premises Academic Cluster with the resources and computational power of the Amazon AWS cloud.

In this project, we aim to connect OnDemand with a fully managed AWS EKS Cluster to support GPU based workloads and users' workflows with high memory requirements. Although the primary objective of this project is to provide the latest GPU resources in the cloud to students through the OnDemand interface, the elasticity and availability of computational resources provided by the cloud enables the project to support a wide range of computational needs on different scales. The support for state-of-the-art GPU resources within Open OnDemand enables users to take advantage of the power of GPU acceleration for their applications such as machine learning, deep learning, natural language processing, and scientific computing.

The Academic Cluster lacks sufficient GPUs to meet the demand of high-enrollment courses like *COMPSCI 109B: Data Science 2: Advanced Topics in Data Science*, which require over 100 GPUs during peak usage periods (Fig. 1).

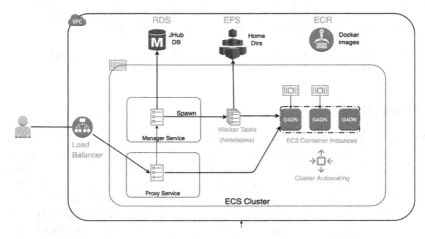

Fig. 1. Architecture diagram of JupyterHub based solution.

Previously, Academic Technology deployed a JupyterHub based solution on AWS that could scale GPU instances as needed. However, this solution was separate from the academic cluster and had its own infrastructure, lifecycle, and support. Additionally, it had several limitations:

a. The JupyterHub solution uses an AWS account that is not protected by Harvard's AWS Cloud Shield (not a direct connection) and requires a Harvard security policy exception each year to run.

b. Additionally, the JupyterHub cluster is based on an ECS cluster that is not optimized for large amounts of virtualized resources such as computing, and storage required to serve dozens of courses and more than a thousand students at any one time. Therefore, we require a flexible and powerful solution like AWS EKS.
c. Moreover, it does not integrate with the existing OnDemand platform where students/courses have a familiar and uniform interface for accessing compute resources and are already working with a variety of applications beyond Jupyter (e.g. RStudio, etc.).

3 Approach

Our goal is to integrate the existing OnDemand solution with AWS and configure the OnDemand application to launch a Jupyter application with access to GPU resources. Access to the course is controlled through Canvas (a web-based, learning management system, or LMS), and only authorized courses will be granted access to the AWS Jupyter application. Additionally, students will not have direct access to the infrastructure; all underlying resources will be hidden from them (Fig. 2).

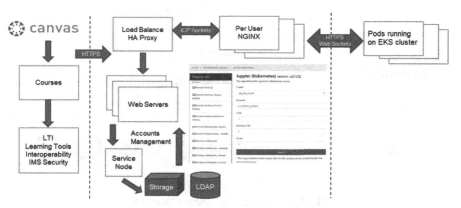

Fig. 2. Integration of Canvas, OnDemand and EKS cluster

Open OnDemand [5] is a web-based portal that provides access to cluster services. Through OnDemand, students are able to upload and download files, submit jobs, and most importantly, run pre-configured interactive applications such as Jupyter or Rstudio. OnDemand simplifies the complexity inherent in accessing and allocating compute resources, which is typically the responsibility of the Academic Cluster's workload manager, Slurm [4]. Although it is commonly used in high-performance computing and Linux-based clusters, most students, and even some faculty, are not familiar with it, so OnDemand provides the necessary high-level interface to take advantage of cluster resources without needing to understand the underlying details.

Kubernetes is a complete open-source container orchestration tool used to automate the deployment, scaling, and management of containerized applications. It is a popular solution for handling container-based workloads and has several compelling features for this project. Key among those features is the overall flexibility and scalability of the platform, as well as the extensive ecosystem of plugins and strong support from multiple cloud vendors in the form of managed services. This provides a strong base to manage resources for OnDemand application jobs in the cloud, which can then be coordinated with Slurm in the Academic Cluster.

Due to the complexity of this project, which involves integrating several components such as OnDemand, Canvas, AWS Elastic Kubernetes Service (EKS. We initially deployed an OnDemand node in the cloud and configured the system to run computational resources on the AWS EKS cluster. This approach helped us conduct a feasibility study and test different services available in AWS. We also evaluated different security solutions, such as AWS Identity and Access Management (IAM) and AWS Cognito and ensured that they aligned with Harvard's security requirements. The diagram below illustrates the high-level architecture of the solution, and we took an iterative approach to implement the current working solution (Fig. 3).

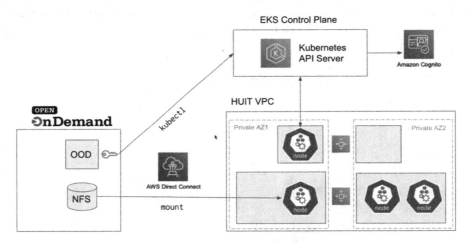

Fig. 3. High-level Architecture Diagram

In Kubernetes, a pod is the fundamental deployment unit that represents a group of containers that are closely connected and share common resources, such as network interface and storage. The entire pod, including all its containers, runs on a single EC2 machine allocated by the AWS autoscaler and shares the same private IP address. The kubelet, the primary "node agent" that runs on each node, communicates with the Kubernetes control plane and Kubernetes nodes. In our solution, the resource request from Kubernetes specifies the minimum and maximum amount of resources that the application container will require in a pod. While Kubernetes includes a reservation mechanism to minimize resource contention, it is limited to CPU [3] and maximum memory, potentially leading to reduced resource utilization. We are trying to optimize the GPU-based resource allocation based on student demand to support the class workload that needs to handle data-intensive and computation-intensive jobs.

4 Solution

4.1 Requirements

The solution is driven based on the following functional requirements:

1. User experience should remain the same as the previous Open OnDemand interface, and the underlying system and infrastructure complexity should be hidden from users.
2. Existing Open OnDemand users should be authenticated to Kubernetes and authorized to access their own servers/containers only.
3. On-premises users' home directories and files should be mounted on their Kubernetes nodes to ensure seamless access and data transfer.
4. Quality attributes like security, availability, reliability, and scalability are also considered during the design phase.

4.2 Implementation

The EKS cluster uses AWS Cognito as an OpenID Connect (OIDC)-compatible identity provider and is set up with two node groups, GPU computation and Kubernetes autoscaler. Each is a logical grouping of nodes that share common attributes, such as instance type, availability zone, and scaling configuration managed by the AWS autoscaling service. Kubernetes autoscaler node group has a minimum capacity of at least one node, while the other node group handles and manages the users' GPU compute nodes used by the EKS cluster. This GPU compute node group template also includes user data or a custom bootstrap script that connects each node provisioned and imaged using this template to the EKS cluster and also mount the on-premise NFS file system to the new node. The auto-scaling node runs a Kubernetes autoscaler pod that has an IAM role to adjust the number of running nodes in the users' computation node group. When a user requests a GPU node from the computation node group, AWS autoscaler checks the available nodes to fulfill the user request. If no nodes are available, Kubernetes autoscaler requests a new node from the computation node group to be attached to the EKS cluster. Once the node becomes ready, Kubernetes auto-scaler assigns the node to the requested workloads. This means that the configured autoscaling group can scale nodes in a node group as needed to optimize the cluster's performance and cost. To reduce the nodes provisioning times, warm pool is configured for the GPU node group (Figs. 4 and 5).

4.3 User Access

Students are expected to access GPU resources by logging into Canvas and using an LTI tool installed in their Canvas course to connect to OnDemand. This is the same process they already use to access non-GPU resources provided by OnDemand. The main difference is that in order to access GPU resources managed by Kubernetes, the user must be able to authenticate with AWS Cognito and then be authorized by Kubernetes RBAC. This part of the process is intended to be handled automatically and hidden from the end user.

AWS Cognito provides federated identities service to users registered in user pool, which provides a unique token credential to the authenticated user via OIDC to grant

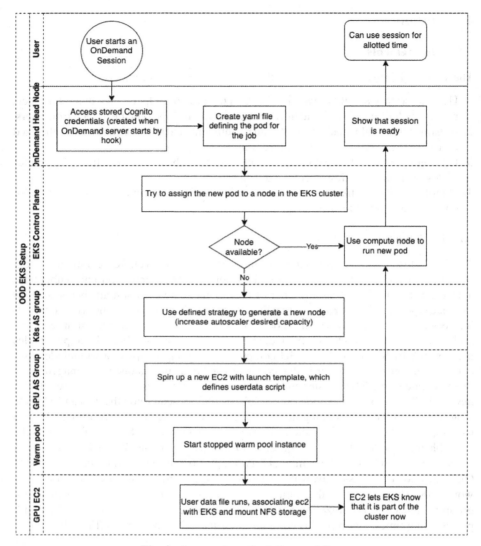

Fig. 4. An overview of solution workflow

access to the AWS EKS. The token identifier provider (IdP) is trusted by AWS Security Token Service (STS) to access temporary, limited-privilege AWS credentials (Fig. 6).

Student accounts are automatically added to the Kubernetes cluster by OnDemand as part of a pre-hook. It needs to initialize root-user credentials, which is executed when the user's per-user Nginx (PUN) process starts. Furthermore, users are created in AWS Cognito user pools as part of the pre-hook workflow. In other words, these accounts are not created until a user accesses OnDemand from Canvas. When a user accesses OnDemand, the pre-hook script checks whether the user exists in Amazon Cognito.

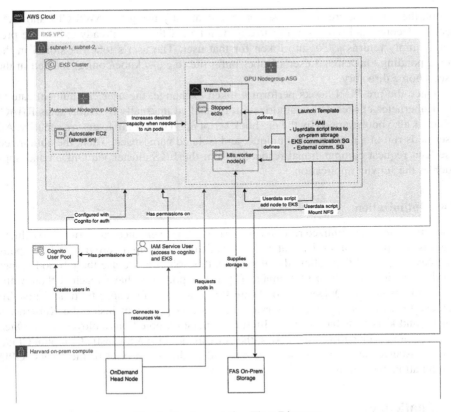

Fig. 5. Implementation Flow Diagram.

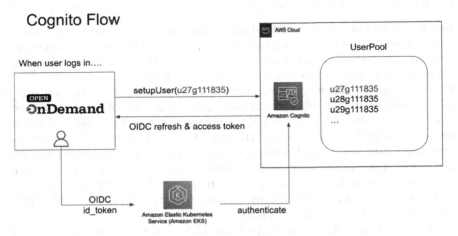

Fig. 6. An overview of Amazon Cognito security workflow

If not, the pre-hook creates the user programmatically using the AWS CLI and IAM service account and returns a user token identifier. If the user already exists, the pre-hook simply returns a Cognito token for that user. The user's token is stored in the corresponding OnDemand user's KubeConfig file (e.g., ~/.kube/config) located in the user's home directory.

Once the pre-PUN hooks perform a token exchange, the user can authenticate to the Kubernetes cluster. User authorization is handled internally by Kubernetes RBAC, which is also bootstrapped by the pre hook script upon user login to ensure security. All user pods run in a user-specific, unique, and isolated namespace. Then, the authorized user can request computational resources from the EKS cluster via OnDemand apps such as the Jupyter application.

4.4 Optimization

The importance of optimized resource usage cannot be overstated, and crucial to achieving this is deploying a service that can automatically clean up (deprovision? kill?) pods that have exceeded their allotted walltime. In this solution, we use the job-pod-reaper service provided by Open OnDemand [1] to kill pods that have reached their wall-time and ensure that OnDemand pods are shut down within a specific time frame. To achieve this, the job-pod-reaper service runs as a Deployment inside the Kubernetes cluster and kills pods based on the lifetime annotation noted on deployed pods. Once the pods are removed from the nodes, the corresponding AWS Elastic Compute Cloud (EC2) instances are scaled down and returned to the warm pool of the Users' GPU computation node group.

5 Challenges

During the development, deployment, and testing, we ran into several challenges.

1. Initially, we used the built-in EKS IAM authenticator, but due to security concerns and policy constraints on the programmatic creation of AWS IAM accounts associated with students, we had to explore alternative solutions like Cognito. Using Cognito, we were able to apply proper policies to those accounts to restrict access.
2. While testing the solution, we noticed that launching a container (Jupyter job) often took 5+ minutes from a cold start (no running instances available for the job to be placed on immediately). One immediate improvement was preloading the docker image on the EC2 instances (Kubernetes nodes). Since the Jupyter docker images were often 10+ GB in size, skipping the image pull saved 1–2 min on average. We also explored the idea of warm pools to further reduce the launch time to ~3 min for a new container; if an instance is already running in the warm pool, a user's job starts immediately. In future work, we will be exploring other solutions like AWS Karpenter to further optimize the runtimes.
3. During stress testing, we ran into the problem of IPv4 address exhaustion. This is not an uncommon issue with Kubernetes solutions. Initially, we were given two subnets of CIDR /24 with 508 usable IPs. Given that each jupyter job in our solution is assigned to a single g4dn.xlarge instance in order to use its GPU, that meant that each

jupyter job effectively consumed 5 IP addresses (kubelet, kube-proxy, aws-node, and nvidia-device-plugin-daemonset, jupyter job). This limited the maximum capacity of the cluster to 101 concurrent users. This was further complicated by the fact that by default, the Amazon VPC CNI plugin automatically attempts to reserve one full ENI of IP addresses so that pods can be immediately assigned an IP address. But in our case, this caused instances to rapidly consume IP addresses. We were able to disable this behaviour and only reserve the minimum required IP addresses per node, but that still imposed a hard limit on the number of possible Jupyter jobs. We worked with the network team to set up two /23 subnets, which allowed us to have 1024 IPs to support a class of ~100 active students with some headroom. For future expansion, we would need to consider an alternative network architecture such as using a private NAT gateway solution.

4. A user's session time is set up during the resource request, which for us is the GPU node.. If the user computation time requires more than the requested time, we need to find a way to enable the extension of the session as needed.
5. EKS nodes have an IAM Role with a permission policy to connect to the EKS cluster. Users on any given node thus will have access to the nodes' set of roles, giving them the ability to make AWS API calls to run other services. We needed to block access to the node's role in order to prevent this.

6 Conclusion

In summary, due to the increasing demand for specialized and specific computational resources in academic courses, which are not readily available through conventional cluster resources, we propose a solution that provides an extensible and user-friendly connection to the AWS-managed EKS cluster. This solution overcomes the limitations of the previously used JupyterHub approach and the deficiencies of traditional resource managers like SLURM by seamlessly integrating an on-premises Academic Cluster and Open OnDemand with the extendable and diverse computational power of the Amazon AWS cloud. Thus, by integrating Open OnDemand with a fully managed AWS EKS Cluster, the solution ensures adherence to secure and scalable infrastructure and policies, offering students a safe and reliable experience via on-demand teaching tools. For future work, we have already started collaborating with Harvard Business School Research Computing services to generalize the solution for their application needs. We plan to open-source the code and improve on documentation for better adoption.

References

1. Settlage, R., Chalker, B.A., Franz, E., Gallo, S., Moore, E., Hudak, D.: Open OnDemand: HPC for everyone. ISC 19. https://par.nsf.gov/biblio/10122554
2. Hudak, D., et al.: Open OnDemand a web-based client portal for HPC centers. J. Open Source Softw. 3(25), 622 (2018). https://doi.org/10.21105/joss.00622
3. Medel, V., Tolón, C., Arronategui, U., Tolosana-Calasanz, R., Bañares, J.Á., Rana, O.F.: Client-side scheduling based on application characterization on kubernetes. In: Pham, C., Altmann, J., Bañares, J.Á. (eds.) GECON 2017. LNCS, vol. 10537, pp. 162–176. Springer, Cham (2017). https://doi.org/10.1007/978-3-319-68066-8_13

4. Simple Linux Utility for Resource Management (SLURM). https://slurm.schedmd.com/
5. Open OnDemand. https://openondemand.org/
6. OnDemand Kubernetes connector. https://osc.github.io/ood-documentation/develop/installat
   ion/resource-manager/kubernetes.html

HPC on Heterogeneous Hardware (H3)

Preface to the Workshop on HPC on Heterogeneous Hardware (H3)

1 Objectives/Topics

The HPC on Heterogeneous Hardware (H3) Workshop was intended as a in-person event in Hamburg, Germany. It provided a platform for pioneering work on algorithmic research, software library design, programming models, and workflow development for increasingly heterogeneous hardware. In the workshop context, such hardware spans from ARM processors featuring long-vector extensions through GPU-accelerated systems to architecture platforms deploying special-function units, FPGAs, or deep learning processors. The workshop consisted of a well-balanced mix of invited talks, peer-reviewed conference contributions, and a panel bringing together worldwide experts in heterogeneous computing.

2 Topics of Interest and Thematic Scope of the Event

A more specific list of topics of interest to focus the submissions and draw specific speakers and invite broad participation of attendees was the following:

1. Heterogeneous algorithms that scale not just in terms of the system size but across diverse hardware kinds.
2. Heterogeneity in data approaches that incorporate mixed-precision storage and compute include data compression as well as hierarchical and randomized projections.
3. Software systems and libraries that support heterogeneous compute hardware and networking.
4. Programming models and tools that incorporate heterogeneity of both on-node compute and cross-node networking.

Perhaps the most challenging aspect was to limit the workshop's scope to the very few thematic areas that currently dominate the efforts of the community. This year, these included the following topics of interest:

– Heterogeneity in programming approaches including language solutions and DSL-friendly (domain specific languages) middleware libraries.
– Heterogeneous workloads that rely on convergence of scientific modeling, data analytics, and scientific AI/ML data models.
– Heterogeneity in data representation including hierarchical, randomized, compressive, and mixed-precision methods.

3 Workshop Organization

Out of the 8 submitted papers, the reviewers selected 6 for in-person presentation. The review process was single-blind with at least 3 reviews per paper and each program committee member reviewing 2 papers from their area of expertise. One of the authors of each of the accepted papers presented a talk with highlights and the latest updates on the specific research from their manuscript.

The workshop opened with an invited talk that aligned very well with the major themes of the workshop.

See below for further details of the talks and presenters.

Organization

Steering Committee

Hartwig Anzt	University of Tennessee, USA
Bilel Hadri	King Abdullah University of Science and Technology (KAUST), Saudi Arabia
Hatem Ltaief	King Abdullah University of Science and Technology (KAUST), Saudi Arabia
Piotr Luszczek	University of Tennessee, USA

Program Committee

Andrey Alekseenko	KTH Royal Institute of Technology, Sweden
Qinglei Cao	University of Tennessee, USA
Pedro Diniz	University of Porto, Portugal
Alfredo Goldman	São Paulo University, Brazil
Mehdi Goli	Codeplay, UK
Jiali Li	University of Tennessee, USA
Neil Lindquist	University of Tennessee, USA
Ravi Reddy Manumachu	University College Dublin, Ireland
Max Melnichenko	University of Tennessee, USA

Outcome of the Workshop

The workshop was well attended with about 50 participants engaging the speakers on the relevant research topics.

The presented talks were as follows:

Keynote talk: *Mixed-precision scientific computing with Tensor Cores on NVIDIA GPUs: Exceeding the performance characteristics of single precision while maintaining numerical accuracy* by Harun Bayraktar, Director of Engineering, Math & Quantum Computing Libraries, NVIDIA

Talk 1: *GEMM-Like Convolution for Deep Learning Inference on the Xilinx Versal* by Jie Lei

Talk 2: *OpenACC unified programming environment for multi-hybrid acceleration with GPU and FPGA* by Taisuke Boku

Talk 3: *Towards Quantum Acceleration of a Classical MCAE Application* by Sophia Kolak

Talk 4: *Observed Memory Bandwidth and Power Usage on Intel FPGA Platforms with oneAPI: A Comparison with GPUs* by Chris Siefert

Talk 5: *Exploring the Use of Dataflow Architectures for Graph Neural Network Workloads* by Sanjif Shanmugavelu

Talk 6: *An Investigation into the Performance and Portability of SYCL Compiler Implementations* by Steven Wright

Based on the presented research findings, we can clearly conclude that the prevalence of hardware and/or software heterogeneity is an increasingly important aspect of running modern workloads: be it high-performance computing, AI/ML, and even quantum computing. The community continues to face challenges of productively obtaining a large fraction of the peak performance. Fortunately, the presented advances in programming models and software libraries help with lowering the barrier to obtaining high levels of efficiency, thus fully exploiting the performance gains that heterogeneity affords its users.

GEMM-Like Convolution for Deep Learning Inference on the Xilinx Versal

Jie Lei[1]([✉])(iD), Héctor Martínez[2](iD), José Flich[1],
and Enrique S. Quintana-Ortí[1](iD)

[1] Universitat Politècnica de València, Valencia, Spain
{jlei,jflich,quintana}@disca.upv.es
[2] Universidad de Córdoba, Córdoba, Spain
el2mapeh@uco.es

Abstract. We revisit a blocked formulation of the direct convolution algorithm that mimics modern realizations of the general matrix multiplication (GEMM), demonstrating that the same approach can be adapted to deliver high performance for deep learning inference tasks on the AI Engine (AIE) tile embedded in Xilinx Versal platforms. Our experimental results on a Xilinx Versal VCK190 shows an arithmetic throughput close to 70% of the theoretical peak of the AIE tile for 8-bit integer operands and the convolutional layers arising in ResNet-50 v.15+ImageNet.

Keywords: Deep learning · Convolution · Direct algorithm · High Performance · SIMD units · Cache Memory

1 Introduction

The convolution (CONV) is a dominant operator for the type of deep neural networks (DNNs) most frequently leveraged in signal processing and computer vision tasks [4,12,13]. For this reason, during the last years there has been an intensive effort to carefully exploit the architecture of modern processors in order to produce efficient realizations of this operator. These implementations rely on the classical algorithm for the direct convolution [3,16], the lowering (or "im2col") approach based on the matrix multiplication (GEMM) [2,6], the Fast Fourier transform (FFT)-based convolution, or Winograd's minimal filtering algorithms [7,10,17].

In this paper, we revisit the GEMM-like algorithms for the direct convolution introduced in [3,16], exploring how to efficiently map them to the Artificial Intelligence Engine (AIE) in the Xilinx Versal accelerator. In doing so, we make the following specific contributions:

– We offer a practical demonstration that the same ideas underlying the high performance realization of the direct convolution on conventional processors, equipped with SIMD (single instruction, multiple data) units and multi-layered memories, carry over to the AIE-enabled Xilix Versal ACAP.

A. Bienz et al. (Eds.): ISC High Performance 2023 Workshops, LNCS 13999, pp. 593–604, 2023.
https://doi.org/10.1007/978-3-031-40843-4_44

- We customize our general design of the direct convolution for the Xilinx Versal VCK190, including a careful mapping of the matrix operands to the various type of memory in this heterogeneous system. In addition, we also conduct a complete experimental analysis for a representative convolutional neural network (CNN): ResNet-50 v1.5+ImageNet.

The rest of the paper is structured as follows. In Sect. 2 we expose the connection between the high performance realizations of the CONV operator and GEMM. In Sect. 3 we present our strategy to map CONV on the Xilinx Versal VCK190, and in Sect. 4 we evaluate the approach. Finally, in Sect. 5 we close the paper with a few remarks and a discussion of future work.

2   Blocking in the Direct Convolution

In this section we follow [3] in order to expose the connection between the convolution operator and the high performance implementations of GEMM in modern instances of the BLAS (Basic Linear Algebra Subprograms) [8].

2.1   High Performance GEMM in Conventional Processors

```
1   for (jc=0; jc<n; jc+=nc) // Loop L1
2     for (pc=0; pc<k; pc+=kc){      // L2
3       // Pack B
4       Bc:=B(pc:pc+kc-1, jc:jc+nc-1);
5       for (ic=0; ic<m; ic+=mc){    // L3
6         // Pack A
7         Ac:=A(ic:ic+mc-1, pc:pc+kc-1);
8         for (jr=0; jr<nc; jr+=nr)  // L4
9           for(ir=0; ir<mc; ir+=mr) // L5
10            // Micro-kernel
11            C(ic+ir:ic+ir+mr-1,
12              jc+jr:jc+jr+nr-1)
13              += Ac(ir:ir+mr-1, 0:kc-1)
14              * Bc(0:kc-1, jr:jr+nr-1);
15  }}
```

```
1   for (pr=0; pr<kc; pr++) // L6
2     C(ic+ir:ic+ir+mr-1,
3       jc+jr:jc+jr+nr-1)
4       += Ac(ir:ir+mr-1,pr)
5       * Bc(pr,jr:jr+nr-1);
```

Fig. 1. High performance algorithm for GEMM. Top-Left: Blocked algorithm; Top-Right: Micro-kernel; Bottom-Right: Packing.

Consider the GEMM $C = A \cdot B$, where $A \to m \times k$, $B \to k \times n$, and $C \to m \times n$. The modern implementations of this kernel (e.g., in AMD AOCL, OpenBLAS, BLIS, etc.) follow GotoBLAS2 [9] to formulate it as a blocked algorithm comprising five nested loops around two packing routines and an architecture-dependent *micro-kernel*; see Fig. 1, top-left.

For the GEMM algorithm in the figure, an appropriate choice of the strides for the three outermost loops, given by m_c, n_c, k_c, (and known as the *cache configuration parameters*,) combined with a certain packing of the matrix inputs into two buffers, $A_c \rightarrow m_c \times k_c$ and $B_c \rightarrow k_c \times n_c$, (Fig. 1, bottom-right), orchestrates a careful pattern of data movements across the memory hierarchy that reduces the number of number of cache misses [11,14]. Hereafter we assume that m, n, k are integer multiples of m_c, n_c, k_c, respectively.

The micro-kernel comprises a sixth loop (L6 in Fig. 1, top-right) that performs a sequence of k_c rank-1 updates on an $m_r \times n_r$ *micro-tile* of C, denoted as C_r, each involving a column of an $m_r \times k_c$ micro-panel of the packed buffer A_c and a row of a $k_c \times n_r$ micro-panel of the packed buffer B_c (blocks A_r and B_r in Fig. 1, bottom-right.) For processors with SIMD arithmetic units, one of the micro-kernel "dimensions" is chosen to perform the accumulation on C_r using SIMD arithmetic instructions, and the special packing of the elements of A, B into the buffers A_c, B_c enables loading their data using SIMD instructions.

2.2 The Convolution Operator

Consider now a CONV operator, $O = \text{CONV}(F, I)$, that applies a 4D filter tensor $F \rightarrow c_i \times h_f \times w_f \times c_o$, on a 4D input tensor $I \rightarrow b \times h_i \times w_i \times c_i$, to produce a 4D output tensor $O \rightarrow b \times h_o \times w_o \times c_o$. Here, b denotes the batch size (i.e., the number of samples); $c_i|c_o$ stand for the number of input|output channels; $h_i \times w_i | h_o \times w_o$ are the input|output height $\times$ width; and $h_f \times w_f$ are the filter height $\times$ width. Furthermore, assuming a padding p along the dimensions h_i and w_i, then $h_o = \lfloor (h_i - h_f + 2p)/s + 1 \rfloor$ and $w_o = \lfloor (w_i - w_f + 2p)/s + 1 \rfloor$.

A simple algorithm that computes the convolution is displayed in Fig. 2. For deep learning (DL) applications, the input and output tensors are generally arranged in memory following either the NHWC or the NCHW layouts, where N specifies the batch dimension; H|W refer to the image height|width; and C correspond to the input|output channels. Also, the filter tensor is stored in either the CRSK (for NHWC) or KCRS (for NCHW) format, where C|K specify the input|output channels, and R|S denote the filter height|width.

```
1  void ConvDirect(I[b][hi][wi][ci], F[ci][hf][wf][co], O[b][ho][wo][co]){
2  for (h=0; h<b; h++)
3   for (i=0; i<ci; i++)
4    for (j=0; j<co; j++)
5     for (k=0; k<wo; k++)
6      for (l=0; l<ho; l++)
7       for (m=0; m<wf; m++)
8        for (n=0; n<hf; n++)
9         O[h][l][k][j] += I[h][l+n][k+m][i] * F[i][n][m][j];
10 }
```

Fig. 2. Simple algorithm for the direct convolution.

2.3   The Direct Convolution is GEMM in Disguise

In essence, the realization of the direct convolution in Fig. 2, consisting of 7 nested loops around a MAC (multiply-and-add) operation, features the same scheme that is present in the naive implementation of GEMM consisting of three nested loops ijk around a MAC. We next revisit [3] to review that, in the case of the direct convolution, it is possible to apply the same techniques that transform the naive GEMM algorithm into a high performance blocked realization.

As a starting point, consider the NHWC layout for the input/output tensors and the filter tensor arranged in an "alternative" RSCK layout. In [3], the work in [16] is extended to reorganize the simple algorithm for the direct convolution following the principles for the optimization of GEMM in current architectures:

- Select the inner loops to saturate computations via a proper micro-kernel.
- Reorder ,the outer loops and block the operands to optimize data reuse.
- Apply a cache-aware layout of the operands.
- Decouple the microkernel dimension from the cache blocking parameters.

The application of these principles to the simple algorithm for the direct convolution result in the reformulated variant in Fig. 3, which exhibits the following properties [3, 16]:

- It preserves the NHWC layout for the input/output tensors.
- It avoids stalls in the micro-kernel due to consecutive writes to the same entry of the output tensor, prevents register spilling and, when possible, accommodates SIMD arithmetic and loads/stores by ensuring access to the convolution operators with unit stride;
- It reduces the memory access overhead by splitting the tensors into smaller blocks that fit into the memory hierarchy; and
- It exposes sufficient thread-level parallelism.

Note the different ordering of the loops for the GEMM and the blocked convolution: L1$\Rightarrow$ L2$\Rightarrow$ L3$\Rightarrow$ L4$\Rightarrow$ L5 for the former vs L3$\Rightarrow$ L2$\Rightarrow$ L1$\Rightarrow$ L5$\Rightarrow$ L4 for the latter. In addition, the packings of $A|B$ into $A_c|B_c$ occur in loops L3|L2 in GEMM while, for the blocked convolution, if necessary, $I|F$ should be packed into two buffers $I_c|F_c$ in loops L2|L3. These changes aim at maintaining a buffer I_c, of dimension $w_{o,b} \times c_{i,b}$ in the L3 cache, and a buffer F_c, of dimension $c_{i,b} \times c_{o,b}$ in the L2 cache. This is referred to as the A3B2C0 variant of GEMM in [5].

2.4   Packing in the Direct Convolution

The GEMM-oriented algorithm for the direct convolution assumes that the filter tensor is arranged in a manner that resembles the packing that is required for the micro-panel of B_c in the GEMM algorithm. For DL inference the filter tensor can be pre-packed and stored in the corresponding memory level. The cost of this transformation is amortized for all inference samples and becomes negligible.

With respect to the packing of the input tensor, the GEMM-oriented algorithm for the direct convolution retrieves the entries of I, from the micro-kernel,

```
1  void ConvDirect_GEMM(I[b][hi][wi][cib], F[hf][wf][ci][co],
2                       O[b][ho][wo][cob]){
3  for (h=0; h<b; h++)
4   for (l=0; l<ho; l++)
5    for (n=0; n<hf; n++)
6     for (m=0; m<wf; m++)
7      for (kp=0; kp<wo; kp+=wob)      // Loop L3, wo = m
8       for (ip=0; ip<ci; ip+=cib)      // L2, ci = k
9        for (jp=0; jp<co; jp+=cob)      // L1, co = n
10        for (ir=0; ir<wob; ir+=mr)      // L5, wob = mc
11         for (jr=0; jr<cob; jr+=nr){      // L4, cob = nc
12          ic = kp+ir; jc = jp+jr; kc = ip;
13          // Micro-kernel
14          for (pr=0; pr<cib; pr++)      // L6, cib = kc
15           O[h][l][ic:ic+mr][jc:jc+nr] += I[h][l+n][ic+m:ic+m+mr][kc+pr]
16                                        * F[n][m][kc+pr][jc:jc+nr];
17 }    }
```

Fig. 3. GEMM-like reformulation of the direct convolution. The comments identify the relationship with the loops inside the GEMM algorithm in Fig. 1.

with a non-unit stride. Fortunately, it is possible to ensure access to I with unit stride from the micro-kernel by packing the entries of I into the $w_{o,b} \times c_{i,b}$ buffer I_c inside loop L2 in Fig. 3; see also [3]. This is equivalent to the packing scheme for the $m_c \times k_c$ buffer A_c in the GEMM algorithm.

To summarize the previous discussion, the direct convolution can be blocked applying some of the same techniques that are present in modern high performance realizations of GEMM.

3 Mapping CONV to the Xilinx Versal VCK190

In this section, after a brief description of the Xilinx platform, we present our strategy to map the CONV operator to this system.

3.1 Xilinx Versal VCK190 ACAP

The Versal VC1902 processor [1] comprises, as main components, (1) a dual-core ARM Cortex-A72 processor plus a dual-core ARM Cortex-R5F processor; (2) a customizable FPGA with 899,840 LUTs (look-up tables); and (3) 400 standalone AIE tiles organized in a 2D array. Furthermore, each AIE tile contains a SIMD arithmetic unit, providing up to 128 MAC operations per clock cycle for (unsigned) integer 8-bit (UINT8) arithmetic. Therefore, a single AIE tile, running at 1.25 GHz (typical speed), can deliver 160 GigaMAC operations per second.

In addition, the Versal VCK190 features a versatile memory with 32 KB of "local" memory per AIE tile; distributed Block and Ultra RAMs with capacity for 4.3 MB and 16.3 MB, respectively; and a global 2-GB DDR4 memory.

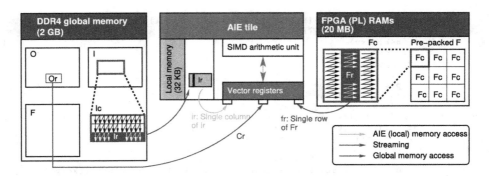

Fig. 4. Data mapping and transfers across the Versal VCK190 memory hierarchy. The transfers from O_r in the global memory, F_r in the FPGA memory, and I_r in the local memory move data directly to the vector registers. The data copy of the micro-panel I_r, from the global memory into the local memory, is carried out by one of the scalar engines (ARM processors).

3.2 Distributing the Data Across the Memory Hierarchy

Our data mapping strategy leverages the cache-friendly blocked algorithm for CONV in Fig. 3, combined with the following distribution of the problem data across the levels of the memory hierarchy (see also Fig. 4):

- The operand F contains the read-only filters for the convolution. The full matrix can be pre-packed off-line into a collection of buffers F_c and kept in the FPGA RAMs, contributing a null cost to the inference process as the same filters are used for many samples.
- Matrix I corresponds to the activation inputs of the CONV operator. This operand is partitioned and packed into a buffer I_c during the execution of CONV in the DDR4 global memory. Also, each individual micro-panel I_r is copied into the AIE local memory. The cost of transferring I_r is amortized by re-using its entries across several iterations of loop L5 in Fig. 1, top-left.
- Matrix O contains the activation outputs of the CONV operator. At each execution of the micro-kernel, a small micro-tile O_r, of dimension $m_r \times n_r$, is first loaded directly from the DDR4 global memory into the AIE tile vector registers, and written back to memory at the end; see Fig. 1, top-right.

At this point, it is worth remarking some differences between our solution and the approach taken when implementing GEMM in a conventional processor:

- From the point of view of hardware, a conventional processor integrates a number of cache levels (usually, between two and three), and relies on a memory controller to orchestrate the data movements across them. In contrast, in the Versal VCK190 the transfers need to be explicitly encoded into the algorithm. This puts an extra burden into the programmer's shoulders, but offers a strict control over the data transfers.

- The Versal system provides streaming access methods for communication with the "outside world." This provides high throughput and lower latency for the FPGA to AIE communication, but is also fundamentally different from the type of communication that occurs between the arithmetic units and the cache/memory levels in a conventional processor.
- From the algorithmic point of view, given that the target is to implement GEMM for DL inference, we can pre-pack the weight/filter matrix F into a collection of buffers residing into the FPGA RAM. Therefore, the packing that occurs within loop L3 of the baseline algorithm for GEMM is unnecessary.

3.3   Design of the Micro-Kernel

Following the general trend toward leveraging low precision arithmetic for DL inference, we selected UINT8 as the baseline datatype for the implementation of the CONV operator in the Versal VC1902. Furthermore, given the capacity and number of accumulator registers in the AIE tile, we set the dimensions of the micro-kernel to $m_r \times n_r = 8 \times 8$; that is, the micro-tile O_r updated inside loop L6 of the micro-kernel comprises 8 entries of 8 columns of O.

Figure 5 displays our micro-kernel for the VC1902. After a few declarations and initializations, the code comprises a loop (Line 18), corresponding to L6, that iterates over the $c_{i,b}$ dimension of the micro-panels I_r, F_r, with an unrolling factor of 16. At each iteration, the loop body multiplies the entries in 16 columns of I_r (128 elements, retrieved in ir0 and ir1) with those in 16 rows of F_r (128 elements, in fr), accumulating the intermediate results on four different registers via eight invocations to the AIE intrinsic mac16() (in Lines 29–42).

Each call to mac16() computes 128 UINT8 MAC operations in one cycle, operating with two vectors: one with 64 elements and the other with 32 elements. As v8uint8 is not supported by the AIE intrinsics, we concatenate two column vectors of the micro-tile O_r into one v16uint8 to perform the MAC operations, as reflected in the accumulator declaration (Line 12).

A single loop iteration retrieves 128+128 elements from memory levels that are close to the arithmetic units, performing $2 \cdot 8 \cdot 8 \cdot 16 = 2,048$ UINT8 arithmetic operations with them. This helps to amortize the cost of memory transfers with enough arithmetic computation, in principle yielding a compute-bound micro-kernel. The high utilization of the accumulator and vector registers (respectively, 100% and 75% of the total resources), along with the appropriate selection of compiler optimization arguments, facilitate to overlap the MAC operations with data transfers.

After the loop is complete, the code "synchronizes" the results with the contents of matrix O in global memory. For that purpose, each execution of the micro-kernel loads a 8×8 micro-tile O_r (Line 46) from global memory and, after updating its contents, stores the results back to global memory (Lines 52). The cost of these data transfers can be amortized provided $c_{i,b}$ is sufficiently large.

```
1   #define conv_mac16(v1,v2,v3, zoffsets) \
2       v1 = mac16(v1, v2, 0, xoffsets, 16, \
3                  xsquare, v3, 0, zoffsets, 2, zsquare);
4
5   void micro_kernel( input_window_int16 * __restrict DDR_IN,
6                      input_window_int16 * __restrict FPGA_IN,
7                      uint8 *Fr,
8                      output_window_int16 *__restrict DDR_OUT){
9
10      // Vectors for cols of Ir, rows of Fr, and accumulators for Or
11      v64uint8 ir0, ir1;
12      v32uint8 fr;
13      v16acc48 Oacc01, Oacc23, Oacc45, Oacc67;
14
15      // Parameters for mac16() intrinsics
16      // Initialization omitted for brevity
17      unsigned int xoffsets, xsquare, zoffsets_0, zoffsets_1, zsquare;
18
19      for (unsigned int pr=0; pr<cib; pr+=16)
20          // Read 2 x 64 = 64 entries of Ir
21          // corresponding to 16 cols with mr=8 UINT8 each
22          ir0 = window_readincr_v64(FPGA_IN));
23          ir1 = window_readincr_v64(FPGA_IN));
24
25          // Repeat four times:
26          //    Read 32 entries of Fr
27          //    corresponding to 4 rows with nr=8 UINT each
28          //    Use the elements of Ir, Fr to update Or
29          fr = *(v32uint8*) Fr[pr/4+0];
30          conv_mac(Oacc01, ir0, fr, zoffsets_0);
31          conv_mac(Oacc23, ir0, fr, zoffsets_1);
32
33          fr = *(v32uint8*) Fr[pr/4+1];
34          conv_mac(Oacc45, ir0, fr, zoffsets_0);
35          conv_mac(Oacc67, ir0, fr, zoffsets_1);
36
37          fr = *(v32uint8*) Fr[pr/4+2];
38          conv_mac(Oacc01, ir1, fr, zoffsets_0);
39          conv_mac(Oacc23, ir1, fr, zoffsets_1);
40
41          fr = *(v32uint8*) Fr[pr/4+3];
42          conv_mac(Oacc45, ir1, fr, zoffsets_0);
43          conv_mac(Oacc67, ir1, fr, zoffsets_1);
44      }
45      // Read Or from global memory
46      v64uint8 O01234567 = undef_v64uint8();
47      O01234567 = window_readincr_v64(DDR_IN);
48
49      // Convert result, add it to Or and write back to memory
50      v64uint8 accV01234567 = concat(ubsrs(acc01,0), ubsrs(acc23,0),
51                                ubsrs(acc45,0), ubsrs(acc67,0));
52      O01234567 = operator + (accV01234567, O01234567);
53      window_writeincr(DDR_OUT, O01234567);
54  }
```

Fig. 5. Simplified version of the micro-kernel for the AIE tile.

4 Experimental Results

The evaluation of the direct algorithm for the CONV operator next was carried out using the Xilinx Vitis 2022.1 developing tool. The AIE transaction-level System C simulator was used to profile the timing, resource requirements, and assembly instructions of the designs, enabling an accurate performance analysis [15].

4.1 Building Blocks

As a starting point for the experimental analysis, we focus on the main components that dictate the performance of the blocked realization of the CONV operator. For that purpose, we first evaluate the micro-kernel in a *stationary* scenario where all data is already "in place". That corresponds to the $m_r \times n_r = 8 \times 8$ micro-tile O_r being retrieved from the global memory; the $m_r \times c_{i,b}$ micro-panel I_r from the local memory; and the $c_{i,b} \times n_r$ micro-panel F_r from the FPGA RAM. Other memory transfer overheads, in particular the cost of copying I_r from the global memory to the local memory, are omitted from this initial study.

The left plot in Fig. 6 displays the throughput rate, in UINT8 MACs/second, attained by the micro-kernel when operating in stationary mode. In this scenario, the $c_{i,b}$ parameter determines the overhead due to loading/storing the micro-tile O_r before/after the execution of loop L6 of the micro-kernel. The plot shows that the micro-kernel attains an asymptotic rate around 110 MACs/cycle, close to the theoretical peak of the AIE tile (128 MACs/cycle).

The blocked direct algorithm for CONV operator requires that, at each iteration of loop L5, a micro-panel I_r is copied from global to local memory, and re-utilized there for all iterations of loop L4; see Fig. 3. The right plot in Fig. 6 compares the cost of this memory transfer versus that of the micro-kernel execution as a function of $c_{i,b}$. While the right plot gives the initial impression that the memory access costs dominate the execution time of the CONV operator, note that the data transfer overhead is amortized over $c_{o,b}/n_r$ iterations of loop L4. We will expose the actual effect of this memory access overhead when considering real convolution layers in the following subsection.

4.2 Convolutional Layers

For the evaluation of the complete convolution algorithm, we selected the convolutional layers in the ResNet-50 v1.5 model. As some of these layers feature the same dimensions, we show only the different ones, listed in Table 1. For the dataset, we chose ImageNet and we set the batch size $b = 1$ (single input scenario). Furthermore, we set the blocking parameters to $c_{o,b} = w_{o,b} = 8192$, and $c_{i,b} = 256$. Note that, in practice, $c_{o,b} \le c_o$, $w_{o,b} \le w_o$, and $c_{i,b} \le c_i$.

Given the large variations between the dimension parameters of the different convolutional layers in ResNet-50 v1.5, in order to evaluate the performance we report the UINT8 arithmetic rate, comparing that with the theoretical peak of the AIE tile. Figure 7 reports the results for this experiment, with the arithmetic throughput rates calculated taking into account the micro-kernel execution in

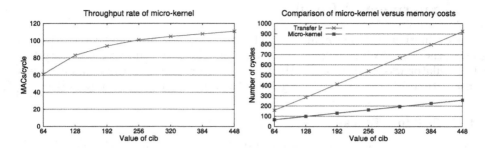

Fig. 6. Impact of the $c_{i,b}$ parameter. Left: Throughput rate of the micro-kernel operating in stationary mode. Right: Cost of micro-kernel versus overhead due to copying I_r from global to local memory.

Table 1. Parameters of the convolutional layers in ResNet-50 v1.5.

Layer id.	c_o	w_o	h_o	w_f	h_f	c_i	Layer id.	c_o	w_o	h_o	w_f	h_f	c_i
C1	64	112	112	7	7	3	C11	1024	14	14	1	1	512
C2	256	56	56	1	1	64	C12	256	14	14	1	1	512
C3	64	56	56	1	1	64	C13	256	14	14	3	3	256
C4	64	56	56	3	3	64	C14	1024	14	14	1	1	256
C5	64	56	56	1	1	256	C15	256	14	14	1	1	1024
C6	512	28	28	1	1	256	C16	2048	7	7	1	1	1024
C7	128	28	28	1	1	256	C17	512	7	7	1	1	1024
C8	128	28	28	3	3	128	C18	512	7	7	3	3	512
C9	512	28	28	1	1	128	C19	2048	7	7	1	1	512
C10	128	28	28	1	1	512	C20	512	7	7	1	1	2048

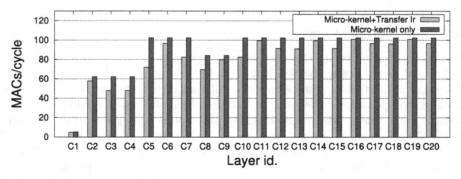

Fig. 7. Performance of the GEMM-like direct algorithm for the CONV operator applied to the distinct convolutional layers of ResNet-50 v1.5+ImageNet.

isolation (stationary mode) as well as that cost plus the overhead due to the data transfers.

The results in Fig. 7 illustrate that, except for the first few layers (C1–C3), the performance of the direct convolution algorithm implemented on the Xilinx AIE attains a throughput rate superior to 60 MACs/cycle when including the data movement overhead. Furthermore, for a significant number of layers the performance is around 90 MACs/cycles (70% of peak). The low performance arithmetic rate observed for some of the layers can be tracked down to two main causes:

- The number of input channels (c_i, see Table 1) is below 256. This is the case, for example, of layers C1–C4 and C8–C9. The reason is that a low value of c_i constraints $c_{i,b}$, as $c_{i,b} \leq c_i$, and results in a micro-kernel with a lower throughput rate, even in stationary mode; see Fig. 6, left. Nonetheless, for those cases with small c_i but large c_o, this problem can be tackled by interchanging the roles of c_i and c_o in the direct algorithm.
- There is a significant overhead due to memory accesses. While not explicitly reported, we can estimate this factor by comparing the cost of the execution with and without considering the data transfers. The overhead is as large as 30% for three of the cases (layers C5, C7 and C8), but in general remains below 12%.

5   Concluding Remarks

We have demonstrated that the same techniques which render high performance from GEMM on a conventional processor, carry over to the AIE tile on the Xilinx Versal. In particular, we refer to an architecture-specific implementation of the micro-kernel, which can be developed using AIE intrinsics, plus a cache-aware layout of the matrix operands and a careful ordering of the nested loops in the convolution operator. The experimental analysis using the convolutional layers in Resnet-50 v1.5+ImageNet shows performance rates which are around 70% of the AIE tile's theoretical peak in UINT8 arithmetic. The analysis exposes that the main limiting factor is the presence of convolution layers with a "small" number of both input and output channels.

Acknowledgments. This project has received funding from the European High-Performance Computing Joint Undertaking (JU) under grant agreement No 955558. The JU receives support from the European Union's Horizon 2020 research and innovation programme, and Spain, Germany, France, Italy, Poland, Switzerland, Norway.

The authors acknowledge funding from European Union's Horizon2020 Research and Innovation programme under the Marie Skłodowska Curie Grant Agreement No. 956090 (APROPOS).

This work was also supported by the research project PID2020-113656RB-C22 of MCIN/AEI/10.13039/501100011033. H. Martínez is a postdoc fellow supported by the *Junta de Andalucía*.

References

1. Ahmad, S., et al.: Xilinx first 7 nm device: versal AI core (VC1902). In: 2019 IEEE Hot Chips 31 Symposium (HCS), pp. 1–28 (2019)
2. Barrachina, S., et al.: Efficient and portable GEMM-based convolution operators for deep neural network training on multicore processors. J. Parallel Distrib. Comput. **167**, 240–254 (2022)
3. Barrachina, S., et al.: Reformulating the direct convolution for high-performance deep learning inference on ARM processors. J. Syst. Arch. **135**, 102806 (2023)
4. Ben-Nun, T., Hoefler, T.: Demystifying parallel and distributed deep learning: an in-depth concurrency analysis. ACM Comput. Surv. **52**(4), 65:1–65:43 (2019)
5. Castelló, A., Quintana-Ortí, E.S., Igual, F.D.: Anatomy of the BLIS family of algorithms for matrix multiplication. In: 30th Euromicro International Conference on Parallel, Distributed and Network-Based Processing (PDP), pp. 92–99 (2022)
6. Chellapilla, K., Puri, S., Simard, P.: High performance convolutional neural networks for document processing. In: International Workshop on Frontiers in Handwriting Recognition (2006). https://hal.inria.fr/inria-00112631
7. Dolz, M.F., et al.: Efficient and portable Winograd convolutions for multi-core processors. J. Supercomput. (2023, to appear)
8. Dongarra, J.J., Du Croz, J., Hammarling, S., Duff, I.: A set of level 3 basic linear algebra subprograms. ACM Trans. Math. Softw. **16**(1), 1–17 (1990)
9. Goto, K., van de Geijn, R.A.: Anatomy of a high-performance matrix multiplication. ACM Trans. Math. Softw. **34**(3), 12:1–12:25 (2008)
10. Lavin, A., Gray, S.: Fast algorithms for convolutional neural networks. In: 2016 IEEE Conference on Computer Vision and Pattern Recognition, pp. 4013–4021 (2016)
11. Low, T.M., et al.: Analytical modeling is enough for high-performance BLIS. ACM Trans. Math. Softw. **43**(2), 12:1–12:18 (2016)
12. Najafabadi, M.M., et al.: Deep learning applications and challenges in big data analytics. J. Big Data **2**(1), 1 (2015)
13. Sze, V., et al.: Efficient processing of deep neural networks: a tutorial and survey. Proc. IEEE **105**(12), 2295–2329 (2017)
14. Van Zee, F.G., van de Geijn, R.A.: BLIS: a framework for rapidly instantiating BLAS functionality. ACM Trans. Math. Softw. **41**(3), 14:1–14:33 (2015)
15. Xilinx: AI Engine tools and flows user guide (UG1079) (2022). https://docs.xilinx.com/r/en-US/ug1079-ai-engine-kernel-coding/Tools
16. Zhang, J., Franchetti, F., Low, T.M.: High performance zero-memory overhead direct convolutions. In: Proceedings of the 35th International Conference on Machine Learning, vol. 80 (2018)
17. Zhao, Y., et al.: A faster algorithm for reducing the computational complexity of convolutional neural networks. Algorithms **11**(10), 159 (2018)

An Investigation into the Performance and Portability of SYCL Compiler Implementations

Wageesha R. Shilpage and Steven A. Wright[✉]

University of York, York, UK
steven.wright@york.ac.uk

Abstract. In June 2022, Frontier became the first Supercomputer to "officially" break the ExaFLOP/s barrier on LINPACK, achieving a peak performance of 1.1×10^{18} floating-point operations per second using AMD Instinct accelerators. Developing high performance applications for such platforms typically requires the adoption of vendor-specific programming models, which in turn may limit portability. SYCL is a high-level, single-source language based on C++17, developed by the Khronos group to overcome the shortcomings of those vendor-specific HPC programming models. In this paper we present an initial study into the SYCL parallel programming model and its implementing compilers, to understand its performance and portability, and how this compares to other parallel programming models. We use three major SYCL implementations for our evaluation – Open SYCL (previously hipSYCL), DPC++, and ComputeCpp – on a range of CPU and GPU hardware from Intel, AMD, Fujitsu, Marvell, and NVIDIA. Our results show that for a simple finite difference mini-application, SYCL can offer competitive performance to native approaches, while for a more complex finite-element mini-application, significant performance degradation is observed. Our findings suggest that development work is required at the compiler- and application-level to ensure SYCL is competitive with alternative approaches.

Keywords: SYCL · High-Performance Computing · Performance Portability

1 Introduction

In the seven decades since the UNIVAC-I digital computer, computing has evolved enormously, fuelled by developments in both hardware and software. As computing power has increased, so too has our reliance on computing as a primary tool in scientific research. The fastest computers in the world today are being employed to help us solve many fundamental questions in the science and engineering disciplines. The High Performance Computing (HPC) research field

© The Author(s), under exclusive license to Springer Nature Switzerland AG 2023
A. Bienz et al. (Eds.): ISC High Performance 2023 Workshops, LNCS 13999, pp. 605–619, 2023.
https://doi.org/10.1007/978-3-031-40843-4_45

is concerned with how these systems, and the software running on them, can be better engineered to provide increased accuracy and decreased time-to-solution.

Historically, the primary metric for assessing the performance of an HPC system has been the number of floating-point operations that can be completed each second (FLOP/s). By this measure, the Exascale-barrier was broken by the Frontier system in June 2022, using nearly 38,000 GPU accelerators to achieve 1.1 ExaFLOP/s[1].

Like many of the recent systems to achieve the #1 ranking, Frontier is a heterogeneous system, with each compute node comprising of both CPUs and GPU accelerators; in the case of Frontier, one 64-core AMD "Trento" CPU, and four AMD Instinct MI250X GPUs. Extracting the maximum level of performance from such systems requires that data is efficiently moved between the host CPU and connected accelerator devices, that algorithms are effectively parallelised and that computation is appropriately distributed across the available hardware. Achieving this is no mean feat, and in some cases might require the use of a vendor-specific parallel programming model.

In order to avoid issues of vendor lock-in and increase developer productivity, a number of language-like tools and frameworks have been developed that are capable of providing the programming semantics that allow us to target heterogeneous architectures from a single codebase. Some of the most commonly used ones are OpenMP [14], OpenACC [13], OpenCL [21], Kokkos [6] and RAJA [1].

The SYCL parallel programming model was developed by the Khronos group in 2014, as another such tool to assist heterogeneous programming [22]. One of the key design goals of SYCL is portability. However, there have been discussions about how performant it is across platforms [4,8]. A 2021 study by Lin et al. addressed this and some other concerns by evaluating historical performance of three major SYCL implementations across a range of platforms [12]. Their study shows the increasing maturity of the compilers, but highlights remaining potential for further improvements.

In this paper, we further evaluate the performance portability of the Open SYCL, DPC++, and ComputeCpp compilers with a focus on mini-applications of interest to the plasma physics community. Our evaluation is motivated by Project NEPTUNE (NEutrals & Plasma TUrbulance Numerics for the Exascale), a UK project to develop a new simulation code to aid in the design of a future nuclear fusion power plant. Specifically, we make the following contributions:

- We evaluate SYCL against OpenMP and CUDA on a simple finite difference heat diffusion code. This serves as a baseline of performance and portability we can expect from SYCL and its implementing compilers;
- We then evaluate SYCL against MPI, OpenMP, Kokkos, CUDA and HIP on a mini-application implementing a finite element method. This evaluation is based on a simple conversion to SYCL and therefore this provides us with an indication of how much optimisation might be required for SYCL to provide performance that is competitive with other approaches;

---

[1] https://www.top500.org/lists/top500/2022/06/.

- Finally, we analyse the performance portability of these two mini-applications using visualisations developed by Sewall et al. [20], showing that for simple codes, SYCL can provide equivalent performance to OpenMP with minimal developer effort, but that for more complex cases, a basic code conversion is not sufficient and additional developer effort is required to bridge the gap.

The remainder of this paper is structured as follows: Section 2 provides an overview of the background and related work; Sect. 3 outlines the methodology of our study; Sect. 4 provides the results of our study; finally, Sect. 5 concludes this paper.

2   Background and Related Work

Since the introduction of IBM Roadrunner in 2008 there has been a shift towards heterogeneous architectures within HPC. However, programming systems with multiple architectures can be challenging, and often relies on vendor-led programming models specifically developed for each architecture (e.g. CUDA on NVIDIA, HIP/ROCm on AMD). Adopting these programming models for large HPC applications can lead to vendor lock-in. To combat this, there are a number of programming models that have been developed that are able to target multiple host and accelerator architectures from a single codebase.

The typically stated goal of these programming models is to achieve "the three Ps", *performance, portability,* and *productivity* [18]. Notable examples are the compiler directive-based approaches OpenMP [3] and OpenACC [13], the C++ template-based approaches Kokkos [6] and RAJA [1], and language extensions such as OpenCL [21]. Many of these have been the target of studies looking at *performance portability* across heterogeneous platforms [5,7,9,10,15,17,23].

Another approach that is beginning to see widespread adoption in HPC is the SYCL parallel programming model [22]. SYCL is a high-level, single-source programming model based on ISO C++17. It was introduced by the Khronos group in 2014, and takes inspiration from, though is independent of, OpenCL. In particular, SYCL sits at a higher level of abstraction to OpenCL, removing much of the "boiler-plate" code that was previously required.

Since its inception, multiple SYCL compilers have been developed, each implementing different subsets of the standard, and targeting different architectures or execution approaches. The programming model has been the subject of a number of recent studies examining its performance portability and the maturity of its implementing compilers [2,5,8,12,19]. In this paper, we build on these previous studies, with a focus on three mainstream SYCL compilers and algorithms of interest to the plasma physics domain.

Open SYCL (previously known as hipSYCL) is an open-source library or SYCL compiler developed at the University of Heidelberg, by Aksel et al.[2]. It is based on the LLVM compiler framework, and one of its defining features is that it

---

[2] https://opensycl.github.io.

is not built on OpenCL. Instead, Open SYCL uses other low-level backends to target different platforms. Open SYCL currently supports an OpenMP backend for CPUs, CUDA and HIP backends for NVIDIA and AMD GPUs, and an experimental Level-Zero backend to support Intel's Level-Zero hardware.

DPC++ is a C++ and SYCL compiler developed by Intel, that forms part of their OneAPI project. They provide two versions of their compiler, one a pre-compiled proprietary implementation[3] and one an open-source fork of the LLVM compiler framework[4]. The compiler can target host CPUs directly, or through an OpenCL runtime, and can target GPUs through CUDA, HIP and Level-Zero.

ComputeCpp was the first fully compliant SYCL 1.2.1 implementation, developed by Codeplay[5]. The compiler is built on the open-source Clang 6.0 compiler, but is distributed as a proprietary compiler with no open-source implementation available. ComputeCpp relies on an OpenCL driver for compilation of kernels and therefore has limited platform support. With the announcement in June 2022 that Intel has acquired Codeplay Software, it is likely that future development effort will instead be focused on Intel's DPC++ compiler.

In addition to these three mainstream implementations there are other projects, like triSYCL and neoSYCL, that are not included in this study.

3   Methodology

This paper seeks to answer three questions regarding the SYCL programming model and its implementing compilers:

1. How does SYCL's performance compare to other parallelising frameworks?
2. How does each SYCL compiler perform relative to other implementations?
3. How much portability is offered by SYCL and by each SYCL compiler?

To address these questions, we evaluate two applications across eleven platforms.

3.1   Benchmarks

Evaluating new parallel programming frameworks is difficult on production-grade applications that often consist of tens of thousands, or hundreds of thousands, of lines of code. Instead, mini-applications are typically used to rapidly investigate performance, portability and productivity, prior to extensive porting efforts. These mini-applications usually implement key kernels or algorithms that are found in production applications, but in only a few thousand lines of code. In this paper we focus our effort on two applications that implement computational methods typically used in the simulation of fluids and plasma.

---

[3] https://www.intel.com/content/www/us/en/developer/tools/oneapi/dpc-compiler.html.

[4] https://github.com/intel/llvm.

[5] https://developer.codeplay.com/products/computecpp/ce/home/.

Heat is a simple mini-application that solves a heat diffusion equation using a finite-differencing scheme, with a 5-point stencil [24]. It was developed at the University of Bristol as part of an OpenMP tutorial course, and therefore consists of only a few hundred lines of code. This limits the optimisation space and gives us a good baseline for the potential performance of any particular parallel programming model. The mini-application operates on a two-dimensional structured grid, and in our study we use a fixed problem size of 10000^2. For our study, implementations are available in OpenMP, CUDA and SYCL.

miniFE also solves a heat diffusion equation, but does so on an unstructured brick-shaped domain, using a finite-element method [11]. miniFE is significantly more complex than Heat, and the SYCL variant used in this paper is a conversion from an OpenMP 4.5 implementation. The relative performance of this simplistic conversion to SYCL will provide us with insight into the optimisation effort that might be required to port an application to SYCL in a performance portable manner. In this paper, we use a 256^3 problem size, and focus our efforts only on the conjugate gradient kernel (since this kernel dominates the performance). We present results for the MPI, OpenMP (with and without target directives), CUDA, HIP, Kokkos and SYCL implementations.

3.2   Evaluating Performance and Portability

The focus of this paper is in evaluating the maturity of the SYCL programming model and its implementing compilers in terms of both the performance of SYCL applications when compared to alternative programming models, and also the performance portability of SYCL applications.

To evaluate comparative performance, we use runtime as the figure of merit; to evaluate the performance portability, we apply the Pennycook metric [18].

$$\Phi(a,p,H) = \begin{cases} \dfrac{|H|}{\displaystyle\sum_{i \in H} \dfrac{1}{e_i(a,p)}} & \text{if } i \text{ is supported } \forall i \in H \\ 0 & \text{otherwise} \end{cases} \tag{1}$$

where H is the set of platforms, a is the application of interest, p is the chosen problem, and $e_i(a,p)$ is the efficiency of an application a solving problem p on platform i (i.e. the ratio of the achieved performance against the best known implementation on the given platform). In this paper we focus on *application efficiency*, where $\Phi(a,p,H)$ represents the *harmonic mean* of the observed efficiency of an application across the selected set of platforms.

However, rather than present the raw performance portability, we instead use the cascade plot visualisations outlined by Sewall et al. [20], and generated using Intel's P3 Analysis Library [16].

3.3   Evaluation Platforms

The results in this paper have been collected using Isambard, at the University of Bristol, and the Intel DevCloud. The CPU platforms are detailed in Table 1, while the GPU platforms are detailed in Table 2. Our evaluation includes the

Intel HD Graphics P630 GPU, which is a mid-range integrated GPU provided on some Intel Xeon Coffee Lake and Kaby Lake CPUs. It is included in our evaluation to demonstrate the portability to Intel *Xe*-HPC GPUs, but we do not expect its performance to be competitive with discrete GPUs.

Table 1. Summary of CPUs used for the platform setup

Name	Clock	Cores (Threads)	Sockets	Memory (GB/s)	Vector type
CLX	2.10 GHz	20 (40)	2	131 (DDR4, 6 ch)	SSE, AVX512
(Intel Xeon Gold 6230, Cascade Lake)					
Rome	2.25 GHz	64 (128)	2	205 (DDR4, 8 ch)	AVX2
(AMD EPYC 7742, Zen 2)					
Milan	2.0 GHz	64 (128)	2	205 (DDR4, 8 ch)	AVX2
(AMD EPYC 7713, Zen 3)					
KNL	1.30 GHz	64 (256)	1	102 (DDR4, 6 ch)	AVX512
(Intel Xeon Phi 7210, Knights Landing)					
ThunderX2	2.10 GHz	32 (128)	2	252 (DDR4, 8 ch)	128 NEON
(Cavium CN9980, ARMv8.1)					
A64FX	1.80 GHz	48 (48)	1	1024 (HBM2)	128-512 SVE
(Fujitsu A64FX, ARMv8.2-A)					

Table 2. Summary of GPUs used for the platform setup

Name	Cores	Memory (GB)	Bandwidth (GB/s)
P100	3840	16	732
(NVIDIA P100 Pascal, CUDA Capability 6.0)			
V100	5120	16	900
(NVIDIA V100 Volta, CUDA Capability 7.0)			
A100	6912	40	1555
(NVIDIA A100 Ampere, CUDA Capability 8.0)			
MI100	120	32	1200
(AMD Instinct MI100, CDNA 1.0)			
HD P630	24	(System-shared) 64	(System-shared) 41.6
(Intel HD Graphics P630, Gen 9.5)			

For each of our evaluations on Isambard, we use version 11.0 of the Clang/L-LVM compiler environment. We use a custom-build of the compiler infrastructure, to ensure all required features are available (e.g. OpenMP target offload directives, CUDA, HIP). All of our results are collected with -O3 and other performance relevant compiler flags. We use OpenMPI version 4.1, except on the ThunderX2 platform, where we use version 3.1. We use version 11.2 of the

CUDA Toolkit, specifying the correct architecture each time. For Kokkos, we use the OpenMP backend for CPU platforms and the CUDA and HIP backends for GPU platforms. The results presented in this paper are the best runtime achieved on each platform, regardless of maximum parallelism achievable, using the best discovered combination of runtime parameters.

For Open SYCL, we build version 0.9.4 of the compiler from source, enabling it to target CPUs and GPUs through OpenMP and CUDA/HIP, respectively.

We use Intel's proprietary DPC++ compiler for the CLX, KNL and HD P630 platforms, and we build DPC++ version 16.0 from source for the AMD and NVIDIA platforms. For ThunderX2 and A64FX, we were able to compile benchmarks using DPC++ but we encountered linking errors that we were unable to resolve and so we omit results from these platforms.

We use version 2.10.0 of the ComputeCpp compiler, which is distributed as a pre-built executable. It is only compliant up to the SYCL 1.2.1 standard, and therefore is dependent on an OpenCL driver for each architecture; because of this, our platform set is limited to CLX, KNL, Rome and Milan CPUs.

4   Results and Analysis

We begin our investigation with the "Heat" mini-application. Since this application is implemented in only a few hundred lines of code, it serves as a good starting point to show the potential performance and portability of the SYCL programming model. We use the OpenMP, CUDA and SYCL implementations present in the HeCBench benchmark repository[6].

We then analyse the performance of miniFE. This application implements a finite element method on an unstructured grid, using 8-point hex elements. The application is implemented in approximately 5000 lines of code, and the SYCL port is based on simplistic conversion from the OpenMP 4.5 implementation of miniFE.

For each application we first present the raw runtime data, and we then analyse the performance portability using visualisations from Sewall et al. [20].

4.1   Heat

Figure 1 depicts the runtime for Heat on eight of the platforms surveyed. This simple evaluation reveals valuable information on platform coverage for SYCL. Crucially, there is at least one SYCL compiler that is able to target each architecture, and SYCL appears to provide performance comparable to OpenMP 4.5. The two most striking features of the data are perhaps the superior performance of the two NVIDIA GPU platforms and the relatively poor performance of the two ARM-based systems (ThunderX2 and A64FX). The V100 is approximately 10× faster than the fastest CPU execution observed, and importantly that performance improvement is seen in both CUDA and Open SYCL/DPC++. The runtimes observed on both ARM platforms are much worse than on the Cascade Lake and Rome CPU systems, likely due to using a custom-build of LLVM

---

[6] https://github.com/zjin-lcf/HeCBench.

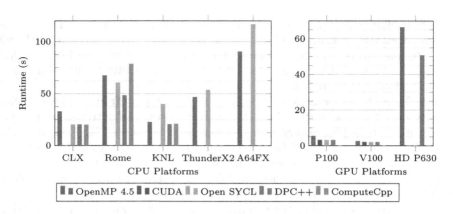

Fig. 1. Raw runtime data for Heat on five CPU and three GPU platforms.

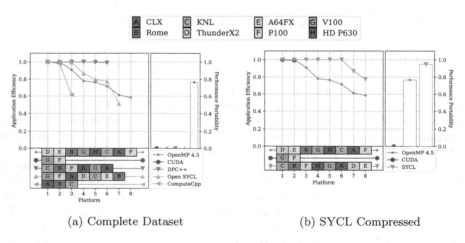

(a) Complete Dataset   (b) SYCL Compressed

Fig. 2. A cascade plot for the Heat application with (a) the complete dataset, and (b) the SYCL data compressed to a single value.

rather than the vendor supplied compiler (which did not support target offload semantics or SYCL).

Figure 2(a) shows how the performance efficiency changes for each programming model as new platforms are added to the evaluation set (in order of decreasing efficiency). For six of the eight platforms evaluated, DPC++ achieves almost perfect efficiency. Both Open SYCL and OpenMP 4.5 follow a similar trajectory, with Open SYCL maintaining a marginally higher efficiency up to the addition of the AMD Rome system. That SYCL is able to outperform OpenMP 4.5 (in particular on GPU platforms) can perhaps be explained by the richer semantics available in the programming model, allowing a greater scope for customisation and optimisation.

To compare the programming models in isolation (away from concerns about individual SYCL implementations), Fig. 2(b) shows a cascade plot where the SYCL data point is taken as the minimum runtime achieved by Open SYCL, DPC++, and ComputeCpp. This analysis further shows the potential of the SYCL programming model, where it is consistently able to achieve equivalent or better performance, and is portable to all of the architectures evaluated. Across the eight platforms, SYCL achieves $\mathcal{P} \approx 0.95$; OpenMP 4.5 achieves $\mathcal{P} \approx 0.77$ and lags SYCL after just three platforms are added to its evaluation set.

4.2   miniFE

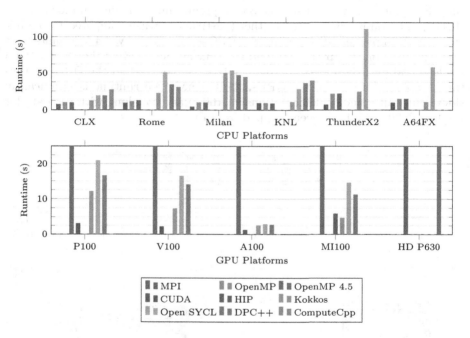

Fig. 3. Raw runtime data for miniFE on six CPU and five GPU platforms.

While Heat provides a good benchmark for the potential of the SYCL programming model and its compilers, its simplicity belies the effort that may be required for larger, more complex applications. The miniFE SYCL port used in this paper is also provided as part of the HeCBench benchmark suite, and is based on the OpenMP 4.5 implementation of miniFE. To provide a more thorough analysis, we compare this against the MPI reference implementation of miniFE, two OpenMP implementations (one with target offload semantics and one without), a CUDA implementation, a HIP implementation, and a Kokkos implementation. Similar to Heat, our evaluation includes the Intel HD Graphics P630 integrated

GPU; while this is not an HPC GPU, it does allow us an insight into the level of support for the Intel *Xe* product line.

Figure 3 shows the runtime achieved by miniFE running on the eleven evaluation platforms. On the six CPU platforms, the reference MPI implementation is the most performant; on the NVIDIA and Intel GPU platforms, the vendor-specific implementations are the fastest (i.e. CUDA on NVIDIA, DPC++ on Intel); Kokkos is the fastest implementation on the AMD Instinct MI100 platform. In contrast to Heat, no portable programming model is as performant as the MPI and CUDA non-portable programming models. However, there is at least one SYCL implementation able to execute on each of the eleven platforms, while OpenMP 4.5 (with target offload directives) is able to target all eleven platforms. As with Heat, there is a performance degradation present on the ARM platforms when using the SYCL programming model, and for miniFE this degradation is exaggerated further (particularly when compared to the reference MPI implementation). Only the DPC++ and OpenMP 4.5 variants have been executed on the Intel GPU, and the runtime achieved by the OpenMP 4.5 implementation (371.3 s) is approximately 5.4× slower than the DPC++ runtime (68.7 s). On each of the GPUs, the OpenMP 4.5 runtime is significantly slower than all other implementations (> 100 s) and so, along with the data for the HD P630, they have been cropped from Fig. 3.

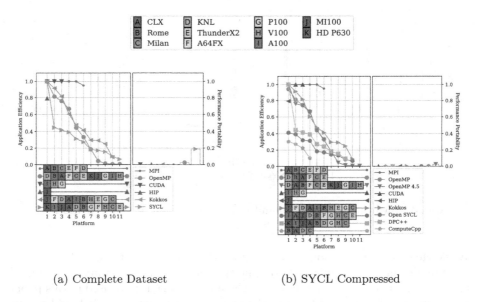

(a) Complete Dataset   (b) SYCL Compressed

Fig. 4. A cascade plot for the miniFE application with (a) the complete dataset, and (b) the SYCL data compressed to a single value.

The performance portability of each miniFE implementation is visualised in Fig. 4(a). The two "native" programming models, MPI and CUDA, both follow the 1.0 efficiency line before abruptly stopping as they reach GPU and non-NVIDIA platforms, respectively. Only the OpenMP 4.5 programming model is able to target all eleven platforms (though the SYCL programming model can achieve this with different compilers for each platform, as shown in Fig. 4(b)). Kokkos and Open SYCL extend to ten of the eleven platforms, respectively, with Kokkos providing better efficiency throughout. DPC++ follows a similar trend to the Open SYCL compiler, but its ability to target the Intel HD Graphics P630 GPU means that its efficiency is generally higher (since it is the most performant implementation on this architecture). For each of the portable approaches, the GPUs and ARM platforms are typically the source of decreased efficiency.

As before, Fig. 4(b) provides the same data but with the SYCL data point taken as the best (minimum) result achieved by either of Open SYCL, DPC++ and ComputeCpp, and the OpenMP data point taken as the best result achieved by OpenMP with or without target offload directives. We can now see that both OpenMP 4.5 and SYCL are able to target every platform in our evaluation set. SYCL's efficiency rapidly drops below 0.5, as soon as the MI100 is added to its evaluation set, but it achieves a $\mathcal{P} \approx 0.19$. OpenMP is similarly portable, but the addition of the GPU platforms (platforms 7-11 in the evaluation set) push its efficiency to near zero, ultimately achieving $\mathcal{P} \approx 0.03$. The Kokkos variant generally achieves a higher application efficiency, but achieves $\mathcal{P} = 0$ as we were unable to collect a data point for the Intel HD Graphics P630 GPU.

Our findings for miniFE run counter to the data seen for Heat in Fig. 2(b). The "performance portability gap" between these two applications is likely not a result of the programming model chosen, but instead an indication that additional effort may be required to optimise the application for heterogeneous architectures. In the case of Heat, the simplicity of the application means that the kernel likely translates reasonably well for each of the target platforms without much manual optimisation effort, regardless of programming semantics. For a significantly more complex application like miniFE, the target architectures must be much more carefully considered in order to optimise memory access patterns and minimise unnecessary data transfers [19].

Figure 5 shows a simplified cascade plot containing only the three portable programming models considered in this study (i.e. OpenMP, Kokkos and SYCL). In this figure, both OpenMP and Kokkos follow the 1.0 efficiency line up to the addition of GPU and CPU platforms, respectively. On CPUs, SYCL is typically less performant than OpenMP; and on GPUs, SYCL is typically less performant than Kokkos, with the exception of the Intel HD Graphics P630 (for which we do not have a Kokkos data point). The platform ordering in Fig. 5 shows that Kokkos and SYCL are typically better at targetting GPU platforms than CPU platforms, while the reverse is true for OpenMP. Overall, when compared only to other portable programming models, SYCL achieves $\mathcal{P} \approx 0.36$, while OpenMP only achieves $\mathcal{P} \approx 0.06$. Although Kokkos achieves $\mathcal{P} = 0$ (due to no result on one of the platforms), if we remove the Intel HD Graphics P630 from our evaluation set, it achieves $\mathcal{P} \approx 0.64$.

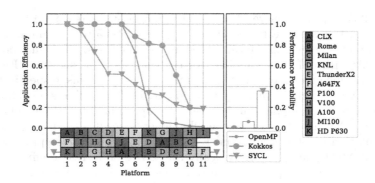

Fig. 5. A cascade plot for the miniFE application considering only the three *portable* programming models (OpenMP, Kokkos and SYCL).

At the most basic level, SYCL provides a similar abstraction to Kokkos, i.e., a parallel-for construct for loop-level parallelism, and a method for moving data between host and device. For this reason we believe that SYCL should be able to provide competitive performance portability to Kokkos. That SYCL achieves approximately half of the performance portability of Kokkos is therefore likely due to limited optimisation efforts at the application-level, and possibly lack of maturity at the compiler-level; this performance gap is likely to close in time.

5   Conclusion

This paper details our initial investigation into the current status of compilers implementing the SYCL programming model in terms of performance and performance portability. Our study is motivated by the growing rate of SYCL adoption within HPC, fuelled by its adoption by Intel for their new *Xe* line of GPUs. Our evaluation is based on three SYCL compilers and two mini-applications that implement methods commonly found in plasma physics simulation applications: one a finite difference method, the other a finite element method.

For a simplistic finite difference heat diffusion mini-application, our results show that SYCL is able to offer performance that is comparable to other performance portable frameworks such as OpenMP 4.5 (with target offload). For well optimised, simplistic kernels, SYCL is able to achieve high performance across a range of different architectures with little developer effort.

On a significantly more complex finite element method application, SYCL leads to a significant loss of efficiency when compared to native approaches such as CUDA and MPI. When compared against other portable programming models, such as OpenMP 4.5 and Kokkos, SYCL fares better, achieving $\mathcal{P} \approx 0.36$. Kokkos is arguably the most performance portable approach considered in this study, achieving $\mathcal{P} \approx 0.64$ (without the Intel HD Graphics P630). It is likely that a focused optimisation effort would improve the performance of the SYCL variant across every platform and reduce the gap between Kokkos and SYCL.

Overall our results (and those of previous studies [4,8,12,19]) show that the SYCL programming model can provide performance and portability across platforms. However, our experience with the miniFE application shows that this performance does not come "for free" and likely requires careful consideration of compilers and compiler options, and a SYCL-focused optimisation effort. As the language and compiler infrastructure are further developed, the burden on developers should decrease considerably.

5.1 Future Work

The work presented in this paper shows an initial investigation into the SYCL programming model using two mini-applications. The most significant performance issues highlighted concern the SYCL implementation of miniFE used in this paper. Since it is a conversion from an OpenMP 4.5 implementation, it has not been subject to the same optimisation efforts as the other ports evaluated. It would therefore be prudent to re-evaluate the application following a focused optimisation effort. Nonetheless, the work in this paper highlights the probable performance gap between a simplistic conversion and a focused porting effort.

Acknowledgements. Many of the results in this paper were gathered on the Isambard UK National Tier-2 HPC Service (http://gw4.ac.uk/isambard/) operated by GW4 and the UK Met Office, and funded by EPSRC (EP/P020224/1).

Access to the Intel HD Graphics P630 GPU was provided by Intel through the Intel Developer Cloud.

The ExCALIBUR programme (https://excalibur.ac.uk/) is supported by the UKRI Strategic Priorities Fund. The programme is co-delivered by the Met Office and EPSRC in partnership with the Public Sector Research Establishment, the UK Atomic Energy Authority (UKAEA) and UKRI research councils, including NERC, MRC and STFC.

References

1. Beckingsale, D.A., et al.: RAJA: portable performance for large-scale scientific applications. In: IEEE/ACM International Workshop on Performance, Portability and Productivity in HPC (P3HPC), pp. 71–81 (2019)
2. Breyer, M., Van Craen, A., Pflüger, D.: A comparison of SYCL, OpenCL, CUDA, and OpenMP for massively parallel support vector machine classification on multi-vendor hardware. In: International Workshop on OpenCL (IWOCL), pp. 1–12 (2022)
3. Dagum, L., Menon, R.: OpenMP: an industry standard API for shared-memory programming. IEEE Comput. Sci. Eng. 5(1), 46–55 (1998)
4. Deakin, T., McIntosh-Smith, S.: Evaluating the performance of HPC-style SYCL applications. In: International Workshop on OpenCL (IWOCL). ACM (2020)
5. Deakin, T., et al.: Performance portability across diverse computer architectures. In: IEEE/ACM International Workshop on Performance, Portability and Productivity in HPC (P3HPC), pp. 1–13 (2019)
6. Edwards, H.C., Trott, C.R., Sunderland, D.: Kokkos: enabling manycore performance portability through polymorphic memory access patterns. J. Parallel Distrib. Comput. (JPDC) **74**(12), 3202–3216 (2014)

7. Herdman, J.A., et al.: Accelerating hydrocodes with OpenACC, OpenCL and CUDA. In: SC Companion: High Performance Computing, Networking Storage and Analysis, pp. 465–471 (2012)
8. Joo, B., et al.: Performance portability of a Wilson Dslash stencil operator mini-app using Kokkos and SYCL. In: IEEE/ACM International Workshop on Performance, Portability and Productivity in HPC (P3HPC), pp. 14–25 (2019)
9. Kirk, R.O., Mudalige, G.R., Reguly, I.Z., Wright, S.A., Martineau, M.J., Jarvis, S.A.: Achieving performance portability for a heat conduction solver mini-application on modern multi-core systems. In: IEEE International Conference on Cluster Computing (CLUSTER), pp. 834–841 (2017)
10. Law, T.R., et al.: Performance portability of an unstructured hydrodynamics mini-application. In: IEEE/ACM International Workshop on Performance, Portability and Productivity in HPC (P3HPC), pp. 0–12 (2018)
11. Lin, P.T., Heroux, M.A., Barrett, R.F., Williams, A.B.: Assessing a mini-application as a performance proxy for a finite element method engineering application. Concurrency Comput. Pract. Experience **27**(17), 5374–5389 (2015)
12. Lin, W.C., Deakin, T., McIntosh-Smith, S.: On Measuring the Maturity of SYCL Implementations by Tracking Historical Performance Improvements. In: International Workshop on OpenCL (IWOCL). ACM (2021)
13. OpenACC-Standard.org: The OpenACC Application Program Interface Version 3.3 (2022). https://www.openacc.org/sites/default/files/inline-images/Specification/OpenACC-3.3-final.pdf
14. OpenMP Architecture Review Board: OpenMP API Version 4.5 (2015). https://www.openmp.org/wp-content/uploads/openmp-4.5.pdf
15. Pennycook, S.J., Jarvis, S.A.: Developing performance-portable molecular dynamics kernels in opencl. In: 2012 SC Companion: High Performance Computing, Networking Storage and Analysis, pp. 386–395 (2012)
16. Pennycook, S.J., Sewall, J., Jacobsen, D., Deakin, T., Zamora, Y., Lee, K.L.K.: Performance, portability and productivity analysis. Library (2023). https://doi.org/10.5281/zenodo.7733678
17. Pennycook, S.J., Hammond, S.D., Wright, S.A., Herdman, J.A., Miller, I., Jarvis, S.A.: An investigation of the performance portability of OpenCL. J. Parallel Distrib. Comput. (JPDC) **73**(11), 1439–1450 (2013)
18. Pennycook, S., Sewall, J., Lee, V.: Implications of a metric for performance portability. Futur. Gener. Comput. Syst. **92**, 947–958 (2019)
19. Reguly, I.Z., Owenson, A.M.B., Powell, A., Jarvis, S.A., Mudalige, G.R.: Under the hood of SYCL – an initial performance analysis with an unstructured-mesh CFD application. In: Chamberlain, B.L., Varbanescu, A.-L., Ltaief, H., Luszczek, P. (eds.) ISC High Performance 2021. LNCS, vol. 12728, pp. 391–410. Springer, Cham (2021). https://doi.org/10.1007/978-3-030-78713-4_21
20. Sewall, J., Pennycook, S.J., Jacobsen, D., Deakin, T., McIntosh-Smith, S.: Interpreting and visualizing performance portability metrics. In: IEEE/ACM International Workshop on Performance, Portability and Productivity in HPC (P3HPC), pp. 14–24 (2020)
21. Stone, J.E., Gohara, D., Shi, G.: OpenCL: a parallel programming standard for heterogeneous computing systems. Comput. Sci. Eng. **12**(3), 66 (2010)

22. The Khronos SYCL Working Group: SYCL 2020 Specification (2023). https://registry.khronos.org/SYCL/specs/sycl-2020/pdf/sycl-2020.pdf
23. Truby, D., Wright, S.A., Kevis, R., Maheswaran, S., Herdman, J.A., Jarvis, S.A.: BookLeaf: an unstructured hydrodynamics mini-application. In: IEEE International Conference on Cluster Computing (CLUSTER), pp. 615–622 (2018)
24. University of Bristol HPC Group: Programming Your GPU with OpenMP: A Hands-On Introduction (2022). https://github.com/UoB-HPC/openmp-tutorial

Observed Memory Bandwidth and Power Usage on FPGA Platforms with OneAPI and Vitis HLS: A Comparison with GPUs

Christopher M. Siefert[1]($\boxtimes$), Stephen L. Olivier[1], Gwendolyn R. Voskuilen[1], and Jeffrey S. Young[2]

[1] Center for Computing Research, Sandia National Laboratories, Albuquerque, NM 87185, USA
{csiefer,slolivi,grvosku}@sandia.gov
[2] College of Computing, Georgia Institute of Technology, Atlanta, GA 30332, USA
jyoung9@gatech.edu

Abstract. The two largest barriers to adoption of FPGA platforms for HPC applications are the difficulty of programming FPGAs and the performance gap when compared to GPUs. To address the first barrier, new ecosystems like Intel oneAPI, and Xilinx Vitis HLS aim to improve programmability for FPGA platforms. From a performance aspect, FPGAs trade off lower compute frequencies for more customized hardware acceleration and power efficiency when compared to GPUs. The performance for memory-bound applications on recent GPU platforms like NVIDIA's H100 and AMD's MI210 has also improved due to the inclusion of high-bandwidth memories (HBM), and newer FPGA platforms are also starting to include HBM in addition to traditional DRAM.

To understand the current state-of-the-art and performance differences between FPGAs and GPUs, we consider realized memory bandwidth for recent FPGA and GPU platforms. We utilize a custom STREAM benchmark to evaluate two Intel FPGA platforms, the Stratix 10 SX PAC and Bittware 520N-MX, two AMD/Xilinx FPGA platforms, the Alveo U250 and Alveo U280, as well as GPU platforms from NVIDIA and AMD. We also extract power measurements and estimate memory bandwidth per Watt ((GB/s)/W) on these platforms to evaluate how FPGAs compare against GPU execution. While the GPUs far exceed the FPGAs in raw performance, the HBM equipped FPGAs demonstrate a competitive performance-power balance for larger data sizes that can be easily implemented with oneAPI and Vitis HLS kernels. These findings suggest a potential sweet spot for this emerging FPGA ecosystem to serve bandwidth limited applications in an energy-efficient fashion.

Keywords: Memory bandwidth · Peak power · FPGA · oneAPI · GPU · Bittware · Intel · Vitis · AMD · Xilinx

A. Bienz et al. (Eds.): ISC High Performance 2023 Workshops, LNCS 13999, pp. 620–633, 2023.
https://doi.org/10.1007/978-3-031-40843-4_46

1   Introduction

Custom hardware architectures promise power- and performance-efficient computation for applications that do not perform optimally on mainstream architectures such as CPUs and GPUs. Field-Programmable Gate Arrays (FPGAs) are one approach to developing custom hardware for such applications, but effectively leveraging FPGAs has traditionally required significant development investment, which has limited their adoption in mainstream computing. Recent advances in high-level synthesis (HLS) have the potential to make custom hardware, including that targeted for FPGAs, easier and faster to design. This advancement is especially of interest to high-performance computing (HPC) where application scale and performance needs lend themselves to custom architectures but practical challenges prevent their adoption. These challenges include the significant complexity of applications, the need for rapid feature improvements, and the reality that HPC application developers tend to be unfamiliar with hardware design languages and principles. If these challenges could be overcome by a high-level synthesis toolchain, it would open the aperture for wider adoption of custom architectures in HPC built around FPGAs. In fact, Intel's oneAPI, a SYCL-based HLS toolchain, and AMD's Vitis toolchain have already made significant inroads for HLS that are usable by HPC developers.

HPC applications that do not map well to conventional architectures commonly exhibit two characteristics: (1) performance that is memory-bandwidth limited and (2) sparse access and compute patterns that do not lend themselves to SIMT architectures like GPUs or CPU architectures with large caches. These applications in particular could benefit from customized accelerator architectures that integrate advanced memory technologies such as high-bandwidth memory (HBM). To that end, in this paper we explore the ability of today's high-level synthesis toolchains to generate kernels capable of saturating HBM bandwidth. We evaluate the performance, power, and bandwidth characteristics of FPGA kernels compared to the same kernels on recent GPUs.

Unsurprisingly, GPUs generally outperform the FPGAs in raw performance. This result is expected given the investment in GPU performance over the past few decades compared to the FPGA which has, until recently, been employed primarily as a prototyping vehicle. However, even given the limits of FPGA performance, this paper shows that FPGAs today can be competitive with some GPUs when the tradeoffs of power and performance are considered together. We do this by looking a measure of how much power is needed to move data on the given computational device, as measured in memory-bandwidth per Watt (GB/s/W). In this metric, we demonstrate that FPGAs are competitive for memory-intensive kernels even with a non-optimized HLS implementation. This finding indicates that HLS toolchains merit further consideration for sparse and memory-intensive HPC applications and kernels.

We outline our FPGA implementation of the STREAM copy benchmark [14] for memory bandwidth measurement in Sect. 2, explaining its usage model on FPGA platforms both with and without HBM. We present computational results in Sect. 3 and review related work in Sect. 4. Finally, we discuss conclusions and future work in Sect. 5.

2   STREAM Copy Implementation on FPGAs

To evaluate and compare FPGA power and performance characteristics relative to GPUs, we employ a modified version of the STREAM [14] benchmark. Our versions are written in SYCL/DPC++ (for Intel FPGAs) and Vitis HLS (for AMD Xilinx FPGAs) and tuned to maximize the memory bandwidth utilization. We use two boards based on Intel Stratix FPGAs: the Intel Stratix 10 SX PAC, a direct Intel product with DRAM, and the Bittware 520N-MX, a reseller product with HBM2. On these FPGAs, we use SYCL's buffer/accessor model for memory allocation and migration, as the explicit Unified Shared Memory (USM) memory model was not supported on our Intel Stratix 10 SX card (and Implicit USM is not supported on any Intel FPGA). The buffer/accessor model performs a host-to-device transfer of the data object on the first use on device and then a device-to-host transfer on buffer deallocation. Neither of these transfers are included in the timings used to calculate memory bandwidth described in Sect. 3, though they certainly could affect the peak power measurements. Our study also includes two AMD Xilinx FPGAs, the Alveo U250 with DRAM, and the Alveo U280 with HBM2. On these FPGAs, we use the buffer object (BO) of the Xilinx runtime (XRT) native C++ API, with calls to its sync operation to perform the untimed data transfers to and from the host.

2.1   Intel Kernel Implementation

Our basic Intel DPC++ implementation of STREAM Copy is shown below.

```
1 q.submit([&](handler &h)[[intel::kernel_args_restrict]]{
2     accessor from(/*args*/,apl<BANK>);
3     accessor to(/*args*/,apl<BANK>);
4     h.parallel_for<>(range<1>(N), [=](id<1> i)
5         [[intel::num_simd_work_items(NWG),
6         sycl::reqd_work_group_size(1,1,WGS)]]{
7             to[i] = from[i];
8         });
9 });
```

In this code snippet, apl<BANK> is shorthand for accessor_property_list < buffer_location <BANK> >, which controls which memory bank is used by the accessor. NWG = 8 is the number of SIMD items to use at a time, WGS = 1024 is the work group size and N represents the vector size to copy. The SIMD width was chosen to get the full 512-bit width on the FPGA load-store units. The from accessor is given the read_only tag and the to accessor has the write_only tag.

Intel Stratix 10 SX PAC. The Intel Stratix 10 SX PAC does not implement explicit user control over memory banks, so BANK in Sect. 2.1 will always be zero, though the entire apl<BANK> could be omitted without changing the generated code. Instead, the four channels of the DDR4 memory on the FPGA are automatically interleaved in 4096 byte increments. This behavior was verified by inspection of the reports automatically generated by the DPC++ compiler.

Bittware 520N-MX. Unlike the Intel Stratix 10 SX PAC, Bittware has chosen not to implement memory interleaving on the 520N-MX. Bittware explains this choice as follows using the term PC (an abbreviation of pseudo-channel) instead of the term BANK that we have used above,

> "By partitioning the PCs, the OpenCL compiler will create a small memory system for each PC that does not interact with other memory systems, which can result in better Fmax and throughput" [8].

In short, Bittware forces the user to manage the 32 memory banks of HBM on the 520N-MX manually. We can still use the code snippet above, except that we need to call it 32 times, once for each bank. For ease of programming our program submits 32 separate kernels to the work queue, though it could also be done with a single kernel. We use C++ templates with integer parameters to generate the 32 kernels and minimize code duplication.

2.2 AMD Xilinx Kernel Implementation

Our Vitis HLS implementation of STREAM Copy for Xilinx is shown below.

```
1 #pragma HLS INTERFACE m_axi port=in bundle=aximm1 /*b1*/
2 #pragma HLS INTERFACE m_axi port=out bundle=aximm2 /*b2*/
3   __builtin_assume( size % 4 == 0);
4   for(int i = 0; i < size; ++i) {
5 #pragma HLS unroll skip_exit_check factor=4
6 #pragma HLS dependence variable=in type=inter false
7 #pragma HLS dependence variable=out type=inter false
8     out[i] = in[i];
9   }
```

In this code snippit, the b1 and b2 variables specify the read/write burst lengths, which is necessary to ensure maximum performance from the memory system. For b1, we set max_read_burst_length=256 and for b2, we set b1, we set max_write_burst_length=256. To conserve resources, we set the "unused" burst length (e.g. the write length for b1) to 2, the minimum possible, as well as the minimum number of outstanding read/writes for the "unused" burst to 1.

In addition to the device code, AMD Xilinx FPGAs need a configuration file, which manually maps kernel "ports" to memory banks (for both DDR and HBM). Like the Bittware 520N-MX detailed in Sect. 2.1, AMD Xilinx does not implement memory interleaving on either the Alveo U250 or Alveo U280 platform. For the Alveo U250 using DDR, we use four replications of the stream copy kernel, one for each of the four DDR banks. This implementation is similar to the Intel implementation described in Sect. 2.1 in that the input and output of each kernel instance reside in *the same* memory bank. For the Alveo U280 using HBM2, we use 16 replications of the stream copy kernel in which the read and write buffers for each replica reside in *different* memory banks. This implementation was chosen because Alveo U280 only allows 32 total memory ports and we wanted to engage all 32 HBM banks.

3   Computational Experiments

To measure memory bandwidth, we consider the copy component of the STREAM benchmark [14] on the platforms described in Table 1. On GPU platforms, we use a version of BabelStream [11] modified to run only the copy benchmark in isolation. On FPGA platforms, we follow the approach described in Sect. 2 and our DPC++ and Vitis HLS implementation of this kernel, detailed in Sect. 2.1 and Sect. 2.2 respectively. The STREAM copy test is repeated 100 times to produce a single estimate of the memory bandwidth. Power measurement is accomplished via another process, which samples the appropriate power management utility and then sleeps for 100 µs before sampling again. Power measurements are obtained using rocm-smi on the AMD GPU platform, nvidia-smi on Nvidia GPU platforms, Bittware's monitor program on the 520N-MX, xbutil on the AMD Xilinx FPGAs, and a stand-alone tool based on the OPAE library [7] on the Stratix 10 SX. The maximum of the sampled power is taken as the peak power for that run. We executed 100 trials of each configuration to calculate the mean value shown at each data point on our plots. One standard deviation error bars are shown on all plots in a slightly darker color, although they may be less easily visible for some datasets with little variation.

3.1   Intel FPGA Memory Bandwidth and Peak Power Measurements

We begin by considering the observed memory bandwidth. As detailed in Sect. 2, the Bittware 520N-MX has 32 banks of HBM, and we launch a separate

Table 1. Platforms used for memory bandwidth testing.

Platform	Host CPU	Accelerator	Memory
MI210	AMD EPYC 7742	AMD Instinct MI210 (GPU)	64 GB HBM2e
A100	AMD EPYC 7452	NVIDIA A100 PCIE (GPU)	40 GB HBM2e
H100	Intel Xeon Plat. 8352Y	NVIDIA H100 PCIe (GPU)	80 GB HBM2e
S10	Intel Xeon Plat. 8256	Intel Stratix 10 SX PAC (FPGA)	32 GB DDR4
520N-MX	Intel Xeon Plat. 8352Y	Bittware 520N-MX (FPGA)	16 GB HBM2
U250	Intel Xeon Plat. 8352Y	AMD Xilinx Alveo U250 (FPGA)	64 GB DDR4
U280	Intel Xeon Plat. 8352Y	AMD Xilinx Alveo U280 (FPGA)	8 GB HBM2

kernel for each HBM bank. We perform data copies ranging from 16 KB up to 12 MB per bank, using from one HBM bank to all 32 banks. Note that number of banks used determines the total memory capacity available, such that increasing the number of banks used enables larger copy sizes. We compare these results from the Bittware 520N-MX with those from the Intel Stratix 10 SX, which uses DDR4 memory and does not have manual control over the memory banks. Figure 1 shows the memory bandwidth results for total copy sizes up to 384 MB using these two FPGA platforms. Please note the use of log scale on the axes. For the Bittware 520N-MX, the optimal number of memory banks to use is a function of the amount of memory copied, with larger memory copies achieving better performance with more HBM banks engaged. The peak memory bandwidth achieved by the Intel Stratix 10 SX is roughly the same as four HBM banks on the Bittware 520N-MX, and for small data copies, the Intel Stratix 10 SX achieves higher memory bandwidth than any option available on the Bittware 520N-MX. Thus, realization of the HBM performance advantage requires two conditions: First, the workload must process a large enough data set to drive bandwidth demand. Second, the data must be distributed among enough HBM banks to together provide the aggregate bandwidth for that demand. Finally, note that the error bars in this graph are small, especially for the larger data copy sizes, indicating little variance over the 100 trials per data point.

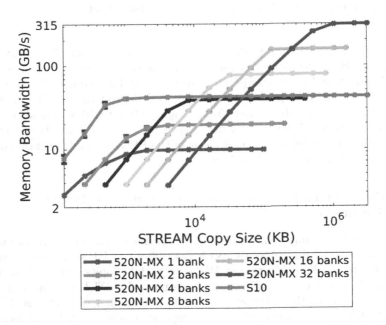

Fig. 1. Observed memory bandwidth as a function of copy size and number of HBM banks used on the Bittware 520N-MX, compared with the Intel Stratix 10 SX. Note log scale axes, and higher is better.

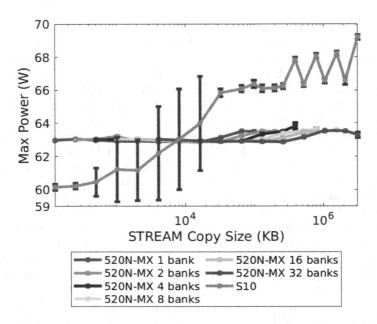

Fig. 2. Observed peak power as a function of copy size and number of HBM banks used on the Bittware 520N-MX, compared with the Intel Stratix 10 SX.

From the perspective of peak power, however, the number of memory banks used by the Bittware 520N-MX and the size of memory copied has very little effect. As shown in Fig. 2, peak power is around 63W for all our tests. Even larger memory copies increase peak power by only a little over half a Watt. The Intel Stratix 10 SX varies a bit more—from roughly 60W to 70W. We also observe some large standard deviations for data copies up to 16 MB using the S10 board. Even so, the modest range of power usage of the FPGAs stands in stark contrast to the GPU results we will show later.

3.2   AMD Xilinx Memory Bandwidth and Peak Power Measurements

We again begin by considering the observed memory bandwidth. As detailed in Sect. 2, the AMD Xilinx Alveo U280 has 32 banks of HBM, for which we can launch 16 separate kernel instances. We perform data copies ranging from 16 KB up to 32 MB per bank, using from a single pair of HBM banks up to 16 pairs of banks. Similar to the Bittware 520N-MX, the number of banks used by the Alveo U280 determines the total memory capacity available, such that increasing the number of banks used enables larger copy sizes. We compare the Alveo U280 results with those from the AMD Xilinx Alveo U250, which uses DDR4 memory. On the Alveo U250, we use four kernel replications. Figure 3 shows that the memory bandwidth achieved by the Alveo U250 is roughly equivalent to that

of the Alveo U280 when using only four HBM banks for most data sizes. For
sufficiently large data sizes, using more HBM banks of the Alveo U280 improves
the observed memory bandwidth.

Unlike the Intel FPGAs described in Sect. 3.1, the size of memory copied
does have an effect on the peak power, especially on the Alveo U250 As shown
in Fig. 4, peak power varies between 33 W and 45 W on the Alveo U280, and
25 W to 60 W on the Alveo U250. That said, these are lower across the board
than the Intel FPGAs and the overall low usage will be very different from the
GPU results shown later.

3.3   Comparing FPGA and GPU Platforms

We now consider the full set of platforms described in Table 1. To maintain
readability, we present only two sets of results for the Bittware 520N-MX, the
full 32 bank case, denoted 520N-MX (32) and a performance "frontier" using the
optimal number of banks for a given copy size, following the data in Fig. 1. We
denote this optimal frontier as 520N-MX (F). We do not use a similar frontier
for the AMD Xilinx Alveo U280 since as shown in Fig. 3, the performance of
using 16 bank pairs is uniformly superior to the other options at most sizes.

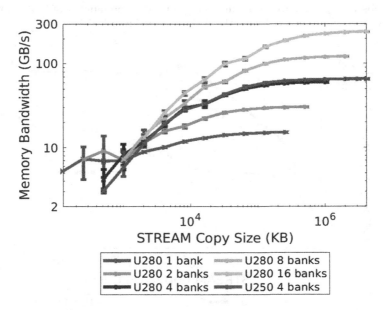

Fig. 3. Observed memory bandwidth as a function of copy size and number of HBM
banks used on the AMD Xilinx Alveo U280, compared with the AMD Xilinx Alveo
U250.

The GPUs deliver substantially more memory bandwidth than the FPGAs,
exceeding a terabyte per second, as shown in Fig. 5. Among the FPGAs, the

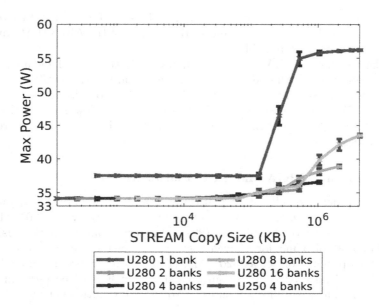

Fig. 4. Observed peak power as a function of copy size and number of HBM banks use on the Alveo U280, compared with the AMD Xilinx Alveo U250.

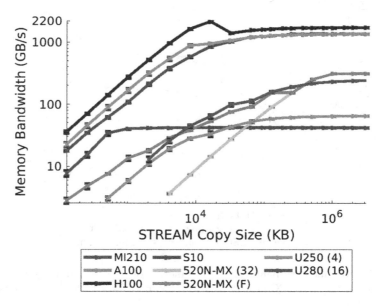

Fig. 5. Observed memory bandwidth Bittware 520N-MX using 32 banks [520N-MX (32)] and optimal frontier of banks [520N-MX (F)] compared with Intel Stratix S10 SX, AMD Xilinx FPGAs, and NVIDIA and AMD GPUs.

Intel S10 board comes closest to the GPU bandwidth performance for small data copies, the AMD Xilinx Alveo U280 comes closest for medium data copies and the Bittware 520N-MX comes closest for large data copies. Nonetheless, the GPU bandwidth advantage holds throughout the range of tested data copy sizes.

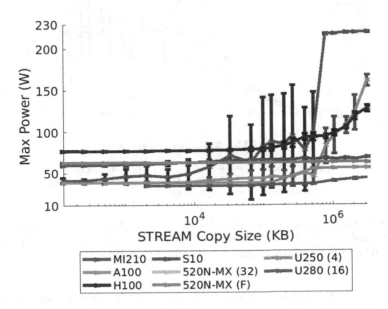

Fig. 6. Observed peak power for Bittware 520N-MX using 32 banks [520N-MX (32)] and optimal frontier of banks [520N-MX (F)] compared with Intel Stratix S10 SX, AMD Xilinx FPGAs, and NVIDIA and AMD GPUs.

The GPU bandwidth advantage comes at the cost of substantially higher peak power usage, as shown in Fig. 6. Viewed at this scale, the lines showing power measurements for the Bittware 520N-MX with using the optimal frontier and using all 32 banks are nearly indistinguishable. The H100 GPU exhibits the highest power usage of all the devices when performing small data copies, but the other GPUs use less power than the FPGAs in this regime. Once the memory copies become larger (in the tens of megabytes range), GPU power usage rises dramatically across all the GPU platforms, while the power usage remains relatively flat for both Intel and AMD Xilinx FPGAs. The effect is particularly pronounced for the MI210 but observed for the other GPUs as well.

We combine these metrics to get memory bandwidth per peak Watt, as shown in Fig. 7. While the GPUs are more power efficient across most of the range, there is clearly an optimal range whereas diminished efficiency is observed for very small or very large copies. For the largest data sizes, the HBM-equipped Bittware 520N-MX and AMD Xilinx Alveo U280 are both relatively close to the AMD MI210 GPU platform in terms of this metric. The DRAM-equipped

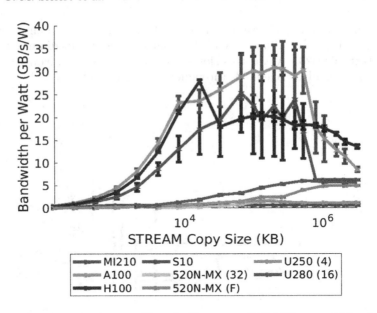

Fig. 7. Observed bandwidth per Watt for Bittware 520N-MX using 32 banks [520N-MX (32)] and optimal frontier of banks [520N-MX (F)] compared with Intel Stratix S10 SX, AMD Xilinx FPGAs, and NVIDIA and AMD GPUs.

Intel Stratix 10 SX PAC and AMD Xilinx Alveo U250 are not competitive with GPUs however. We summarize these results focusing on the furthest right data point—384 MB copied—in Table 2.

4   Related Work

The coupling of FPGAs with HBM technology has sparked recent investigations into the suitability of such platforms for high performance scientific computing. Several have focused on using the roofline model of performance analysis [10,16,19], for which bandwidth is of course one factor. Mayer et al. adapt the HPC Challenge benchmark suite for FPGAs using OpenCL [15]. Some application efforts have focused on problems involving sparse matrix operations [17,18,20] whose irregularity can be challenging for GPUs. One computational science effort using oneAPI for Intel Stratix FPGAs is the StencilStream code generation pipeline, demonstrated in the context of shallow water discontinuous Galerkin simulations [9], but it currently does not target HBM. Similar to scientific computing, high performance data analytics has also been considered as a target area for FPGA systems with HBM [13]. The Shuhai tool [12] of Huang et al. supports performance analysis of HBM-equipped FPGAs by measuring memory bandwidth and latency effects due to low level characteristics such as refresh interval and address mapping policies.

Table 2. Advertised and observed memory bandwidth and GB/s/W at 384 MB memory copy size. S10 maximum memory bandwidth is extracted from the Intel DPC++ compiler reports.

Platform	Advertised BW (GB/s)	Observed BW (GB/s)	GB/s/W
MI210	1638.4 [3]	1366	6.21
A100	1555 [5]	1375	8.54
H100	2000 [6]	1734	13.60
S10	76.8	32	0.61
520N-MX	410 [4]	323	4.95
U250	77 [1]	66	1.17
U280	460 [2]	242	5.55

5 Conclusions and Future Work

The memory performance benefits of HBM coupled with the productivity benefits of high level programming models like DPC++ and Vitis HLS are advancing FPGA technology toward consideration as an alternative to GPUs for memory-intensive HPC applications. This direction is especially of interest to HPC centers and users who consider power usage as a factor in their choice of architecture. Our work demonstrates that while GPUs exhibit the fastest execution for memory intensive kernels, FPGAs are competitive with the memory bandwidth per Watt of AMD GPUs at large data sizes. As noted by Siefert et al. [18], the higher cost of kernel launches on FPGAs relative to GPUs almost certainly contributes to the performance gap observed at small data sizes. These latency limitations for PCIe-based FPGAs are likely to be improved in the near future via new protocols like Compute eXpress Link (CXL). We look forward to reevaluating future FPGA platforms with a focus on including peak bandwidth and data transfer overheads with CXL. We also look forward to evaluating newer generations of Intel FPGAs such as Agilex. To further our goal of assessing their readiness for HPC applications, we are also commencing evaluations of inter-FPGA data movement using MPI.

Acknowledgment. Sandia National Laboratories is a multimission laboratory managed and operated by National Technology and Engineering Solutions of Sandia, LLC., a wholly owned subsidiary of Honeywell International, Inc., for the U.S. Department of Energy's National Nuclear Security Administration under contract DE-NA-0003525. This written work is authored by an employee of NTESS. The employee, not NTESS, owns the right, title and interest in and to the written work and is responsible for its contents. Any subjective views or opinions that might be expressed in the written work do not necessarily represent the views of the U.S. Government. The publisher acknowledges that the U.S. Government retains a non-exclusive, paid-up, irrevocable, world-wide license to publish or reproduce the published form of this written work or allow others to do so, for U.S. Government purposes. The DOE will provide public access to results of federally sponsored research in accordance with the DOE Public Access Plan.

References

1. Alveo U250 data center accelerator card. https://www.xilinx.com/products/boards-and-kits/alveo/u250.html. Accessed 13 June 2023
2. Alveo U280 data center accelerator card. https://www.xilinx.com/products/boards-and-kits/alveo/u280.html. Accessed 13 June 2023
3. AMD Instinct MI210 accelerator. https://www.amd.com/en/products/server-accelerators/amd-instinct-mi210. Accessed 15 Mar 2023
4. Bittware 520N-MX PCIE card with Intel Stratix 10 MX FPGA. https://www.bittware.com/fpga/520n-mx/. Accessed 15 Mar 2023
5. NVIDIA A100 tensor core GPU: Unprecedented acceleration at every scale. https://www.nvidia.com/content/dam/en-zz/Solutions/Data-Center/a100/pdf/a100-80gb-datasheet-update-nvidia-us-1521051-r2-web.pdf. Accessed 15 Mar 2023
6. NVIDIA H100 tensor core GPU. https://www.nvidia.com/en-us/data-center/h100/. Accessed 15 Mar 2023
7. Open programmable acceleration engine. https://opae.github.io/latest/index.html. Accessed 15 Mar 2023
8. Bittware 520N-MX gen 3x16 BSP release notes (2021). release 1.8.1
9. Alt, C., et al.: Shallow water DG simulations on FPGAs: design and comparison of a novel code generation pipeline. In: Bhatele, A., Hammond, J., Baboulin, M., Kruse, C. (eds.) ISC High Performance 2023. LNCS, vol. 13948, pp. 86–105. Springer, Cham (2023). https://doi.org/10.1007/978-3-031-32041-5_5
10. Calore, E., Schifano, S.F.: Performance assessment of FPGAs as HPC accelerators using the FPGA empirical roofline. In: 2021 31st International Conference on Field-Programmable Logic and Applications (FPL), pp. 83–90 (2021). https://doi.org/10.1109/FPL53798.2021.00022
11. Deakin, T., Price, J., Martineau, M., McIntosh-Smith, S.: Evaluating attainable memory bandwidth of parallel programming models via BabelStream. Int. J. Comput. Sci. Eng. **17**(3), 247–262 (2018). https://doi.org/10.1504/IJCSE.2017.10011352
12. Huang, H., et al.: Shuhai: a tool for benchmarking high bandwidth memory on FPGAs. IEEE Trans. Comput. **71**(5), 1133–1144 (2022). https://doi.org/10.1109/TC.2021.3075765
13. Kara, K., Hagleitner, C., Diamantopoulos, D., Syrivelis, D., Alonso, G.: High bandwidth memory on FPGAs: a data analytics perspective. In: 2020 30th International Conference on Field-Programmable Logic and Applications (FPL), pp. 1–8 (2020). https://doi.org/10.1109/FPL50879.2020.00013
14. McCalpin, J.D.: Memory bandwidth and machine balance in current high performance computers. IEEE Comput. Soc. Tech. Committee Comput. Architect. (TCCA) Newsl. **2**, 19–25 (1995)
15. Meyer, M., Kenter, T., Plessl, C.: Evaluating FPGA accelerator performance with a parameterized OpenCL adaptation of selected benchmarks of the HPC Challenge benchmark suite. In: 2020 IEEE/ACM International Workshop on Heterogeneous High-Performance Reconfigurable Computing (H2RC), pp. 10–18 (2020). https://doi.org/10.1109/H2RC51942.2020.00007

16. Nguyen, T., Williams, S., Siracusa, M., MacLean, C., Doerfler, D., Wright, N.J.: The performance and energy efficiency potential of FPGAs in scientific computing. In: 2020 IEEE/ACM Performance Modeling, Benchmarking and Simulation of High Performance Computer Systems (PMBS), pp. 8–19 (2020). https://doi.org/10.1109/PMBS51919.2020.00007
17. Parravicini, A., Cellamare, L.G., Siracusa, M., Santambrogio, M.D.: Scaling up HBM efficiency of Top-K SpMV for approximate embedding similarity on FPGAs. In: 2021 58th ACM/IEEE Design Automation Conference (DAC), pp. 799–804 (2021). https://doi.org/10.1109/DAC18074.2021.9586203
18. Siefert, C., Olivier, S., Voskuilen, G., Young, J.: MultiGrid on FPGA using data parallel C++. In: 23rd IEEE International Workshop on Parallel and Distributed Scientific and Engineering Computing (2022). https://doi.org/10.1109/IPDPSW55747.2022.00147
19. Siracusa, M., et al.: A comprehensive methodology to optimize FPGA designs via the roofline model. IEEE Trans. Comput. **71**(8), 1903–1915 (2022). https://doi.org/10.1109/TC.2021.3111761
20. Zeni, A., O'Brien, K., Blott, M., Santambrogio, M.D.: Optimized implementation of the HPCG benchmark on reconfigurable hardware. In: Sousa, L., Roma, N., Tomás, P. (eds.) Euro-Par 2021. LNCS, vol. 12820, pp. 616–630. Springer, Cham (2021). https://doi.org/10.1007/978-3-030-85665-6_38

Evaluating Quantum Algorithms
for Linear Solver Workflows

Sophia Kolak[1,2], Hamed Mohammadbagherpoor[1], Konstantis Daloukas[3],
Kostas Kafousas[3], Francois-Henry Rouet[3], Yorgos Koutsoyannopoulos[3],
Nathan Earnest-Noble[1], and Robert F. Lucas[3(✉)]

[1] IBM Quantum - IBM T.J. Watson Research Center,
Yorktown Heights, NY, USA
[2] Department of Computer Science, Carnegie Mellon University,
Pittsburgh, PA, USA
[3] Ansys, Inc., Canonsburg, PA, USA
robertflucas@gmail.com

Abstract. We normally think of implicit Mechanical Computer Aided
Engineering (MCAE) as being a resource intensive process, dominated
by multifrontal linear solvers that scale super linearly in complexity as
the problem size grows. However, as the processor count increases, the
reordering that reduces the storage and operation count for the sparse
linear solver is emerging as the biggest computational bottleneck and
is expected to grow. Reordering is NP-complete, and the nested dissection heuristic is generally preferred for MCAE problems. Nested dissection in turn rests on graph partitioning, another NP-complete problem.
There are quantum computing algorithms which provide new heuristics
for NP-complete problems, and the rapid growth of today's noisy quantum computers and associated error mitigation techniques leads us to
consider them as possible accelerators for reordering. This review reports
on the evaluation of the relative merits of several short depth quantum
algorithms used for graph partitioning, integration with the LS-DYNA
MCAE application, and using the initial results generated on IBM quantum computers to bring to attention critical focus areas based on the
methods used within.

1 Introduction

In the past few years, quantum computing has had a significant upturn - in both
its development, and industrial interest. When looking at the development of
quantum systems, it is easy to appreciate how quickly the field has developed
in the past decade. For example, the current industry superconducting qubit of
choice, the Transmon, was first demonstrated less that two decades ago [28]. In
the time since the transmon's inception, it's gate fidelities and coherence times
have grown orders of magnitude. Roughly one decade after the realization of
the qubit itself, or three years after the transmon coherence grew to 60 μs [7],
quantum systems were made available via cloud access in 2016 - being the first

A. Bienz et al. (Eds.): ISC High Performance 2023 Workshops, LNCS 13999, pp. 634–647, 2023.
https://doi.org/10.1007/978-3-031-40843-4_47

point in history when non-specialists could practically test the potential benefits from the systems. Since then, a variety of physical realizations are now available via cloud access, with many of them surpassing a scale in which we can classically simulate these systems, with associated *system* capabilities also rapidly developing. With this rapid growth of quantum hardware, the broader industry has taken an interest in understanding how it may help their clients' needs. The potential for quantum computers to improve computing capabilities in the unknown, and potentially near-term future leads to two important questions: when is the appropriate time to begin to actively invest in a quantum initiative and in what ways?

The answer to this question is different depending on the nature of a given software product. In addition to the type of software a company produces, there is the question of which problems quantum algorithms are currently well equipped to solve. Although quantum computing can in theory provide solutions more efficiently to NP-Complete problems than the classical heuristic algorithms used today [16], the present reality of both quantum hardware and software limits stake-holders to a few specific use cases, which are often much smaller than the scales needed by industry.

We begin the paper by providing context on Ansys as a company, quantifying their relative need for quantum computing according to the size of their bottlenecks and the expected growth in data volume and the performance of quantum systems. In Sect. 2 we describe the Ansys technological offering and client relevant workflows, seeking where there are computational bottlenecks. We identify graph-partitioning (reordering) as the strongest candidate for quantum migration, over presently existing algorithms for solving this problem. In Sect. 3 we layout some of the different methods available to be used for graph partitioning and give a quick introduction to practical aspects of these algorithms. In Sect. 4 we highlight how the quantum algorithms in question are expected to scale with problem size (judging by circuit width and depth), and assess the expected quality in both classical simulations of quantum algorithms and direct quantum experiment on IBM Quantum hardware. We leverage the parameters from noise free simulations to get a rapid assessment of quantum hardware capabilities. Using this information, we finish the paper with a discussion and potential next steps in Sect. 5. Based on the hardware demo results we highlight some of key milestones which would need to be achieved for full integration, and discuss the best course of action for Ansys in light of these findings.

2   Possible Quantum Integration Pathways

Ansys is a software company that provides engineering simulation solutions that enable organizations to design and test virtual prototypes of products, systems, and materials. Ansys software is used by engineers and designers in a range of industries, including aerospace, automotive, construction, consumer goods, electronics, semiconductors, energy, healthcare, and more. Ansys' software suite

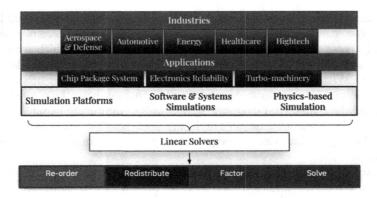

Fig. 1. A breakdown of the main industries Ansys works with, and the services they provide. Across this wide range of industries and simulation types, linear solvers are required. Within the linear solver pipeline, reordering (one sub-step) is a ubiquitous bottleneck, limiting the efficiency of the services at the top of the stack. The process is to Reorder, Redistribute, Factor, and then Solve.

includes a range of products that allow engineers to simulate and analyze different physical phenomena, such as structural mechanics, fluid dynamics, electromagnetics, signal/power integrity, and thermal management. These tools enable engineers to optimize the design of their products and systems, reduce physical prototyping costs, and accelerate time-to-market. Figure 1 shows the general breakdown of the Ansys client environment – from the fundamental need for physics-based simulation up to many of the relevant client industries. Furthermore, the figure outlines many of the relevant computational steps which must be taken for these industrial applications. For the purpose of this study, we remained focused on pathways which impact the entirety of Ansys' clients to maximizes the potential revenue impact. We have highlighted two key challenges which become classical computational bottlenecks across a broad range of Ansys' client workflows, and are thereby strong candidates to explore for quantum integration. Some of these simulations already take days to complete, and are expected to take longer in the coming years as the users' models grow in complexity. A future impact analysis may benefit from considering the needs of specific simulation use cases (e.g. Material Science) to determine other, more tailored, pathways and assess their potential.

2.1 Linear Solvers

Linear solvers are not only pervasive, but present a super-linear computational bottleneck in Ansys programs. This is unsurprising, as on classical computers the process of linear equation solving (finding the vector x, for the matrix A such that $Ax = b$), for a sparse A matrix is $O(n^{1.5})$ for planar systems of equations, $O(n^2)$ for three-dimensional ones, and $O(n^3)$ for dense non-Sparse A matrix,

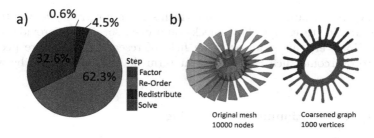

Fig. 2. a) LS-DYNA linear solver computing time breakdown for one load step in an implicit finite-element simulation. One first recursively partitions the graph (i.e., reordering), then redistributes the matrix, followed by factoring, and finally triangular solves. b) An impeller, when its graph is coarsened from 10,000 to 1,000 nodes, as an example of how this impacts its representation. In the subsequent analysis, we consider the graph of each object coarsened from 10,000 to as few as 25 nodes.

where n is the dimension of the matrix [24]. While researchers have devised highly efficient algorithms and parallelization strategies for reducing the work involved, solving linear equations still scales polynomially with the dimension of the matrix. When the matrix A remains relatively small or has some special properties, the linear solver will finish in a reasonable amount of time. Ansys, however, is already dealing with massive matrices, which may be sparse or dense. Sparse matrices coming from Finite Element or Finite Volume discretizations, e.g., in structural mechanics or fluid dynamics, can have several hundred millions or even billions of rows and columns. Dense matrices from Boundary Element discretizations, e.g., in electromagnetic field simulations, can have a few hundred thousand rows and columns, sometimes a few millions. Today these operations can take days, but as Ansys' use cases become larger and more complex (as expected in the near future), finding a solution could take weeks, and in some cases, may be effectively uncomputable via classical methods. As such, these solvers were identified early on as the high-level target for quantum migration.

Although there are potential scaling benefits to integrating quantum linear solvers with Ansys' quantum software needs, the quantum algorithms for doing so present major challenges in the both today's noisy quantum computers era and beyond. The two main quantum algorithms for solving linear equations are either fault tolerant [19] or variational [4]. In practice unfortunately, both approaches have problems. When considering fault tolerant approaches (e.g., HHL [19]), we are faced with two main concerns. First, this approach is unlikely to be implemented in the near term due to the lack of existence of a suitable fault tolerant quantum computer. Second, there are issues with experimental implementation of some associated technology (e.g., qRAM and I/O bottlenecks) which bring into question whether these algorithms can be implemented today or in the near future.. Given these points and the inability to implement these algorithms at scale on today's quantum hardware, we exclude this from our main discussion. Potentially nearer-term approaches like Variational Quantum Linear

Solver (VQLS) [4] suffer from circuits which still do not transpile well to native quantum architectures, I/O bottlenecks, and even so, do not provide an exact solution. However, this is an on-going field of research [23], where people are seeking to overcome such issues for near term devices and should be watched closely.

2.2 Graph Partitioning/Re-Ordering

Since solving linear equations *in its own right* does not have an obvious practical implementation in the near future, we took a closer look at the speed of each step within the solver pipeline, which revealed that the re-ordering of sparse matrices is what dominates highly parallel workloads, as seen in Fig. 2a. Ansys must perform this reordering in order to efficiently perform sparse Gaussian elimination, a key component of reaching a final solution. Reordering matrices to minimize computational complexity has been an active field of research for over 60 years [22]. Nested dissection of the adjacency graph associated with the matrix has emerged as the best practical algorithm for reordering matrices derived from mechanical MCAE models [13]. Nested dissection involves recursive graph-partitioning, which is itself an NP-complete problem classically solved using heuristic approximations. Notably this is an issue for Ansys customers *today*, not tomorrow.

Since the sparse matrices Ansys factors can range to billions equations, and because linear solvers are ubiquitous bottlenecks across many MCAE codes, an improvement in this major sub-step in their solvers would have a massive effect on the overall performance of their simulations. We therefore choose to investigate the efficacy of near-term quantum approaches to graph-partitioning, a key component in linear solvers, as opposed to the process as a whole.

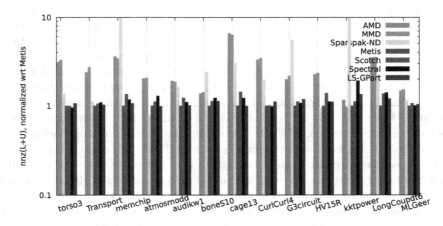

Fig. 3. A comparison of different reordering algorithms. The 14 test matrices are from the SuiteSparse Matrix Collection [8]. The initial data is from P. Ghysels et al. [14]. Ansys' LS-GPart reordering software was added to the comparison [21].

This presents an exciting opportunity for quantum computing. Progress has stalled on classical heuristics for nested dissection as depicted in Fig. 3 [21]. The figure compares 7 ordering heuristics for 14 matrices from different applications; the baseline is the Metis nested dissection package from the late 1990's [18]; the figure shows that no significant progress (in terms of quality of the reordering, i.e., number of operations and memory footprint of the linear solver) has been made in recent years. Quantum heuristics are comparatively young, and relevant hardware tests are only beginning. Considering the specific needs of Ansys' client workflows and connecting this to the IBM Quantum Development road-map [1], we next consider some critical focus points which could greatly reduce the time until real user problems can be tested for potential benefits.

3   Quantum Graph-Partitioning Methods

Quantum graph-partitioning works by first formulating the problem as a Quadratic Unconstrained Binary Optimization (QUBO) problem, and then solving this QUBO with a quantum algorithm. In the following sections we explore the options for partitioning Ansys graphs according to the method diagram in Fig. 4. An important consideration, outside the scope of this review, is how to optimally prepare a graph to be partitioned by a quantum system - namely the process of coarsening a graph ahead of partitioning or potential for quantum features in the processing of uncoarsening a graph.

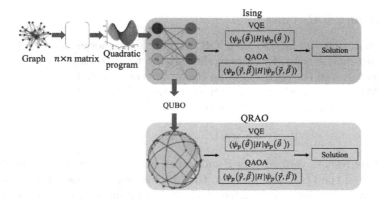

Fig. 4. Method diagram showing the general process one must go through in order to run graph partitioning problems on a gate-based quantum system Both methods take in a graph, in this case, a representation of one of the physical objects simulated by Ansys (described further in Sect. 4.1), and produce solutions of the same form. Note that both methods follow identical steps initially, converting the graph to a matrix, the matrix to a quadratic program, and then finally the quadratic program to a QUBO. The distinction between these methods presents itself in the circuit generated, or the correspond measurements needed.

3.1   Encoding Methods Used for Quantum Optimization

Generally speaking, there exist a variety of methods for encoding optimization problems into a quantum primitive, usually in the form of sampling a circuit distribution [12,15,30]. In Fig. 4 two encoding options which we applied to an Ansys graph partitioning problem are shown: an Ising Encoding [20] and a Quantum Random Access Encoding (QRAC) [30]. The Ising model is equivalent to Quadratic Unconstrained Binary Optimization (QUBO) [15], and is the traditional method of mapping optimization problems to gate-based quantum hardware [11]. Alternatively one translates a QUBO into a QRAC and get a more efficient measurement basis - the underpinning aspect of the Quantum Random Approximate Optimization (QRAO) algorithm [12]. QRAO in particular allows larger problems to be encoded with fewer qubits, making this solution more useful in the near-term. However, as we will detail in the next section, for the specific realization of experiment [12] these encoding benefits are lost for the balanced graph partitioning cost function provided by the Ansys use case. Since the start of our review, researchers have updated the QRAO method to guarantee an encoding benefit of $2\times$, even when using a balanced cost function [27].

Once an encoding method is chosen, an end-user must ultimately select which quantum circuit they will run. For the purpose of our demo, we highlight two possible candidates: A hardware efficient ansatz (HEA) approach with the Variational Quantum Eigensolver (VQE) [25], or a QAOA [11] ansatz which is directly made based on the provided graph.

3.2   Quantum Circuits

After generating the QUBO or a QRAC, you have chosen the qubit mapping and measurement basis. From here there is the need to choose the initial state of parameters and the corresponding circuit ansatz. The initial circuit generated for a QAOA circuit is given by repetition of an evolution between your 'problem' and a 'mixer' Hamiltonian in the form:

$$|\gamma, \beta\rangle = U_{\beta,\beta_1} U_{\gamma,\gamma_p} \dots U_{\beta,\beta_1} U_{\gamma,\gamma_1} |\psi_0\rangle$$

where β represents your mixing Hamiltonian and γ your problem Hamiltonian. The depth of the QAOA ansatz can then be increased in the number of repetitions of layers p, where in the asymptotic limit of infinite p, it is shown that this converges to the optimal solution of the desired cost function [11]. For initial circuit analysis, we will consider the impact of the repeating layers p on the circuit depth.

Alternately one can use different HEAs which are heuristic in their nature and one can design any sort of ansatz which is best mapped to the quantum hardware. These ansatzes have the benefit of being able to be extremely shallow in their circuit depth, but when using these methods, there is another level of optimization which goes beyond the parameter optimization of the ansatz, but choosing the ansatz itself. There are some early studies which try to characterize these approaches, using various forms of entropy [9]. Furthermore, these methods are prone to getting stuck in local minima and even having the parameter gradient vanish exponentially – either from circuit-induced [6], or noise-induced [29].

3.3   Warm-Starting Quantum Circuits

Quantum variational algorithms such as QAOA and VQE are utilized to solve the combinatorial optimization problems by finding the minimum energy to the corresponding formulated Hamiltonian. These algorithms combined with classical optimizers are always dependent of the initial values for the optimizer and the initial states for the quantum circuit on the Hilbert space which effect the algorithm's performance to find the minimum energy to the problem. Applying a warm-start technique that can initiate the initial value/sate to the quantum circuit would be able to improve the convergence of these algorithms to solve the problem accurately. A warm-start QAOA technique was presented in [10] in which it replaces the binary variables with the continuous variables to relax the optimization problem and solve it classically that improves the performance ratios in polynomial time. Then it uses the solution to the relaxed problem to find the initial state to the QAOA algorithm. By applying the warm-start technique combined with the QAOA algorithm, a better result with higher fidelity can be achieved. Similar approaches can be used for the VQE algorithm to either initiate the parameters of the variational circuit or modify the variational circuit to help the optimizer to converge to the correct value to find the minimum energy of the problem. A new ansatz modification technique is introduced in [26] where the variational circuit is build in a discrete approach based on the property of the problem Hamiltonian and the corresponding Pauli string. In principle this could be applied to improve our 'unfair VQE Warm-start', but this is beyond the scope of this paper.

4   Experimental Setup and Results

4.1   Experimental Setup

To test this method of graph partitioning, we use real Ansys graphs of physical objects from both mechanical and electromagnetic simulations. Images of the two objects used in the analysis are shown in Fig. 2b. Note that the number of vertices in these graphs ranges from 0.6M–34.9M, making their raw size too large for both QAOA or QRAO to run on current quantum hardware. In order to conduct preliminary experiments, we instead use coarsened versions of these graphs, for 25, 50, 100, 1K, and 10K nodes, respectively. The effects of graph coarsening are demonstrated in Fig. 2b, which shows the difference in resolution when an Impeller is coarsened from 10K nodes to 1K. While coarsening does reduce the level of detail in the object graph, it still maintains the general topology and properties of the original object. This allows us to test smaller versions of real graphs on quantum hardware today, while retaining as much of the object's

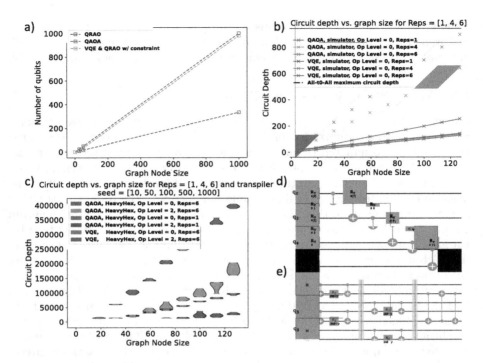

Fig. 5. a) Required number of qubits for a given graph size, for different encoding parameters. Of particular note: Ansys' desired graph partitioning with constraints does not benefit from the present QRAO encoding. b) Circuit Depth as a function of different graph node sizes, with varying levels of compilation and increased circuit depth. As an example of the importance of the problem – this figure took approximately 1 day to complete with a recent Apple MacBook Pro. c) The repeated structure of a HAE and QAOA ansatz used for our VQE and QAOA demonstrations. (This sort of repeated structure particular benefits from dynamic circuit transpilation capabilities). Due to its heuristic nature, the HEA can nicely conform to hardware topology constraints but also has issues when scaling to larger sizes (e.g. barren plateaus). d) Example structure in a VQE circuit. e) Example structure in a QAOA circuit.

original integrity as possible. Coarsening the graph, partitioning the coarsened graph, and uncoarsening the partition (a.k.a., *projecting*, or *interpolating*), is at the heart of so-called *multilevel partitioning* [2,5], which has been the most popular technique for partitioning large graphs in the past three decades. Most graph partitioners reduce the initial graph to a few tens or hundreds of vertices. By coarsening and uncoarsening properly, following a hierarchy of levels, they achieve very high-quality partitions.

With these graphs, we then conduct two series of experiments. The first is designed to test the efficacy of the selected algorithm (QRAO) on real Ansys graphs. As mentioned in Sect. 3.1, QRAO uses quantum random access codes (QRACs) to encode a maximum of 3 qubits per node, for a slight trade off in accuracy. In order for this position to be recovered with high probability, however, two nodes that share an edge cannot be encoded on the same qubit. This means that the encoding ratio, which can range from 1–3, is variable depending on graph topology. As such, we study the compression ratio achieved for these graphs, which allows us to measure the number of necessary qubits according to graph size/number of nodesand observe the impact of adding the balancing constraint. We also measure the required processing time for each step in the graph partitioning, as this is a relevant additive factor in tracking the overall algorithmic run-time.

The second series of experiments involves real-hardware demonstrations, and allows us to evaluate the quality of quantum hardware partitions as we increase the size of the graph being studied. Specifically, we measure how well these algorithms conform to simulated expectations and compare the accuracy of the hardware solutions against the exact solution. However, as hardware sizes continue to increase, these benchmarking approaches will no longer work. To this end, we suggest alternate long term benchmarks to assess the trustworthy-ness of a quantum run, and how to measure the corresponding accuracy against alternative, classical methods such as those found in METIS [18].

4.2   Results

Encoding and Scaling Results. To begin, we startup by first determining theoretical scaling for the given approaches, as seen in Fig. 5. Firstly, we measure the relative encoding efficiency of QRAO against QAOA, both with and without our constraints in Fig. 5a. Since QAOA requires a 1:1 mapping between nodes and qubits, it requires the same number of qubits to compute a solution for a graph as the number of nodes in the graph. In contrast, QRAO requires only one-third the number of qubits to solve the same problem for Ansys graphs, when a balancing constraints is not included. However, as the reordering process requires a graph to be bisected by considering the balancing constraint, the corresponding encoding benefits are lost. In the outlook, we highlight what this means for an Ansys integration but choose to focus on the Ising encoding for initial hardware testing and validation.

With the Ising encoding method selected, we now wish to evaluate which quantum circuit will be ideal to run for the given problem on a given hardware architecture. To do this, we evaluate how a quantum circuit depths depend on both the graph size and the transpilation method used for HEA [17] or the graph-informed ansatz of QAOA [11]. Specifically, we use a HEA circuit with *TwoLocal* entanglement, or a p = 1 realization of a QAOA circuit. As seen in Fig. 5b, the circuit depth grows much more rapidly for a QAOA circuit compared to the HEA ansatz, making it more unlikely to have a successful evaluation on quantum hardware.

Hardware Results. Results from hardware demos, Fig. 6, will measure accuracy, and max size computable on current quantum hardware. For the purpose of our hardware comparison, we want to note that we choose to focus on a 'quality' metric for comparative result. Though the required time for computation is quite important for ultimate comparison, the practical nuances of getting an accurate required compute time (utilizing the state-of-the-art techniques vs what is available via cloud providers) makes this comparison difficult to properly judge. To this end, we refrain from elaborating in this work and kept this for future investigation.

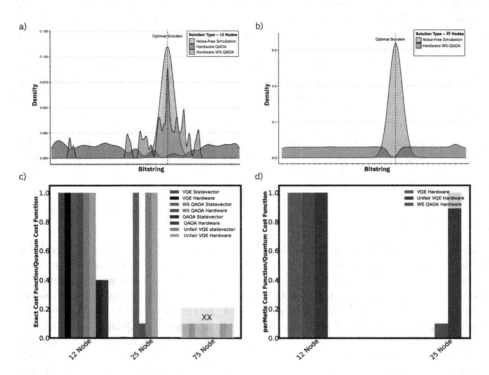

Fig. 6. Quantum hardware results comparison to noise free simulations. From this we can see that quantum hardware has an increase count of bit strings. a) The result of noise-free simulation, QAOA and WS-QAOA for 12 node graph. b) The result of noise-free simulation and WS-QAOA for 25 node graph. c) A plot comparing the solutions of hardware to exact solution calculated by CPLEX. *= this is a benchmark of the circuit and is not a valid comparison for VQE since we do not yet have a proper iterative test. Specifically, we manually tuned a one rep = 1 HEA ansatz (in the assumption such an ansatz may find the minimum). Due the slowness of statevector simulations, we are opting to run the VQE algorithm on the quantum hardware directly. In some sense, this is an accomplishment in its own right – though it does not provide direct value for someone wishes to use this for an application. XX = We can't do these - which necessitates a longer term benchmark. Statevector simulations are impossible, regardless of what compute power you put behind it which makes a 75 node exact solution to become impractical. Namely, it took over 5 h to simulate this on a laptop. d) A more appropriate long-term in which we compare our solution to Metis. This is the benchmark which can be easily used beyond 50 node graphs. For the method of comparison we compare both the Metis and Quantum Hardware cost functions.

5   Outlook

From our exploration, we have found that for beneficial quantum graph partitioning (reordering) at larger scales, current circuit fidelities require more extensive error mitigation protocols than used here. Though we limited our use of error mitigation to readout error mitigation [3], this is more a matter of the availability of certain software features, more-so than fundamental limitation and will be addressed in subsequent work. For this work, we focused our encoding methods to Ising Encoing, and QRAC encoding. For quantum circuits we focused on structured QAOA circuits and one example of a arbitrary HEA quantum circuit. Furthermore, we showed that using a warm start was essential for our QAOA circuits to converge to the proper solution. However, as we increase the size of the graph the QAOA circuit scale sufficiently fast to make our initial attempts at 25 node partitioning non-trivial. Furthermore, we show that in principle one can get substantially shorter circuit depths but still achieve good results with our 25 node 'unfair warmstart'. Though this cannot be practically used at larger scales, there may be means, such as the VQE Hot Start [26], which can enable larger graph partitioning. Furthermore, though the Quantum Random Access Code implementation used in our testing did not have encoding benefits when including the balancing constraints – a recent update to the algorithm makes it possible to get at least a factor of two of savings [27]. Each of these factors will be considerably important when trying to understand how to achieve useful quantum advantage for linear solvers. For immediate next steps, we will seek to achieve a software interface which will enable a more complete characterization of the impact of quantum features being used in nested dissection. Furthermore, we need to more completely evaluate expected runtimes as quantum systems increase in size and quality. Given the rapid development of the underlying hardware, we will need further study to better predict when the error mitigation overhead of near-term quantum systems will be sufficiently low that there can be practical (at-scale) industry workflow investigations. To gain the most from both the pending software interface and our ability to properly judge impact of quantum features in nested dissection workflows, we will need to deeply engage with the quantum community to guide tools and features to their needs for research and development, and work towards adding quantum-based comparisons [21]. For explicit next steps in our work we need to work on developing warm start methods for VQE or improving circuit depth of a QAOA circuit.

Acknowledgements. The authors acknowledge use of the IBM Quantum devices for this work. The authors are also thankful to Bryce Fuller, Stefan Woerner, Rudy Raymond, Paul Nation and Antonio Mezzacapo for insightful discussions and Johannes Greiner, Stefan Woerner and Paul Nation for a careful read of the manuscript.

References

1. https://www.ibm.com/quantum/roadmap
2. Barnard, S.T., Simon, H.D.: A fast multilevel implementation of recursive spectral bisection for partitioning unstructured problems. In: Proceedings of the Sixth SIAM Conference on Parallel Processing for Scientific Computing, PPSC 1993, Norfolk, Virginia, USA, 22–24 March 1993, pp. 711–718. SIAM (1993)
3. Van Den Berg, E., Minev, Z.K., Temme, K.: Model-free readout-error mitigation for quantum expectation values (2020). https://doi.org/10.48550/ARXIV.2012.09738. https://arxiv.org/abs/2012.09738
4. Bravo-Prieto, C., LaRose, R., Cerezo, M., Subasi, Y., Cincio, L., Coles, P.J.: Variational quantum linear solver. arXiv preprint arXiv:1909.05820 (2019)
5. Bui, T.N., Jones, C.: A heuristic for reducing fill-in in sparse matrix factorization. In: Proceedings of the Sixth SIAM Conference on Parallel Processing for Scientific Computing, PPSC 1993, Norfolk, Virginia, USA, 22–24 March 1993, pp. 445–452. SIAM (1993)
6. Cerezo, M., Sone, A., Volkoff, T., Cincio, L., Coles, P.J.: Cost function dependent barren plateaus in shallow parametrized quantum circuits. Nat. Commun. **12**(1), 1–12 (2021)
7. Chang, J.B.: Improved superconducting qubit coherence using titanium nitride. Appl. Phys. Lett. **103**(1), 012602 (2013)
8. Davis, T.A., Hu, Y.: The university of Florida sparse matrix collection. ACM Trans. Math. Softw. **38**(1), 1–25 (2011). https://doi.org/10.1145/2049662.2049663
9. Du, Y., Hsieh, M.H., Liu, T., Tao, D.: Expressive power of parametrized quantum circuits. Phys. Rev. Res. **2**(3), 033125 (2020)
10. Egger, D.J., Mareček, J., Woerner, S.: Warm-starting quantum optimization. Quantum **5**, 479 (2021)
11. Farhi, E., Goldstone, J., Gutmann, S.: A quantum approximate optimization algorithm. arXiv preprint arXiv:1411.4028 (2014)
12. Fuller, B., et al.: Approximate solutions of combinatorial problems via quantum relaxations. arXiv preprint arXiv:2111.03167 (2021)
13. George, A.: Nested dissection of a regular finite element mesh. SIAM J. Numer. Anal. **10**(2), 345–363 (1973)
14. Ghysels, P., Li, X.S., Chávez, G., Liu, Y., Jacquelin, M., Ng, E.: Preconditioning using rank-structured sparse matrix factorization. In: SIAM Conference on Computational Science and Engineering (2019)
15. Glover, F., Kochenberger, G., Du, Y.: A tutorial on formulating and using QUBO models (2018). https://doi.org/10.48550/ARXIV.1811.11538. https://arxiv.org/abs/1811.11538
16. Grover, L.K.: A fast quantum mechanical algorithm for database search. In Proceedings of the 28th ACM Symposium on the Theory of Computing, pp. 212–219 (1996)
17. Kandala, A., et al.: Hardware-efficient variational quantum Eigensolver for small molecules and quantum magnets. Nature **549**(7671), 242–246 (2017)
18. Karypis, G., Kumar, V.: A fast and high quality multilevel scheme for partitioning irregular graphs. SIAM J. Sci. Comput. **20**(1), 359–392 (1998)
19. Lloyd, S.: Quantum algorithm for solving linear systems of equations. In: APS March Meeting Abstracts, vol. 2010, pp. D4–002 (2010)
20. Lucas, A.: Ising formulations of many np problems. Front. Phys. **2**, 5 (2014)

21. Lucas, R.F., et al.: Implicit analysis of jet engine models on thousands of processors. In: Sparse Days (2019)
22. Markowitz, H.M.: The elimination form of the inverse and its application to linear programming. Manage. Sci. **3**(3), 255–269 (1957). http://www.jstor.org/stable/2627454
23. Montanaro, A., Pallister, S.: Quantum algorithms and the finite element method. Phys. Rev. A **93**(3), 032324 (2016)
24. Pan, V.: Complexity of algorithms for linear systems of equations. In: Spedicato, E. (ed.) Computer Algorithms for Solving Linear Algebraic Equations. NATO ASI Series, vol. 77, pp. 27–56. Springer, Berlin (1991). https://doi.org/10.1007/978-3-642-76717-3_2
25. Peruzzo, A., et al.: A variational eigenvalue solver on a photonic quantum processor. Nat. Commun. **5**(1), 4213 (2014). https://doi.org/10.1038/ncomms5213
26. Polina, B., Arthur, S., Yuriy, Z., Manhong, Y., Dingshun, l.: Hot-start optimization for variational quantum Eigensolver (2021). https://doi.org/10.48550/ARXIV.2104.15001. https://arxiv.org/abs/2104.15001
27. Teramoto, K., Raymond, R., Wakakuwa, E., Imai, H.: Quantum-relaxation based optimization algorithms: theoretical extensions. arXiv preprint arXiv:2302.09481 (2023)
28. Wallraff, A., et al.: Strong coupling of a single photon to a superconducting qubit using circuit quantum electrodynamics. Nature **431**(7005), 162–167 (2004)
29. Wang, S.: Noise-induced barren plateaus in variational quantum algorithms. Nat. Commun. **12**(1), 1–11 (2021)
30. Wiesner, S.: Conjugate coding. ACM SIGACT News **15**, 77–78 (1983)

Exploring the Use of Dataflow Architectures for Graph Neural Network Workloads

Ryien Hosseini[1]([✉]), Filippo Simini[1], Venkatram Vishwanath[1],
Ramakrishnan Sivakumar[3], Sanjif Shanmugavelu[3], Zhengyu Chen[1,2,3],
Lev Zlotnik[3], Mingran Wang[1,2,3], Philip Colangelo[3], Andrew Deng[1,2,3],
Philip Lassen[3], and Shukur Pathan[1,2,3]

[1] Argonne Leadership Computing Facility, Argonne National Laboratory,
Lemont, IL, USA
{rhosseini,fsimini,venkat}@anl.gov
[2] Groq, Mountain View, CA, USA
{rsivakumar,sshanmugavelu,lzlotnik,pcolangelo,plassen}@groq.com
[3] SambaNova Systems, Palo Alto, CA, USA
{edison.chen,mingran.wang,andrew.deng,shukur.pathan}@sambanova.ai

Abstract. Graph Neural Networks (GNNs), which learn representations of non-euclidean data, are rapidly rising in popularity and are used in several computationally demanding scientific applications. As these deep learning models become more prevalent in practical applications, their performance during inference becomes increasingly critical. GNNs have been shown to suffer from hard memory and computational bottlenecks on traditional hardware platforms (i.e. GPUs) due in part to their reliance on non-contiguous data structures. While dataflow architectures used by emerging hardware accelerators provide a potential solution to alleviate these issues, end-to-end GNN models are generally not yet supported by these platforms. Thus, it is not currently possible to directly compare the performance of GNNs on traditional GPUs with these hardware accelerators. In this work, we analyze the performance of operators relevant to modern GNNs on three platforms: NVIDIA A100 GPU, Groq GroqChip1, and SambaNova Reconfigurable Dataflow Unit (RDU). Specifically, we first profile several modern GNN models on traditional GPUs to determine the operators, fused kernels, and message passing layers most relevant to these architectures. Then, we systematically benchmark and analyze the performance for each of these levels of abstraction on each hardware platform. Our analysis shows that (1) due to their reliance on non-contiguous data, GNNs suffer from cache inefficiency on conventional GPUs (2) dataflow architectures, due in part to their cache-less design, are able to implicitly optimize for operators pertinent to GNNs and, (3) the RDU and GroqChip1 platforms enable significant inference speedup compared to traditional GPU on pertinent subsets of end-to-end GNN networks. Our open source code is available at https://github.com/ryienh/gnn-ops-benchmark.

A. Bienz et al. (Eds.): ISC High Performance 2023 Workshops, LNCS 13999, pp. 648–661, 2023.
https://doi.org/10.1007/978-3-031-40843-4_48

Keywords: Graph-based Machine Learning · Graph Neural Networks · Machine Learning and Systems · Dataflow Architectures

1   Introduction

Graph Neural Networks (GNNs), which can directly learn representations on non-euclidean data, are showing promising applications in diverse domains such as traffic prediction, fraud detection, and drug discovery [30]. While these models have been shown to be successful in controlled scientific settings, a large gap still exists between the development and training of such models and their real world deployment [6]. One of the major obstacles to efficient deployment of GNNs in production is the performance of the inference tasks: Many domains require low-latency inference of user data, often at very small batch sizes. However, as the number of parameters in state-of-the-art architectures continue to increase, inference performance, in terms of time-to-solution, can become progressively problematic. GNNs have been shown to suffer from hard memory and computational bottlenecks on traditional hardware platforms due in part to their reliance on non-regular data structures [3,17]. One possible solution to this issue is the use of emerging hardware platforms for model deployment. Such platforms, or *hardware accelerators*, provide specific optimizations for runtime performance of deep learning models [25,26]. However, hardware support for end-to-end applications requires substantial engineering and manufacturing effort [25]. Thus, a method for assessing the performance of specific applications can help hardware developers assess the viability of development of particular models on their platforms and guide the prioritization for bring-up of particular workloads. Such a method can also help application developers assess the viability and promise of hardware accelerators for their models of interest.

In this paper, we analyze the viability of a specific class of hardware accelerators, that is, *dataflow architectures* [9], for GNN inference workloads. Toward this, our objective is to evaluate the inference performance of state-of-the-art GNNs on two emerging dataflow platforms: GroqChip1 [1], and SambaNova Reconfigurable Dataflow Unit (RDU) [21,22]. Since end-to-end GNN support is not yet available on these platforms, we carefully analyze the performance of key building blocks of such networks at three levels of abstraction: operators, fused kernels, and graph convolution layers. By doing so, we help assess the viability of accelerating GNNs using dataflow architectures before significant engineering effort is put into supporting GNNs on these platforms. Additionally, our resulting profile of relevant operators, fused kernels and layers may be used by other dataflow platforms to begin building support for GNNs. To our knowledge, we are not aware of an existing work to evaluate lower level subsets of deep learning workloads across accelerator platforms where end-to-end implementations are yet to be made available. Although GNNs are used in several computationally demanding scientific applications [30], detailed performance analysis about GNNs are largely unknown, both on traditional GPUs as well as on emerging hardware accelerators [17]. Through detailed comparison and analysis of GNN applications on NVIDIA A100 GPU, GroqChip1, and SambaNova RDU platforms we conclude that (1) due to their reliance on non-contiguous data, GNNs suffer from cache inefficiency on conventional GPUs, (2) the cache-less design of dataflow architectures results in implicit speedup of operators relevant to state-of-the-art GNNs, and (3) GroqChip1 and RDU platforms both show potential to substantially accelerate the inference of the diverse GNN models evaluated, suggesting that dataflow architectures can mitigate the bottlenecks observed on GPUs thanks to the higher efficiency of their fused kernels and convolution layers. By providing support for such models, these hardware accelerators can significantly benefit GNN-based applications.

2   Background

In this section, we overview challenges of benchmarking deep neural network (DNN) performance on emerging hardware platforms, detail GNN algorithms at a high level, and introduce the two emerging platforms used for analysis in this work: the GroqChip1 and SambaNova RDU.

Benchmarking Deep Learning Models Across Emerging Hardware Platforms. Robust and fair benchmarking of DNNs across hardware platforms generally present several challenges. Namely, hardware platforms often support different software frameworks, rely on diverse system level architecture designs, and optimize at different levels of the compute stack [25, 26]. Thus, when support for full applications (e.g. GNN models) are not available, careful consideration is required to collect relevant performance data. Since end-to-end GNN architectures are not yet supported on many emerging hardware platforms, we carefully analyze performance of subsets of GNNs. This approach is perhaps most similar to [17], though we look at subsets at three levels of abstraction, namely operators, fused kernels, and graph convolutions, rather than just the operator level. It is important to note that many existing benchmarking frameworks additionally focus on *training* regime issues such as accuracy performance tradeoffs [5, 7, 10]. However, given that our analysis is for the *inference* regime, we limit our analysis to runtime latency. Benchmarking compound operators, or what we refer to as *fused kernels*, requires special nuance. Traditional GPU based acceleration relies on explicit allocation (and deallocation) of kernels in order to efficiently run parallelizable operations [27]. In order to launch and execute a traditional kernel, non-trivial kernel overhead, such as reading data from memory to register, instruction fetch cycles to load kernel implementation, etc., is introduced [23]. Thus, in practice, compound operations that are found to be used commonly in workloads of a specific domain may be *fused* into a single kernel, wherein the one-time costs of launching said kernel need occur only once [13, 27]. In this work, we call this single kernel operation a *fused kernel*. However, this so-called kernel fusion requires substantial ad-hoc engineering effort, as a new kernel must be written which combines the effect of the two or more kernels being fused [13]. In this work, we either manually fuse or use an existing fused kernel implementation for all compound operations on A100. The GroqChip1 and RDU systems avoid this issue, as these dataflow architectures do not rely on explicit kernel allocation [1, 21]. Thus, in addition to any runtime speedups, dataflow architectures have the added benefit of implicit kernel fusion.

Graph Neural Networks. Graph neural networks, or GNNs, can be viewed as a generalization of common neural network algorithms, such as convolution, to non-euclidean graph-like data. While traditional deep learning applications such as computer vision operate on organized grid-like structures, other tasks, for example particle simulation, protein folding, traffic prediction, social-networks etc. have data that is more naturally organized into graphs. Thus, the development of GNNs, which can learn useful representations directly on these graphs, has substantially expanded the application domains of deep learning. At the heart of GNNs is the message passing operation, wherein neighboring nodes of a graph are iteratively updated based on differentiable and permutation invariant functions [30]. Most variations of this message passing scheme add features such as non-linearities, feature-wise modulations, etc. [30], but keep the general concept of iteratively updating representations of a given node v based on the representations of its neighbors $u \in N(v)$. One advantage of GNNs is their comparative computational efficiency with respect to traditional DNNs. Since the message passing algorithm operates directly on graphs, sparse inputs often require far less computation than with traditional DNNs operating on their euclidean-mapped sparse counterparts [30]. To this end, operators that perform common mathematical operations relevant to deep learning (e.g. matrix multiplication, transpose, etc.) on sparsely formatted data have been introduced in many deep learning frameworks, such as Pytorch Geometric [12]. Our model profiling work outlined in Sect. 4 demonstrates the use of such operators in the tested end-to-end networks. However, it is important to note that many of these sparse operators are not yet supported on emerging hardware platforms, including RDU and GroqChip1. Thus, we rely on the conventional operators in these cases (e.g. matrix multiplication, rather than sparse matrix multiplication). Moreover, the performance benefits of dataflow architectures found in Sect. 5 are in spite of the lack of support for such operators. Thus, future work by such platforms to support sparse operators will likely increase performance of end-to-end networks here even further.

GroqChip1. The Groq's GroqChip1 architecture is designed to take advantage of dataflow locality in machine learning (ML) and deep learning (DL) operators [1]. Its decoupled access-execute dataflow structure enables exploiting several levels of parallelism such as data, instruction-level, memory concurrency, and model parallelism. This simple functionally-sliced microarchitecture enables deterministic low latency execution of workloads by eliminating any reactive components like caches and branch predictors. GroqChip1 is organized into two symmetrical hemispheres, called the east and west hemispheres. Each hemisphere is organized into two matrix execution modules (MXMs), one switch execution module (SXM), and 44 memory (MEM) slices, and both hemispheres share the 16 vector execution modules (VXMs) in the middle [1, 15]. Data movement between these functional slices is orchestrated by streams, which are the logical resources for moving vectors between functional slices and stream registers are the logical resources for tracking the position and timing of streams.

RDU Platform. The SN 10 RDU is a coarse-grained reconfigurable architecture (CGRA) [19] based architecture, which provides a reconfigurable hardware accelerator platform for deep learning and high-performance computing (HPC) workloads [21].

The 7-nm CMOS SN10 RDU contains 50 km of interconnects and 40 billion transistors [22]. SN10 RDU contains four tiles that can be configured by software to either operate independently or as a larger logical tile. SN10 RDU delivers 300 BF16 TFLOPs of compute and is rated to provide 320 MB of on-chip memory with 150 TB/s memory bandwidth [22]. The on- to off-chip communication is handled by a address generation and coalescing unit (AGCU) [21].

Due to RDU's system level reconfigurability, SN10 RDU can implement ML applications in a spatial way on hardware, i.e. process the kernels on chip without data access from off-chip. As depicted in Fig. 1a, the kernel-by-kernel execution on CPU/GPU executes one operation at a time and materializes the entire intermediate data off-chip, which requires high off-chip bandwidth for performance. In contrast, dataflow execution on RDU enables high computation resource utilization and gets the effect of kernel fusion with minimal memory transfer costs, and without requiring specialized ad-hoc kernel fusion implementations by a team of engineers [21].

The SambaNova in-house compiler, SambaFlow, captures the ML application as a compute graph with parallel patterns and explicit memories, and systematically lowers the graph to a logical dataflow pipeline that exploits data, task, and hierarchical pipeline parallelism [21]. Figure 1c shows dataflow execution on RDU that concurrently executes multiple layers of an example model as a dataflow pipeline. Intermediate results are produced and consumed entirely onchip, which lowers off-chip bandwidth requirements.

 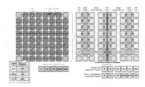 

(a) Dataflow for typical NVIDIA GPUs, such as A100 (b) Dataflow for GroqChip1 Platform (c) Dataflow for RDU Platform

Fig. 1. Dataflow/architecture comparison of NVIDIA GPU, GroqChip1, and RDU platforms

3   Related Work

Profiling Deep Learning Applications Across Hardware Accelerator Platforms. The majority of work done on profiling deep learning applications on hardware accelerator platforms has focused on end-to-end model performance. For instance, Reuther *et al.* focuses on introducing several commercially available accelerator platforms and reports application benchmarks where available [25]. Other works, such as Blott *et al.* robustly analyze specific operators such as Convolutional Neural Networks (CNNs) and recommend specific optimizations for particular accelerator frameworks [4]. Additionally, hardware oriented literature contains work that evaluates the effect of specific on-chip features, such as interconnect tools, on deep learning performance [2]. Additional work, such as *ParaDNN*, propose frameworks to evaluate workloads by parameterizing end-to-end models in order to evaluate platforms at different memory and computational workloads [28]. We adapt a similar parameterization scheme as *ParaDNN*, but apply it to operators, fused kernel, and layer-level analysis, rather than end-to-end applications. To our knowledge, no work exists which evaluates lower level operators across accelerator platforms where end-to-end implementations are not available.

Performance Benchmarks on Nvidia GPU Platforms. Performance benchmarks of deep learning workloads on Nvidia GPUs are comparatively better explored compared to emerging hardware platforms. Many benchmark frameworks focus on end-to-end performance of applications [28]. Other work has specifically explored performance of kernel fusion [14], wherein the effect of explicit kernel fusion for compound operators is explored in detail. Recently, benchmarking specific to GNNs has also been of significant interest, wherein state-of-the-art GNNs are parameterized and extended in order to analyze their performance on GPU [3,11,17]. Notably, [17] benchmarks operators relevant specific to GNNs. These recent efforts are further detailed in the next section.

Profiling GNNs and Sparse Operators. Recently, as the popularity of GNNs have increased, so has work to accelerate the sparse operators relevant to their training and inference. For example, Wang *et al.* proposes a method of improving performance of sparse operators on the NVIDIA CUDA platform by explicity translating these operators to dense counterparts where the GPU optimization is more advanced [29]. Finally, in [3,17] end-to-end GNN models are profiled for sparse operators in order to evaluate the degree to which individual operators contribute to the total runtime of such end-to-end models. Specifically, [17] applies a parameterized approach similar to *ParaDNN* [28] for individual operators relevant to GNN models in order to systematically test performance of A100 GPUs. We use a similar parameterization scheme for operators and fused kernels and apply it across multiple hardware accelerator platforms.

4   Methods

We present our benchmarking framework for assessing an emerging hardware platform's ability to support a given application workload without end-to-end support. Although our focus is on GNNs, this approach can be generalized to other deep learning architectures. We distinguish between mature (NVIDIA

A100) and emerging (GroqChip1 and RDU) hardware platforms, with the former having established end-to-end support and the latter showing potential for outperforming mature platforms but requiring additional hardware or software features. Our goal is to create microbenchmark indicators for lower-level operators relevant to the targeted applications, which can be used to evaluate the suitability of an emerging hardware platform for accelerating the target applications. We create microbenchmark indicators at the operator, fused kernel, and message passing layer levels. To ensure fair performance comparisons, we use the Pytorch Geometric framework, built on Pytorch, as a single software framework. We report median and standard deviation runtime values from at least 100 runs for each operator and fused kernel microbenchmark and mean values from 300 data points for each layer microbenchmark. We also seed non-deterministic algorithms and generate error bars, with a performance difference of less than 0.000021 s observed for all operators and fused kernels when varying the seed.

Profiling End-to-End Architectures for Relevant Operators. The methodology for our profiling methodology begins with selecting a set of target applications, K, and a set of emerging platforms, Θ, along with a mature platform, Φ. The target applications are chosen by the user based on their domain of investigation, and the emerging platforms represent new or upcoming hardware architectures. For this work, we choose K to be a set of state-of-the-art GNN architectures summarized in Table 2, namely $K = \{$Principal Neighbourhood Aggregation (PNA) [8], Graph Isomorphism Network (GIN) [32], GraphSAGE [16], and Crystal Graph Network (GCNet) [31]$\}$. We choose $\Theta = \{GroqChip1, RDU\}$ and $\Phi = \{A100\}$. Using the mature platform, standard tools such as Pytorch profiler and NVIDIA Nsight are used to calculate the runtimes for all target applications at different levels of abstraction, and the top $L = 3$ fused kernels and $Q = 5$ operators are selected as the final microbenchmarks, summarized in Tables 1 and 2. The selected microbenchmarks collectively account for 68.7%, 81.1%, 79.2%, and 69.4% of total end-to-end runtime on A100 for PNA, GIN, GraphSAGE, and GCNet, respectively. Note that emerging platforms may not yet support all microbenchmarks This is taken into account in the analysis.

Operator Microbenchmarks. The next step in our benchmarking framework involves systematically assessing the performance of each selected operator, $p_i^{ops} \forall i \in \{1, ..., Q\}$, see Table 1. For each p_i^{ops}, we start with the most common input combinations of the end-to-end applications, as determined by the profiling results of the target applications. Then, parameters are varied based on the theoretical memory capacities of all $\theta \in \Theta$. This *memory aware microbenchmarking* is valuable because (1) it allows for performance analysis at regimes near significant memory boundaries on each system, and (2) provides performance insights for future end-to-end applications which, as discussed by Wu *et al.* [30], may likely contain many more parameters than current models. Additionally, other parameters which have a significant impact on memory optimization infrastructures (e.g. indexed dimensions), are also varied. For this study, we define *significant theoretical memory cutoffs* as the rated L2 cache on the A100 platform (40 MiB),

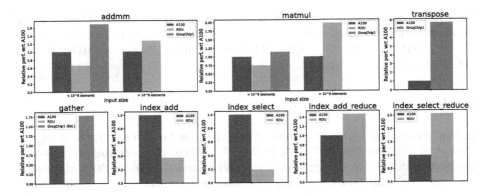

Fig. 2. Relative performance with respect to A100 of the various operators, defined as the mean of the ratio between the A100 runtime over the runtime of the system considered. Higher bars represent better performance. The reported relative performance is averaged over the common range of sizes.

and the rated SRAM on the GroqChip1 (220 MB) and RDU platforms (320 MB) (Fig. 2).

In this study, we evaluate the following operators:

1. `torch.matmul` consists of a matrix-matrix multiplication.
2. `torch.transpose` swaps two dimensions of a tensor.
3. `torch.gather` collects the elements of an input tensor specified by an index along a given axis, for example `out[i,j] = input[i,index[i,j]]`.
4. `torch.index_select` collects the elements of an input tensor along the axis specified by an index, for example `out[i,:] = input[index[i],:]`.
5. `torch.index_add_` accumulates the elements of a source tensor along an axis specified by an index, for example `input[index[i],:] += source[i,:]`.

Fused Kernel Microbenchmarks. We next move up a layer of abstraction and create microbenchmarks for $\mathbf{p}_i^{fused} \forall i \in \{1, ..., L\}$, see Table 1. For these operators, we follow the same procedure outlined in the previous section. While GroqChip1 and RDU do not require explicit kernel fusion as the equivalent effect of kernel fusion is handled automatically by the architecture, we explicitly fuse A100 kernels wherever possible.

Layer Based Microbenchmarks. Finally, we create microbenchmarks for $\mathbf{p}_i^{layer} \forall i \in \{1, ..., |K|\}$, running with parameters exactly as used by their original applications, see Table 2. However, certain hyperparamters to these end-to-end models, most notably batch size, are generally decided by user needs during inference time. Due to our focus on real-time GNN inference, we fix a the batch size of each layer to 1, reflecting the need to calculate single predictions in real time. Future work should examine the effect of varying input batch size on each layer microbenchmark. In order to evaluate the performance of layers in a real-world setting, inputs for each microbenchmark were sourced from a dataset used by the authors of the respective models in their original publications. Thus, realistic graph properties (e.g. sparsity, node and edge features) are tested. Specifically, we use MNIST [11] for PNA, QM9 [24] for GIN and GCNet, and IMDB-MULTI [18] for GraphSAGE.

5 Results

In this section, we highlight results of applying our benchmark methodology to the set of GNN models described in Sect. 4, analyze the performance based on the system designs of the three systems, and evaluate these results with respect to theoretical end-to-end applications performance on the emerging platforms.

Table 1. Results for operator and fused kernel microbenchmarks. Operators prepended with `torch.` are the exact operators defined by Pytorch and Pytorch Geometric [12, 20]. Fused kernels without the `torch.` prefix are defined in Sect. 4. Performance numbers are the mean of all tested input sizes, averaged over 100 runs. In addition to performance numbers, average-case L2 cache hit rates for the A100 GPU are also provided.

	Mean ($\pm$ Std) Runtime Ratios		L2 Hit % (A100)
	$\frac{A100}{GroqChip1}$	$\frac{A100}{RDU}$	
Operators			
torch.gather	1.782 ± 0.796	0.002 ± 0.001	62.75
torch.index_add_	–	0.374 ± 0.106	82.09
torch.index_select	–	0.191 ± 0.025	70.02
torch.matmul($\leq 10^8$ el.)	1.142 ± 0.395	0.746 ± 0.349	88.58
torch.matmul($> 10^8$ el.)	–	1.976 ± 0.675	89.56
torch.transpose	7.748 ± 0.381	–	93.59
Fused Kernels			
torch.addmm ($\leq 10^8$ el.)	1.683 ± 0.148	0.661 ± 0.271	86.72
torch.addmm ($> 10^8$ el.)	–	1.274 ± 0.606	88.07
index_add_reduce	–	1.462 ± 0.293	79.02
index_select_reduce	–	2.563 ± 0.713	63.04

Operator Level Performance Analysis. The operators chosen p^{ops} are summarized in Table 1. As described in Sect. 4, all operators are parameterized and tested over several input combinations, and are visualized in Fig. 3. Figure 3 demonstrates that the GroqChip1 shows comparable or better runtime performance than the A100 platform on all tested[1] microbenchmarks. Due in part to comparatively larger on-chip memory, the speedup improves as peak memory exceeds the 40 MiB cache size of the A100 platform and A100 performance

---

[1] GroqChip1 currently supports all operators in Table 1. Operators not tested are due to lack of multi-chip support, which render benchmarking at scale impractical.

Table 2. Mean runtime of layer-based benchmarking on A100 and GroqChip1 over 300 runs. All layer implementations are as defined in Pytorch Geometric [12]. GroqChip1 runtime values are fully deterministic and therefore do not include error bars.

| Application | Layer | Mean Runtime (ms) (± Std) | | Runtime Ratio |
		A100	GroqChip1	$\frac{A100}{GroqChip1}$
PNA	PNAConv	79.052 ± 1.540	**0.1297**	609.500
GIN	GINConv	0.188 ± 0.0385	**0.0028**	67.143
GraphSAGE	SAGEConv	$0.263 \pm .040$	**0.0275**	9.564
GCNet	GCConv	0.298 ± 0.024	**0.0027**	110.370

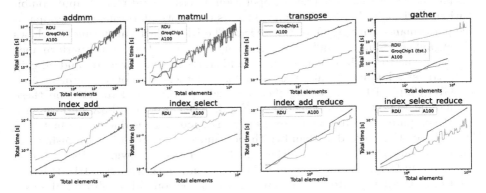

Fig. 3. Runtime of the operators considered as a function of total input elements. Input types are FP16 for all tensors, except index tensors that are of type INT64.

subsequently drops off. However, for certain operators, most notably `matmul`, A100 performance is competitive, likely due to explicit memory optimizations for such operators. Figure 3 shows that RDU performance compared to A100 on single operators varies significantly depending on the operation. For example, the `matmul` operator shows comparatively better performance, especially for larger input sizes. However, for others, such as `index_select` and `index_add`, performance is worse. Roofline analysis [33] indicates that the RDU system is not compute bound on these operators, but rather may suffer from unoptimized kernel implementations.

Operator L2 Cache Hit Rates. Table 1 also includes the average-case Nvidia A100 L-2 cache hit rate for all operators. For the purposes of analysis, we can classify each operator into those who are *GNN specific* and those that are relevant to more general deep learning workloads. Specifically, we classify `gather`, `index_add`, and `index_select` as GNN specific operations, and `matmul` and `transpose` as more general operators. Although this classification can be subjective, we believe that these distinctions are straightforward for our chosen operators; given the absence of the GNN specific operators in most other classes of deep learning architectures and the use of matrix multiplication and transpose in common general deep learning operators such as convolution and attention. As shown in Table 1, the L2 hit rates for all GNN specific operators are lower than the more general operators. This empirically supports our earlier claim that GNN specific operators are comparatively cache inefficient due to their reliance on non-contiguous data. Thus, the cache-less design of both dataflow architectures should implicitly optimize for this issue. Specifically, GroqChip1 is able to perform especially well on GNN operators, namely gather, despite similar theoretical FLOPS ratings between the GroqChip1 and A100 platforms.

Fused-Kernel Level Performance Analysis. The fused-kernel compound operators, p^{fused}, are also summarized in Table 1. Similar to the p^{ops} results, visualizations of each fused-kernel operation across several tested input combinations is visualized in Fig. 3. Figure 3 shows that both platforms have comparable performance with A100 for the addmm. The RDU platform specifically shows significant speedup (30–40%) at larger input sizes, where A100 performance drops off due to on chip memory limits and starts to suffer from on and off chip data transfer latency. While, the other fused kernels are not yet implemented on GroqChip1, RDU shows significant speed ups compared to A100 on these compound operators. As depicted in Fig. 3, RDU provides 2-3X performance boost compared to A100 on index_select_reduce. This is due to the fact that RDU hides the large data bandwidth demand of the operation by fusing the operation on-chip. That is, the RDU on-chip memory bandwidth (150 TB/s) is significantly faster than A100's off-chip High bandwidth memory (HBM) bandwidth (2TB/s). By automatically fusing the kernel on chip, substantial speed up results. The performance of RDU on index_add_reduce is similar, with a 30–50% performance boost, depending on the input size.

Fused Kernel L2 Cache Hit Rates. Similar to our operator level analysis, we report fused kernel L2 cache hit rates for the A100 platform. Again, we distinguish between GNN specific fused kernel layers, namely index_add_reduce and index_select_reduce and a general fused kernel, addmm. Again, we believe that this distinction is straightforward given the use of the addmm operator in many general DNN architectures, such as in feed-forward network layers with bias, and the absence of index_add_reduce and index_select_reduce in non-GNN workloads. Similar to our operator level analysis, we find that GNN specific fused kernels have comparatively lower L2 cache hits and are thus less cache efficient. Thus, we again conclude that the cache-less design of dataflow architectures should implicitly optimize for these kernels.

Layer Level Performance Analysis. The microbenchmarks results for all p^{layer} are summarized in Table 2. The GroqChip1 significantly outperforms the A100 for all layers tested. Moreover, the speedup for all p^{layer} are higher than in p^{ops} microbenchmarks. Thus, as with p^{fuse}, the lack of kernel overhead in the GroqChip1 platform contributes significantly to performance at higher levels of abstraction. Microbenchmarks for $\mathbf{p}_i^{layer}$ are not yet supported on the RDU platform. However, given the analysis of fused kernel results, we conclude that implicit kernel fusion may similarly lead to significant speed ups for $\mathbf{p}_i^{layer}$ microbenchmarks. Future work should empirically verify this claim.

Implications for End-to-End Performance. The results of our study demonstrate that as the level of abstraction of a microbenchmark increases, so does the relative speedup of the tested emerging hardware platforms (GroqChip1 and RDU) compared to the A100 platform. This indicates that end-to-end performance of the tested GNN models on these emerging hardware platforms can likely outperform the mature platform significantly.

6   Future Work

Our work focuses on microbenchmarking at the operator, fused kernel, and layer levels, excluding other levels of the performance stack, such as scheduling and pipeline performance. Future work should consider including these analyses and expanding the list of evaluated operators and fused kernels to enhance end-to-end performance prediction. Our study demonstrates the usefulness of microbenchmark indicators in predicting end-to-end performance on a mature hardware platform. By definition, emerging platforms cannot be used to verify this claim. However, if, as recommended based on our analysis, GroqChip1 and RDU provide support for GNNs in the future, work should be done to verify that end-to-end speedup for the tested GNN models holds.

7   Conclusion

In this work, we assess the performance of GNNs on emerging hardware platforms in the inference regime by testing relevant operators, fused kernels, and layers on the GroqChip1 and RDU platforms against an NVIDIA A100 baseline and provide novel performance insights regarding inference of these networks on each respective platform. Our high-level conclusions are as follows:

1. Both GroqChip1 and RDU platforms show competitive performance for operators related to GNNs despite no explicit sparse optimizations, and show significant inference performance speed up for these operators. For example, the RDU platform provides 2-3X performance improvement compared to A100 on index_select_reduce, a key building operation of the sparse operators such as sparse-dense matrix multiplication. The GroqChip1 provides an 11X performance boost on a single layer of the GraphSAGE convolution.
2. We empirically show that operators relevant specifically to GNNs are comparatively cache inefficient on A100. Thus, the cache-less design of dataflow architectures implicitly optimize for GNNs.
3. Due in part to systems and hardware features that result in automatic kernel fusion and memory optimization, dataflow architectures such as GroqChip1 and RDU platforms present an exciting opportunity to accelerate the inference of GNNs compared to well-established systems such as A100 GPUs.

Thus, we conclude that dataflow architectures such as GroqChip1 and RDU have the potential to significantly accelerate GNNs inference workloads and our analysis can offer insights as to which GNNs building blocks, i.e. operators, fused kernels, should be optimized in order to improve performance of GNN workloads on such platforms.

Funding Information. This research used resources of the Argonne Leadership Computing Facility, which is a DOE Office of Science User Facility supported under Contract DE-AC02-06CH11357.

References

1. Abts, D., et al.: Think fast: a tensor streaming processor (tsp) for accelerating deep learning workloads. In: 2020 ACM/IEEE 47th Annual International Symposium on Computer Architecture (ISCA), pp. 145–158 (2020)
2. Awan, A.A., Jain, A., Chu, C.H., Subramoni, H., Panda, D.K.: Communication profiling and characterization of deep-learning workloads on clusters with high-performance interconnects. IEEE Micro **40**(1), 35–43 (2019)
3. Baruah, T., et al.: GNNmark: a benchmark suite to characterize graph neural network training on GPUs. In: 2021 IEEE International Symposium on Performance Analysis of Systems and Software (ISPASS), pp. 13–23. IEEE (2021)
4. Blott, M., et al.: Evaluation of optimized CNNs on heterogeneous accelerators using a novel benchmarking approach. IEEE Trans. Comput. **70**(10), 1654–1669 (2020)
5. Blott, M., Halder, L., Leeser, M., Doyle, L.: QuTiBench: benchmarking neural networks on heterogeneous hardware. ACM J. Emerg. Technol. Comput. Syst. (JETC) **15**(4), 1–38 (2019)
6. Chen, Z., Cao, Y., Liu, Y., Wang, H., Xie, T., Liu, X.: A comprehensive study on challenges in deploying deep learning based software. In: Proceedings of the 28th ACM Joint Meeting on European Software Engineering Conference and Symposium on the Foundations of Software Engineering, pp. 750–762 (2020)
7. Ciżnicki, M., Kierzynka, M., Kopta, P., Kurowski, K., Gepner, P.: Benchmarking data and compute intensive applications on modern CPU and GPU architectures. Procedia Comput. Sci. **9**, 1900–1909 (2012)
8. Corso, G., Cavalleri, L., Beaini, D., Liò, P., Veličković, P.: Principal neighbourhood aggregation for graph nets. In: Advances in Neural Information Processing Systems, vol. 33, pp. 13260–13271 (2020)
9. Culler, D.E.: Dataflow architectures. Annu. Rev. Comput. Sci. **1**(1), 225–253 (1986)
10. Dang, V., Mohajerani, K., Gaj, K.: High-speed hardware architectures and fair FPGA benchmarking of CRYSTALS-kyber NTRU and saber. In: NIST 3rd PQC Standardization Conference (2021)
11. Dwivedi, V.P., Joshi, C.K., Laurent, T., Bengio, Y., Bresson, X.: Benchmarking graph neural networks. arXiv preprint arXiv:2003.00982 (2020)
12. Fey, M., Lenssen, J.E.: Fast graph representation learning with PyTorch geometric. arXiv preprint arXiv:1903.02428 (2019)
13. Filipovič, J., Madzin, M., Fousek, J., Matyska, L.: Optimizing CUDA code by kernel fusion: application on BLAS. J. Supercomput. **71**(10), 3934–3957 (2015)
14. Gale, T., Zaharia, M., Young, C., Elsen, E.: Sparse GPU kernels for deep learning. In: SC20: International Conference for High Performance Computing, Networking, Storage and Analysis, pp. 1–14. IEEE (2020)

15. Gwennap, L.: Groq rocks neural networks. Microprocessor Report, Technical report (2020)

16. Hamilton, W., Ying, Z., Leskovec, J.: Inductive representation learning on large graphs. In: Advances in Neural Information Processing Systems, vol. 30 (2017)

17. Hosseini, R., Simini, F., Vishwanath, V.: Operation-level performance benchmarking of graph neural networks for scientific applications. arXiv preprint arXiv:2207.09955 (2022)

18. Ivanov, S., Sviridov, S., Burnaev, E.: Understanding isomorphism bias in graph data sets (2019)

19. Karunaratne, M., Mohite, A.K., Mitra, T., Peh, L.S.: HyCUBE: A CGRA with reconfigurable single-cycle multi-hop interconnect. In: Proceedings of the 54th Annual Design Automation Conference 2017, pp. 1–6 (2017)

20. Paszke, A., et al.: PyTorch: an imperative style, high-performance deep learning library. In: Advances in Neural Information Processing Systems, vol. 32 (2019)

21. Prabhakar, R., Jairath, S.: SambaNova SN10 RDU: accelerating software 2.0 with dataflow. In: 2021 IEEE Hot Chips 33 Symposium (HCS), pp. 1–37. IEEE (2021)

22. Prabhakar, R., Jairath, S., Shin, J.L.: Sambanova sn10 RDU: a 7 nm dataflow architecture to accelerate software 2.0. In: 2022 IEEE International Solid-State Circuits Conference (ISSCC), vol. 65, pp. 350–352. IEEE (2022)

23. Qiao, B., Reiche, O., Hannig, F., Teich, J.: From loop fusion to kernel fusion: a domain-specific approach to locality optimization. In: 2019 IEEE/ACM International Symposium on Code Generation and Optimization (CGO), pp. 242–253 (2019)

24. Ramakrishnan, R., Dral, P.O., Rupp, M., von Lilienfeld, O.A.: Quantum chemistry structures and properties of 134 kilo molecules. Sci. Data 1, 1–7 (2014)

25. Reuther, A., Michaleas, P., Jones, M., Gadepally, V., Samsi, S., Kepner, J.: Survey and benchmarking of machine learning accelerators. In: 2019 IEEE High Performance Extreme Computing Conference (HPEC), pp. 1–9. IEEE (2019)

26. Reuther, A., Michaleas, P., Jones, M., Gadepally, V., Samsi, S., Kepner, J.: Survey of machine learning accelerators. In: 2020 IEEE High Performance Extreme Computing Conference (HPEC), pp. 1–12. IEEE (2020)

27. Wang, G., Lin, Y., Yi, W.: Kernel fusion: an effective method for better power efficiency on multithreaded GPU. In: 2010 IEEE/ACM International Conference on Green Computing and Communications & International Conference on Cyber, Physical and Social Computing, pp. 344–350. IEEE (2010)

28. Wang, Y.E., Wei, G.Y., Brooks, D.: Benchmarking TPU, GPU, and CPU platforms for deep learning. arXiv preprint arXiv:1907.10701 (2019)

29. Wang, Y., Feng, B., Ding, Y.: TC-GNN: accelerating sparse graph neural network computation via dense tensor core on GPUs. arXiv preprint arXiv:2112.02052 (2021)

30. Wu, Z., Pan, S., Chen, F., Long, G., Zhang, C., Philip, S.Y.: A comprehensive survey on graph neural networks. IEEE Trans. Neural Netw. Learn. Syst. 32(1), 4–24 (2020)

31. Xie, T., Grossman, J.C.: Crystal graph convolutional neural networks for an accurate and interpretable prediction of material properties. Phys. Rev. Lett. 120, 145301 (2018). https://doi.org/10.1103/PhysRevLett.120.145301

32. Xu, K., Hu, W., Leskovec, J., Jegelka, S.: How powerful are graph neural networks? arXiv preprint arXiv:1810.00826 (2018)

33. Yang, C.: Hierarchical roofline analysis: How to collect data using performance tools on intel CPUs and NVIDIA GPUs. arXiv preprint arXiv:2009.02449 (2020)

OpenACC Unified Programming Environment for Multi-hybrid Acceleration with GPU and FPGA

Taisuke Boku[1,2(✉)], Ryuta Tsunashima[2], Ryohei Kobayashi[1,2],
Norihisa Fujita[1,2], Seyong Lee[3], Jeffrey S. Vetter[3], Hitoshi Murai[4],
Masahiro Nakao[4], Miwako Tsuji[4], and Mitsuhisa Sato[4]

[1] Center for Computational Sciences, University of Tsukuba, Tsukuba, Japan
{taisuke,rkobayashi,fujita}@ccs.tsukuba.ac.jp
[2] Degree Programs in Systems and Information Engineering, University of Tsukuba,
Tsukuba, Japan
tsunashima@hpcs.cs.tsukuba.ac.jp
[3] Oak Ridge National Laboratory, Oak Ridge, USA
{lees2,vetter}@ornl.gov
[4] RIKEN Center for Computational Science, Kobe, Japan
{h-murai,masahiro.nakao,miwako.tsuji,msato}@riken.jp
https://www.ccs.tsukuba.ac.jp/

Abstract. Accelerated computing in HPC such as with GPU, plays a
central role in HPC nowadays. However, in some complicated applications with partially different performance behavior is hard to solve with a
single type of accelerator where GPU is not the perfect solution in these
cases. We are developing a framework and transpiler allowing the users
to program the codes with a single notation of OpenACC to be compiled
for multi-hybrid accelerators, named MHOAT (Multi-Hybrid OpenACC
Translator) for HPC applications. MHOAT parses the original code with
directives to identify the target accelerating devices, currently supporting
NVIDIA GPU and Intel FPGA, dispatching these specific partial codes
to background compilers such as NVIDIA HPC SDK for GPU and OpenARC research compiler for FPGA, then assembles binaries for the final
object with FPGA bitstream file. In this paper, we present the concept,
design, implementation, and performance evaluation of a practical astrophysics simulation code where we successfully enhanced the performance
up to 10 times faster than the GPU-only solution.

Keywords: GPU · FPGA · Programming framework · OpenACC ·
MHOAT

1 Introduction

GPU is the main player as a powerful accelerator on supercomputers, especially
for ultra-large scale systems to achieve a high performance/power ratio. Over
half of the world's top-10 machines in TOP500 List are equipped with GPUs.
However, GPU is not a perfect accelerating device in such cases with:

© The Author(s), under exclusive license to Springer Nature Switzerland AG 2023
A. Bienz et al. (Eds.): ISC High Performance 2023 Workshops, LNCS 13999, pp. 662–674, 2023.
https://doi.org/10.1007/978-3-031-40843-4_49

- poor degree of uniform parallelization lower than core count
- frequent conditional branches
- frequent internode communication, etc.

On the other hand, FPGA (Field Programmable Gate Array) becomes attractive as another candidate for accelerator [6,14,15]. The advantages of introducing FPGAs in HPC applications are:

- true codesigning system to be specialized for the target application
- pipelined parallel execution not in SIMD-manner
- high-end FPGAs are equipped with their own high-speed optical links for parallel FPGA environment
- relatively low power consumption compared with GPU

However, in most traditional research to employ FPGA in HPC applications, it is shown that the absolute performance of FPGA implementation is lower than GPU. Therefore, we should employ FPGA in problems where some parts of the entire computation are unsuitable for GPU. Even if a small fraction of the application cannot be improved, it makes the limit of performance even with a high performance of GPU according to the Amdahl's Law.

We have been researching the coupling of GPU and FPGA together toward highly efficient accelerated computing under the concept of CHARM (Cooperative Heterogeneous Acceleration with Reconfigurable Multidevices) [4,8] where both devices compensate with each other by different performance characteristics (Fig. 1). In this concept, we name such a computing framework with multiple types of accelerators as *multi-hybrid* computing.

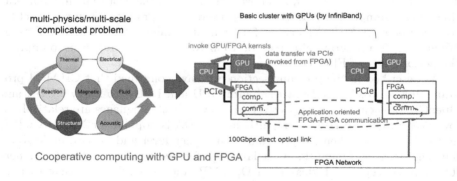

Fig. 1. Concept of CHARM

In previous works, we have researched the programming method and framework to apply the CHARM concept and developed the first practical application code. In [5], we presented an astrophysical application that implies heavy computation part where GPU acceleration does not work well, and we ported that part to Intel Arria10 FPGA to achieve up to 10 times faster performance with the programming of OpenCL High Level Synthesis (HLS). Then in [8] we successfully combined that OpenCL code for FPGA and CUDA code for GPU to assign two devices appropriately where each one achieves higher performance than the other. In the latter work, we found that it is possible to combine partial binary modules compiled by CUDA compiler for NVIDIA GPU and OpenCL compiler for Intel FPGA (Intel FPGA SDK for OpenCL [1]) without any conflict on symbols and modules. The overall performance of the entire code improves up to 17 times faster than GPU-only code. This multi-hybrid code was also ported to Intel oneAPI [3] environment for more sophisticated device controlling and data management without any performance loss, as reported in [7].

However, these works are complicated for general HPC users, requiring a mixture of CUDA and OpenCL programming. To solve this problem, we have been developing a comprehensive framework for a single language solution to offload appropriate code parts to multi-hybrid devices based on OpenACC. We initially considered using OpenCL both for GPU and FPGA as the basic notation of accelerator offloading since both devices support this language framework. However, OpenCL is still relatively low for application users and too complicated to mix in multi-hybrid accelerator programming by them. Therefore, we decided to use OpenACC as the higher level of the basic framework.

2   MHOAT - Single Language Coding for CHARM

The language processing environment we developed is named MHOAT (Multi-Hybrid OpenACC Translator) to hire several backend compilers for GPU and FPGA to allow users to code simply in OpenACC with a small directive expansion. The preliminary work was reported in [13] with the prototype implementation on tiny sample codes. In this paper, we report a practical example of actual code compiled by MHOAT and its functionality enhancement of MHOAT itself. We also apply a programming method to increase spatial parallelism to improve the performance of FPGA.

As described in the previous section, we have confirmed that CHARM programming is possible and practical with GPU and FPGA to apply CUDA and OpenCL for each device, respectively. However, both languages are relatively in low level for general HPC users, although CUDA is popular for NVIDIA GPU, and it is ideal for them to program with higher level and easy-to-understand language such as OpenMP. As a language for accelerators, OpenACC inherits many concepts and ideas from OpenMP, and it is relatively easy to port OpenMP codes to OpenACC toward easy GPU acceleration for general users. Although the language is available only for NVIDIA GPUs, these GPU families dominate the market, and many applications have been developed. If a user can program only with OpenACC both for GPU and FPGA, it is ideal for the CHARM programming framework.

Since creating a single compiler to cover every type of accelerating device is challenging, we need several backend compilers for all supported devices and a top-level language processing system to analyze the program modules assigned to appropriate devices based on user definition. Therefore, in the basic compilation framework of multi-hybrid OpenACC programming, we need the following process flow as shown in Fig. 2.

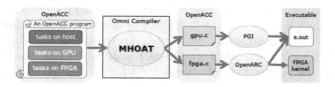

Fig. 2. Basic flow of single OpenACC code to process by backend compilers

The essential job of the MHOAT process is to separate tasks described in OpenACC pragma, such as *kernels* or *loop* to offload the target loop block to the accelerators. Here, we introduce an original pragma extension named **target_dev** to identify which accelerator is the target of that part, as shown in Fig. 3. We use **accomn** pragma instead of **acc** to identify that feature is our original extension (*omn* comes from our project name Omni for our compiler development). Currently, two device families, *GPU* and *FPGA*, can be specified as target devices.

```
#pragma accomn target_dev(GPU)
#pragma acc kernels
for(i=0; i<N; i++)    // this loop is offloaded to GPU
...
#pragma accomn target_dev(FPGA)
#pragma acc kernels
for(i=0; i<M; i++)    // this loop is offloaded to FPGA
...
```

Fig. 3. Extended directive **accomn target_dev** to target the accelerators

Then, MHOAT splits the source code into several files to be processed by the backend compilers, as shown below.

– Reading the program file and parsing the OpenACC directives for offloading to devices, especially with the specification of target accelerators,
– Separating the program fragments dispatched to the target backend compilers according to the target devices, and
– Assembling partially compiled binary objects created by these compilers into a final object file with several supportive run-time routines.

Currently, there is no commercial compiler for OpenACC on FPGA, and we only have HLS compilers by Intel or Xilinx for OpenCL, standard C, or C++. One of the solutions for OpenACC compilation is OpenARC [10] by Oak Ridge National Laboratory. It is a research compiler for multiple target devices, including GPUs and FPGAs. However, the device handling and data management policy is limited, and we like to extend more aggressive features on the system, for example, implying the fast DMA transfer mechanism between GPU and FPGA, which we originally developed. Therefore, we use the function of OpenARC to translate OpenACC to OpenCL only for FPGA. For GPU compilation, we can use the traditional compiler, NVIDIA SDK for HPC by PGI and NVIDIA [2].

Based on this design, we developed a prototype of a meta compiler for multi-hybrid OpenACC compilation, named MHOAT (Multi-Hybrid OpenACC Translator). Figure 4 shows the entire construction of MHOAT. Here, two backend compilers, NVIDIA SDK for HPC for NVIDIA GPU and OpenARC compiler for Intel FPGA, are invoked in the process flow. We have confirmed that the symbols and objects do not conflict between these compilers, so the binary of x86 host CPU can be easily assembled. For the partial compilation of OpenACC kernels dispatching to FPGA, the OpenARC compiler generates an OpenCL source code as the target file. We compile it by Intel FPGA SDK for OpenCL to create the target bitstream file (aocx file) to download to FPGA.

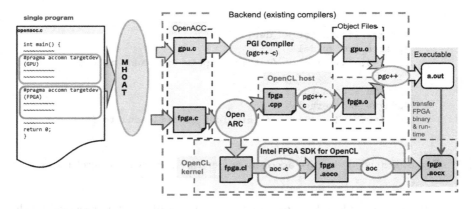

Fig. 4. Compilation flow of MHOAT with NVIDIA and OpenARC backend compilers

The current version of MHOAT does not support device-to-device direct data movement. Data handling should be treated as ordinary data directive in OpenACC as the relationship between the host CPU and the accelerating device. Therefore, when the data created by GPU is referred to on FPGA, it should first be synchronized with CPU memory, then synchronized with CPU and FPGA device memory. Introducing a feature to handle device-to-device data transfer is our future work.

3   OpenACC Coding for High Performance on FPGA

While pipeline parallelism is the base of performance gain on FPGA, there is a limit to the number of operations in the pipeline according to the target application. It is required to enlarge the number of operations per clock by exploiting spatial parallelism. A primary and efficient method is loop unrolling. However, the applicability is limited, especially due to the memory bandwidth bottleneck if high Byte/FLOP is required. To achieve a higher level of parallelization in coarse grain, we introduce multiple kernels to apply domain decomposition, like MPI programming on distributed memory architecture. That is a simple solution to enhance the performance to exploit a large amount of computing elements in the same manner as traditional HPC programs. The difference is how to connect multiple computation kernels within an FPGA. Intel FPGA SDK for OpenCL provides a feature named Channel to create a communication pipeline buffer for any pair of contact points of two kernels. The user can define an arbitrary number of Channels.

OpenARC provides a feature to program Intel Channel, which can be directly transformed into OpenCL code with Channel function. However, the current version of OpenARC supports only the default parameters on Channel attributes, and we need more flexibility for performance tuning (described later).

In Intel FPGA SDK for OpenCL, it is recommended to use Single Work-Item kernel to exploit pipeline parallelism rather than NDRange for spatial parallelism used for GPU usually. To exploit high performance with pipelining, we implement multiple kernels (in this study, eight identical kernels), and connect them by Channels. To program it, the code should be written as shown in Fig. 5.

```
      void fpga(...) {
#pragma accomn target_dev(FPGA)
      int channel1[1];
      int channel2[1];
      ...
#pragma acc data copy(a[:N], b[:N]) pipe(channel1[:1], channel2[:1])
{
#pragma acc serial pipein(channel1) pipeout(channel2) async(0)
      for(i=0; i < N/2; i++)
      ...
#pragma acc serial pipein(channel2) pipeout(channel1) async(1)
      for(i=N/2; i < N; i++)
      ...
} // acc data end
#pragma acc wait
...
}
```

Fig. 5. Multiple kernels by Single Work-Item, connected by Channel

Here, two kernels taking the first and latter half of data run asynchronously, and data are copied through two Channels, *channel1* and *channel2*. **serial** pragma is specified, but actually, these loops are pipelined by the FPGA compiler.

As described before, the overall performance of an FPGA is limited by the number of actual operations per clock and the frequency. In several cases, the compiler cannot estimate the behavior of the loop, especially on the dependency between operations, and it makes very conservative solutions where setting the pipeline pitch (single-stage latency) is too long. It is reflected in low clock frequency to limit the performance. In HPC applications, a typical case is a sort of reduction operation where a number of data are finally accumulated to finalize a scalar number or vector. If the calculation is complicated with several elements, it may happen more than expected.

Currently, we could not find a concrete solution to tell a reasonable estimation of pipeline latency to the compiler, so the final solution is to go back to the old-fashioned low-level description - Verilog HDL. It is similar to using *asm* construct in C language to escape to assembler coding to solve the problem partially. In our case of the target practical application shown in the next section, we could not solve this problem and introduce a function written in Verilog HDL to avoid too much long latency. However, we also did it in the previous works with CUDA and OpenCL descriptions, so this is not a fundamental problem of OpenACC coding. In our MHOAT solution, invoking functions written in Verilog HDL is possible.

4   Practical Application Example - ARGOT

As the first target application, we implement ARGOT (Accelerated Radiative transfer on Grids using Oct-Tree) [11] code developed in the Center for Computational Sciences, University of Tsukuba. It is a fundamental astrophysics simulation code to analyze how the first objects such as stars and galaxies were created in the universe about 500,000 years after the Big Bang. That is quite a short term in more than 13,000,000,000 years of its history. The most important source of these objects' creation is the radiation and the collection of tiny dust clouds. Radiation spread from a baby star or spatially spread in the universe affects other small objects to make their growth. There are two kinds of radiation calculated in the ARGOT code.

- Radiation spread from each Point Source (object) as shown in the left hand of Fig. 6. It can be calculated similarly to the gravity calculation where tree-code is applied like ordinary computation in astrophysics. This computing is named the ARGOT method.
- Radiation spread from long distance objects to be treated as potentially existing ones to go across the space field as shown in the right hand of Fig. 6. The calculation is similar to Ray-Tracing, where many light arrows cross the field and hit objects. This computing is named the ART (Authentic Radiation Transfer) method [12].

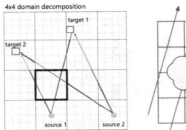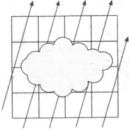

Fig. 6. Two methods of radiation transfer: ARGOT (left) and ART (right) methods

Remind that ARGOT *code* is for the entire application program while ARGOT *method* is a part of the computation in the code. So that ARGOT *code* mainly consists of ARGOT *method* and ART *method* computations as well as other additional physical phenomena.

Through the past work [5], we found the GPU acceleration does not work effectively on ART method calculation while it is suitable for ARGOT method like tree-code on GPUs. There are two main reasons. 1) Memory access pattern in ART method is almost random where the HBM memory of GPU does not work effectively, and 2) each radiation arrow to pass the target space is too short for the SIMD operation of the GPU core. Both features are critical to GPU performance, so GPU cannot improve ART method calculation. The serious problem is that approximately 90% of the computation cost on the GPU-only version of ARGOT code is consumed for ART method. That means we cannot accelerate the entire ARGOT code with GPUs only. We implemented the ART method part to Intel Aria10 FPGA, and achieved about ten times faster performance than GPU (NVIDIA P100). That is an excellent achievement of FPGA applied to HPC applications. Since GPUs are still applicable for ARGOT method much better than FPGA, we decided to apply the CHARM concept to the ARGOT code, as shown in Fig. 7.

5   Performance Evaluation

5.1   ARGOT Code Implementation for MHOAT

There are several versions of ARGOT code for CPU (with OpenMP) and GPU (with CUDA and OpenACC). All of them are parallelized by MPI for large scale computing in domain decomposition manner. However, this paper evaluates only a single node without MPI.

As described in the previous section, we applied a multi-kernel solution for domain decomposition within an FPGA on ART method calculation to exploit the coarse grain parallelism. Eight kernels are running in parallel and connected by Intel Channel with each other. We define a long macro description to implement a kernel and use it eight times to duplicate them so that the effort for the

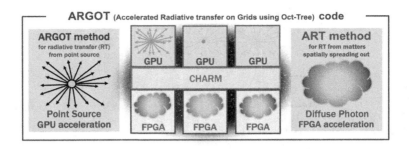

Fig. 7. ARGOT method and ART method mapping to GPU and FPGA in CHARM concept for ARGOT code

multi-kernel solution is easy. For inter-kernel communication, we need to apply a much deeper pipeline buffer on Channel communication than the default parameter set. However current version of the OpenARC compiler has no feature for optional Channel parameter settings. Therefore, we modify this part of OpenCL code generated from OpenACC by OpenARC compiler with a sort of 'patch script' after compilation.

Since the memory access pattern of ART method is almost random, we allocate all temporal data for target space in BRAM (Block RAM), which is a kind of SRAM implemented with the same calculation logic circuit. However, since the capacity of BRAM is limited to just 28 MByte, we keep all the data in DDR DRAM outside of FPGA, and transfer them according to the calculation progress. It means that we use BRAM as an addressable cache. That is another coding technique to enhance the FPGA performance.

As described before, the current MHOAT does not support the device-to-device data synchronization feature. However, in the ARGOT code, the data amount transferred between GPU and FPGA is negligible, with less than 1% of execution time, and it does not impact the performance.

5.2 Performance Evaluation

The target platform consists of two sockets of Intel Xeon E5-2690 v4 as host CPUs, NVIDIA Tesla V100 (32 GiB HBM2, PCIe Gen3×16), and Intel Stratix10 GX2800 FPGA (BittWare 520N card, PCIe Gen3×16).

Figure 8 shows the overall performance comparison of the MHOAT solution on ARGOT code compared with GPU-only code in OpenACC, GPU-only code in CUDA, and GPU + FPGA code with CUDA + OpenCL. That is the case with $32 \times 32 \times 32$ grid, a relatively small size problem of ARGOT code where the GPU performance bottlenecks by ART method calculation. The floating point operation is in single precision. Each bar implies the computation time for ARGOT method (GPU), ART method (GPU or FPGA), and Others (miscellaneous tasks mainly working on CPU with OpenMP).

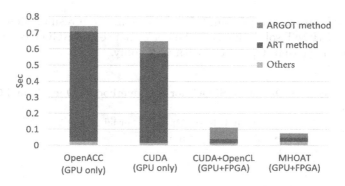

Fig. 8. ARGOT code execution time (1 step) with four styles of programming

At first, we confirmed that the performance gain by CHARM programming is significantly higher than GPU-only cases, and MHOAT achieves the best performance. The ART method calculation performance on GPU is poor because the excellence of GPU architecture does not fit, so the ART method part dominates the computation time. For the GPU-only cases on ART method, the efficiency of OpenACC is slightly higher than CUDA, and it still shows the CUDA coding with detailed tuning is better than OpenACC. On the other hand, the ARGOT method calculation on GPU is improved in OpenACC. We have yet to analyze the reason, but it has a good effect on the MHOAT solution.

Table 1. Breakdown of execution time (sec./step)

	OpenACC (GPU-only)	CUDA (GPU-only)	CUDA+OpenCL (CHARM)	MHOAT (CHARM)
ARGOT method	0.033	0.074	0.071	0.026
ART method	0.686	0.559	0.028	0.026
Others	0.023	0.015	0.014	0.023
Total	0.742	0.649	0.113	0.075

Table 1 shows the detailed execution time for each computation part in all cases. In the main computation for ARGOT method and ART method, the MHOAT solution is the best. However, the miscellaneous tasks take a long time on MHOAT. In total, MHOAT still keeps the advantage over the CUDA+OpenCL coding. When we see the two bars in the right hand, it is clearly saying that the CHARM solution dramatically improves the performance of this application. Especially by MHOAT, 1) ART method on FPGA has no performance difference between OpenCL and OpenACC thanks to an efficient compilation on OpenARC, and 2) ARGOT method calculated on GPU is better in MHOAT because that performance is better in OpenACC than CUDA as shown in two bars in the left hand. In conclusion, these results show the excellence of the MHOAT solution where the performance of ARGOT code execution is 9.9 times faster than OpenACC with GPU-only.

Table 2. Source Line Of Count (SLOC) for ART method on OpenCL and OpenACC

	OpenCL host	OpenCL kernel	OpenACC
SLOC	263	945	900

Finally, we examined the source code line counts. The difference between the naive CUDA+OpenCL coding and MHOAT OpenACC coding for multi-hybrid computing is shown in Table 2. Here, SLOC (Source Line Of Code) for OpenCL is 1208 lines, with 263 for the host (CPU) and 945 for the kernel (FPGA). On the other hand, OpenACC in MHOAT counts just 900 lines. Simply the source line count is reduced to 75%. Moreover, the user has to understand OpenACC notation only for easy programming, even for CHARM.

6   Discussion

The concept of CHARM is to provide multi-hetero accelerating environment on supercomputers where a single kind of accelerator, such as GPU, does not effectively work partially in the code, while other parts have no performance problem. That problematic parts bottleneck the total execution performance according to the Amdahl's Law. On multi-physics applications especially, that is a practical problem. Thus, a different kind of accelerator, such as FPGA, could support and compensate these parts. If the entire code can be accelerated only by GPU, there is no problem, and GPUs have been used for such cases so far.

MHOAT requires users to specify the computation parts to offload to GPU or FPGA. On the other hand, Intel oneAPI allows any computation part to offload to GPU and FPGA. This is because oneAPI assumes offloading any kernel dynamically for load balancing over multiple devices. However, running the same kernel code on both is impractical because the performance characteristics are wholly different depending on the devices. In our concept, a user must choose the devices how to run each kernel according to its computation behavior. The performance result of ARGOT code clearly proves it. Therefore, it is unnecessary to compile all loops (kernels) for FPGA, and perform it only for them to run on that device.

Another issue is the footprint of the logic circuit of an FPGA device. Since it is critically limited, there is only room to compile some of the loops for FPGA in a complicated code. In this viewpoint, we should limit the kernels on FPGA to only the necessary ones. In conclusion, explicitly limiting the target kernels for FPGA is a necessary and sufficient condition in the CHARM concept.

7 Conclusions

In this paper, we described our concept of CHARM, where multi-hybrid heterogeneous computing is a powerful solution for multi-physics simulations such as complicated astrophysics ones. While GPU is the most powerful and efficient solution as a representative accelerating computing device, it is imperfect. On the other hand, FPGA is relatively weak on HPC applications compared with GPU, but the performance characteristics and architecture behavior are almost opposite from GPUs. Thus, we combine both devices to compensate for each other in performance. We developed MHOAT for a single notation programming framework with OpenACC to support easy programming. In the first practical application of astrophysics, we achieved approximately ten times higher performance on MHOAT-coded astrophysical simulation driven by GPU+FPGA than traditional GPU-only solution with OpenACC.

Our future works imply the node-parallel extension of ARGOT code with MPI. It is easy to work because the original OpenACC version of ARGOT code is already written for MPI, and nothing by MHOAT inhibits it. We have already done with parallelized CHARM code with CUDA+OpenCL [9] where we showed a good performance improvement with a parallel environment with GPU+FPGA. The current version of OpenARC used in MHOAT needs several enhancements, such as more flexible Channel usage, automatic spatial parallelism improvement such as loop unrolling, etc. Our final goal for ARGOT on CHARM is to run the program on the full scale of our CHARM-base cluster Cygnus [4].

Acknowledgements. This work is supported by JSPS KAKENHI (Grant Number 21H04869). The Cygnus utilization is supported by the MCRP 2022 Program by the Center for Computational Sciences, University of Tsukuba.

References

1. Intel FPGA SDK for OpenCL. https://www.intel.com/content/www/us/en/software/programmable/sdk-for-opencl/overview.html
2. Nvidia HPC SDK: A comprehensive suite of compilers, libraries and tools for HPC. https://developer.nvidia.com/hpc-sdk
3. oneAPI: A new era of accelerated computing. https://www.intel.com/content/www/us/en/developer/tools/oneapi/overview.html#gs.smg356
4. Boku, T., Fujita, N., Kobayashi, R., Tatebe, O.: Cygnus - world first multi-hybrid accelerated cluster with GPU and FPGA coupling. In: 2nd International Workshop on Deployment and Use of Accelerators (DUAC2022) (2022)
5. Fujita, N., et al.: Accelerating space radiative transfer on FPGA using OpenCL. In: 2018 International Symposium on Highly-Efficient Accelerators and Reconfigurable Technologies (HEART 2018) (2018). https://doi.org/10.1145/3241793.3241799
6. Hill, K., Craciun, S., George, A., Lam, H.: Comparative analysis of OpenCL vs. HDL with image-processing kernels on Stratix-V FPGA. In: 2015 IEEE 26th International Conference on Application-specific Systems, Architectures and Processors (ASAP2015), pp. 189–193 (2015)

7. Kashino, R., Kobayashi, R., Fujita, N., Boku, T.: Multi-hetero acceleration by GPU and FPGA for astrophysics simulation on intel oneAPI environment. In: Proceedings of International Conference on High Performance Computing in Asia-Pacific Region (HPCAsia2022) (2022)

8. Kobayashi, R., et al.: Multi-hybrid accelerated simulation by GPU and FPGA on radiative transfer simulation in astrophysics. J. Inf. Process. **28**, 1073–1089 (2020). https://doi.org/10.2197/ipsjjip.28.1073

9. Kobayashi, R., et al.: GPU-FPGA-accelerated radiative transfer simulation with inter-FPGA communication. In: 2023 International Conference on High Performance Computing in Asia-Pacific Region (HPCAsia2023) (2023)

10. Lee, S., Kim, J., Vetter, J.S.: OpenACC to FPGA: a framework for directive-based high-performance reconfigurable computing. In: 2016 IEEE International Parallel and Distributed Processing Symposium (IPDPS2016), pp. 544–554 (2016)

11. Okamoto, T., Yoshikawa, K., Umemura, M.: ARGOT: accelerated radiative transfer on grids using oct-tree. Monthly Not. Roy. Astron. Soc. **419**(4), 2855–2866 (2012)

12. Tanaka, S., Yoshikawa, K., Okamoto, T., Hasegawa, K.: A new ray-tracing scheme for 3D diffuse radiation transfer on highly parallel architectures. Publ. Astron. Soc. Jpn. **67**(4), 1–16 (2015)

13. Tsunashima, R., et al.: OpenACC unified programming environment for GPU and FPGA multi-hybrid acceleration. In: 13th International Symposium on High-level Parallel Programming and Applications (HLPP2020) (2020)

14. Tsuruta, C., Miki, Y., Kuhara, T., Amano, H., Umemura, M.: Off-loading let generation to peach2: a switching hub for high performance GPU clusters. ACM SIGARCH Comput. Archit. News **43**(4), 3–8 (2016)

15. Zohouri, H.R., Maruyama, N., Smith, A., Matsuda, M., Matsuoka, S.: Evaluating and optimizing OpenCL kernels for high performance computing with FPGAs. In: Proceedings of the International Conference for High Performance Computing, Networking, Storage and Analysis (SC 2016), pp. 35:1–35:12 (2016)

Author Index

Printed in the United States
by Baker & Taylor Publisher Services